I Confess!

I Confess!

Constructing the Sexual Self in the Internet Age

Edited by THOMAS WAUGH and BRANDON ARROYO

McGill-Queen's University Press

Montreal & Kingston · London · Chicago

© McGill-Queen's University Press 2019

ISBN 978-0-7735-5910-3 (cloth)
ISBN 978-0-7735-5939-4 (paper)
ISBN 978-0-2280-0064-8 (ePDF)
ISBN 978-0-2280-0065-5 (ePUB)

Legal deposit fourth quarter 2019
Bibliothèque nationale du Québec

Printed in Canada on acid-free paper that is 100% ancient forest free (100% post-consumer recycled), processed chlorine free

Funded by the Government of Canada / Financé par le gouvernement du Canada Canada Council for the Arts / Conseil des arts du Canada

We acknowledge the support of the Canada Council for the Arts.

Nous remercions le Conseil des arts du Canada de son soutien.

Library and Archives Canada Cataloguing in Publication

Title: I confess! : constructing the sexual self in the internet age / edited by Thomas Waugh and Brandon Arroyo.
Other titles: I confess! (2019)
Names: Waugh, Thomas, 1948– editor. | Arroyo, Brandon, 1982– editor.
Description: Includes bibliographical references and index.
Identifiers: Canadiana (print) 20190137355 | Canadiana (ebook) 20190137541 | ISBN 9780773559103 (cloth) | ISBN 9780773559394 (paper) | ISBN 9780228000648 (ePDF) | ISBN 9780228000655 (ePUB)
Subjects: LCSH: Internet users—Sexual behavior. | LCSH: Sex customs. | LCSH: Internet—Social aspects. | LCSH: Mass media—Social aspects. | LCSH: Arts and society. | LCSH: Online identities. | LCSH: Self.
Classification: LCC HQ31 .I5 2019 | DDC 306.70285—dc23

Contents

Foreword: Falling in Love with Johnnie Ray: Sixty Years of Telling Sexual Stories | ix
KEN PLUMMER

Introduction | 3
THOMAS WAUGH AND BRANDON ARROYO

PART ONE SCIENTIA SEXUALIS
Activism

1 The Treachery of Rape Representation | 29
TAL KASTNER AND UMMNI KHAN

2 More Than Just Selfies: #Occupotty, Affect, and Confession as Activism | 49
ANDIE SHABBAR

3 Against Authenticity: The Feminist Turn in N. Maxwell Lander's Video Work | 65
NAOMI DE SZEGHEO-LANG WITH N. MAXWELL LANDER

4 Blogging Affects and Other Inheritances of Feminist Consciousness-Raising | 83
ELA PRZYBYLO AND VERONIKA NOVOSELOVA

5 "YES I'M GAY": The Mediality of Coming Out | 107
   SILKE JANDL

   ### Author, Subject, and Audience

6 "Aren't You Worried about What People Might Say? What People Might Do?": Lady Gaga and the "Heeling" of Queer Trauma | 129
   JACOB EVOY

7 Letters to Nina Hartley: Pornography, Parrhesia, and Sexual Confessions | 136
   INGRID OLSON

8 Femininities of Excess: The Cinematic Confessions of Rituparno Ghosh | 158
   SHOHINI GHOSH

9 The Videomaker and the Rent Boy: Gay-for-Pay Confessional in *101 Rent Boys* and *Broke Straight Boys TV* | 177
   NICHOLAS DE VILLIERS

10 Confessions: Watching the Masturbating Boy (Excerpts) | 193
   INTERVALS, AN ANONYMOUS COLLECTIVE

   ## PART TWO ARS EROTICA
   ### Pornographies

11 Like a Prayer: Confessing My Beatific-Cum-Demonic Visions of Men (and God?) | 237
   CONNOR STEELE

12 Camming and Erotic Capital: The Pornographic as an Expression of Neoliberalism | 245
   ÉRIC FALARDEAU (translated by JORDAN ARSENEAULT)

13 Confessions of a Masked Pornographer: Reorienting Gay Male Identity via Bodily Confession | 263
    BRANDON ARROYO

14 Sadean Confessions in Virginie Despentes's Punk-Porn-Feminism | 300
    VALENTINA DENZEL

15 *Fuck Yeah Levi Karter!* and New Authenticities | 318
    DANIEL LAURIN

16 Circuitous Pleasures, Guilt, and Pain: *Nymph()maniac* and the Pornographic Hard Code | 338
    JUSTINE T. MCLELLAN

17 Porn Fast | 353
    SHAKA MCGLOTTEN

Documentaries

18 "I Confess: I Was the Girl in the Shadows" | 371
    REBECCA SULLIVAN

19 Queer Auto-Porn-Art: Genealogies, Aesthetics, Ethics, and Desire | 378
    THOMAS WAUGH

20 On Not Seeing All: *The Incomplete*, Sexual Play, and the Ethics of the Frame | 408
    SUSANNA PAASONEN

21 To Queer Things Up: Sexing the Self in the Queer Documentary Web Series | 423
    SARAH E.S. SINWELL

22 A Man with a Mother: *Tarnation* and the Subject of Confession | 436
    DAMON R. YOUNG

Transmedia

23 Looking, Stroking, and Speaking: A Queer Ethics of MAP Desire | 453
ANONYMOUS

24 Playing Confession: Gaming, Autobiography, and the Elusive Self | 473
STEPHEN CHARBONNEAU

25 From a "Disappeared Aesthetics" to a "Trans-Aesthetics": Derek Jarman and Ming Wong's Image-Based Technologies of the Self | 489
MILAN PRIBISIC

26 Writing Intimacy: Fantasy, New Media, and Confession in Marie Calloway's *what purpose did I serve in your life* | 504
ELEANOR TY

27 *Hentai* Confessions: Transgression and "Sexual Technologies of the Self" in Akihiko Shiota's *Moonlight Whispers* | 515
RON S. JUDY

28 Porno-Graphing: "Dirtiness" and Self-Objectification | 533
ANNAMARIA PINAKA

29 Shut Me Up in Grindr: Anti-confessional Discourse and Sensual Nonsense in MSM Media | 549
TOM ROACH

Figures | 573
Contributors | 581
Index | 591

Foreword

Falling in Love with Johnnie Ray: Sixty Years of Telling Sexual Stories

KEN PLUMMER

Things are moving fast. Things are moving faster. On a queer day you can see forever, and ever, and ever ... or at least you can look.
• Martha Gever, John Greyson, and Pratibha Parmar (1993)

So these are the times and the tales of our lives
Contested. Contingent. Creatively striving.
Progressing. Regressing. Sometimes surviving.
Incorrigibly plural. Intransigently vast.
These are the tales of how we order our past.
• Ken Plummer (2008)

Johnnie Ray was, I think, my earliest gay love. Few recall him today, but I fell in love with him when I was about eight, watching ITV in England as he topped the most popular variety show of the 1950s, *Sunday Night at the London Palladium*. He was a dark-haired, handsome young man with looks to kill as he crooned his sentimental heart out. Wearing his smooth black suit, oh how he would move. This was before Elvis Presley and rock and roll. He wore a hearing aid, and when he sang his love songs, his hand caressed that side of his head. And his hips shivered and slivered. It seems a little queer, perhaps, that a grown man now in his seventies can recall this so vividly. Yet as I write, he reappears in my mind (fig. 00.1). This recall is helped these days by being able to scan for YouTube images of such memories. Singing his songs (which I hadn't thought of for years) – "The Little White Cloud That Cried" and, sexy beyond belief, "Oh What a Night It Was!" – he was a little potential gay boy's dream come true. And it was the 1954 film *There's No Business Like Show Business* (also starring Marilyn Monroe and Ethel

00.1
Breaking little gay hearts all over England. Publicity still of Johnnie Ray, 1952.

Merman in glorious CinemaScope and DeLuxe Colour), where he appeared as the good priest son in a show-business family, that confirmed my eight-year-old adoration. I cut out photos of him from newspapers and magazines.

And then, I knew not why, he was arrested on something called a morals charge. (I did not know what that meant, but I knew it was not good news.) A little later he vanished, presumed dead. My first love was tragic and gone. But I was heartless, as many others soon replaced him: the young Tommy Steele (whom I fell in love with in *The Tommy Steele Story* when he sang "Butterfingers"), the young and oh-so-sexy Cliff Richard (when he sang the sentimental and quasi-religious "Shrine on the Second Floor"), and most of all, Billy Fury (when he turned his back and showed his tight-trousered rear on *Oh Boy!*). Elvis was also a hit, but a poor relative to these three. And I was dimly aware of many others: even, as it happens, Montgomery Clift in the film *I Confess* (which would have made me seven!). It was not their singing or their acting skills I was going for, but their looks.

These images are still powerful, and I have recollected them fairly readily. I am recalling days from my junior school through the first and second years of secondary school, when I was aged between seven and twelve. They suggest to me *the visibility of the "sexual," or maybe the romantic, at very early ages.* I was, it seems, "falling in love" with beautiful media men all over the place.

By contrast, a little later, the film *Victim* (1962) was the first X-rated film I went to see – straight after school one day, so I did not have to explain it to my parents, who would have been at work. The year was 1962; I would have been fifteen. I went with a school pal who may well have been gay too, but we watched together in silence, went home, and never ever spoke about the experience again. The film starred Dirk Bogarde, and that was enough for me to want to see it. I had liked him in the *Doctor* films, which were very popular then (*Doctor in the House*, *Doctor at Sea*), and he was without doubt the best-looking actor on the block. But there was also something mysterious about the film. Why was it an X film? Who was the Victim? Homosexuality was never explicitly stated – it was an unmentionable topic at that time – but I could see from the newspapers that it was causing a controversy of some kind. I was quite used to this, as I had been growing up on a series of controversial films and books about sex – *Lady Chatterley's Lover*, *Room at the Top*, *Look Back in Anger* – but this seemed to be different. And it seemed to be about homosexuality.

And indeed it was! Imagine, knowing nothing about it at all, hardly even the word, and entering this cinema (the Odeon, in Wood Green, London) and this film. I had been having these feelings for Johnnie Ray, Billy Fury, and the like (and come to think of it, quite a few fifth formers at school), but the idea that I was gay, queer, or anything like that (whatever that might have meant) was simply outside my realms of understanding. The limits of my world were indeed the limits of my language.

But with *Victim* (fig. 00.2), what a story I learned. Young men hang themselves if they are gay. Older men have their careers ruined if they are gay. Blackmail is everywhere in this world. Watch out for the police and possible imprisonment. Look out for a furtive little world of men who seem to be utterly scared and wide open to every kind of abuse. Look at your garage door and find "Queer" written all over it. Better to marry and try to conceal it. Vivid, striking, and in black and white, this film had a gritty story to tell and told it well. And Dirk Bogarde – what was he doing in all this? First, he played the leading homosexual role. Second, he was one of the victims – of various attacks. But thirdly, in an admittedly muted fashion, he came out to his wife (Sylvia Syms) and kind of wanted to change the world. Oh, how brave! He was my handsome victim – and hero!

I started furtively to find out more and more about the film, about Dirk Bogarde's views: after all, to play such a role, he had to at least be sympathetic to

00.2
A sexually tormented Dirk Bogarde. Poster for *Victim*, dir. Basil Dearden, 1961.

homosexuality. And hold on – didn't that mean the whole crew behind the film was possibly sympathetic? Wasn't it indeed a crusading film against the ways in which homosexuality was treated in society – as a crime, as a sickness, and a "blackmailers" charter? My world of understanding was dramatically shifting.[1]

Now, and for quite a long while to come, I searched out all the films and scraps of information I could find about queer matters. As a newspaper delivery boy, I often saw nasty, cruel headlines about these people. But now I scanned in more detail, for more new films that might be like *Victim*, noting local and famous cases of people charged with "suspicious" behaviours and finding also that there was a much wider public discussion going on: some people were trying to change the law. Meanwhile, I watched Shirley MacLaine hang herself in William Wyler's *The Children's Hour* …

Much later, in my college days, I recall seeing the play *The Boys in the Band* by Mart Crowley when it opened in London in 1968 at the Wyndham's Theatre. It was a significant talking point: the first overt West End play about queers. I was full of admiration for such a bold dramatic event. I bought the book to study the play, and I saw it twice. What a breakthrough, I thought. Two years later, in a flurry of activist activity linked with my early days in the Gay Liberation Front, I stood outside a cinema in Fulham picketing audiences and trying to stop them going to see the film of *The Boys in the Band*. Only a short while earlier, I had thought it wonderful, a world of queers now made visible. And here I was now picketing it because apparently it was a terrible film, full of bad stereotyping and awful images of gays. So I picketed, and started to learn that things I could see as very good at one moment could rapidly turn into things I could see as really bad at another.[2]

And so here I was, a little boy becoming a young man, entering the magical worlds of films, drama, and sexual storytelling aided by various screens along the way. But bigger things were waiting for me: I was by now entering adult life.

A Story of My Stories

> What is a life? How indeed can we know a life? What is the link between telling a life and living a life? What are the ways of telling a life? How does "writing a life" differ from a telling? How does a life's telling link to a culture and its history? How does the reading of a life link to the telling of a life? And to truth? Are all lives to be told equally or are some better to tell?
> • Ken Plummer ([1983] 2001)

Such questions have perpetually haunted me over the past sixty years or so, even as they have simultaneously become more prominent in public culture. Telling sexual stories is part of a very long history of confessional cultures in the West from Augustine to Foucault that now sits very easily with the ravages of modern capitalist individualism, the "selfie," and the continuing era of confession. With a long history of such stories, I can by now gather up (or even "curate," in the currently fashionable term) a few of my past stories into *a short story of my stories.*

And So. In the Beginning, there was Johnnie Ray. But this is only one of many, many sexual stories I have told over the years. It all started with having to grapple with these issues at a young age as I dealt with my own (now very traditional) *coming out stories*, back in the 1950s and '60s, when being queer was shrouded in stigma, secrecy, shame, and sickness. Not to mention illegality. A little later, going to graduate college, I turned to asking the more research-oriented questions of how to get others to tell their sexual stories. I interviewed other gay people initially: on their relationships, their communities, and their coming out at the very moment (1967) when the homosexual law was changing in England (these were my *stigma stories*, as well as my *sociological stories*). In this earliest work, I followed the well-known research rules for interviewing people and gathering data. Writing a few early papers based on the stories told to me, I became dissatisfied. And so my thesis became more theoretical, cutting a lot of the basic data out.

The early 1970s were also a time of political turmoil; my earliest research days were sharply and abruptly modified through the arrival of the early Gay Liberation Front (GLF) movement (*activist stories*). Here I was challenged to think about the conditions under which people get a voice and how are they silenced. What can be said and what cannot be said? Why could gay people start to speak at this very moment and not much before? And it led me to grasp the importance of public statements of being out, which till then had been more or less non-existent (*personal stories, political stories*).

By the mid-1970s I had taken the usual career path for an academic life. I needed to get a grant and do "real post-doc research." This I duly did. My new research was into stigmatized sexual diversities; with a colleague, I made preliminary investigations into the *life stories* of "transvestites" and "transsexuals," "sadomasochists," "pedophiles," and "prostitutes" (all the terms have changed!). Eventually this broadened into an even wider concern: the politics of gender and the conflicts between sexual liberation and gender liberation (*gender politics stories*). All this, it might be added, was before the ideas of Foucault on sexualities burst on the scene (in the UK around 1978: *Foucauldian stories!*). I soon found the research was messy and chaotic and served me as an apprenticeship in doubting (my *research tales*). It led me to find the data I had gathered deeply worrying. What kind of truth was I getting at? Audiences were certainly more interested in the stories I had than any abstractions, but all the time I was wondering about the status of these stories, including my own. I started to talk more and more about the methods of research, leading me to write *documents of life* in the late 1970s. This study emphasized the importance of life story as a basis for humanistic research where ethics and reflexivity would become key issues (my *reflexive stories*). My doubts grew; I worried about the complexities, multiplicities, contingencies of what people say about their lives as I moved into the even grander questions of epistemology and ontology. What indeed is a life, can it ever really be told, what is the status of what someone says about their life? In all this, I was never alone: I joined a vast conversation on such matters, and the chorus grew almost deafening.

Gradually the book *Telling Sexual Stories* started to take shape. My concern was becoming less with the actual content of texts (of what sexual stories said) and more with the historical, cultural, economic, and political conditions under which stories could be told and shaped – and what the consequences might be of telling some stories rather than others. I was getting more and more engaged with problems of the politics and sociology of narrative. I had known almost from the start, way back in the 1970s, that there could never be any simple or straight telling of a sexual story (or indeed any story): call this queer if you like (*queer stories? reflexive stories? critical stories?*). My doubts grew about a social-science enterprise that seems to rely overwhelmingly on people giving information about their lives to interviewers: material that is always and inextricably, indelibly, inevitably problematic. There simply are no "pure" stories to be told. The humanities have long recognized this, and there is much the social sciences could learn from them.

Moving on and looking back, I can see I have always been writing on the edge of *the autobiographical*. Involvement in social research always impinges on one's life. I can, for example, now see that the stages of my own coming out in the mid-1960s were an inspiration for the "stage model of coming out" (sensitization, signification, subculturalization, and stabilization) that I developed for my book *Sexual Stigma* (1975). It made sense to me personally. I also came out in my lecturing way back in the 1960s, and have been out in that environment ever since. Even so, it took ten or so more years before I let the personal directly and visibly become part of my writing (*autoethnographic stories*). By the late 1980s, I was more willing to let my own story intrude into my writing. Inspired by feminist trends towards self-reflection, I did this first at the large *Homosexuality, Which Homosexuality?* conference (Van Kerkoff 1989) in Amsterdam in 1987 (in a paper never published), and I did it again in the opening vignettes of my book *Telling Sexual Stories* in 1995. By the late 1990s, I was regularly letting the personal and the reflexive intrude into what I was saying. When I was invited by Janice Irvine to write a more personal account, it developed into "Queers, Bodies and Postmodern Sexualities" (2003), and when I wrote for *The Sage Handbook of Qualitative Research*, I made my tensions around humanism and queer an organizing theme (2011a). Writing an introduction for a study on narrative perspectives on the gay and lesbian life course, I introduced it with a statement of my early sexual life and coming out (2009). And most recently, a major life-threatening illness led me to think long and hard about my multiple sickness bodies, the important role of illness stories, the use of auto/ethnography, and the rise of narrative medicine (2012) (*illness stories*). The point of this little publications list (!) is to suggest that I have been busy writing tiny fragments of a queer research life for more than forty years. They are all written at angles, and none tells the whole story. But I have increasingly found myself taking two strands: a more personal one, and a more overtly political one. They were connected. By the time I was writing *Cosmopolitan Sexualities* (2015a), an appendix was necessary to contain my self-reflections (*cosmopolitan stories*). Although my private self has always been hanging around on the edges of my writing, increasingly it has come out and become its own voice. And here is also where I ventured a short poem about Peggy Lee and my life to briefly capture it all (2015a).

And now, as I enter the later stages of an aging – and ultimately dying – life, the autobiographical puzzles of generation and time, illness and death are becoming ever more prominent and pervasive. The questions for life storytellings keep rolling on. As I became more involved with these stories, so I was also becoming increasingly aware of their problems: of *the fragility of storytelling and the infinitude of stories*.

The Generational Problem of Sexual Storytelling

So here we are: that was then and here is now. Having spent some seventy significant, short years on this fast-moving, hurling, spinning globe in a multi-universe of storytelling, I continue – as we all are – compelled to live in the newness of the present. Our multiple stories of the past continue in the present to keep moving us inexorably on to some kind of future. And as we move, so our stories start to congeal in generational forms. As I get older, the significance of generations for social organization becomes more and more striking: "All sexualities dangle from an age perspective. They are situated in age standpoints" (2015a, 165). As I have said elsewhere,

> When I was a young man, I only had a couple of decades of my own life: everything was new and exciting and many of the old ideas given to me by my elders had to be rejected: this was by now the 1968 generation of baby boomers after all. But now I have at least six decades to incorporate and so whilst I am still very excited by the new, I can also sense clearly just how the very new so soon becomes the very old. When I started my research, I was active in the (soon and now long defunct) Gay Liberation Front; these were

probably the pivotal moments of my life. Gagnon and Simon's *Sexual Conduct* was published in 1973, and Foucault's *History of Sexuality* in 1976. During my research there developed the famous feminist "sex wars" – linked to the Barnard Conference and Carole Vance's volume *Pleasure and Danger*. In the late 1970s, I wrote about the paedophile panics of the time: a battle which has proceeded unabated. And after my research ended, in 1981, AIDS came to thwart, haunt us, and change sexual meaning forever. Queer theory did not arrive till a full decade later – at roughly the same time as computers became widespread (but long before the Internet) …

All of this is now a generation or three away from me, but it does not die. It lives on both in me and those of my generation in the present moment. We cannot unlive this and we are the carriers of history. And now in 2014 [the year in which I was writing this] the world I live in is very different indeed from the world of my research. New generations are possibly surprised when they read Jeffrey Weeks's book *The World We Have Won* (2008), where he traces the history of gay change and liberation in England over his life, which roughly parallels mine, and sees profound changes that have transformed sexual possibilities. Indeed, we have both witnessed this change over the short span of sixty years of our lives. The sexual world has changed massively over the past half century and each generation brings different understandings to this complicated whole. (2015b, 339)

I have just charted my own generational life over the past sixty years through a range of epiphanic sexual confessional stories that have engaged and preoccupied me. I suspect my interest in all this peaked in my book *Telling Sexual Stories*, published in 1995 – a generation ago but written between 1985 and 1993 and hence approaching two generations ago. Whatever I had to say in that moment, the world has surely moved on. The current generation brings three new issues (at least) to this past construction: digitalism, globalization, and a neoliberalism linked to extreme inequalities, endless commoditization, and a continuing individualism. They were just starting as ideas really in the early 1990s. Now they are part of the air we breathe. Nobody can really write or think about sexualities these days without taking such key ideas very seriously.

And so too we start to see a growing awareness of what has been called "media generations" (Bolin 2017). There is a whole project here: pausing and reflecting on the many visual issues of the past that move as ghosts today, on the "new visual sexual world" that Madonna and Michael Jackson created when MTV first appeared in 1981, or the rise of queer bookshops and film festivals in the 1970s, the New

Queer Cinema in 1991, the first digital porn, on and so forth. But let me linger on one of these truly critical moments: the time of AIDS. I was part of the AIDS generation that started around 1981. If this book were being assembled in the 1980s, it would most certainly have been packed with many accounts of AIDS, sickness, and dying self-stories and the rise of the visual as a political act. For this was the time of a silence, a noise, and a growing visibility. In that era, AIDS swamped all sexual debate and created its own visual of the Person With AIDS (PWA). As HIV became the central feature of gay life, reorganizing all in its wake, so a new visual imagery came into being – from films to photos to protest and activism. Dwelling in a culture of ubiquitous death and dying, grief and mourning, it regenerated the by-then fading activisms of the 1970s. As the activists started to become highly professionalized (through new organizations and AIDS work as well as academic work), they worked, ironically, in closer and closer relationships with governments and the state. International links became more and more prominent as international conferences were held and the United Nations became engaged through the auspices of UNAIDS. And it all became much more visual – a visual activism was being brought into prominence: the generation of Act Up. Radical cultural writings, such as that of art critic Douglas Crimp, argued for cultural practices actively participating in the struggle against AIDS (1987). Yet thirty years on, this cultural awareness has almost gone completely missing: it has once again become a silence.

Well-established personally and academically in my own gay life by the 1980s, I was shaken by AIDS. It changed the way I moved about in the gay world, and it generated grief as friends died. As part of the AIDS generation, I look back with anger at the ways in which such a major historical moment of gay history has (within a quarter of a century) largely been obliterated. Not only did that time bring dying, disease, and pain: it also was a major force for enormous energetic activism. It helped open up queer cultural critique. It also brought fear that this might indeed be the very end of the homosexual – the death of the gays. And while it is marvellous that gay people did indeed bounce back, it would be very sad if this past got lost. And yet it does seem that a new generation has managed to construct a history that works to obliterate this very past. As Castiglia and Reed remark in their recent study of queer memory, "The years following the onset of the AIDS epidemic witnessed a discursive operation that instigates a cultural forgetting of the 1960s and 1970s, installing instead a cleaned-up memory that reconstitutes sanctioned identity out of historical violence" (2012, 40).

And so we are starting here a new journey of trying to grasp *the narrative memories of generations, the visual generations,* the *media generations*. To repeat, all sexualities – and their images – dangle from an age perspective. We are all situated in age standpoints.[3] We need to take our stories and our images and make sense of them developmentally (with diachronic time) and simultaneously (with synchronic time). *Diachronic or chronological sexualities* understand generations as always flowing through age cohorts. We might think about them through an escalator imagery: people come and go clustered together on different starting steps, even as differing groups follow on new steps behind. We ask how different "different visual generations" and sexual generations move into different identifiable if inchoate life stages, developmental stages, life histories, and age cohorts. We can trace them simply through, say, the 1930s, the 1960s, the 1980s, and on to the new … Usually this a linear model, but it can be a cyclical or even regressive one. It often flags "progress" (linear-progressive time). By contrast, *synchronic sexualities* suggest much more complex and challenging ideas of time, asking how we live in "simultaneous time" where "visual moments" of the past might mingle with the visual moments of now, with issues of memories and memorializing," "ghosts," "imagined utopias and dystopias," "hope," and "futures." This view is exemplified by Avery Gordon's claim that "to study social life one must confront the ghostly aspects of it" ([1997] 2008, 7). It suggests a multiplicity matrix helix of flux, flowing chaos, and the rhizomes of repressed life. Here we have the messy sexual narratives, memories, embodiments, identities, silences, and conflicts of different generations living simultaneously together. Ultimately, we have to ask how the different visual and sexual pasts, presents, and futures dwell in the fragile ever-changing moment. A key question now becomes: How do the sexual stories and visual imageries of the past continuously dwell in the sexual present? And how might the contradictions and complexities arising from age differences in this history stop us seeing reality too simply while helping aid our understandings of what is going on? Any of our stories takes on a denser form once it is placed within a generational standpoint.

And So the Story Never Ends

In this foreword I have glanced backwards a little, taking myself as the merest, tiniest of blips in the grand historical flows of generational confessional narratives and using my story as a basis for reflecting on some the complexities of the storytelling this book raises. For within this book you will find a multitude of exciting, emerging signs of new generational communities at work as authors tell their representational tales of desire, pornography, feminism, race, sex work, rent boys, feminism, coming out, queer, transgender, and the rest. The ghosts of some of these stories were alive and fighting in the 1970s (indeed, I researched rent boys and "coming out" in the 1960s, trans in the '70s), but here they inevitably assume new forms, shapes, politics. Some texts are scrutinized from a range of different generations and across cultures. Older ones, like Derek Jarman's *Blue* and Akihiko Shiota's *Moonlight Whispers* from the '90s, mingle with many from today. But we can also find new generational shapes that would have been very hard to anticipate in the '60s and '70s: just how could we have anticipated the new generational "digital sexualities" or the new "mediality" as a mode of coming out? Many striking new things are happening. Film, media, and digital studies hardly existed for the generations of sixty years ago: now they are omnipresent with their own growing (and often clichéd) languages and texts. With journals like *Porn Studies* and others, we might even say the days of confessional sexual narratives have become routine and institutionalized. This new world highlights the embodiment of the erotic visual and its routine presence as part of the everyday.

And so here and now we have this wonderful trail-blazing collection to lay down markers and herald what the editors suggest may well be a Third Sexual Revolution. The invitation of *I Confess*, is to look and see a new generation bringing new stories and new hopes for a new and better world.

NOTES

1 In August 2017, to celebrate the fiftieth anniversary of the Sexual Offences Act, 1967, the BBC produced an intriguing radio play, *Victim*, by Sarah Wooley, about the making of this film.
2 I have more recently seen a new production in London, and it has stood the test of time. I now think it is a really good and timely play!
3 I discuss the idea of generational sexualities in Plummer 2010.

REFERENCES

Bolin, Göran. 2017. *Media Generations: Experience, Identity and Mediatised Social Change*. Abingdon: Routledge.
Castiglia, Christopher, and Christopher Reed. 2012. *If Memory Serves: Gay Men, AIDS, and the Promise of the Queer Past*. Minneapolis: University of Minnesota Press.
Crimp, Douglas. 1987. "AIDS: Cultural Analysis/Cultural Activism." Special issue, *October* 43 (Winter): 3–16.
– 2002. *Melancholia and Moralism: Essays on AIDS and Politics*. Cambridge: MIT Press.
Gever, Martha, John Greyson, and Pratibha Parmar, eds. 1993. *Queer Looks: Perspectives on Lesbian and Gay Film and Video*. London: Routledge.

Gordon, Avery. [1997] 2008. *Ghostly Matters: Haunting and the Sociological Imagination.* 2nd ed. Minneapolis: University of Minnesota Press.

Plummer, Ken. 1975. *Sexual Stigma: An Interactionist Account.* London: Routledge.

– ed. 1981. *The Making of the Modern Homosexual.* London: Hutchinson.

– 1995. *Telling Sexual Stories: Power, Change and Social Worlds.* London: Routledge.

– 2001. *Documents of Life: An Invitation to Critical Humanism.* 2nd ed. London: Sage.

– 2003. "Queers, Bodies and Postmodern Sexualities." *Qualitative Sociology* 26, no. 4 (Winter): 515–30.

– 2008. "Outsiders, Deviants and Countercultures: Subterranean Tribes and Queer Imaginations." In *1968 in Retrospect: Amnesia, Alterity*, edited by Gurminder Bhambra and Ipek Demir. London: Palgrave.

– 2009. "On Narrative Pluralism." In *The Story of Sexual Identity: Narrative Perspectives on the Gay and Lesbian Life Course*, edited by Phillip L. Hammack and Bertram J. Cohler, vii–xiv. New York: Oxford University Press.

– 2010. "Generational Sexualities, Subterranean Traditions, and the Hauntings of the Sexual World: Some Preliminary Remarks." *Symbolic Interaction* 33, no. 2: 163–91.

– 2011a. "Critical Humanism and Queer Theory: Living with the Tensions." In *The Sage Handbook of Qualitative Research*, 4th ed., edited by Norman Denzin and Yvonna Lincoln, 195–207. London: Sage

– 2011b. "Postscript 2011: "Moving On." In Denzin and Lincoln, *The Sage Handbook of Qualitative Research*, 208–11.

– 2012. "My Multiple Sick Bodies: Symbolic Interaction, Auto/Ethnography and the Sick Body." In *Routledge Handbook of the Body*, edited by Bryan S. Turner, 75–93. London: Routledge.

– 2015a. *Cosmopolitan Sexualities: Hope and the Humanist Imagination.* Cambridge: Polity Press.

– 2015b. "Afterword: Liberating Generations: Continuities And Change in The Radical Queer Western Era." In *Ashgate Companion to Lesbian and Gay Activism*, edited by David Paternotte and Manon Tremblay, 339–55. Farnham: Ashgate.

Taylor, Chloe. 2010. *The Culture of Confession from Augustine to Foucault: A Genealogy of the Confessing Animal.* London: Routledge.

Van Kerkoff, M., et al. 1989. *Homosexuality, Which Homosexuality?* London: Gay Men's Press.

I Confess!

Introduction

THOMAS WAUGH AND BRANDON ARROYO

Sexual Revolutions

We confess! We stole our title for our book on confessionality within the Third Sexual Revolution from a wonderful film made here in Quebec in 1953 and from its director, Alfred Hitchcock, who in turn had stolen it from the Catholic sacrament. As *I Confess*'s tormented priest who will not betray the secret of the confessional, Hitchcock cast the era's greatest male star. Queer Montgomery Clift did not have to act very hard to play tormented and, as biographers have repeatedly revealed, would probably have benefited from a few confessionals of his own. It was the era of what we can now safely call the Second Sexual Revolution – following the *First* Sexual Revolution of the post–World War I decades, the era of women's suffrage, flappers, Prohibition, and Mae West ("When ev'ry night the set that's smart is in- / truding in nudist parties in / studios, / anything goes," as Cole Porter put it in 1934). *I Confess* came out the same year as the second Kinsey report, *Sexual Behavior in the Human Female* (five years after the even more scandalous volume based on the confessions of human males), and with unbelievable felicitousness, the same year as the first issue of *Playboy*. Both confession and sexual revolution were in the air.

Quebec's most prestigious theatrical and film director, Robert Lepage, also borrowed Hitchcock's film, not only for his title but also as the setting for his great first feature *Le Confessionnal* (The Confessional) in 1995 (figs. 0.1 and 0.2). This retro potboiler offered its own torments, narrating confessions of teenage pregnancy, suicide, lies, betrayal, fraternal melodrama, and false genealogies. And 1995 was a watershed year in other ways too: it was the year the Arroyo family subscribed to America Online and, looking back, it was the dawn of the popular internet age, when the development of the internet reached its full commercialization in the United States. This is the moment from which the cataclysmic

0.1 Above
Montgomery Clift embodying the Second Sexual Revolution. Poster for *I Confess*, dir. Alfred Hitchcock, 1953.

0.2 Right
The torments of a retro potboiler in a watershed year. Poster for *Le Confessionnal*, dir. Robert Lepage, 1995.

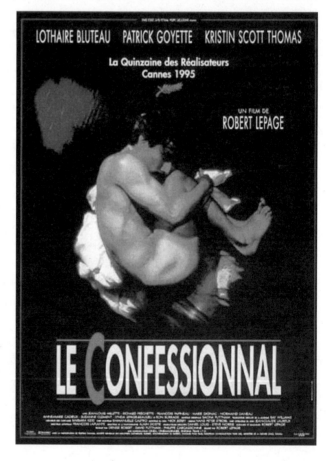

cultural and social shifts we are documenting and interpreting in this book, the Third Sexual Revolution, crystallized in the acts and rituals of confession that are the staple of our twenty-first-century lives, can be conveniently dated.

Hugh Hefner died in September 2017 as we were assembling this book, an ironic and symbolic reminder of the continuities and ruptures over the decades that our thirty-two or so authors are pondering here. Even more on our minds since Hefner's passing, however, are the proliferating sexual-harassment scandals rocking both West and East: behaviours of distinctly carnal bodies swept up into the most ethereal corners of the virtual universe, concretized by confessional voices and testimonials in dozens of social media, by both alleged perpetrators and victims. These upheavals, and all the alarming contradictions and disturbing questions they raise, confirmed to us the timeliness and urgent pertinence of our anthology about constructions of the self within the *Third* Sexual Revolution, the cataclysmic paradigm shift sparked by the introduction of the internet a quarter century or so ago. The shift's ominous implications of surveillance and control and its utopian glimmers of community and liberation were both immediately palpable. As well, 1995 was the year of publication of contributor Ken Plummer's epochal book *Telling Sexual Stories: Power, Change and Social Worlds*, which did not touch on the internet but whose diagnostic power has maintained itself over several decades despite the technological revolution that enabled this Third Sexual Revolution.

Histories

But enough felicitous chronological synchronicity. It is now time to flesh out the historical context in which we are producing this book. We are of course speaking first of the immediate political environment in which a tweeting American presidency imposes its paranoia and polarization, nuclear escalation, and ecocide over our social world, in which increasing numbers of our friends are pharma-harnessed to PrEP and hormones and living with heightened threats of sero-criminalization, in which sex panic, shame, juventophobia, and censorship have dictated a situation in which two of our contributors have opted for anonymity and another has withdrawn. We return to this situation a bit later.

We are speaking also in more general terms of a cultural moment where confessionality symptomatizes larger and more ominous politico-cultural tendencies – as well as the utopian glimmers that many of our authors insist on. Confession, by which we mean to include the proliferating moving-image practices of self-referencing, first-person and/or autobiographical stories, testimonies, or performances, is the thread between the Second and Third Sexual Revolutions that demands this attention. And since Michel Foucault makes clear that sex is the "privileged theme of confession," there is no doubt that our inquiry's starting point must be sexuality, which we push beyond queer-straight binaries towards an inclusive, diverse, and far-reaching spectrum of identities, desires, and related representational practices.

The transformational energy of the Second Sexual Revolution introduced us to newly recognized voices and practices of long-silenced sexual, gender, and racial minorities. These voices soon transformed cinema, television, and the emerging moving-image art scene. They turned scattered individuals on the fringes of society into recognizable communities and a new cultural force. During the 1980s, however, with the loss of many of those voices to the AIDS crisis, and the ideological destruction of collective empowerment in favour of individual accomplishment during the Reagan-Thatcher-Mulroney regimes, one might have thought that the revolution would slow down. But in fact the ever-expanding pornography industry, in dialogical relation with the inextinguishable and continuous sex/porn wars and women's growing sexual self-enfranchisement, kept alive confessional voices that maintained the revolution's critical mass.

The digital revolution and the confessionalization of culture, launched in earnest in the 1990s, sparked new energies and aftershocks, triggering its own Third Sexual Revolution, leading to galactic techno-cultural economies of sexual representation that ancestors and pioneers – not only Kinsey and Hefner but also Fred Halsted and Barbara Hammer – had never dreamed of. These twenty-first-century sexual-cultural economies clearly corroborate and extend Foucault's prophetic probings into the interwoven operations of confession, desire, identity, truth, and power, what one of our authors has called the "first person industrial complex" (chapter 10) and another "confession porn" (chapter 9).

Confession is the primary modality of the internet. It is the force that maintained its impetus through the conversion from analog to digital, and it remains at the centre of people's interactions within online culture. We go there to confess, and to hear others confess. Comment boards, amateur pornography, Snaps, YouTube videos, and all social media – not to mention the gamut of the digital arts – are all fuelled by confession. This extraordinary, paradigm-shifting proliferation of first-person voices and imagery penetrates all moving-image formats in both high and low culture, inflected by subaltern and identity political movements as well as hegemonic backlashes, deploying both traditional and new media and platforms. *I Con-*

fess!'s aim is to give the confessional culture of the Third Sexual Revolution complex and interdisciplinary focus, both historical and critical, from its inception in vestigial analog forms to its most contemporary incarnation.

Perhaps the most fascinating aspect of millennial confessionality is the way it exists within the *in-between* spaces and across inherited boundaries of culture and ideology. The Third Sexual Revolution's culture of confession presides over what Brian Massumi has termed a post-ideological era (1995, 104), where the social divisions that we thought were created by race or sexuality or class actually disguise the mechanisms of neoliberal capitalism. Confession has become the last space for individual self-actualization, the enduring fantasy where we can imagine that we exist outside of the neoliberal ethos. For example, pornworld confessionality offers new ethnographies of pornography performers and sex workers, extending to soft-core, G-rated social platforms like Facebook, Instagram, and YouTube and expressing multiple sides of the self, private and public – affective labour that is as much about relationality as profit. Confessionality also creates a political environment where the contradictions are compellingly rife: first-person discourses of sexual diversity mask currents of sexual conformity, getting mired in sexual political correctness, advocating assimilation, instilling fear, and confirming racial and gender stereotypes. Such contradictions and panics within popular culture stretch across the entire landscape of moving-image culture from pornography sites (chapters 14, 15, 19) to Grindr (chapter 29) to the art house (chapters 8, 14, 16, 19, 20, 22, 25) to the rock concert (chapter 6) and the art gallery (chapters 1, 25, 26, 28). We believe that these complex issues need to be addressed head on and situated within their complex historical context.

A thirty-four-year disparity in the ages of *I Confess!*'s two editors has turned out to be an asset – we hope – in producing a collection of essays looking historically both back and forward. Born in the year of the first Kinsey report, Waugh lived through the Second Sexual Revolution, which happened even in rural Ontario, saw *Deep Throat* in its first run in Times Square, and marched in the third or fourth edition of what was then called the Christopher Street Liberation Day Parade as a graduate student in the early 1970s. Arroyo, born in New York City the year of the Barnard Conference on Sexuality, the 1982 pro-sex feminist upheaval that challenged the patriarchal logjam of the Second Sexual Revolution and arguably ushered in symbolically its delayed *bad girl* tsunami, is a millennial who never turns off his devices, emerged into adulthood as digital gay chatrooms were the new normal, and produced a doctoral dissertation full of the "I" word.

We confess: we also have a pedagogical relationship, of which creating this collection has truly brought out the reciprocal dimensions (Waugh has been introduced to Chris Crocker, Arroyo to the politicized version of feminist "bad girls," a term that had formally been reserved to describe certain females whom Arroyo went to Catholic school with in his youth). More concretely, our intergenerational, transnational dynamic, and other dynamics of difference as gay men (WASP Bach and Pasolini fan versus Nuyorican, Tweeting Kanye West fan), have enabled our networking and recruitment of the exciting multigenerational and multicultural roster you are about to explore. The oldest is seventysomething, youngest is twentysomething, and these voices come to us everywhere from Delhi to Salt Lake City.

Theories: "I Have Nothing to Admit"

Arroyo has never really understood all the hype that much of western society projects onto the idea and practice of *coming out of the closet* to another person. Perhaps this is due to his own happenstantial and inconsequential experience of *coming out* to his mother. (In contrast, Waugh's involved a dramatic snail-mail epistle in 1976 and a subsequent shift of familial tectonic plates [Waugh 2015].) Mrs Arroyo simply asked her sixteen-year-old son if his best male friend was his boyfriend. He told her that he was not, because "he's straight." Like many parents, she was not so much cluelessly trying to find out if Arroyo was gay but was merely waiting for him to confirm her suspicions. This "foundational" confessional practice of *coming out* that is situated as the primary linchpin confirming an alliance with a gay identity was for Arroyo more ordinary than revolutionary.

So, while mainstream media and popular gay-rights groups have been working for half a century or more to situate this one-on-one confessional declaration as an essential confirmation of a pop "Born This Way" ethos, this rhetoric ignores the intense affective interactions that people have with media objects long before *coming out* to another human being. The relationships that we foster with and through media texts and platforms are often a part of our first solo sexual experiments; they help to facilitate our first in-person sexual encounters, work as outlets for our sexual desires, and foster opportunities for us to confess aspects of ourselves to ourselves and to other people – including strangers. If we are to take a holistic approach to confession, it is essential that as scholars we not be held captive by the traditional notions of confession prioritizing face-to-face contact with another human, which de-emphasizes the wide range of confessional approaches that are continually enacted through various media platforms.

Arroyo's generation is perhaps the last that does not take these types of sexualized confessional interactions with media forms for granted. He is of a generation that came of age in an awkward transitional period where memories before the popular internet age are sometimes faint and sometimes vivid, and the emergence of the internet coincided with an immediate pubescent hormonal tumult. He remembers his family excitedly testing out their first AOL CD-ROM, delivered in the (snail) mail – their gateway to the internet in 1995. At thirteen, he could not have imagined then just how profound an impact this technology would have on him and his family dynamic. The same AOL chatrooms where his father talked with other sports fans would later on in the evenings transform into the chatrooms where he would have his first conversations with other gay people. He never needed to confess to these anonymous usernames that he was gay; it was a matter of fact. Legitimizing the worthiness of this machine based on its ability to facilitate his confessions elevated its status in his mind as an important new addition to the family – like a new pet. Ensuring time with the computer away from the rest of the family was an essential priority, because he wanted not only to ensure time for emotional confession through typing but also to engage in a type of sexual confession through watching pornography. Confession – at its core – is an admission, and being able to admit to one's own sexual pleasures by enjoying it being reflected in pornography is its own type of self-admission – a confession. These experiences with pornography before *coming out* are surely part of what made Arroyo's subsequent declaration to his mother so anticlimactic. How could it match up to his first encounters with pornography on the web? He still remembers watching the erotic loop of two "perfect" Bel Ami boys making love to each other. The libidinal intensity of this moment for him represents a lingering memory lasting longer than most of his own face-to-face confessions. In comparison, his confession to his mother was much less visceral. For Waugh, the equivalent libidinal intensity was thumbing through the glossy-paper *Young Physique* magazine in the mid-1960s!

Part of what keeps this experience so alive for Arroyo is that the interactive nature of the internet triggers a more immediate recognition of how one's sexual desires are part of a global circulation of affects shared, experienced, and indulged via transnational digital platforms. The dominant terminology at the time – *Amer*ica Online, the *World* Wide Web – testify to the affective geography embedded within the framework of the internet. Of course, this idea of global connectedness via technology did not begin with the internet. Discourses around the telegraph, telephone, radio, television, and home video, ad infinitum, all preceded what was to come with the internet. Even after many pornographic experiences with the internet, another of Arroyo's lingering memories is staying up past midnight on an October night in 2000 just so he could listen to (and record on audio tape!) the premiere of Radiohead's third album *Kid-A*, on New York City's 92.3 K-Rock station. Sharing a collective moment of musical bliss with fellow New Yorkers from the privacy of his bedroom was an experience of non-internet connectedness. What connects this primal scene with Radiohead to pornographic experiences is an active awareness in the indulgence of pleasure along with masses of people connected by technology. What in the past would have been isolated experiences fostered by a networked community (e.g., a bootleg music tape, or *Young Physique* circulated among a brown-paper-bag brigade) now incorporates simultaneity as part of the erotic aspects of the internet. It is this drive towards immediacy and simultaneity within digital networks that moves us away from fetishizing the precious material collections of analog archivists and instead encourages us to indulge in the erotics of floating through a digitized morass.[1] This shift in erotic sensibilities prompted by the expanded connectivity of the internet realizes Gilbert Simondon's assertion that "the opposition drawn between culture and technics, between man and machine, is false and has no foundation" (2017, 16). Simondon's declaration is literalized in the ergonomics of masturbating in front of a computer. It takes little effort to situate a three-pound screen connected to a massive hard drive as the phallic representation of aroused genitals. The proximity of the two leave little room for interpretation. Being so physically and affectively invested in this pornographic moment mirrors what Arthur Kroker situates as Gilles Deleuze and Félix Guattari's own "epochal confession for the age of hyper-modern: the confessional statement of 'bodies without organs'" (1992, 108).

Ultimately, when confession is situated as a practice working to reveal the "true" interiority of a subject, it presupposes that discourse can function to effectively narrow and control our understanding of a subjectivity. However, for Deleuze and Guattari, such a concept merely describes the "'black hole' of dead subjectivity" (Kroker 1992, 110). For them, this idea is a dead end. The intention behind "bodies without organs" is precisely to de-emphasize these types of stagnant notions of subjectivity centred around interiority, and to argue instead that the body is in tune with an external realm of social intensities. Deleuze expands on this idea when he explains that "there is nothing to explain, nothing to understand, nothing to interpret. It can be compared to an electrical connection. A body without organs" (1977, 114). This is how we can come to understand confession as something that exists outside of our body and as a fully incorporated part of wider social affects. After all, this must be the case if the confessional act of *coming out* has attained such prominence in the first place. *Coming out* does not reveal anything revelatory about an individual; confessions merely work to swallow one's subjectivity into a wider gay narrative. It is the community, not the individual, that is reinforced by *coming out*. In this era of over-exposure and hyper-confession, we are seemingly reaching a point of exhaustion regarding the utility of confession. (See chapters 5, 6, and 23 for complementary takes on types of *coming out*.) Confession is practically coming out of our pores! Even before our current era, one can feel Deleuze expressing impatience with the state of confession in his own time: "As for the bunch of you, you are still busy provoking, publishing, making up questionnaires, forcing public confession ('admit, admit …'). Why should we? What I anticipate is just the opposite: an age of clandestine-ness. Half voluntary and half obligatory, which will shelter the new born desire, notably in politics … Thus I have nothing to 'admit'" (1977, 115).

This liberating declaration of having "nothing to admit" speaks to the contradictory fait accompli of confessional practice today – a ubiquitous part of our modern media aesthetic that has all too often been ignored. "I have nothing to admit" can be understood as *I Confess!*'s figurative slogan working to transition our mindset from a Foucauldian understanding of a medieval/Victorian notion of confession ordained by disciplining institutional powers like the church, the medical field, and the law to a broader understanding of confession as an intuitive part of a control society valorizing technological liberation – while those same technologies actively work to limit radical possibility. Situating confession within this control framework is crucial to understanding the dynamic power of confession to guide us into this digital-networked period where we situate the Third Sexual Revolution. To imagine that our understanding of confession can remain stagnant within this transitional moment is incongruent with progress. An affective conception of confession not only helps us to account for the wide variety of media platforms that our authors attempt to cover in this book but also helps us remain aware of the multitude of ideologies intersecting within these multi-media formations. In an essential passage, Massumi makes clear that "affect hold[s] a key to rethinking postmodern power after ideology. For although ideology is still very much with us, often in the most virulent of forms, it is no longer encompassing. It no longer defines the global mode of functioning power. It is now one mode of power in a larger field that is not defined, overall, by ideology" (1995, 104). Chapters from Jacob Evoy, Andie Shabbar, Ela Przybylo and Veronika Novoselova, Connor Steele, Shaka McGlotten, Susanna Paasonen, Stephen Charbonneau, and Tom Roach, as well as Waugh and Arroyo, actively

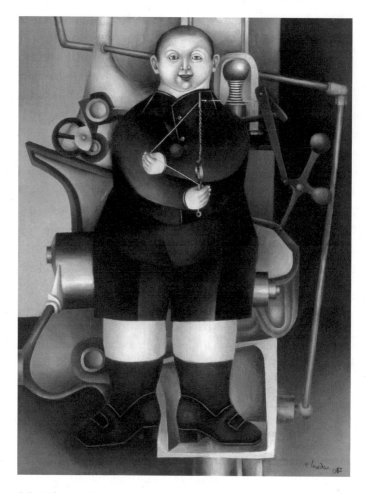

0.3 A "boy without sex" blending seamlessly into his technological environment: *Boy with Machine*, oil on canvas, Richard Lindner, 1954. Estate of Richard Lindner via Artists Rights Society (ARS), New York. https://www.arsny.com/. Courtesy Thomas Ammann Fine Art AG, Zurich.

engage with this theoretical turn of confession as it is approached through a variety of media platforms, and wrestle with the confluence of ideologies at play within their textual makeup and social assemblage.

When writing about Richard Lindner's painting *Boy with Machine* (fig. 0.3), Deleuze and Guattari describe the boy in the foreground as an "enormous undifferentiated object" with "no tongue. No teeth. No larynx. No esophagus. No belly. No anus ... the full body without organs" (1983, 7–8). Kroker takes the next logical step and declares the figure "a boy without sex" (1992, 104). These characterizations should not be understood as attempts to dismiss humanity, but instead as allegories illustrating how desires that we think of as being inherent to our physical makeup are actually part of a wider circulation of affects contributing to Deleuze and Guattari's concept of "desiring-machines." Desiring-machines connote the ideological, social, or technological assemblage in which desires circulate. And while the boy in this painting can be understood as being in a state of affective exchange with the technological world around him – thanks to his inhuman characteristics and his blending into the mechanical background – the one aspect that remains unaccounted for in this image is his voice. This character's audible absence helps us to recognize that the spoken voice in contemporary media is what carries confession into the Third Sexual Revolution.

In our contemporary mediascape, we have transitioned from *Boy with Machine* to what we could call *boy in machine*. The ubiquitous outline of a screen framing a confessional voice is a quality embodied as a foundational aspect of YouTube content – a phenomenon addressed in greater detail in this collection by Silke Jandl. Making the voice a crucial part of *boy in machine* would account for the humanity of the subject while simultaneously acknowledging the technological platform through which it is delivered. The reason *Boy with Machine* is an ideal example of a "body without organs" is due to its inability to talk back. This collection conversely dares to take on the talking subject, and all the contradictions that arise from such subjects. Because no matter how much writers in this collection might want to detail the subversive aspects of the confessions they are analyzing, dealing with subjects that can talk back will always frustratingly reflect back to us the limited range of possibilities and discourses available within our neoliberal social structure.

Perhaps most importantly for our purposes, we account for – and prioritize – the sex within "a boy without sex." Kroker surely was not dismissing copulation (he most likely intended "without sex" to mean without genitals) but rather meant "a boy without sex" as a provocation to explain how both affect and a "body without organs" are intriguingly caught in between the sexual self and its delivery through a wide range of media platforms. As Kroker explains it: "The social machinery of desiring-production, having completed its consummatory feast, finally speaks ... This is the confession of all the humanoids, of beings half-flesh/half-metal, who, speaking from *within* the closed, liquid textuality of technology, ruminate longingly, and romantically, on a past in their telematic future" (1992, 108, original emphasis).

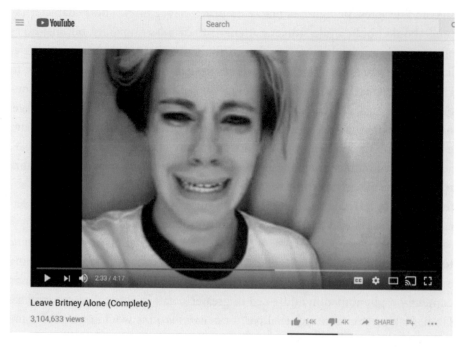

0.4 Chris Crocker becoming the *boy in machine* in his viral video "Leave Britney Alone," YouTube, 2007.

One subject that fits well into this mould of *boy in machine* is the viral YouTube sensation Chris Crocker. Crocker came to the plugged-in world's attention in 2007 after he took to YouTube to react against the negative attention that social and mainstream media heaped upon Britney Spears after her lacklustre MTV Video Music Awards performance that night. The anger he expressed as a fan of Spears toward those criticizing her helped to dissolve the line between a fan and a celebrity. Crocker became a celebrity in his own right when this video, titled "Leave Britney Alone," accumulated eleven million views in just two weeks. The virality of the video took Cocker's yelling, crying, and pleading out of context and turned his image into a type of floating signifier that would be circulated, mocked, and parodied throughout the mediascape. The over-exposure of indexical markers like tears led to the questioning of their genuineness. His subsequent forays into talk-show guest, singer, documentary subject, and pornographic performer exemplify the ways in which a *boy in machine*'s "half flesh/half-metal" subjectivity is continually/productively rendered as a trans individual in flux.

I Confess! lands squarely at the intersection where *boy in machine* resides.

Our Book

Few studies keep up with the ways in which moving-image visual culture and the internet have moved beyond the traditional academic cloisters and boundaries of cultural analysis (e.g., boundaries of sexual identities, nation and geo-political region, gender, class, pre/post-AIDS). We are proud to capture within the same analytic scrutiny the utter promiscuity of the net's sexual revolution, both licit and illicit, analog and digital, documentary and fiction, queer and straight, North and South, subversive and hegemonic, text and flow, trauma and *jouissance*, panopticon and marketplace, surveillance and empowerment, narcissism and community, art-cinema artifacts and ephemeral series/clusters/flows, traditional one-way-delivery packages and interactive encounters. We are equally proud of our international assemblage of scholars, both emerging and established, and their eclectic and interdisciplinary mix of methodologies – often within the same chapter! By and large, however, most of our authors privilege textual analysis – as applied, of course, to the always-evolving platforms of the sexual mediascape – rigorously anchored both theoretically and materially/historically (and confessionally where appropriate; several of our chapters are themselves engaging first-person presentations). *I Confess!*'s debt to cultural studies and performance studies as well as traditions of cinema and media studies goes without saying, as do its benefits from recent advances in queer, gender, sexuality, and affect studies. We're happy, though, that our authors are sometimes open to cross-pollinations from the social sciences, and in one case, *legal studies* (chapter 1). Together they offer a mix of scale and voice and language, from short personal pieces, frankly confessional, to those of greater scholarly and theoretical ambition, confronting four-letter words and four-syllable words, Lady Gaga and Gilles Deleuze. We are happy with this vivid reminder that twenty-first-century scholarship in the humanities, social sciences, and fine arts is also transformed by the animus of confession. Whether these assets ensure a crossover audience, the watchword of our and all publishing pitches, is up to you, dear reader: please share with your next Grindr hookup or pizza-delivery girl, or inquisitive mother.

As the table of contents makes clear, we divide our twenty-nine chapters (including this introduction), all original essays, in homage to Foucault, between *scientia sexualis* and *ars erotica*, very roughly separating discourses of knowledge, sobriety, and empiricism from those of aesthetics, affect, and desire. Under "Scientia Sexualis," we have the sections "Activism" and "Author, Subject, and Audience," approximating a dialectic of relationality and pragmatism. Under "Ars

Erotica," we have "Pornographies," "Documentaries," and "Transmedia," loosely assembling histories of arousal, sexual didacticism, and technological flux and innovation, respectively. This said, however, we must emphasize that these sections are not ironclad; they flow into each other, and voices from one section echo or anticipate and contradict those from another.

The historical scope of *I Confess!* is approximately the past quarter-century (early 1990s to 2018), as we have said. This time period covers the turn of the popular internet age, so even those essays addressing localized or non-digital moving image culture in traditional platforms and venues – from the film festival to the art gallery – will situate their object in relation to the ineradicable onslaught or presence of the net. Although we focus on Euro-American culture and the Global North, inflected, as in Foucault, by the heritage of Judaeo-Christian confessionality and *scientia sexualis*, the volume encompasses, at least as control studies, other cultural contexts, notably South Asian and East Asian (chapters 8, 26, and 27). While the thriving new journal *Porn Studies* has exemplified the entrenchment of internet studies and sexuality within academia, our book's originality lies in the way we bridge pornography and the spectrum of "licit" sexual discourses, and in the way we bridge "queer" and the entire undifferentiated spectrum of twenty-first-century human sexualities. (More than half of our chapters have fallen into place as queer or queer-ish.) That's not to mention the multitude of mediascapes these discourses travel through.

We are proud to join the chorus of other excellent anthologies and monographs from the past decade that ponder the current landscape or its histories, echoing them in our own way in dissecting the new digital sexual culture and its political context. In chronological order, we are thinking especially of several rich collections: Linda Williams's *Porn Studies* (2004), Brinda Bose and Subhabrata Bhattacharyya's *The Phobic and the Erotic: The Politics of Sexualities in Contemporary India* (2007), Thomas Hubbard and Beert Verstraete's *Censoring Sex Research: The Debate over Male Intergenerational Relations* (2013), Tim Dean, Steven Ruszczycky, and David Squires's *Porn Archives* (2014), and David Halperin and Trevor Hoppe's *The War on Sex* (2017). We are also thinking of germinal monographs including Katrien Jacobs's *Netporn: DIY Web Culture and Sexual Politics* (2007), Tim Dean's *Unlimited Intimacy: Reflections on the Subculture of Barebacking* (2008), Linda Williams's *Screening Sex* (2008), Feona Attwood's *porn.com: Making Sense of Online Pornography* (2009), Sharif Mowlabocus's *Gaydar Culture: Gay Men, Technology and Embodiment in the Digital Age* (2010), Susanna Paasonen's *Carnal Resonance: Affect and Online Pornography* (2011), Noah Tsika's *Pink 2.0: Encoding*

Queer Cinema on the Internet (2016), and John Mercer's *Gay Pornography: Representations of Sexuality and Masculinity* (2017). We insist on the unconventional strategy of praising and listing "the competition" in this way because they have inspired us in the challenging job of gathering together this book over five years of pleasure, stimulation, and headaches. We are also indebted to the roster of brave and inventive artist-confessers evoked and invoked by our authors, from (the necessarily) anonymous to Lars von Trier, from Virginie Despentes to Isaac Leung, from Nina Hartley to Colby Keller.

The Politics of Confession

All books are political, ours included, and most scholarly anthologies of any merit bear the scars of political struggle, whether knowingly or non-, visibly or invisibly. We would be remiss in not making transparent the scars that have accumulated on the skin of this book on its long path to production, since we believe they are inextricable from its potential impact, and its mandate to confront sexual confessionality in the arts and media, historically and theoretically, over the past generation.

It is a cliché of acknowledgments in scholarly books for authors to thank peer-review readers for their helpful comments, and we thank our three readers sincerely and enthusiastically for their hard work and insightful feedback on our very large volume, and, in the case of two of the readers, for their gratifying and heartwarming support for our risk-taking venture. (One graciously came out to us, John Mercer of the Birmingham City University, no doubt in keeping with our confessional theme.) Another reader opposed the publication of our book unless we removed our two excellent anonymous chapters, both not coincidentally dealing with adolescent sexuality and intergenerational desire: respectively, chapter 10, "Confessions: Watching the Masturbating Boy (Excerpts)," and chapter 23, "Looking, Stroking, and Speaking: A Queer Ethics of M[ature] A[ttracted] P[erson] Desire." This reader's opposition was around anonymous authorship, as well as certain ethical and intellectual concerns posed by the chapters.

Much discussion and negotiation followed, but as you can see from what is in your hands, inclusion, risk, and truth prevailed. As academics, we are used to making compromises every day of our lives, but some are strategic and integrable within the flow of the "take a deep breath, pick yourself up, dust yourself off, and start all over again" of everyday work and life. Others are absolutely and unequivocally not.

This was clearly in the latter category, since urgent issues in the academic field of sexuality studies and in the real world of sexuality politics are at stake. We are honoured by the first anonymous reader and Professor Mercer's attention to and trust of our arguments for including these two indispensable essays – and of course to McGill-Queen's University Press's editor-in-chief Jonathan Crago and the Publication Review Committee for their recognition of the importance of the issues raised by this hurdle, and for listening so carefully to us.

We would like to justify and contextualize the inclusion of anonymous work in our book, and to remind readers of its fundamental pertinence to the book you are reading and to the politics of confession in the real world. An anthology on sexual representation in 2019 should challenge and provoke alongside its more traditional intellectual and scholarly objectives. We wryly noted to the publisher that we should perhaps be happy that we have achieved the objective of provocation – to the extent of jeopardizing the whole publication! Here we want to bring you, the reader, into the conversation, exploring the misunderstandings around ethics and scholarship that surfaced since they strike us as symptomatic of an underlying crisis in sexuality studies – and of course pointing to the rot in the entire peer review/scholarly publishing industry (notwithstanding the incontrovertible effect that it has also had in improving our book).

We initially thought our original brief reference to the "current political climate" was a self-evident justification for the admittedly exceptional practice of anonymous authorship in an academic anthology, but it clearly was not. Working within the bubble of a progressive and inclusive university setting with a gay president and several trans* faculty, with an exciting and growing sexuality/queer studies program and community, we were asleep at the switch. We have been reminded how precarious academic freedom around sexual/gender freedom and expression is, as whistleblowers from Jane Gallop to Laura Kipnis have already repeatedly argued, beginning in the 1990s. They are seconded in this book by Khan and Kastner's chilling account of gender politics on the neoliberal campus and artworld (chapter 1), and by Falardeau, Arroyo, McLellan, Charbonneau, Pinaka, and Roach around confessionality in the worlds of pornography, art cinema, games, the art marketplace, and social media, respectively.

Our contributor "Intervals" is hardly exaggerating in using the word "totalitarian" to describe this context. Of course their tone is polemical, appropriate in personal and essayistic political writing – not to mention civil disobedience – and we welcome this tone throughout our volume's coverage of a whole spectrum of sexual confessionality in media and the arts. From this collective author's critique of the post–Sexual Revolution feminist-dominated therapy and youth protection industries, to other authors' challenge to feminist blogging, Grindr, Lars von Triers, and Colby Keller, we hope we have left a lot of knickers in knots – productively so, of course.

Thanks to various sex panics around the globe since the Second Sexual Revolution of the 1960s, we have witnessed a proliferation of criminalization of sexual minorities and "outer circle" sexual activities in our increasing carceral states (Rubin 1984). In Canada and the United States, this tendency includes the criminalization of 1) consensual sex work among adults; 2) consensual sexual activities by HIV+ individuals, sometimes even those having disclosed their serostatus; 3) sexting teenagers (the many famous cases of "Romeo and Juliet" criminals inscribed for life in sex-offender registries); 4) individuals intentionally or accidentally possessing sexual representations or nude photos of people under the age of eighteen; and of course, 5) individuals harbouring the *desire* for intergenerational sexual activities (we emphasize "desire" as opposed to practices such as non-consensual assault). We respect the wishes of our contributors to opt for anonymity and to keep safe during these dark times.

Our dissident reader claimed that these authors' "refus[al] to claim their work" could "destabilize the foundation upon which our field is constructed and the traditions of scholarly rigor and accountability." These chapters are potentially controversial, and they are intended to be such. Sexual stigma and criminality are a thread through many of our chapters, and we are proud to have in our book these two anonymous writers among the many witnesses to the turbulence of our era. University presses have a long and distinguished history through the twentieth and twenty-first centuries of publishing anonymous and pseudonymous witness-authors, from dissidents in the Soviet Union to on-the-ground witnesses of twenty-first-century conflicts in the Middle East.[2] It is far from unheard of for anthologies like Taormino et al.'s *The Feminist Porn Book: The Politics of Producing Pleasure* (2013) to include pseudonymous authors who fear retribution, stigma, and criminalization. (Among the contributors to that book are pseudonymous but identifiable "pornstars" as well as more private individuals with well-camouflaged legal identities: "Ms Naughty," "Sinnamon Love," "Dylan Ryan," "Jiz Lee," and others.) We like the implied solidarity with sex workers that resonates throughout our book, not only in this authorship strategy but also specifically in chapters 7, 9, 12, 14, 15, 16, and 26. In fact our own book uses pseudonyms elsewhere, for both a contributor and subject. Moreover, M[inor] A[ttracted] P[erson] adult voices (to use the term preferred by author 23) are frankly and boldly heard in such recent US and Canadian anthologies as the scholarly *Porn Archives* (Duke University Press 2014) and the well-received trade collection *Queers Were Here* (Biblioasis 2016).

Professor Mercer explicitly endorsed both the content of the chapters as well as the proposal to retain the anonymity of their authors in publication:

> I think the inclusion of these two contributions, whilst they will raise eyebrows (and certainly chapter 10 and chapter 23 will challenge the sensibilities of many readers as is their intention), act[s] as a useful and timely reminder and caution against privilege and complacency. Our hard won liberal freedoms of speech/expression/scholarship are neither universal nor are they eternal and there are still many places in the world where the freedoms to write about sexuality are not available to scholars or anyone else for that matter. Anonymity in the context of this collection reminds us that there is an element of risk attached to the endeavour that these authors are engaged in and that some of the topics that this excellent collection gathers together are undoubtedly risky. It strikes me that this is their strength ... It seems to me singularly ironic that someone who claims anonymity in order to write a waspish review then has the temerity to throw shade at someone who for the most obvious reasons chooses to publish anonymously ... irony of course is lost on some!

In short, we support our two authors' legitimate fear of persecution, legal and extra-legal. While neither acknowledges any infraction whatsoever of any offenses under Canadian or American criminal codes, the "current political climate" is fraught with much danger for the authors, ranging from passive omnipresent surveillance, both corporate and governmental, to pernicious stigma in the academic market/workplace,[3] to vigilante harassment including media lynching (remember the US broadcast-TV program *To Catch a Predator* [2004–07]) and internet entrapment/harassment). Moreover, let us mention the American International Megan's Law, in force since the Obama administration, whereby all registered sex offenders have their passports stamped with a "unique identifier" – a provision decried by both civil-liberties organizations and Jewish groups who evoke the 1938 Nazi provision for a "J" stamp in Jewish passports as the sole known precedent.

Our dissident reader went on to suggest that the inclusion of anonymous contributors could somehow compromise the other twenty-eight authors in the volume. We strongly disagreed and conferred with our contributors, summarizing the negative report and offering a final opportunity for each to withdraw from the book. While almost all of our authors articulated a strong solidarity with the co-editors' judgment, two female contributors asked to see the contentious chapters. Of these, one responded, "Thank you a lot for sending the essays over. I read them, I think they are great, daring, works, and I would love to be part of the anthology of which I am too very proud." The other took seriously the reader's contention about two anonymous authors' "contamination" of the other contributors and withdrew her chapter, informing us she would be coming up for tenure shortly and could not take any chances. Ironically, the topic of this seemingly straight, white-presenting feminist from a US metropolitan area was the work of Marlon Riggs, the brave queer African-American video artist whose work had been vilified, stigmatized, and panic-attacked by Republican campaigners in the 1992 presidential election. We could repeat Mercer's dictum about irony, but let's just acknowledge how heartbroken we are to have Riggs missing in action from our book.

Illustrations are another litmus test of both the risk-taking and astuteness of analysis within the current culture, and we hope that our readers will take *I Confess!*'s visual thread as seriously as our contributors (albeit in black and white only, given the economics of book publishing in 2019). In your hands is not only a scholarly anthology on confessionality but an artifact of visual confessional culture: we are proud to illustrate each chapter to the hilt allowed by our budget. Our dissident reader shares our commitment to visual evidence and was unsurprisingly "greatly troubled" by the inclusion of chapter 10's illustrations, which included a small sampling of anonymously and securely received outline images, "eviscerated" and decriminalized by what the Intervals collective calls the "cutout" method (or non-indexical silhouettes), presented as evidence.[4] Intervals is playfully and defiantly deconstructing the infamous paradox of contemporary research in sexual representation, frequently commented on in the literature, whereby scholars researching the sexual [self-]representation of and by "under-eighteens" automatically incriminate themselves by even so much as accidentally looking at the evidence, let alone analyzing it (regardless of whether the age of consent is sixteen, as is the case in Canada, or fourteen, as is the case in Germany and Italy and many other jurisdictions). Here the co-editors have perhaps compromised, but on condition of transparent disclosure. Intervals' chapter offers only four frame grabs, two from a licit (non-pornography) fiction film discussed by the author(s), and two from illicit materials, which neither the author(s) nor we have seen, of course, using the cutout-silhouette method and outlining neither nudity or erogenous zones, which we strongly agree contribute to the chapter's argument.

Even more surprising was our dissident reader's harsh reaction to a footnote and brief reference list in chapter 23, maintaining it "has only the most basic academic justification for what is otherwise primarily a first-person narrative detailing erotic behaviors involving minors. Most problematic, however, is footnote 7 and the list of links, neither of which have any academic purpose whatsoever. The links are not only to footage of minors, but footage originally uploaded to YouTube of and for non-sexual purposes. Given the narrative in this chapter, this is literally the sharing of the author's arousal material (which depicts minors) used for masturbation. This is disguised as scholarship and is not academically justified, explained, or supported."

The offending note and reference list provided four search terms and four public links to the self-produced and self-uploaded teen martial-arts videos discussed by the author. (The scholarly bibliography for this now fine-tuned chapter offers a much-increased number of sources including publications from several reputable university presses alongside Foucault.) Moreover, the reader's word "involving" is as misleading as it is libellous. The categorical dismissal of the author's good faith, academic purpose, and justification, and his "disguised scholarship" offends and baffles us. We find very apt this author's personal reflection on the eroticizing "détournement" of benign YouTube materials by sexual minorities as a key phenomenon in confessional internet culture as well as in homosocial masculinity (anticipated, of course, by baby boomer heterosexual males who learned to masturbate with Eaton's catalogue bra ads). In general, providing the reader with access to the public, legally available, and benign corpus analyzed in the chapter strikes us as a standard academic practice for scholars of visual media. This involves, in our minds, fewer substantive ethical issues than a porn scholar referencing a gonzo hetero rape scene from the pornography archive (standard practice in *Porn Studies* and the new literature in the field). Harm cannot conceive to be done (this side of Andrea Dworkin, that is) to individual subjects in such access to published images, whether teenage kickboxers or Eaton's catalogue models – that is, in the study of freely available recorded commercial or YouTube moving image media. The author would be remiss in not providing the links, and we refused to delete them.

We need in conclusion to acknowledge our dissident reader's comment on a section of chapter 5 dealing polemically with the denial of masturbation in western culture. He finds "inaccurate and irresponsible" the following sentences: "To be scholars of the masturbating boy, then, we must confess that we are masturbators. We must introduce this most unlikely instrument of scholarly objectivity, because otherwise we are likely to flee from the research object due to anxieties resulting from the uncertainties and shame surrounding our own solitary sexual practices." Our dissident reader saw this passage as a defence of the arousal and self-gratification of the authors upon the image of the masturbating boy. However, we think that in addition to offering a diagnosis of an academic culture in denial, the author is providing fair if admittedly rhetorical comment on many scholars' denial of their own bodies and erotic practices, and we take the comment to heart. In fact, we affirm being inveterate and incorrigible self-defilers ourselves. Moreover, we strongly believe all our authors have fulfilled our mandate in a transparent, engaging, and ethical way, as well as in a bravely "confessional" way that acknowledges desire and the body as fundaments of understanding and pedagogy, community, and social justice and transformation. Jane Gallop has hit the nail on the head more than a few times: "I happen to be both a feminist and someone whose professional relations are sexualized. It is because of the sort of feminist I am that I do not respect the line between the intellectual and the sexual ... the power of desire and knowledge ... It is no more possible to really teach without at times eliciting powerful and troubling sensations than it is to write powerfully without producing the same sort of sensations. Teachers and writers might better serve the claims of knowledge if we were to resist not sex but the impulse to split off sex from knowledge" (Gallop 1997, 11,100).

We invite you, dear readers, to judge for yourselves.

Finally, we would like to register our heartfelt gratitude to our funders, the Concordia University Office of Research and Faculty of Fine Arts as well as the Social Sciences and Humanities Research Council of Canada, who have all supported some pretty kinky stuff over the years in the name of truth, knowledge, creativity, justice, and empowerment. To stalwart and resourceful research assistants Ferrin Evans and David Leblanc, and brilliant translator Jordan Arseneault. To our loyal, long-term research partner Maria Nengeh Mensah and Cultures du témoignage, Université du Québec à Montréal. And to our trusting and magnanimous publisher McGill-Queen's University Press and its team of humane and fastidious professionals. The volume in your hands or on your screen is the fourth very, very heavy object with the Waugh name the press's delegate, the strong rugbyist Jonathan Crago, has cheerfully carried down the field. Arroyo would particularly like to thank his mother and father for enduring the long and winding road of their son's academic journey. Waugh would also like to thank his consanguineal family, and both co-editors fervently express their indebtedness to their chosen families for their love, challenges, and support.

NOTES

1 Arroyo expands on this idea of erotics being embedded in our clicking from website to website in Arroyo 2016.
2 "Academic authorship." *Wikipedia*, wikipedia.org/wiki/Academic_authorship.
3 For more on academic stigma, harassment, and silencing, see Hubbard and Verstraete's 2013 *Censoring Sex Research: The Debate over Male Intergenerational Relations*. For more on the "current political climate," see Halperin and Hoppe's *The War on Sex* (2017).
4 A similar method was used to reference without fully and culpably transmitting archival visual materials in Waugh's 2004 scholarly collection *Lust Unearthed*.

REFERENCES

Arroyo, Brandon. 2016. "From Flow to Float: Moving through Porn Tube Sites." *Porn Studies* 3, no. 3, 308–10.

Attwood, Feona. 2009. *Porn.com: Making Sense of Online Pornography*. London: Peter Lang.

Bose, Brinda, and Subhabrata Bhattacharyya, eds. 2007. *The Phobic and the Erotic: The Politics of Sexualities in Contemporary India*. Kolkata: Seagull.

Dean, Tim. 2008. *Unlimited Intimacy: Reflections on the Subculture of Barebacking*. Chicago: University of Chicago Press.

Dean, Tim, Steven Ruszczycky, and David Squires, eds. 2014. *Porn Archives*. Durham: Duke University Press.

Deleuze, Gilles. 1977. "I Have Nothing to Admit." *Semiotext(e)* 2, no. 3: 111–16.

Deleuze, Gilles, and Félix Guattari. [1972] 1983. *Anti-Oedipus: Capitalism and Schizophrenia*. Translated by Robert Hurley, Mark Seem, and Helen R. Lane. Minneapolis: University of Minnesota Press.

Gallop, Jane. 1997. *Feminist Accused of Sexual Harassment*. Durham: Duke University Press.

Gilmour, Richard, and Robin Ganev. 2016. *Queers Were Here: Heroes and Icons of Queer Canada*. Windsor: Biblioasis.

Halperin, David, and Trevor Hoppe, eds. 2017. *The War on Sex*. Durham: Duke University Press.

Hubbard, Thomas, and Beert Verstraete, eds. 2013. *Censoring Sex Research: The Debate over Male Intergenerational Relations*. Walnut Creek, CA: Left Coast Press.

Jacobs, Katrien. 2007. *Netporn: DIY Web Culture and Sexual Politics*. New York: Rowan & Littlefield.

Kroker, Arthur. 1992. *The Possessed Individual: Technology and the French Postmodern*. Montreal: New World Perspectives.

Massumi, Brian. 1995. "The Autonomy of Affect." *Cultural Critique*. 31, no. 2: 83–109.

Mercer, John. 2017. *Gay Pornography: Representations of Sexuality and Masculinity*. London: Tauris.

Mowlabocus, Sharif. 2010. *Gaydar Culture: Gay Men, Technology and Embodiment in the Digital Age.* London: Routledge.

Paasonen, Susanna. 2011. *Carnal Resonance: Affect and Online Pornography.* Cambridge: MIT Press.

Rubin, Gayle S. 1984. "Thinking Sex: Notes for a Radical Theory of the Politics of Sexuality." In *Pleasure and Danger: Exploring Female Sexuality*, edited by Carole S. Vance, 267–93. London: Pandora.

Simondon, Gilbert. [2005] 2017. *On the Mode of Existence of Technical Objects.* Translated by Cecile Malaspina and John Rogove. Minneapolis: Univocal.

Taormino, Tristan, Constance Penley, Celine Parrenas Shimizu, and Mireille Miller-Young. 2013. *The Feminist Porn Book: The Politics of Producing Pleasure.* New York: CUNY Press.

Tsika, Noah. 2016. *Pink 2.0: Encoding Queer Cinema on the Internet.* Indianapolis: University of Indiana Press.

Waugh, Thomas. 2004. *Lust Unearthed: Vintage Gay Graphics from the Dubek Collection.* Vancouver: Arsenal Pulp.

– 2015. "My Coming Out: 'I'm Afraid This Letter Is Going to Cause You Both a Lot of Pain.'" *Montreal Gazette*, 8 August. https://montrealgazette.com/life/my-coming-out-im-afraid-this-letter-is-going-to-cause-you-both-a-lot-of-pain.

Williams, Linda, ed. 2004. *Porn Studies.* Durham: Duke University Press.

– 2008. *Screening Sex.* Durham: Duke University Press.

Part One
Scientia Sexualis

Activism

1

The Treachery of Rape Representation

TAL KASTNER AND UMMNI KHAN

On 3 June 2015, performance artist Emma Sulkowicz released an online installation piece titled *Ceci n'est pas un viol*, which translates into English as *This Is Not a Rape*. The work consists of several sections: descriptive text, along with reflection questions on the home webpage; a video accessed via a link on the webpage; and an open comment forum at the bottom of the webpage. The linked video features a sexual encounter between two people, played by Sulkowicz and a man whose face is obscured, screened from the vantage points of four simultaneous surveillance-style videos. At first the sex appears consensual, but the activity soon turns rough and seemingly unwanted by Sulkowicz's character. The explanatory text on the home page states that the video is "consensual but may resemble rape." It explicitly denies that this piece is "about one night in August, 2012" and insists that *Ceci n'est pas un viol* is "about your decisions, starting now. It's only a reenactment if you disregard my words. It's about you, not him."

Notwithstanding the caveats – or, indeed, partly because of them – the piece invokes Sulkowicz's publicized allegations of a rape in a Columbia University dorm room in August 2012. After a university investigation, the accused student was found "not responsible." *Ceci n'est pas un viol* also echoes back to Sulkowicz's high-profile senior thesis, the "Mattress Performance," or *Carry That Weight*, an endurance performance art piece created in part to protest the university determination. *Carry That Weight* involved multiple elements, but most famously, Sulkowicz hauled a mattress resembling those in the Columbia college dorms with her wherever she went on campus in her senior year. The title *Ceci n'est pas un viol* also alludes more broadly to René Magritte's famous painting, *La trahison des images* (The Treachery of Images), which features a realistic depiction of a pipe, under which are the words "Ceci n'est pas une pipe" (This is not a pipe) (fig. 1.1). In doing so, the title calls attention to the debates and interpretations that

1.1 *The Treachery of Images*, oil on canvas, René Magritte, 1929.

Magritte's painting and related drawings inspired – most notably, perhaps, Michel Foucault's essay of the same name.[1]

These intertextual links to previous events, creative works, and scholarly commentary, and the multiple ways that *Ceci n'est pas un viol* adamantly insists that it is "not about" a contested allegation of sexual assault, highlight the fraught relationship between representation and reality in legal and cultural discourse. Among other things, the process foregrounds the instability of narrative framing, and the politics involved in determining the bounds of context, including legal context. The piece also interpellates its audience within its performance, addressing the viewer directly, imposing legal conditions for full participation in the form of an online agreement, and offering a site for comments. Further, the artist's comments warn that the viewer who disregards Sulkowicz's wishes and intentions will be implicated in "participating in [Sulkowicz's] rape." In light of the challenge of discerning intention that the piece explores and exploits, the warning also mirrors the structure of confession in its potential coercion of the viewer.

This chapter analyzes the ways in which *Ceci n'est pas un viol* stages the treachery of rape representation in legal and cultural mediums. We begin by providing background context on the significance of confession within the socio-legal imaginary. Through a legal lens, we identify how expressions of truth/self-revelation/guilt and consent/coercion – as manifested in confession and the contractual mode of agreement – necessarily implicate social and legal constraint. Through a cultural lens, we deconstruct how the text addresses not just the violence of representation but also its failure to ever adequately signify sexual assault. Our analyses of both discourses (and the overlap between the two) points to the semiotic instability between fact and fiction, earnestness and irony, accusation and confession, performer and audience, consent and coercion, sex and rape, and the experience of rape and its representation, with which art and law each struggle. Throughout the analysis, we examine confession as a product of coercion (as it is often produced in the legal context) and as a site of revelation, deception, exhibition, and/or empowerment (as it often functions in cultural narratives). We conclude by considering how the process of framing and signifying rape implicates the challenges of drawing boundaries not only within the law but also between art and experience and between law and society.

Confession: A Compelled and Attenuated Revelation

Before analyzing *Ceci n'est pas un viol*, we briefly review competing cultural and legal valences of confession to make salient the role of confession in Sulkowicz's performance art. As a formative cultural starting point, confession as exemplified by St Augustine suggests a conceptual model of revelation and thus a process of representation of truth that in turn serves as the basis for judgment.[2] In this narrative of confession, a profligate sinner, through a process of voluntary self-reflection, comes to recognize and express his sins. This earnest process (in Augustine's case involving sexual behaviour) thereby enables a presentation of authentic self that ultimately merits redemption.[3]

This narrative of confession as a freely given, authentic, and redemptive revelation of a coherent self, which provides a legitimate basis of judgment, continues to have a powerful hold on western imagination. This is so notwithstanding the actual coercion that so deeply informs the practice of confession, historically and in contemporary life. From the Inquisition to current-day interrogation rooms, the violent process of extracting legal confessions belies the narrative of authenticity through self-revelation.

Contemporary scholarship speaks to the limits of confession as a mode of truth telling, especially in the courtroom.[4] Studies have shown that individuals asked to judge the reliability of others' confessions are hard pressed to accept that a confession may be false (Kassin, Meissner, and Norwick 2005). This is so even when suspects are held in conditions involving psychological and physical pressures, including long hours of exhausting questioning, misrepresentations, psychological manipulation, implied promises, and/or threats by interrogators, to name a few common techniques that typically lead an innocent person to say whatever will end the interrogation process (Bikel 2010). The overwhelmingly persuasive power of confession on legal factfinders such as juries further complicates the ostensibly revelatory nature of this dynamic (White 1997). In addition, the presence of cognitive biases more generally points to the revelatory limitations of self-reflection.[5] In this way, as a result of the often-obscured coercive framework that precipitates their expression, confessions themselves implicate the treachery of representation. A reframing of the narrative of confession to include the social and legal context quickly reveals the role of constraint and coercion, which *Ceci n'est pas un viol* also arguably – if perhaps incoherently – invokes.

Treachery, Denial, and Intertextuality

Ceci n'est pas un viol implicitly engages the question of confessional framing through its invocation of a preceding event and its expressed denial of its relation to that event. The constraints and possibilities of context, and their implications for representation, also manifest through intertextuality and the process of allusion in which the piece engages. Thus, as noted in the introduction, *Ceci n'est pas un viol* takes up the issue of framing of its own meaning in part by making an intertextual link to the painting below.

It bears noting that the repetition of the words "Ceci n'est pas un(e) … " does not straightforwardly parallel Magritte's work. As if warning the viewer, the painting is called "La Trahison des images," while the image of the words "Ceci n'est pas une pipe" makes up part of the painting itself, handwritten, as Foucault ([1968] 1983, 15) states, "in a steady, painstaking, artificial script, a script from the convent, like that found heading the notebooks of schoolboys, or on a blackboard after an object lesson!"[6] Sulkowicz thus titles the piece by mimicking the image of stylized words found within the art-object itself, not the formal title of the painting that could be found on a museum's identification card and would serve to both represent and shape a viewer's understanding of the painting. In addition, Sulkowicz, like Magritte, includes another title-like image in Sulkowicz's own creative work. When you open the webpage, the first lines appear as follows:

Ceci N'est Pas Un Viol
Emma Sulkowicz
June 2015

A___'s S___t

Underneath, this text (which suggests a term paper heading, perhaps as contemporary analogue to Foucault's imagined schoolboy's notebook entry) presents a "Trigger Warning," followed by an ostensible explanation of what *Ceci N'est Pas Un Viol* is and is not about (see appendix for the full text). But what does "A___'s S___t" signify? Its positioning at the top and centre of the text invites us to read it as a title identifying the webpage as the "artist's statement," a potentially revelatory expression. But because of the redaction suggested by the underscoring between the characters "A" and "'s," and "S' and "t," the meaning invites interpretation. As with Magritte's painting of the words "Ceci n'est pas une pipe," "A___'s S___t" creates a semiotic tension between the gesture toward representation and revelation, and one that challenges its intelligibility. Both pieces create a jarring dissonance between the title-like signifier and the rest of the art-object.

In Magritte's painting, the simplicity of the words "Ceci n'est pas une pipe" heightens the incongruity of the image of a pipe directly above the statement. Magritte's painting thereby compels the viewer to experience the gap between language and objects, and thereby between the signifier and the signified. At the same time, as Foucault ([1968] 1983, 37) states, "Ceci n'est pas une pipe exemplifies the penetration of discourse into the form of things; it reveals discourse's ambiguous power to deny and to redouble." The statement "Ceci n'est pas une pipe" is both true and untrue. In common parlance, one could easily say that "this" – the image above the words – *is* [of] a pipe. The statement, in this sense, is false. And yet neither the painting nor the words are an actual pipe.[7] As Magritte himself stated, "The famous pipe. How people reproached me for it! And yet, could you stuff my pipe? No, it's just a representation, is it not?" Magritte calls attention to the very tension his painting makes salient in making his point: "So if I had written on my picture 'This is a pipe,' I'd have been lying!" (Torcyner 1979, 71). In contrast to Magritte's deceptively simple phrase "Ceci n'est pas une pipe," Sulkowicz's redacted title highlights its opacity. Consisting of a sequence made of letters, underscores and an apostrophe, the meaning is literally illegible even if the audience suspects it knows how it relates to the rest of the work. Sulkowicz does not merely stage the tension between representation and the thing it strives to stand in for (the signified), but asserts the perpetual mystery of representation. It is a fill-in-the-blank word puzzle that foregrounds the question of whether it can definitely be solved.

This slipperiness of representation further unfolds in the sentences following "A___'s S___t." The text repeatedly asserts that the video is "not about" rape in general, or about Sulkowicz's alleged rape in particular. But what do all these negations signify? Arguably, *Ceci n'est pas un viol* constitutes the most significant denial, given its status as title of the project. Similar to Magritte's semiotic strategy, the website forces us to think about literal and common-sense meanings. It seems, straightforwardly, that "Ceci" is not literally a "viol." Ceci is a website, a digital document, and a representation, along with an invitation for comment, though the denial of what it is doing and/or depicting forces the viewer to consider the extent to which it is an act or representation of rape. Halley (2008, 78) discusses the impossibility of disaggregating rape and representation, suggesting, "rape, though real and really, really bad, is also inevitably *ideological* – and thus, that rape as representation sticks like glue to rape as event." The art project thus attests to the impossibility of ever conveying the phenomenon of rape without getting mired in the politics of representation, or distorted by the filter of the audience. Indeed, Sulkowicz has expressed frustration in trying to explain the alleged rape during Columbia's investigation. In an interview with *New York* magazine, Sulkowicz said, "One of the three judges even asked whether Paul [the alleged assailant] used lubricant, commenting, 'I don't know how it's possible to have anal sex without lubrication first'" (Grigoriadis 2014). Sulkowicz also noted that the investigators kept up a barrage of questions regarding the technical details of the position of their bodies during the rape: "At one point, I was like, 'Should I just draw you a picture?' So I drew a stick drawing" (Grigoriadis 2014). Verbal explanation apparently proved insufficient to communicate the experience to this audience, a challenge no doubt compounded by the allegedly painful nature of the experience. As Elaine Scarry has famously noted, "Whatever pain achieves, it achieves in part through its unsharability, and it ensures this unsharability through its resistance to language" (1984, 4). Thus Sulkowicz mobilized drawing, a visual medium, in attempting to share the experience, and make it coherent and credible to the investigators. This effort, as we know, failed, as measured by the university's response.[8]

In this light, the video contained in *Ceci n'est pas un viol* can be understood as an elaboration on the "stick drawing" – one that visually demonstrates the process by which consensual activity and vaginal penetration can segue into violent assault and anal penetration (even without lubrication!). Sulkowicz's insistence that "*ceci n'est pas un viol*" can thus serve as an ironic, but pragmatic, "legal loophole" protecting her from a claim of defamation from her alleged rapist (Nair 2015b), while at the same time conveying a political indictment of the investigation's effective inability to recognize the perpetration of a rape.[9] The ironic resonance of this indictment draws attention to the perpetual vagaries of representation – whether through language, pictures, or videography – and the challenge of whether it can ever accurately re/present a rape.

The other negations expressed by the piece further complicate the issue of representing rape. The statement "Everything that takes place in the following video is consensual but may resemble rape" introduces the possibility of multiple counter-narratives. On the most literal level, it can be read as an assurance to the viewer that while the video may look like it is capturing a rape, the actors in the video had consented to play the fictional scene. It also suggests that the depicted scenario could be understood as kinky role-playing, where the participants had agreed to the sexual encounter ahead of time. In this narrative, withdrawal of consent would not be expressed in conventional terms through struggle or the word "no," but rather through an agreed-upon "safe word" or "safe gesture" that the audience would not be privy to (kaliochaos 2015). This possibility thereby introduces yet another framing of a viewer's understanding of the scene depicted.

Another possible interpretation of this negation refers back to Sulkowicz's original complaint of sexual assault at Columbia. In the video, four camera angles show a couple engaged in sexual activity that turns violent in a way that seems to re-enact Sulkowicz's claims of rape (figs. 1.2 and 1.3). By insisting this is not a rape or about rape, the statement could actually be interpreted as a confession by Sulkowicz that the 2012 rape accusation was unfounded and/or a denial of Sulkowicz's own guilt in implicating the viewer. As implausible as these interpretations might seem, the piece nonetheless opens up these possibilities, particularly because, as discussed below, it provides a comment forum reflecting the views of many who understood the video as a confession that Sulkowicz's sexual assault accusation had not been truthful but, rather, was a publicity stunt.

A more plausible interpretation of the negation that the video is "not about rape" suggests that the accused assailant genuinely misread the signs.[10] For example, perhaps the crime of "rape" did not occur because he was under mistaken belief in Sulkowicz's consent.[11] The statement could thus be read as an acknowledgment by Sulkowicz that the 2012 accusation would not be recognized by a patriarchal legal framework that privileges the assailant's perspective over the victim's subjective experience (if the mistake in consent is deemed "reasonable"). In this way, Sulkowicz draws on Catherine MacKinnon's (1989, 146) insight that "anything sexual that happens often and one cannot get anyone to consider wrong

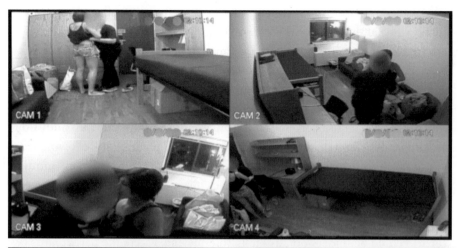

1.2 *Top* Complicating the issue of representing rape. Screen capture, *Ceci n'est pas un viol* (This Is Not a Rape), Emma Sulkowicz, 2015.

1.3 *Bottom* Visual symbolism invoking the different significations of "lying" in the bed, screen capture, *Ceci n'est pas un viol* (This Is Not a Rape), Emma Sulkowicz, 2015.

is intercourse not rape, no matter what was done." In other words, MacKinnon highlights the fact that when an adjudicating body has determined that a sexual assault *has not happened* (as was done at Columbia in Sulkowicz's complaint), then no matter how violent, unwanted, or coerced the incident may be, it is rendered "sex" rather than "rape" within patriarchal ideology and, of course, the law.[12] Taking this one step further, as MacKinnon has done, the piece potentially suggests that the violence of rape is not unlike the male dominance and aggression in so-called "ordinary" or "normal" sex. Thus *Ceci n'est pas un viol* gestures toward a radical feminist critique of normative sexuality, as well as its entrenchment in the law.[13]

In the parts of the text that address the audience directly, Sulkowicz extends this feminist critique to hint at the issue of responsible viewing, voyeuristic violence, and collective responsibility. On the one hand, as Long Chu points out, "Sulkowicz dares her voyeurs to re-up their own affective investments in her traumatic scene by flirting with the pornographic" (2017, 304). On the other hand, Sulkowicz warns, "If you watch this video without my consent, then I hope you reflect on your reasons for objectifying me and participating in my rape." The statement suggests that the viewer – through the watching – may be guilty, an accessory to rape. Accordingly, "Ceci" may very well be a kind of symbolic "viol": the viewer/voyeur's potential "viol" of the artist. The danger of vicariously participating in the artist's rape is particularly treacherous, as it is unclear how one might obtain Sulkowicz's consent to watch the video. One journalist analyzing the piece, who decided not to watch the video, explained Sulkowicz's instructions this way: "Had I watched, I wouldn't have watched it as pornography, and I wouldn't have watched it to cast judgment; I would have observed the act and probably felt heartbroken for her. That's the only way to watch the video with her consent. Any other form of viewing – viewing for pleasure or disgust – is non-consensual" (Brink 2015). This interpretation of the instructions, however, remains speculative and does not find grounding in the text, as nowhere does Sulkowicz decree the specifics of *how* one is supposed to watch the video. Indeed, she even expresses tolerance for ambivalent feelings in response to the piece. While her "Trigger Warning" suggests that people should "proceed with caution" or even "exit the website" if they get too upset, it also qualifies this statement: "However, I do not mean to be prescriptive, for many people find pleasure in feeling upset."

While Sulkowicz does not clarify how to consensually interact with the video, the webpage explains, albeit elliptically, how *not* to watch it: "Do not watch this video if your motives would upset me, my desires are unclear to you, or my nuances are indecipherable." These three fraught conditions recall the challenges of deciphering the title. In addition to complicating legibility through the artist's own nuances, Sulkowicz urges us throughout her text to contemplate our own motivations and feelings. The piece claims it is not about rape but about "your decisions, starting now ... It's about you, not him." Further down the text states, "Look – I want to change the world, and that begins with you, seeing yourself." The questions Sulkowicz provides also encourage further self-reflection. Thus, one might conclude that Sulkowicz desires us to turn the gaze back onto ourselves, as audience members, as we interact with the piece, and if we do so, then our motives will not upset Sulkowicz. But the last condition that directs us not to watch the video if the artist's "nuances are indecipherable" sets the audience up for failure. The uncertain word-puzzle subtitle, "A___'s S___t," highlights the impossibility of grasping Sulkowicz's nuances. Following the logic then, anyone who watches the video must necessarily be violating this condition and Sulkowicz's consent, thereby participating in Sulkowicz's rape. Again, the piece suggests the possibility of an entrapment, and in doing so, operates as a forced confession of guilt of the viewer. This in turn prompts a reading of the disclaimer "Ceci n'est pas un viol" as a means of self-protection for the artist.

In gesturing toward possibilities of self-reflection and revelation in the context of the unstable framework of confession in the law, the piece questions how properly to determine innocence or guilt. Not only does it suggest more than one possible implication of confession and coercion in relation to the artist and the artist's subject but the piece further invokes an ideal of self-revelation through confession in its relation to the viewer. As stated, at the bottom of the webpage, below the link to the video, is an open comment forum. By allowing the audience members to share their reactions, the piece at times serves to document what can be read as a confession of misogyny by some of those posting. In doing so, the piece speaks directly to the viewers' motives. The ongoing conversation on the comments section is beyond the scope of this essay, but it is worth noting that comments continue to be posted, and they engage ongoing debates regarding things like sexual assault, pornography, gender relations, race, immigration, and politics. Many posts consist of discriminatory and sexually violent diatribes, as well as claims that the video "proves" Sulkowicz was lying about being sexually assaulted in 2012. By creating an inviting stage for the viewer to engage in misogynistic self-exposure, the text redoubles the earlier insistence that *Ceci n'est pas un viol* is "about your decisions, starting now ... It's only a re-enactment if you disregard my words. It's about you, not him." But by inviting the viewer to react to the video footage through the open comment section, the piece provokes disclosure, even though the responses may seem entirely voluntary (perhaps even to the participant). Thus, while the piece invites a radical critique, as per MacKinnon, it also engages in the seduction of the viewer by encouraging self-incrimination – framing the viewer, if not coercing the viewer into confession. Yet at the same time, by providing the viewer with "a few questions to help you reflect," and inviting the viewer to engage in comments while being "mindful of what you desire to gain,"[14] in a context likely to provoke uncircumspect responses, the piece also ironically engages the possibilities of authentic self-reflective confession. It both taps into and troubles the narrative of confession as authentic revelation or a representation of one's true self.

Contract as Coercion

Related to the question of authentic consent, *Ceci n'est pas un viol* grapples with and underscores the conundrum of consent in a context of coercion. The piece invokes the framework of contract through formalities of consent central to American contract law. It does so through the use of so-called "wrap" language that ostensibly verifies the viewer's consent to the terms of the transaction prior to using the product or service.[15] *Ceci n'est pas un viol* incorporates this ubiquitous mode of assent to formally (if not substantively) elicit consent.[16] It is a common feature of contemporary American life that individuals – particularly online – formally accede and are thus bound to terms that they cannot realistically understand.[17] In this case, the online terms take the following form: below the text on the introductory webpage, a link to the video appears stating "This is the video," followed by a virtual play button. Immediately below it is a statement that reads: "By clicking PLAY, I hereby verify that I am at least 18 years of age or that I have a parent's/guardian's permission to watch this video. I have read the above text and understand what it means for me to click PLAY." Functioning as so-called "terms of use," the non-negotiable deal between the artist and viewer invokes the structure of a contract of adhesion – a take-it-or-leave it transaction in which an individual must accept the terms as imposed or forgo the transaction (Kessler 1943). In doing so, this structure manifests the coercion at times enabled through contract, or the positing of non-negotiable terms as a manifestation of agency and choice.

An appreciation of the way the piece engages the structure of contract, and in the process comments on it, requires an understanding of the tensions inherent in contract as a vehicle of agency and autonomy. In the United States, contract has long been imagined as an exercise in agency and free will.[18] With the turn toward emancipation in the nineteenth century, contract figured culturally in contrast to slavery as a worldview that idealized self-ownership and voluntary exchange. The act of entering into a contract also served as "the very symbol of freedom" (Stanley 1998, x). This narrative continues to resonate into the present day as legal doctrine posits parties as free agents who are capable of negotiating terms and reaching an agreement that reflects both parties' wishes, and judges routinely examine contract terms to ascertain parties' intent.[19] This traditional paradigm of contract involves "dickered-for" or meaningfully considered terms, which create enforceable obligations.[20]

At the same time, in a manner analogous to the myth of confession, the traditional story of contract elides the framework of coercion in which it operates. The idea of contract as an expression of individual choice and freedom, like the traditional vision of American society, presumes fair play, equal bargaining power, and a level field. In reality, however, contract has served to naturalize disparities in access and resources. Thus, for example, given the limited power of the labourer in the post-bellum free market, Southern planters imposed terms on freedmen replicating in substantial part the controls of slavery, including mandating personal conduct. Along similar lines, employers changed and violated contract terms to the detriment of freedmen (Stanley 1998, 42–3, 45). Thus, notwithstanding the limited power of the labourer, the ability to enter into contract with respect to one's wage labour – even on severely constrained terms – represented free will and freedom from slavery in the social and legal imaginary. The ideological function of contract in the nineteenth century thus demonstrates the suppression of a collective awareness of constraint and the reinforcement of inequities in a way that carries forward into the American treatment of contract in the present day.

Today, non-negotiable fine print epitomizes the potential for contract to reinforce and naturalize disparities in power through formal markers of consent and agency.[21] In the United States, non-negotiable fine print pervades and shapes nearly all aspects of contemporary life, from social-media terms of use to financial transactions. Compelled to accept these terms in order to transact, individuals cede meaningful rights and legal protections without the possibility of negotiation. Thus, for example, terms of use may limit rights to privacy, a trial, or even recourse from harm.[22] At the same time, viewed as part of the contract, at least in the American legal framework, these terms signal consent and thereby marshal the power of legal enforceability.[23] This is so notwithstanding the ways in which transactions implying consent through so-called "wrap" agreements, or fine print accompanying an online transaction, stretch the notion of informed, unconstrained choice on which contract doctrine relies.[24]

Ceci n'est pas un viol engages this very question of the structural limits on consent. On a rhetorical level, the website troubles the boundaries between consent, coercion, and seduction by presenting the viewer with a Pandora's box. On the one hand, the website beckons the audience to watch the video by providing teasers that both "deny and redouble" allusions to rape. It implores the viewer to participate thoughtfully: "Look – I want to change the world, and that begins with you, seeing yourself." This statement further entices the audience by suggesting that if one engages self-reflectively, then by watching the video one might participate in a noble endeavour to "change the world." On the other hand, the website warns the viewer away: "If you watch this video without my consent, then I hope you reflect on your reasons for objectifying me and participating in my rape." Yet it positions the viewer like Pandora – who could resist opening the box / clicking on play? Sulkowicz has adamantly and repeatedly asserted it's "not about rape" – but most viewers will of course want to judge for themselves. Indeed, the framing of the video encourages them to do so.

By prompting the viewer to "Look" at the video, whether in connection with self-reflection or voyeuristic pleasure, the text both insists on engaging the artist's consent and complicates the possibility of a viewer's authentic agreement in the deal as presented. As suggested, the piece confounds the viewer – among other things, through its highlighted elisions and redactions, as well as its disclaimer that it is not "about one night in August" (an assertion, as noted, that once made, belies itself). At the same time, to carry out the implicit imperative of the piece to look and reflect, the viewer is invited to click on a play button accompanied by terms that ascribe motives to the viewer.

Thus, the terms highlight the near-impossibility of meaningful consent epitomized by the ubiquitous phenomenon of that standard form contract. As stated, the terms accompanying the "play button" compel an acknowledgment – by way of formal representation – that the viewer "understand[s] what it means ... to click play," but are presented in a context of rhetorical and representational games and elisions. Indeed, Sulkowicz goes further to leverage the power typically granted to the contract drafter in online transactions. The language engages the legal structure as a shield to protect the artist from legal action resulting from the expressive content. Specifically, the imposed verification by the viewer of being "at least 18 years of age" or having "a parent's/ guardian's permission to watch" the video ostensibly aims to protect the artist against accusations of distributing sexually explicit materials to minors. In doing so, the piece not only manipulates a viewer to assert (or lie) about their adult status but also opens up the possible interpretation that Sulkowicz is in fact producing a form of pornography. In what might be seen as an analogue to the structure of confession in the law, the piece uses the framework of contract and disclaimer to implicate the viewer and the artist. It thereby manifests the ways in which the structures of law shape and frame representation and self-revelation.

Conclusion

The video runs a bit over eight minutes, and nearly the entire second half depicts Sulkowicz's character alone in the room after the encounter remaking the bed, replacing the black bedding with white, and lying in it. Through this visual symbolism and the visual pun that invokes the different significations of "lying," the piece invites assessment of Sulkowicz's role and responsibility in framing the work. By reinvoking the mattress, but this time as a metaphor for a white canvas, the piece transforms the material reality of sexual assault into abstracted representation, which becomes subject to the manipulation and polysemy highlighted in the piece's allusions and formal framing devices. In contrast to the *Carry That Weight* performance piece, which attested to the concrete material reality of this lived event (the tangible aftermath of which could not be ignored, like a large blue mattress being hauled around campus), *Ceci n'est pas un viol* invites its audience to question the stability of apparent narratives, not least the narrative of facts posited by the earlier piece. Enacting the role of seducer, whether in sexual or visual terms or through the structures of confession or contract,[25] Sulkowicz draws us into her political-creative project. Mobilizing the screen as its medium of communication – a metaphorical invocation of the confessional, the material intermediary that enables a process of ostensible revelation – the piece invites judgment both of the artist and of the viewers' commentary. By implicating the artist, the audience, and the broader social context, not least the law, the piece demands that we look critically at the shaping of self, agency, consent, and coercion through the socio-legal structures that frame our world.

Appendix

Ceci N'est Pas Un Viol
Emma Sulkowicz
June 2015
A___'s S___t

<u>Trigger Warning:</u> The following text contains allusions to rape. Everything that takes place in the following video is consensual but may resemble rape. It is not a reenactment but may seem like one. If at any point you are triggered or upset, please proceed with caution and/or exit this website. However, I do not mean to be prescriptive, for many people find pleasure in feeling upset.

Ceci N'est Pas Un Viol is not about one night in August, 2012. It's about your decisions, starting now. It's only a reenactment if you disregard my words. It's about you, not him.

Do not watch this video if your motives would upset me, my desires are unclear to you, or my nuances are indecipherable.

You might be wondering why I've made myself this vulnerable. Look – I want to change the world, and that begins with you, seeing yourself. If you watch this video without my consent, then I hope you reflect on your reasons for objectifying me and participating in my rape, for, in that case, you were the one who couldn't resist the urge to make *Ceci N'est Pas Un Viol* about what you wanted to make it about: rape.

Please, don't participate in my rape. Watch kindly.

A special thank you to everyone who made *Ceci N'est Pas Un Viol* possible, especially my actor (*********), my director (Ted Lawson), and those I love who have guided and supported me.

* * *

- Here are a few questions to help you reflect.
  - Searching:
  - Are you searching for proof? Proof of what?
  - Are you searching for ways to either hurt or help me?
  - What are you *looking* for?
- Desiring:
  - Do you desire pleasure?
  - Do you desire revulsion? Is this to counteract your unconscious enjoyment?
  - What do you *want* from this experience?
- Me:
  - How well do you think you know me? Have we ever met?
  - Do you think I'm the perfect victim or the world's worst victim?
  - Do you refuse to see me as either a human being or a victim? If so, why? Is it to deny me agency and thus further victimize me? If so, what do you think of the fact that you owe your ability to do so to me, since I'm the one who took a risk and made myself vulnerable in the first place?
  - Do you hate me? If so, how does it feel to hate me?

* * *

This is the video:

NOTES

1 Foucault's discussion ([1968] 1983, 15) addresses two drawings that resemble but are not identical to the painting, demonstrating the negotiability of the context invoked through the process of allusion.

2 In book 5 of his *Confessions* ([AD397–400] 2009), for example, Augustine poses the rhetorical question, "Is it not thus, as I recall it, O Lord my God, Thou judge of my conscience? before Thee is my heart, and my remembrance, Who didst at that time direct me by the hidden mystery of Thy providence, and didst set those shameful errors of mine before my face, that I might see and hate them."

3 Notably, Augustine's *Confessions*, recognized as perhaps the western world's earliest known autobiography, tells the story of a man's search for truth and self-judgment through self-reflection, leading ultimately to his conversion to Christianity (or, in this context, an acceptance of the law). The significance of the ritual of confession to a number of religious traditions, not least certain Christian practices, also manifests the way in which the notion of authentic self-expression may not only be possible, but serves as a path to judgment by the law and justice. See, for example, the first line of *Confessions*, book 2: "I will now call to mind my past foulness, and the carnal corruptions of my soul; not because I love them, but that I may love Thee, O my God. For love of Thy love I do it; reviewing my most wicked ways in the very bitterness of my remembrance, that Thou mayest grow sweet unto me"; "Amidst these offences of foulness and violence, and so many iniquities, are sins of men, who are on the whole making proficiency; which by those that judge rightly, are, after the rule of perfection, discommended, yet the persons commended, upon hope of future fruit, as in the green blade of growing corn."

4 See Babcock and Hadaegh's documentary, *Scenes of a Crime*, released 16 April 2011; White 1997; Benforado 2010; Lassiter et al. 2001 ("The findings regarding the fundamental attribution error and salience effects lead to the conclusion that observers routinely fail to appreciate fully the causal influence of external factors or pressures on another individual's behavior and that the problem is compounded when those situational forces are rendered even less visible or salient by virtue of observers' visual perspective" [197]).

5 Studies show how culture and worldview, along with more specific perspectival framing, impact assessment of self and other. See Kahan, Hoffman, and Braman 2009; Benforado 2010.

6 Foucault's discussion focuses on a drawing by Magritte that depicts the pipe floating above a drawing of the famous painting precariously balanced on an easel. Foucault's discussion (7–8) notably engages the role of the frame and questions the ambiguous context clues created by the relationship of the images in the drawing(s).

7 And further complicating the interplay, Foucault makes note ([1968] 1983, 12) of how the

shape of the script of the word "Ceci" ("This") itself mimics the shape of the image of the pipe.

8   Sulkowicz insisted that the mattress performance would cease only if the alleged assailant was expelled, or if he left the university. See McDonald 2014.

9   Nair points to the heightened socio-legal significance of anal sex in the American imaginary, especially the way in which conventional presumptions impact its legibility. As Nair points out, "the larger cultural narratives about the act [anal sex] still mostly define it as something that only not-nice girls do. Or … as something that can only be forced upon nice girls, during rape." Thus, the claim that consensual vaginal sex turned into assaultive anal sex fits well within the prevailing gendered and heteronormative ideology (Nair 2015a).

10 For an overview of the common law definition of rape, see Lafave 2003, section 17.1(a) at 605–6. Rape is typically defined as non-consensual sexual intercourse that is committed by physical force, threat of injury, or other duress.

11 For a paradigmatic case of "acquaintance" rape showing that securing rape convictions in most US jurisdictions requires proof of more than just non-consensual sexual intercourse with a person who resists verbally, see Commonwealth v. Berkowitz 641 A.2d 1161 (Pa. 1994). See discussion of case and of the defence of "reasonable mistake" in Kahan 2010. See also Rusk v. State 406 A.2d 624 (Md. Ct. Spec. App.1979) and State v. Rusk, 424 A.2d 720 (Md. 1981) for a range of framings by judges of an encounter alleged to be rape differing on the characterization of force and consent.

12 See MacKinnon 2016, 431, for an updated radical feminist analysis of current rape law.

13 Compare Kahan 2010 for data suggesting that individuals' understandings of sexual encounters are shaped by cultural values (e.g., a hierarchical worldview, as opposed to an egalitarian one) more than by gender.

14 Sulkowicz 2015.

15 Cognizant of the variety of web interfaces used to procure manifestations of consent, contract scholars and some courts nonetheless refer to online agreements that purport by their terms to bind a user rather than requiring a particular action as "browsewrap" (Preston and McCann, 2011, 1). See also Hines v. Overstock.com, Inc., 668 F. Supp. 2d 362, 366 (E.D.N.Y. 2009), *aff'd*, 380 F. App'x 22 (2d Cir. 2010) (citing Southwest Airlines Co. v. BoardFirst, L.L.C., No. 06-CV-0891-B, 2007 WL 4823761, at *4 (N.D. Tex. Sept. 12, 2007)). So-called "clickwrap" agreements require a user to click prior to proceeding further in an order or service. See Hoffman v. Supplements Togo Mgmt, L.L.C., 18 A.3d 210, 219 (N.J. Super. Ct. App. Div. 2011). Browsewrap agreements do not require a user to take any affirmative action concerning the terms of agreement but rather purport by their terms to bind a user. Hines v. Overstock.com, Inc., 668 F. Supp. 2d 362, 366 (E.D.N.Y. 2009), *aff'd*, 380 F. App'x 22 (2d Cir. 2010) (citing Southwest Airlines Co. v. BoardFirst, L.L.C., No.

06-CV-0891-B, 2007 WL 4823761, at *4 (N.D. Tex. 12 September 2007)). These categories have been acknowledged as oversimplifications of the variety of website interfaces but are used by courts, if not dispositively, to construe the form of transaction. See, for example, Hoffman, 18 A.3d at 219. Though courts refer to "clickwrap" and "browsewrap" agreements, suggesting different degrees of consumer action and manifested agency, the distinction between "clickwrap" and "browsewrap" on its own does not render browsewrap agreements unenforceable. See Swift, 805 F. Supp. 2d at 915. Courts' determinations hinge on "whether a website user has actual or constructive knowledge of a site's terms and conditions prior to using the site." Hines, 668 F. Supp. 2d at 367. T per se; "What Is a Clickwrap Agreement? – Definition from Techopedia," 2016.

16 Legal scholars increasingly acknowledge that much of the non-negotiable terms consumers confront cannot be meaningfully processed by individuals, leaving them with a choice to accede or walk away (Korobkin 2003; Eisenberg 1995). Fine-print disclosures "are functionally unreadable (or at least indigestible) for consumers with bounded cognitive capacity – i.e., everyone" (Wilkinson-Ryan 2014).

17 See discussion in Kastner 2016.

18 See Stanley 1998, x.

19 Notwithstanding courts' so-called "objective" approach to contract since the nineteenth century, judges continue to invoke the rhetoric of a "meeting of minds" between parties: "In order to create a binding contract there must be a meeting of the minds as to the essential terms of the agreement." May v. Wilcox, 182 A.D.2d 939, 939-40 (N.Y.S. 2d 1992).

20 See ConocoPhillips Alaska, Inc. v. Williams Alaska Petroleum, Inc., 322 P.3d 114, 129 (Alaska 2014) (equating "dickered-for terms" with those deemed "sufficiently important"); Bowen v. Young 507 S.W.2d 600, 605 (Tex. Civ. App 1974) (granting "'dickered' aspects of the individual bargain," which go "so clearly to the essence of the bargain," the power to override words of disclaimer in a purchase agreement).

21 See discussion of how powerful parties can mobilize the myth of consent to constrain the agency of individuals in Kastner 2016.

22 See Radin 2014, 4–10.

23 For a comparative analysis of non-negotiable fine print, see Kastner 2016.

24 See Kastner 2014; Kim 2014.

25 See Bar-Gill 2013, 6–7.

REFERENCES

Augustine. [AD397–400] 2008. *Confessions*. Translated by Edward Bouverie Pusey. Peabody, MA: Hendrickson.

Babcock, Grover, and Blue Hadaegh, dirs. 2011. *Scenes of a Crime*. Documentary.

Bar-Gill, Oren. 2013. *Seduction by Contract: Law, Economics, and Psychology in Consumer Markets*. Oxford: Oxford University Press.

Benforado, Adam. 2010. "Frames of Injustice: The Bias We Overlook." *Indiana Law Journal* 85, no. 4: 1333–78.

Bikel, Ofra. 2010. "The Confessions." *Frontline* documentary, PBS, 9 November. https://www.pbs.org/wgbh/pages/frontline/the-confessions/.

Brink, Rebecca Vipond. 2015. "Emma Sulkowicz's 'Ceci N'est Pas Un Viol': An Explainer." *The Frisky*. 5 June. http://www.thefrisky.com/2015-06-05/emma-sulkowiczs-ceci-nest-pas-un-viol-an-explainer/.

Eisenberg, Melvin Aron. 1995. "The Limits of Cognition and the Limits of Contract." *Stanford Law Review* 47, no. 2 (January): 211.

Foucault, Michel. [1968] 1983. *This Is Not a Pipe*. Translated and edited by James Harkness Berkeley: University of California Press.

Grigoriadis, Vanessa. 2014. "Meet the College Women Who Are Starting a Revolution against Campus Sexual Assault." *The Cut*. 21 September. https://www.thecut.com/2014/09/emma-sulkowicz-campus-sexual-assault-activism.html.

Halley, Janet. 2008. "Rape in Berlin: Reconsidering the Criminalisation of Rape in the International Law of Armed Conflict." *Melbourne Journal of International Law* 9, no. 1: 78–124.

Kahan, Dan M. 2010. "Culture, Cognition and Consent: Who Perceives What, and Why, in Acquaintance Rape Cases." *University of Pennsylvania Law Review* 158, no. 3: 729–813.

Kahan, Dan M., David A. Hoffman, and Donald Braman. 2009. "Whose Eyes Are You Going to Believe? Scott v. Harris and the Perils of Cognitive Illiberalism." *Harvard Law Review* 122, no. 3: 837–906.

kaliochaos. 2015. "Safe Words and Safe Gestures." *Kali Chaos BDSM*. 22 June. https://kalichaosbdsm.wordpress.com/2015/06/22/safe-words-and-safe-gestures/.

Kassin, Saul M., Christian A. Meissner, and Rebecca J. Norwick. 2005. "'I'd Know a False Confession If I Saw One'": A Comparative Study of College Students and Police Investigators." *Law and Human Behavior* 29, no. 2: 211–27.

Kastner, Tal. 2014. "How 'bout Them Apples? The Power of Stories of Agreement in Consumer Contracts." *Drexel Law Review* 7, no. 1 (Fall): 67.

– 2016. "'I'm Just Some Guy': Positing and Leveraging Legal Subjects in Consumer Contracts and the Global Market." *Indiana Journal of Global Legal Studies* 23, no. 2: 531. doi:10.2979/indjglolegstu.23.2.0531.

Kessler, Friedrich. 1943. "Contracts of Adhesion – Some Thoughts about Freedom of Contract." *Columbia Law Review* 43, no. 5 (July): 629.

Kim, Nancy S. 2014. "Situational Duress and the Aberrance of Electronic Contracts." *Chicago-Kent Law Review* 89, no. 1: 265.

Korobkin, Russell. 2003. "Bounded Rationality, Standard Form Contracts, and Unconscionability." *University of Chicago Law Review* 70, no. 4: 1203–95. doi:10.2307/1600574.

Lafave, Wayne R. 2003. *Substantive Criminal Law*. 2nd ed. Eagan, MN: Thomson/West.

Lassiter, Daniel G., Andrew L. Geers, Patrick J. Munhall, Ian M. Handley, and Melissa J. Beers. 2001. "Videotaped Confessions: Is Guilt in the Eye of the Camera?" *Advances in Experimental Social Psychology* 33, no. 1: 189–254.

Long Chu, Andrea. 2017. "Study in Blue: Trauma, Affect, Event." *Women and Performance: A Journal of Feminist Theory* 27, no. 3: 301–15.

MacKinnon, Catharine A. 1989. *Toward a Feminist Theory of the State*. Cambridge: Harvard University Press.

— 2016. "Rape Redefined." *Harvard Law and Policy Review* 10, no. 2: 431.

McDonald, Soraya Nadia. 2014. "It's Hard to Ignore a Woman Toting a Mattress Everywhere She Goes, Which Is Why Emma Sulkowicz Is Still Doing It." *Washington Post*. 29 October. https://www.washingtonpost.com/news/morning-mix/wp/2014/10/29/its-hard-to-ignore-a-woman-toting-a-mattress-everywhere-she-goes-which-is-why-emma-sulkowicz-is-still-doing-it/.

Nair, Yasmin. 2015a. "Anal Sex and Its Discontents: Emma Sulkowicz, Lawrence v. Texas, and the Histories of a Sex Act." 28 May. http://www.yasminnair.net/content/anal-sex-and-its-discontents-emma-sulkowicz-lawrence-v-texas-and-histories-sex-act-subscribe.

— 2015b. "Emma Sulkowicz's Rape Video: Some Thoughts." [June]. http://www.yasminnair.net/content/emma-sulkowiczs-rape-video-some-thoughts.

Preston, Cheryl B., and Eli W. McCann. 2011. "Unwrapping Shrinkwraps, Clickwraps, and Browsewraps: How the Law Went Wrong from Horse Traders to the Law of the Horse." *Brigham Young University Journal of Public Law* 26, no. 1: 1.

Radin, Margaret Jane. 2014. *Boilerplate: The Fine Print, Vanishing Rights, and the Rule of Law*. Princeton: Princeton University Press.

Scarry, Elaine. 1985. "The Body in Pain." New York: *Oxford University Press*.

Stanley, Amy Dru. 1998. *From Bondage to Contract: Wage Labor, Marriage, and the Market in the Age of Slave Emancipation*. Cambridge: Cambridge University Press.

Sulkowicz, Emma. 2015. "Ceci n'est pas un viol." http://www.cecinestpasunviol.com/.

Torczyner, Harry. 1979. *Magritte: Ideas and Images*. New York: Harry N. Abrams.

"What Is a Clickwrap Agreement? Definition from Techopedia." 2016. *Techopedia.com*. https://www.techopedia.com/definition/4243/clickwrap-agreement.

White, Welsch. 1997. "False Confessions and the Constitution: Safeguards against Untrustworthy Confessions." *Harvard Civil Rights-Civil Liberties Law Review* 32, no. 1: 105–57.

Wilkinson-Ryan, Tess. 2014. "A Psychological Account of Consent to Fine Print." *Iowa Law Review* 99, no. 4.

2

More Than Just Selfies: #Occupotty, Affect, and Confession as Activism

ANDIE SHABBAR

The #Occupotty selfie campaign began in 2013 after a series of trans discriminatory "bathroom bills" were introduced in the United States and Canada that sought to make it illegal for trans people to use the bathroom of their choice.[1] Posted to social media sites such as Instagram, Facebook, and Twitter, #Occupotty selfies encompass both still photos and short videos in which trans people take images of themselves in the gender bathroom of their birth-assigned sex. Images tagged with #Occupotty also include "selfies" that do not picture a person or represent an identifiable self, an important point I will explore further. Both satirical and sombre, these images serve to represent different experiences of being trans in public restrooms as well as the desire to participate in collective political action. Like other selfie movements on social media, the hashtag is a critical aspect of the campaign's momentum and visibility. Not only does a clever hashtag enable the rapid circulation of images to public audiences, it also brings images together to create a visual mosaic of difference and community activism. While the content and style of #Occupotty selfies vary, a popular trope is to visually contrast one's gender presentation to cisgender actors who pose as patrons in the bathroom. For example, trans activist Michael Hughes from Minnesota staged a series of selfies that show him standing in front of the bathroom mirror staring sullenly into his camera phone while a conventionally feminine woman can be seen in the background. The disparity between the two, a bearded and butch Hughes alongside a woman applying lipstick, as one of his images depicts, frames the following caption that is embedded in most of his images: "Republicans want to put me in the restroom with her, because I was assigned female at birth – do I look like I belong in women's facilities? #occupotty #wejustneedtopee #letmypeoplepee #translivesmatter" (fig. 2.1). The direct address to the viewer, which solicits the answer no, makes a strong political statement. What is more, by including the occupotty hashtag within the image, Hughes participates in and incites others to join the

2.1 Trans Twitter activist Michael Hughes utilizing visual evidence to point out the awkwardness of his male presentation within a female public restroom. #Occupotty, Twitter, 2015.

campaign and confess to their own experiences of being trans in public bathrooms. #Occupotty, therefore, is an activism that rests on the mobilization of confession. However, as I argue, this particular act of confessing is not so much concerned with telling the "truth" of one's gender but rather harnesses confession as an *affective tool* to generate collective political action.

By presenting a radically different approach to confession that takes affect as its starting point, the constraining and exhaustive aspects of confession – the interplay between truth and sex and knowledge – this paper instead generates a politically useful adaptation of confession, questioning the conventional understanding of its function as disciplinary. I turn to the #Occupotty selfie movement to ask: How are confessional images mobilized by activists as a political tool? What new and affirmative potentials do social media bring to the act of confessing? And, can confession, as a collective form of activism, be unyoked from the production of truth and identity? To address these questions, I argue for an understanding of confession that takes into account both its affective intensity and its potential as a collective assemblage.

As an assemblage, #Occupotty brings together singular confessions to form a multiplicity of confession capable of doing activism in ways that exceed the limitations of identity politics. The problem with a politics of identity is that it often demands rights and recognition based on an essentialist claim that there exists an authentic interior and true self that needs to be recognized and acknowledged by others. As many feminist and queer scholars have critiqued, essentialist identity politics limit what counts as a particular identity, thereby erasing and excluding outsiders from its political endeavours. By turning away from questions of truth and identity, and looking toward the affective dimensions of confession, I aim to shed light on how confessing can be utilized as a tool to challenge the identificatory regimes that undergird gender policing in public bathrooms. This is not to say that confession is no longer imbued with relations of power or that it is not used as a primary technique in the production of knowledge. What I hope to impart to the reader is an argument that explores how we can deploy confession in unexpected ways to transform relations of power and our understanding of sexual subjectivity as it relates to political autonomy. First, however, it is necessary to understand how confession is theorized as an *individualizing* disciplinary mechanism so that we can then reimagine how it may be deployed as a *collective* tool for political action.

Discipline and Confession

From Facebook status updates to Christian penance, we are a society that incites confession at every turn. We tell the "truth" of ourselves and of others everywhere all the time to bring into light what is thought to hide deep within. However, as Foucault tells us in *The History of Sexuality*, vol. 1, confession is an act that *produces* the subject ([1976] 1990, 61). Confession does not represent the truth of something that already exists: rather, it produces that which it names. In this sense, confession is a disciplinary technique and an effect of power that forms the subject through a discourse of knowledge that links truth and sex. Telling the truth of sex, which is to say acknowledging one's own actions and thoughts about sex, is essential to the production of identity and the status of one's subjectivity (ibid.). Confession modifies the subject by setting one free, unburdening one from the "secret inside," but it does so through a relation of domination. Foucault explains that confession must be performed in the presence (or virtual presence) of an authoritative other who prescribes and receives the confession in order to either punish or liberate the subject from what they conceal (1978, 62). This aspect of confession – the freedom from the repressive weight of "the secret" – spirals pleasure and power such that "the pleasure of knowing the truth, of discovering and exposing it, the fascination of seeing and telling it, of captivating and capturing others by it, of confiding in its secret, of luring it out in the open" conceals the dynamics of power embedded therein (71). Whether we are confessing ourselves or witnessing others' confessions, the act of telling the "truth," Foucault contends, is so deeply embedded in our society and in the modern subject that it is no longer perceived as something that is coerced but as voluntary, which serves to conceal the weight of its disciplinary force (60).

Further, Foucault argues that there is always an authority figure, an interlocutor, to whom we confess, and this figure is the benefactor of our pleasure. In Foucault's words, "The agency of domination does not reside in the one who speaks (for it is he who is constrained), but in the one who listens and says nothing; not in the one who knows and answers, but in the one who questions and is not supposed to know. And this discourse of truth finally takes effect, not in the one who received it, but in the one from whom it is wrested" (62). This passage illustrates the domination at the heart of confession. If subjectivity is conferred through confession, it is done so by taking hold of the subject in a hierarchical relationship that masks control with a discourse of pleasure. What is more, confession is a procedure of individualization that guarantees *oneself* by virtue of telling the truth *about* oneself. At stake in this process of individualization is the location of the subject within societal structures such that "truth" becomes tied to identity. Ultimately, Foucault's critique of confession is that it creates a discourse of knowledge whereby sexuality and identity are presented as givens – truths that have been repressed and that once confessed will set the subject free. The notion that there exists an inner truth is, Foucault exclaims, "the internal ruse of confession" ([1976] 1990, 59); it is an illusion that obscures the ways in which our knowledge of sexuality is produced through disciplinary power.

Unlike Foucault's approach to confession, this essay begins from an ontology of affect that takes confession as a site of *potentiality* insofar as confession is mobilized for political transformation. This commitment does not dismiss the disciplinary aspects of confession; instead, it is interested in imagining *new* applications in a society evermore saturated by confession. My argument, that the #Occupotty movement is formed through a multiplicity of confession that we, as viewers and participants, encounter *all at once,* conceptualizes confession as a *depersonalized force* that is capable of activating and intensifying political engagement through its *affective* dimensions. This perspective necessitates a shift in our attention from the confessing *subject* to the *movement* of confession. The movement of confession in #Occupotty, I claim, is an event that decentres the subject along with truth and identity so as to collapse the distinction between "subject" and "object." The movement of confession forms a rhizome in which a unity, *a* subject, does not exist. As Gilles Deleuze and Félix Guattari explain in their magnum opus, *A Thousand Plateaus*: "There are no points or positions in a rhizome, such as those found in a structure … There are only lines" ([1980] 1987, 6). In other words, there is no one identity, political message, or selfie image that is representative of #Occupotty. As follows, my approach to #Occupotty as a confessional movement is collective in kind, affirmative in nature, and affective in force.

My use of the term *affect* is largely informed by Deleuze's philosophy including his collaborative work with Guattari. Briefly, affect is the capacity to affect and be affected. It is a sensate relationality and intensity that puts a body into motion.[2] Importantly, Deleuze argues that affects operate independently of emotions. For Deleuze, affects are non-personal becomings, material contagions, and instincts of the flesh (Deleuze 1981, 39).[3] Brian Massumi further elucidates Deleuze's distinction between affect and emotion: "Affect is most often used loosely as a synonym for emotion. But … emotion and affect – if affect is intensity – follow different logics and pertain to different orders" (2002, 27). Massumi continues: "An emotion is a subjective content, the sociolinguistic fixing of the quality of an experience which is from that point onward defined as personal. Emotion is qualified intensity, the conventional, consensual point of insertion of intensity into semantically and semiotically formed progressions, into narrativizable action-reaction circuits" (2002, 28).

In short, affect is a *virtual* intensity, and emotion is that intensity *actualized*. Affects are pre-personal, whereas emotions are seated in particular discursive histories. In this way, "the affective is not about empathy or emotive identification, or *any* form of identification for that matter" (Massumi 2002, 40, emphasis added). The #Occupotty selfie, for example, generates affect not through an identification with its content or an emotional interpretation of it but through relations with its form, function, and materiality. The selfie generates "lines of flight," forming a connective tissue between the selfie and viewer that folds new bodies into the #Occupotty rhizome. The movement's expansive reach and political momentum intensifies not through a structure of identification but through *a structure of feeling*. At first glance, it may seem like an odd pairing, a theory of affect and the topic of confession; while the former decentres the subject (and object distinction), the latter is concerned with subject-formation. It is precisely this theoretical disjuncture that sparks in me the desire to bring confession and affect together to see what this new conceptual framework – assemblage – can *do*.

Selfies or Usies?

From blogs and vlogs (video logs) to tweets and status updates, and what some view as a "selfie obsessed" culture, there is no denying that online confessions permeate the fabric of our society. But are these social expressions of the "self" just acts of vanity, as some suggest? Are they a way to confess to others what is hiding away deep inside only to be set free once published online? Or, conversely, are selfies, posted and shared on the internet, entered into a web of knowledge-power, a cultivation of *usies* that aim to collectivize rather than individualize? While there is no one answer, the last suggestion is often quickly dismissed and its collective and subversive potentials denied. For example, even in an overtly political selfie campaign such as #Occupotty, there is a concerted effort by those reporting on it to focus on the "leaders" of the movement or to highlight the identity of the person who "started it." Even here, I name two of the most prominent figures of the movement and isolate their images from the rest for analysis. However, unlike news coverage and community journalism that report on the campaign, I aim to do so without privileging their selfies over others or detaching them from the rhizomatic web in which they belong and where their virality is produced. The selection of images reproduced here is guided by an ethical consideration for those who have posted selfies using the hashtag Occupotty but who have not, for whatever reasons, chosen to make their personally identifiable information public. The reason for this notation is to underline the importance of conceiving of #Occupotty as an assemblage. While I do believe the movement can be reducible to its parts, with each selfie carrying its own political weight, my focus of this essay is to discuss how #Occupotty forms an *assemblage of confessions* that displaces the very possibility of truth and identity.

    Assemblage (*agencement*) is a concept introduced by Deleuze and Guattari that relates closely to the rhizome. Described by Deleuze as a "general logic" (quoted in Nail 2017, 21), assemblages are the arrangement or fitting together of discrete elements to form a constellation with a new function. Crucially, an assemblage is not a unity comprised of various parts that all work together like the inseparable organs of a human body. Indeed, an assemblage is what Deleuze and Guattari call a Body without Organs (BwO) (1987, 150). Assemblages are not organizing or prioritizing systems like the human body that requires all of its organs to function (the heart requires the brain, the brain requires the lungs, and so on). Unlike the assemblage, in a unity such as the human body, there is no room for recombination or emancipation without destroying the unity in the process (Nail 2017, 23). For Deleuze and Guattari, assemblages are more like machines. They are formed through a mixture of elements that are interchangeable and aggregate. When new elements are added to the mix, the assemblage changes (Nail 2017, 23). In this way, assemblages are multiplicities that transform, recombine, and change in function with the introduction of new discrete elements, which can also be considered as their own multiplicities (or assemblages). What is important about an assemblage, then, is not its heterogeneous elements but the *relations between them*, since it is precisely these relations that produce the assemblage's potential to affect and be affected (Deleuze and Guattari 7). For example, Deleuze and Guattari contend that a book, as an assemblage, can never be taken as a final product. Its elements – paper, ink, the printing process, literacy, glue, and so forth – bring the book together to function as a text, but we can never know what the book will become or what it will do in the future. When brought into relation with wood and gasoline, for instance, the book no longer functions as a production of ideas; its materiality is what matters most as the book enters into a becoming-kindling for fire. The importance of assemblage theory is that it emphasizes relationality, connectivity, and fluidity. In an assemblage, nothing is ever fixed or stable; there is no essence, only difference (8–9). What would it mean to consider #Occupotty as an assemblage? Already, we have been doing just that. Thus far, I have suggested that the movement forms through a composition of heterogeneous selfies that, when in relation, function as a collective tool of activism. Now I would like to take a closer look at two of its discrete elements – not to give them privilege but to illustrate how discrete selfies both transform and are transformed by the #Occupotty assemblage.

Michael Hughes and Brae Carnes are two activists who have taken centre stage in media coverage of the bathroom selfie movement. Prior to Hughes's first selfie, posted in March 2015, Carnes, a trans woman from Victoria, British Columbia, shared one of the first bathroom selfies in 2013 using the hashtag WeJustNeedToPee. Unlike the majority of #Occupotty selfies, Carnes's images include sleek and stylized photographs, and some "selfies" are shot from a secondary camera that the viewer is unable to see. In these images, it is not immediately obvious that a secondary camera took the photograph; it is only when the viewer closely inspects the perspective and composition of the image that its staging becomes noticeable (fig. 2.2). Still, Carnes holds her hot-pink phone in front of her as if she is taking the image. That the cell-phone remains central to the photograph attests to the importance of #Occupotty images being perceived as selfies. The aesthetic of a selfie photo gives the impression that the image was taken spontaneously and stealthily, and, in this instance, seemingly unbeknownst to the other patrons pictured in the bathroom. I suggest that this particular aesthetic of the selfie photograph renders it a mode of confession whereby a secret is shared only between the viewer and "selfieographer." And, this secret, in the case of the #Occupotty movement, is only knowable through its hashtag.

What is interesting about bathroom selfies like Carnes's and Hughes's is that *they perform confession* to *resist the incitement to confess*. That is to say, taking bathroom selfies in the "wrong bathroom" and then tagging them with the hashtag Occupotty emphasizes to the viewer the oppressive effects of both concealment and exposure. The selfies attempt to underline the importance of *not* being subject to confession and *not* having to tell the "truth" of oneself whenever one goes to the bathroom. It is somewhat curious, then, that the cisgender actors in the photographs do not appear to notice Carnes or Hughes, nor is there any indication from the scene that Carnes or Hughes are perceived by others as not belonging, and yet both ask the viewer: "Does it look like I belong here?"[4]

This particular question of belonging, shared by both activists, has unwittingly invoked criticism of the movement from some non-binary and gender nonconforming people who retort: "If you clearly belong in *the other* bathroom, then *where* do *I* belong?"[5] This query is entirely different from the rhetorical question Carnes and Hughes pose. "*Where* do I belong" instead of "Do I look like I belong *here?*" indicates that the problem goes beyond presenting as a man or woman and then subsequently being forced to use the bathroom of the opposing gender.[6] The former question gestures toward the concern that there is a larger discursive issue that needs to be addressed on a structural level as well as through individual bathroom policies. There is, of course, a third "solution" to the "bathroom problem" that Carnes and Hughes do not invoke – which is making gender-neutral bathrooms available and commonplace in everyday public space. The proposal for more gender-neutral bathrooms in addition to non-discriminatory legislation acknowledges that not all trans or gender non-conforming people adhere to normative presentations of gender. The reaction to Hughes and Carnes from

#Occupotty, Affect, and Confession | 57

2.2 Casual activism as part of the WeJustNeedToPee campaign: Brae Carnes, WeJustNeedToPee, Instagram, 2015.

those who do not and do not want to conform to a gender presentation of *either* male or female illustrates the fundamental importance of considering the #Occupotty movement as a *multiplicity* of selfies and political statements regarding public bathrooms. Moreover, the reaction highlights the dangers of singling out individual activists and their *particular gender identities* as representative of the whole movement as well as generalizing the oppressive effects of anti-trans legislation. This is precisely the reason I have chosen to focus on the hashtag Occupotty and not WeJustNeedToPee. Though the latter quickly communicates to the viewer what the image is about (and the political value of this should not be underestimated), it indicates that the "bathroom problem" has a straightforward fix: the government needs to sanction non-discriminatory laws so that trans people can use the bathroom that *corresponds* to their gender identity. While legislative change like this is undoubtedly a political gain, it does not address the "problem" for those who do not have a facility that "corresponds" to their gender. Whereas the second hashtag, Occupotty, signifies the need for an active political response: to occupy and reclaim the oppressive space of *gender segregated* public bathrooms as a form of resistance to cisgender *and* heteropatriarchal structures that uphold the gender binary system. In sum, the two hashtags carry different political messages: WeJustNeedToPee addresses lawmakers as a plea for equal

(equal to cisgender people) rights and recognition, whereas #Occupotty incites trans, queer, and non-binary people to take up space in ways that subvert the gender system altogether. Thus, #Occupotty moves away from the desire for state acknowledgment insofar as it does not ask for permission or acknowledgment from the government or public; rather, it incites civil disobedience. In this way, #Occupotty mobilizes the confessional selfie as a direct action in which the selfie acts as a catalyst for *collective* activism rather than as a production of subject-formation or individual identity representation.

*Dis*identification and Confession

In addition to conventional self-portrait images like those produced by Carnes and Hughes, the bathroom selfie movement is populated with thousands of images that stretch the boundaries of what constitute a selfie and further, a confession. For example, on Instagram, #Occupotty encompasses images that include group photos, street protests, art activisms outside of the bathroom, Internet memes on bathroom politics, public bathroom signposts, image clippings of news articles, seemingly random pictures of cats and dogs, bathroom graffiti, and political cartoons that critique the bathroom bills. Though each image is linked to an individual user account, when brought together under #Occupotty, the images form a collective response that *dis*identifies the movement from any one particular user or identity.

In *Disidentifications: Queers of Color and the Performance of Politics* (1999), José Esteban Muñoz theorizes "disidentification" as a survival tool for minoritarian subjects who face systemic violence and oppression in a majoritarian sphere. To disidentify is a tactical strategy that enables one to negotiate the constraints of dominant ideologies that punish subjects who do not conform to normative configurations of subjectivity – namely, white heteronormativity. For example, Muñoz contends that the normativizing forces of whiteness and heterosexuality erect phobic barriers around race and sexuality in ways that construct queerness as "a white thing" (9). Consequently, queers of colour are barred access to their sexual identity in ways that white queers are not. Significantly, both Carnes and Hughes, to whom the media attribute the #Occupotty movement, are both white. Disidentification, Muñoz proposes, enables queers of colour to identify with both queerness and ethnos despite racialized phobias coming from both domains (11). To disidentify, one must not assimilate within *nor* entirely reject dominant images of identity. That is, the disidentified subject refuses attempts to conform to the dominant ideology – indeed, this subject emerges from its initial failure to conform – and at the same time the subject resists adopting a counter-identity (11). The problem with counter-identification, Muñoz explains, is that it over-determines and validates the authority of the dominant ideology through its symmetrical opposition (11). As a political strategy, disidentification is not dismissive of identity politics, nor is it apolitical; it is a tactic that works *within and against* the dominant ideology to wrest free of it a new subject position with increased agency.

#Occupotty does not identify with a particular trans identity, nor does it seek to create a symmetrical counter identity. It enacts a mode of disidentification that works within and against the production of a singular identity. For instance, when taken as a whole, #Occupotty is undoubtedly an act of political resistance to anti-trans bathroom legislation. However, its resistance is not tied to one particular identity, nor does the movement crystallize around one particular political focal point. As an assemblage, #Occupotty does not have a beginning or end point; there is no one primary issue or goal. Furthermore, its selfies perform sexuality in diverse ways, and sometimes these performances do not immediately correspond to bathroom politics. #Occupotty's visual detachment of selfies from identity is expressly *anti-assimilationist* and thus endeavours to reclaim, both actually and virtually, a hostile and violent public space through *inattention* to identity. The incitement from phobic bathroom patrons, policy makers, or even other activists to confess to an *individualized* experience of sexuality aims to buttress dominant images of who qualifies as trans. For example, when Carnes's and Hughes's selfies are viewed *in isolation* from the movement, it becomes possible to read their expressions of trans identity in ways that authenticate hegemonic representations of trans subjectivity. To expand on this point, both of their selfies explicitly enact a counter-identification by symmetrically opposing gender-discriminatory legislation. The two activists counter the demand that trans people use the "right bathroom" by illustrating how this rule would place trans people in the "wrong bathroom." Their either/or approach – right versus wrong (bathroom), I don't belong here, I belong over there – does not challenge the gender dichotomy but only the way in which it is imposed. Accordingly, their selfies risk being appropriated in ways that oversimplify the "bathroom problem" – whom it affects and what its solution should be. Importantly, I am not critiquing Carnes' or Hughes' political endeavours; I am attempting to point out the ways in which their emphasis on identity makes the images vulnerable to exploitation while also excluding those who do not share a similar gender presentation or trans identity. Their selfies are not less politically effective than those that go beyond identity, but they do serve different political ends. Indeed, disidentification may not be the best strategy of resistance and survival for Hughes or Carnes or for other trans people more generally. As Muñoz states, "At times, resistance needs to be pronounced and direct; on other occasions, queers of colour and other minority subjects need to follow a conformist path if they hope to survive a hostile public sphere. But, for some, disidentification is a survival strategy that works within and outside the dominant public sphere simultaneously" (1999, 5). Besides, when tagged with #Occupotty, Carnes's and Hughes's selfies become part of the rhizome of disidentification, an assemblage that decentres the "self" from selfies, enabling them to work in more expansive ways. It is only when bathroom selfies are taken as individualized confessions that these issues arise. #Occupotty enables subjects who were previously excluded from the "bathroom debates" (i.e., not represented on either side) to take action against structural oppression regardless of whether or not their experience of oppression is acknowledged in the public sphere.

The act of disidentification in which images are no longer tied to an identity or seek acknowledgment from an other gives #Occupotty access to the public sphere through a mode of confession that subverts its usual dialectical hierarchy of recognition. To reiterate, Foucault argues that confession requires submission to an authoritative other who has the hierarchical power to either punish or forgive ([1976] 1990, 61). #Occupotty elides this relation of domination by producing confessional images that do not link the confession back to *a* self. In a similar vein, writing on trans video blogs on YouTube, Tobias Raun (2012) argues that trans vlogs, like #Occupotty selfies, do not belong to a confessional culture in the Foucauldian sense. However, Raun argues, unlike #Occupotty selfies that evade the disciplinary forces of confession through disidentification, trans vlogs subvert domination by telling one's experience at one's own request (169). Contrasting the ways in which trans people are subject to routine and forced confession in juridical and medical fields to their chosen performances of confession on YouTube, Raun avers that trans vlogs "become a resilient collective effort to intervene in and negotiate dominant public discourses on trans identity that often victimize and/or pathologize the trans person" (169). On a different wavelength, #Occupotty brings a politics of difference into the public arena not only to challenge constricting narratives of trans identity but to *question* identity *en masse*. For Raun, trans vlogs provide a degree of public visibility for trans people who are often denied visual representation in the social sphere. In contrast, #Occupotty uses the power of *invisibility* as a mode of disidentification that performs a "bulwark against the effects of dominant publicity" (Muñoz 1999, 169).[7] Namely, by not spotlighting identity, #Occupotty enacts invisibility as a safeguard against a hostile

2.3
The immediacy of #Occupotty scribbled on a bathroom stall. Instagram, 2017.

and voyeuristic public but makes its political potential visible to those in proximity to its politics. Or, put another way, #Occupotty forms an intimate public. Lauren Berlant (2011) introduces the concept of an intimate public to describe a political counter-site in which constituency is based not on identification but *affective affinity*. Just as disidentification is a survival strategy for Muñoz, the intimate public functions as a strategy for Berlant. She explains that intimate publics are sites that loosely hold people together through emotion and affect rather than identification and commitment (2011, 226). She maintains that intimate publics tell stories of survival and trauma. Likewise, #Occupotty is an intimate public of survival, but in place of telling individual "truths" of trauma, the movement collectivizes the affect of trauma through a public display of images that are not reducible to one another. In this way, #Occupotty "loosely holds people together" by weaving the affective threads of disidentification *in between* patterns of identification and counter identification.

Like bathroom selfies, bathroom graffiti is another political tool that mobilizes activism through an affective aesthetic of disidentification. Bathroom graffiti, as I have argued elsewhere, messes up the heteronormative landscape and acts on bodies in ways that build a sense of community without attaching confession to a particular identity (Shabbar 2016, 85). One obvious way this is achieved is through anonymity. Whereas social-media videos and images can arguably be traced back to a user and thus a creator/confessant, bathroom graffiti leaves no such trace. When one encounters bathroom graffiti in public restrooms, there is an immediacy of potential felt through our bodies as we come into proximity with its *materiality*. The unique stylistics of each graffiti inscription alters our somatic experience of the public bathroom space in one way or another, but always in ways that cannot be known in advance. In this register, the crucial question is not *who* wrote it or *why*, or even *what* it says? But more pressingly, the question is *what* it *does*? That is, how does it change the oppressive space of gender-segregated bathrooms? How does it produce the conditions for subsequent confessions to follow? There are a number of images of bathroom graffiti tagged with #Occupotty (fig. 2.3). While not hugely popular, as images that circulate online these "selfies" are unique in their capacity to perform disidentification for the simple fact that the person who wrote the graffiti, the one who confessed, is not necessarily the person who posted and tagged the image. Because the identity of the graffiti writer is opaque, the inscription, both as written in the bathroom and as pictured online, evokes not a sense of identification but an affective affinity. What I am suggesting is that bathroom graffiti performs disidentity through the production of affect, and this affect is not attributable to any one identity or group. As such, bathroom graffiti is another performance of disidentification that, like #Occupotty selfies, challenges individual/collective, representational/performative, and public/private binaries that underpin both the social space of public bathrooms *and* the disciplinary forces of confession.

As the #Occupotty movement mobilizes confession as a collective political tool, its potentials go beyond identificatory regimes that reduce the complexity of subjectivity to a static and simplified identity. #Occupotty performs a tactical *mis*recognition that challenges oppressive configurations of minoritarian identity in the public sphere. As Muñoz says of disidentification, the #Occupotty movement is not anti-identity; it is an "anti-identitarian identity politics" (1999, 76) that critiques "weak" identity pluralism and calls for "an engagement with the *question of identity*" (164, emphasis in original). The bathroom selfie movement mobilizes confession in ways that do not rely on a model of identification and that question the necessity of activisms grounding in identity. Instead, the #Occupotty movement softens the hard lines of identity-driven bathroom politics and through its *affective force* of disidentification opens up new potentials for collective political transformation.

NOTES

1. The most popular bill during the emergence of #Occupotty in 2015 was the North Carolina Public Facilities Privacy and Security Act, otherwise known as House Bill 2 or HB2. The bill sanctions state discrimination against LGBTQ people by not recognizing gender identity and sexual orientation as markers of classes of people who deserve protection against discrimination. In effect, the law prohibits trans people from using public bathrooms that correspond to their gender identity. In Canada, in 2013 Conservative senator Donald Plett amended Bill C-279 that proposed adding gender identity to the Canadian Human Rights Act, removing the trans-inclusive provision, thus exempting "sex-specific" facilities, including public bathrooms, from discriminatory protection.
2. Here a body refers to both human and non-human bodies.
3. For example, one place where we see Deleuze articulate affect apart from emotion is in his analysis of the painter Francis Bacon. Deleuze suggests that "there are no feelings in Bacon: there are nothing but affects; that is, 'sensations' and 'instincts,' according to the formula of naturalism. Sensation is what determines instinct at a particular moment, just as instinct is the passage of one sensation to another, the search for the 'best' sensation (not the most agreeable sensation, but the one that fills the flesh at a particular moment of its descent, contradiction or dilation" (1987, 39).
4. While not pictured here, Carnes, like Hughes, captions selfies on several occasions with the query, "Does it look like I belong here?"
5. See ZangPiePearl 2015.
6. In the subreddit forum TrollXChromosomes, users discuss the exclusionary politics of "passing" and criticize images tagged with the WeJustNeedToPee hashtag specifically for reproducing normative ideas and images of trans identity.
7. The complexity of oppression necessitates that different tools be deployed at different times for different purposes. My suggestion that invisibility is a powerful strategy of resistance does not aim to ignore the importance of visibility and recognition. While space does not permit an adequate discussion on the subversive potentials of invisibility, the following authors theorize the political potentials of non-visibility: For theories of escape see Papadopoulos et al. 2008; for "the right to opacity," see Glissant 1990; and for a politics of imperceptibility, see Deleuze and Guattari 1987; Braidotti 2006.

REFERENCES

Berlant, Lauren. 2011. *Cruel Optimism*. Durham: Duke University Press.
Braidotti, Rosi. 2006. "The Ethics of Becoming Imperceptible." In *Deleuze and Philosophy*, edited by Constantin V. Boundas, 133–59. Edinburgh: Edinburgh University Press.
Deleuze, Gilles. 1981. *Francis Bacon: The Logic of Sensation*. Translated by Daniel W. Smith. Minneapolis: University of Minnesota Press.

Deleuze, Gilles, and Félix Guattari. [1980] 1987. *A Thousand Plateaus: Capitalism and Schizophrenia*. Translated by Brian Massumi. Minneapolis: University of Minnesota Press.

Foucault, Michel. [1976] 1990. *The History of Sexuality*. Vol. 1, *An Introduction*. Translated by Robert Hurley. New York: Vintage Books.

Glissant, Édouard. 1990. *Poetics of Relation*. Translated by Betsy Wing, Michigan: University of Michigan Press.

Massumi, Brian. 2002. *Parables for the Virtual: Movement, Affect, Sensation*. Durham: Duke University Press.

Muñoz, José Esteban. 1999. *Disidentifications: Queers of Color and the Performance of Politics*. Minneapolis: University of Minnesota Press.

Nail, Thomas. 2017. "What Is an Assemblage?" *Substance* 46, no. 1: 21–37.

Raun, Tobias. 2012. "DIY Therapy: Exploring Affective Self-Representations in Trans Video Blogs on YouTube." In *Digital Cultures and the Politics of Emotion: Feelings, Affect and Technological Change*, edited by Athina Karatzogianni and Adi Kuntsman, 165–80. Palgrave Macmillan.

Papadopoulos, Dimitris, Niamh Stephenson, and Vassilis Tsianos. 2008. *Escape Routes: Control and Subversion in the Twenty-First Century*. Chicago: University of Chicago Press.

Shabbar, Andie. 2016. "Queer Bathroom Graffiti Matters: Agential Realism and Affective Temporalities." *Rhizomes: Cultural Studies in Emerging Knowledge* 30: 80–92.

ZangPiePearl. 2015. "I Saw This and It Made Me Think of the Woman […]" *Reddit*. Accessed July 2015. Link expired. https://www.reddit.com/r/TrollXChromosomes/comments/2ytjot/i_saw_this_and_it_made_me_think_of_the_woman_who/.

3

Against Authenticity: The Feminist Turn in N. Maxwell Lander's Video Work

NAOMI DE SZEGHEO-LANG
WITH N. MAXWELL LANDER

Naomi

On a hot summer's day in June 2006, I rounded the corner onto Toronto's Queen Street West and into the Gladstone Hotel. In many ways, it was a day like any other: friends had asked me to join them at an event, and I agreed without knowing much about it. As soon as I entered the Feminist Porn Awards (FPAs),[1] I could tell I was witnessing a watershed moment in the city's sex-positive feminism. The Gladstone's ballroom was packed full of feminists and queers, and the air was thick with sweat and laughter. I was overwhelmed by the high-energy excitement that surrounded me. That first year's event was a modest undertaking, a single night of discussion and screenings where the speakers shared their experiences of creating more woman-friendly porn, more conscientious porn, and less oppressively stereotypical porn.[2] I stood near the back of the room, with an almost-ex-lover on my left and a soon-to-be-new-lover on my right. I caught only every other word of the conversation, straining to hear more over the crowd's chatter, but I knew the event had been a long time coming.

Though I attended the FPAs each year after that, the awards remained the bulk of my engagement with feminist porn. Years later, when I performed in my first porn scene, I realized I was still largely unaware of the robust histories I was aligning myself with. I had already been modelling in nude and erotic shoots, mostly for feminist photographer N. Maxwell Lander – who, incidentally, was the aforementioned "soon-to-be-new-lover" and who had since become my partner – but I had not considered performing in video work until Max and his co-director, Beau Charlie, decided to shoot, edit, and submit something to the 2011 FPAs on a tight timeline of just one week. A small group of friends banded together in support of the project, and I ended up performing with Max's best friend Billy.

It was only after that short, *Maybe He's Gifted*, was released and after I had become closer with some of the key players in the FPA scene at the time that I felt compelled to bridge the study of pornography with my academic background in cultural studies and women's studies. My own queer coming of age brought me into a feminism that declared itself to be sex-positive and gender transgressive, but it was not so long ago that feminism and pornography were seen to be altogether incommensurable. The Sex Wars of the 1970s, '80s, and '90s popularized the view that all things pornographic were and are inherently "women's issues," and the frontrunners of anti-porn feminism vocally publicized the far-reaching evils of porn.[3] While grounded in the material impacts of systemic oppression and economic coercion, narratives that focus solely on violence, desperation, and rape in the industry ignore all the positive and non-violent interactions had by those performing in porn. Still, the force of anti-porn opposition propagated the idea that all porn is necessarily and unequivocally anti-feminist and anti-woman.

Since the early 1970s, pro-porn, anti-censorship, and sex-positive feminists have been challenging these dominant views, and conversations around women's engagement with porn have become increasingly nuanced. Influential feminist sex workers such as Annie Sprinkle, Candida Royalle, Susie Bright, and Nina Hartley have continued to reiterate that neither viewing porn nor performing in it is inherently bad for women, men, or anyone else; rather, it is the intersecting conditions both inside and outside of the industry that impact one's experience (e.g., Bright 2011; Comella 2010; Royalle 2005; Sprinkle 1998). Recent years have seen an increase in publications from current and former sex workers, which often focus on labour conditions – particularly of racialized performers, trans performers, performers with disabilities, and other marginalized performers – and how the industry can better support these workers (e.g., Lee 2015; Ray 2014; Taormino et al. 2013). The performers and performer-producers featured in these anthologies articulate a politics of sexual labour through their experiential knowledges, advocating for ways to address gendered, racialized, and sexualized dynamics (Lee and Sullivan 2016; Webber 2015).

These interventions have caused mainstream discourse to more seriously consider the possibilities of incorporating feminist politics *into* porn production. Sitting in conversation with alternative porn genres that include woman-positive porn, alt-porn, indie porn, and queer porn, the term *feminist porn* has been taken up to describe sexually explicit, erotic works that interrupt dominant, exploitative production standards. At its best, feminist porn refigures normative imperatives of off-screen sex (e.g., that its labour goes unrecognized, that it be unmonetized) and refuses normative elements of dominant, mainstream porn (e.g., that male viewers be centred, that women be objectified, and that the processes of production be glossed over or erased). Early iterations of feminist porn often placed it within a logic of *authenticity*; through the efforts of early pin-up sites like Suicide Girls and NoFauxxx, representing authentic scenarios, authentic bodies, and authentic orgasms became emblematic qualities of feminist porn. This emphasis on authenticity has since been disputed and nuanced, with feminist porn makers foregrounding the development of ethical production standards (e.g., Scott 2016; Stryker 2015; Taormino et al. 2013), critiquing the demand for authenticity (e.g., Ashley 2016; Raphael, cited in Ms Naughty 2015), and finding other ways of preventing static or stable notions of what feminist intervention does or could look like. Still, the notion of authenticity continues to haunt narratives surrounding feminist porn.

Admittedly, my own scenes have never been about authentic sex for me. For *Maybe He's Gifted*, Billy and I discussed our artistic goals, our desire to engage in embodied experimentation, our vanity, and our investments in aesthetic possibilities, but the scene was never part of a broader desire we had for one another. Do our motivations count as "authentic," even if the particulars of our sexual dynamic were not? And what of porn performers who earn a living working in an industry that relies on creating and/or engaging in fantasy? Are they inherently unable to create feminist-minded change simply because their scenes are not "authentic" enough?

These are some of the questions I explored with my now ex-partner, N. Maxwell Lander, when we sat down in a Toronto apartment on a chilly fall day. Five years had passed since we filmed *Maybe He's Gifted*, and our politics and relationships to feminism and porn had shifted since those early days of engagement. Max and I now have a friendship that is based in honesty, trust, intellectual conversation, artistic collaboration, and a series of messy, painful affective pasts. In this experimental piece of writing, Max and I navigate our multifaceted history through a combination of interview, personal narrative, and content analysis of Max's pornographic video work. Through Max's role as artist and creator, and my role as performer and collaborator, we contemplate the varied makings of sexual selves through art, porn, feminism, and queer aesthetics.

In my reading, Max's work rejects the focus on authenticity and tends instead towards a fragmented, immersive, and highly stylized aesthetic that conscientiously obscures any coherent notion of erotic "truth." Though Max's repertoire is small in number, his moving-image pieces show a clearly developed vision – a vision that plays with the relationship between bodies and technology, narrative, and politicized representation to construct inauthentic yet highly intentional relationships to time, sex, sound, and selfhood. Throughout our conversation, I identify a counterlogic in Max's work, one that denies authenticity by way of visual confession and pushes back on the historically feminist imperative to narrativize experience in order to legitimate it.

Real Unreal: *Maybe He's Gifted* (2011)

Maybe He's Gifted (MHG) is a four-and-a-half-minute short that opens on two performers, Varina and Billy, sitting in a dark, smoke-filled living room. Their dress and visual aesthetic evoke '90s butch/femme dynamics, yet the atmospheric, synth-infused soundtrack is decidedly current. The scene is dreamlike and non-linear: frames are alternately layered, broken, pulled out of focus, and hyper-focused on the minutia of intimate detail. Varina pairs her short dark hair and pale skin with a black and white polka-dot swing dress, beige thigh-high stockings, and peep-toe heels, and Billy balances her ginger complexion and facial piercings with a classic white t-shirt and black suspenders.

The camera alternates between close-ups of eyes, mouths, hands, and feet, and wider shots of bodies that are pressing up against one another in playfully earnest exploration. When Varina and Billy move from the living room into the hallway, the smoke clears for a backlit make-out session. The light behind them almost becomes a third character in the scene, peering out from between the performers. As the couple moves into the bedroom, the lighting becomes cleaner and brighter as clothes come off and a black latex glove is snapped onto Varina's hand.

In many ways, the short is as much music video as it is porno. The soundtrack – "Pathetik Party" by Erdbeerschnitzel – is front and centre, drowning out any noise that might be coming from the human bodies. The only time the track fades away is when performer Billy orgasms and her vocalizations echo resolutely in the foreground. Rather than focusing on delivering a narrative presentation of "authentic" desire or sex, MHG draws the viewer into a multisensory experience that is unfolding on screen; the pulsing music, light flares, glitches, and camera angles are just as integral to the story as the human performers are.

MAX: MHG was a real experiment, both of form and representation. At the time, I saw very few accessible representations of queer bodies and queer sex, let alone ones that were created by visual artists who were explicitly trying to make artistic pieces. Today, watching two thin, white, able-bodied queers is far less interesting than it once might have been, because we have so much more content out there now, but at the time there was a real dearth of anything non-mainstream and queer in a politicized and overtly sexual sense (with a few notable exceptions, like Shine Louise Houston's work, for example). Because it was the first time I was making porn, I was looking for a roadmap or a formula, but I didn't actually *have* a roadmap or formula – it's like I asked, "How do you make a porn? Well, I guess you get two people together and they have sex on camera and then you make it look pretty." Later, I realized art-porn could be literally anything you eroticize, but when I was making MHG, I wanted to show actual sex, including a real orgasm, and even though I played around with the visual aesthetics in postproduction, adding glitches and visual fragmentation, I believed it should be at least somewhat authentic in its representation of what had happened in my apartment that day.

NAOMI: I want to talk more about this idea of using fragmentation as an aesthetic choice. You often use close-up shots to isolate specific body parts in your work, and you make cuts that interrupt the kind of long-hold shots that are typical of porn (and many kinds of video) shoots. Aside from it being an aesthetic preference, I wonder what kind of political implications this might have, especially because most of your performers are female-identified. Conversations about media representations of women have often included some kind of critique of the tendency to fragment, and subsequently objectify, women's bodies (see Attwood 2004). I think your work, though, manages to resist that equation and create a different kind of aesthetic that isn't about treating women as non-agential objects. In *Hard Core*, Linda Williams writes about moving-image porn as reflecting a desire to gain sexual knowledge through witnessing a kind of visual confession. In contrast to "mainstream fictional narrative and soft-core indiscretion," Williams argues, hard-core pornography "obsessively seeks knowledge, through a voyeuristic record of confessional, involuntary paroxysm, of the 'thing' itself" (1989, 49). Your work resists the principle of "maximum visibility" Williams takes up in her work, and it is decidedly not hard-core. Though you include tight frames, often of naked body parts, the eroticism of your work is built through a combination of lighting, soundscapes, and manipulation/interruption of linear narrative progress.

MAX: All of my films have involved a number of conversations with performers beforehand about what they wanted to do, what they wanted to avoid, what aesthetics they enjoyed, what they liked about porn, and what they didn't like about porn. I've always felt like when you're shooting people's bodies, you should probably let them do whatever they want with said bodies. Hard-core or not, performers have always guided the content of my work. *Fragmentation* is a tricky term for me when talking about visual imagery, because I think another way to look at it is that it's about pulling focus – either term could be applied to the same shot. I could shoot a close-up of your lips, and it could either be that I've disembodied that pair of lips or that I've pulled focus towards that pair of lips. Of course, I'm not sure there would be an inherently visible difference between a sexual image that looks exploitative and one that looks empowering, because nudity can be both of those things; it can be exploitative and empowering at the same time. While the viewer's personal experiences and their interpretation of what they're seeing has a lot to do with how it will be received, I think that in film, when you have a larger narrative and more contextualization, you can actually manipulate to some degree whether a scene feels more empowering or whether it feels more exploitative.

NAOMI: I think that question brings us back to some of the conversations around "feminist" porn or "woman-positive" porn, where context and narrative become important parts of the discussion. Very often we hear about *narrative* and *emotional connection* being markers of what makes porn "woman-friendly," along with more realistic representations of sexual scenarios. While the pornographic fantasy remains intact in feminist porn, it is a remarkably different fantasy from that of patriarchal porn; it's often assumed that all women who watch porn want to see more intimacy in their scenes, that an unfolding narrative and building connection is what's erotic for women – as if women's desires are monolithic, as if a storyline somehow equals sexual empowerment while lack of one equals coercion, and/or as if performers never experience intimate exploitation in narrative scenes.

MAX: I've never felt invested in narrative storytelling, not with any of my work. Of course, some women and some people of all genders would like to see more narrative in their pornography, because that's what makes it erotic to them. That's totally great, and that porn should exist for those people, but those aren't my turn-ons and I'm not going to be the one to make that style of porn. Overall, though, audience response to MHG has been really positive. I'm sure a large part of that is because the performers are conventionally attractive, but I think another reason is because I was making work that still followed some of the conventions that were popular in feminist porn at the time. In the months following MHG's release, I had more exposure to and involvement in porn industry realms, and I had many more conversations with industry folks and porn performers. One result of that

The Feminist Turn in Lander's Video Work

3.1 Aesthetic overload: *'98 Bit*, dir. N. Maxwell Lander, 2012.

was I found myself really wanting to push back against some of the most common audience expectations. I wanted to push the genre more and experiment with different kinds of (lack of) narrative. That's when I created *Emile*, and then shortly after that I did *'98 Bit* (fig. 3.1).

Meditative Excess: *Emile* (2012) and *'98 Bit* (2012)

Emile and *'98 Bit* show two extremes of Lander's experiments with genre and style. Both feature solo performances and an aesthetics of excess, yet they have distinct approaches: *Emile* is a slow, meditative, romantic piece that is over the top in its overstated erotic gravitas, while *'98 Bit* is a loud, bright, and campy film that is over the top in its parodic enactment of gender and porn stereotypes. Unlike more traditional cinemas of excess, which tend to present descriptive scenarios of superfluous and hedonistic behaviour (see Black 2014; King 2009), these films employ a form of aesthetic excess that uses sensorial overload to interrupt the coherence of mainstream representations and porn tropes.

Emile features rich sepia tones, soft lighting, and a luxurious soundtrack that is replete with orchestral inflections. The visuals are sharp and clean, but the air is thick with a meditative melancholy: The opening shot reveals performer Geena sitting on a windowsill, drinking coffee and having a morning cigarette. When Geena exhales, a close-up on her mouth reverses to show her suck the curl of smoke back in through her full lips. Taking place in the intimate space of the bedroom, the scene is one of eroticized domesticity; the solo performance cuts between the textures of bed linens, the angles of Geena's face, and her hand between her own legs as she masturbates. Similar to Billy's climax in MHG, Geena's orgasmic sounds take centre stage as the music fades into the background, if for only a moment. Unlike in MHG, however, Geena's "orgasm" was reshot several times, and her vocalizations were cut together between actual orgasm sounds and performed approximations. This is not evident in the final product alone, which blends multiple tracks together seamlessly.

In a disparate approach, '98 Bit features fast cuts, neon colours, and up-tempo electronic music. This piece marks a shift for Lander's work from an aesthetic of heightened reality to one of decidedly humorous hyperreality. The six-minute short is styled like a late 1990s music video with a cyberpunk sensibility, and its camp aesthetic simultaneously pokes fun at the conventions of mainstream jerk scenes and stripping routines. Performer Jinxy is dressed in exaggerated attire. She wears a full-sleeved, white fishnet crop top with no bra and a stark white harness. As she is coated with brightly coloured glow-in-the-dark paint, she spreads the fluid over her breasts and stomach and plunges her toes into a pile that has accumulated on the floor. She slides on white stiletto pumps, followed by large pink dildo. She strokes the dildo emphatically and eventually "ejaculates" hot-pink paint directly onto the camera lens.

These two moving-image portraits were produced in the same year – just weeks apart – and their markedly different styles manage similar effect: *Emile* speaks back to the luxury and romanticism that is often expected from "woman-friendly" porn by inflating their presence, while *'98 Bit* pushes back on porn conventions by emphasizing the spectacle of the cum shot, replacing bodily fluids with fluorescent and synthetic materials and explicitly removing ties to the supposedly authentic body/orgasm/scenario.

MAX: In creating both *Emile* and *'98 Bit*, I took a lot of inspiration from music videos. Most of the porn I've watched has generic background music that fades away as soon as the hard-core fucking starts, but I think that music really sets the mood of porn almost as much as visual components, if not more, so sound elements are especially important to me. That's why I tend to source the music first and cut the visuals once I have a soundtrack.

NAOMI: The interplay of sound and visual cues is really striking in your work, because the different elements play off each other and enhance the overall aesthetic. Soundscapes don't tend to get nearly as much attention in porn studies as visual components do, but as Mowlabocus and Medhurst write, "The music that features in pornography ... often frames the pornographic text, providing a bridge between the text and the cultures in which it might be consumed" (2017, 212). It sounds like you were having some fun with the whole field of porn, and even though you were challenging a serious kind of romantic porn (with *Emile*) and an excessive kind of jerk porn (with *'98 Bit*), it's also clear that you are invested enough in feminist porn communities to stay in conversation with them rather than writing them off or taking your work elsewhere. I wonder, would you say you were actively gearing your work towards a particular kind of audience as you were making it? Did you have an awareness of the cultures or subcultures in which your porn films are consumed as you were producing them?

MAX: Not intentionally, no. I suppose MHG was consciously trying to follow the format of what I thought feminist porn was supposed to be at the time, but as my understandings of "feminist porn" changed, I found that many other producers and performers were struggling with the same questions I was.[4] As I said, *Emile* and *'98 Bit* were more about challenging feminist porn conventions by accentuating the ways that stereotypes and tropes were still operating there. Although I'm critical of some of the work that comes out of feminist porn spaces, I'm also invested in lots of folks who are doing work in feminist/alternative/art/indie porn worlds. Part of that for me though means I will continue to experiment and push back. To that end, *'98 Bit* is conscientiously over the top. It's ridiculous. I enjoy sensory overload as both an artistic and erotic practice, so it's personally satisfying to think that the music would fall in line with a series of flashing images that are quick-paced, or that the music would build with the fucking or the jerking off instead of fading away. In my mind, creating sensory overload just heightens the hot factor, and isn't that ultimately the point of porn?

NAOMI: What I hear in your reflections is that when we talk about gauging an "authentic" representation, there's the question of *are models performing sex acts that are authentic to their off-screen sex and desires?* But then there are also the questions of *does the sex act on screen look the same or similar to how it might look off camera?* And *is the scenario plausible to begin with?* Often, cultural production of, for, and by marginalized folks takes up confessional-style frameworks that make embodied experiences visible through practices of truth-telling and/or authenticity (see Goldstein 1999; Edelman 2015). Rather than getting hung up on specific details that may be fact/fiction or truth/lies, I wonder if we might continue to shift our communal goals towards addressing the ethics of production and support of the workers. While that shift is occurring for many feminist porn makers, there's still a long way to go.

MAX: I agree that the ethics and behind-the-scenes production elements matter a great deal, and I'm also not sure if our collective initial thoughts about what formal, visual, explicit representations make porn into a "feminist" or "alternative" or whatever else piece are as relevant anymore. The point of porn is to engage in erotic fantasy, right? There's a difference between a kind of fantasy that exists within a plausible alternate-reality and that which exists in a decidedly implausible scenario. There's nothing inherently wrong about fantasy that isn't plausible, but I think the key thing is that we need to focus on porn literacy so that people can recognize the difference between those realms and not confuse everyday worlds with imagined ones.

NAOMI: Porn literacy, as a form of broader media literacy, is extremely important. The conversations that have been happening around feminist porn – including conversations about why we need feminist interventions in the first place and why we need intersectional performers in decision-making roles – have contributed in leaps and bounds to porn literacy. Now that "feminist porn" is being recognized in more mainstream outlets, there is, arguably, more of a commercial market for feminist work as well. In my experience, the impacts of this shift are thorny. On the one hand, more consumers are demanding feminist work. Great, right? On the other hand, I think more people are recognizing that what we've come to think of as "authentic" in porn is often (re)produced as just another kind of aesthetic, and that aesthetic is becoming commodified just like everything else.

MAX: That commodification or commercialization is part of my desire to keep changing and experimenting with different mediums and aesthetics – my attempt to resist getting caught up in the capitalist wheel of what sells. My favourite part of making art has always been post-production, where I get to play around with aesthetic a lot. In moving-image work, there are also many opportunities to geek out about tech. My professional growth is often fuelled by boredom – I tend to get bored when I do the same kinds of work for an extended period of time – so I'm always trying to learn new techniques and get into new kinds of media. Lately

The Feminist Turn in Lander's Video Work

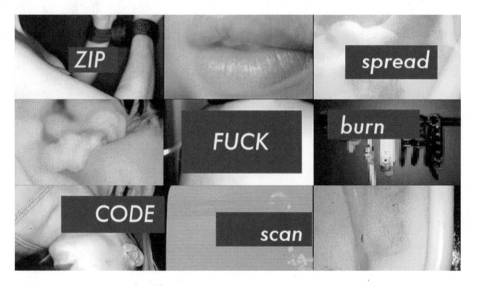

3.2 Utilizing multiple screens to disrupt the traditional unidirectional consumption of most pornographic content, *Porn Game*, dir. N. Maxwell Lander, 2014.

I've been exploring darker themes and visuals, experimenting with newer technologies including virtual reality, 360° photography, and wearable technologies. *Porn Game* is the project that really started me down that path.

Manifest Interactive-Destiny: *Porn Game* (2014)

Porn Game (fig. 3.2) makes use of emerging technologies to explore user-driven narratives and interactivity between porn makers and porn viewers. A sort of choose-your-own-adventure of the porn world, *Porn Game* is a two-screen full-motion videogame, where one screen (a television, monitor, or projected image) acts as a viewing device and the other (a tablet, smartphone, or Raspberry Pi[5]) acts as a game controller. Developed as part of a Dames Making Games game jam,[6] *Porn Game* disrupts the unidirectional consumption of most pornographic content.

Viewers/players are presented with the controller and are tasked with navigating their way through a series of clips, guided by a computer overlord. The game opens with a voice-over from the faux-sentient narrator, who demands participants work to please her:

Welcome, User. I've been waiting for you. It gets so lonely in this binary world, and a machine has wants. So, let's play a game. I'm sure you like games – especially this kind. Oh, don't go all coy on me; I am in control of your browser history, you know. Think of it as an "I've scratched your back, you scratch mine" scenario. Now, I know you fairly well (please refer to my previous statement about your browser history), but how well do you know me? Can you guess what titillations will please me? The choice is yours on how you get there. Oh, and one thing to bear in mind? I tend to get glitchy and upset when things don't go my way. Good luck!

From there, the player selects one of nine images. Obscured pictures of body parts hint at rope bondage, handcuffs, and bubble baths, and some include word text – *spread*, *burn*, *zip*, *fuck*, *code*, *scan* – but no other guidance is offered. The player's choice either meets the desires of the robotic mistress, in which case the viewer is rewarded with a steamy sex clip, or fails to satisfy her demands, in which case the viewer is punished with missing files, image glitches, and decidedly unsexy sounds that include static noise and nails dragging on chalkboards. The game continues until the player reaches one of five potential endings, comprised of two "winners" and three "failures" – one "bondage" inspired squirting orgasm, one "romance" inspired writhing orgasm, and three loud, interrupted, and grating clips that each include some version of the message "You missed the point; try again."

MAX: At its core, *Porn Game* is an investigation into the ways in which we access and engage with porn. Usually, porn is consumed in a unidirectional process – one or more people will go online or watch a film – but with this piece, I was trying to experiment with other kinds of user interaction. With human–human sex, you actually have to negotiate scenes, put some energy into your exchanges, and do *something* (even if it's a limited something); there is a degree of effort involved. *Porn Game* was an attempt to interrupt the usual assumptions about porn, which include that it's a medium that is, and should be, all about the reward of the viewer. I really liked the idea of creating a scenario where the consumer has to work for their viewing experience. I also liked thinking about building in an element of punishment and failure, because to me that is also a part of sex.

NAOMI: What I'm hearing is that you wanted to continue blurring the line between more accurate or realistic representations of sex and the fantasy of porn worlds. The interactive component of *Porn Game* means that the film is partially co-authored by the consumer, and the format of a video game allows for viewer engagement that exists somewhere between a traditional pre-recorded porn scene and a "live show" or cam chat – although in this case, it's an AI on the other end of the interaction. I'm curious about the possibilities of interactive media as they relate to porn and fantasy. I imagine that advances in technology are always going to be used to make and/or engage with porn, but I think many of us don't often get to see those experiments unless we are already "in the know." There are virtual reality (VR) porn projects in the works, and we've seen Google Glass used in porn parody videos.[7] What kinds of technology inspired this project for you? And how did you decide to create the narrative branches using the clips you did?

MAX: *Porn Game* was actually designed to test a piece of software that was developed to allow people to make branching (e.g., multi-narrative, non-linear) video-based interactive content, so I wanted to make good use of the possibilities that software opened up. The premise of the game is that the computer is an AI trying to piece together something it thought would be both recognizable and "sexy" to humans – these video clips are files the computer sourced through its various networks. As the viewer/player, you are trying to decipher what the computer wants you to do to it, and the computer communicates with you by rewarding or punishing you with footage it thinks you will like or dislike. Until we can actually train AIs to do this kind of work in real time (a process that is well underway but hasn't yet been achieved), I had to imagine what that interaction might look like. I wanted to put together a varied set of clips, bodies, and settings to resist the idea that this AI is a singular being with a physical form.

NAOMI: Because the clips are pieced together from your existing footage – some from *Emile*, some from unreleased work – and combined with newly shot images, this piece further emphasizes the erotic potentials of themes that run through your work, including fragmentation, atmospheric manipulations, and uneven soundscapes. The variety of source material not only positions the AI as taking on multiple human forms at once but it also resists common porn tropes that are upheld through the rehearsal of certain kinds of visual repetition. The clips are edited together in a way that collapses multiple performers into one, embracing a postmodern aesthetic that destabilizes the coherence of bodies or identities and resists any singular notion of "truth." The format of *Porn Game* speaks to another important layer of technological advancement, and more specifically, it raises questions for me about the application of game technologies to erotic video content. As games scholar Patrick Jagoda (2014, 193) explains, the incorporation of game mechanics into "traditionally non-game activities" is becoming more and more common through processes of *gamification*. As more people have access to the base means of production for film, and as more people become interested in making feminist (or supposedly feminist) sexy, erotic content, we get to experience the sometimes-messy but always interesting impacts of *abundance* in representation.

MAX: It's funny to think about how much conversations around porn and representation have changed, even over the last few years. Feminists and queers have been engaging with sexual media for a really long time. They've been having these kinds of conversations for a really long time. Because of digital media, though, the conversations have changed, and they've changed quickly. Video content and the internet, social media and the way porn circulates across different platforms – those are all relatively new parts of the conversation. When we were making *MHG* and my other early films, there were things to think about that were as simple as recognizing it was really hard to find real dyke sex anywhere. There were only one or two sources for ongoing, reliable content of dykes and genderqueer folks, so it was really easy for us to do something about that lack.

NAOMI: Access to queer representation really has changed so much. Even though there were some early indie and queer porn sites out there, they were islands. They were not as widely disseminated; they were harder to find unless you already knew what you were looking for. The FPAs started pre-Facebook (launched to the public in 2006), pre-Twitter (launched in 2006), pre-Instagram (launched in 2010), and before other social-media platforms that are so important now for disseminating porn in general, but also for developing feminist, queer, and indie porn and alternate kinds of representation in particular. Because there is more diversity of content now, we're able to move beyond the base questions of representation (i.e., mere *existence*) and push and challenge those representations to be way more nuanced. To be ever more thoughtful and conscious of the representational work they are accomplishing.

MAX: Social media is definitely convenient for getting the word out about projects, and many of us use it for self-promotion, but it's also a bit of a mixed bag. It can host really surface-level interactions, which can be hard for those of us who want to make change. I know that all I have to do is put up a semi-nude photo of a model and I'll get two or three times as many likes as I would for anything else I post. That's fine sometimes, but the "likes" don't necessarily lead to monetary support for artists, and that is a problem. After I released my first couple of films, I was getting a lot of positive feedback from audiences, but I found that I was uncomfortable with something in the dynamic. I realized much later that the whole experience of interacting with strangers at the FPAS felt weirdly invasive – kind of like interacting with strangers online. My work wasn't commercial, but it was still being consumed by mass-ish audiences. Not only that, but the most validated aspects were not the kinky queer ones that I found most interesting and challenging, but they were the elements that reflected the most conventional forms of beauty or eroticism. That's when I knew I needed to take a step back from spaces organized around "feminist porn" and explore different realms.

NAOMI: For so many of us, I think spaces of queer and/or feminist promise and potential become a let-down when they fail to meet the impossible demands we inevitably put on them. We can't pull these conversations apart from the broader communities and the broader politics that exist around porn and art or feminism and queerness or representation and mediation – even if and when we find ourselves burnt out and frustrated by the specifics of any given initiative. It raises the question for me of how we might move away from a type of "feminist porn" that is being solidified into a genre and move it back to a feminist political project and dynamic goal that finds its way into every part of the work. I also wonder how we might make our feminist politics visible in our work without relying on elements that have become conventions of feminist porn. That's why your work to me is an important contribution to the field. The interactive component of *Porn Game* decentralizes the narrative and the top-down kinds of representation that we're used to, and it moves beyond fragmentation into productive incoherence. *Emile* and *'98 Bit* challenge audiences to approach larger-than-life jerk scenes with a reflexive sense of humour. And *Maybe He's Gifted* shifts aesthetic engagements with romance, art, and queer sex to imagine erotic worlds framed otherwise. In the always-unfinished project of feminist world-building, we need to spend less energy worrying about authenticity and more time revelling in unapologetic queer fantasy.

NOTES

1 In early 2017, the Feminist Porn Awards announced they would be changing their name to the Toronto International Porn Festival (TIPF). A statement explained that even though the TIPF continues to hold the same values, goals, and spirit as the FPAS in the past, the event has evolved into a type of gathering that is better reflected by their new name. Because this chapter considers events that occurred from 2011 to 2014, the authors have chosen to maintain the acronym FPAS as a reflection of the time period being discussed.

2 Roundtable members included Candida Royalle, Tristan Taormino, Dana Dane, Angela Phong, Abiola Adams, and Jen Bowers.
3 See, for example, Dworkin (1982), MacKinnon (1987), and MacKinnon and Dworkin (1985).
4 For reflective contemplations on the changing role of feminist porn, as well as further insight into complex processes of defining, identifying, and categorizing feminist porn, see Gallant (2017), Noble (2012), and Penley et al. (2013).
5 A Raspberry Pi is a stripped down, single-board computer that is able to perform basic computing functions with no frills. The Raspberry Pi Foundation released their first model in 2012, focusing on the possibilities for teaching basic computer science to young people and those in developing countries, but the technology has since gained popularity across computer programming, game development, and robotics fields.
6 Dames Making Games (DMG) is a feminist "not-for-profit videogame arts organization" in Toronto that provides training, workshops, mentorship, production space, and social networking primarily for "genderqueer, nonbinary, femmes, Two Spirit people, and trans and cis women" (www.dmg.to). A "game jam" is an intensive and highly interactive event hosted by DMG where participants often workshop and create games of their own.
7 In 2013, porn performers James Deen and Andy San Dimas starred in a comedy-sketch trailer for the first porn film made with Google Glass. For more information about the trailer, see MiKandi (2013). Though we hesitate to promote any of Deen's work, given his history of sexual violence, the technological mark is notable. For more information about the rape and abuse allegations launched against Deen, see Sunderland (2015) and Gira Grant (2015).

REFERENCES

Ashley, Vex. 2016. "Porn – Artifice – Performance – and the Problem of Authenticity." *Porn Studies* 3, no. 2: 187–90.

Attwood, Feona. 2004. "Pornography and Objectification." *Feminist Media Studies* 4, no. 1: 7–19.

Black, Izzie. 2014. "*The Wolf of Wall Street* and the New Cinema of Excess." *Agents and Seers*. 8 April. https://agentsandseers.wordpress.com/2014/04/08/the-wolf-of-wall-street-and-the-new-cinema-of-excess.

Bright, Susie. 2011. *Big Sex Little Death: A Memoir*. Berkeley: Seal Press.

Comella, Lynn. 2010. "Nina Hartley's Adult Film Career Has Been Long, Distinguished and Trailblazing – and It's Far from Over." *Las Vegas Weekly*. 6 October. https://lasvegasweekly.com/as-we-see-it/2010/oct/06/nina-hartleys-adult-film-career-has-been-long-dist/.

Dworkin, Andrea. 1982. *Pornography: Men Possessing Women*. London: Women's Press.

Dworkin, Andrea, and Catharine A. MacKinnon. 1985. *The Reasons Why: Essays on the New*

Civil Rights Law Recognizing Pornography as Sex Discrimination. New York: Women Against Pornography.

Edelman, Elijah A. 2015. "The Cum Shot: Trans Men and Visual Economies of Ejaculation." *Porn Studies* 2, nos. 3–2: 150–60.

Gallant, Chanelle. 2017. "Why I Started the Feminist Porn Awards Ten Years Ago (and What I Got Wrong)." *Huffington Post*, 10 January. http://www.huffingtonpost.com/entry/why-i-started-the-feminist-porn-awards-ten-years-ago_us_587559afe4b0f8a725448343.

Gira Grant, Melissa. 2015. "How Stoya Took On James Deen and Broke the Porn Industry's Silence." *Guardian* (UK), 4 December. http://www.theguardian.com/culture/2015/dec/04/how-stoya-took-on-james-deen-and-broke-the-porn-industrys-silence.

Goldstein, Lynda. 1999. "Raging in Tongues: Confession and Performance Art." In *Confessional Politics: Women's Sexual Self-Representations in Life Writing and Popular Media*, edited by Irene Gammel, 99–116. Carbondale: Southern Illinois University Press.

Jagoda, Patrick. 2014. "Gaming the Humanities: Digital Humanities, New Media, and Practice-Based Research." *Differences: A Journal of Feminist Cultural Studies* 25, no. 1: 189–215.

King. Mike. 2009. *The American Cinema of Excess*. Jefferson, NC: McFarland & Co.

Lee, Jiz, ed. 2015. *Coming Out Like a Porn Star: Essays on Pornography, Protection, and Privacy*. Berkeley: ThreeL Media / Stone Bridge Press.

Lee, Jiz, and Rebecca Sullivan. 2016. "Porn and Labour: The Labour of Porn Studies." *Porn Studies* 3, no. 2: 104–6.

MacKinnon, Catharine A. 1987. *Feminism Unmodified*. Cambridge: Harvard University Press.

MiKandi. 2013. "First-Ever Google Glass Porn." YouTube.com. 23 July. https://youtu.be/Xxt24JoLlPE.

Mowlabocus, Sharif, and Andy Medhurst. 2017. "Six Propositions on the Sonics of Pornography." *Porn Studies* 4, no. 2: 210–24.

Ms. Naughty. 2015. "The Feminist Porn Conference, University of Toronto, 5–6 April 2014." *Porn Studies* 2, nos. 2–3: 292–96.

Noble, Bobby. 2012. "'F*cking the Record': On Year 7 of the Feminist Porn Awards." *No More Potlucks* 22: n.p. http://nomorepotlucks.org/site/fck-ing-the-record/.

Penley, Constance, Celine Parreñas Shimizu, Mireille Miller-Young, and Tristan Taormino. 2013. "Introduction: The Politics of Producing Pleasure." In *The Feminist Porn Book: The Politics of Producing Pleasure*, edited by Tristan Taormino, Constance Penley, Celine Parreñas Shimizu, and Mireille Miller-Young. New York: Feminist Press at CUNY.

Ray, Audacia, ed. 2014. *Prose and Lore: Memoir Stories about Sex Work*. Issue 3. New York: Red Umbrella Project.

Royalle, Candida. 2005. *How to Tell a Naked Man What to Do: Sex Advice from a Woman Who Knows*. London: Piatkus/Little, Brown.

Scott, Karly-Lynne. 2016. "Performing Labour: Ethical Spectatorship and the Communication of Labour Conditions in Pornography." *Porn Studies* 3, no. 2: 120–32.

Sprinkle, Annie. 1998. *Post Porn Modernist: My Twenty-Five Years as a Multimedia Whore*. San Francisco: Cleis Press.

Stryker, Kitty. 2015. "An Open Letter to the Feminist Porn Awards." 25 March. http://kittystryker.com/2015/03/25/an-open-letter-to-the-feminist-porn-awards.

Sunderland, Mitchel. 2015. "'I Thought, I'm Going to Die Here': Joanna Angel Accuses James Deen of Assault." *Broadly*, 3 December. https://broadly.vice.com/en_us/article/9ae7e3/i-thought-im-going-to-die-here-joanna-angel-accuses-james-deen-of-assault.

Taormino, Tristan, Constance Penley, Celine Parreñas Shimizu, and Mireille Miller-Young, eds. 2013. *The Feminist Porn Book: The Politics of Producing Pleasure*. New York: Feminist Press at CUNY.

Webber, Valerie. 2015. "Public Health Versus Performer Privates: Measure B's Failure to Fix Subjects." *Porn Studies* 2, no. 4: 299–313.

Williams, Linda. 1989. *Hard Core: Power, Pleasure, and the "Frenzy of the Visible."* Berkeley: University of California Press.

MEDIAGRAPHY

N. Maxwell Lander, dir. 2012. *Emile*.

– dir. 2012. *'98 Bit*.

– dir. 2014. *Porn Game*.

N. Maxwell Lander and Beau Charlie, dirs. 2011. *Maybe He's Gifted*.

4

Blogging Affects and Other Inheritances of Feminist Consciousness-Raising

ELA PRZYBYLO AND VERONIKA NOVOSELOVA

We have used our feelings as our best available weapon – hysterics, whining, bitching.
• Kathie Sarachild (1968)

Affect is channelled within and across media with political consequences.
• Imogen Tyler, Rebecca Coleman, and Debra Ferreday (2008)

Hysterics, whining, bitching, as the excerpt from Kathie Sarachild's address on consciousness-raising in the late 1960s attests, have been central tools in the feminist arsenal for decades. Feelings, and methods for propelling these feelings into collective action, have formed a core element of feminist organizing and theorizing since at least the women's liberation movement.[1] It is not an overstatement to say that feelings constitute the energy and lifeblood of feminist movements. As a form of knowledge that is enfleshed and lived rather than "cold" and disembodied (Gordon [1997] 2008, 8; Williams ([1977] 2009), feelings also come to circulate in central ways in contemporary online and offline feminisms in the interconnected social landscape that includes trending hashtags, mass street demonstrations, blog comments sections, classroom discussions, crowdfunding campaigns, circulating online selfies, and guerrilla art installations. In this chapter, we draw on feminist and queer theory on affect, feminist media studies, and feminist historiography, to examine the affective confessional strategies of feminist consciousness-raising and feminist blogging. We find that feminist consciousness-raising and feminist blogging, while defined by different historical contexts and grounded in different theories, are akin in their affective mobilization of the method of "confessing."

Drawing on feminist philosopher Chloë Taylor's (2009) outline of various historical iterations of the confessional, we argue that both blogging and consciousness-raising adapt the confessional for feminist purposes.

As feminist editor and blogger Samhita Mukhopadhyay has reflected, in the 2000s and 2010s, feminist blogs became the "consciousness-raising groups of our generation" (qtd. in Johnson 2013, para. 19; Loza 2014). In this co-authored piece, we examine the uses and applicability of feminist consciousness-raising to the making of contemporary online feminisms. In doing so, we are specifically interested in how, both historically and in the present, feminisms have been invested in a confessional politics, one that confesses to the feminist community, be it at a small meeting or online to an unknown number of participants. As a particular incarnation of confessionality, certain aspects of consciousness-raising continue to exist today in online feminist engagements. Looking at feminist media such *xoJane* (2011–16) and *Jezebel* (launched 2007), we explore the contemporary inheritances of the consciousness-raising technology, with an eye to thinking about how it produces particularly sexed, racialized, and sexual subjects.

Further, we explore the affective structures of the feminist confessional – that is, what feelings the confessional fosters both in the confessant and the confessed to, and how these feelings coalesce and fracture the imagined feminist audience. Consciousness-raising, we hold, continues to offer unique contributions to feminist cultures and the concomitant modalities of subject-making that emerge. We argue that consciousness-raising is a feminist technique that enabled a personalized discourse stemming from the "I" and "we," a collective generation of feminist feeling, and a navigation of privilege and difference that is in full bloom in online feminist cultures today. At the same time, we build on the critiques of "free" online labour (Terranova 2004; Pybus 2015) to understand how circulations of feminist affect are appropriated for their economic value. We suggest that the increasing commercialization of blogging formats has an impact on the ways in which feminist testimonies are commissioned, manufactured, and distributed along social networks. Critiquing what Laura Bennett (2015) termed "the first-person industrial complex" – the monetization of self-exposure and autobiographical narratives of trauma – we draw attention to the ways in which confessional essays become a part of a commodified exchange in digital media. We are interested in how the confessional, as it surfaced first in feminist consciousness-raising and more recently in feminist blogging, draws on "emotional knowledge ... derived from a broadly common historical experience" (Berlant 2008, viii).

This chapter begins with a discussion of the affective registers of feminist consciousness-raising of the women's liberation movement, examining both primary and secondary texts on this mode of feminist making. Drawing on Taylor's Foucauldian outline of the structure of the confessional and genealogy of confessionals, we consider what confessing evoked for feminists and in the service of feminism, and how feminist interventions in confessing strove to alter the very power structures of the confessional itself. Second, we establish continuity between feminist consciousness-raising of the women's liberation movement and present-day online feminisms by considering how the confessional functions in online feminist spaces today, and what affects it travels with. The feminist confessional, we suggest, has never stopped being important to feminist engagement, and while we examine online feminist media expressions of confessionality in particular, the feminist confessional mode is an abundant site of creativity and political action across mediums of protest. We suggest that feminist confessional narratives across online media continue to play an important role in building feminist communities and mobilizing feminist affect; we also maintain that the specificity of digital environments, characterized by instantaneous and "viral" distribution of information, brings new forms of producing and consuming confessions. Finally, we conclude by engaging with Jia Tolentino's recent (2017) article on the end of the era of the personal essay, arguing for the continuing importance of feminist confessional methods to political action.

Consciousness-Raising, the Feminist Confessional, and Insubordinate Affects

In brief, "consciousness-raising is the name given to the feminist practice of examining one's personal life in light of sexism" consisting of "personal testimony and emotional analysis" (Gornick [1971] 2000, 287–8). Feminist consciousness-raising, also known by the acronym CR, was first adopted by the group New York Radical Women in the late 1960s at the suggestion of Anne Forber, the term being promulgated by Kathie Sarachild shortly after and gaining further momentum under the group the Redstockings (Echols 1989, 83; Shreve 1989, 10). As feminist historiographers have noted, consciousness-raising was a method drawn from the Civil Rights Movement's commitment to nonviolent resistance grounded in "telling it as it is." This practice, in turn, draws on the method of rural Chinese reform from the 1940s of "speaking bitterness" in the face of state-sanctioned oppression (Echols 1989, 84; Norman 2006, 44; Shreve 1989, 9). Feminist CR was based in putting into words one's personal life as a "political action to tell it like it is" from the standpoint of the marginalized social group called "women"

(Hanisch [1969] 2000, 113). Until the mid-1970s (Crow 2000, 13), CR, through making the personal political, or seeing one's personal experiences as part of a fabric of patriarchal oppression, was a central technique of the women's liberation movement in America. In the early 1970s, at least one hundred thousand women in the United States were estimated to partake in CR groups (Shreve 1989, 6).

Consciousness-raising consisted of bringing forth, through group talk, personal and autobiographical life details in pursuit of a gender-based class consciousness. In confessing and detailing experiences of oppression related to gender, sexuality, work, racialization, education, and family, CR brought into clarity both similarities of experiences and their differences, with the goal of reframing personal life as political and seeing as systemic the operation of everyday experiences of sexism (Sarachild 1970). In practice, these discussions could involve sex, menstruation, marriage, normative beauty standards, pregnancy, orgasm, rape, work and family-based sexism, and mothering (Cornell 2000, 1034). In the sense that gender-based class consciousness was emphasized, it is arguably the *similarity* of experiences – "a collage of similar experiences" (Allen [1970] 2000, 279) – that was stressed over the differences, often muting the dissimilar and uneven experiences of womanhood as they intersected with racialization in particular. Driven by a desire to forge a ground for thinking about the systematicity of gendered oppression, and the primacy of women's oppression above and beyond other forms of injustice, the "Redstockings Manifesto" (Morgan 1970), for example, spelled out that women were "an oppressed class," with "male supremacy [being] the oldest, most basic form of domination [and] all other forms of exploitation and oppression (racism, capitalism, imperialism, etc.) [as] extensions of male supremacy" (1). Ellen Willis, a member of New York Radical Women and co-founder of Redstockings, wrote in retrospect, "We were acting on the unconscious racist assumption that our experience was representative, along with the impulse to gloss over racial specificities" (Willis 1982, 11). Indeed, CR groups tended to be predominately white and middle class and were grounded in a form of "women's experience" that rested on the presumed neutrality of whiteness and cisgender-womanhood (Shreve 1989, 12–13; Hesford 2013, 179–80). On the other hand, others have argued that while similarity of experience was sought, the very format of group-based feminist confessing, where "everyone's voice was to count as equally important in the group," also created a site for disagreement (Cornell 2000, 1033). Crucially, CR was grounded in a subversive approach to knowledge-making that situated women in the position to produce knowledge about their lives and their experiences as women, challenging the androcentric and sexist tradition of women being objects rather than subjects of analysis (Echols 2002, 92).

While CR is often discussed as a primarily white feminist tool of investigation, Brian Norman has pointed out that it was also at play in black feminist circles in the United States. Norman discusses the role of CR for the Black Women's Liberation Group of Mount Vernon, formed in the late 1960s and led by Pat Robinson, which was active until the early 1970s and made up of working-class and poor women (Norman 2006, 40). In distinction to many white-dominated feminist groups that practised CR, the Black Women's Liberation Group demanded that racism and class be interrogated in conversation with gender-based consciousness towards a "race-conscious sisterhood" (Norman 2006, 38; Norton 1970).

Historiographers such as Kimberly Springer (2005) argue that black feminism in the United States developed apart from white feminism for multiple reasons, including white women's inability to recognize their own role in anti-black racism and privilege (29). Other historiographers have argued that this story of white and black feminist separateness has in itself been harmful, since black women, such as lawyer Florynce (Flo) Kennedy, were central to the sparking and making of the women's liberation movement and acted as bridge-builders between the Black Power and women's lib movements (Gore, Theoharis, and Woodard 2009; Norman 2006; Randolph 2015). It is clear that black feminists developed CR on intersectional terms, since they had to speak to their experiences of sexism as interlocking with racism, colonialism, and class (Bambara 1970; Combahee River Collective [1977] 1982).

The sharing of personal life details in a group environment toward larger social change can be usefully understood as a historically situated form of confessing. In *The Culture of Confession from Augustine to Foucault* (2009), feminist philosopher Chloë Taylor draws attention to the shifting modes of what it means to confess, what the confessional is, and how it has functioned across historical periods through antiquity, Catholicism, psychoanalysis, and more recent Foucauldian formulations. Feminist confessionals such as CR add to this repertoire a particular, historically situated mode of confessing. In the confession of the minutiae of individual oppression, CR functions through its group dynamic to reposition feelings of blame and unhappiness away from the individual to patriarchy and its systemic and pernicious effects on individual women. Catharsis takes place not only through making public previously personal content that one might have found shameful under the principles of misogynistic self-loathing but also through relocating feelings of blame from the individual to the systemic and institutional. A confession in this sense refers to "statements which claim to explain the being of the subject who is speaking ... which are told despite claims of repression, or with difficulty and shame," and which upon sharing transform the subject in some way: confession is not merely about speaking wrong-doings but also about bringing into speech how one has been wronged (Taylor 2009, 8). In this Foucauldian sense, feminist consciousness-raising, in speaking gender-based injustice, seeks to undertake the transformation of both the individual and the group to politically based awareness. Affectively, as Sara Ahmed has mentioned in her work on the feminist killjoy, consciousness-raising does not consist of "affective conversion" from unhappiness to happiness but rather a conversion from seeing unhappiness as a personal plight to framing unhappiness as a collective feeling rooted in political consciousness (2010, 584–5). To be unhappy along these lines is to be out of line with dominant life trajectories as they are hinged to heteronormative futurity. "Feminism involves political consciousness of what women are asked to give up for happiness," Ahmed writes: reproduction, subordination to male desires, and assimilation to capitalist manners of being (585). "Feminism involves a sociality of unhappiness," in which consciousness-raising, "generating talk about the collective nature of suffering that is concealed and reproduced," was a central tool (589).

At the same time, Taylor, drawing on Foucault, argues that "speaking the truth about the self is a privileged form of subject formation"; self-reflective discourse "is thus a crucial technique both of domination and self-care," the two being interwoven (Taylor 2009, 9). Consciousness-raising, as a confessional group practice, offered opportunities for self-invention and para-patriarchal identity creation while also functioning as a disciplinary technology itself. Eliciting mandatory confessing from its subjects, CR functioned to conform women *into* particular types of feminist subjects. This form of feminist subjecthood was often grounded in attachments to whiteness and in the taken-for-granted privileges of white womanhood it afforded, as well as in cisgenderhood and the presumed "obviousness" of what constituted womanhood. While a vocabulary was in place in white-dominated feminist groups, at least nominally, for stipulating multiple oppressions such as class-based oppression, "white skin privilege," and "(imperialist) nation privilege" (Sarachild 1970, 80), many have argued that, in focusing on gender-based oppression, subtleties pertaining to the intersections of oppression as well as the effects of privilege were lost. The confessional thus functioned in many instances to confirm certain experiences (primarily gender-based oppression against women), disciplining women into recognizing this oppression *as* oppression at the cost of deprioritizing other life experiences and identities.

Importantly, affect played a crucial role in the method of feminist consciousness-raising. Kathie Sarachild's key primary text, "A Program for Feminist 'Consciousness-Raising,'" presented at the First National Women's Liberation Conference outside Chicago on 27 November 1968, outlined the role of feelings in the CR method: "We always stay in touch with our feelings ... In our groups let's share our feelings and pool them. Let's let ourselves go and see where our feelings lead us. Our feelings will lead us to ideas and then to actions. Our feelings will lead us to our theory, our theory to our action, our feelings about that action to a new theory and then to new action" (1970, 78). Sarachild goes on to outline a skeletal plan for CR that would include, chronologically: "bitch session" groups to share "our bitter experiences" and the feelings emerging from them, "relating and generalizing individual testimony," "classic forms of resisting consciousness" such as "rugged individualism," and then a plan for overcoming oppression (79). Similarly, in 1970 Pamela Allen (2000) articulated the significance of "opening up" and talking about feelings even while "society alienates us from our feelings" (277). Her expression of CR involved opening up, sharing, and establishing similarities of experience, analyzing the reasons and causes for women's oppression, and finally abstracting – at which point new ideologies were developed. For Sarachild and for Allen, feelings get voiced as reality and as the basis not only for CR but for transformative action. In bell hooks's words, for feminists this involved recognizing the "depths of their intimate wounds" such that, in addition to politicizing the individual and the group, CR as a confessional tool also "served as a healing ritual," providing the sustenance needed to take direct action against heteropatriarchy (hooks 2000, 8).

Also, CR was grounded in an affective making-conscious, or in today's parlance "being woke," though often primarily along gender-based lines[2] – that is, in "awakening the latent consciousness that we and all women have about our oppression" (New York Consciousness Awakening Women's Liberation Group 1969). Yet these methods of staying with one's feelings, building collective feelings, and using them as a platform for action draw on the strategies of civil rights organizing and other social justice movements. Norman (2006) discusses how CR used as blueprints the Chinese method of "speaking bitterness" as well as Martin Luther King Jr's outline for nonviolent resistance (44), while Randolph (2015) notes that it was black feminists like Flo Kennedy who introduced these and other organizing tactics to the women's liberation movement. Notably, this "awakening" and building of affect-based knowledge had a different significance for black feminist groups such as the Mount Vernon group since it involved recognizing the inability of separating one's gender-based discrimination from race and class-based injustice.

Anger, in particular, formed a constitutive affect of the CR method. "Simmering for years, like a back-stage volcano," consciousness-raising provided groups with the momentum to erupt "all over the place," as one account elucidates: "at home, at work, in the streets, in restaurants, subways, at parties, in bed ... it spurted out all over everything, redhot" (Arnold [1970] 2000, 283). "Affect" makes sense here as an operative term above and beyond feelings and emotions, because while feelings are assumed to belong to their subjects, the feeling-based politics articulated by feminists in CR groups, and in the women's liberation movement more broadly, were seen less as belonging to subjects than as belonging to the conditions women experienced under patriarchy. Such a "non-subject-centred" model of feeling is thus best framed as "affect" (Ahmed 2010, 574n2; Sedgwick 2003). Specifically, it was imagined that the process of CR could substantively change the general affect of American life, not only for the women who partook in CR but also for the public and society more broadly, through a "linking network of feminist analysis and emotional up-chucking" that "suffuse[d] the political-social air of American life" (Gornick [1971] 2000, 287). In this sense, as Norman has argued, both CR and the CR document generated a "we" stemming from individual and shared experience (2006, 41).

Also, affect is mobilized both in-group and beyond to form intimacy and feelings of "sisterhood" (Allen [1970] 2000, 278). Sisterhood here emerges as a *feeling* of solidarity toward other women. It also, as has been critiqued, is a feminist fantasy often resting on the erasure of racial and class difference and relying on exclusion of transgender women. Springer, looking at black feminist organizing of the women's movement, argues that "the concept of sisterhood, as proposed by the majority of white feminists, meant that all women were the same, regardless of economic or social differences. Yet this definition erased the discrimination that black women faced based on their racial differences from white women. The result was an elision of women's differences in the interest of a common women's movement agenda" (Springer 2005, 28). In this reading, CR emerges as a technique not only of building affective unity but also of affective exclusion, of imagining sisterly feelings on an unstable ground and at the expense of many women. Ahmed discusses how in feminist circles, "some bodies more than others can be attributed as the cause of unhappiness [...] such as] the figure of the angry black women [who] ... may even kill feminist joy ... by pointing out forms of racism within feminist politics" (2010, 583). In such ways, even while affect was mobilized toward building "sisterhood," it rested on structures of white subjectivity and on the development of hegemonic ways of being feminist and gender-conscious.

Sisterhood was also too often understood as "cisterhood" and rested on a permissible ignorance around transgender issues and on the permissibility of excluding transgender women from categories of womanhood and sisterhood (Stryker 2017, 127–38). Although recent scholarship by Cristan Williams (2016) and Finn

Enke (2018) has suggested that there were examples of feminist and lesbian feminist communities that were invested in trans-inclusionary practices and in protecting trans women from hatred, CR was centrally interested in analyzing gender on binary and often biologically determinist lines. Sisterhood was thus often imagined as primarily cisgender-based, and CR took the shape of raising consciousness around gender oppression on specific terms.

Having considered some key aspects of consciousness-raising in regards to the confessional and affect, in the following section we turn to contemporary online feminisms, and specifically blogging, to think about the inheritances of the tool of consciousness-raising. In the *Erotics of Talk*, Carla Kaplan (1996) suggests that the communicative ethics of consciousness-raising had been replaced in the 1990s by that of performativity. Similarly, hooks has argued the CR fell out of favour as small groups of feminists dismantled, as feminism became depoliticized in the 1980s through "lifestyle feminisms," and as feminist engagement migrated to the institutionalized worlds of women's studies classrooms (2000, 9). We disagree with Kaplan and hooks in that we believe that the confessional has never gone out of operation as a feminist tactic but has remained prominent in multiple modes of feminist world-making in North America over the decades, even while CR has been phased out. Yet, drawing on hooks, "When feminist movement renews itself … enabl[ing] a mass movement to end sexism … consciousness-raising will once again attain its original importance" (2000, 11). It is thus in recent years, with the palpable intensification of feminist struggles, that the confessional as a method for building consciousness has become increasingly present and relevant. We see the central function of the confessional in online feminist engagements as a reinvention and reinterpretation of the CR method that speaks to the renewed intensity of feminist action in an unjust world.

We argue that consciousness-raising, while no longer practised in the format popular during the era of the women's liberation movement, continues to be central to contemporary feminisms online in that both are rooted in a feminist politics of solidarity-making through confessing. Drawing on Taylor (2009) again, we could say that the feminist blogosphere, especially in its autobiographical genre, offers a new iteration of the confessional, a new opportunity for feminists to enact, in Foucauldian terms, both self-care and disciplinary tactics on communities of feminists broadly imagined. In the next section we demonstrate that the feminist method of the confessional continues to have a focal role in feminist thinking and organizing, even as the contexts and conditions under which confessionality takes place have shifted.

#Raw #Honest #Manufactured #Commercialized: Feminist Blogging and Corporatized Confessionals

As a form of autobiographical writing, blogs facilitate self-disclosure while engendering flows of affect through circulations, both orchestrated and spontaneous, of texts, images, and mixed-media artifacts. Candid accounts of daily life are at the heart of personal blogging (Qian and Scott 2007). Among the plethora of digital self-publishing formats that enable the dissemination of the personal, diary-style blogging, and the varied textual communities and social networks around it, stand out for their mediated confessionality.

Mediated communication gives rise to a collaborative and intersubjective authorship in which "the blogger's voice, while self-created and self-creating, is never complete in itself" (Fitzpatrick 2007, 177). Such collective authorship is made possible by commenting, constant mutual linking, and migrations of content between platforms; these networked processes enable affective and relational exchanges that are the major motive for reading personal blogs (Huang, Chou, and Lin 2008). Although the "traditional" stand-alone format of blogging reached its peak of popularity in the mid-2000s and lost some of its popular appeal by the mid-2010s, the affective pull of networked self-publishing has become stronger, as evidenced by the rise of Facebook, Twitter, Instagram, and other social-media platforms thriving on the instantaneous transmissions of the personal.

Feminist scholars turn to women's confessional blogs to highlight the ways in which online environments afford networked spaces for individual self-reflection, aid in the creation of supportive communities, and catalyze collective political action under the discursive banner of "the personal is political" (Lövheim 2011; Taylor 2011). Feminist bloggers' first-person narratives are said to reinvigorate and creatively reshape the legacies of the women's liberation consciousness-raising while producing alternative, oppositional knowledge. In her research on personal sex blogs, Elizabeth Anne Wood (2008) suggests that mediated self-exposure is "consciousness-raising 2.0" (480) or a continuation of a long-standing feminist practice of collective empowerment through sharing resources and information. Mommy blogs, built around confessions of joy as well as of the struggles, pressures, failures, and disappointments brought by the demands of maternity, have also been analyzed in terms of renewed consciousness-raising that troubles the dominant ideologies of motherhood (Anderson and Grace 2015; Petersen 2015; Van Cleaf 2015). This sentiment of empowerment is reflected by bloggers Courtney E. Martin and Vanessa Valenti, who celebrate the transformative power of feminist blogging in the collaboratively produced *#FemFuture: Online Revolution* report. Martin and Valenti argue that the blogging format "constitutes both a 'communications arm' for the contemporary feminist movement and an inexhaustible force continually radicalizing and challenging its institutionalization" (2013, 3). Importantly, the report has been critiqued as drawing on, without properly crediting, the online labour of women of colour bloggers and erasing differences of race, class, and geographic positioning among feminists (Johnson 2013; Loza 2014).

Although disclosing intimate details might increase a blogger's vulnerability to unwanted attention (Wood 2008), the key assumption remains that the benefits of confessional consciousness-raising for reconstituting the public discourse outweigh the risks that come with public exposure. Still another assumption, operative in the literature on feminism 2.0, is that the public testimonies are necessarily in service of transformative politics. What is often missing from feminist discussions of mediated, confessional consciousness-raising is an analysis of the digital economy and its effects on feminist self-making. The digital economy is for the most part driven by the immaterial labour of users who forge and amplify affective connections through producing, reworking, remixing, sharing, and archiving digital content (Terranova 2004). As Pybus (2015) puts it in her work on affect and personal digital archives, "every keystroke, every link, every comment that people generate can be extrapolated for surplus value" (238). Even among feminists, labour extrapolation operates along lines of race, class, and geographic location such that white American feminists often draw personal surplus value from other feminist voices including and especially those of women of colour (Johnson 2013; Loza 2014). By sharing their life-stories and narratives of everyday life, users reinforce the centrality of intimacy and affect in both the digital economy and the production of contemporary citizenship (Poletti 2011). As the following analysis of popular media demonstrates, women's narratives of suffering and their confessions of conflicted feelings, both couched in feminist discourses of CR and postfeminist discourses of individual empowerment, become instruments for generating revenue rather than pathways to collective political action.

To address the commercialization of mediated confessionality, we look at *xoJane*[3] (fig.4.1), an American online lifestyle magazine launched in 2011 and defunct as of 2016, which was founded by Jane Pratt, a publisher and journalist known for previously producing *Jane* and *Sassy* teen magazines. Unlike explicitly feminist online media such as *Bitch*, *EverydayFeminism*, or *Ms. Magazine*, *xoJane* was branded as a women's lifestyle blog without clear reference to feminist politics; yet it would be wrong to call *xoJane* postfeminist if we take Angela McRobbie's (2004) definition of postfeminist as a process of undoing feminist gains through positively framing

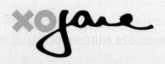

4.1 *xoJane*'s front page illustrating the aesthetics of amateur photography and DIY remixing of digital content, 2016.

women's movements but ultimately discarding contemporary feminist politics as no longer necessary. Rather than postfeminist, *xoJane* was implicitly feminist – it was known and referred to as "feminist" by networked publics, its contributors often self-identified as feminist, and its commentators regularly invoked intersectionality, rape culture, slut shaming, and other conceptual tools rooted in feminist thought. In this sense, *xoJane* was similar to *Jezebel* (launched 2007), another lifestyle website that provides a feminist-friendly space without being explicitly positioned and branded as feminist media (Novoselova 2015; Wazny 2010). Yet *xoJane*'s articulations of feminism were often narrow and consistently exploited personal misery rooted in structural inequalities for monetary gain.

To establish and solidify affective relations to its networked audience, *xoJane* solicited personal narratives from its readers, who were paid a small honorarium for their content (US$50, according to Tolentino 2017). Some writers submitted autobiographic narratives anonymously; for those who published under their own names, it was an opportunity to drive traffic to their blogs, increase sales of their books, or secure publishing deals, as was the case with *xoJane* writer Cat Marnell. Yet the benefits of such publicity were distributed unequally, as confessional essays written by women of colour were less likely to be picked up by major publishing presses (Brown 2015).

One of the key differences between feminist blogging and online feminist magazines such as *xoJane* or *Jezebel* is the relative editorial freedom afforded by personal blogs and the presence of editorial demands for shareable and clickable content on commercial platforms. Both *xoJane* and *Jezebel* are hybrid media that maintain a DIY look and an intimate, informal feel of a personal blog while generating revenue for a corporate media platform. Although *xoJane* was owned by Time Inc. and produced by a team of professional publishers, it resembled, drew on, and exploited amateur aesthetics and relational affects of feminist confessional blogging (fig. 4.1).

In contrast to edited and carefully stylized illustrations in traditional women's magazines, pieces on *xoJane* were often accompanied by personal photography. A popular representational form on *xoJane* was the selfie, a photographic genre associated with self-portraits captured by digital hand-held devices. Distinctively performative, selfies' "corporeal sociability" enacts a "see me showing you me" communicative gesture (Frosh 2015, 1609–10), propelling emotional attachments along social networks. In addition to digital self-portraits, *xoJane* contributors established affective links with audiences by submitting their low-resolution childhood photos. Pointing out the paradoxical effects of low-resolution images shared by mediated audiences, Hito Steyerl argues that "the circulation of poor images feeds into both capitalist media assembly lines and alternative audiovisual economies" (2009, para. 26). Drawing on Steyerl, Smith-Prei and Stehle (2016) suggest that the distribution of low-resolution visuals is aligned with the "awkward," discontinuous feminist politics of synthesizing counter-cultural rebellion with commercial circulations and feminist self-branding. By sharing their awkward and mundane childhood moments captured on camera, *xoJane* contributors participated in the production of feminist intimate publics (Berlant 2008) glued together by playfulness, immediacy, and confessionality.

The attempt to elicit confessions is especially visible in *xoJane*'s pitching guidelines that echoed a feminist rhetoric of self-knowledge and lived experience; they emphasized the importance of radically authentic, unfiltered narratives for drawing in the networked audience: "We're especially interested in personal stories told from a raw, honest perspective. Our audience craves stories about personal experiences. It helps to always be brutally honest and radically transparent. Don't fake anything. At *xoJane*, women themselves are the experts – our advice comes from having lived through an experience" (*xoJane* 2014, paras. 1–2).

Like reality shows with their confessional rooms that have become a staple of TV programming, autobiographical essays have become the currency of commercial feminist media. In *xoJane*, the widely read and heavily commented on "It

Happened to Me" (IHTM) section illustrated the problematics of feminist confessions in the context of "viral" digital media. A number of IHTM pieces were infused with feminist politics as they located personal experiences within wider power structures; topics in this category included body image, eating disorders, reproductive rights, dating violence, and experiences of harassment ("It Happened to Me: I'm a Lesbian Teacher in Rural Illinois and Every Day Is a Struggle"); the section also included topics traditionally coded as feminine, such as relationships and beauty ("It Happened to Me: My Boyfriend Lives with His Ex-Wife"); other types of personal narratives covered shocking and traumatic experiences ("It Happened to Me: I Survived a Home Invasion on the South Side of Chicago"), and occasionally amusing stories ("It Happened to Me: I Was Chased by a Stampede of Goats").

In 2014 *xoJane* published an essay entitled "It Happened to Me: There Are No Black People in My Yoga Classes and I'm Suddenly Feeling Uncomfortable with It," authored by Jen Polachek, under the pseudonym Jen Caron, reflecting on her encounter with privilege and difference upon seeing a black woman in a yoga class. Juxtaposing her thin, white body with a body of a black woman whom she describes as "heavy set," Polachek failed to see her own bias and the act of othering by making several problematic assumptions about that woman's thoughts and feelings. Polachek confesses feeling unease, helplessness, shame, and alienation: "I was completely unable to focus on my practice, instead feeling hyper-aware of my high-waisted bike shorts, my tastefully tacky sports bra, my well-versedness in these poses that I have been in hundreds of times. My skinny white girl body. Surely this woman was noticing all of these things and judging me for them, stereotyping me, resenting me – or so I imagined … I thought about how that must feel: to be a heavyset black woman entering for the first time a system that by all accounts seems unable to accommodate her body. What could I do to help her?" She describes her feelings of disempowerment and loss upon realizing her complicity in racism: "I got home from that class and promptly broke down crying. Yoga, a beloved safe space that has helped me through many dark moments in over six years of practice, suddenly felt deeply suspect" (Polachek [Caron] 2014a, n.p.).

The frenzied reception of this piece by *xoJane* commentators and the wider feminist public exemplifies the "viral" effects of commercialized confessions. Within hours, Polachek's confession generated waves of outrage due to her blatant racism, "white girl" naiveté, and fatphobic rhetoric. Following intense harassment and hate mail, Polachek deleted her accounts from social media, returning to the networked sphere later with a piece in *Hypocrite Reader* magazine where she reflected on the naiveté, insensitivity, and reckless confessionality of her IHTM story:

"I was punished for a confession, a transgression of public and private spaces: I exposed readers to personal thoughts that should have stayed private, and in turn, I am denied any remaining shroud of privacy" (Polachek 2014b).

Polachek's admission of white privilege is an "unhappy confession" that attempts to absolve the speaker from her responsibility to enact anti-racism (Lockard 2016). In her essay on the non-performativity of anti-racism and the politics of admissions, Ahmed argues that well-intentioned declarations of white guilt "do not do what they say" (2004, 50) in the sense the admissions of racism are intended to point out that one is conscious of one's biases and thus is not a racist. Confessions of bias are intended to be seen as a good practice in itself and as "moves to innocence" that absolve one's guilt (Coates 2015, 97; Tuck and Yang 2012, 3). Ahmed (2004) suggests that such declarations afford illusory ways out of being racist, yet provide no tools for addressing inequities.

What we find the most interesting here is not Polachek's piece – well-intentioned but lacking depth and critical, intersectional engagement with racism – but the tendency of *xoJane* and similar media to publish increasingly controversial pieces framed as a way to facilitate a feminist discussion. Given the feminist sensibilities of *xoJane*'s user base and the increasing visibility of intersectional feminism in the digital sphere more broadly, the disapproval and outrage were predictable, but so were hundreds of comments that generated page views, social-media shares, and returning site visits. Commentators not only took apart Polachek's argument but mocked and shamed the author. Some of *xoJane*'s commentators displayed disdain towards the medium, yet they came back to the website over and over, often professing their enjoyment of the commentariat community. As one *xoJane* commentator tellingly stated, "The comments and everyone in them are THE ONLY reasons I get onto this site." In Internet lingo, this practice has been termed hate-reading, defined by *Urban Dictionary* as "an online activity in which one visits a website … for the express purpose of ridiculing – or indulging one's disdain for – the author and/or the content on the site" (2012).

Another example of feminist media that mobilizes confessional politics to draw in readers – and profits – is *Jezebel* (fig. 4.2), a blog initially owned by Gawker Media and subsequently bought by Univision Communications, covering fashion, lifestyle, and celebrity and launched in 2007. Like *xoJane*, it attracts an audience of women who tend toward feminist perspectives. In 2016, *Jezebel* published an anonymous confession, regarded by some readers as a satire, based on its humorous tone and grotesque sexism, entitled "My Daughter Forced Me to See Women as People" and tagged with "dad feminism." In this piece, the author admits to having a range of highly sexist attitudes towards women, attitudes that he claims

4.2 Rather than earnestly reacting to the essays, a commentator playfully anticipates a heated discussion in the comment section of *Jezebel*, 2016.

were challenged by interactions with his daughter. He writes, "When I look at my daughter I don't see a woman. I see myself. And that's why I think she should be legally allowed to vote and own property, and have access to equally-good soccer fields (even though women's sports are objectively as bad as the idea of war)" (Man 2016, para. 3).

Throughout the essay, the author, identified by the pseudonym "A Man," makes demeaning comments directed at women while applauding what he understands to be a reflection of masculinity in his daughter: "Luckily, my daughter is growing up to be a brilliant, handsome young man [*sic*], and I think that speaks quite well of me. I love my daughter so much that I don't even care if some other, worse bitches are also elevated by this confession: I am a feminist, because I see myself in my little girl" (paras.10–11). Offering no analysis or introspection, this piece brings forward anti-feminist clichés only to repackage them as confessions for a feminist audience. Yet the audience, it seems, has grown weary of such confessional spectacles, as few people attempted to argue earnestly with the author in the comments section and a number of commentators remarked on the "clickbait" qualities of this piece.

Slate's contributor Laura Bennett characterized *xoJane*'s IHTM section and some of *Jezebel* as belonging to the "First-Person Industrial Complex," a set of media practices and institutional values that produce "the push to ensure that every story, no matter how narrow, will find an ardent audience of cheerleaders (or hate-readers) and a corresponding number of clicks – to dress up the personal in the language of the political" (2015, 9). Bennett quotes Jia Tolentino, Jezebel's former features editor, saying that "writers feel like the best thing they have to offer is the worst thing that ever happened to them" (para. 9). Former IHTM editor Mandy Stadtmiller published a piece entitled "It Happened to Me: How I Became a First-Person Human Trafficker" (2015) in *New York Magazine*, admitting that many young women whose confessions she published on *xoJane* were unprepared for the consequences of such public disclosures. Initially convinced that such stories were "agents of liberation," Stadtmiller saw her work in commissioning authors to share and elaborate on their most intimate and traumatic memories as at "the forefront of a revolution." Her narrative reveals how attempts at networked consciousness-raising lend themselves to commercialization, turning personal suffering into a pursuit of clicks.

Confessions, whether infused with a feminist sensibility or not, can be used for profit in digital media, driven by the affective bonds of users who perform the free labour of sharing and commenting. While mediated confessional narratives display the characteristics of consciousness-raising and are couched in emotive feminist language, the question remains when and how such confessions aid social change, and when their benefit is solely with platforms and their monetization strategies. As Tolentino (2017) has written, "Web sites generated ad revenue in direct proportion to how many 'eyeballs' could be attracted to their offerings." "Eyeball" capitalism thus becomes an integral element of the design and circulation of online feminist confessional writing, functioning not only to reach out affectively to imagined communities but also as click-bait in the pursuit of revenue generation. In this sense, then, the confessionality of the online feminisms we examined is unlike that of the CR method directed more explicitly at social action and change. Even while feminist engagement has intensified in recent years and intersectionality has become available for mainstream use as a political framework, feminism – as hooks (2000) recognized – is available for resale. While the feminist confessional has a rich history of making the personal political, it also seems to be a genre newly connected to neoliberal viral regimes of generating income through clicks, likes, comments, and networks.

Confessional End Times?

Affective dimensions of intimate publics, such as those circulating in the feminist blogosphere as described above, provide a new frame for confessional politics. Affordances of the virtual engender intimate feminist publics that engage in confessional consciousness-raising through networked actions such as commenting, hashtagging, and media-making. Mobilizing affects of networked audiences, feminist confessions go viral, overflowing the spaces for which they were written. Viral confessions are consumed, shared, tweeted, and commented on by both feminist and anti-feminist publics. Jasbir Puar suggests that the concept of virality evokes both information sharing and bodily contamination "while pointing more positively to the porosity, indeed the conviviality, of what has been treated as opposed" (2013, 42). Distributed through transnational connectivity enabled by corporate media platforms, viral narratives of trauma and oppression generate feelings, spur discussions, and transform collective consciousness. Yet as our analysis of *xoJane*'s "It Happened to Me" and *Jezebel*'s "dad feminism" piece demonstrates, the effects of such virality are ambivalent in light of broader networked processes such as the commercialization of blogging and the appropriation of confessional methods for commercial goals.

While the confessional as a mode of politics and relating has gone viral in the feminist media sphere, Jia Tolentino (2017), *Jezebel*'s former editor and a staff writer at the *New Yorker*, has recently argued that the era of the personal essay is over. Tolentino maintains that the online feminist personal essay took off in 2008 following the publication of Emily Gould's piece "Exposed" in the *New York Times Magazine*, about her experiences with confessional writing on the internet, and that it died in November 2016 after the US presidential elections, at which time "personal-essay subjects ... seemed to hit a new low in broader social relevance." As she argues, the "ultra-confessional essay, written by a person you've never heard of and published online, that flourished until recently ... now hardly registers" (para. 3) and that this change happened as "navel-gazing" became an inadequate tool for tackling broader social injustice in the wake of Donald Trump's election.

Given that *xoJane* folded in 2016 and *Jezebel* has reduced the number of confessional pieces it publishes, we might as well agree with Tolentino (2017) that the peak of the first-person narrative has passed as the publishing market has become over-saturated with women's confessions of adversity. Yet while the first-personal narrative appears to be in decline, the personal continues to be the dominant currency of the digital economy. Rather than dying out as a method, the women's liberation movement's central method of consciousness-raising continues to circulate, and especially so online and through social media, in the manner in which feminists tell their lives, render them political, mobilize affect, and seek collective community-making around experiences. Although, according to Tolentino, "the personal is no longer political in quite the same way it was," the affective dimensions of what is personal, private, and individual have shifted dramatically in new media environments alongside a new recognition of state-sanctioned injustice. As such, we do not think that the centrality of the confessional for feminist mobilizing is a concluded story, although we are hesitant to speculate on what the futures of feminist confessionality might be.

Feminist blogging's inheritances of consciousness-raising include both speaking at power and the fostering of affective connectedness as a way to attest to shared feelings of unhappiness rooted in social inequities. It is through confessing that forms of solidarity including coalitional politics can be made and managed. Yet in contrast to the locally grounded CR groups that proliferated in the early 1970s, online networks blur private confessions and public commentary within a landscape of digital feminism. This hypervisible publicness of today's confessing means that feminisms are increasingly seen and increasingly voiced, yet also potentially co-optable and sellable. Even though, as we have been arguing, the affective politics of consciousness-raising are present in online feminisms, what has changed is the new corporatized digital environment that has put first-person confessionality in service of the digital economy while affording corporate environments the power to hold sway over the future of feminist confessionality.

NOTES

1 Throughout we foreground the term "women's liberation movement" above that of "second wave feminism" when referring to the feminist movements of the 1960s and '70s. While both terms are in use and accurate, we follow feminist historians such as Victoria Hesford (2013), who opt for the former term because of its energizing sound and its sceptical approach toward the idea that there were and are only ever several "waves" of feminism. "Waves" also tend to elide the multiplicity of feminist movements and in particular the work and revolutionary actions of feminisms of colour including black feminisms, Indigenous feminisms, and Latinx feminisms. Further, using the wave metaphor leaves us

at a loss as to the contemporary feminist moment: are we in the fourth wave, the third wave, numerous waves simultaneously? This parsing out of waves in turn does a disservice to our argument that present day feminisms cycle the feelings and methods of the women's liberation movement, namely consciousness-raising, while making them their own. See Astrid Henry's (2012) work for a discussion of the waves metaphor.

2 "Being woke" or "staying woke" refers to being conscious of social injustices and in particular anti-black racism in the United States. These phrases are commonly associated with the #BlackLivesMatter movement. For one example of its usage, see, for instance, Sady Doyle (2014).

3 Founded in 2011, the site operated until December 2016, when Pratt left Time Inc.

REFERENCES

Ahmed, Sara. 2004. "Declarations of Whiteness: The Non-Performativity of Anti-Racism." *Borderlands* 3, no. 2. http://www.borderlands.net.au/vol3no2_2004/ahmed_declarations.htm.

– 2010. "Killing Joy: Feminism and the History of Happiness." *Signs* 35, no. 3: 571–94.

Allen, Pamela. [1970] 2000. "The Small Group Press." In *Radical Feminism: A Documentary Reader*, edited by Barbara Crow, 277–81. New York: New York University Press. Originally published in 1970 in *Free Space: A Perspective on the Small Group in Women's Liberation*. New York: Times Change Press.

Anderson, Wendy KZ, and Kittie E. Grace. 2015. "'Taking Mama Steps' toward Authority, Alternatives, and Advocacy: Feminist Consciousness-Raising within a Digital Motherhood Community." *Feminist Media Studies* 15, no. 6: 942–59.

Arnold, June. [1970] 2000. "Consciousness-Raising." In Crow, *Radical Feminism: A Documentary Reader*, 282–6. New York: New York University Press. Previously published in 1970 in *Women's Liberation: Blueprint for the Future*, edited by Stookie Stambler. New York: Ace Books.

Bambara, Toni Cade. 1970. Preface to *The Black Woman: An Anthology*, edited by Toni Cade Bambara, 7–12. New York: New American Library.

Bennett, Laura. 2015. "The First-Person Industrial Complex." *Slate*. 14 September. http://www.slate.com/articles/life/technology/2015/09/the_first_person_industrial_complex_how_the_harrowing_personal_essay_took.html.

Berlant, Lauren. 2008. *The Female Complaint: The Unfinished Business of Sentimentality in American Culture*. Durham: Duke University Press.

Brown, Stacia L. 2015. "The Personal Essay Economy Offers Fewer Rewards for Black Women." *New Republic*, 18 September. https://newrepublic.com/article/122845/personal-essay-economy-offers-fewer-rewards-black-women.

Coates, Ta-Nehisi. 2015. *Between the World and Me*. New York: Spiegel and Grau.

Combahee River Collective. [1977] 1982. "A Black Feminist Statement (1977)." In *All the Women*

Are White, All the Blacks Are Men, but Some of Us Are Brave: Black Women's Studies, edited by Gloria T. Hull, Patricia Bell Scott, and Barbara Smith. Old Westbury: Feminist Press.

Cornell, Drucilla. 2000. "Las Greñudas: Recollections on Consciousness-Raising." *Signs* 25, no. 4: 1033–9.

Crow, Barbara, ed. *Radical Feminism: A Documentary Reader*. New York: New York University Press.

Doyle, Sady. 2016. "The True Story of How Teen Vogue Got Mad, Got Woke, and Began Terrifying Men Like Donald Trump." *Quartz*. 19 December. https://qz.com/866305/the-true-story-of-how-teen-vogue-got-mad-got-woke-and-began-terrifying-men-like-donald-trump/.

Echols, Alice. 1989. *Daring to Be Bad: Radical Feminism in America, 1967–1975*. Minneapolis: University of Minnesota Press.

– 2002. *Shaky Ground: The Sixties and Its Aftershock*. New York: Columbia University Press.

Enke, Finn. 2018. "Collective Memory and Transfeminist 1970s: Toward a Less Plausible History." *TSQ: Transgender Studies Quarterly* 5, no. 1: 9–29.

Firestone, Shulamith, and Anne Koedt, eds. 1970. *Notes from the Second Year: Women's Liberation*. New York: Radical Feminism.

Fitzpatrick, Kathleen. 2007. "The Pleasure of the Blog: The Early Novel, the Serial, and the Narrative Archive." In *Blogtalks Reloaded: Social Software-Research and Cases*, edited by Thomas N. Burg and Jan Schmidt, 167–86. Vienna: Social Software Lab.

Frosh, Paul. 2015. "The Gestural Image: The Selfie, Photography Theory, and Kinesthetic Sociability." *International Journal of Communication* 9: 22.

Gordon, Avery. [1997] 2008. *Ghostly Matters: Haunting and the Sociological Imagination*. Reprint of first edition. Minneapolis: University of Minnesota Press.

Gore, Dayo F., Jeanne Theoharis, and Komozi Woodard, eds. 2009. *Want to Start a Revolution? Radical Women in the Black Freedom Struggle*. New York: New York University Press.

Gornick, Vivian. [1971] 2000. "Consciousness." In Crow, *Radical Feminism: A Documentary Reader*, 287–300. New York: New York University Press. Originally published 10 January 1971 in *New York Times Magazine*.

Gould, Emily. 2008. "Exposed." *New York Times Magazine*. 25 May. https://www.nytimes.com/2008/05/25/magazine/25internet-t.html.

Hanisch, Carol. [1970] 2000. "The Personal is Political." In Crow, *Radical Feminism: A Documentary Reader*, 113–16. New York: New York University Press. Originally published in 1970 in Firestone and Koedt, *Notes from the Second Year: Women's Liberation*.

Hemmings, Clare. 2010. *Why Stories Matter: The Political Grammar of Feminist Theory*. Durham, NC: Duke University Press.

Henry, Astrid. 2012. "Waves." In *Rethinking Women's and Gender Studies*, edited by Catherine M. Orr, Ann Braithwaite, and Diane Lichtenstein, 102–18. New York: Routledge.

Hesford, Victoria. 2013. *Feeling Women's Liberation*. Durham: Duke University Press.

hooks, bell. 2000. *Feminism Is for Everybody: Passionate Politics.* Cambridge: South End Press.

Johnson, J.M. 2013. "#FemFuture, History, and Loving Each Other Harder." *Diaspora Hypertext: Black Femme History and Futures.* 12 April. https://dh.jmjafrx.com/2013/04/12/femfuture-history-loving-each-other-harder/.

Kaplan, Cara. 1996. *The Erotics of Talk: Women's Writing and Feminist Paradigms.* Oxford: Oxford University Press.

Lockard, Claire A. 2016. "Unhappy Confessions: The Temptation of Admitting to White Privilege." *Feminist Philosophy Quarterly* 2, no. 2: 1–20.

Lövheim, Mia. 2011. "Young Women's Blogs as Ethical Spaces." *Information, Communication and Society* 12, no. 3: 338–54.

Loza, Susana. 2014. "Hashtag Feminism, #SolidarityIsForWhiteWomen, and the Other #FemFuture." *Ada: A Journal of Gender, New Media, and Technology* 5. https://adanewmedia.org/2014/07/issue5-loza/.

Man, A [pseud.]. 2016. "My Daughter Forced Me to See Women as People." *Jezebel* 26 August. https://jezebel.com/my-daughter-forced-me-to-see-women-as-people-1785522086.

Martin, Courtney E., and Vanessa Valenti. 2013. "#FemFuture: Online Revolution." *Barnard Center for Research on Women* 8. http://bcrw.barnard.edu/wp-content/nfs/reports/NFS8-FemFuture-Online-Revolution-Report-April-15-2013.pdf.

McRobbie, Angela. 2004. "Post-Feminism and Popular Culture." *Feminist Media Studies* 4, no. 3: 255–64.

Miguel, Cristina. 2016. "Visual Intimacy on Social Media: From Selfies to the Co-Construction of Intimacies through Shared Pictures." *Social Media + Society* 2, no. 2. http://journals.sagepub.com/doi/full/10.1177/2056305116641705.

Morgan, Robin. 1970. "Redstockings Manifesto." http://history.msu.edu/hst203/files/2011/02/Morgan-Redstockings-Manifesto.pdf.

New York Consciousness Awakening Women's Liberation Group. 1969. https://www.cwluherstory.org/organizing/national-womens-liberation-conference.

Norman, Brian. 2006. "The Consciousness-Raising Document, Feminist Anthologies, and Black Women in 'Sisterhood Is Powerful.'" *Frontiers* 27, no. 3: 38–64.

Norton, Eleanor Holmes. 1970. "Women in Black Liberation." In *Sisterhood Is Powerful: An Anthology of Writings Women's Liberation Movement*, edited by Robin Morgan, 398–9. New York: Vintage.

Novoselova, Veronika. 2016. "Digitizing Consumer Activism: A Thematic Analysis of Jezebel.com." In *Defining Identity and the Changing Scope of Culture in the Digital Age*, edited by Alison Novak and Imaani Jamillah El-Burki, 140–4. Hershey, PA: IGI Global.

Paasonen, Susanna, Ken Hillis, and Michael Petit. 2015. "Introduction: Networks of Transmission: Intensity, Sensation, Value." In *Networked Affect*, edited by Ken Hillis, Susanna Paasonen, and Michael Petit, 1–24. Cambridge: MIT Press.

Petersen, E. J. 2015. "Mommy Bloggers as Rebels and Community Builders." *Journal of the Motherhood Initiative for Research and Community Involvement* 6, no.1: 9–30.

Polachek, Jen. [Jen Caron, pseud.] 2014a. "It Happened to Me: There Are No Black People in My Yoga Classes and I'm Suddenly Feeling Uncomfortable with It." *xoJane*. 28 January. https://archive.vn/jDYpn.

— 2014b. *Hypocrite Reader* 38. http://hypocritereader.com/38/shame-and-the-internet.

Poletti, Anna. 2011. "Coaxing an Intimate Public: Life Narrative in Digital Storytelling." *Continuum: Journal of Media and Cultural Studies* 1: 73–83.

Puar, Jasbir K. 2013. "Homonationalism as Assemblage: Viral Travels, Affective Sexualities." *Jindal Global Law Review* 4, no. 2: 23–43.

Pybus, Jennifer. 2015. "Accumulating Affect: Social Networks and Their Archives of Feelings." In *Networked Affect*, edited by Ken Hillis, Susanna Paasonen, and Michael Petit, 235–47. Cambridge: MIT Press.

Qian, Hua, and Craig R. Scott. 2007. "Anonymity and Self Disclosure on Weblogs." *Journal of Computer Mediated Communication* 12, no. 4: 1428–51.

Randolph, Sherie M. 2015. *Florynce "Flo" Kennedy: The Life of a Black Feminist Radical*. Chapel Hill: University of North Carolina Press.

Sarachild, Kathie. [1968] 1970. "A Program for Feminist 'Consciousness-Raising.'" In Firestone and Koedt, eds., 78–80, *Notes from the Second Year: Women's Liberation*. Originally presented at the First National Women's Liberation Conference outside Chicago, 27 November 1968.

Sedgwick, Eve Kosofsky. 2003. *Touching Feeling: Affect, Performativity, Pedagogy*. Durham: Duke University Press.

Shreve, Anita. 1989. *Women Together, Women Alone: The Legacy of the Consciousness-Raising Movement*. New York: Penguin.

Smith-Prei, Carrie, and Maria Stehle. 2016. *Awkward Politics: Technologies of Popfeminist Activism*. Montreal: McGill-Queen's University Press.

Springer, Kimberly. 2005. *Living for the Revolution: Black Feminist Organizations, 1968–1980*. Durham, NC: Duke University Press.

Stadtmiller, Mandy. 2015. "Happened to Me: How I Became a First-Person Human Trafficker." *New York Magazine*, 21 September. http://nymag.com/thecut/2015/09/happened-to-me-happened-to-me.html.

Steyerl, Hito. 2009. "In Defense of the Poor Image." *E-flux* 10. https://www.e-flux.com/journal/10/61362/in-defense-of-the-poor-image/.

Stryker, Susan. 2017. *Transgender History: The Roots of Today's Revolution*. New York: Seal Press.

Taylor, Anthea. 2011. "Blogging Solo: New Media, 'Old' Politics." *Feminist Review* 99, no. 1: 79–97.

Taylor, Chloë. 2009. *The Culture of Confession from Augustine to Foucault: A Genealogy of the "Confessing Animal."* New York: Routledge.

Terranova, Tiziana. 2004. *Network Culture: Politics for the Information Age*. New York: Pluto Press.

Tolentino, Jia. 2017. "The Personal Essay Boom Is Over." *New Yorker*. 18 May. http://www.newyorker.com/culture/jia-tolentino/the-personal-essay-boom-is-over.

Tuck, Eve, and K. Wayne Yang. 2012. "Decolonization Is Not a Metaphor." *Decolonization: Indigeneity, Education and Society* 1, no. 1: 1–40.

Tyler, Imogen, Rebecca Coleman, and Debra Ferreday. 2008. "Commentary and Criticism." *Feminist Media Studies* 8, no. 1: 85–99.

Urban Dictionary. 2012. S.v. "hate-reading." Posted 30 January. https://www.urbandictionary.com/define.php?term=hate-reading.

Van Cleaf, Kara. 2015. "Of Woman Born to Mommy Blogged: The Journey from the Personal as Political to the Personal as Commodity." WSQ: *Women's Studies Quarterly* 43, no. 3: 247–64.

Wazny, Katelyn M. 2010. "Feminist Communities Online: What It Means to Be a Jezebel." *B Sides*: 1–23. http://ir.uiowa.edu/cgi/viewcontent.cgi?article=1012&context=bsides.

Williams, Cristan. 2016. "Radical Inclusion: Recounting the Trans Inclusive History of Radical Feminism." TSQ: *Transgender Studies Quarterly* 3, nos. 1–2: 254–8.

Williams, Raymond. [1977] 2009. "Structures of Feeling." In *Marxism and Literature*, 128–35. Oxford: Oxford University Press.

Willis, Ellen. 1982. "Sisters under the Skin? Confronting Race and Sex." *Village Voice Literary Supplement* no. 8 (June): 10–12.

Wood, Elizabeth Anne. 2008. "Consciousness-Raising 2.0: Sex Blogging and the Creation of a Feminist Sex Commons." *Feminism and Psychology* 18, no. 4: 480–7.

xoJane. 2014. "*xoJane* Pitching Guidelines." *Scoop.It!* 13 November. https://www.scoop.it/t/writing-by-a-k-andrew/p/4031671363/2014/11/13/xojane-pitching-guidelines.

5

"YES I'M GAY": The Mediality of Coming Out

SILKE JANDL

Innumerable examples of videos containing the term "My Sexuality" show that YouTube has become a space where vloggers and audiences discuss their sexuality. As a consequence, coming out on YouTube has become exceedingly popular, as the official YouTube blog pointed out in February 2015: "Coming out videos are a large and important part of YouTube culture: there are more than 36,000 videos related to the subject on the platform today, the sum of which have received more than 300m views. Last year alone, we saw ~9,600 coming out stories shared on YouTube – a 20% increase from the year before" (Lanning and Huang 2015). And because a significant number of highly popular YouTubers have come out as gay or bisexual in vlog form, this number has undoubtedly risen since then. Many of these YouTube stars have discussed their decision in some detail in their autobiographies as well. The interconnectedness between the depiction of personal issues regarding sexuality on YouTube and the discussion of these same issues in published books warrants an analysis of the impact that mediality has on the sexual discourse within the YouTube media sphere. My area of focus is the semi-professionally shot vlog, filmed and produced by full-time YouTubers who have gained fame primarily among teenagers and millennials.

YouTube videos are by definition multimodal, unifying visual, verbal, and interactive media forms. As Ruth Page and Bronwen Thomas observe in the introduction to their anthology *New Narratives: Stories and Storytelling in the Digital Age*, "Much online discourse is hybrid in nature, blending the written word with [the] near-instantaneous … In particular the narratives that emerge in Web 2.0 environments where personal expression is inextricably interwoven with dialogue (for example, through the use of conversational metacommentary) require paradigms that account for both their interpersonal and expressive qualities"

(Page and Thomas 2011, 4). Interestingly, this kind of interweaving is also a characteristic feature of the books that YouTubers have written in the recent past, and links them intrinsically to the online content they produce.

Moreover, YouTubers increasingly operate transmedially, engaging with their audiences on various social-media platforms as well as in movie productions, on radio shows, and in books.[1] This dispersion of information across media can be seen as a form of transmedia storytelling, as Henry Jenkins proposes in *Convergence Culture* (2006). Even though Jenkins focuses primarily on fictional world building and argues that "most often, transmedia stories are based not on individual characters or specific plots but rather complex fictional worlds," transmedia storytelling in the context of YouTube personalities revolves around the life story of a specific YouTuber. As Page points out, "It is not only fictional stories that are created in web 2.0 environments. In increasing measure, individuals use web 2.0 technologies to document their lives, telling anecdotes on personal blogs, discussion forums and in fragmented forms through microblogging or social network sites" (2010, 219). Thus, despite the fact that vlogs are typically non-fictional snippets of a YouTuber's private life, the expansion in the form of engagement on other social-media sites, and more recently their venturing into the realm of printed books, can very well be subsumed under Jenkins's concept of transmedia storytelling.

Many of the transmedial interfaces between books and YouTube videos are perhaps best characterized as adaptations. However, as Linda Hutcheon points out, it is important to "expand the traditional focus of adaptation studies on medium-specificity and individual comparative case studies in order to consider as well relations among the major modes of engagement: that is, it permits us to think about how adaptations allow people to tell, show, or interact with stories. We can be told or shown a story, each in a range of different media" (2006, 22). Determining the key functions of medium-specific choices YouTubers make with regard to the book-to-video relation is essential in gaining an understanding of the transmedial phenomenon of YouTubers' book publications.

To illustrate how the medium or media employed can affect how sexuality is talked about and how it might be received, I focus on YouTuber Shane Dawson and how he deals publicly and transmedially with questions about his sexuality.[2] I specifically investigate Dawson's autobiographical book *I Hate Myselfie*, published in 2015 before his coming out as bisexual, and *It Gets Worse*, published afterwards in 2016. Dawson's three tie-in short films to the books are also of interest, while his coming-out video is at the centre of my analysis.[3] This line of argument illustrates the extent of influence that transmedia storytelling and mediality have on the sexual discourse on YouTube and also demonstrates the need for such a discourse in the first place. The increasing representation of a variety of gender and sexual identities is crucial especially for younger viewers, as "media characters who share similarities with an individual can produce changes in the individual's self-perception" (Gomillion and Giuliano 2011, 331). YouTubers often inspire positivity and empowerment in their viewers and over the past decade have become significant role models for teenagers all over the world. Their claiming non-heterosexual identities with increasing confidence in front of millions of subscribers and readers thereby contributes to a decrease in marginalization and a normalizing of non-binary sexual and gender identities. The transmedial dimension of this discourse not only illustrates the interest in an inclusive representation of sexuality but also aids in effectively reaching a wider audience while providing a larger number of different perspectives on the complex and sometimes still controversial issue of sexual orientation and identity.

"YES I'M GAY": Coming Out on YouTube

Coming out as non-heterosexual seems to be rather normal on YouTube. Dodie Clark, for example, explains that within the YouTube community, "Everyone knew I was freaking bi because everyone's freaking bi" (2016). Relating the story about a Grindr date, Dawson too speculates, "Maybe he was a YouTuber in the closet too?! Maybe they were ALL YouTubers in the closet! I'm pretty sure there are hundreds of them" (Dawson 2016a, 115). These examples illustrate how normal non-heterosexuality is taken to be among some YouTuber groups.

YouTube vloggers have, however, avoided discussing their sexuality with their audience for a long time, apart from notable exceptions like Tyler Oakley and Hannah Hart. This is significant because audiences feel they know YouTubers quite intimately through their vlogs. Only recently have long-term YouTubers felt compelled to share details of their sexuality with their fans. For some YouTubers like Connor Franta, writing an autobiographical book seems to have accelerated the decision to come out on the platform. Writing a book most definitely had such an effect on Joey Graceffa, who has stated that he had initially planned to come out to his audience via his book (2015c). However, three days before the book's publication date, he uploaded a music video hinting in the visual narrative that he was gay (2015b). The video's story ends in a kiss between Graceffa and another male and has subsequently been taken by many fans as his coming out, which he confirmed two days later in a vlog (2015c).

Discussing sexuality, whether or not it is binary, has become something of a trend among YouTubers, at least since early 2015. The words "my sexuality" bring up more than a million videos on YouTube.[4] The number of views increases exponentially if the title indicates confessions about non-binary gender identities or non-heterosexual desires. The promised increase in traction for YouTubers who engage in discussions about sexuality in a confessional manner has led to several forms of queerbaiting. Some YouTubers have posted videos with often-misleading titles and thumbnails[5] that insinuate confessional-type videos about sexuality or about fanships[6] of same-sex YouTubers to attract more viewers.[7] Queerbaiting in itself "has decidedly negative connotations" (Brennan 2016, 190) that imply "that any suggestion of queerness … is labelled as shameful" (191). However, YouTubers who exploit the surging interest in non-heterosexual identities via queerbaiting thereby trivialize the practice into just another form of clickbait. The effectiveness of such gaybaiting and queerbaiting tactics is nevertheless evidence of the lack of representation of non-heterosexual identities among "Big YouTubers" and may well reflect a craving for more videos on the topic in general. Especially in the context of community-oriented YouTubers, potentially positive associations with confession can be observed regardless of the topic. Whether YouTubers open up about their mental health, physical illness, or sexuality, loyal viewers are tendentially quick to express acceptance and support. Indeed, cultivating a loyal fan base via confessions of any sort has proven effective for media producers off YouTube as well.[8]

"I Wish I Was Gay": Coming Out as Bisexual

Dawson's "I'm bisexual" video (fig. 5.1) exhibits many of the characteristics of coming-out videos on YouTube. The video was filmed on a webcam, which results in an uncharacteristically (for Dawson) unpolished video with poor image and sound quality. The lighting, angle, and even his clothes are below the usual standard on his channel. The comparatively poor quality of the video functions as a visual signposting of honesty and immediacy, as he establishes in the video: "And I didn't want to turn on my like camera, my lights and my – I didn't want to do my hair, I just wanted to turn on my computer and talk to you guys, because that's what I have done since 2008 when I started this channel. And I just want to be honest" (Dawson 2015c). Similarly, Connor Franta in his coming-out video emphasizes, "I'm sitting here, in front of you, with no script, no plan, no fancy editing

The Mediality of Coming Out

5.1 Shane Dawson's emotional coming-out video, "I'm Bisexual," Shane Dawson TV, YouTube, 2015.

and I'm just gonna be really honest" (Franta 2014). The quality brings to mind the beginnings of vlogging when YouTubers were filming and editing on laptops rather than with expensive high-quality cameras, microphones, lighting, software, and set design. Thus, purposefully creating a video that is reminiscent of early-day vlogging also evokes the genuineness and sincerity those vlogs appeared to inherently represent. Poor video quality in coming-out videos functions as an indicator of honesty and authenticity and is intended to bridge the gap between creator and viewer that professional equipment and sophisticated video production sometimes cause. Opting to showcase vulnerability in a way that could be imitated by anybody with minimal equipment and internet access makes these videos easy to relate to, which in turn makes YouTubers accessible role models. This "relatability" is crucial, as "children, adolescents and young adults often emulate their favorite media figures as well as adopt the media figures' values and personality characteristics" (Gomillion and Giuliano 2011, 344). As a result, the videos helped not only LGBTQ+ viewers to "feel as though it [i.e., their sexual orientation] was acceptable" and to "view their identity more positively" (ibid., 346); they may even have helped "alleviate some of the psychological difficulties" prevalent among non-heterosexual individuals (350). Most importantly, however, the rising number of positive representations of LGBTQ+ people across media "can cause heterosexuals to espouse more positive attitudes toward this group" (350), and thus "may be an important first step toward reducing societal prejudice against the GLB community" (351).

Creating audiovisual markers of authenticity is also crucial for the motivation of publicly coming out to an audience. For many full-time YouTubers, this motivation lies in the desire to help their subscribers. They frequently cite the intention of being helpful in their videos and do so even more explicitly in their book publications. Grace Helbig, for example, states in *Grace's Guide* (2014), "I sometimes consider myself to be the Internet's awkward older sister. I may not have ALL the answers, but I've got my own advice, opinions, and theories to help get you through this arbitrary piss den called life" (10). In coming-out videos, helping others to come to terms with their own sexuality is fairly pronounced. Connor Franta made "this video for anyone, who needs it" and tried to encourage those who struggle with their sexuality (2014). Joey Graceffa, stating that helping is a core motivation for his coming out on YouTube, also sees himself as part of a bigger picture: "And I am just so excited to live in this world and be one of those people to push and help to make this [being gay] more acceptable" (2015c).

Homosexuality is not only accepted but almost fashionable, at least in some YouTube vlogger communities, due to the large and increasing number of openly gay and successful YouTubers. Being bisexual, on the other hand, is often not taken as seriously as a sexual orientation.[9] Dawson states that he is "making this video because I feel like a lot of you guys might be confused and scared, and you're not talking to people about it"; he wants his video to provide support (Dawson 2015c). He also repeatedly expresses his wish to be gay rather than bisexual: "You know I always wish that I was gay, that I was just 100% gay for so many reasons, you know. Number 1, that means I would know who I was. Number 2, it would be a lot easier for me to be accepted by people" (2015c).

Dawson ascribes a certain amount of confidence to those who are gay; Joey Graceffa's exclamation "YES I'M GAY"[10] is only one expression of this confidence. A source of confidence for homosexuals, at least in the YouTube context, stems from the numerous coming-out videos that those struggling with their sexuality can turn to, as Dawson observes: "There is a lot of coming-out videos of people who are gay or lesbian or – and they are so confident and they are like, you know, I've known since I was five, you know, I've always been gay. The Ingrid[11] video is fucking the best video I've ever seen. I loved it. But it made me cry because I'm not that. I don't know who I'm 100%. And I know that a lot of you guys may feel the same way" (Dawson 2015c). By comparison, YouTube videos dealing with coming out as bisexual are rare and are often accompanied by hate comments and explicit "bi-bashing" to a much larger extent than coming-out-as-gay videos.[12] Dawson is highly aware of this: "I know a lot of people make fun of bisexual people. I've made fun of them in the past obviously projecting, because people, are like oh, you're just gay, you're just in denial" (2015c). There are many more gay role models to look up to and gain confidence from than there are bisexual role models. Dawson states that this lack of representation is another reason he decided to talk about his sexuality publicly on his channel.

Dawson's envy of those who knew they were homosexual "since they were five" (2015c) seems to have triggered memories of a story about him in kindergarten which he subsequently included in *It Gets Worse*:

When I was in kindergarten I had my first crush, or should I say, first crushes … I walked into class, and I took a look around. My eyes stopped on what was the most beautiful girl I had ever seen in my five years of living … I walked up to her and tried to introduce myself, but before I could a boy with spiked, gelled hair and a douchebag face swooped in to steal my thunder. It was in that moment that my world got more confusing. The boy looked up at me and said, "Go away, fat ass," and instead of crying, I just stared at him, completely awestruck. All the feelings I had for the girl I started having for the boy … I sat down at an open desk and started to panic. I had two crushes: one on a boy and one on a girl. (Dawson 2016a, 8–9)

While this story is supposed to illustrate that bisexual desires were evident early on in Dawson's life, he says, "It would be years before I was ready to confront my feelings. I went through the next fourteen years holding them in and pretending that I was completely straight" (2016a, 12). Significantly, he draws connections between his mental and physical problems (like obesity, eating disorders, and depression), the repression of his sexuality, and his religious upbringing: "I love my family, but that was not accepted, it was like; no, you can't do that. God will not accept that. So I just shut it down. And I just repressed it. And … I got real fat, and I ate all the feelings. And I was morbidly obese … I started really hating myself and really being ashamed, and scared … I turned to eating disorder, I turned to, you know, to just depression" (2015c). Indeed, compared to the general population, LGBTQ+ individuals reportedly have an increased likelihood of both physical and mental problems, as well as comorbidity (see, for example, Hafeez et al. 2017). He therefore feels that coming out as bisexual to his family, friends, and subscribers is necessary because "I don't want to hate myself anymore. I don't want to be sad all the time" (Dawson, 2015c). His statement also implies that coming out publicly can, on a personal level, be the starting point of a healing process, allowing a reassessment of indoctrinated values and expectations. More generally, such discussions about non-heterosexuality can aid in the attempt to destigmatize sexualities that are perceived as deviant.

"More about Me": Autobiographical Books as Transmedial Expansions

The shift in perspective when it comes to sexual norms and values is also reflected in Dawson's autobiographical books. His first, *I Hate Myselfie: A Collection of Essays*, was an instant *New York Times* bestseller, as was his second, *It Gets Worse*. Both books promise to reveal more intimate details about his personal life than his videos do. In the introduction to *I Hate Myselfie*, he immediately differentiates his online persona from his private self when he explains his title: "For the record, I don't really hate myself, but I do hate the way I portray myself online. Hence, myselfie … Online I'm this loud, outrageous confident guy who acts like nothing bothers him and he has the whole world at his fingertips. In reality I'm a shy, quiet guy who would rather spend his nights lying in bed watching Netflix than being a valuable member of society" (Dawson 2015a, 3).

In *The Art of Self-Invention*, Joanne Finkelstein argues that "to participate in society we cultivate a public persona, a manner of being in the world that works to sustain our engagements with others" (2007, 2). Dawson embodies Finkelstein's notion of participation when he distinguishes between the persona that he projects onto the world – even if it is from the comfort of his home – and the private person who may choose to spend time alone rather than with others. However, his declaration is somewhat problematic, as it suggests that he presents a persona online rather than an authentic self – yet it is the promise of authenticity that draws audiences to vlogs.

Nevertheless, he insists, "In this book, you'll get to see the real me, not the 'me' you see on YouTube" (Dawson 2015a, 4). His second book similarly asserts that "you will get to know even more about me than you did in my last book … mainly because I've learned so much more about myself since writing it" (2016a, 4). The books thus undertake to do what transmedia storytelling does for fictional universes: namely, to provide more personal information, more intimate details, more stories and anecdotes. As fan engagement with YouTubers and other celebrities on social media shows, fans crave more than they get in a single medium.

Vlogging, as a quintessentially personal, intimate, and revealing form of video, perfectly fulfills the appetite for more and highly personal content and has therefore become indispensable, even for those YouTubers whose channels focus on different genres, such as sketch comedy, gaming, or book reviews. Although vlogs by definition represent an intimacy and authenticity that is rarely achieved as immediately and to the same extent in other media, fans still crave more. Thus books, tweets, and Tumblr and Facebook posts become transmedial expansions of a YouTube personality brand. It is a staple in the introduction of many YouTubers' book publications to promise more real and authentic depictions of their life. Nevertheless, several examples, especially in the coming-out context,[13] suggest a degree of loyalty to vlogging. This is no coincidence or surprise, since vlogging is the medium through which YouTubers can engage best and most intimately with viewers.

More than most other YouTubers, Dawson embraced the medium specificity of the printed book. Unlike any other YouTubers' autobiographically influenced books, Dawson's do not include any photographs beyond their cover art. Photographs, as Marie-Laure Ryan suggests, "thanks to their technological objectivity ... offer a much more convincing testimony of the objects or events they represent than images created by the human hand, or even verbal descriptions" (Ryan 2010, 16). Dawson's two autobiographical short films adapted from *I Hate Myselfie* provide an emphasis on the visual beyond the book. The multimodality that is the hallmark of most YouTubers' books, thus, is also present in Dawson's book, although to a much lesser extent. Both of his books feature fifteen to twenty fan illustrations, one at the beginning of each of his chapters, including also a short biographical note about the fan artist, thus combining visuality and interactivity in the print medium.

"I HATE MYSELFIE – SHORT FILM": Adapting Gender and Sexuality

Both of Dawson's books were accompanied by short films released on his main YouTube channel. The two short films connected to the first book are more or less faithful adaptations of two of the book's chapters, "My High School Musical" (Dawson 2015a, 15–28) and "Prom" (2015a, 209–24). What is interesting about the choice of these two chapters and their filmic realization is that they effectively enforce a perception of Dawson's heterosexuality. Yet, the book on the whole, even though it does not deal with bisexuality or homosexuality per se, presents a more complex sexual identity. The opening of the chapter "Two First Kisses" (2015a, 29–40) elucidates how Dawson plays with preconceived notions about his sexuality in a humorous and ultimately foreshadowing manner: "When I tell people my first relationship was when I was twenty-one they assume I grew up Amish. They also assume I'm an insanely repressed, closeted homosexual. Considering I'm only twenty-six, there's still plenty of time for me to explore my gay side … The saddest part is that not only did I experience my first relationship at twenty-one, it was also the age when I had my first kiss. I swear I'm not Amish. The gay thing is questionable" (2015a, 29).

In light of Dawson's coming out as bisexual, the humorous intent of the allusions to possible homosexuality also invite speculation about his state of mind regarding his sexual identity at the time of writing. While such speculation is possible and most likely intended in *I Hate Myselfie*, both short films focus exclusively on Dawson's heterosexual desire rather than providing a more complex image of his sexuality. Since these short films are compressed into twelve- to fifteen-minute videos, depicting complexities of sexual orientation is not a priority, and the romantic connotations of the plot are kept to a minimum. As Linda Hutcheon states, "Adaptation – that is, as a *product* – has a kind of 'theme and variation' formal structure or repetition with difference. This means not only that change is inevitable but that there will also be multiple possible causes of change in the *process* of adapting made by the demands of form, the individual adapter, the particular audience, and now the contexts of reception and creation" (2006, 142).

The first short film promoting the book, "I HATE MYSELFIE" (all caps) (2015b), is based on the last chapter, "Prom," and deals with Dawson's experience at a school dance. While much of the dialogue and narration are transposed verbatim from the book into the short film, allusions to Dawson's possible homosexuality, abundant in the written text, have been eliminated completely. However, homosexuality is a crucial theme in the short film, as Dawson's prom date Kelley is an outspoken lesbian. It is significant, however, that even though the short film has to make concessions in other areas, it includes an extra scene showing Kelley's coming out to the fictionalized Dawson. The scene functions primarily to characterize him as a sympathetic character. Even though Dawson is shown as being exceptionally understanding and supportive of his friend's coming out, there are numerous moments in the short film and book chapter that spell out Dawson's disappointment that Kelley was not romantically interested in him.

The very last scene of the short film is also an extra scene that is introduced by the present-day narrating Dawson: "And that's the story of my prom. And I know

The Mediality of Coming Out | 117

5.2 Dawson and his prom date in the last scene of the short film dramatizing episodes from Dawson's book, Shane Dawson TV, YouTube 2015.

what you guys are thinking: did those crazy kids get wasted and throw their sexual orientations to the side just for one night? Oh yeah" (2015b). It then cuts from the framing narrator to a scene of the teenage Dawson with his prom date in bed, him grunting suggestively on top of her. (See the screenshot from Dawson's short film in figure 5.2.)

While the scene does not contain much dialogue, it includes a punch line when Kelley says, "Yeah, I'm definitely a lesbian" (2015b). Clearly the entire scene is intended to be perceived as a joke, especially since Dawson has spoken and written about not having sex until long after high school, in part also because of his Christian upbringing. He addresses this upbringing in connection with sex in *I Hate Myselfie*, when he talks about his first girlfriend in college: "At the time I was pretty religious and the thought of having sex before marriage made my guilty Christian penis crawl back inside my guilty Christian body" (2015a, 33).

The final scene in the short film as well as several other allusions to Dawson's unsuccessful pursuit of potential girlfriends implicitly promotes the portrayal of heterosexual desires, as does the short film "I HATE MYSELFIE 2" (2015d). This second short film deals with Dawson's experience of participating in a high-school musical alongside his crush. However, after being unable to ask her out on a date, he does not pursue his interest in the girl further, and the narrative shifts away from the romantic connotations towards the comedic and dramatic aspects of the high-school musical. Even though Dawson depicts his sexual and/or romantic interest in girls in both short films, he really has no chance of "getting the girl" in either of them. Including these love interests in spite of the impossibility of an actual relationship serves to strengthen his declaration of love to his girlfriend at the time of writing, which he includes in a different chapter of his book to combat abundant online speculations about his sexuality.

After Coming Out: *It Gets Worse*

Almost a year passes between Dawson's coming-out video and his second book. Reflecting on that year, he finds that "the biggest thing that has happened is that I discovered who I truly am and came out as bisexual" (Dawson 2016a, 4). The positive impact Dawson hoped his coming out would have has apparently come to pass, as "this last year has been a journey of self-discovery and also an attempt at self-love. If there's one thing I've learned about myself since my last book, it's that I don't hate myselfie" (4). This impact is even more clearly spelled out by Dawson's character in the accompanying short film, who says, "But this year has been one of the best of my life: I've come to terms with my sexuality, I've dealt with my severe anger and depression" (2016b).

Dawson has made his sexuality a recurring topic in his videos. Some might even accuse them of queerbaiting, although the increased representation of bisexuality as well as more serious discussions about queer issues can be beneficial to viewers questioning their own sexuality. As Connor Franta has pointed out in his coming-out video, seeing and hearing about other people's experiences can help to normalize the viewer's own feelings and desires that might not seem normal in certain political or familial environments (Franta 2014). Viewers turn to YouTubers for reassurance that their experiences are normal and acceptable, and the fact that they talk about a variety of topics connected to sexuality, ranging from first same-sex kisses[14] to depression and eating disorders stemming from repressed sexuality[15] to showcasing a same-sex relationship and presenting it as desirable[16] provides comfort and encouragement for many who are otherwise still discriminated against.

Dawson primarily uses humour to normalize his own bisexuality, a key component in the short film "IT GETS WORSE." This short film is not an autobiographical adaptation of an individual book chapter, as the previous two short films were. Rather, it is a fictionalized exploration of core themes in Dawson's second collection of essays in the form of a horror story. The medium of the horror short film also allows the exploration of concerns not alluded to in the book.

5.3 Dawson and Monson in the "Make a Shane Dawson Video Thumbnail" photobooth, Shane Dawson TV, YouTube 2016.

Thus, the short film is a prime example of transmedia storytelling: it adds to the personal narrative of the core medium. Additionally, adhering to medium- and genre-specific conventions helps to make this short film "a unique contribution to the unfolding of the story" (Jenkins 2007).

"IT GETS WORSE" exaggerates expectations and accusations that YouTubers face from their fans. Accordingly, the short film mocks the presumed narcissism that YouTubers are often accused of by setting the short film in Dawson's fictional estate filled with countless books in every room and innumerable framed portraits of Dawson in every corner of the mansion. The short film also self-reflexively responds to reproaches for gay baiting, an aspect that is already introduced as a joke in Dawson's welcome address to his party guests: "Dearest friends, YouTube colleagues who I make out with for views, thank you so much for coming" (2016b). It is more explicitly visualized later by having Dawson's character show up at the "Make a Shane Dawson Video Thumbnail" photo booth, where he grabs Drew Monson, his friend and frequent collaborator, with the exclamation "Uh-oh, collab time!" He then takes hold of Drew's shoulders, looks into the camera to dictate "Title: My New Boyfriend??" and kisses Monson for the thumbnail photo. (See screenshot from Dawson's "IT GETS WORSE," fig. 5.3.)

The horror short film enables Dawson to explore other questions and concerns that have not made it into his book. Thus his breakup and continued public friendship with his former girlfriend Lisa Schwartz is a key aspect of this short film and allows him to address accusations of having exploited the relationship in a satirical manner. The unfolding of the plot, then, is intended to indicate that the friendship continually presented in vlogs on both YouTubers' channels is genuine and sincere rather than a ploy for views.

The plot revolves around a killer who eliminates all the party guests to eventually force Dawson to revive a character he used to portray in his videos. The resulting overarching message of the short film directed at viewers seems to be that, with an audience of millions, the content produced for YouTube will never please everyone. It is also speaks to the pressure that YouTube comments can put on creators, which is an issue that from a marketing perspective is perhaps better kept in the realm of fiction. The function of this short film as a transmedia extension is thus to add to the collection of autobiographical essays layers that might be controversial, to address accusations humorously as well as an entertaining reprimand directed at overzealous fans.

Interestingly, Dawson's horror short film seems in many ways more honest and revealing than his usual content and even his autobiographical essays. The realm of fiction seems to grant him the freedom to criticize and address a multitude of issues he steers clear of in non-fictional and serious contexts. In some ways, the short film contains more of the revelatory content that viewers seek in various media than the book provides. Yet both are dealt with in such different ways, revolving around the thoughts, opinions, and creativity of one personality, that they ultimately complement each other.

Conclusion

The contemporary entertainment industry increasingly turns to transmedia storytelling and transmedia marketing. YouTuber creators are well versed in navigating various social-media sites to build and maintain their personality brands, and for many it has become necessary to transcend the core medium of YouTube videos and expand onto social-media applications like Snapchat, Twitter, and Instagram to provide more information for devoted fans in real time. Their scope has widened further with the wave of books released by YouTubers since late 2014. A substantial number of these are autobiographical, playing into the demand for sharing ever more personal information.

Overall, the YouTube aesthetic has become dependent on the willingness of those who wish to be successful on the platform to comply with the incessant demand for confessions of all kinds. It is evident that the promise of emotionality, drama, and confession in a video draws large quantities of viewers. While this popularity has resulted in the emergence of so-called "drama channels,"[17] it has also led YouTubers to frame bits of information about themselves so as to make them seem like confessions in the attempt to maximize views. Ultimately this trend leads to several questions that will, no doubt, be crucial in future investigations in this area. Perhaps the most pressing is what authenticity means in a context in which personality branding determines the content and style of an online creator, resulting in the representation of a branded persona rather than a person.[18] Further, as the distribution of content over various media platforms already creates different engagement types,[19] the media experience provided by content creators is becoming increasingly complex and varied. Therefore, questions concerning canonicity will be of imperative relevance. Lastly, the emerging practice of using information derived from metadata to refine personal performances online is certainly an aspect worth investigating further.

Shane Dawson's coming-out story illustrates how discussions about sexuality might adjust to or make use of media and genre specific conventions. Thus the vlog provides the immediacy, honesty, and authenticity the medium has become associated with. The autobiographical book emphasizes credibility and promises coherence and closure. The short films, on the other hand, foreground entertainment values and serve promotional purposes. Accordingly, in the discourse on sexuality, vlogs have been used to initiate conversations via confessions; the books then seek to explain and legitimize crucial points in the ensuing conversation, while the short films are best suited to expand, exemplify, and visualize select facets. The transmedia story of Dawson's sexuality thus engages honest, serious, and satirical perspectives, providing fans with a complex notion of sexuality. It does, however, raise the question of what role mediality plays in the distribution of confession-like revelations and the creation of contemporary personality brands. While the different media clearly contribute to the brand in their own way, it seems increasingly impossible, or at least reductive, to examine the books that YouTubers write without considering their output on other media.

Coming-out stories, due in part to their inherently personal nature, have garnered much attention. The surge of coming-out stories on YouTube has enabled discussions on queer issues, including the problem of bi-bashing even in LGBTQ+ communities, and the controversy of queerbaiting in contemporary media output. In observing certain online communities, it becomes clear that being gay on YouTube is occasionally represented as an inherently positive utopia, glossing over the fact that the acceptance and tolerance that dominate those communities do not necessarily translate into real-life environments. While this theme is sometimes taken up in YouTubers' memoirs,[20] there is a definite tendency to embrace non-heterosexuality among prominent YouTube vloggers, which plays well with the emphasis on self-help and advice in most of their book publications.

In the promotion of YouTubers' books, the promise of providing more intimate insights than are available online is a strategy based on the established perception of celebrity memoirs as being confessional and revelatory. However, emerging from a style of content creation (i.e., vlogging) largely built on the discussion of personal details and therefore arguably confessional in nature, this promise does not ultimately hold up. As I have argued, Shane Dawson's coming out between book releases exemplifies that YouTubers prefer the vlog medium when it comes to communicating personal and, in particular, sexuality-related issues.[21] While confessional content is fleshed out to some degree in their book publications, YouTubers are unlikely to hold back confessions to be revealed in their books. This is due to a sense of obligation that stems from the relationship vloggers cultivate with their viewers, which is based on (perceived) authenticity and sincerity. There are several more reasons why YouTubers, so far, favour vlogs over books in this respect. First, vlogging allows the YouTuber complete control over when and how content is presented. Additionally, there is a sense of immediacy as well as instant feedback. Lastly, and significantly, a larger audience will engage with a video freely available on YouTube, while only relatively affluent and devoted fans will purchase a book that, given the fast-paced changes in online environments, may already be outdated by the time of publication.[22]

The hostility in comment sections across the internet has made many YouTubers careful about what they do or do not share online. As a result, they have sometimes cultivated an almost contradictory relationship with their viewers over the years. On the one hand, they build their personality brand on the promise of authenticity, often achieved by the display of intimacy and vulnerability. Yet it has taken several years, in some cases even a decade, of building up communities through vlogging about seemingly everything online before some YouTubers discuss their sexual orientations with these communities. The fact that many of the "big YouTubers" have since engaged with the topic transmedially is not only an expression of the rise of media-transcending communication but also a contribution to the much-needed mainstream representation of non-heterosexual identities in a positive way. YouTubers, because of their ambivalent roles as virtual friend and idol, have a significant impact on the perception of non-heterosexuality.[23] Given their immense and growing popularity among teenage viewers, their transmedial engagement with sexuality may in fact play a role in normalizing non-heteronormative identities. Consequently, analyzing their fictional and non-fictional books and videos not only allows insights into the role of the medium and the possibilities of transmedial expression but also advances the conversation and ultimately aims at destigmatizing non-heterosexual identities.

NOTES

1. See, for example, the movie *Camp Takota* (2014), directed by Nick Riedell and Chris Riedell, New York City: VHX, 14 February 2014, digital distribution, http://www.camptakota.com/; or *Dirty 30* (2016), directed by Andrew Bush, Santa Monica, CA: Lionsgate, 23 September 2016, digital distribution, http://dirtythirtymovie.com/, both produced, written, and starring YouTubers Hannah Hart, Mamrie Hart, and Grace Helbig. See also *Not Cool* (2014), directed by and starring Shane Dawson, Englewood, CO: Starz Digital Media, 23 September 2014, digital distribution, http://notcoolthemovie.com/. Notable also is BBC Radio 1's cooperation with YouTubers all over the world. See "The Internet Takeover," BBC Radio 1, http://www.bbc.co.uk/programmes/b055k5n3.
2. American YouTuber Shane Dawson was among the first YouTube personalities to call being a YouTuber his job. Starting in 2008, he made a name for himself with comedy videos and music-video spoofs, today garnering over twenty-seven million subscribers across his YouTube channels, as well as more than five billion views.
3. Given the fast-paced changes on YouTube in general and for individual YouTubers in particular, it seems important to point out that I am writing this in late 2016. I can of course only speak to the content Dawson has created up to this point.
4. This estimate is based on a search in May 2018; for examples, see Savannah Brown, https://www.youtube.com/watch?v=L1qLhs8ORCE; noodlerella, https://www.youtube.com/watch?v=eZNQ1KnayNo; Evan Edinger, https://www.youtube.com/watch?v=I41cBuTMhD0; Dodie Clark, https://www.youtube.com/watch?v=ke5EDEk9vvI; Ricky Dillon, https://www.youtube.com/watch?v=KFA4hsSDbhc.
5. A thumbnail is the image that viewers see before they click on a video and is supposed to be representative of the content. Ever since it became possible for larger YouTubers to choose and manipulate this image, it has become more and more important in advertising a video and in enticing viewers to watch it.
6. There are several popular same-sex fanships (i.e., relationships between two YouTubers that fans imagine are real, or like to speculate about). Among the most prominent and long-standing are the shipping of British YouTubers Daniel Howell and Philip Lester, as well as that between Troye Sivan and Tyler Oakley.
7. See, for example, the discussion of Joe Sugg's problematic thumbnail, baiting viewers with

Photoshopped pictures of him and his roommate and fellow YouTuber Caspar Lee kissing, thus playing into a long-standing fanship even though the video in fact was about announcing Sugg's graphic novel. Jazza John, "Is Joe Sugg Gay Baiting?" YouTube, Jazza John, 5:19, 8 February 2015, https://www.youtube.com/watch?v=6o3LRZeYB4g&feature=youtu.be.

8   Josh Homme's emotional apology following an incident of violence in late 2017 is just one such example. http://www.nme.com/news/josh-homme-photographer-hospital-2170193. Even though the video and written apologies have since been taken down from all of the band's social-media accounts, the markers of emotionality in Homme's confession/apologies have certainly aided in the quick recuperation of the band's reputation following the media outrage.

9   See, for example, bisexual YouTuber Ashley Mardell, who has made several videos on the topic of "bi-bashing," for example, the collaborative video "(some) BISEXUALS EXPLAIN DATING (some) LESBIANS." YouTube, Ashley Mardell, 12:46, 19 June 2016. https://www.youtube.com/watch?v=Cn2gzxkxe0c.

10 Graceffa 2015c.

11 YouTuber Ingrid Nilsen came out as gay in an emotional video in June 2015. Her video went viral and has so far garnered fifteen times as many views as an average video of hers.

12 See, for example, Ashley Mardell's video poem "YOU'RE NOT GAY ENOUGH," YouTube, Ashley Mardell, 7:27, 30 January 2015, https://www.youtube.com/watch?v=qO_Dk_Z2zRM.

13 Franta, Graceffa, and Dawson all chose to come out in vlogs rather than in their autobiographical books, even though their books and coming-out videos were released in relative proximity to one another.

14 See, for example, James Hill, "First Time I Kissed a Boy?" YouTube, Jimmy0010, 7:26, 25 September 2016, https://www.youtube.com/watch?v=5WrtHCErUh8.

15 See, for example, Shane Dawson's "I'm Bisexual" (2015b) and also *It Gets Worse* (2016a).

16 Consider some of Graceffa's titles for videos with his boyfriend: "Our Love Story!," "Best Date Ever!," "Drunk in Love!," "Best Boyfriend!," or "Proud Boyfriend!"

17 "Drama channels" are primarily devoted to discussing and/or perpetuating gossip rather than providing creative content.

18 Some YouTubers have already discussed how they have felt that they trapped themselves in their persona, and how their content has been shaped by the expectations that their branding has produced. See, for example, Lousie Pentland's 2016 video, https://www.youtube.com/watch?v=rwrNa1s2Mwk.

19 These types range from casual viewers (i.e., viewers who occasionally watch videos by a content creator) to the "notification squad" (i.e., those viewers who get notified as soon as a creator has uploaded and who will attempt to watch and also comment on the video

immediately) to hardcore fans who will venture beyond one platform to engage with creators on all available platforms, buy merchandise, go to live events, etc.

20 See, for example, Tyler Oakley, who discusses his father's difficulties in coming to terms with Oakley's homosexuality in *Binge* (2015).

21 For a more detailed discussion of Graceffa's and Franta's intermedial coming out, see my 2017 article "Intermedial Sexuality: How YouTubers Negotiate Coming Out and Gender Identities."

22 Dawson's coming out as bisexual shortly after the release of his first book quickly made the book seem outdated. Similarly, Anna Akana's 2017 book *So Much I Want to Tell You* was outdated upon publication, as it includes several sections and numerous references and allusions to a relationship that ended between the final draft and publication.

23 For example, danah boyd has described her interaction with a female teenager who "found a community of other queer girls in a chatroom" and "found their anonymous advice to be helpful. They gave her pointers to useful websites about coming out, offered stories from their own experience, and gave her the number of an LGBT-oriented hotline if she ran into any difficulty coming out to her conservative parents" (boyd 2014, 52). This sense of "community" is enhanced by YouTubers who simulate a close relationship with their mass audiences.

REFERENCES

Akana, Anna. 2017. *So Much I Want to Tell You: Letter to My Little Sister*. New York: Ballantine Books.

boyd, danah. 2014. *It's Complicated: The Social Lives of Networked Teens*. New Haven: Yale University Press.

Brennan, Joseph. 2016. "Queerbaiting: The Playful Possibilities of Homoeroticism." *International Journal of Cultural Studies* 21, no. 2 (2018): 189–206.

Dawson, Shane. 2015a. *I Hate Myselfie: A Collection of Essays*. New York: Keywords Press.

– 2016a. *It Gets Worse: A Collection of Essays*. New York: Keywords Press.

Finkelstein, Joanne. 2007. *The Art of Self Invention: Image and Identity in Popular Visual Culture*. London: I.B. Tauris.

Franta, Connor. 2015. *A Work in Progress: A Memoir*. New York: Keywords Press.

Gomillion, Sarah C., and Traci Giuliano. 2011. "The Influence of Media Role Models on Gay, Lesbian, and Bisexual Identity." *Journal of Homosexuality* 58, no. 3, 330–54. https://doi.org/10.1080/00918369.2011.546729.

Graceffa, Joey, with Joshua Lyon. 2015. *In Real Life: My Journey to a Pixelated World*. New York: Keywords Press.

Hafeez, Hudaisa, Muhammad Zeshan, Muhammad A. Tahir, Nusrat Jahan, and Sadiq Naveed.

2017. "Health Care Disparities among Lesbian, Gay, Bisexual, and Transgender Youth: A Literature Review." *Cureus* 9, no. 4. http://doi.org/10.7759/cureus.1184.

Helbig, Grace. 2014. *Grace's Guide: The Art of Pretending to Be a Grown Up.* New York: Touchstone.

Hutcheon, Linda. 2006. *A Theory of Adaptation.* New York: Routledge.

Jandl, Silke. 2017. "Intermedial Sexuality: How YouTubers Negotiate Coming Out and Gender." *Sibéal E-Journal – (In)Visible Lines* no. 2: 10–19. https://issuu.com/sibealnetworkjournal/docs/sibe__al_journal_issue_2/1?ff=true.

Jenkins, Henry. 2006. *Convergence Culture: Where Old and New Media Collide.* New York New York University Press.

Jenkins, Henry. 2007. "Transmedia Storytelling 101." *Confessions of an ACA Fan: The Official Weblog of Henry Jenkins.* 22 March 2007. http://henryjenkins.org/2007/03/transmedia_storytelling_101.html.

– 2011. "Transmedia Storytelling 202: Further Reflections." *Confessions of an ACA Fan: The Official Weblog of Henry Jenkins.* 1 August 2011. http://henryjenkins.org/2011/08/defining_transmedia_further_re.html.

Lanning, Carly, and Christine Huang. 2015. "YouTube Trends Explainer: Coming Out on YouTube." *YouTube Trends.* 19 February 2015. http://youtube-trends.blogspot.co.at/2015/02/youtube-trends-explainer-coming-out-on.html.

Oakley, Tyler. 2015. *Binge.* New York: Simon & Schuster.

Page, Ruth. 2010. "Interactivity and Interaction: Text and Talk in Online Communities." In *Intermediality and Storytelling,* edited by Marina Grishakova and Marie-Laure Ryan, 208–31. Berlin, New York: De Gruyter.

Page, Ruth, and Bronwen Thomas. 2011. Introduction to *New Narratives: Stories and Storytelling in the Digital Age,* edited by Ruth Page and Bronwen Thomas, 1–16. Lincoln: University of Nebraska Press.

Ryan, Marie-Laure. "Fiction, Cognition, and Non-Verbal Media." In *Intermediality and Storytelling,* edited by Marina Grishakova and Marie-Laure Ryan, 8–26. New York: De Gruyter.

MEDIAGRAPHY

Clark, Dodie. 2016. "I'm Bisexual Woo." YouTube, doddlevloggle. Video, 5:55, 23 May. https://www.youtube.com/watch?v=SXJnkNA2z38.

Dawson, Shane. 2015b. "I HATE MYSELFIE." YouTube, Shane Dawson TV. Video, 12:49, 2 March. https://www.youtube.com/watch?v=nGFyoRhSrV8.

– "I'm Bisexual." 2015c. YouTube, Shane Dawson TV. Video, 14:35, 7 July. https://www.youtube.com/watch?v=PPdE3rbqf_Q.

– "I HATE MYSELFIE 2." 2015d. YouTube, Shane Dawson TV. Video, 15:49, 8 August. https://www.youtube.com/watch?v=zFyrWj8jeUk.

– "IT GETS WORSE." 2016b. YouTube, Shane Dawson TV. Video, 21:22, 19 July. https://www.youtube.com/watch?v=TIMpp7l65gg.

Franta, Connor. 2014. "Coming Out." YouTube, Connor Franta. Video, 6:27, 8 December. https://www.youtube.com/watch?v=WYodBfRxKWI.

Graceffa, Joey. 2015. "Don't Wait." YouTube, Joey Graceffa. Video, 4:32, 16 May. https://www.youtube.com/watch?v=Kcwo_mhyqTw.

– "YES I'M GAY." 2015. YouTube, Joey Graceffa. Video, 11:58, 18 May. https://www.youtube.com/watch?v=z1PoNhYb3K4.

Pentland, Louise. 2016. "Finishing with Sprinkle of Glitter." YouTube, Sprinkleofglitter, 16:58, 1 September. https://www.youtube.com/watch?v=rwrNa1s2Mwk.

Author, Subject, and Audience

6

"Aren't You Worried about What People Might Say? What People Might Do?": Lady Gaga and the "Heeling" of Queer Trauma

JACOB EVOY

On a cold and snowy night in February 2013, my friends and I were walking arm in arm, laughing and singing all the way back to our hotel, having just left Lady Gaga's Born This Way Ball. As we walked, I was amazed by the transformation that had somehow occurred among my friends. Oddly enough, all of this revolved around the pair of heels I'd decided to wear to the concert. This chapter examines our experiences before, during, and after Lady Gaga's concert through the lens of Ann Cvetkovich's *An Archive of Feelings* (2003), which positions trauma as being felt within our everyday experiences. Additionally, I argue that Lady Gaga was able to help in the creation of a public trauma culture, thereby permitting an acting-up of those in attendance that served, among my friends, to work towards a "heeling" of the everyday homophobia that we experience and/or are aware of and to which we can easily fall victim.

I'd saved up to buy a ticket, the day of the concert finally arrived, and I journeyed to Toronto from the conservative city of London, Ontario, to attend the concert with five self-identified gay men. Of course, the main topic that had come up in our preparations for the concert was what we were all going to wear. I suggested that we each choose a different Gaga look for the concert, as I had previously done with a group of friends for Gaga's 2011 Monster Ball in Ottawa. For the Monster Ball, I mimicked what Gaga wore to MTV's Total Request Live in August 2008 (Schutte and Godley 2011). My outfit had consisted of a dancer's body suit, tights, black heels, red gloves, and a red infinity scarf draped around my head and covering my shoulders. After seeing my previous outfit, my friends decidedly rejected the idea of imitating Gaga's fashion. When we arrived at our hotel and were taking the elevator up to our room, they discussed my past concert outfit and inquired as to what I would be wearing later that night. "I'm not wearing anything outlandish," I replied. "All I'm wearing is a tank, skinny jeans, and a pair of high heels." Their faces dropped.

My friends were unable to move past my chosen attire. They pestered me with countless questions throughout the day leading up to the concert. "Will you be able to dance? Will you be comfortable? Can you walk in them? What about the ice? What about the snow?" Question after question came and went as I assured them that I am more than comfortable in heels and able to walk and dance in them without any problems. Finally, their real concern came forth when one friend, whom I shall refer to as Charlie, asked, "Aren't you worried about what people might say? What people might do?" Here was the issue underlying their questions and discomfort around my wearing heels. They feared not only the reactions I might be faced with by being a presumed man wearing heels but also the possibility that they might face some danger through their association with me. By my wearing something as simple as high heels, they felt I would be putting myself as well as those with me in danger of homophobic abuse.

The discomfort and fear of being seen with a presumed man wearing high heels was caused by my friends' shared affective orientation towards heels being worn by a presumed man. In her discussions of affect and emotion, Sara Ahmed argues that objects have specific emotional affects. It is not, she maintains, the object that produces happiness or any other emotion, but the connotations that are attached to the object and to possessing said object that causes happiness or any other emotion (Ahmed 2010, 32). Ahmed further states that "when happy objects are passed around, it is not necessarily the feeling that passes. To share such objects (or have a share in such objects) would simply mean you should *share an orientation toward those objects as being good* … In other words, we anticipate that happiness will follow proximity to this or that object" (2010, 37–8, 41; emphasis in original).

Ahmed's concept of affect as a shared orientation towards a specific object can be seen quite clearly in my friends' reactions to my heels. High heels can possess many different affects depending on the situation. Heels may have the affect of perhaps sexiness, class, formality, or even shame, compliance, or self-hatred, in the context of feminist ideological readings of dress codes of compliance, fuckability, and availability – but solely when being worn by someone presumed to be a woman. When placed on a presumed male body, however, the affect of the heels becomes discomfort, strangeness, shame, and fear – as was clearly evident in my friends' reactions. The shared orientation to the heels being worn by someone presumed to be male was one of shame and fear that the heels would open us all to the possibility of attack.

A presumed man wearing heels (fig. 6.1) is not viewed as "normal" even among my friends. Part of their shared negative orientation towards my wearing heels stems from what Judith Butler describes in her formative chapter "Imitation and

Lady Gaga and the "Heeling" of Queer Trauma | 131

6.1
Jacob Evoy, February 2013. Outfit with heels worn by the author to Lady Gaga's Born This Way Ball.

Gender Insubordination" (1991). Butler argues that while there are obvious risks, such as potential homophobia, with coming out as a gay or lesbian, there are also risks associated with the identification of "gay" and "lesbian." Butler puts forth the argument that when gay men and lesbian women come out as such, they walk out of one closet and into another. By taking up the label of "gay" or "lesbian," we place ourselves within a box that has its own limitations and expectations. My wearing of heels broke my friends' ideas and understandings of viewing me as a gay man as I (rather fabulously) failed to uphold traditional masculinity in both my appearance and actions. Instead, my donning of perceived feminine clothing marked me and my body as non-normative and open to potential attack. The failure to uphold traditional gender norms or the way my friends expected a gay man to act and dress not only marked my own body as open to attack but expanded to our group as a whole. They recognized that my heels placed them as possible targets of homophobic abuse. My friends' reactions are quite telling. Not only do they help demonstrate the norms and barriers gay men place upon themselves, they also indicate how the trauma of homophobia is felt and, as Cvetkovich argues, "connected to the textures of everyday experience" (2003, 3–4). Furthermore, the shame of being associated with a presumed man wearing heels brings forth questions about the connections between shame, queer culture, and queer identity. As Nikola Stepić has noted, "Shame, queer culture and queer identity are inextricably linked, as identity is not only a matter of cultural history, but also of taste. The aura of low culture, of camp as legitimized bad taste, still pervades queer culture and denotes its icons, legends and stars as somehow inherently shameful, precisely because shared culture becomes the locus of the marginalized, shamed identity" (2017, 76).

Even as devoted Gaga fans, my friends were still ashamed to be associated with someone breaking gender norms, although they were aware of Gaga's own history of breaking both fashion and gender norms. They internalized this shame as something that a gay man is not meant to be/do, while simultaneously preparing to attend a concert that celebrated the very breaking of the norms they were ashamed of and feared.

I was not willing to take my friends' suggestions to simply wear flats and so left for the concert in my heels. As we walked to the subway, only one friend chose to walk with me; Charlie and the others lagged behind, too afraid to be associated with a perceived man in heels. On the subway, my one friend and I sat together chatting and hypothesizing about what Gaga had in store for us. From the subway, we made it to the Air Canada Centre and were surrounded by Gaga's Little Monsters. As we went through the security check, a guard complimented me on my shoes, which earned him a wink and smile. We finally arrived at our seats and after months of anticipation, the show began.

Lady Gaga put on an incredible performance. My friends and I sang at the top of our lungs, danced our asses off, and had a wonderful time. Between songs, Gaga often engaged the audience through speaking about the current state of LGBTQ rights and acknowledging the homophobia we experience daily. She emphasized throughout the entire Born This Way Ball the importance of accepting ourselves for who we are, loving ourselves, and letting our inner monster fly. It was amidst these messages and the songs that I noticed a change in my friends' behaviour. We danced together, placed our arms around each other, and put our paws up as we embraced the Little Monsters that we are.

Gaga had managed something quite extraordinary. She had gathered a group of gender and sexual deviants into the Air Canada Centre to create a space where we celebrated ourselves and our differences from those who awaited us outside the arena. Gaga transformed the Air Canada Centre, usually home of the Toronto Maple Leafs and Toronto Raptors, into a queer space. J.J. Halberstam defines queer space as "the place-making within postmodernism in which queer people engage and ... the new understandings of space enabled by the production of queer counterpublics" (2005, 6). Halberstam's notion of queer space can be applied to Lady Gaga's Born This Way Ball as the notoriously hyper-heterosexual and hyper-masculine space of the hockey arena was transformed into a space for a queer public that combated the norms typically enforced within the heteronormative space of the hockey arena. As someone who grew up in a typically Canadian "hockey family" and spent the weekends of my childhood being dragged from one hockey arena to another, I was overjoyed by the transformation of the space. I used to dread and hate having to go watch my brother play hockey. I was always the little femme who, no matter what I did, could not protect myself from other families' stares and comments about my "girlish" behaviour. Gaga, however, was able to transform a space that once filled me with fear into one where queer people celebrated our difference and formed a counterpublic to the hegemonic public's notions of gender and sexuality.

Within the space of the Air Canada Centre, Gaga and those in attendance formed what Cvetkovich has referred to as a trauma culture, which she conceptualizes as "public cultures that form in and around trauma" (2003, 9). The Born This Way Ball was a celebration of breaking with what society tells us not to be and not to do. The arena was filled with gender and sexual deviants who had come to openly celebrate our differences. While the atmosphere was celebratory, it was simultaneously marked by knowledge of what waited us outside the arena. But in its transformation of space, the concert provided an opportunity for us all to let out our inner monster and to take pride in our differences. Gaga's transformation of the space, her music, her spoken words, along with all of those in attendance collectively created a public that provide a venue for us to work through our various traumas. "Queer performance," Cvetkovich writes, "creates publics bringing together live bodies in space, and the theatrical experience is not just about what's on stage but also about who's in the audience creating community" (2003, 9). Through our collective transformation of the concert space and formation of a trauma culture, those in attendance created a space that performed the work of therapy as we collectively acted up in response to our various traumas.[1]

When the concert ended, my friends and I walked home arm in arm as we navigated the slippery streets of Toronto. The next morning, my friend Charlie, the one who had been the most visibly apprehensive of my chosen attire, came and sat on my bed. We discussed the concert and how much fun it had been. Charlie, who had previously been so nervous about simply being associated with a presumed man wearing heels, asked, "Jacob ... would I be able to try on your shoes?" With a smile reaching from ear to ear, I replied, "Yes!"

Charlie put on the heels and instantly fell over back onto the bed – a symbolic falling from normativity. We all had a good laugh as he struggled to get up again and walk across the room. After Charlie, all of my friends (or those whose feet would fit) tried on the heels and attempted a catwalk-like strut across the hotel room. It was a hilarious and incredible experience as everyone took a turn either falling on the bed or making it across the room, arms in the air as if they had scored a touchdown, to everyone's laughter and applause. After a more successful attempt at crossing the room, Charlie exclaimed, "Well, I'm going to have to practice quite a bit before Gaga's next concert so I can join you and wear heels too."

The experience of my friends trying on the heels resembles José Esteban Muñoz's discussion of Kevin Aviance, queerness, and loss. Aviance performed on a raised box in the middle of the dance floor surrounded by "a certain stratum of New York gay men ... Their dance style is aggressive yet rigid ... they do not let themselves flow" (Muñoz 2009, 77). As Aviance takes the stage, he "uses gestures that permit the dancers to see and experience the feelings they do not permit themselves to let in. He and the gestures he performs are beacons for all the emotions that the throng is not allowed to feel" (78). Like the men in New York nightclub, my friends did not allow themselves to feel certain emotions nor allow their bodies to move in certain ways. They had made themselves fit into the idea of how they thought a "gay man" should dress, move, and feel. Over the course of our trip, however, there was a transformation as my heels went from something to be feared to something that brought joy and laughter. This transformation was made possible by the queer public culture created within the space of Gaga's that acknowledged our pain, permitted us to embrace our non-normative selves, and to celebrate our inner monsters.

NOTE

1 I use the term "act up" deliberately in this scenario, as acting up can refer to a multitude of actions and feelings that are often dismissed or viewed as negative ways of responding to trauma. I follow Cvetkovich in her criticism of the idea of "working through" trauma. In *An Archive of Feelings*, she writes, "I refuse the sharp distinction between mourning and melancholy that leads Dominick LaCapra, for example, to differentiate between 'working through,' the successful resolution of trauma, and 'acting out,' the repetition of trauma that does not lead to transformation. Not only does the distinction often seem tautological –

good responses to trauma are cases of working through; bad ones are instances of acting out – but the verbal link between acting out and ACT UP [AIDS Coalition to Unleash Power] indicates that activism's modes of acting out, especially its performative and expressive functions, are a crucial resource for responding to trauma" (2003, 164).

REFERENCES

Ahmed, Sara. 2010. "Happy Objects." In *The Affect Theory Reader*, edited by Melissa Gregg and Gregory J. Seigworth, 29–51. Durham: Duke University Press.

Butler, Judith. 1991. "Imitation and Gender Insubordination." In *Inside/Out: Lesbian Theories, Gay Theories*, edited by Dianna Fuss, 13–31. New York: Routledge.

Cvetkovich, Ann. 2003. *An Archive of Feelings: Trauma, Sexuality, and Lesbian Public Cultures*. Durham: Duke University Press.

Halberstam, J.J. 2005. *In a Queer Time and Place: Transgender Bodies, Subcultural Lives*. New York: New York University Press.

Muñoz, José Esteban. 2009. *Cruising Utopia: The Then and There of Queer Futurity*. New York: New York University Press.

Schutte, Lauren, and Chris Godley. 2011. "Lady Gaga's MTV Evolution." *Hollywood Reporter*, 26 August. http://www.hollywoodreporter.com/gallery/lady-gagas-mtv-evolution-227977/2-trl-august-12-2008.

Stepić, Nikola. 2017. "Spectacles of Shame: Ryan Murphy as Curator of Queer Cultural Memory." *Collection of Paper of the Faculty of Philosophy* 47, no. 3: 71–86.

7

Letters to Nina Hartley: Pornography, Parrhesia, and Sexual Confessions

INGRID OLSON

Nina Hartley is a pornography star, sexual-freedom activist, and sex educator (Hartley 1999; 2013). Her pornography career began in 1984, and the following year she created the Nina Hartley fan club. Although internet technologies enabled electronic mail, she received postal letters from fans into the twenty-first century. Personal letters can be understood as "the intimacy of heart and mind speaking to heart and mind across distance" (Kenyon 1992, viii). Fan letters can invoke hermeneutic and epistemic issues of sexuality and gender (Cook 1996; Garlinger 2005). That is, confidential correspondence between confessant and confessor permits the letter-writer to disclose circumspect questions of interpretation and knowledge of sexual identity, practices, and desires. There is a connection between "letter writing with the physical body" and with sexuality specifically (Bower 1997, 57). Pornography can be understood as representations of physically intimate sexual acts, and epistolarity recognizes the connection between letter writing with the physical body.

Foucault observes that we all have an "immense curiosity about sex, bent on questioning it, with an insatiable desire to hear it speak and be spoken about" (Foucault [1976] 1990, 77; Williams, citing Foucault, 1989, 2). The intimacy of Hartley fan club letter writers' "open-heartedness" and "speaking freely" regarding sexuality is commensurate with Foucault's ([1981–82] 2001, 366) work on parrhesia. The subject's truthful enunciation in parrhesia is an "ontological commitment" (Foucault [1982–83] 2010, 379). Through the act of speaking truth to another, "the individual constitutes himself and is constituted by others as a subject of a discourse of truth" (Foucault [1983–84] 2008, 3). This chapter examines a selection of Hartley's fan letters as a particular kind of sexual confession that speaks the truth of the pornography spectator's "knowledge-pleasure" (Foucault [1976] 1990).

Nina Hartley

Nina Hartley has been described as a "trailblazer," an "outspoken feminist, sex educator and advocate for sexual freedom," and "a guiding force for a generation of feminist porn stars" (Comella 2010). Born in Berkeley in March 1959, as a teenager Hartley identified as a feminist and was influenced by the 1970s feminist phrase "my body, my rules," a call for liberated women to enjoy their sexuality (Hartley 2013, 228). As a young adult, she intentionally and enthusiastically sought a career in adult films, an opportunity for her to make a life out of having sex (personal conversation, 2013). It would be fair to add that Hartley's physical appearance also contributed to her successful pornography career. An attractive, white, blond, blue-eyed woman with a voluptuous figure, she fits pop-culture stereotypes of Marilyn Monroe and the California girls of Beach Boys songs. She immediately captured the attention of many mainstream, heterosexual-identified, male pornography viewers.

Hartley is now an established pornography icon. She has performed in hundreds of films, starting with the videotape *Educating Nina* (Anderson, dir.) in 1984 and still performing more than three decades later in *Couple Seeks Third, 8* (Pornstar Platinum, 2018).[1] She has won numerous adult film awards, most recently a 2017 XBIZ award for Specialty Release of the Year (XBIZ Awards). Media and technologies represent the (re)shaping of connectivities and relationships between bodies and sexualities; the trajectory of Hartley's career begins with the development of VCR and, later, DVD and internet technologies. The year of Hartley's premiere, 1984, saw the rise of the videotape era and the subsequent explosion of pornography production for the home-entertainment industry. The technological advance of videotape pornography is significant (Alilunas 2016; Greenberg 2008; Kleinhans 2006; Melendez 2004; Salgado 1989), particularly in feminist analyses, as it increased women's access to viewing pornography (Juffer 1998).

Letters to a Porn Star

The Nina Hartley fan archive is located at the Center for Sex and Culture (CSC) in San Francisco. The CSC is a non-profit organization that, in addition to a non-public sexuality archive, provides resources for sexuality studies researchers, hosts events related to sex and culture such as art exhibits and readings, and maintains an extensive lending library on sexualities. The Hartley fan-mail archive is carefully preserved, most of the letters in their original envelopes. Most are salacious:

invitations for personal sexual encounters and, of course, letters of confession. The letters I categorize as confessional are explicit sexual fantasies or memories describing the authors' desires involving Hartley and/or others. The pornography viewer's engagement with a breadth of varied explicit sexual practices invites an assessment of their sexual knowledge, desires, and (dis)identifications (Muñoz 1999; Stryker 2006; Sycamore 2006). The connection of pornography to confession has garnered recent academic attention (Duff 2010), and selections from Nina Hartley's fan-mail archive can be understood as a repository of confessions responding to representations of sexualities (Davidson 2001). Fans of pornography, like other subculture fans, sometimes correspond with a celebrity and write letters of adoration, devotion, education, and confession; this chapter's analysis is based on my reading of hundreds of Hartley's fan letters. The Hartley archive represents the desire of fans to be close to Hartley. A desire to feel close to a celebrity is not new or unique to pornography, of course. However, due to the explicit sexual content of pornography, the fan mail often consists of specific content. The letters respond to an unspoken invitation to porn viewers, an opportunity to correspond with and confess sexual desires, practices, and memories to a porn star.

In the following section I examine samples of text from several of Nina Hartley's fan letters that can be interpreted as a form of confession. The fantasy of film pornography can be somewhat paradoxical; the pornographic story can be "both a legitimate form of culture and a fictional, fantastical, even allegorical realm … mythological and hyperbolic"; its characters and activities are not real, and yet they are (Kipnis 1996, 163). That is, while pornography storylines are fictitious, the performers are real people performing actual sexual acts on camera for the entertainment of the viewer.

A 1995 letter from Jack tells Nina she has "helped [his] sex life" because he is "not afraid to try new and different ways" of having sex. He adds that his girlfriend also enjoys Hartley's movies and, through viewing them, "has learned to be more relax[ed] and enjoy sex more." This may not seem a significant confession, particularly when addressing a pornography star, yet for many persons, it can be. Similarly, John wrote to Nina in 1995 to say that he and his wife had experienced a "fairly conservative" sex life before they started watching her videos. He declares, "We have since opened up and have reached heights we never could have without your help." Fred from Pennsylvania tells Hartley in an undated letter that he "enjoy(s) watching a woman who can exuberantly enjoy fucking for the pure sensual pleasure of it – and in your case, it's nice to know that you are not just acting."

Hartley received a postcard, also undated, with a famous black-and-white photograph of Marilyn Monroe. The author does not include a name or use language that indicates a specific gender identification. I originally assumed the postcard to be from a male writer due to a reference to "Other guys"; however, it is possible that this correspondence is from a female fan. The postcard starts: "Happy Valentine's day." The anonymous author claims to be "too shy to send [Hartley] anything else than a post card." The card thanks her for her help in "seeing the beauty of female genitals and oral sex! Other guys and girls have always told me going down on women was gross," but Hartley has changed the writer's mind. The message closes with the wish to someday "wind up with my head between your thighs" to return "some of the pleasure" received from Hartley. "I hope this made you smile, even a little bit. Have a nice day. Love, Me."

These letters articulate the ease, casualness, and comfort most authors experienced in acquiring and viewing pornography at home. Their letters reveal, generally, the idea of pornography as a source of permission-giving: the letters from Jack and John mention becoming less conservative and more open to trying new things, and feeling more relaxed about sexuality. Similarly, the anonymous writer confesses to exploring oral sex with women despite earlier advice to the contrary.

Many of the fan letters are more salacious. In a 1997 letter, Michael states that he is "very disappointed" with the anal sex portion of Nina's video *Guide to Alternative Sex*. He states that he loves anal sex and clarifies: "I don't mean putting my penis in my wife's anus. I mean putting sex toys in my anus. In fact, there is a toy in there right now and I often wanted to have this done to me, so I bought my wife a dildo + harness but she won't do it to me." Michael closes by asking Nina why her video did not include anal intercourse.[2] Particularly, why did she not "do anything anal to the men?"

This confessional letter deserves attention for its intersection with ideas of normative gender roles, particularly masculinity, and sexual practices. Michael writes that he is "very disappointed" in that the sole focus of the video's anal sex is on women, not men, being penetrated anally. The author raises a significant point; mainstream pornography at that time was produced largely by heterosexual men for the entertainment of heterosexual men, a reality that frustrates him. His letter draws attention to the fact that a video titled *Guide to Alternative Sex*, while including anal sex as a topic, adheres to a heteronormative narrative where "penetration" = women. Michael desires anal penetration; he has invited his wife to assume the role of penetrator. Moreover, it could be argued that to some extent he is in the role of sex educator here: he expresses his disappointment in Hartley's "alternative sex" video and informs her (and us) that he is a married man frustrated by his wife's lack of interest in penetrating him. For most heterosexual persons, his interest would likely be interpreted as a shift in gender roles and the sexual practices associated with traditional heterosexual roles. The author's seriousness and dedication to anal sex as a practice that can be equally enjoyed by men is arguably represented through his use of a sex toy for anal penetration while writing his letter to Hartley.

These texts provide some diverse examples of Hartley fan letters that take the form of a kind of sexual confession. In the next section, I introduce Foucault's work on parrhesia in relation to the "open-heartedness" about sexuality of letter-writers in Hartley's fan club.

Parrhesia

Foucault's definition of parrhesia is an "ethics of speech," an "opening the heart" ([1981–82] 2001, 137) to free, frank discussion in which everything is revealed. It is a "modality of truth-telling" in which the speaker "is recognized by others as speaking the truth" ([1983–84] 2008, 2–3). Through the act of speaking truth to another, "the individual constitutes himself and is constituted by others as a subject of a discourse of truth" (3). The idea of parrhesia as a discourse that reveals everything entails the ethical concern in that there is a moral quality required from every speaker (2001, 366). Openness is a rule for verbal conduct in addressing the soul of the other because it is "the practice of spiritual direction" (164).

Foucault states, "The objective of *parrhesia* is to act so that at a given moment the person to whom one is speaking finds himself in a situation in which he no longer needs the other's discourse" (379). This is achievable because "the other's discourse was true." Truth is a vital component in parrhesia; discourse must be pure and ready to be embraced by the subject. The goal is that "the truth, passing from one to the other in *parrhesia*, seals, ensures, and guarantees the other's autonomy" (379). This passing of truth becomes a dialectic of virtue where the person giving advice is reminded and emboldened by the truth they share with the other – it is valuable to both (361).

It is important to highlight that the subject gains autonomy from truthful discourse; it is a genuine sharing of thought, not a prescribed set of rules with predetermined parameters. Foucault states that parrhesia occurs under a "rule of prudence" (317); this prudence concerns the what, where, and when – the conditions with which we engage in discourse (384).

Parrhesia is a discourse that is truthful: the language cannot be artificial, rhetorical, or seductive. A significant issue around discourse that Foucault addresses is flattery, which he views as a method for a subordinate person to "win over" the power he meets with superiors (375). The idea of winning over is of course contrary to the true discourse of parrhesia. Parrhesia is anti-flattery, in that "unlike what happens in flattery, he speaks to the other in such a way that this other will be able to form an autonomous, independent, full and satisfying relationship to himself" (379). The objective of flattery is dependence and the use of rhetoric or seduction to win over others; it is "the opposite of the true and healthy guidance of souls" (379).

Parrhesia's goal is instead autonomy and independence. In an integral, robust technique of the self, Foucault argues for a transformational autonomy: self-creation. The ability to create one's own body, thought, and soul must be reconciled with the definition of power as action on an action. That is, autonomous individuals transform themselves concurrent with, or subsequent to, the power relations acting upon their transforming action. This transformation does not negate self-knowledge or parrhesia, and it is possible and accommodating for these techniques to occur concurrently.

Tom Roach (2012) examines Foucault's later philosophy on the concept of friendship, paying some attention to parrhesia. In an interview, Foucault described the biopolitical imperative that forces confession as "a formidable tool of control and power" (Roach 2012). Unlike authors who adhere to an "historical imperative to speak of sex" there are opportunities for what can be described as an anticonfessional discourse (20). Succinctly, Roach observes that although it can be exciting to hear disclosures of "shameful fantasies or perverse inclinations," Foucault offers us a consideration of a discourse of friendship that is not confessional (23).

What I want to posit here is Foucault's idea of confession as a system of "regulation and surveillance" alongside friendship as an anticonfessional discourse that provides a "metamorphosis from confession to *parrhesia*" (Roach 2012, 21–3). Moreover, I suggest the relationship between Hartley and her fans is a kind of long-distance friendship where "truth is linked to sex"; it is this connection that allows an understanding of the Hartley letters as parrhesia (23).

The description of parrhesia that Roach provides includes the interactive relationship whereby the speaker "simultaneously guides himself and another," reminding the speaker of their own need for "self-mastery" (2012, 24). The relationship between oneself and another is important in considering the porn star–fan relationship discussed here. Contrary to Platonism's "recollection" model and Christianity's monastic "self-renunciation" model in considering care of the self, the Hellenistic model "privileges self-transformation": the relationship of the self to the self (25). *Parrhesiastic* discourse is performative in that it "forces the subject to understand both himself and the world in a relational manner" (27). Self-transformation is possible through parrhesia because "the self becomes the subject of true discourse and is transformed in the truth's enunciation" (28).

I leave this brief explication of parrhesia here. The inclusion of parrhesia in a discussion of the concept of confession and Hartley's fan mail is to suggest a discourse delivered to the addressee that can be interpreted as truthful and transformative.

Confessional Texts

In Alfred Hitchcock's 1953 film, *I Confess*, a church caretaker kills a man while committing robbery; the caretaker wears a priest's cassock during the crime. The caretaker returns to the church and confesses the murder to the priest, then returns home. He tells his wife about the murder and confession, saying the truth of his crime is safe because the priest is forbidden to reveal confessional information. The next day, witnesses report seeing a priest leaving the crime scene, leading police to make him the prime suspect of their investigation.

What is the relationship between the interlocutors of a confession? As Dennis Foster observes in *Confession and Complicity in Narrative*, confession is an act that usually "involves a narrator disclosing a secret knowledge to another; as a speaker to a listener, writer to reader, confessor to confessor" (Foster 1987, 2). For Foster, confession implies not just a relationship but a reciprocal dialectic. A "full confession" is an act that "would presumably require that a private knowledge be revealed in a way that would allow another to understand, judge, forgive, and perhaps even sympathize" (2).

For the recipient of the confession, the possibility of flattery or narcissism exists upon "find(ing) oneself confirmed in another's text" (13). This an idea that opens up Hartley's positionality in her reading of the fan letters. I can state with certainty that Hartley is delighted by the fan letters she receives; she retained more than fifteen years of these letters in pristine condition. I would not judge her reception of the letters as narcissistic or vulnerable to flattery. Contrary to the idea of flattery or narcissism, open, honest correspondence enables the reader to form an autonomous, independent interpretation and to avoid seductive language. (See the discussion of flattery in the preceding section on parrhesia.)

The Hartley fan letters lie between a Foucauldian understanding of "the exigent nature of confession as a discipline" (Cryle 2001, 127) and the idea of a letter as unsolicited correspondence that is sent from an autonomous author. In most cases, the fan authors have not had personal contact with Hartley; no prior relationship exists beyond spectatorship. Foucault writes that confession is "a self-referential utterance which requires a relationship with another" (Taylor 2009, 7). However, he defines confession as "a ritual of discourse where the subject who speaks corresponds with the subject of the statement" (Foucault [1976] 1990, 82–8). He further clarifies that this correspondence occurs within a "relationship of power, since one doesn't confess without the presence, at least the virtual presence, of a partner who is not simply an interlocutor but the agency that requires the confession" (83). Foucault includes in his discussion "the practice of autobiographical writings" that can be delivered "to another in one's imagination" (Taylor 2009, 7).

I take the idea of the addressee as a "virtual presence" that can receive confession through writing as permitting the interpretation of (some of) Hartley's fan mail as confession. Imagining Hartley as a virtual presence invites a questioning of the characteristics, and perhaps categorization, of oral, written, film/video, and digital confession. Historically, confession "originates in an oral culture"; it is a "private verbal exchange" (Brooks 2000, 95). There are varied modalities of confession; it can be the written word: letters or documents. More recently, however, confession can be recorded and communicated. Advances in media technologies have enabled the communication of confession via radio, television, videotape, the Internet, and other digital technologies. While usually a private communication, in some circumstances confession has moved from the discreet context of religious practice or private dwelling to apologies and disclosures in the public realm (Bauer 2008).

Who is permitted to hear confession? As in Hitchcock's *I Confess*, alluded to above, religious authorities are recognized as qualified and experienced in hearing confession. Christian confession, in which addressing the listener is "similar to prayer" where the listener is God (Brooks 2000, 95), dates back to Augustine's *Confessions* (Taylor 2009). The historic understanding of confession introduces the question of whether we can imagine Nina Hartley, a porn star and sex educator, as an expert or authoritative addressee for sexual confession. Bjorn Krondorfer observes the requirement of an audience for confession, as in Foster's description of confession. The historic confessions of men reveal "their sins, their shame, their shortcomings, their deceptions, their desires" (Krondorfer 2010, 2).

Religious confession "allows men to talk about their intimate selves, their flawed and sinful selves, without having to condemn themselves entirely" (3). While the Hartley letters do not necessarily make declarations of sin, shame, or deception, they reveal the letter-writers' intimate selves.

What are the restraints on confession? Diversity can play a role in one's ability to write confessionally. Age, class, dis/ability, education, ethnicity, gender, "race," religion, sexual orientation, and a sense of entitlement to address another regarding oneself may limit access to revealing the intimate self (Krondorfer 2010, 7). The Hartley fan archive includes a number of letters that can be categorized under the heading of diversity. In Zamir's (2013) articulation of the uniqueness of porn, he states that its "therapeutic potential lies in its power to show individuals that they are not alone" (85). The letter-writers I include can be understood as the spectators searching for a pornographic representation of someone like themselves and, conceivably, looking for representations of their own penis (Fung 1991).

This chapter puts forth the idea that Nina Hartley's fan letters can be understood as a particular kind of sexual confession. I suggest that these letters – describing sexual identifications, practices, and desires – are confidential correspondence sent without obligation to a recipient whom the author trusted with their intimate disclosure. An important distinction in adjudicating confession is the interpretation of the utterance as either coerced, solicited, or given freely, if it is possible to reconcile the concept of consent with confession. Briefly, regarding pornography spectatorship, virtual presence, and the writing of letters, I include some of Foucault's relevant work.

Foucault references the Stoics with relation to the importance of reading and listening, and the idea that writing what one has observed can be understood as a way of preserving it. I take a liberal interpretation of "reading" here to include viewing pornographic film/video. While pornography spectatorship can be thought of as a passive audience activity, the spectator will garner something from the text (Foucault [1981–82] 2001, 334–8). That is, in listening and watching the film, viewers are attentive to what they regard as significant information (351). Citing Seneca, Foucault discusses the importance of writing to give "body (*corpus*) to what has been obtained by reading" (359). Writing, in this context, is part of "the exercise of the self" (359). The "techniques and ethics of reading and writing are bound to true discourse, and subsequently, to the concept of *parrhesia*" (372). Foucault intends these passages to give direction to students and theorists in developing their learning skills. I suggest, however, that the progression from the pornography spectator viewing and listening to pornographic film(s), and subsequently writing their thoughts to Hartley, is a defensible interpretation of this skill.

The Porn Star–Fan Relationship

Kipnis (1996) describes the pornographic story as "a fictional, fantastical, even allegorical realm." Pornography fans, however, are real people, sometimes divulging in letters "shameful fantasies or perverse inclinations" (Roach 2012, 23). I include sections from numerous texts from the Hartley fan archive to provide tangible examples of Hartley's fan mail, and to support my analysis above.

The first two letters were written in 1997 and 1998, respectively, a period when film pornography had advanced from videotape to DVD and onto internet adult websites. In the letter dated August 1997, the fan notes that he found Hartley's fan club address on the internet. By the late 1990s, email correspondence was common and accessible, yet these authors chose to send a letter by post.

The limitations of a chapter permit the use of only several pieces of Hartley fan correspondence. These letters were selected to represent the Hartley archive because, like much of that archive, they articulate admiration, attraction, and devotion. The authors openly and honestly share their sexual desires and specific fantasies involving Hartley, through a kind of confession.

The first letter is an example of a Hartley fan articulating a specific sexual fantasy, told through the author's idea for a Hartley pornographic film he has conceived of directing. This letter can be interpreted as a sexual confession in the form of the writer describing his direction of a fantasy scenario. In his letter of 19 August 1997 (fig. 7.1), Robert tells Nina that he served as a tank gunner in the US Army during Operation Desert Storm in Iraq. He describes how he had a photograph of Hartley "standing with [her] gorgeous ass to the camera and looking over [her] right shoulder." Robert had the photograph "wedged in between the firing trigger and gun camera computer box in the M1A1 tank" he served in. The picture of Hartley's "hot body" kept him "company through the long hot days and cold nights in the desert." Robert wishes he could direct a pornographic movie starring Hartley. He shares his Desert Storm fantasy scenario, describing how Hartley would be "wearing nothing but an Army cap and bandana straddling the 120mm cannon of the M1A1 tank with a sweaty GI in your mouth and one pumping in and out of your pussy from behind while your tits rub against the

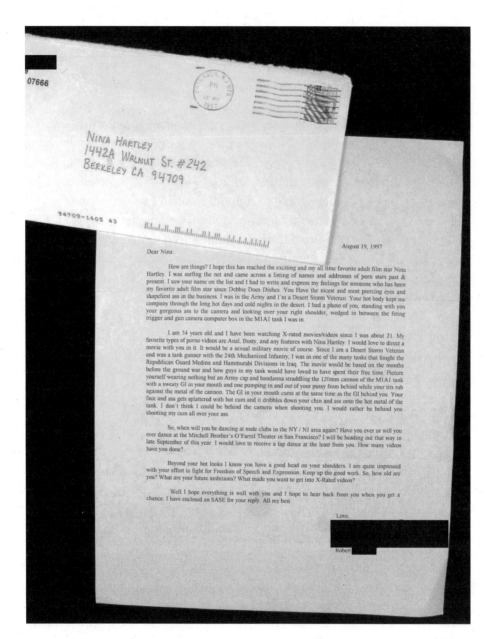

7.1 Desert Storm M1 tank fantasy, letter from Robert, 19 August 1997. Photograph, Ingrid Olson, 2012.

metal of the cannon. The GI in your mouth cums at the same time as the GI behind you. Your face and ass get splattered with hot cum and it dribbles down your chin and ass onto the hot metal of the tank." Robert then confesses that he does not think he could be "behind the camera when shooting you. I would rather be behind you shooting my cum all over your ass."

In closing his letter, Robert tells Hartley that he realizes beyond her "hot looks" she has "a good head on her shoulders," and he commends her activism on "Freedom of Speech and Expression." I include explicit excerpts from Robert's letter because it represents a kind of sexual confession, and because, in this article's attention to the spectator's engagement with pornography, the fantasy of directing a pornography scenario represents the transition of the viewer from spectator to (potential) creator of pornography. Moreover, because Robert's letter reveals a sexual fantasy through the would-be eyes of the director, he is not involved physically; he directs where and what kind of sexual scenario the tank crew has with Hartley. So, while Robert states that this particular fantasy is his chance to direct a Hartley pornographic film, it is curious that he does not include himself in the sexual scenario until it occurs as an afterthought. Additionally, Robert's is a very personal conceptualization in that the scenario takes place entirely on the type of US Army battle tank in which he served during war in Iraq. That is, the M1 tank becomes sexualized as the performer's stage in the scenario including Hartley splayed on the gun barrel. Robert uses the generic term "GI" to describe the men having sex with Hartley. Presumably the men he includes in the fantasy scenario are not friends from the military, or they are but he did not feel it necessary to include their names.

Finally, Robert describes the photograph of Hartley located inside the tank – an aspect that I believe says much more than a casual reader might consider. Robert served as a gunner in an armoured vehicle in a war on the other side of the planet from his home. In his letter he includes information on his military unit and particular Iraq war battles he participated in (I have omitted his last name for anonymity). My point is that Robert, like many soldiers before and after him, was then far from home and in danger of being killed. For Robert as the gunner in a battle tank, the location of Hartley's photograph – "wedged in between the firing trigger and gun camera computer box" – meant that it was in his field of vision most of his waking hours in Iraq. And, given Robert's confession of his fantasy of directing a pornographic film featuring Hartley, it would seem she was in his thoughts beyond that photographic image. As Robert tells Hartley in his letter, the photograph gave comfort through long hot days and cold nights.

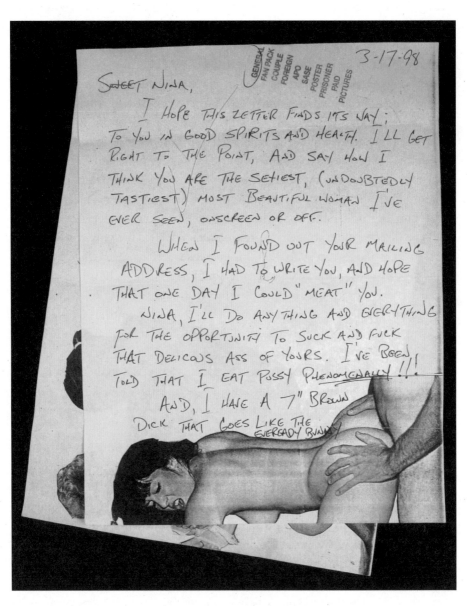

7.2 Letter from Trace, 17 March 1998, p. 1. Photograph, Ingrid Olson, 2012.

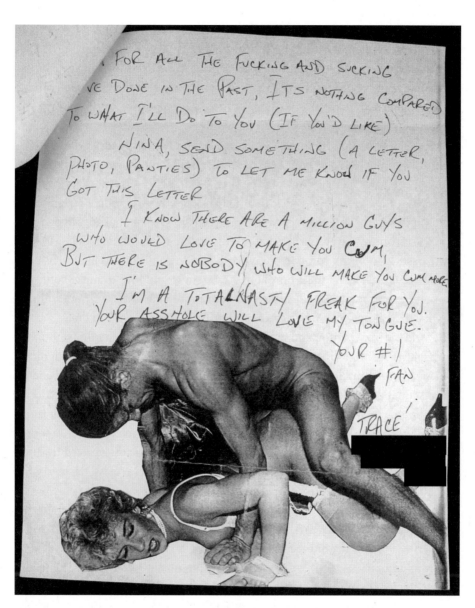

7.3 Letter from Trace, 17 March 1988, p. 2. Photograph, Ingrid Olson, 2012.

I suggest that declaration to Hartley says quite a lot about the relationship between self and confession.

A two-page letter from Trace dated 17 March 1998 (figs. 7.2 and 7.3) is unique in that the stationery itself has been transformed into a pornographic text. That is, each of the two pages of stationery has a photocopy of a different sexually explicit magazine photograph of a man-woman couple engaged in intercourse. Trace's equally explicit text is written on these pages: pornographic literary text on pornographic visual text.

Trace tells Nina that he thinks she is "the sexiest (undoubtedly tastiest) most beautiful woman" he has "ever seen, onscreen or off," and hopes that one day he could "meat" [sic] her. He continues, "Nina, I'll do anything and everything for the opportunity to suck and fuck that delicous [sic] ass of yours. I've been told that I eat pussy phenomenally!!! And, I have a 7" brown dick that goes like the eveready [sic] bunny." Trace writes that "all the fucking and sucking" he has "done in the past" is "nothing compared to what I'll do to you (if you'd like)." His confession recognizes that "there a million guys who would love to make you cum, but there is nobody who will make you cum more." He closes his letter, "I'm a total nasty freak for you. Your asshole will love my tongue. Your #1 fan."

Beyond the imagination and time involved in creating pornographic stationery, Trace's letter is interesting for its confession that he possesses a "7" brown dick"; he describes the physical dimensions of his penis and declares his sexual energy and sustainability: the "eveready bunny." Also interesting is his unabashed declaration that he possesses a sexual prowess and enthusiasm for Hartley, a pornography star, that she has perhaps never experienced; he will make her "cum more" than anyone. That is, the confession of Trace's letter can be interpreted through his speaking sexual truth of his enthusiasm and expertise as a sexual partner, what Foucault describes as "transformational autonomy."

There are letters in the Hartley archive from fans that represent diversity, including Trace's letter above. While most of the Hartley letters are from heterosexual-identified men, she did receive letters from a small number of women fans.

A woman named Carole wrote a succinct, single-page letter (fig. 7.4) encouraging Nina to "do more amateur videos" and "especially using a strap-on to fuck the women." Carole wants to see representations of women "with unique sex abilities like being fist fucked," or women with "special physical features like big clits or distended pussy lips." Her focus on specific genitalia is interesting. She does not elaborate on why she desires these particular pornographic scenes or how they are of interest to her; we are left to speculate. Perhaps she was bored or dis-

7.4 Letter from Carole regarding strap-on and fisting scenes.
Photograph, Ingrid Olson, 2012.

mayed from viewing "perfect," normative, pornographic women's bodies. It is also possible that, similar to Fung's (1991) idea of the viewer "looking for his penis," Carole hoped to view pornographic representations of women with genitalia similar to her own. Her letter steers toward specific issues of embodiment – genitalia –and the idea of normative bodies.

Carole's desire to view scenarios of women being "fist fucked" is interesting as a kind of sexual confession. The sexual act of fisting – vaginal or anal penetration by, and thrusting with, a fist – would seem to constitute the idea of what Foucault ([1954–84] 1997) described as "new possibilities of pleasure" (165). That is, using the thrusting movement of a fist, a bodily motion often associated with physical aggression, as an instrument of sexual pleasure, inverts its interpretation as a violent act and disrupts many persons' understanding of penetrative sexual acts. Unlike the use of dildos or other sex toys, fisting is a bodily connection; fisting represents a personal, intimate connection, an alternative to penile penetrative sex that is non-procreative. Fisting is a sexual act that is usually capable of being sustained in terms of time beyond penile penetrative sex acts. For some persons, fisting invites considerations of sexual penetration with greater endurance and size (clenched fist), possibly making it an appealing alternative to what might be considered normative heterosexual or homosexual sex practices.

Carole confesses her desire to view representations of "special physical features like big clits or distended pussy lips." This attraction can be interpreted as confessing a kind of adoration or fascination for particular bodies. Carole's letter discusses physical features that, while not a reference to disability, are usually not seen, and, for persons with genitalia similar to that Carole describes, it is possible they would feel some discomfort or be open to viewing those explicit representations. As the text of Carole's letter does not refer to her own genitalia, it is not known if her desire is a personal interest or fetish, or a wish to see pornographic representations of bodies similar to her own. And her desire to see Hartley engaging in fisting scenarios can be interpreted as a confession of seeking non-normative, non-procreative sexual practices.

Similarly, in a letter pertaining to embodiment and sexualized bodies (fig. 7.5), a man who refers to himself as "Davey One Step" asks Nina, "Would you ever screw a guy with one leg?" Davey's letter deserves attention here for several reasons. First, he refers to himself more than once as "Davey One Step," presumably disclosing that he is comfortable with having only one leg. Second, he asks Nina if she would have sex with a man with one leg. Third, he states that he has urged his girlfriend to engage in "lesbianism," regretting that she would only be interested in lesbian sex with Nina, as this limits the possibility of his girlfriend hav-

> Nina,
>
> You are the supreme erotic movie goddess. There's never been better on the blue screen. I heard you was studyin nursein back in the days. I have dreams that I'm in the Hospital and your my nurse. Me and my Girlfriend watch your flix all the time She gets turned on watchin you. I always ask her to try lesbianism she says only if you can get Nina Hartley to do it with me. Oh well I guess in another life. Send me some info on how to join your fan club and Please send an Autographed Picture signed to Davey "one step". I know your in "Girls will be Boys 4" but have you done any other recent flix
>
> Stay cool Baby!
>
> Love ya,
>
> Davey "one step"
>
> P.S. Would you ever screw a guy with one leg. Once you do ya never go back

7.5 Davey "One Step" writes of embodiment and sexualized bodies. Photograph, Ingrid Olson, 2012.

ing sex with another woman to one person. And fourth, Davey cites Hartley's 1992 video *Girls will be Boys 4*, a film Hartley starred in with an all-female cast – perhaps another reference to his interest in "lesbianism." Although we do not have a complete, sexual portrait of Davey, it is reasonable to interpret his letter as not only a confessional of his own desires, but a glimpse into his girlfriend's consideration of a "lesbian" encounter with Hartley. And perhaps, a suggestion that Davey's questioning of Hartley having sex with a man with one leg might be considered as part of his own sexual transformation.

As articulated above on confessional texts, the porn star-fan relationship can be understood through the trajectory of the fans' viewing and listening to Hartley's film, reflecting on what is significant in the texts for them, and then writing a fan letter, a form of true discourse (Foucault [1981–82] 2001). Foucault (137) defines parrhesia as an opening of the heart, a frank, honest discussion where all is revealed. Parrhesia, as a discourse of truth, is interactive: the speaker constitutes themselves through a dialectic of virtue (379). The authors above experience a transformational autonomy because the self becomes the subject of true discourse (Roach 2012, 28). The porn star-fan relationship between Hartley and her fans can be thought of as a kind of friendship, one in which the author trusts that the recipient is an expert in issues of sexuality. As such, the relationship could permit an anticonfessional discourse, a "metamorphosis from confession to *parrhesia*" (23).

Conclusion

The intellectual objective of *I Confess!* is to examine the construction of the sexual self through moving-image media. This chapter's contribution is an analysis of constructions through confessions in the cumulative fan-mail archive of pornography star Nina Hartley.

In my introduction I presented the idea that as "sex becomes more and more an object of expertise, the techniques of sexualities are received within the power relation of confessor and confessant" (Taylor 2005, 57). I suggest that Hartley's status as a porn icon, sex educator, and author locates her as a sex expert, and so it is reasonable to interpret her fan mail archive as a repository of sexual confessions. The letters from Hartley's fans are a particular kind of sexual confession: authors describing sexual identifications, practices, and desires to a porn star addressee.

Hartley's emerging porn career was concomitant with technological media advances, yet the confessions are written letters, not the spoken word that "invites attention to the ear" (Tambling 1990, 73). But in a Foucauldian (1978) context of sexual confession, the "virtual presence" of Hartley in the lives of these pornography spectators represents not just an interlocutor "but the authority who requires the confession, prescribes and appreciates it" (Duff, citing Foucault 2010, 688).

Confession can be understood as an act that "involves a narrator disclosing a secret knowledge to another; as a speaker to a listener, writer to reader, confessor to confessor" (Foster 1987, 2). I have posited the definition of "full confession" as an act requiring that "a private knowledge be revealed in a way that would allow another to understand, judge, forgive, and perhaps even sympathize" (2). The Hartley letters represent a trajectory from fans viewing and listening to her pornographic film texts to writing to the porn star based on their engagement with the text: a transformation from confession to parrhesia.

NOTES

1 I was unable to find a reference for the director of this film, even including personal correspondence with Nina Hartley, who could not recall the director's name.
2 At least one of her Adam & Eve "*Guides to*" sexual-instruction videos specifically addresses anal sex.

REFERENCES

Alilunas, Peter. 2016. *Smutty Little Movies: The Creation and Regulation of Adult Video*. Oakland: University of California Press.

Bauer, Susan. 20018. *Art of the Public Grovel: Sexual Sin and Public Confession in America*. Princeton: Princeton University Press.

Bower, Anne. 1997. *Epistolary Responses: The Letter in 20th-Century American Fiction and Criticism*. Tuscaloosa: University of Alabama Press.

Brooks, Peter. 2000. *Troubling Confessions: Speaking Guilt in Law and Literature*. Chicago: University of Chicago Press.

Comella, Lynn. 2010. "Nina Hartley's Adult Film Career Has Been Long, Distinguished and Trailblazing – and It's Far from Over." *Las Vegas Weekly*, 6 October. http://lasvegasweekly.com/as-we-see-it/2010/oct/06/nina-hartleys-adult-film-career-has-been-long-dist/.

Cook, Elizabeth. 1996. *Epistolary Bodies: Gender and Genre in the Eighteenth-Century Republic of Letters*. Stanford: Stanford University Press.

Cryle, Peter. 2001. *The Telling of the Act: Sexuality as Narrative in Eighteenth- and Nineteenth-Century France*. Newark: University of Delaware Press.

Davidson, Arnold. 2001. *The Emergence of Sexuality: Historical Epistemology and the Formation of Concepts*. Cambridge: Harvard University Press.

Duff, Brian. 2010. "Confession, Sexuality and Pornography as Sacred Language." *Sexualities* 13, no. 6: 685–98.

Foster, Dennis. 1987. *Confession and Complicity in Narrative*. Cambridge: Cambridge University Press.

Foucault, Michel. [1976] 1990. *The History of Sexuality.* Vol. 1, *An Introduction.* Translated by Robert Hurley. New York: Vintage Books.
— 1980. *Power/Knowledge: Selected Interviews and Other Writings.* Edited by Colin Gordon. New York: Pantheon Books.
— [1980] 1993. "About the Beginning of the Hermeneutics of the Self: Two Lectures at Dartmouth." *Political Theory* 21, no. 2: 198–222.
— [1966–84] 1996. *Foucault Live: Interviews, 1966–84.* Edited by Sylvère Lotringer. New York: Semiotext(e).
— [1954–84] 1997. *Ethics: Subjectivity and Truth.* Edited by Paul Rabinow. Translated by Robert Hurley. New York: New Press.
— [1954–84] 2000. *Essential Works of Foucault.* Vol. 1. Edited by James Faubion. New York: New Press.
— [1981–82] 2001. *The Hermeneutics of the Subject: Lectures at the Collège de France, 1981–1982.* Translated by Graham Burchell. New York: Picador.
— [1983–84] 2008. *The Courage of Truth (The Government of Self and Others II): Lectures at the Collège de France, 1983–1984.* Translated by Graham Burchell. New York: Palgrave Macmillan.
— [1982–83] 2010. *The Government of Self and Others: Lectures at the Collège de France, 1982–1983.* Translated by Graham Burchell. New York: Palgrave Macmillan.
Fung, Richard. 1991. "Looking for My Penis: The Eroticized Asian in Gay Video Porn." In *How Do I Look? Queer Film and Video*, edited by Bad Object-Choices, 145–68. Seattle: Bay Press.
Garlinger, Patrick. 2005. *Confessions of the Letter Closet: Epistolary Fiction and Queer Desire in Modern Spain.* Minneapolis: University of Minnesota Press.
Greenberg, Joshua. 2008. *From Betamax to Blockbuster: Video Stores and the Invention of Movies on Video.* Cambridge: MIT University Press.
Hartley, Nina. 1999. "Using Porn to Bridge the Mind–Body Gap." In *Porn 101: Eroticism, Pornography, and the First Amendment*, edited by James Elias, Veronica Diehl Elias, Vern L. Bullough, and Gwen Brewer, 203–6. Amherst: Prometheus Books.
— 2006. *Nina Hartley's Guide to Total Sex.* New York: Avery.
— 2013 "Porn: An Effective Vehicle for Sexual Role Modeling and Education." In *The Feminist Porn Book: The Politics of Producing Pleasure*, edited by Tristan Taormino et. al, 228–36. New York: Feminist Press at the City University of New York.
Juffer, Jane. 1998. *At Home with Pornography: Women, Sex, and Everyday Life.* New York: New York University Press.
Kenyon, Olga. 1992. *Eight Hundred Years of Women's Letters.* Stroud, UK: Allan Sutton.
Kipnis, Laura. 1996. *Bound and Gagged: Pornography and the Politics of Fantasy in America.* Durham: Duke University Press.
Kleinhans, Chuck. 2006. "The Change from Film to Video Pornography: Implications for

Analysis." In *Pornography: Film and Culture*, edited by Peter Lehman, 154–67. New Brunswick: Rutgers University Press.

Krondorfer, Bjorn. 2010. *Male Confessions. Intimate Revelations and the Religious Imagination*. Stanford: Stanford University Press.

Melendez, Franklin. 2004. "Video Pornography, Visual Pleasure, and the Return of the Sublime." In *Porn Studies*, edited by Linda Williams, 401–27. Durham: Duke University Press.

Muñoz, José. 1999. *Disidentifications. Queers of Color and the Performance of Politics*. Minneapolis: University of Minnesota Press.

Roach, Tom. 2012. *Friendship as a Way of Life: Foucault, AIDS, and the Politics of Shared Estrangement*. Albany: State University of New York Press.

Salgado, Richard. 1989. "Regulating a Video Revolution." *Yale Law and Policy Review* 7, no. 2: 516–37.

Stryker, Susan. 2006. "(De)Subjugated Knowledges: An Introduction to Transgender Studies." In *The Transgender Studies Reader*, edited by Susan Stryker and Stephen Whittle, 1–17. New York: Routledge.

Sycamore, Mattilda. 2006. *Nobody Passes: Rejecting the Rules of Gender and Conformity*. Emeryville, CA: Seal Press.

Tambling, Jeremy. 1990. *Confession: Sexuality, Sin, the Subject*. New York: St Martin's Press.

Taormino, Tristan, Celine Parrenas Shimizu, Constance Penley, and Mireille Miller-Young, eds. 2013. *The Feminist Porn Book: The Politics of Producing Pleasure*. New York: Feminist Press at the City University of New York.

Taylor, Chloe. 2005. "Alternatives to Confession: Foucault's 'Fragments of an Autobiography.'" *Symposium: Canadian Journal of Continental Philosophy* 9, no. 2 (Spring): 55–66.

– 2009. *The Culture of Confession from Augustine to Foucault: A Genealogy of the "Confessing Animal."* New York: Routledge.

Williams, Linda. 1989. *Hard Core: Power, Pleasure and the Frenzy of the Visible*. Berkeley: University of California Press.

XBIZ Awards. 2017. "XBIZ Awards 2017 Winners." *XBIZ Awards*, 6 October. xbizawards.xbiz.com/winners.php.

Zamir, Tzachi. 2013. "Pornography and Acting." In *Pornographic Art and the Aesthetics of Pornography*, edited by Hans Maes, 75–99. London: Palgrave Macmillan.

MEDIAGRAPHY

Anderson, Juliet, dir. 1984. *Educating Nina*. Videotape. California: Cinderella Productions.

Couple Seeks Third, 8. 2018. DVD. Los Angeles: Pornstar Platinum

Hitchcock, Alfred, dir. 1953. *I Confess*. Film. Burbank: Warner Bros.

8

Femininities of Excess: The Cinematic Confessions of Rituparno Ghosh

SHOHINI GHOSH

After his premature passing in 2013, the famous Bengali filmmaker Rituparno Ghosh (1961–2013) became a queer icon, leaving behind a body of work that has immense significance for those invested in undoing the heteronormative. Ghosh's coming out as queer was both incremental and spectacular. A regular winner of National Film Awards, he was one of India's best-known regional filmmakers. When he died unexpectedly, he left behind no autobiography but a trail of confessionals that included his films, replete with autobiographical references. A series of editorials titled "First Person," written for a weekend magazine, had acquired over the years a devoted following and come closest to being his memoirs. Most importantly, his public self-presentation was a critical mode of confession. This essay is a series of reflections on how Rituparno Ghosh's star persona – circulating through a relay of films, writings, public and cinematic appearances – produced a set of counter-normative confessionals around body, desire, intimacy and the performance of gender. Rituparno's retrieval and embodiment of a femininity of excess is perhaps his most dissident confessional.

Meeting Rituparno

The word "tomboy" is going out of fashion, but that's what I called myself when I was growing up in Calcutta. Except for two afternoons when I had to attend an art school with a gendered dress code, I always wore clothes worn by boys. Once when someone said that I should dress "appropriately," my mother told me not to worry. She said I was a tomboy and had a right to wear what made me happy. But the city was not anything like my parents. As I walked down the streets, I would be pursued by comments, inevitably from men – "Hey, is that a girl or a boy?" This was the standard heckler's taunt aimed at boyish girls and girlish boys.

8.1 Rituparno Ghosh, the public intellectual. Courtesy Shohini Ghosh.

I didn't know anyone else like me outside the world of fiction. Occasionally, I caught glimpses of those who seemed gender non-conforming. These welcome visitations assured me that other worlds existed. At the time I had no idea that during those same years, another girlish boy was growing up in the city, who, several decades later, would become one of my closest friends and my reason for loving the city again after I had chosen to leave.

His parents had named their sons Shouroneel and Indraneel. Shouroneel did not like his birth name, so he named himself Rituparno. He would grow up to be one of the country's most acclaimed filmmakers. Before his life and career came to a premature end following a massive heart attack, he had become one of Calcutta's most influential public intellectuals (fig. 8.1). After we became friends in 2006, Rituparno wanted to make an explicitly queer film set against the conflict in Kashmir. Apart from directing, it was decided, he would also act in the film. He was going to play the role of a Bengali journalist who in the course of writing an investigative story becomes close to a Kashmiri detainee. With the intimacy between the two men begins an excavation of the complex political situation in Kashmir. Our idea was to show what India looked like from the vantage of Kashmir and what gender normativity looked like from the perspective of the queer. Despite our enthusiasm, the film never got made but it taught us many lessons.

When we went to Bombay to cast for the role of the Kashmiri militant, a number of actors showed interest because everyone wanted to act in a Rituparno film. But once they heard about the script, they begged to be let off. Barring two actors, one a top Bengali actor who was a close friend of Rituparno's, no one wanted to play the role of a man who gets sexually involved with another man. We also discovered that even those who considered the possibility were reluctant to play the role of the feminine man. With rare exceptions, the on-screen feminine man had mostly been treated with derision. It would be left to Rituparno the actor to bring the apparitional queer feminine man out of the shadows and onto the screen.

Rituparno's body of twenty feature films marks a critical departure from the majority of films made in the 1980s that, with some significant exceptions, displaced the female protagonist from any position of centrality. In Rituparno's films, women returned to the centre of cinematic narratives. For this reason, even the top actresses of Bombay were eager to work with him. It is possible to see Rituparno's considerable body of cinematic work as explorations in femininities. In the four films in which he has featured as a protagonist, his own body becomes a site of experimentations. In this essay I draw attention to *Jeevan Smriti* (Selective Memories, dir. Ghosh 2013), a documentary on the life of Bengal's greatest literary figure, Rabindranath Tagore.[1] Reading *Jeevan Smriti* as a queer text, I highlight Rituparno's emplacement in the film and his embodiment and performance of a femininity of excess that become, as I argue, a sensorium of provocative confessionals.

The Rise of Rituparno Ghosh

Rituparno Ghosh was entirely a self-taught filmmaker. He never attended a film school nor apprenticed with a filmmaker. His work in the advertising industry, where he quickly acquired a reputation for writing witty taglines, served as a training ground for his filmmaking. His first theatrical release *Unishe April* (19 April, 1994) received popular and critical acclaim and also won the National Film Award. He went on to make a series of important films including *Dahan* (Crossfire, 1977), *Bariwali* (The Lady of the House, 2000), *Titli* (The First Monsoon Day, 2002), *Shubho Mahurat* (The Auspicious Moment, 2003), *Chokher Bali* (Passion Play, 2003), *Raincoat* (2004), *Antarmahal* (The Inner Chambers, 2005), *The Last Lear* (2007), *Shob Choritro Kalponik* (All Characters Are Imaginary/Afterword, 2009), *Abohomaan* (The Eternal, 2010), and *Chitrangada* (The Crowning Wish, 2012). Rituparno's films revived a flagging industry and saw the return of urban audiences to the theatres. Over the two decades that he made films, he also wrote a popular television series around the songs of Tagore, edited a popular Bengali magazine called *Anandalok* (1997 to 2004), hosted two successful TV shows, *Ebong Rituparno* (And Rituparno) and *Ghosh & Company*, and from 2006 to 2013 edited *Robbar* (Sunday), a weekend supplement of the newspaper *Pratidin* (The Daily) in which he wrote his weekly editorial "First Person." The immense popularity of "First Person" became the driving force behind the sales of the weekender.[2] In the absence of a formal autobiography, the "First Person" editorials, now compiled into two volumes, come closest to being Rituparno's memoirs.

Despite his remarkable achievements, Rituparno's journey in filmmaking was not easy. With the release of *Antarmahal* in 2005, a film about sexual hypocrisy and religious dogma, he became the *enfant terrible* of the Bengali film industry. The Bengali middle class was outraged by the many provocations that the film extended – in particular, its juxtaposition of sex and religion. The uninhibited centrality of sex in the film earned Rituparno the moniker Ritu-porno, punning on pornography and insinuating sexual deviance.

When I first met Rituparno, he had made the less controversial *Dosar* after *Antarmahal* but was poised to explore darker, more transgressive themes. I had found *Antarmahal* refreshingly audacious and encouraged him to move further in that direction. I was heavily immersed in my own research and writing on films and sexuality, much of which I shared with him. He had an insatiable curiosity about international debates on sexuality and a keen interest in queer cinemas emerging across the world. But Rituparno did not allow his provocative experimentations to alienate him from popular audiences. He alternated his cinematic experiments with non-contentious films that served to reassure his audiences and producers. Until the end, he managed to soften the blow of his more dissident films by following them up with ones that had a ready popular appeal. At the time of his death, however, he was deeply invested in pushing the conventional boundaries of cinema. He wanted to make only films that were cinematically inventive. In a recorded interview with me, he says, "I don't want to make that many films anymore. I take long breaks. I sit on a subject and think of how I could present it in the most unconventional way possible. The conventional is the easiest. But this is not being unconventional for the sake of being unconventional but being able to judge whether by being unconventional there can be an added dimension to [the film]. This is a new journey I have embarked upon and I want to see where it takes me" (S. Ghosh 2013).

Rituparno was a skilled and prolific writer. Words and ideas flowed effortlessly out of him. The actress and filmmaker Aparna Sen remembers Rituparno once telling her that whenever he saw a blank piece of paper, he had an urge to fill it with words. Rituparno admits that he had allowed his writing skills to become an obstacle to cinematic experimentation; the ease with which he wrote dialogue-driven scripts made him lazy. But now he was determined to change that. What were the implications of such a change? He said that he now wanted to make films that one would have to watch in order to experience. One would no longer be able to go home and describe the film through its story. The story would be in the telling of it.

The Queer Tetralogy

The films *Arekti Premer Golpo* (Just Another Love Story, dir. Kaushik Ganguly 2011), *Memories in March* (dir. Sanjoy Nag, 2011) *Chitrangada* (dir. Ghosh 2012) and *Jeevan Smriti* (Selective Memories, dir. Ghosh 2013) form a significant tetralogy of Bengali queer films – a kind of a first in Bengali cinema. Rituparno, who wrote the scripts for *Memories in March, Chitrangada,* and *Jeevan Smriti,* featured in all four films. In playing these roles, Rituparno brought his own star persona, popularized through magazines, TV chat shows, internet circulation, rumour, and gossip, into the realm of the cinematic.

Arekti Premer Golpo was an important film for Rituparno, as it was his acting debut and dealt with a subject close to his heart. It was a feature-length remake of a television film titled *Ushnotar Jonno* (Warm for Her/For the Sake of Warmth, 2002) directed by Kaushik Ganguly.[3] Telecast on ETV *Bangla* as part of a TV series titled "Stories of Domesticity," *Ushnotar Jonno* was a fearless exception in a resolutely heteronormative series. Starring two of Bengal's stellar actresses (Rupa Ganguly and Churni Ganguly), the film features Chapal Bhaduri, the famous female impersonator of the Jatra (the traditional Bengali theatre), about whom Naveen Kishore made the documentary titled *Performing the Goddess* (1999).[4] The protagonists in *Ushnotar Jonno* undertake complex journeys into the labyrinthine world of erotic desires where masculinities and femininities are detached from biological bodies (S. Ghosh 2012b). Appearing exactly a decade later, *Arekti Premer Golpo* restages the story with several critical departures from the original telefilm. It replaces the two women with men and moves homophobia from residing within the protagonists to the larger social world they inhabit. The film captures the intricate texture of everyday homophobia. Yet the world of the lovers is not threatened by external forces alone. They battle their own demons, like lovers in any other story. The film unfolds on two parallel narrative tracks. The first is about the love story between Abhiroop (Rituparno), the filmmaker, and Basu (Indraneil

Sengupta), his married cinematographer. The second parallel track – the film within the film – is Abhiroop's recreation of Chapal Bhaduri's life as a female impersonator. Rituparno, who plays the younger Chapal Bhaduri, says:

> In the contemporary story, I played the young gay filmmaker who is making a film on Chapal Bhaduri. In the second track, I played Bhaduri as a young man ... I had to play two feminine men, but very differently. I had to do justice to the role of Chapal because he was acting as himself in the film. If I tried to imitate him, I would run the risk of turning the character into a travesty. I refused to copy his mannerisms and used only his very distinctive voice as a signature of his feminine side. If you heard Chapal on the phone, you wouldn't know whether it was a man or a women speaking. I retained that ambiguity. (S. Ghosh 2012a)

Excited to be making a debut in another director's film, Rituparno participated enthusiastically in its writing and styling. In *Memories in March*, he plays a gay man who builds a relationship with his dead boyfriend's loving but homophobic mother. Inspired by Rabindranath Tagore's dance drama of the same name, Rituparno's *Chitrangada* is about a dancer who wishes to change his body according to the desires of his innermost self.

The theatrical release of the first three films of the tetralogy made issues of gender and sexuality the subject of household conversations in Bengal. The decision to cast Rituparno as a queer protagonist embodying a diversity of femininities heightened public dilemmas around queerness. Audiences were forced to confront their own conflicted relationship with Rituparno, who was the object of both public admiration as well as homophobic insinuation. By the time *Chitrangada* was released, Rituparno had managed – through his films, writings, interviews, and television appearances (livestreamed and shared through social media and the internet) – to make queer issues central to public debates in Bengal.[5]

Queer Becomings, Queer "Sen-sations"

The "respectable" intellectual achievements of Rituparno Ghosh were accompanied, especially in the last decade of his life, by a number of unconventional personal choices. The most public and provocative was the dramatic transformation of his physical appearance. Through a combination of diet, makeup, cosmetic surgery, and abdominoplasty, Rituparno began to sculpt his body.[6] Rituparno, says Aparna Sen, can only be understood in the light of his films, writings, scholarship, eccentric lifestyle, and sexuality: "It was as if he was creating himself from scratch in his own laboratory" (Datta, Bakshi, and Dasgupta 2016).

When Rituparno was a young boy, he ruined his eyesight wearing oversized glasses in an attempt to look like actress Aparna Sen in *Joy Jayanti* (Hail Jayanti, dir. Sunil Basu Mullick 1971), a Bengali reworking of *Sound of Music* (1965, dir. Robert Wise). After Rituparno's death, Sen, then editor of the magazine *Prathama*, brought out a special issue in his memory. The issue carried a long email I wrote to Sen in the immediate aftermath of Rituparno's death. An extract from the letter reads:

> You never took the films in which you acted seriously but Ritu and I did. This has been our longstanding disagreement with you. But since I have your attention now, let me state that you – as an actress, person and filmmaker – influenced him more than you realize. More than perhaps even he realized. Ritu held in high regard your sense of aesthetics, ability to manage home and work, your non-parochial worldview and disdain for conventional morality. Most of all, he admired your ability to feel compassion. Ritu genuinely believed that if anyone consistently supported his gender and sexual choices in the Bengali film industry, it was you. Of course he had many complaints against you, ones that are reserved for those closest to our hearts. (S. Ghosh 2013b)

Rituparno first met Aparna Sen when he went to show her a script that he had written. That film was never made, but a deep friendship was born. Sen made possible Rituparno's first theatrical release, *Unishe April* (1994). She acted as the film's primary protagonist and, since nobody else would risk backing an unknown filmmaker, she co-founded the company Spandan in order to produce and distribute the film. The idea for his second film, *Dahan* (Crossfire, 1997), also came from Sen. Yet Sen's influence over Rituparno preceded their first formal meeting. In 2005, I wrote a proposal for a documentary on Sen that never got made. The film was to be driven by the affective cinephilia of two fans: one who desired her and the other who desired to be like her. In short, it was about Aparna Sen, Rituparno, and me. One passage from the proposal read:

> Rituparno is one of my closest friends. We both love cinema and spend hours every morning talking about our lives and films. Aparna Sen slides in and out of our conversations. We discuss her as a common friend, an industry

professional and an iconic star who had left a deep impression on our adolescent minds. Rituparno grew up adoring Aparna Sen's star persona and wanting to be a Diva like her. One day, the teen Rituparno spotted the actress buying flowers from the street below. He rushed down and stood next to her. Then he did something unbelievably cheeky. He started repeating whatever she was saying to the flower-seller. Boys in Calcutta often mimic women to mock feminine affectation. But this young boy was queer. He was not mocking but fashioning himself after her. He was becoming her.[7] (Ghosh 2005)

Rituparno, who was content with the gender pronoun "he," had desires of "becoming" that were far more complex than the common perception that he wanted to become a woman.[8] Rituparno would often say that between the two opposing words "men" and "women" lay a vast expanse inhabited by many incarnations of the *ardhanareshwara*.[9]

Since Rituparno's passing, there has been much celebration of him as a queer icon. His posthumous hailing as an adored and unquestioned queer icon is riven with irony. While he was a source of strength and inspiration to innumerable queer individuals, LGBTQ groups rarely expressed public support for him during his lifetime. On the contrary, until a year before he died, these groups were either indifferent or hostile to him and tended to dismiss him as a celebrity sensationalist who was hijacking the LGBT platform. During a trip to Calcutta in 2010, I happened to catch a talent contest on a Bengali TV channel. A young boy was making everyone laugh uproariously by mimicking Rituparno through an act he called, "porno-porichoy," which, apart from punning on a famous Bengali primer, loosely translates as "introducing porn."[10] Male effeminacy was the butt of the joke. One of the jury members visibly enjoying the hilarity was an actress who had found national acclaim through Rituparno's films. Homophobia was so omnipresent that no one seemed to notice.

Until about a year before he died, Rituparno had little public support from either the intelligentsia or queer activists in Calcutta. In a widely watched TV show in 2009, he confronted Mir, a prominent television anchor and comedian whose formidable arsenal of spoofs included an impersonation of Ghosh's femininity. In show after show, Mir parodied Rituparno's gestures and speech, adding imaginary lines laced with homophobic sexual innuendoes. In a widely watched and much discussed show on *Ghosh & Company*, Rituparno chastised a bemused and unbending Mir for his sneering mimicry of male femininity (Biswas 2009). "It is not only me that you are mocking," says Rituparno, "but all feminine men who suffer social opprobrium everyday without the protection of celebrity." The "face-off" attracted much public attention. Mir was lavished with comforting words while Rituparno was chided for being harsh. An unrepentant Mir took revenge in subsequent shows through heightened homophobia while audiences became hysterical with laughter. Not a single eminent person or LGBTQ group issued any public statement protesting the brazen homophobia that Mir had displayed. But Rituparno's articulate and dignified protest was lauded by many who suffered daily humiliation for being gender non-conforming.

A city of moral paradoxes, Calcutta continues to maintain a deep ambivalence around queer sexuality. The seething undercurrent of homophobia in the city has been skilfully captured by Aveek Sen in a description of his waiting at a doctor's chamber with three staid middle-class couples:

> Lulled by the air of collective trust and shared mortality in the room, I noted that my lips were feeling dry. So I took out a chap-stick from my satchel and anointed them. Immediately, there was electricity in the air. Six pairs of eyes fastened on me with a look of perfectly consensual disgust. It was just a matter of seconds. But a whole gamut of expressions and little movements animated the faces and bodies of the men and women. In the women, there was derision first, then curiosity, and finally amusement with their husband's radiant discomfort …The men were more seriously chap-struck. I had quite inadvertently touched a raw nerve in them, from where sprang a strange, pungent mixture of shock, loathing and what I can only describe in retrospect as a fear of contagion. (Sen 2007)

The city's fear of the queer always cast a shadow over Rituparno's life.[11] For large numbers of people, Rituparno was a worthy and legitimate heir to Satyajit Ray's cinematic legacy but an unworthy inheritor of his much-admired masculinity. If Ray had the poise, voice, and comportment of a "real man," then Rituparno was his cruel caricature. Therefore, when Rituparno made his acting debut, the audiences were forced to confront their own discomfort around his gender non-conformity because the films had become inextricable from the filmmaker. After the release of *Just Another Love Story*, Rituparno received innumerable messages applauding his performance, but many others spewed venom. One phone text read: "You are perverted. You deserve to die." But the fire that burnt him also fashioned him into a fierce fighter. Like a phoenix, he rose from the ashes each time with greater determination and with his life and work conveyed the significance of my favourite line from *Chitrangada*: "*Jaar jeta shobhaab, shetai to shabhabik*"

(Whatever comes naturally to someone is what is natural; or, Whatever comes normally to someone is what is normal).

"Nyakaa": The Excessively and Undesirably Feminine

The descriptor most commonly used by Rituparno's detractors is *nyakaa* (pronounced nayh-kuh), a common and uniquely Bengali expression to describe someone who exudes an air of excessive and performative affectation. *Nyakaa* is a pejorative and derisive term directed at women and feminine men. In the case of feminine men or boys, the idea of excess does not apply, because to merely be feminine is often enough to earn for them to qualify as *nyakaa*. When Rituparno started going to school, the word was routinely hurled at him. As he grew older, he began to retort, "I am not *nyakaa*, I am feminine. Don't you know the difference between the two?" (R. Ghosh 2012). He devoted an entire issue of *Robbar* to discussing the *nyakaa*. The perception of the *nyakaa*, he wrote, is of a person who, even in ordinary circumstances takes recourse to excess – is excessively shy, gets excessively angry, and is generally excessively sensitive. He unpacked the term to show how popular usage had severed the word from its etymological roots in the word *nek* (honest, upright.) and turned it into a term of disapproval for certain behavioural excesses and affectations of which being feminine (*meyeli*) was one.

The idea of excessive femininity is somewhat unattractive if not abhorrent to many Bengali women trying to shed the baggage of gender conformity. Aparna Sen, for instance, is mystified that Rituparno and I have liked so many of her popular films because she feels that a large number of the characters she played were *nyakaa* and had nothing to do with how she saw herself as a woman. Ironically, many of the actresses who played the *nyakaa* heroine on screen were in their real lives nothing like their screen counterparts. For the modern Bengali woman, excessive femininity verging on the *nyakaa* was baggage to be permanently discarded. The powerful women characters in Rituparno's films, played by a range of talented actresses, rarely strayed into the terrain of the excessive, even when the narrative unfolded through a melodramatic mode. The aspirations of the modern Bengali woman, which included a desire to jettison from her personality the mannerisms of the *nyakaa*, found rich and varied expression in Rituparno's films. But for Rituparno, the derided excess of femininity had an unstated appeal. In the films in which he appears as a queer protagonist, he frequently retrieves and reinscribes on his body this discarded and much disapproved performance of feminine excess. Passages in the queer tetralogy bear witness to this, but perhaps most notable is *Jeevan Smriti* (2013), his documentary on Rabindranath Tagore.[12]

Tagore was a powerful and persistent presence in Rituparno's life.[13] He says, "If Satyajit Ray taught me to be disciplined, then it was Tagore who taught me non-normativity" (S. Ghosh 2013a). Rituparno inherited Tagore's love for the *Vaishnav Padabali* (Vaishnava Collection of Songs), inspired by which, at the age of sixteen, Tagore had written *Bhanushingho Thakurer Padabali* (Songs of Bhanushingho), adopting a feminine voice to explore the yearning of Radha for her lover Krishna.[14] Rituparno also admired Tagore's fearlessness in writing *Nashtanirh* (The Broken Nest), about a married woman's romantic involvement with her brother-in-law. Rituparno believed that, in writing the novella, Tagore confirmed the rumours about his relationship with his sister-in-law, Kadambari Devi (S. Ghosh 2013a). Satyajit Ray's most acclaimed film, *Charulata* (1964), was adapted from this novella. During the research for his documentary on Tagore, Ray had come across the original manuscript of *Nashtanirh* and noticed that Tagore's marginal notations linked the name of Kadambari to that of Charu, the novel's central character (Seton 1971).

Rituparno's cinematic engagement with Tagore extends beyond the films that were adapted from his works – namely, *Chokher Bali*, *Noukadubi* (The Boatwreck, 2010), and *Chitrangada*. Writing about the painful consequences of choosing to live a life that defied social conventions, Rituparno declared, "But I am very lucky that one immortal never abandoned me, my Rabindranath." This experience finds expression in the predicament of the female protagonist of Rituparno's *Ashookh* (The Ailment, 1999). In *Ashookh*, Tagore's poetry opens the doors to the subjectivity of the female protagonist. When she is abandoned by her lover, it is Tagore, whose giant portrait hangs over her bed, who consoles her: "He was her sole companion; almost a surrogate lover."[15] The photograph, Rituparno points out, is of the young man, not that of the older Tagore found in almost all Bengali households. "Bengalis treat Tagore with a lot of reverence," he once said, "but for me he is too close for only reverence." Over the years, he found himself increasingly drawn to the young Rabindranath.

When Rituparno was commissioned to make a documentary on Tagore, he settled on a treatment markedly distinct from that of Ray's 1961 documentary. Ray's film was detailed and rich but disinterested in approach. Arriving fifty years later, Rituparno's portrait is a personal one. In an interview on his relationship with Tagore, Rituparno says, "I could have made a competent, smart, and intelligent film on Tagore that people would receive well. But I thought that, in this lifetime, I would get only one chance to make a film on Tagore. In that case, is it enough to just make a smart and intelligent film? As for what I have made, I am not sure that it will count as a work with high artistic merit, but it is certainly one that is close to my heart" (Bandyopadhyay and Ghosh 2016).

Jeevan Smriti journeys across several significant moments in Tagore's life through fictional recreations accompanied by voice-overs delivered by multiple narrators, suggesting perhaps the impossibility of arriving at a singular or definitive vision of the poet's life. Rituparno's everyday intimacy with Tagore is cinematically woven into the texture of *Jeevan Smriti*, where the filmmaker and his subject meet across multiple spatial and temporal thresholds. Rituparno's "chance encounters" with Tagore at different stages of his life become the most audacious cinematic trope used in the film. The fictional Tagore, played by four different actors, is haunted by the visitations of the filmmaker. This idea plays out in several sequences but most notably in one sequence in which Rituparno and his crew enter the palatial ancestral home of the Tagores in Jorasanko, Calcutta, triggering a series of chance encounters.

The camera is placed on one end of a spacious veranda in the expansive colonial-style home of the Tagores. The side of the balcony that leads into the inner rooms is lined with tall shuttered wooden doors. At the opposite end from the camera, looking directly at the viewer, is a large portrait of Rabindranath Tagore. The sun shining through the thin wooden blinds have cast a pattern on the floor. The sound designer leans across the railing, perhaps to record live sound. A tramcar noisily trundles past. Rituparno enters the frame with a crew member, who draws his attention to the portrait of Tagore. Rituparno is dressed in a loose-fitting jacket worn over a pair of pants with a long scarf draped over his shoulders. He wears dark glasses and long silver earrings, with a messenger-bag slung over his right shoulder. Back on the veranda, it is hard to tell the visitors from the crew members. Rituparno peers into the camera of a still photographer.

The crowds begin to thin, and Rituparno is alone on the veranda. Music floods the soundtrack as he turns to face the door behind him. In a reverse shot, he can now be seen from inside the room, through the glass on the wooden door. He walks towards the door, comes close, and peers inside. Another reverse shot reveals a young dreamy boy – Rabindranath – sitting on a four-poster bed (fig. 8.2). A voice on the soundtrack says: "One cloudy afternoon, thrilled by the break occasioned by the darkening sky, I went into one of the inner rooms and stretched out on the bed with a slate in my hand. I wrote: '*Gahana kusuma kunj maajhe*' [Deep amidst the blossoming bower] … Having composed this line, I felt exhilarated."

Rituparno opens the door and stares at the boy, who is annoyed at the intrusion. As a smiling Rituparno steps into the room, the child takes his slate and

8.2 Encountering the young Rabindranath Tagore in *Jeevan Smriti*. Rituparno Ghosh, 2013.

turns to leave. The musical strains return, this time with voices singing the famous song from *Bhunushingho Thakur Padabali*: "*Gahana kusuma kunj maajhe…*"

> Deep amidst the blossoming bower,
> The sweet, soft strains of the flute do hover
> Leaving behind fear and shame, come,
> Come to me, my beloved …

As the words and music of the song fill the soundtrack, a large wooden door swings open and four pairs of feet cross the threshold to another room. Rituparno is accompanied by a sound-recording duo and another crew member. Rituparno has changed from his androgynous clothes to those markedly more feminine, His flowing purple and magenta robes and long black *dupatta* are worn with long earrings that touch his shoulders. His lipstick is dark and his eyes are lined with kohl. Unlike those of his accompanying crew members, his movements are languid, slow and deliberate. He smiles as he points out patterns of sun and shade on the floor. The camera holds his bare feet in close-up as they move in dance steps across the sunlit patterns. As he moves closer to the window, the light streaming through the slanted blinds falls on his face. The camera lingers on his close-up as he looks out of the window. He sees Rabindranath, now a handsome young man, sitting cross-legged on the floor of the veranda, writing on a wooden desk, smiling, lost in another world. Gazing at Rabindranath, Rituparno also smiles. The sequence keeps returning to close-ups of an enchanted Rituparno who looks as though he has sighted his much-awaited lover.

This lyrical and intense cinematic encounter is created through a clever use of shot-reverse-shots and eye-line matches. Distinct from the casual disposition of the other crew members, Rituparno's deliberate and choreographed movements – the gaze, the walk, the smile, the gestures – enact a femininity that through its excess embodies the quest and deportment of the *abhisharika* – the desiring heroine who goes in search of her lover.[16]

I earlier stated that Rituparno's actresses were never burdened with performing an excessive femininity, but *Jeevan Smriti* marks a departure.[17] Take, for instance, the following sequence. Young Rabindranath (Samadarshi Dutta) has returned from England without a law degree to meet with a cold reception from his father. The voice-over narration states, "Rabi had brought immense treasures home, which no one appreciated except for Kadambari, his sister-in-law." The line segues into a sequence in which young Rabindranath sings one of his new compositions to Kadambari (Raima Sen) on the sprawling terrace of the Jorasanko house. Rabindranath reclines on the floor while Kadambari, seated across from him, gazes at him lovingly. She looks happy and radiant in his company. Over the sound track, the young Rabindranath's song alternates with the narrator's voice that states, "They find their soul mates in each other. She is his muse. And yet he names her Hecate, after one of the witches in Macbeth, whose spell he could never escape." The visual sequence is driven by long, lingering close-ups of Kadambari who, while glancing coquettishly at her beloved Rabi, performs a series of languid movements choreographed around several everyday household objects. In this short sequence, Sen embodies a performative excess rarely seen in Rituparno's female protagonists.

A sequence from the short film *The Making of Jeevan Smriti*[18] shows that the excess has travelled from the body of the filmmaker to that of the actress. Rituparno, wearing lipstick, eye makeup, long earrings, and a colourful turban, enacts the entire ensemble of gestures and glances for Raima Sen. In the next sequence she reproduces his performance with absolute precision, while his voice – strong and authoritative – keeps directing her movements. Here, the performance of feminine excess travels affectively from the body of the director Rituparno to that of the actress. Through a relay of affects, Rituparno becomes, as it were, the surrogate lover of the young Rabindranath.

The Energetic Underlife of Failure

Rituparno's queer enactments have often been read too literally as biographical confessions. In public, Rituparno shared little about his experiments with the body, so its elaborate public self-presentation became the subject of multiple spec-

8.3 Ritu and the author (*left*). Courtesy Shohini Ghosh.

ulations. *Chitrangada* in particular is often read as an autobiographical film about Rituparno's experience of undergoing sexual reassignment surgery. While none of the queer characters Rituparno played were autobiographical, many of the situations that they find themselves in emerged from his own experiences. More importantly, perhaps, they were sculpted from a plenitude of desires. The amorphous terrain of desire may elide words; therefore confessions may not always take the form of verbal admissions about the self. Rituparno's cinematic confessions lie within the folds of affective enactments – to be felt, to be sensed. In *Jeevan Smriti*, the persona of Rituparno is fashioned from forbidden, even unspeakable desires of embodying a discarded and derided femininity of excess that becomes the affective conduit through which he presents himself as an object of desire to *his* object of desire – the young Rabindranath Tagore.

In this chapter, I have confessed to what was a point of tension between Rituparno and me arising from our different aspirations around enactments of femininity (fig. 8.3). He was interested in performances of femininity, I in a reworking of it. He was interested in excess, I in restraint. As someone who saw his first cuts, I tended to try to limit what I saw as performative and emotional excess, but very often I would fail, as in the case of *Jeevan Smriti*. This to me was a productive failure, because it now compels me to re-engage with femininities of excess.

In a manner of speaking, *Jeevan Smriti* also failed – to capture popular imagination. Rituparno's performative self-representation in the film confounded many. If the criticism of *Jeevan Smriti* was muted, it was because his untimely passing was still being mourned. That the film will have a vibrant social life in the future I have no doubt, but at the moment we have to see this enterprise in the light of Judith Jack Halberstam's theorizing of failure as a queer art (Halberstam 2013). For Halberstam, failure can be a performance of dissent and refusal, and so we are invited to discover its energetic underlife. Rituparno's determined transgression in exploring less popular performances of femininities is redolent with possibilities. Through the elaborate choreography of movement and gesture, what remains is the lasting image of Rituparno himself. We gaze at Rituparno … male, female, trans become immaterial.

NOTES

1 *Jeevan Smriti* (Selective Memories, 2013) and *Satyanweshi* (The Truth-Seeker, 2013) were the last films Rituparno made. *Satyanweshi* was completed by Rituparno's cast and crew members (*Outlook*, 9 September 2013, 58–9). *Jeevan Smriti/Selective Memories* was commissioned by the Ministry of Culture to celebrate the 150th anniversary of Tagore's birth.

2 For a wide-ranging discussion of Rituparno's work, see Datta, Bakshi, and Dasgupta 2016.

3 The title, with a subtle shift, reconciles two meanings. In the opening credits, the title first appears as two words: "*Ushnotar Jonno*," literally, "for warmth's sake," or "for intimacy's sake." The title then splits into three words, "*Ushno Taar Jonno*," with an emphasis on *Taar*," which refers to a gender-neutral third person. The shift allows for a twin reading. The first meaning privileges desire over the person desired, while the second reading reverses the emphasis.

4 Chapal Bhaduri is one of Bengal's most celebrated female impersonators who spent a lifetime playing the roles of women and goddesses in Jatra. It is said that Bhaduri (who adopted the stage name of Chapal Rani, or Chapal Queen) was so compelling that even the Bengali matinee idol Uttam Kumar insisted on meeting this charismatic actress after a performance. He was surprised, it is said, to discover that Chapal Bhaduri was a man. This incident may well be part folklore, but it points nevertheless to the kind of stardom that Chapal Rani enjoyed.

5 The two decades during which Rituparno made his films witnessed sweeping transformations in the mediascape. The 1990s and 2000s saw the liberalization of the economy, a

dismantling of state-run media, rapid proliferation of satellite TV channels, and an expansion in IT infrastructures. The decade also witnessed a robust public debate on issues of sexuality amidst moral panics and calls for censorship. The theatrical release of Deepa Mehta's film *Fire* in 1998 triggered a nation-wide public debate on homosexuality. The 2000s were significant for the "coming out" of queer sexuality, with LGBTQ activism gaining visibility over demands to decriminalize homosexuality. By the middle of the first decade of the new millennium, the silence around queer sexuality had been decisively broken. There were queer groups, writers, activists, academics, filmmakers, and an increasing number of spaces where friendship, solidarity, and political engagement were being nurtured. On 2 July 2009, the Delhi High Court decriminalized non-heterosexual sex among consenting adults. The scripting and shooting of *Just Another Love Story* coincided with this landmark judgment, which was later overturned but then restored in 2018.

6   For a detailed discussion of how he changed his appearance, see my interview with Rituparno in *Marie Claire* (S. Ghosh 2012a).

7   The funding proposal was written in response to a call put out by a prominent LGBT organization in New York. The proposal was shortlisted but rejected after much debate because the primary protagonist, Aparna Sen, was not a lesbian! This is a perfect example of a global North inability to understand queerness not through identity but desire.

8   While professions and occupation are often gendered in Bengali as in *nayak* (hero or actor) and *nayika* (heroine or actress), the third person pronoun is not gendered. For instance, the word *shey* (which in English would be either "he" or "she") is gender neutral and could therefore refer to a person of any gender. This has worked to the advantage of erotic ambiguity as in the title *Ushno Taar Jonno*.

9   In Hindu mythology, the Ardhanareshwar is an androgynous half-man/half-woman image of the god Shiva and his consort Parvati.

10 *Borno Porichoy* (An Introduction to Alphabets) is a popular Bengali primer written by Ishwarchandra Vidyasagar, a famous scholar and social reformer.

11 Rituparno said he most identified with the character of Binodini (played by Aishwarya Rai) in *Chokher Bali* "because she stands on the threshold of transformation. Binodini becomes a widow when widow remarriage has been legislated by the British but has yet to find social acceptance. There is a tragic isolation in being caught in the half-light of legitimacy. I feel a strong sense of identification with that" (S. Ghosh 2012a).

12 Speaking about his approach to *Jeevan Smriti*, Rituparno says, "I never had the discipline to do documentaries. I am basically a storyteller and while making this documentary I felt that I didn't have to shift from that point … There were [several] authorities on Rabindranath and I didn't feel I needed to add any new information on him. When I am connecting with Rabindranath, it is on a personal level. The interesting thing is that for Satyajit Ray, Rabindranath was memory. Ray had interacted with Rabindranath. But for

me, Rabindranath is history. His contemporaneity with Rabindranath was also an obstacle for Ray. That is why his documentary feels objective to me … as if he forcibly detached himself from Rabindranath." See Sengupta 2012.

13 Rabindranath Tagore (1861–1941) is a towering literary figure in Bengal. Born on 7 May 1861 in the Jorasanko mansion in Calcutta, Rabindranath had little formal education. The Tagore family was at the forefront of the Bengali Renaissance, and Rabindranath became its most illustrious member. A prolific writer from childhood, he wrote novels, short stories, essays, memoirs, and poetry and composed two thousand songs known as Rabindrasangeet, or "Songs of Tagore," which include the national anthems of India and Bangladesh. In 1913 he was awarded the Nobel prize for literature for his collection of poems, *Gitanjali*. At sixty, he took to drawing and painting, exhibiting across the world. In 1915, he was given a knighthood by the British, which he renounced after the notorious Jallianwala Bagh massacre in 1919.

14 The *Vaishnava Padavali* (Vaishnava Collection of Songs) emerged from a movement in medieval Bengal that opposed the tyranny of upper-caste practices. Accompanied by an efflorescence of songs and poetry, a recurring theme in the Vaishnava literature is the legendary love of the Hindu mythological figures Radha and Krishna. In several versions, Radha is depicted as a married woman who is older than Krishna and also related to him. The term *padavali* literally means "gathering of songs." Going against the classical language of Sanskrit, the Vaishnava songs and poetry were composed in local languages or derivatives of literary languages like Brajabuli, used by Vidyapati in the fourteenth century. Inspired by the *Vaishnava Padavali*, Rabindranath at the age of sixteen wrote *Bhanushingho Thakurer Padabali* (Padavali of Bhanushingho), a collection of Vaishnava lyrics first anthologized in 1884. Rabindranath had assumed the pseudonym Bhanushingho – the "Sun Lion."

15 Looking back, I feel that I stopped Rituparno from elaborating on the idea of Tagore as an imagined, surrogate lover and pushed him to say that he was more like a friend.

16 In the *Natya Shastra* (the classical Sanskrit treatise for the performing arts), the *abhisarika* is one of eight heroines (*Ashta-Nayika*) who are classified according to their relationship to their lovers. The *abhisarika* is the one who daringly leaves the boundaries of the home desiring union with her lover. In traditional poetry, Radha is the romantic *abhisarika* who, in order to meet Krishna, overcomes obstacles like storms, snakes, and the dangers of the deep woods. For an elaboration on the leitmotif of the *abhisharika* in Rituparno's films, see the introduction and "Invoking Love, Death and an Elsewhere" in Datta, Bakshi, and Dasgupta 2016.

17 Since what is excessive is also in the realm of the subjective, there are bound to be disagreements with my observation.

18 https://www.youtube.com/watch?v=sqA_7Qs1Mmo.

REFERENCES

Bandyopadhyay, Ranjan, and Rituparno Ghosh. 2016. "*Aamar Rabindranath.*" Milton Music. https://www.youtube.com/watch?v=8Lf5pzcBK8w.

Biswas, Kaushik. 2009. "Rituparno Ghosh and Mir, Part 4." https://www.youtube.com/watch?v=iTd7LcTiIo8.

Datta, Sangeeta, Kaustav Bakshi, and Rohit K. Dasgupta. 2016. *Rituparno Ghosh: Cinema, Gender and Art*. New Delhi: Routledge.

Ghosh, Rituparno. 2012. "First Person: Nyaka." *Robbar*, 5 May. Kolkata: Sambad Pratidin.

Ghosh, Shohini. 2005. Film proposal. In the possession of the author.

— 2012a. "I Get Respect Even When I Am the Target of Homophobia." *Marie Claire*, December 2012.

— 2012b. "Forbidden Love and Passionate Denials: A Dialogue on Domesticities and Queer Intimacy." In *Handbook of Gender*, edited by Raka Ray, 429–40. New Delhi: Oxford University Press.

— 2013a. *In Conversation with Rituparno Ghosh*, Part 1. AJK Mass Communication Research Centre, Jamia Millia Islamia.

— 2013b. *Prothoma*, 15 July 2013: 85–87.

Halberstam, Jack (Judith). 2011. *The Queer Art of Failure*. Durham: Duke University Press.

Sen, Aveek. 2007. "Preludes." In *The Phobic and the Erotic*, edited by Brinda Bose and Subhabrata Bhattacharyya, 1–16. Calcutta: Seagull Publishers.

Sengupta, Reshmi. 2012. "Rituparno's Rabindranath." *Telegraph India*, 24 July. https://www.telegraphindia.com/1120724/jsp/entertainment/story_15762862.jsp

Seton, Marie. 1971. *Portrait of a Director: Satyajit Ray*. New Delhi: Vikas Publishing.

9

The Videomaker and the Rent Boy: Gay-for-Pay Confessional in 101 Rent Boys *and* Broke Straight Boys TV

NICHOLAS DE VILLIERS

> Gay men and straight men do not live in separate worlds, but instead witness, perform, and even sometimes inhabit what is ostensibly one another's relationship to homosexuality.
> • Jane Ward (2015)

> I gave him some money, he promised to be at the rendezvous an hour later, and of course never showed. I asked myself if I was really so mistaken (the received wisdom about giving money to a hustler in advance!), and concluded that since I really didn't want him all that much (nor even to make love), the result was the same: sex or no sex, at eight o'clock I would find myself back at the same point in my life; and since mere eye contact and an exchange of words eroticizes me, it was that pleasure I paid for.
> • Roland Barthes ([1979] 1992)

In "The Ethics of Intervention: Dennis O'Rourke's *The Good Woman of Bangkok*," Linda Williams explains how the making of O'Rourke's documentary explicitly hinges on the procurement of its Thai sex worker subject. This crucial "interaction with a prostitute in her capacity *as prostitute*" raises a range of complex ethical issues that "go to the heart of questions about the contemporary documentary's intervention in the realities it films" (Williams 1999, 180; Williams's italics). In the film, the Thai sex worker Aoi understands and critiques the bargain of O'Rourke's interventionist filmmaking (his attempt to "save" her from "the life"). In the intimate hotel-room interviews, "the film consists of a man buying some aspect of her behavior. As in the relation of prostitution, the power inequity between client and whore remains the same," but Aoi "criticizes the arrogance of the participant-observationist" who flatters himself that he can save her (Williams 1999, 182). Williams compares this situation with the feminist "saving" of the stripper and porn model Linda Lee Tracy in Bonnie Klein's 1982 *Not a Love Story*, arguing that Klein's film is in fact "less honest and less ethical" than O'Rourke's: "Whereas O'Rourke's purchase of his subject is made overt in his ongoing negotiation with her, Klein's purchase of Tracy is covert" (185).

In this essay, I follow Williams's suggestion that there can be no pure ethical relation in documentary filmmaking and consider the uneasy complicity established between the videomaker and the "rent boy" in two contemporary reality-television-style documentaries where differences of sexual identity, class, and sometimes race are made explicit. The documentary *101 Rent Boys* (dirs. Fenton Bailey and Randy Barbato, 2000) and the reality television program *Broke Straight Boys TV* (dir. Mark Erickson and Damian McKnight, 2015) promise revealing behind-the-scenes views of male sex workers (hustlers and porn actors), many who identify as "straight" but "gay-for-pay." I develop an ongoing conversation in porn studies and queer theory about the meanings of "gay for pay." By analyzing the shifting and blurring genre boundaries between documentary, reality television, and pornography, I argue that the intimate motel room interviews and reality television techniques in these examples create a hybrid mode of *confession porn* or *gay-for-pay confessional*. These specific case studies build on those in my book *Sexography: Sex Work in Documentary* (de Villiers 2017), but here I am interested in the fact that a porn studio has "branched out" into producing reality television, and what the formats may have in common.

I advance a theory of confessional and counter-confessional performance for the camera by the interviewed subject, who must negotiate both loaded questions and stigma. I argue that contemporary filmmakers and videomakers modulate and extend (rather than breaking with) a long tradition in sexology of scrutinizing the psychology and sexual orientations of male sex workers rather than their material conditions of existence – even while financial motivations are foregrounded within these specific examples (Kaye 2003). I advocate shifting our approach from scrutinizing the motives of those who sell sex (or have "gay-for-pay" sex on camera) to scrutinizing the ethics and motives of the filmmakers and the "knowingness" and fascination of their mostly gay male audiences.

101 Rent Boys

In a technique parallel to O'Rourke's use of intertitles to explain the cinematic situation and contract in *The Good Woman of Bangkok*, Fenton Bailey and Randy Barbato open their made-for-television (World of Wonder/Cinemax) documentary *101 Rent Boys* (fig. 9.1) with an explanatory note: "We like to think of ourselves as normal people, a world apart from your everyday street hustler ... We think about money, love and sex. We worry about our families, our bodies, our jobs. We dream of the future. So do they." Their words underscore a classic problem in attempts to "humanize" sex workers: invoking an us/them difference, the filmmakers suggest that they did not originally think of hustlers as normal people with dreams and worries like their own (or like those of their non-sex-worker audience subsumed in that "we"). They then explain the contract of the interviews: "Over the course of a year, we interviewed 101 male escorts from Los Angeles ... and we paid them each $50 for their time." This statement sets the stage for the performative nature of confessional interviews for cash, and we see snippets of the interviewees commenting on this situation: "Instead of having sex, just here exposing myself on television. I don't know which is worse ... oh well"; "You're gonna pay me *on camera?*"; "Why are you recording that?"; "It's so demeaning"; "Another day at the office"; "$50 doesn't get my pants off." (Here the subjects are analyzing and potentially shaming the filmmakers explicitly about the ethics of the transaction.)

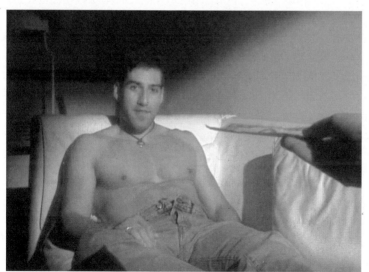

9.1
A rent boy confesses to the viewer and is paid on camera. DVD still from *101 Rent Boys*, dir. Randy Barbato and Fenton Bailey, 2000.

Bailey and Barbato's film makes use of several cinéma vérité conventions that highlight the physical relationship between the video crew and the interviewee in front of the camera. One man asks, "Just look straight that way?" and in another scene, an off-camera hand wipes sweat off an interviewee's brow. Jonathan Kahana argues that in the American tradition (for example, in *Primary*), "The signature moment of the *cinéma vérité* image was and is the close-up or zoom-in to a telltale expressive feature, the twitch or fidget that betrays the subject's discomfort, by which the viewer's gaze is trained on the everyday psychopathology of the camera's subjects" (Kahana 2008, 291). Kahana notes that this search for telltale expressivity and intimacy was well suited to American television and anticipated "reality television." In *101 Rent Boys*, editor William Grayburn often highlights pauses in the interviewees' testimony, encouraging the audience to interpret them as pregnant pauses signalling shame or stigma. The filmmakers also create the documentary equivalent of psychological voice-over by dubbing interview dialogue over images of the subjects' nervous facial expressions and crying. This editing style is in tension with the moments of MTV-style rhythmic editing with close-ups of body parts, tattoos, and faces, accelerated footage of cars on Santa Monica Boulevard, and the soulful dance music refrains of "Land of the Living" (*Lisa Marie Experience*, 1996 vinyl).

The mise-en-scène of the interviews is mostly bare-bulb, unflattering lighting in motel rooms, with an almost camp "urban pastoral" American motel aesthetic (Sontag 1966, 279). Shots of interviewees are punctuated with close-ups of tacky décor, lamps, neon, and empty beds (approaching Gilles Deleuze's cinematic *espace quelconque*, "any-space-whatever" [Deleuze [1983] 1996, 109–11]). For the interviewed subjects, the motel room is precisely "another day at the office" in the "business doing pleasure with you," but for the filmmakers it becomes a makeshift confessional booth. We are often reminded of how awkward the situation is: the interviewees frequently call attention to their body microphones and the fact that the sound recordist is a woman, Janet Urban, implying a rather old-fashioned idea of speaking differently in mixed company versus the homosocial code of men only, speaking freely about sex together.

Sometimes the subjects appear grateful for the opportunity for remunerated conversation with "people who take the time to know you instead of just wanting a piece of meat." This sentiment apparently flatters us, the sympathetic audience, as well as the curious filmmakers. The voices behind the camera are stereotypically recognizable as "gay voices" (this production is by the same people who brought us *The Eyes of Tammy Faye* [2000b], narrated by RuPaul), which acts as a reminder of the specific *positionality* of the investigators.

We hear upsetting testimony about personal relationships – including loss of lovers due to AIDS or drug addiction, negatively affecting the interviewees' ability to put on a happy face for clients. These accounts underscore the reality that sex work is a form of affective labour. During these emotional moments, we hear the filmmakers ask, "Are you gonna be okay?" "Do you ever think you're in the wrong business?" But the filmmakers sometimes choose this moment to hand over the cash, potentially demanding *a performance of degradation*. (Arguably, the hustler "sob story" is itself a form of affective labour, even though some clients, like Barthes in "Soirées de Paris," complain about it.)

The filmmakers use intertitles to organize the pseudonymous and numbered testimonial interviews (interviewees hold up a piece of paper with a number and are also given t-shirts with their number) around particular topics, presumably drawn from a standard questionnaire: Losing it; The First Trick; Gay; Acting the Part [i.e., cowboy]; Straight; Sex; Best Assets; Love; Turn-Ons; Turn-Offs; Homeless; Mom and Dad; Watersports; Pain; Weird Shit; Drugs; Dreams; The Future; Prejudice and Pride; Alone (3 Minutes). The interviewees give a wide range of responses to these prompts, especially with regard to their own sexual identity/orientation: "gay to me is: are you happy?"; "I don't know if you'd call me gay; I like queens"; "most hustlers I think are straight"; "I'm not homosexual, not bisexual, even heterosexual ... Let's just put it this way: I am sexual"; "Buy-sexual: they buy, you're sexual." The parts they play are also distinguished in terms of class, ethnic, and racial fetishes (cowboy, rough trade, black hetero stud, etc.). Cirus Rinaldi has noted how the position of some hustlers lower in a hierarchical system serves to maintain a market of what he terms "*lumpen-erotic racial(ized) services*" (Rinaldi 2013a, 2013b). Through this concept, he refers to the "consumption" of male sex work as a form of production of classed, sexualized, and racialized bodies and subjectivities. Part of this class hierarchy is reflected in the condescending attitude of the filmmakers toward their subjects. When asked what he wants to be when he grows up, a gruff cowboy is insulted and says, "What you're telling me is you don't really think I'm a grownup." This is yet another patronizing moment that lays bare the tension of this relationship.

For a historical antecedent to the filmmakers' questionnaire, we can juxtapose it with the schedule of questions and responses gathered in the study *Male Prostitution* (1993) by criminologist Donald J. West with Buz de Villiers, featuring several hundred "intimate" interviews with street-based workers conducted at a London drop-in youth centre called Streetwise starting in 1988, with comparisons to off-street workers including self-employed masseurs and agency workers. The dust jacket invites us to discover "little known details" of the trade and its workers, including "sexual orientation; the drift into homelessness; entry into prostitution; fees and charges and transactions that turn sour; threats of blackmail, violence, and murder; prostitutes as lovers; models and escort services; legal and criminology issues; unusual, rare, and interesting client requests; personal fears, desires, and interests of male prostitutes" (West 1993). West emphasizes constraints in interviewees' responses to questions about sexual orientation, sexual behaviour, sexual feelings, and social identities (as well as questions of who is in control: the rent-boy or the "punter"). Sometimes he openly expresses scepticism of the accuracy of their testimony, especially those identifying as straight but gay-for-pay, viewing their statements as constrained by homophobia and the scripts of normative masculinity, aka machismo (1993, 22–6; 32).

Middle-class sexologists and later gay liberation writers have shown a particular preoccupation with the sexual orientation, sexual identity, and sexual practices of the male hustler, and this subject continues to preoccupy filmmakers making documentaries about male sex workers (Kaye 2003, 47). West is aware of certain ethical problems in his gathering of interview material – does paying the interviewees a small inducement (£10) encourage a form of prostitution or lying, or are his probing questions upsetting – that might cast doubt on the researchers' motives (West 1993, 4–5). He rationalizes away the fact that a few of the young men "had to be interviewed wearing dressing gowns" as the result of "their only set of clothes ... being washed in the Centre's machine" (5). There is some unacknowledged irony in the demand for "stripped bare" frankness in interviews while the subjects are practically stripped bare.

These very same ironies and ethical problems are foregrounded in Bailey and Barbato's *101 Rent Boys*, but the male sex workers here more pointedly provide the sceptical critique of the interview situation and the (male) whore stigma. In the "Prejudice and Pride" segment, they address common misconceptions: that hustlers are all the same, jaded, dirty, immoral, unworthy of love, trash, and that they should feel humiliated or degraded. One observes that people look down on them "because they would be ashamed if they did what I did. I don't choose to be ashamed. Does that make sense?" Interviewee Tony Valenzuela explains that he moved to LA to pursue a career as a writer, but people assume escorts have no intellect. He argues that the "biggest lie and myth about this work" is in the hypocritical prejudice of people who don't realize the "hundreds of other ways they prostitute themselves. They [just] don't unzip their pants or whatever." Another remarks, "You want humiliating and degrading? Be a cater waiter." (For a critique of the use of prostitution as a metonym for the critique of capitalism, see the interview with Melissa Gira Grant in Gerrard 2014.) Valenzuela's "older gentlemen" clients "presume that I have some kind of a broken background and that I need to be saved, saved from this horrible lifestyle of being a call boy, which is also ironic to me that they call call boys all the time, yet don't have any respect for those of us who are making a living as an escort. I come off as not needing to be saved and they don't like that." (Recall Aoi's message to O'Rourke in *The Good Woman of Bangkok* when he tries to get her to agree to leave the sex industry if he buys her a rice farm.)

At the end of *101 Rent Boys*, the interviewed subjects are given three minutes alone with the camera running, approximating Andy Warhol's practice of walking away from the camera in his Screen Tests, or the camera "confessional" of MTV's *The Real World* (1992–present). The subjects comment on how preposterous they find the documentary itself: "What the fuck, tell you my personal shit?" "You got me looking naked, stupid, on this TV show? I want some more money." They highlight the way the filmmakers have underpaid them for the verbal and bodily confessions they have performed for the camera. Their public confessional performance is a mediatized version of what Michel Foucault and Judith Butler term "exomologesis": penitent self-verbalization for another (Foucault [1982] 1997, 249; Butler 2003, 113).

I turn now from the made-for-television documentary that still retains elements of cinéma vérité to "porn reality television," which is more knowingly artificial (where the self-conscious staging of confession is part of the "brand"). The power imbalance in my second example is explicitly part of the deal and is framed as such (rather than something the critic must expose).

Broke Straight Boys TV

The confessional-booth reality television conventions of *The Real World* are particularly prominent in *Broke Straight Boys TV* at first available via paid subscription to the LGBT narrowcasting Here TV YouTube channel (fig. 9.2) but now available for free at http://www.brokestraightboys.tv. The series promises an "uncensored look at the personal lives of people who make porn" – specifically, gay-for-pay porn stars working for the studio Broke Straight Boys. We are told, "Every straight guy has a price," but the show asks, "At what cost?" Episode titles like "The Revolving Door" highlight the fact that their porn careers are fleeting.

The series is essentially an extended "behind the scenes" infomercial for Blu-Media Corp, featuring the mansion of CEO Mark Erickson in Colorado where the reality series is filmed (with a porn studio nearby). The mansion operates like a

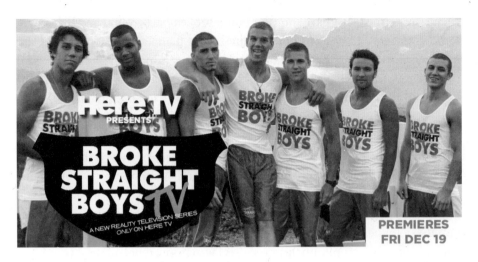

9.2 Advertising *Broke Straight Boys* on Here TV, Twitter post, 2 December 2014.

"frat house" complete with a "house mother" (Sabrina Erickson) and "house rules" that insist that the performers can't have sex with anyone off camera – a kind of Spartan save-it-for-the-battlefield mentality that the performers liken to the army or prison – institutions with which they are often familiar.

The reality-television format of the series resembles *The Real World* but also *The Jersey Shore*, *Big Brother*, *Survivor*, and *Top Model*: dorm-like cohabitation (under the stress of both work and company-sponsored hedonism), competition for attention and resources, disciplinary panopticism and biopolitical management (including blood tests for STDs), and the confessional-booth "aside" (now ubiquitous in mockumentary television like *The Office*). One of the stars, Kaden Alexander, mostly parodies the "porn-star confessional" format, but there are a number of close-up interviews with a red curtain backdrop that suggest the enduring appeal of what I call "confession porn," marked by prurience and the performance of authenticity, transgression, and disgust (Hester 2014).

Gay-for-pay porn stars and other sex workers are frequently suspected of lying when they insist that they are straight and just have sex with men for money, echoing the history of suspicion and duplicity surrounding homosexuality and "the closet." Aware of this fact, the producers of the show frequently probe the young, mostly white, "jock" men about their orientations and their motivations for doing "gay" porn. Simply put, the money is much better than what they can earn acting in heterosexual porn, and they typically use the money to support their families or pay off court fees (even this latter aspect is part of the cross-class mystique of rough trade).

What we see on display throughout the series is the paradoxical *epistemology of the straight but gay-for-pay closet*. In one episode, we travel with Paul Canon to visit his family to get their reaction to his profession. (His brother insists that he defends him to his friends as not gay, but later we learn that Paul is perhaps bisexual as he is having a secret affair with one of the other *Broke Straight Boys* performers, Damien Kyle.) Jimmy Johnson's girlfriend makes an uncomfortable visit to the house to remind him of his obligation to his children and to reprimand him for his alleged infidelity and not caring about his public reputation. Sergio Valen is filmed talking to his girlfriend about her family's reaction to learning that he acts in gay-for-pay porn. We also see Kaden rejected by a potential girlfriend on a date when she learns what kind of porn he does.

BluMedia CEO Mark Erickson and *Broke Straight Boys* producer Damian McKnight explain in an interview with *The Daily Dot* how gay porn performers

> will question if the guys are really gay ... we've seen our gay performers hit on our straight performers, and it just doesn't happen for them. (*Laughs*). But the straight men actually are very supportive of the gay performers. A lot of the straight performers really look up to the gay men, because they understand the scrutiny and the homophobia they have to deal with. Once the family members find out, they undergo the same scrutiny and experience the same issues that gay men do when they're first coming out. (Dickson 2014)

The interviewer asks a follow-up question about how aware of the potential consequences of doing gay-for-pay porn the performers are before they are on camera, to which Erickson and McKnight respond, "We talk with each model in the casting process, and let them know this is one of the largest gay-for-pay sites out there. We tell them it's not a matter of if they find out, it's when they find out, but I don't think they're fully aware of what could happen beforehand. That's not to say they're stupid. A lot of these guys are really smart." They explain how they will support the models if they have problems with rejection by family members because "these models spend anywhere from a week to two weeks with us every month. We become very close to them. We try to foster a sense of family with them. It's a dysfunctional family, it's a family that has sex with each other. But it's a family nonetheless" (Dickson 2014).

This "family" model of business is reminiscent of *Madonna: Truth or Dare* (1991), in which the singer appropriates the language of drag-house mothers to explain her relationship to the mostly gay male dancers who are her employees on her Blond Ambition tour. In her commissioned "behind the scenes" documentary, Madonna compares intimate confessional discourse with a game of truth or dare, revealing how "truth is a token of exchange in a game of seduction" (Cvetkovich 1993, 164).

Along with the personalities and struggles of the performers, *Broke Straight Boys* illuminates the evolution of the internet porn business model (CTO Bryce Thomason addresses the problem of competing with piracy) and the fans' desire for behind-the-scenes photography, social media interaction, and opportunities to meet the *Broke Straight Boys* performers on tour at Gay Pride festivals across the country (as we learn from the COO Shannon Prewitt). The model approximates the "Star System": personality-driven, behind-the-scenes content that simultaneously reinforces and transgresses distinctions between public and private and boundaries between producers, performers, and audiences (and the nebulous labour of maintaining a "social media presence").

BluMedia Group also runs JustUsBoys.com, an online community featuring porn reviews and discussion boards, with a non-pornographic offshoot community forum site emptyclosets.com, designed for underage gay, bisexual, and questioning users. In their interview with the *Daily Dot*, Erickson and McKnight also discuss the appeal of gay-for-pay for gay male audiences (offering a typical developmental psychology model of "imprinting"):

> A lot of gay men's attraction to what they like develops at an earlier age. And a lot of those guys happen to be jocks, straight guys, football players, soccer players, this really masculine ideal for what we believe is beautiful. So with that, you start an attraction to straight men, because they're the guys who are unreachable … These are guys who live straight lives, and there's something about seeing guys reach outside of their comfort zones and their boundaries that is so hot. They're the guys you always wished you could get with. (Dickson 2014)

Browsing through the fan reviews and forums about *Broke Straight Boys*' actual porn content yields a wide range of consumer "motivations" for viewers of gay-for-pay porn (and sometimes a kind of Brechtian scepticism regarding "authentic" performance).

In his important study of the gay-for-pay porn phenomenon, Jeffrey Escoffier explains,

There is no irrefutable evidence establishing that these men are really straight or gay. However, all sexual conduct in the video porn industry is an example of situational sexuality inasmuch as the performers are often required to engage in sexual acts for monetary compensation that they would not otherwise choose to perform and with partners for whom they feel no desire. (2003, 531).

Escoffier highlights how "identitarian assumptions" often shape the production and reception of gay-for-pay porn, and how pornography has a remarkable "documentary effect" despite being highly choreographed and scripted (552). Such insights about situational (homo)sexuality do not, however, stop armchair sexologists from searching for evidence of the "real thing."

One of the evidentiary gimmicks used by *Broke Straight Boys* TV is bringing in a polygrapher to administer a lie-detector test to the performers, ostensibly asking them if they have broken any of the house rules, but this includes asking if they have had sex with men, including each other, off camera. The producers are remarkably credulous about the technology and the accuracy of the responses, using it to inform their decisions about who stays and who leaves the house and their employment. But they also make use of another fallible method, "gaydar," to screen new talent with video-chat interviews to discern which applicants are "really straight" or "actually gay." To work for the company, all performers must say they are straight, although some learn over the course of shooting that they enjoy sex with men.

Broke Straight Boys TV is quite illuminating regarding the choreography of sexual personas and sexual scripts used by the producers and performers. We even see motivational (or sarcastic) hand-written notes by the bed where porn scenes are filmed: "Cowboy up! It only hurts for a minute"; "The things I'll do for $ money $"; "Bromance WTF"; "Still not digging it"; "Why?☺"; "You have to try everything once." The overarching script, of course, is being a "broke straight boy."

The popularity of *Broke Straight Boys* on gay porn blogs and message boards and BluMedia's successful foray into television suggest that indeed many gay male producers and consumers enjoy seeing straight men perform financial need (broke-ness), submission to the dictates of the director, and non-identitarian homosexual sex on camera. Some consumers apparently invest in the "real" masculinity of the performers and their disidentification with gay identity. Footage of first-timers walking off the set early in the series plays to viewers' fascination with the performer's disgust, even when the director asks, "What if I give you a little money?" This is one of those moments when Williams's notion of *ethical impurity* in documentary is particularly relevant.

Warm-up interviews are a conventional framing device in gay-for-pay pornography, with the porn director generally unseen behind the camera, asking young men about their orientations, experience, and willingness to experiment with men on camera (Bozelka 2013). We can compare this convention to the documentary and reality-television interviews in *101 Rent Boys* and *Broke Straight Boys TV*. What is unique about the *Broke Straight Boys* brand of gay-for-pay porn is the staged negotiation of the financial contract on camera.

John Paul Stadler summarizes two main interpretations of the genre (or, perhaps, "mode"[1]) of gay-for-pay porn. The first is a *homophobic* interpretation that attempts to police boundaries between gay and straight, to disambiguate the ambiguous, and that decries "an eroticism of homophobic homoeroticism not because it is homophobic, but because it is not homophobic *enough*," insisting that the straight performer must actually be gay. The second is a queer *utopian* reading that doesn't do away with the identity categories of gay and straight but evokes a nostalgic gay fantasy of a time when lust for men did not cohere in a minority identity, thus pointing to the constructedness not just of homosexuality but also of heterosexuality (Stadler 2013). Each of these interpretations tellingly relies on the other:

> To rigidify, there must be ambiguity. To ambiguate, there must be rigidity … Just as gay-for-pay favors indeterminacy, so too gay male desire might reside not in one interpretation or the other, but in a conflicted joining of the two. Gay-for-pay provides a glimpse into not just the fantasy of gayness, but also that of straightness, bound as these identity formations are to one another and to the narratives and technologies we use to get off. (2013, n.p.)

The reciprocal effects of straight male and gay male understandings of each others' homosexual activities are further explored by Jane Ward in her timely book *Not Gay: Sex between Straight White Men* (Ward 2015). Ward is sceptical of overly exceptionalizing, accidental, "situational homosexuality" explanations of frequent, organized, and often-deliberate sexual behaviour between straight men, and incredulous toward arguments pointing to disgust and repulsion as proof that an activity is not sexual (Ward 2015; Singal 2015). While she mostly addresses non-commercial sexual encounters, her penultimate chapter discusses the pseudo-amateur fraternity hazing porn website *Haze Him*. Ward suggests that "the boys in

Haze Him, most likely gay or 'gay for pay' actors, know enough about the exceptionalizing logics that facilitate sex between straight men to be able to engage in believable not-gay sex on screen" (Ward 2015, 180–1).

Ward argues for a reading of the relationship between hetero-masculine and gay approaches to homosexuality that "recognizes that homophobic disidentification and dramatic displays of repulsion and endurance are what imbue homosexual activity with heterosexual meaning, and that these theatrics are up for grabs, so to speak – available not only to straight men but also to gay-identified men who may put them to erotic uses" (185–6). Ward also discusses the scripts that govern rare instances of interracial sex in *Haze Him* – which tend to highlight otherness rather than fraternal similarity. A related issue is raised in *Broke Straight Boys TV* when the one black performer, Kaden Alexander, and the black photographer Damian Christopher react to white performer Damien Kyle's insistence that he will not film a scene with a "coloured" performer. (The scene suggests that sexual racism is different from the other kinds of limits the performers place on what acts they will or won't perform with other men.) Ward justifies her emphasis on straight white men as a way of understanding their privileged sense of normality and the freedom this gives them to be heteroflexible in comparison to pathologizing accounts of black men on the "downlow." *Broke Straight Boys TV* differs from *101 Rent Boys* in this respect especially; the boys are chosen for precisely their alleged "normality" as (mostly) white straight men.

Rentboy Negotiations

What I find provocative about *101 Rent Boys* and *Broke Straight Boys TV* is the way they encourage us to think about the ethics of documentary intervention (like O'Rourke for Williams). They do so not by pretending to establish an equitable, brotherly, dialogic interview situation between the non-sex-worker filmmakers and their paid sex-worker subjects but by highlighting the power imbalance and force relations that inhere in the documentary situation (including differences of class, sexual identity, and race), and by foregrounding the possibility of interviewees resisting and mocking the probing confessional format.

The 2015 Department of Homeland Security raid on Rentboy.com shows that the authorities involved in the raid clearly believed they could shock readers of the report with (prurient) sexual details of the services offered to users of the male-escort platform while accusing Rentboy.com of operating an "online brothel." Several feminist sex-worker activists pointed out the double standard in the way that trafficking and victimhood were not invoked in the Rentboy.com case in the same way as is common in discussions of female sex workers. But they acknowledged how the coverage of the raid by mainstream gay publications like *The Advocate* showed that those involved in the raid misjudged the public climate of support for LGBT civil liberties and for the gay, bisexual, straight, trans and cisgender, etc. sex workers who used Rentboy.com to advertise their services, share information, and safely screen clients (Grant 2015; cf. *The Advocate*'s "In the Wake of Rentboy Arrests, Decriminalize Sex Work?," Ring 2015, and "How the Rentboy Indictment Threatens Our Community's Safety," D'Adamo 2016). This response seems a hopeful sign that the gay community is starting to combat the assimilationist amnesia that has ignored the prominent role of hustlers and trans sex workers in fighting police harassment at pivotal moments in the LGBT histories of New York, San Francisco, and Toronto.

As the examples of "confession porn" discussed here reveal, the resonance between queer and/or sex-worker negotiations of the interactive interview – involving both performance and performativity, coming out as *executing* one's identity as well as *describing* it, making the viewer who is engaged in the on-camera confession the documentary referent along with the speaker (Waugh [1997] 2011, 235) – can best be understood in the context of the shared history of LGBT and sex-worker communities, including the role of documentary in their historiography (Shah 2012). Perhaps the naïve epigraph to *101 Rent Boys* can be resignified with this interdependency and indeterminacy in mind: your everyday street hustler knows "we" gay tourists might like to think of ourselves as normal people living in a world apart from sex workers, but from the perspective of the rent boy, getting solicited for an erotic confessional performance on camera is just another day at the office (and worth more than $50).

NOTE

1 I thank Daniel Laurin for raising this question of whether gay-for-pay porn is a "genre" or a "mode" (personal correspondence).

REFERENCES

Barthes, Roland. [1979] 1992. "Soirées de Paris." In *Incidents*, edited by François Wahl and translated by Richard Howard, 49–73. Berkeley: University of California Press.
Bozelka, Kevin John. 2013. "The Gay-for-Pay Gaze in Gay Male Pornography." *Jump Cut* 55 (Fall). http://ejumpcut.org/archive/jc55.2013/BozelkaGayForPay/index.html.
Butler, Judith. 2003. *Giving an Account of Oneself*. New York: Fordham University Press.

Cvetkovich, Ann. 1993. "The Powers of Seeing and Being Seen: *Truth or Dare* and *Paris Is Burning*." In *Film Theory Goes to the Movies*, edited by Jim Collins, Hilary Radner, and Eva Preacher Collins, 155–69. New York: Routledge.

D'Adamo, Kate. 2016. "How the Rentboy Indictment Threatens Our Community's Safety." *Advocate*, 19 February.

Deleuze, Gilles. [1983] 1996. *Cinema 1: The Movement-Image*. Translated by Hugh Tomlinson and Barbara Habberjam. Minneapolis: University of Minnesota Press.

de Villiers, Nicholas. 2017. *Sexography: Sex Work in Documentary*. Minneapolis: University of Minnesota Press.

Dickson, E.J. 2014. "'Broke Straight Boys' Reality Show Trailer Examines the World of 'Gay-for-Pay' Porn." *Daily Dot*, 5 July. http://www.dailydot.com/entertainment/broke-straight-boys-porn/.

Dorais, Michel. 2005. *Rent Boys: The World of Male Sex Workers*. Translated by Peter Feldstein. Montreal: McGill-Queen's University Press.

Escoffier, Jeffrey. 2003. "Gay for Pay: Straight Men and the Making of Gay Pornography." *Qualitative Sociology* 26, no. 4 (Winter): 531–55.

Foucault, Michel. [1982] 1997. "Technologies of the Self." In *Essential Works of Foucault*. Vol. 1, *Ethics, Subjectivity, and Truth*, edited by Paul Rabinow, 223–51. New York: New Press.

Gerrard, David Burr. 2014. "'Do What You Love' – Oh, but Not That! On Recognizing Sex Work as Work." Interview with Melissa Gira Grant. *The Awl*, 6 March. http://www.theawl.com/2014/03/do-what-you-love-oh-but-not-that-on-recognizing-sex-work-as-work.

Grant, Melissa Gira. 2015. "How Sex Workers' Rights Made the Mainstream." *RH Reality Check*, 11 September. http://rhrealitycheck.org/article/2015/09/11/sex-workers-rights-made-mainstream/.

Hester, Helen. 2014. *Beyond Explicit: Pornography and the Displacement of Sex*. Albany: State University of New York Press.

Kahana, Jonathan. 2008. *Intelligence Work: The Politics of American Documentary*. New York: Columbia University Press.

Kaye, Kerwin. 2003. "Male Prostitution in the Twentieth Century: Pseudohomosexuals, Hoodlum Homosexuals, and Exploited Teens." *Journal of Homosexuality* 46, nos. 1–2: 1–77.

Minichiello, Victor, and John Scott, eds. 2014. *Male Sex Work and Society*. New York: Harrington Park Press.

Morrison, Todd G., and Bruce W. Whitehead. 2007. *Male Sex Work: A Business Doing Pleasure*. Binghamton, NY: Harrington Park Press/Haworth.

Rinaldi, Cirus. 2013a. "Il sociologo come cruiser. Riflessioni intorno ai mondi sociali dei clienti e dei marchettari." In *I clienti del sesso. I maschi e la prostituzione*, edited by A. Morniroli and Oliviero, 95–110. Naples: Intra Moenia.

– 2013b. "Razza, genere e sessualità nelle arene del sex working maschile. Implicazioni auto-etnografiche." In *Razzismi, discriminazioni e confinamenti*, edited by M. Grasso, 175–88. Rome: Ediesse.

Ring, Trudy. 2015. "In the Wake of Rentboy Arrests, Decriminalize Sex Work?" *Advocate*, 25 August.

Sedgwick, Eve Kosofsky. 1990. *Epistemology of the Closet*. Berkeley: University of California Press.

– 1993. *Tendencies*. Durham: Duke University Press.

Shah, Svati. 2012. "Sex Work and Queer Politics in Three Acts." *S&F Online* 10, nos. 1–2 (Fall 2011/Spring 2012). http://sfonline.barnard.edu/a-new-queer-agenda/sex-work-and-queer-politics-in-three-acts/.

Singal, Jesse. 2015. "Why Straight Men Have Sex with Each Other." Interview with Jane Ward. *New York Magazine*, 5 August. http://nymag.com/scienceofus/2015/08/why-straight-men-have-sex-with-each-other.html.

Sontag, Susan. 1966. *Against Interpretation and Other Essays*. New York: Anchor Books.

Stadler, John Paul. 2013. "Dire Straights: The Indeterminacy of Sexual Identity in Gay-for-Pay Porn." *Jump Cut* 55 (Fall). http://ejumpcut.org/archive/jc55.2013/StadlerGayForPay/index.html.

Ward, Jane. 2015. *Not Gay: Sex between Straight White Men*. New York: New York University Press.

Waugh, Thomas. [1997] 2011. *The Right to Play Oneself: Looking Back on Documentary Film*. Minneapolis: University of Minnesota Press.

West, Donald J. 1993. *Male Prostitution*. In association with Buz de Villiers. New York: Harrington Park Press/Haworth.

Williams, Linda. 1999. "The Ethics of Intervention: Dennis O'Rourke's *The Good Woman of Bangkok*." In *Collecting Visible Evidence*, edited by Jane Gaines and Michael Renov, 176–89. Minneapolis: University of Minnesota Press.

MEDIAGRAPHY

Bailey, Fenton, and Randy Barbato, dirs. 2000a. *101 Rent Boys*. Los Angeles: World of Wonder. Originally produced for Cinemax.

– dirs. 2000b. *The Eyes of Tammy Faye*. Los Angeles: World of Wonder.

Broke Straight Boys TV. 2014. Episodes 101–8. Here TV Premium, YouTube.

Bunim, Mary-Ellis, and Jonathan Murray. 1992–present. *The Real World*. TV series. New York: Viacom.

Keshishian, Alek. 1991. *Madonna: Truth or Dare*. Santa Monica, CA: Lionsgate Home Entertainment.

Klein, Bonnie Sherr. 1981. *Not a Love Story: A Film about Pornography*. Montreal: National Film Board of Canada.

O'Rourke, Dennis. 1991. *The Good Woman of Bangkok*. Sydney: Home Cinema Group.

10

Confessions: Watching the Masturbating Boy (Excerpts)

INTERVALS, AN ANONYMOUS COLLECTIVE

Dangerous Confessions

Much of what passes for confession these days is untainted by any hint of discomfort. The church pews empty, confession has turned into a genre of the "first person industrial complex" where trauma is a form of currency, and "writers feel like the best thing they have to offer is the worst thing that ever happened to them" (Bennett 2015). Not only can "anyone's personal troubles ... now serve as a front-page story couched as a banal morality tale with a happy ending" (Denzin, cited in Plummer 1995, 107), but like a celebrity sex-tape, sexual confessions can propel a career forward (Hajda 2017). Indeed, this book, *I Confess!*, is predicated on the professional and institutional success of confession as a mode of sexual identity and gender performance. Dangerous, risk-taking, self-implicating confessions are rare these days.

This essay will mark a place where dangerous confessions continue to intersect. Here the confessional sexual self-expression of boys *meets* the confessional masturbatory-archival practices of adult male desire that *meet* the eliminationist institutional confessions of Euro-American law enforcement that *meet* with and are sustained by a rarely confessed academic, artistic, and activist complicity. We hope with this essay to re-form this chain of meetings into a circle, linking the reader with the masturbating boy to institute a new and corrective cultural feedback loop.

We require a phenomenological excursus: a rushing forward to the object of our research that affords us an experience rich enough to challenge these assumptions. The aim of this essay, therefore, is not to prove a thesis but to provide an experience. We want to confront the reader with representations, or at least their descriptions, that have until very recently been kept off the record – out of sight out of mind – denied, confiscated, and destroyed.

Boys make pornography, recording and distributing images and video of their nudity and masturbation through social networks such as Twitter, Snapchat, Kik, Omegle, and Chatroulette, among others. These are the sexual self-representations that serve as the confessions of *puerile desire*, not only playful but also orgasmic. Documented and made real, these confessions go beyond a mute and inoperative acknowledgment of boys' desire that first appeared in Alfred Kinsey's statistical tables in 1948 (Kinsey, Pomeroy, and Martin 1948), and have for the past forty years have been reduced to whispers under the continuous panic about child sexual abuse and the demonological figure of the pedophile (Jones 1990; Kilpatrick 1987).[1] Introducing agency, the sexual self-representations of boys cannot be wholly captured by the concept of exploitation. Rather, they reveal, as if for the first time, the activity of boys devoted to their own sexual pleasure, pleasure as they want and experience it.

These confessional self-representations offer a new opportunity for scholarship to matter-of-factly address the widespread sexual practices of boys with established methods of descriptive analysis. However, the public is prohibited from examining the materials documenting the masturbating boy. We are prevented from opening ourselves as viewers (and world citizens) to this phenomenon; instead, a prohibition employing invasive police state tactics treats these images and videos as nothing more than confessions of criminal conduct, both the making ("self-exploitation") and the viewing ("child exploitation material"), ensnaring both the youths themselves (Miller 2015) and the pornography cultures in which these documents maintain their continued existence.

Do constitutionally protected rights to scholarly access to these materials, like those in Canada, mean anything if academics and academic publishers fail (or refuse) to bring these materials before the eye so they can be addressed and understood? (Casavant and Robertson 2007, 18). When thousands of men (and boys) are being threatened and thrown into jail for *looking* at pictures, do academics and activists have a right to feign an "ethical" objectivity that is indistinguishable from complicity with an authoritarian prohibition? Can it be so simple?

Scholars in the humanities often find themselves waist deep in theory. Our theory is rather simple: *look*. Our method simultaneously engages and disengages us from the image. The image, simultaneously seen and unseen, becomes available to us in a new way. We are no longer blind and need no longer remain mute.

And we have reason to look. We must address ourselves to the analytic challenge outlined by Foucault vis-à-vis the relation between state power and child sexuality. In 1978, Foucault predicted the rise of a "new legislative framework" aimed at protecting "certain vulnerable sections of the population" involving a "new medical power" centred on "a conception of sexuality" but especially the "relations between child and adult sexuality." The child, granted a sexuality by psychiatry that is immediately withdrawn from circulation under the sign of inevitable trauma ("the child must be protected from his own desires"), will serve as a perpetual justification for the legislator of the "society of dangers":

> We're going to have a society of dangers, with, on the one side, those who are in danger, and on the other, those who are dangerous … And what we will have there is a new regime for the supervision of sexuality; in the second half of the 20th century it may well be decriminalized, but only to appear in the form of a danger, a universal danger, and this represents a considerable change. I would say the danger lay there. (Foucault [1978] 1996a, 270)

We propose a return to the *masturbating boy*, the figure of the "onanist" who historian Julian Bourg observes "lay at the very origins of [Foucault's] history of sexuality project" (Bourg 2007, 213). The masturbating boy, positioned in the torsion between "adult sexuality" and "childhood innocence," who effortlessly and enthusiastically embraces social media as sexual media, has brought the puerile orgasm into view with his self-representation.

Established norms of porn studies may not be enough to address this figure. Indeed, books like *Porn Studies* (2004), edited by Linda Williams, and *The Feminist Porn Book*, edited by Tristan Taormino et al. (2013), operate as if boy pornography doesn't exist – neither the material nor the intense policing of it.

Lynn Comella says of the porn studies discipline, "The objective here is not to search for some hidden 'truth' about pornography (e.g., is it harmful or empowering?). Rather, the goal is to establish a better vantage from which to observe, engage with, and make sense of how discourses and practices are organized within specific cultural contexts, including by whom and with what effects" (2014, 69).

But what "better vantage" can be taken from a position of blindness enforced by a prohibition? If we cannot see it, how can we possibly understand the extent to which the "discourses and practices" produced and maintained by the prohibition are specifically cultural, i.e., historically bound and not universal?

Comella's position as quoted here is inadequate. There *is* a hidden "truth" about pornography: until we affirm it in the sense of permitting it to appear, we cannot see it; and if we cannot see it, we will never understand it. Even specialists investigating child pornography understand this: "Undisputedly, there is a great value to seeing the content of the images. After all, it is difficult to really know what something is unless you have actually seen it" (Ferraro and Casey 2004, 9). Child safety expert John Carr once confessed, "We cannot have a grown up conversation about a problem if the facts are being concealed, no matter how noble the motive" (Carr 2013a).

Let us take the point of view of US Supreme Court justice Potter Stewart, who famously said of pornography, "I know it when I see it." Let us admit that we may know it only if we have seen it. And let us also admit the difficulty in approaching and understanding what we see. Let us therefore be open to a sustained encounter with what we have not seen, what we have been prohibited from seeing, even with what we may ourselves resist seeing.

We begin this essay with an examination of present attitudes toward boys' masturbation and sexual expression. The essay then reflects on different modes of the representation of boys' sexuality and the challenges of accessing and understanding the sexual representation of boys. The essay concludes with an examination of actual sexual self-representations of boys and a call for an independent archive of boys' sexual representation.

Masturbatory Reading and the Masturbating Boy

In its admitted insistence on drawing out the erotic qualities of the images under consideration, this text revels in "the overheated mind of the masturbator" (Greenblatt 2004). But we believe that a masturbatory reading is required to bring scholarship forward. The possibility of scholarship depends on the ability of scholars to manage their anxieties surrounding the research object. Anxiety shuts down our thought processes, narrows our point of view; it makes us laugh nervously, become too serious, or even refuse to engage.

To be scholars of the masturbating boy, then, we must confess that we are masturbators. We must introduce this most unlikely instrument of scholarly objectivity, because otherwise we are likely to flee from the research object due to anxieties resulting from the uncertainties and shame surrounding our own solitary sexual practices. Our language itself must enact in this confession, refusing the safety of the "scientific" language by engaging the language of the sexual imagination, interposing penis with cock, testicles with balls, anus with asshole, ejaculate with cum.

And we must confess something else. If double entendres make it hard to avoid coming to certain conclusions, the personal physiological implications of viewership of sexual performance may be even more difficult to confront. Scholarship requires the viewer to accept these and other affective valences produced through interaction with the text. We are experiencing a shift in our collective relationship to masturbation. Masturbation is no longer the "private vice that escapes the gaze of civilization" (Laqueur 2003, 226). With the internet, the great confessional of the twenty-first century, its secrets are spilling out everywhere. Indeed, it is the basis of this essay that even the masturbation of boys is being brought into view, through their practices of sexual self-representation, including partner-to-partner sexting but also through other forms of participation in online pornographic cultures, especially through social media. The normalization of masturbation and its surging online representation should mark the beginning of boys' entry into sexual culture.

But fear draws from a deep well. We may believe that we have moved beyond the 1990s when US surgeon general Joycelyn Elders was forced to resign because she thought "masturbation was an appropriate subject for classroom discussion" (Levine 2003, 185). But sex educators continue to struggle to get masturbation on the curriculum (Scott 2017), and in America abstinence-only education in which masturbation is never mentioned remains a powerful presence (Carroll 2017). The sudden visibility of boys' masturbation online has only provoked a new crisis, the broader features of which can be linked to the atmosphere of anxiety established in the 1970s by concerns about child sexual abuse (Malón 2009, 18). It seems we are still mired in a generalized anxiety about the realities of boys' ordinary sexual behaviour. Seeing it only makes us more nervous.

Let us work through this anxiety by training ourselves to see what has been prohibited behind the gate marked "sexual abuse" by looking to the sexual representations made by boys themselves. Let us contemplate a desiring being, complete with sexual practices of his own: the *masturbating boy*:

> The first time I masturbated, I was 11 years old. I remember our sixth grade teacher telling us something about the topic in class, and I decided to go home and try it. I was bookish and took it to be a kind of scientific experiment. I closed the door to my room and fiddled with my erection for a while, but nothing happened. Somehow I got the idea to fuck my pillow with my hand in the right spot. This produced the surprising result.

This is not only a confession of one of our sources. It pushes the reader into a personal confrontation: Is the reader prepared to accept the presence of an orgasmic eleven-year-old boy? Is that really what this essay is about?

"Astonished" anti-porn sociologist and self-described radical feminist Gail Dines positions her own contribution to the panic precisely here: "Astonishingly, the average age of first viewing porn is now 11.5 years for boys" (Dines 2010, blurb). Again: "Nowadays the average age for first viewing porn is just eleven years" (xi). And again: "As noted, boys see their first porn on average at eleven years of age" (xxi). Dines wants mothers to feel horror that boys might "come out of the womb with a homing device for GagFactor.com" (xxviii), but we take a different lesson from her obsession with eleven-year-olds: a boy's adventure with masturbation and pornography does not begin "in adolescence" or with "sexual maturity" or "after puberty."[2] According to an expert, "Masturbation becomes goal-driven around age 10. Boys in particular are trying to get to the point of orgasm" (Zamosky 2011). We reject the sexualization approach that situates boys' sexual desire and practice as nothing but symptoms of the ills of society – bad impulse control, bad media, bad touch, etc. (Erooga and Masson 1999, 10). The seed of orgasmic practice is planted somewhere within the region of childhood itself. The "awakening" into sexuality does not divide childhood from adulthood but bridges these two territories. Boys' arousal, masturbation, and orgasm in response to sexually explicit visual inputs are not the desecration of boyhood but an important part of it. The porn may be new, but the instinct is not.

Although Thomas Laqueur emphasized that anti-masturbation entrepreneurs targeted girls too (Laqueur 2003, 202), we want to introduce a working distinction between boys and girls. Males and females inhabit different coordinates in the discourses surrounding sexuality, masturbation, pornography, sexting and sexual self-representation, rape and sex offenses. The masturbating boy has experiences of his own, and as males we leave advocacy for the masturbating girl to women and girls. We think the politics are very different.[3]

To begin with, males and females experience masturbation and pornography differently. Masturbation statistics convincingly show that males learn masturbation earlier on average and masturbate more often. The University of Michigan Health Services webpage states, "By age 15, almost 100% of boys and 25% of girls have masturbated to the point of orgasm" (Viglianco-VanPeld and Boyse 2009). In one study, "half [of boys] said they masturbated at least twice a week, but only 23% of girls reported the same frequency" (Rochman 2011). Male masturbation is more likely to involve pornography, another area of difference: "Young men are more likely than their female peers 'to use porn, to do so repeatedly, to use it for sexual excitement and masturbation, to initiate its use (rather than be introduced to it by an intimate partner), to view it alone and in same-sex groups, and to view more types of images'" (Crabbe and Corlett 2010).

A recent study by the Burnet Institute discovered that for Australian youth, "the median age of first viewing is 13 years for boys and 16 years for girls," with "around

80 percent of young men [watching] weekly" and "nearly two-thirds" of women viewing "monthly" (Morgan 2017). According to one study, 93 per cent of boys but only 62 per cent of girls reported exposure to pornography before the age of eighteen. The same study reports that 69 per cent of boys but only 17 per cent of girls reported looking at porn because they wanted sexual excitement. The report states, "Girls were significantly more likely than boys to report never looking for pornography on purpose, indicating they were involuntarily exposed" (Sabina Wolak, and Finkelhor 2008). These differences lead to gendered distinctions in how masturbation and pornography are managed, as researcher Debby Herbenick notes: "We know that quite a few women 'police' men's sexual behavior, including getting upset if they find their partner is masturbating – and even more upset if they feel their partner is masturbating to porn" (Eaves 2016).

The masturbating boy is not especially supported by the media, educational institutions, or political organizations. Nor is he celebrated by the "rainbow polity" (Sullivan 2016) of adults enjoying their non-reproductive pleasures in parades that fill the streets to overflowing with diverse sexual orientations. The masturbating boy is too common to be a protected class. Instead, his masturbation and pornography use serves in the public imagination as another aspect of the increasingly discounted tyrannical heterosexual male suffering from the symptoms of "toxic masculinity."[4] In looking away from the masturbating boy, we collectively deny the sexual desire and pleasure practices of boys – unless they act upon it in strange and unexpected ways. Then we arrest them. The masturbating boy returns as a "person of interest," a suspect of some wrong-doing rather than a citizen-participant in sexuality.

Research into "youth offenders committing sex offenses against other children found that 93 percent of the offenders were male" (Human Rights Watch 2013). According to the US Department of Justice, "The greatest number of offenders from the perspective of law enforcement was age 14" (Snyder 2000; Classically Liberal 2009; Skenazy 2016).[5] The gender inequality in arrest rates for sexual offences points to significant gendered differences in the experience of sexual desire. Male desire is harder to manage. After all, it is not only "monsters" who run afoul of sex laws.

And yet many people find it difficult to view boys' relationship to masturbation and pornography positively, as a viable method of self-management of desire. For example, some vocal sex-phobic feminists treat boys' online sexual behaviour as an emerging danger to women and girls. Dismissively claiming that boys "go to pornography for an ejaculation," Gail Dines treats boys' masturbation to pornography as nothing but orgasmically reinforced ideological indoctrination into the hatred of women. Following the old anti-porn adage that "pornography is the theory, and rape the practice" (Robin Morgan, cited in Nathan 2007, 51), Dines asserts that pornography is just the depiction of hate: "The man [in porn] makes hate to the woman's body" (Avard 2010). This contaminates boys' very "sexual identity" (Dines 2010, xi). Dines refuses to treat boys' pornography use as an authentic life experience, instead characterizing it as if it were the beginning of a degenerative disease: "If you're exposed to it at age 11 or 12, you're jaded by 20" (Avard 2010). Dines's narrative could have come out of an anti-masturbation tract from 200 years ago.

Sexting, part of the visibility of boys' arousal and masturbation, intensifies the atmosphere of risk. Males flashing strangers has been translated to the internet, with the ubiquitous and dreaded "dick pic" (Saint Thomas 2017). If online journalism is any indication, females appear generally resigned to managing it with eye-rolling rejection and biting humour. One female commentator made this dramatic announcement to the internet: "Attention all men: Women do not enjoy unsolicited dick pics," and "Please stop sending me pictures of your dick" (Bahadur 2015). Another asks, "Does he know how ugly those things are?" (not4urmother 2017). And not every woman is amused:

> When Eric Gray was 17, he took a picture of his penis and texted it to a 22-year-old woman he fancied, asking, "Do u like it babe?" Gray, whose lack of social skills had led to a diagnosis of Asperger's syndrome, may have thought he was courting the woman. She thought he was harassing her and contacted police, who thought he was distributing child pornography. Last week, the Washington Supreme Court upheld Gray's conviction on that charge, which makes him a perpetrator as well as a victim, guilty of exploiting himself. (Sullum 2017)

Although some online feminist writers admit of sexting that "society and our laws are struggling to figure out how to manage this new way of expressing desire" (Marniel Goldenberg quoted in Schroeder 2015), given the divergence of interest between males and females, other writers situate boys' relation to sexual self-representation within a sex-phobic feminist critique that describes it primarily as a "non-consensual sharing of sexual images by teens [that] is part of a broader culture in which sexual surveillance of women without their consent is endemic" (Chemaly 2015). Worrying about the effect of sexting and pornography on girls, women can typecast boys as sexual predators: "Boys pass around nude photos of classmates to older boys in exchange for alcohol. We hear about 'slut pages,' where nude photos sent to one boy are posted publicly on social media (technically a crime)" (Westwood 2016). According to Michelle Drouin, sexting among teens is just a "new form of intimate partner abuse" (Dewey 2015). Boys' demands for sexts draw girls into a "sexting addiction" that causes "catastrophic mental breakdowns" in "its victims – predominantly girls" (Hind 2017).

Dines's call for "a massive public health awareness campaign" was answered by US senator Todd Weiler (Rep. Utah), who successfully headed efforts to classify pornography in Utah as a "public health crisis" (Romboy 2016). He described porn use by boys as an "epidemic" comparable to drugs. And, as if on cue, Weiler said, "I'm concerned that the average age of first exposure to hardcore sex videos on the Internet is now the age of eleven" (Anderson 2017).

Even advocates of improved sex education denigrate boys' pornography use. In an article advocating the teaching of sexual love, intimacy, and masturbation to children, Philippe Brenot says of porn (according to him, "an artificial vision of sex") that "nothing could be more damaging than these images devoid of explanation." This position is misleading, to say the least, and continues the tradition of using hyperbolic claims to appeal to an audience's worst expectations about pornography and the sexual practices of boys.[6]

And things get worse. A father discovering his fourteen-year-old son's porn searches noted they "seemed both naïve and potentially troublesome, and he worried that his son might unintentionally violate child-pornography laws by looking for images of girls his own age" (O'Leary 2012). When boys look for pornography involving people their own age, their masturbatory practice pushes them into the domain of law enforcement and psychiatry.[7] What comes naturally to boys presents an extraordinary risk to them: "'Child pornography is illegal' is hardly straightforward for students at this age; those laws can mean that if a teenager sexts their SO [significant other] a naughty picture, both they and the recipient could potentially spend a lifetime on the sex offender registry" (Guappone 2016).

A British psychotherapist, Heather Wood, reporting a fifty-to-one ratio of boys to girls referred to her by the authorities for therapy related to porn-related "offenses," says, "I regularly see boys as young as 12 who have convictions for looking at child porn because they did not realise they had crossed the line ... Because most parents are so uncomfortable with a child's developing sexuality, few warn them about porn before they see it – or can face up to the fact they might be watching it" (Wood 2013). The irony of "regularly" convicting twelve-year-olds for masturbating to a picture of a twelve-year-old is breathtaking. But it is the unthinkable quality of child pornography itself that has had an unexpected effect: parents can't imagine their own sons with sexuality. In protecting boys, parents have ended up in a bubble of their own where mothers are invited by online mommy media to be terrified of their son's masturbation: "At some point all boys do it, and at some point most moms accidentally witness it. *Terrifying but true*" (Mamiverse Team 2014, italics in original).

It is remarkable that fifty years after sexual-liberation movements in America there remains a lack of realism about boys' sexuality and a lack of courage to talk to boys about their sexual lives. The panic about sexual abuse has obliterated the lines between informing, initiating, and abusing. Nobody wants to be accused of asking a boy sexual questions. Instead of supporting the masturbating boy, we surround him with panic narratives involving existential dangers about pornography, "self exploitation," "intimate partner abuse," even suicide, at the thought of being caught doing what "almost 100%" of boys do. Without effective political rights, without any organizational support, we cannot expect the masturbating boy to advocate on his own behalf for the right to masturbate to pornography or engage in online pornographic culture.

But boys aren't remaining silent either. Through internet technologies, boys are confessing the story of their pleasure through forms of sexual self-representation that go beyond institutionalized categories like "child exploitation material" or "child abuse images" – categories constructed by those in the "child protection space" to maintain a prohibition that brooks no exceptions. By challenging these categories, boys themselves introduce a twist in the narrative, giving us an opportunity to see things differently. To address the sexual health of boys and make sure they are safe is not irrational, but have the critics and doom preachers ever treated the masturbating boy as anything other than a threat, anything other than a problem, anything other than a victim? Can't we see boys as they are, in the ordinariness of their pleasure seeking, at the point of orgasm?

Can't we simply look at the masturbating boy?

Boys' sexual self-representation calls for widespread investigation but not necessarily by law enforcement or psychiatry. We believe the narrative has shifted sufficiently to call for these images to be examinable within a critical culture. In addition to the problem of "exploitation," we must allow ourselves to recognize the presence of agency, participation, and pleasure, key terms that the discourse of the "innocent victim" has until now shut out.

Such an examination means overcoming the embargo on access. As Steven Ruszczycky writes, "The central problem remains, however, that child pornography is still a genre defined by its legal prohibition" (2014, 408). But the prohibition of child pornography is grounded in a concept of exploitation that was never intended to manage self-representation. When the masturbating boy represents himself, he disrupts, through his willingness and pleasure, the "sacred boundary" that constitutively structures "abuse" and distinguishes it from an ordinary, everyday sexual encounter (Klotz 2014, 295).

We believe it is time for researchers to treat the masturbating boy as an anthropological subject, no longer located a priori behind the high walls of an institutionalized prohibition. We need to replace scholarly inhibition with openness to the self-driven, self-structuring, and self-chosen sexual practices of boys. We need to reject complicity with law-enforcement agencies, reject their offers to limit our investigations to representations they choose – the worst pornography has to offer – and reject too their limited interpretive matrix exemplified by the COPINE scale (the child pornography measurement schema originating in Ireland and the UK in the 1990s) that grades images on an ascending scale from 1 to 10 (Stapleton 2010, 39–40). We need to overcome the fear that makes us abandon the masturbating boy to rigid, institutionalized language that resounds with demonological presences, irrecoverable losses, horrifying traumas, and absolute and transcendent evils. No other category of representation in media and cultural studies is permitted to function like this. Let's instead develop language that is free and supple and appropriate and true, or at least richer and better trained to pick up the nuances and intricacies of what we can actually see.

Some readers may resist the claim that there are meaningful distinctions that go beyond the institutionalized language of "child exploitation material" and "child abuse images." We of course do not want to abandon what has been learned about sexual assault and exploitation. But we feel the material itself speaks to other experiences that have thus far been overlooked, minimized, or explicitly rejected. We believe that child protection is compatible with a shift away from a limited perspective grounded in a few privileged terms. We advocate a new scholarly perspective that is open to the fullest complexity of the representations in question, a perspective that is not exhausted by one or two viewings any more than by none. Opening to this territory, we will become capable of traversing and mapping it, recognizing that its dimensions and depths require high-resolution grayscale and colour, not only black and white.

This essay will pursue its visual analysis by examining a film that offers exceptions to the rule of the absolute prohibition on representations of boys' sexuality.

The Sexting Revolution

Technology is giving young people the opportunity to sexually express themselves, an opportunity to which boys especially are responding with enthusiasm. This new genre of sexual representation is shared privately and publicly by youth themselves, against systems of censorship and surveillance and against all expectations of those advocates of children's safety who presume the sexual innocence of their targets of defence. "This is a variation on a theme that we haven't seen. It's unbelievable," said Ernie Allen, CEO of the US National Center for Missing and Exploited Children (Eichenwald 2005).

In 2005, the *New York Times* exposé of teen pornographer Justin Berry brought teen "cam whore" culture out of the basement into the studios of television talk-show host Oprah Winfrey. Before the studio audience, journalist Kurt Eichenwald, previously best known for his reporting on the Enron scandal in 2002, implored out of fear of the pedophile menace conspiring to ravish the nation's children that "every webcam in every child's room in America should be thrown out today" (Oprah Winfrey Show 2006).

But the cameras were not thrown out. In fact, since then they have proliferated beyond all imagining via the cell-phone. About 88 per cent of teens between the ages of thirteen and seventeen possess a cell-phone (with or without a camera), making them potential participants in online cultures of sexual self-representation (Lenhart 2015). According to a recent digital trends study, "The average age for a child getting their first smart phone [invariably *with* a camera] is now 10.3 years" (Influence-Central 2017).

As news reports testify, many youths use cell-phones to record themselves in various states of undress and nudity, arousal, and sexual behaviour. There is ongoing controversy about the prevalence of sexting (partly due to differences in defining sexting behaviour). A Pew Study found only 4 per cent of cell-owning teens aged twelve to seventeen had sent "sexually suggestive nude or nearly-nude photo or videos of themselves," with 15 per cent of cell-owning teens having received them (Lenhart 2015, 4). Measuring "sending or showing sexual pictures of themselves," one study found 7 per cent of teens thirteen to eighteen had done so in the past year (Ybarra and Mitchell 2014, 757). A study conducted via telephone survey found 9.6 per cent of youths aged ten to seventeen had sexted (sent or received) "sexually suggestive" representations in the past year (Mitchell et al. 2012, 6).[8] A more recent study found 54 per cent of college students admitted to sexting in their teen years, 28 per cent with still or moving images (Strohmaier, Murphy, and DeMatteo 2014). The discrepancy between 9.6 per cent and 28 per cent may be due to the former number representing an annual amount, with the latter number representing the cumulative amount. But the numbers have not yet settled on the sexting phenomenon.

Taking this cumulative number against the estimated 21 million youths in the United States aged between thirteen and seventeen in 2010 (*Nations Encyclopedia* 2017), we would expect (at 28 per cent) that perhaps as many as 5.9 million people will produce sexually explicit still or moving images during their adolescence (over a five-year period). If each producer were to create only ten representations, we would expect over the next five years that teenagers would produce nearly sixty million pornographic still or moving images of themselves, or about twelve million representations per year total.[9] Dividing that number in half along gender lines, we get a conservative estimate of six million sexts per year produced by boys alone. In contrast, consider that in 1995 the UK police knew of only seven thousand sexual representations of children *in total* (Carr 2013b). Boys alone will produce about 857 times this amount every year, and we can expect this amount will only increase.[10] (Such statistical extrapolations become even more mind-blowing when one intersects them with the real statistics of draconian sentences widely imposed for possession of child pornography. For example, in 2017, Henrik Nocolai Styles received a sentence of 365 years for child pornography offences in the United States, based on charges of possessing 150 images of boys and of making contacts with boys via the dark net under the name "VA Dad4Yung" in a chat room called "GayDads4Sons" [Bowes 2017].)

Teen sexting is normalizing, as research psychologist David DeMatteo explains: "We were struck by how many of those surveyed seemed to think of sexting as a normal, standard way of interacting with their peers" (Hoder 2014). Only 1 per cent of those who admitted to sexting experienced a negative consequence (Strohamaier, Murphy, and DeMatteo 2014). "A large-scale study found no correlations between sexting and sexual risk behaviors or psychological health" (Karaian and Van Meyl 2015, 24). Even though the danger of sexting, according to psychologist Barbara Greenberg, is that "other people might be aroused by seeing a provocative photo of them" (Hoder 2014), "a growing body of research suggests that, on average, engaging in sexting does not produce subsequent negative *attitudes* towards the behavior despite knowledge that one's image may be redistributed, presumably because negative consequences do not inherently flow from the behavior" (Karaian and Van Meyl 2015, 29).

Within little more than ten years, teen sexual self-representation has escaped from the shadowy bedroom into the quasi-public space of social media, where the real risk now is that an anonymous other might be aroused by it – an effect many young people don't seem to be bothered enough by to stop their sexting behaviour. It is a remarkable transformation.

Yet it is difficult to understand boys' sexual relationship to culture if we are not able to respond as directly as possible to the kinds of sexual self-representations they produce and distribute. If we can't see, we can't know, and we can't say.

Cinematic Confessions 2: The Masturbating Boy

Even though archives of boys' sexual representations are practically forbidden, we find the stories of boys' masturbation leaking out into cinema. In this section we will see how confessions of sexual desire and masturbatory performance are situated in the body of the boy, sidestepping the themes of horror and exploitation, while at the same time interrogating the audience about its own involvements and motivations, through a very important European short film, *Hazel* (2012).[11]

Here we see sexual performance as self-discovery played out. This film carries us beyond the solipsistic pleasures of masturbation into the dynamics of the interactive present in which what is mirrored upon the screen transmits signals of desire that implicate the audience. Set in a cartoon version of Switzerland in the 1970s, the film begins with twelve-year-old Hazel (Maxime Mori) opening his eyes as if sexually awakening. He immediately begins to dance in a remarkable thirty-four-second sequence.

The initial shots establish Hazel's dancing as perhaps a bit too enthusiastic and expressive for a straight boy. But these soon give way to a suggestive gyration of the hips that make the dance more explicitly transactional. Hazel reaches out and looks seductively to the camera as if the audience were his dance partner. He holds himself and sways his hips, then grasps his buttocks, then looks again to the audience. Suddenly, after he grasps his buttocks once more, his mother (Manuella Biedermann) pulls the plug on the record player, stopping the music.

She later reports the dance to Hazel's therapist (Jacqualine Ricciardi) as if it were a sexual act. The lewd therapist prompts Hazel to "confess": "Is it a masturbatory fantasy that has taken hold on your body?" This dancing boy is a masturbating boy, a boy queered by his evasive gender performance, his fantasy about a man (Tiber Sesti), and the implications for the audience drawn into the boy's metaphorically sexual performance.

After the therapist's attempt to convert him to heterosexuality fails, Hazel takes a frozen treat from the freezer and sits on the kitchen counter opposite his mother. He sucks the phallic treat enthusiastically. His mother cries out, "I'm warning you,

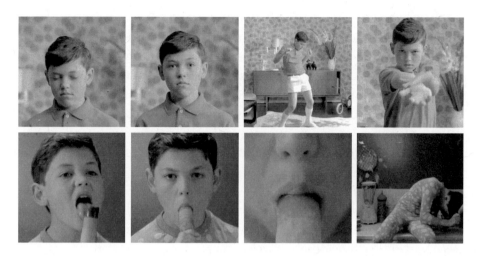

10.1 Hazel sexting us, performing for us. *Hazel*, dir. Tamer Ruggli, 2012.

stop that right now!" When he refuses to stop, she throws a cup at him. But he only looks angry and defiantly continues to suck. The film closes with Hazel removed from all the family photos, and the audience is left to contemplate whether they too would prefer to erase Hazel from their consciousness. *Hazel* amplifies the erotic potentiality of the boy by presenting his body directly, through dancing and sucking. In doing so, the director poses difficult questions to the audience.

The first part of the film warmly invites a sympathetic audience to support Hazel as a boy awakening to his queer sexual identity. Hazel's desire is at first easy to accept because although his dancing is a metaphor for masturbation, there are no definite mechanics of sexual behaviour taking place, and his fantasy for a man belongs to a dream world.

But the audience's security shatters in Hazel's final scene, where his invitations to the audience are shorn of their ambiguity as he sucks the frozen treat as if it were a phallus. The disturbed behaviour of Hazel's mother emphasizes this possible reading. The ease with which we might register the desire of a twelve-year-old boy when it is hidden behind the metaphor of dancing and a sexual orientation reading gives way to anxiety when that same boy acts in a more explicitly sexual manner. Ruggli presents us with a twelve-year-old boy who wants to suck cock. This is something many people would feel uncomfortable with, even those who claim to support boys who identify as gay. Will the audience accept not only the queer boy's sexual *orientation* but also the desires, fantasies, and behaviours that logically follow from it?

But the film (fig. 10.1) goes still further. With the erection virtualized as a colourful treat, Hazel's sucking obeys tropes of first-person pornography, as if he were fellating the erection of the audience. In a way, *Hazel is sexting us*, dancing for us, sucking for us, performing for us from the security of his home. The cinema camera becomes a webcam and the film a tiny video on our private screen. Hazel's masturbatory dance is expressive, communicative. Looking into the camera in a sustained way and gesturing toward us, he involves us, intensifying his invitation with self-touching. Looking at Hazel's body and its movements, are we drawn by his gestures to engage his image with a fantasy of our own? Do we masturbate to the masturbating boy?

In raising these possibilities, *Hazel* not only invites the audience to sympathize with Hazel's self-pleasure but shows us why many in the audience will find it hard to support him. Getting close to Hazel means addressing feelings, desires, and experiences we have collectively put off-limits.

Interlude: The Forensic Gaze and the Cutout Technique

We have referred to the problem with "ethical" research. But we cannot ignore the difficulties with encountering the masturbating boy and his self-representations. We need a kind of showing that simultaneously (1) challenges the reader to confront the corporeality of the masturbating boy, (2) enables recognition that is the basis of scholarly and journalistic verification, (3) respects the privacy of young people, (4) acknowledges that not every representation has been produced or distributed ethically, and (5) protects the audience from law enforcement. In this section we cross the investigative philosophy of police authorities stamping out child pornography with the white-out technique we find in *Hazel*.

Hazel offers something more than a depiction of a boy's desire. We also find in the film a cutout technique for leveraging our insights about the forensic gaze. When his father abandons the family, Hazel's mother uses white correction fluid to "erase him forever from our lives." The father is already conspicuously absent from the family photos, having been replaced by a white shape. Later, when Hazel's mother cannot handle her son's sexuality, she does the same to him, covering his eyes and mouth, blinding and silencing him. In the final frame of the film (fig. 10.2), we see Hazel obscured by the white fluid.

According to Europol, "The most innocent clues can sometimes help crack a case. The objects are all taken from the background of an image with sexually explicit material involving minors" (Europol 2017). When the police examine rep-

 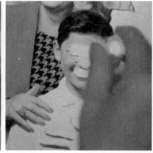 

10.2 Mother uses white correction fluid to "erase him forever from our lives." *Hazel*, dir. Tamer Ruggli, 2012.

resentations of boys in sexual situations, they do not see them as we do. They have a *forensic gaze* that draws attention away from sexually engaged bodies to the periphery and background – a newspaper lying on a table, a license plate of a vehicle seen through a window, an amusement park wristband, an electrical socket. The periphery and background arise from what has been unthought and unexpected by the producer and represent the unconscious of the image. This is where clues may be found pointing to the location or identity of those depicted.

Like the forensic gaze, our attention once Hazel has been whited out is drawn to the periphery: we see only his clothes, hair, his mother, a toy dog, and the wallpaper behind them; Hazel's body is missing. His sexuality is covered up – not only his homosexual orientation but his orientation toward sexual pleasure itself.

And yet the will to erase something completely produces an intriguing effect: we can see what has been censored, not exactly bodies but shapes, exchanging full indexicality for another kind of access. The more precisely the body is removed, the more clearly what has been censored comes into view (as in this book!). Paradoxically, perfection in censorship produces a view of the very thing prohibited, while protecting the privacy of those depicted.

In Defence of Our "Legitimate Purpose"

Now that we are preparing to look more closely at the bodies of boys, let us briefly attend to the norms and laws modulating access. We look briefly at three arguments commonly levelled against viewership of boy pornography (exploitation, market, and revictimization), the assumptions of the US Court decision *New York v. Ferber* that struck down First Amendment protections for child pornography, and the Canadian "legitimate purpose" defence that allows for an exemption to the blanket prohibition.

The sexual self-representation of boys puts heavy pressure upon the assumptions that "behind every picture there's pain" and "every picture is a crime scene where a real child is abused or exploited," which are commonly bandied about by those battling child pornography (UK Database 2012). Leaving aside for the moment whether boy pornography in general is necessarily exploitative (or not), with respect to sexual *self*-representations exploitation transmutes into self-exploitation. We believe that "self-exploitation" is conceptually incoherent and offends a reasonable person's notion of criminal and moral responsibility. It is possible to harm one's interests but not to exploit one's self ("self-abuse" is a term that was thrown out with the anti-masturbation panics).

"University of Utah law professor Paul Cassell, a former judge, claimed that consumers of child pornography drive the market for the production of child pornography, and without people to consume this stuff there wouldn't be nearly as many children being sexually abused" (Sullum 2011). The question of markets in boy pornography is too complex to handle in a summary fashion. However, two points are germane for our discussion. First, sexting by its very existence proves that boys are not only subject to a pornography market but are also producers and consumers in their own right. Second, so long as researchers do nothing to encourage the production of new boy pornography, scholarly use of the existing corpus of sexual representations of boys cannot be said to *drive* a market for it. The claim by Bartlett-Hughes that "any act of downloading fuels the market" is a hyperbolic slogan, not sedate legal opinion (2010, 24). Jacob Sullman further underlines this point:

> Steve Maresca, the assistant state attorney who prosecuted Vilca, tells the *Times* "these children are victimized, and when the images are shown over and over again, they're victimized over and over again." That claim seems even more problematic, since any such injury would require (at the very least) that victims know when people are looking at images of them. (Sullum 2011)

Justin Patchin, a professor of criminal justice at the University of Wisconsin and cyberbullying expert, said with respect to sexting, "I don't think it should be a criminal offense where there is no victim" (Miller 2015). Whatever the metaphysics of spectatorship may be – whether simply viewing an image is capable of producing harm in someone depicted, even when they don't know about it – it is reasonable to think that, with respect to representations that contain no victim, the *re*victimization hypothesis cannot be accepted without further argumentation and evidence.

If the metaphysical properties of representations enabled them to "revictimize" those depicted, one would expect terrorist and Holocaust imagery to be subject to this claim. However, research into terrorist war crimes and crimes against humanity are not restricted because of claims of "revictimization" (or market, or exploitation). On the contrary, researchers examine these representations to establish what has taken place and make them available to the public for the purpose of education. This is true even when the villains and victims are boys. Because journalists and researchers are permitted to observe these representations, they are able to verify the reporting of other journalists, thus collectively arriving at something approximating the truth. As citizens, we can compare reports or seek out the representations ourselves. There is no law that prohibits researchers from downloading, possessing, reviewing, and reporting on these documents.

Let us now turn to the decision outlawing child pornography in 1984 and consider the Canadian "legitimate purpose" defence.

The 1984 *New York v. Ferber* decision is important because it grounded all subsequent developments in the conditions of not only child pornography production and dissemination but also the socio-political experience of pedophiles who became and continue to be the targets of boundless investigations. It is summarized, unsurprisingly, in a book titled *Investigating Child Exploitation and Pornography*: "*Ferber* held the states have a compelling interest in protecting children; that child pornography is inextricably intertwined with child exploitation and abuse because it is both a record of the abuse and it encourages production of similar materials; and that child pornography has very little social, scientific, political, literary, or artistic value" (Ferraro and Casey 2004, 16).

Today we find this reasoning less sure. In the case of sexual self-representations, the undoing of the concepts of abuse (as self-abuse, i.e., masturbation) and exploitation (now self-exploitation, i.e., an absurdity) puts irremediable pressure upon the claims of *Ferber*. The self-representations of boys' arousal and masturbation is not in itself "a most serious crime and an act repugnant to the moral instincts of a decent people" (Free Speech Coalition, cited in Weinstein 2016, 46). The shifting ground does not negate concerns about exploitation. Rather, it shifts the discussion: what are we protecting minors from – exploitation or their own sexuality and sexual expression?

The point is, sexting and sexual self-representation radically destabilize the assumptions surrounding child pornography law (Ryder 2003; Karaian and Van Meyl 2015; Crofts and Lee 2013). And in doing so, sexting opens up realms formerly felt to be closed: social, scientific, political, literary, and artistic value. And, we might also add, historical value, as these records accumulate upon the hard drives of young people themselves, serving as part of their personal archive of sexual expression. It turns out these expressions may be protected by the First Amendment in the United States. Mary Anne Franks, a University of Miami law professor, wrote:

> Sexual activity that does not even involve another person – such as taking a sexually explicit photo of yourself – should not ever be a crime. In fact, criminalizing such expression likely violates the First Amendment. Child sexual exploitation laws were clearly designed to address the exploitation of children by adults, not teenagers exploring their sexuality on their own or with a willing peer. (Miller 2015)

Alongside Justin Patchin (Miller 2015), we find many experts expressing the following train of thought: sexual self-representation (insofar as it) implies no exploitation and implies no victim implies a defence under the First Amendment. It's a radical transformation in the conditions of the sexual representation of boys, which until very recently was viewed as universally exploitative, regardless of what was depicted. Consider another opinion, expressed in a paper claiming to examine and critique assumptions that distort and limit discussions of pornography's ethical implications: "None of [the] definitions [contained in this paper] includes child pornography, which we believe is beyond the justification of any moral system and which has long been deemed illegal and thus excluded from any constitutional protections for expression" (Wyatt and Bunton 2009, 1).

We think this attitude is untenable. The unfolding conditions of sexual representation of young people necessitate a reappraisal of the law and attitudes within human sciences. Scholars may therefore decide to look at what has been prohibited. We have no space to examine US exemptions but can report that they are insignificant. Let's therefore turn to the Canadian "legitimate purpose" defence that provides broader and more meaningful access to the sexual representations of people under the age of eighteen:

> No person shall be convicted of an offence under this section if the act that is alleged to constitute an offence
> (a) Has a legitimate purpose related to the administration of justice or to science, medicine, education or art; and
> (b) Does not pose an undue risk of harm to persons under the age of eighteen years.

(Canadian law cited in Casavant and Robertson 2007, 18)

Let's get straight to the point: does this essay have a "legitimate purpose"? Yes. See accompanying text box for our statement.

> "Legitimate Purpose"
>
> The "risk of harm to persons under the age of eighteen years" includes not only the possibility of harm arising from exploitation and sexual abuse but also harm from a systematic denial of the sexual capacity of young people, the criminalization of their sexual activity and sexual representations, and a denial not of political (i.e., voting) rights and, as we have seen, even the right to register their opinions through scholarship critically examining the prohibition on youth sexuality.
>
> We argue that the prohibition on access to the sexual self-representations of young people denies scholarship access to phenomenological experiences that would reveal the physical, social, and psychical capacities of young people and, more importantly, enable a shift in awareness among experts and the adults who are in positions not only to protect and guide young people but also to misunderstand, needlessly restrict, criminalize, and punish them for their normal sexual behaviours.
>
> The fact that sexting has disrupted the logic of the prohibition justifies the claim that the current approach to prohibiting child pornography has been grounded in a limited view of young people's capacity for sexual experience and behaviour. We believe it is the duty of scholarship to venture into the domain of the sexual self-representations of young people to find out directly what is taking place there.
>
> These representations can no longer be broadly defined as nothing more than evidence of abuse and exploitation. They are anthropological records of human sexual behaviour, and therefore evidence that supports and justifies objective research into the sexuality of youth.
>
> Since boys exhibit a greater interest in pornography than girls, the prohibition on access also disproportionately criminalizes and obfuscates the sexual behaviour of boys. Since a determining proportion of authorities in traditionally gender-streamed positions to police youth sexuality are

women (as teachers, social workers, psychologists, etc.), we risk the hypothesis that there may be contained in this matter a question of gender inequality.

Lastly, we would like to point out that in *R. v. Sharpe* the Supreme Court of Canada found that possession of such material poses no reasonable risk of harm to children if it is self-created recordings of lawful sexual activity (Casavant and Robertson 2007, 13; Karaian and Van Meyl 2015, 20), what legal commentator Bruce Ryder called "harmless representations of the sexuality of children and youth" (Ryder 2003, 109). The networked nature of sexting (i.e., its inherent distribution) is not the result of scholarship but something that scholarship has a right to examine.[12]

We would have liked to fulfil our obligation to reduce the risk of harm to young people by applying methods that reduce the risk of identification through works of scholarship alone, i.e., through the cutout method. We believe therefore that our essay falls within the requirements of the "legitimate purpose" defence but resign ourselves under protest to the compromise dictated by our peer review, our editors, and our publisher, substituting second-hand description for cutout imagery except in two exceptional images below.

Research Methods

INTERVALS does not directly handle sexual representations of boys but requests and receives documents (file name lists, still images, rich descriptions, transcripts, and so forth) prepared by anonymous sources, which have been edited to our specifications (i.e., with the cutout method). These materials are then enriched by follow-up questions to our sources. Drafts are circulated through encrypted channels among INTERVALS researchers, who make their contributions. These notes and commentaries are integrated seamlessly into the text. All correspondence between INTERVALS and anonymous sources is destroyed upon completion of the research, and all temporary identities are scrubbed. For security reasons, our international collective maintains no persistent public digital identity, social media presence, or email account, and does not participate openly on any website or forum.

10.3
Cutout image of sexual self-representation within the requirement of "legitimate purpose." Unidentified frame.

As They Are: The Sexual Self-Representations of Boys

With this section we establish the visibility of boys' sexual self-representations for the first time in scholarship. We begin by describing nine sexts as well as reproducing one that we have received in cutout format, moving on to explore the broader spectrum of boys' online sexting behaviour that does not fit into the usual interpretive frameworks offered by mainstream sexting discourse. The everyday sexts the public reads about in news reports are described below, in these cases depicting, we are told, eight different boys between the ages of twelve and fourteen showing their erections (fig. 10.3).

The erections in these images have not been taken by accident. The boys have posed specifically to capture their erections in images. In three of the images, we can see the cameras the boys used reflected through the bathroom mirror. In the other photos, the boys aimed the camera toward their bodies. The cameras are not always visible, but we can tell by the angle of an arm or the perspective that the boy himself took the image. These are the images of boys flashing their dicks to strangers online. These are the sexual self-representations of boys.

Two images were produced by a boy of about fourteen or fifteen years old. In the first image of the series, we see the boy as we would encounter him in public, fully clothed and desexualized. This is the boy as we might know him through institutionalized relations: at home, at school, at church, as parents, as teachers, as authority figures. In the second image we see the boy depersonalized, nothing but an erection. Boys, like adult men, commonly focus their cameras on their erections, getting a free security bump by leaving out their faces; hence the term "dick pic" rather than "body shot." But this depersonalization reveals something deeply personal. This is the boy as we might know him in a sexual encounter.

These images are part of the selfie and sexting culture that emphasizes the body as a proper subject of communication. We can see that they are not mute victims of a pornographic culture alien to themselves but are active and surprisingly conversant participants. Since we are speaking of *culture*, these images will be influenced by others. But their poses and aesthetic choices are determined not only by corporate pornography and adults but also by the ephemeral practices, styles, and coded expressions typical of youth culture. Since this culture has been forbidden public exposure, we are documenting through verbal description this youth culture for the first time.

We note that we see nothing surprising. The only apparently notable fact about the images is the ages of the people who made them. But that in itself is notable. The common-sense view is that these boys are "too young" to be involved in pornography, that they are "not ready" for sexuality (and that they are in great danger from sexuality). We would then expect their representations to reflect their being "too young" and "not ready." The boys might attempt to represent sexuality in an unusual, partial, inadequate, or deformed way. Something about the images would strike us as strange or even frightening or dangerous.

But in looking at these images, we see not a bad copy of sexuality but simply sexuality. These are not broken, warped, partial, deformed, or deranged images of sexuality. Whatever these boys had to learn, they learned it. Sexual expression is not something too complicated, beyond their comprehension or capacity to configure, capture, and post to the internet. Instead of beginning with assumptions about boys' readiness, we should begin with what we see: boys showing what they wanted to make visible. In attending to the surface of what we see – rather than the depths of what we might assume, our prejudices – we see boys who are sexually aroused.

These are images we *have to* get used to. At least six of the images were taken in what appear to be bathrooms. To stop sexting at its production stage, either young people would have to be deprived of access to networked cameras (on laptops, tablets, and smart phones) or they would have to be deprived of their privacy in the bathroom. Neither of these actions can be reasonably expected. Because of this, the battle against sexting must shift to distribution, when the images have already been circulated, with the police attempting to put horses back in barns. As the years go by, we will see many more of these images, not less.

And we think these are images we *should* get used to. If boys are themselves the primary source of the sexual representation of boys, producing millions of images and videos per year, policing shifts from specifiable outcast communities and "pedophile rings" to the general population. Every boy online is vulnerable not only to sexual predators but to invasive policing.

These are the kinds of images boys get arrested for. When young people are caught by the police with their own sexts, in many jurisdictions they may be charged with sexually exploiting themselves. This absurdity can carry serious consequences. In two cases, boys have faced up to ten years in prison (Miller 2015; Farivar 2017).[13] We've already noted that the prosecution of young people for "self-exploitation" offends our intuitions about wrongdoing, making the same person the perpetrator and the victim, an illogical contradiction. Sexual expression widely taken as pleasurable is treated as if it were intrinsically harmful, and the boys are subjected to painful and disruptive police interventions. Even if we feel it would be better if boys didn't sext, given that sexting is basically just visible masturbation – a habit notoriously difficult to refrain from – is it reasonable to expect that boys will even be *capable* of stopping their sexting behaviour?

Why do we impose serious consequences upon boys for something that is both (to a great extent) compulsive and harmless? We find the boy prosecuted for what the man looking at his images may do. Karaian and Van Meyl point out that in the absence of any victims or abuse or any other source of harm in sexting, teenagers are held accountable because child pornography is supposed to "promote cognitive distortions, fuel fantasies that incite offenders, [and] enable grooming of victims" (*R v. Sharpe*, para. 103, cited in Karaian and Van Meyl 2015, 24). "Thus, the legal risks of sexting … flow from the claim that teens ought to be held criminally responsible for the *potential* risk of harms that their images *may* facilitate at some unknown point in the future" (24).

What "fantasy" is being "fuelled" here – that men might get erections in sympathetic response to the erections of boys? What "cognitive distortion" is at stake here – that a man might come to believe that pubescent boys want to jerk off? What possible danger do these images present in terms of grooming – that a boy might see something he has already seen, be induced to do what he already does? (We are speaking here of the masturbating boy, not the baby in the crib.) And still, as ambiguous as these dangers are, they serve as the foundation for the way the Supreme Court of Canada has constructed the risk of child pornography.

Karaian and Van Meyl note that even though the Supreme Court of Canada effectively legalized private teen sexting in Canada with the *R. v. Sharpe* decision in 2001, "present day social, political and extra/legal debates surrounding teenage sexting in Canada tend not to acknowledge the constitutionality of this subset of teenagers' consensual sexual expression" (Karaian and Van Meyl 2015, 20). Can the reader recall the constitutionally protected expression of any other group attracting so much flimflam? If teens are at risk from "irresponsible sexting," why can't we establish norms and technologies that make responsible sexting possible?

The reader is invited to gaze upon the bodies of these boys and consider whether they recognize defensible self-expression. Are we not viewing boys as they really are when the power of absolute censorship is temporarily lifted? Men, isn't this also how we are, and how we were? This is what boys "want to say." They are expressing something deeply felt and near to their heart. For decades we have ignored, censored, and rejected this expression, treating it as nothing or a deviation or a moral horror. Now we can see it as expression *now that we can see it*.

And now that we can see it, we find it to be different from the news reports. Mainstream discourse surrounding boys' sexual self-representation is dominated by themes of (1) predatory threats and (2) (potentially threatening) heteronormative relations.[14] Absent from discussion is acknowledgment of queer and voluntary participation in porn culture for its own sake. A brief overview of the range of boys' sexual self-representations reveals how complex the terrain really is.

In research from PornResearch.org, we find pornography use "within an ongoing relationship" as only one of eleven reasons given by porn audiences for viewing (Smith, Barker, and Attwood 2015, 277). Likewise, the sexual self-representations of boys have many possible origins, reasons, purposes, and audiences. They cannot be reduced to only two categories. Let's examine some representations that until now have gone unreported.

That boys sometimes just want to make porn, irrespective of any particular audience, can be corroborated by pondering a few videos whose descriptions we have received through the channels described above. In a video titled *YuroTube – Hot Dutch (or Belgian) with Good Dick*, a boy of about twelve years says (in translation), "This is a porno video" while showing his erection. A video titled *how to wank* features a boy of about twelve silently mouthing "how to wank" while masturbating to a clear cumshot. In another how-to video, a boy shows his audience how to make a sex toy out of a diaper and a mason jar, which he demonstrates by fucking it (*13yo – Homemade anus with diaper – fucking, peeing, moaning, dirty talking (Sound)* HOT). Based on descriptions we have received securely and anonymously, these are not sexts to a girlfriend but to the pornographic public domain, the audience of people "out there" who (like the boys themselves) enjoy porno and find masturbation and sex topics fascinating.

A significant number of boys' sexual self-representations involve queer boys, or queered narratives arising from heterosexual boys bending the rules a little by participating in networks of desire that are intrinsically queering because they are open to indeterminate permutations of desire. In *Tommy13Snapchat*, a video-sequence of Snapchat stills and video captures, we see Tommy has added the title "Cum all over me," suggesting he wants a male to ejaculate "all over" him. Another boy, in *IMG_1941*, about fourteen years old, lying on his back with his legs up, moans, "Oh yeah, baby, I love you so much. Oh, fuck me harder. Oh yeah. Oh yeah. Fuck me," before ejaculating into his own face and mouth. Unless he's thinking of a girl with a strap-on dildo, this boy is thinking of a male fucking him. And then there's the sub-genre of gay boy bibcams (i.e., boys in bedroom webcams), with titles like "OWC 11yo Gay Boy Plays – 20m27s." Interactive use of caption cards is not unknown, for example, "L2TC 28/4/2014 Gimme some fuckin requests!" (fg.10.4). These boys are looking for males, not females.

Putting a wrinkle in the narrative of innocent boys victimized by deceptive men, some boys are even aware of the underground boy pornography scene. In a video titled "Awards (2016) [BV4]", an erect twelve-year-old boy says, "I'm your boy toy. For all those boy lovers out there on BV4" (aka *BoyVids4*, an underground boy pornography website). What it means for boys to visit underground child pornography sites is a future topic for our ongoing research and reflection. The point is that boys are not universally unaware that their representations circulate among strangers (i.e., men) attracted to boys.

Even when boys focus on girls, they often know their videos have a wider audience. This might be the hardest thing for older generations to grasp. This boy's sexual videos are just part of his sexual identity and practice. They are not necessarily communications to specific people. Nor are they perfectly heterosexual communications, for they know their audience is coloured by wider circles of desire. Sexual networks, if they are open, are by definition queer, because anyone (of any gender, any age, any self-identification) can join and link up representations in whatever way they wish. Boys participating in these networks choose to

10.4 Queer boys participating in interactive networks of desire:
L2TC 28/4/2014 Gimme some fuckin requests!

give up on the strict policing of sexual orientation, leaving themselves open to view by all in exchange for the opportunity to view whoever they want, irrespective of the law, social norms, or the expectations of parents and authority figures. Under these conditions the boy's "self is ontologically multiple, different from itself, radically variegated" (Roach 2012, 36). Youth sexting subculture resists the institution of fear established by discourses of risk (of irrevocable losses) and threats (originating from unknown others), with what Karaian and Van Meyl refer to as "queer time," an attitude that recognizes "'the positive face of risk as excitement and pleasure' and even self-actualization" in the expenditure of non-reproductive pleasure (Karaian and Van Meyl 2015, 30).

Boys use Twitter to show their penises (both soft and erect) and masturbation (in still image and short-video formats), including cumshots. Networks that develop around the sexual self-representations of boys are composed of queer boys looking for boys and men, straight boys looking for girls and women, gay-identified men attracted to teens, pederastic boy porn traders, males from the East Asian and Arabic gay scenes that continue to include man-boy relations, pseudo-females (men pretending to be women), and adult hard-core porn feeds (of various orientations).[15] Boys on Twitter use their accounts to attract sexual interest, leading some to webcam encounters on Kik or other video streaming services. For these boys, *social media is sexual media*, part of complex masturbatory practices that involves the creation of a sexual identity, negotiation with prospective masturbatory partners, and the exchange of sexts (on and off Twitter).

These boys are not the tortured victims of sexual bondage, tied down and forced to perform for a camera controlled by men, something we can see in *Who Took Johnny?*, the sensationalist television documentary (about an Iowa boy's presumed kidnapping) that rocked the US mediascape in 2014, now freely available on YouTube. The sequences we have presented are not reducible to fear, exploitation, horror, or pedophile madness. (This is true even if the conditions of production and distribution in some cases might raise important questions.) These are boys revealing practices of pleasure that derive from their own bodily drives, their own inner feelings, their fantasies, desires, curiosity, and their experiences and love of masturbation. Perusing this archive of described materials, we might see boys as they are, as they want to be seen.

Empiricism means that when we begin by looking we begin in a place of truth. The machinic resurrection of a boy's sexual behaviour confronts us with facts that force us to move beyond the unreliable testimony and interested police reports. It is in the multitude and repetition of boys' production of orgasm that puerile sexuality becomes real, becomes indisputable. After the thousandth repetition, our will to deny what we see becomes exhausted, and we find ourselves finally able to confess what we knew all along: "Yes, this exists. This happens. This belongs to our world." A breakthrough in consciousness transforms abstract knowledge of sexuality into a concrete sense of its practical potentiality in the bodies of the boys in our lives. Only when we recognize that orgasm belongs to the boys we know will we be able to engage that part of them with reason, compassion, and love.

Conclusion: In Defence of the Masturbating Boy

The representations discussed here are a drop in the ocean of images produced each year. And yet these few images challenge many assumptions circulating amongst experts and non-experts alike about the sexuality and sexual representation of boys. We have shown that the genre of sexual self-representations of boys is an authentic literature of child sexuality. It shows us the ways that desire and pleasure can be for boys. It tells stories different from what we may have heard. This is "writing" that is becoming part of the record, as statements of fact, of the deepest desires, and silly moments too, sometimes meaningless and fleeting but today captured and memorialized, standing as monuments to formerly forgotten, lost, and rejected childhoods.

Orgasm is for boys. If the reader has reached the point where they can look calmly and with curiosity at an image of a masturbating boy, a great deal has been achieved, for the strict prohibition on access to these representations has forced us all to effectively deny sexual pleasure to young people, to deny seeing it as possible or meaningful, to deny anyone could recognize it or believe in it or defend it.

And there is reason to defend it. In 2016, Britain passed legislation to foist an age-verification system upon the internet industry and the general public in the name of protecting children from "inappropriate material," i.e., legal pornography. If large commercial legal adult pornography sites – like Pornhub.com – don't implement a UK government-approved age verification system, they will be blocked using the same technology originally used to block child pornography and then expanded to file-sharing sites (akin to the so-called "Great Firewall of China"; one of the ironies of living in a "free society" is its increasing resemblance to authoritarian states). This move was joined by Ennocence, a French pressure group, that tried to make regulating "Tube sites" (YouTube-like porn sites) an issue in France's 2017 presidential election (AFP 2017). And the large commercial sites are only the beginning. Next in the crosshairs are social media accounts that swap porn (Carr 2017).

The whack-a-mole war on internet porn may be hopeless, but it will be fought on the no-man's-land of the masturbating boy, who will continue to be the target of institutionalized fear-mongering. The aim is to deprive children (read: boys) their access to pornography, the only reliable education in sexual pleasure offered to boys in an abstinence-only "child protection" space that pathologizes male desire while converting every sexual expression of boys into "sexualization" and "child exploitation material."

John Carr, member of the executive board of the UK Council on Child Internet Safety and one of the ideological architects of the UK policy, had this to say about the problems arising from a lack of reliable information:

> If the child protection community – indeed if the general public, the voters, do not have reliable information about how well or otherwise we are doing in trying to combat these horrific crimes against children we are all being deprived of a vital tool which ought to be shaping key policy decisions. Else-

where that would be called a "democratic deficit." When it comes to the protection of children it is completely unacceptable. (Carr 2015)

We agree. If we are forced for ideological reasons to resort to fixed terminologies that lead us away from what is depicted in boys' sexual representation and the actual circumstances of its production, then citizens will not have reliable information and will not seek the right policies. Ignoring the masturbatory and self-representational practices of boys, treating their pleasure as unimportant or as nothing more than a danger to girls, acting as if pornography is an evil to them, or describing their self-representations as nothing but "horrific crimes against children," all constitute another kind of democratic deficit and should also be completely unacceptable.

Online, boys are voting (and confessing) with their dicks. We should be pragmatic and listen to what they are telling us they want: normalization of masturbation, access to pornography, and the decriminalization of sexting. "Protecting the children" needs to include protecting boys' access to sexual pleasure, which includes their ability to participate in pornographic culture in ways that fairly balance risk and reward. Sexting is objectively the safest sex ever devised, and is today normalizing as an integrated part of masturbatory practice for boys (even while it is being heavily policed). Addressing the sexual self-representation of boys should not be limited to inflating risks and dangers; it should also be emphasizing pleasure and self-expression. We have seen that this expression is complex and challenges the logic of exploitation that dominates thinking about boy pornography.

We believe it is time for scholarship to catch up to the radical developments in the sexual self-representation of boys. To do so will require courage and a will to innovate. In the cutout method, scholarship has one reliable technique for securing access. That method does, of course, remove much of what these images have to say. But the images are no longer absolutely silenced. In 1997, the sexologist Frits Bernard wrote of the literature pertaining to child sexuality as "generally speaking, theoretically driven, meaning that it is not based on facts" (Bernard 1997, 3). It may be possible in the near future to speak of evidence-based scholarship in the new sub-discipline of boy pornography studies, or of sexology grounded in a visual anthropology of boys' actual sexual behaviour rather than in theory, dry statistics, and half-forgotten memories that make it so easy to overlook the sexual interests of boys. There may even be sexologists who are no longer afraid to inquire into boys' ejaculation.

These transformations in scholarship have become necessary as the absurdity of protecting boys from sexual self-exploitation meets the dangerous terminal politics of an absolute prohibition defended by increasingly totalitarian police-state tactics aimed at a sexual minority, their ways of thinking, perceiving, and masturbating. Sarah Goode writes, "When individual people become so corrosively vilified, not because of what they *do* but because of what they *are*, it is certainly time that sociologists and other students of culture study this phenomenon" (2010, 47).

The sexual representations of boys are not only pornography. They are literally the only way to see the sexual behaviour of boys. It's like the telescope: you need to look through it to see the planets. You need to see boys having sex to know what it means for boys to have sex. Astronomers today cannot rely on copies of Ptolemy's star charts made a thousand years ago, with epicycles that dance around its contradictions. That's not science. We have seen the consequences of upholding the prohibition on access to the sexual representations of boys, to their corporeal confessions. It leads to analyses that to a considerable degree are out of step with the evidence.

We advocate, therefore, as the very basis of scholarship on the subject of the sexual lives and self-representation of boys, the development of an independent, scholarly archive in which boy pornography can be deposited, catalogued, and made available to academics, journalists, artists, and activists. And analyzed and understood within the context of the first-person industrial complex in which we all live, confess, masturbate, and desire.

NOTES

This chapter is comprised of excerpts from the collective's book-in-progress, which ponders and investigates such issues as exploitation and self-exploitation, feminism and state power, sexting and social media, gender politics within the abuse industry, the pornographic public domain including boy pornography culture and its markets and mythologies, and the challenges and methodologies of researching and referencing these areas under totalitarian prohibition. This chapter has been edited by the co-anthologists for reasons of length and clarity.

1 On a terminological note, we prefer the term *pederasty* to *ephebophilia* or *hebephilia* to indicate men attracted to pubescent boys, in part because the term links to historical man-boy sexual cultures meaningfully distinct from heterosexual regimes, such as those in ancient Greece or Renaissance Florence (Rocke 1996). For lack of better options, we use

the term *pedophile* to indicate men attracted to prepubescent boys but also to acknowledge the discourse of fear surrounding the relations between adults and children. Together, pederasts and male homosexual pedophiles make up the community who often self-designate as *boy lovers*.

2 This coincides with recent research which indicates White and Hispanic American boys enter puberty around ten years old, with pubic hair appearing around eleven and a half (Herman-Giddens et al. 2012). African American boys develop somewhat earlier.

3 For example, sexologist Betty Dodson links female sexual repression and lack of self-motivation and self-possession to the inability to obtain orgasm (Dodson 2013, 31) resulting from having "grown up without childhood masturbation" (30). For girls and sex play, see Lamb 2002. For girls resisting sexualization, see Duits and Van Zoonen 2011.

4 Toxic masculinity is the idea that "all that repressed emotion, all that anger, all those tears – held back since early childhood, because 'boys don't cry'– has to go somewhere, whether outwards, in the form of aggression and violence, or inwards, as depression, or ultimately suicide: the biggest killer of men under 45" (Cosslett 2017).

5 And it isn't necessarily because the boys deserved it. Andrew Heller writes, "Although some of these [youth] offenses are violent and very harmful to their victims, others are illegal not because they are coercive or harmful, but because the participants are under the age of consent" (Heller 2013, 235).

6 One recent study concluded that the "research is sparse and leaves more questions than answers" (Owens et al. 2012, 115): "Collectively, these studies suggest that youth who consume pornography may develop unrealistic sexual values and beliefs. Among the findings, higher levels of permissive sexual attitudes, sexual preoccupation, and earlier sexual experimentation have been correlated with more frequent consumption of pornography. Researchers have had difficulty replicating these results, however, and as a result the aggregate literature has failed to indicate conclusive results" (116). Other researchers note: "For a topic of considerable public policy interest, the impact of Internet pornography exposure on young people has been subjected to little social scientific research" (Sabina, Wolak, and Finkelhor 2008, 693). These statements put in question the claim that "nothing could be more damaging" than masturbating to pornography.

7 Needless to say, we find calls to safeguard girls and boys from self-surveillance (i.e., sexting) by means of state-surveillance politically dangerous.

8 The authors distinguish "sexually suggestive" and "sexually explicit," claiming only the latter would run afoul of child pornography laws, but we disagree with this sentiment, as child pornography law is notorious for capturing everything conceivably sexual in representations of young people.

9 Ten representations is a highly conservative estimate. An analysis of nine boys' sextual out-

put ranged from between twenty and 252 representations (images and videos), with an average of seventy-eight sexts per boy. Plugging that number into our calculations, we get forty-six million sexts per year produced by boys.

10 "In the last two years [2012], nearly 26 million child abuse images have been confiscated in England and Wales. The total comes from just five of the 43 police forces in England and Wales which were able to check their records" (*UK Database* 2012).

11 Funded by Swiss public arts agencies, *Hazel* was screened at the following festivals of short or queer films outside of Switzerland, among others: Amiens, Palm Springs, Cork, Saguenay, Los Angeles Outfest, Berlin Interfilm, Wiesbaden.

12 See the discussion of "networked privacy" in boyd 2012 and Karaian and Van Meyl 2015, 29.

13 "Charging documents list [the sixteen-year-old boy] as both the culprit (as an adult) and the victim (as a minor), simply for snapping a nude photo of himself in the mirror and sending it to his girlfriend … [The boy] faced up to 10 years in prison, if convicted [and] also could have been labeled sex offenders for life" (Miller 2015). "The Washington Supreme Court has upheld the conviction under state child porn laws of a 17-year-old boy who sent a picture of his own erect penis to a 22-year-old woman. The case illustrates a bizarre situation in which [the boy] is both the perpetrator and the victim of the crime. Under state law, [the boy] could face up to 10 years in prison for the conviction" (Farivar 2017).

14 This roughly corresponds to the distinction of Ringrose and Barajas between "outside-unknown" and "inside-known" (Karaian and Van Meyl 2015, 21n9).

15 Almost entirely absent is true pedophile pornography: prepubescent boys are almost never seen on Twitter, except perhaps in networks composed entirely by protected accounts and thus invisible to public inspection.

Without authoritative publishers (like newspapers or journals) or stable distribution points (like youtube.com), without stable filenames (due to renaming) or stable file sizes (due to variations in cropping, re-encoding, and re-sizing), without specific dates or geo-locations (due to lack of EXIF data), without access to PhotoDNA-type technologies that produce fingerprints from the contents (as contrasted with hashes), without a single public or scholarly repository where all of this can be established, without being able to make the material available themselves, how can researchers reference boy pornography as research material? For now we offer file name, date where known, file type (file size), time.

REFERENCES

AFP. 2017. "Porn 'Tube' Sites Threaten Children and Actors, Critics Say." *Deccan Chronicle*, 28 January. http://www.deccanchronicle.com/world/america/280117/porn-tube-sites-threaten-children-and-actors-critics-say.html.

Anderson, Mike. 2017. "After Declaring 'Public Health Crisis,' Lawmaker Wants to Pave Way for Pornography Lawsuits." *KSL*, 2 January. https://www.ksl.com/?nid=148&sid=42757842&title=after-declaring-public-health-crisis-lawmaker-wants-to-pave-way-for-pornography-lawsuits.

Avard, Christian. 2010. "Gail Dines: How 'Pornland' Destroys Intimacy and Hijacks Sexuality." *XYonline*, 29 June. http://xyonline.net/content/gail-dines-how-"pornland"-destroys-intimacy-and-hijacks-sexuality.

Bahadur, Nina. 2015. "This Is How Women React to Dick Pics." *Huffington Post*, 11 February. https://www.huffingtonpost.ca/entry/women-react-to-dick-pics-with-horror_n_6661402?ec_carp=8206467080471929363.

Bartlett-Hughes, C. 2010. "Respondent's Factum." *R. v. Robert Katigbak* in the Supreme Court of Canada. Court File No. 33762.

Bennett, Laura. 2015. "The First-Person Industrial Complex." *Slate*, 14 September. http://www.slate.com/articles/life/technology/2015/09/the_first_person_industrial_complex_how_the_harrowing_personal_essay_took.html.

Bernard, Frits. 1997. "Tabooed Child Sexuality." In *Pedophilia Unbound: Theory, Research, Practice*, edited by Frits Bernard. Originally published by Foerster Verlag. http://www.shfri.net/trans/bernard/bernard.cgi.

Bourg, Julian. 2007. *From Revolution to Ethics: May 1968 and Contemporary French Thought*. Montreal: McGill-Queen's University Press.

Bowes, Mark. 2017. "Danish Man Living in Dinwiddie Sentences to Serve 25 Years for Graphic Collection of Child Porn." *Richmond Times-Dispatch*, 2 September. https://www.richmond.com/news/local/central-virginia/danish-man-living-in-dinwiddie-sentenced-to-serve-years-for/article_67d5bcad-915f-549b-acb5-85383258a20a.html.

boyd, danah. 2012. "Networked Privacy." *Surveillance and Society* 10, no. 3–4: 348–50.

Carr, John. 2013a. "A Sad, Sad Moment." *Desiderata*, 2 June. Blog. https://johnc1912.wordpress.com/2013/06/02/a-sad-sad-moment/.

– 2013b. "Tackling Online Child Sex Abuse Images." *Desiderata*, 11 June. Blog. https://johnc1912.wordpress.com/2013/06/11/tackling-online-child-sex-abuse-images/.

– 2015. "A Big Step Forward." *Desiderata*, 6 January. Blog. https://johnc1912.wordpress.com/2015/01/06/a-big-step-forward/.

– 2017. "A Big but Solvable Problem." *Desiderata*, 20 January. Blog. https://johnc1912.wordpress.com/2017/01/30/a-big-but-solvable-problem/.

Carroll, Aaron E. 2017. "Sex Education Based on Abstinence? There's a Real Absence of Evidence." *New York Times*, 22 August. https://www.nytimes.com/2017/08/22/upshot/sex-education-based-on-abstinence-theres-a-real-absence-of-evidence.html.

Casavant, Lyne, and James R. Robertson. 2007. *The Evolution of Pornography Law in Canada*. CIR 84-3E. Ottawa: Library of Parliament of Canada, Senate, Law and Government Division.

Chemaly, Soraya. 2015. "Twelve Reasons Why Gender Matters to Understanding Teenage Sexting." 11 November. https://www.huffpost.com/entry/12-reasons-why-gender-matters-to-understanding-teenage-sexting_b_8523142.

Classically Liberal. 2009. "There Is a Fury and Sadness Inside That I Cannot Express." *Classically Liberal*, 16 September. Blog. http://freestudents.blogspot.ca/2009/09/there-is-fury-and-and-sadness-inside.html.

Comella, Lynn. 2014. "Studying Porn Cultures." *Porn Studies* 1, no. 1–2: 64–70.

Cosslett, Rhiannon Lucy. 2017. "At Last Men Are Joining Our Conversation about Toxic Masculinity." *Guardian* (UK), 6 September. https://www.theguardian.com/commentisfree/2017/sep/06/men-joining-feminist-conversation-toxic-masculinity-chris-hemmings-robert-webb.

Crabbe, Maree, and David Corlett. 2010. "Eroticising Inequality: Technology, Pornography and Young People." Domestic Violence Resource Center Victoria. 16 November. http://www.dvrcv.org.au/knowledge-centre/our-blog/eroticising-inequality-technology-pornography-and-young-people.

Crofts, Thomas, and Murray Lee. 2013. "'Sexting,' Children and Child Pornography." *Sydney Law Review* 35, no. 1: 85–106.

Dewey, Caitlin. 2015. "The Sexting Scandal No One Sees." *Washington Post*, 28 April. https://www.washingtonpost.com/news/the-intersect/wp/2015/04/28/the-sexting-scandal-no-one-sees/.

Dines, Gail. 2010. *Pornland: How Porn Has Hijacked Our Sexuality*. Boston: Beacon.

Dodson, Betty. 2013. "Porn Wars." In *The Feminist Porn Book: The Politics of Producing Pleasure*, edited by Tristan Taormino et al., 23–31. New York: Feminist Press.

Duits, Linda, and Liesbet Van Zoonen. 2011. "Coming to Terms with Sexualization." *European Journal of Cultural Studies* 14, no. 5: 491–506.

Eaves, Ali. 2016. "Study: Only 57 Percent of Straight Men Masturbate Regularly." *Men's Health*, 9 March. https://www.menshealth.com/sex-women/how-common-is-masturbation.

Eichenwald, Kurt. 2005. "Through His Webcam, a Boy Joins a Sordid Online World." *New York Times*, 19 December. http://www.nytimes.com/2005/12/19/us/through-his-webcam-a-boy-joins-a-sordid-online-world.html.

Erooga, Marcus, and Helen Masson, eds. 1999. *Children and Young People Who Sexually Abuse Others: Current Developments and Practice Responses*. London: Routledge.

Europol. 2017. "Stop Child Abuse – Trace an Object." *Stop Child Abuse*, 1 June. https://www.europol.europa.eu/stopchildabuse/.

Farivar, Cyrus. 2017. "Teen Sends Dick Pic to 22-Year-Old Woman, Now He's a Child Pornographer." *Ars Technica*, 15 September. https://arstechnica.com/tech-policy/2017/09/teen-sends-dick-pic-to-22-year-old-now-hes-a-child-pornographer/.

Ferraro, Monique Mattei, and Eoghan Casey. 2004. *Investigating Child Exploitation and Pornography: The Internet, Law and Forensic Science*. Amsterdam, Elsevier.

Foucault, Michel. [1978] 1984. *The History of Sexuality.* Vol. 3, *Care of the Self.* New York: Penguin Books.

— [1978] 1996a. "The Danger of Child Sexuality." In *Foucault Live: Collected Interviews, 1961–1984*, edited by Sylvère Lotringer; translated by Lysa Hochroth and John Johnston, 264–74. New York: Semiotext(e).

— [1982] 1996b. "History and Homosexuality." Translated by Lysa Hochroth and John Johnston. In *Foucault Live: Collected Interviews, 1961–1984*, edited by Sylvère Lotringer, 363–70. New York: Semiotext(e).

Goode, Sarah D. 2010. *Understanding and Addressing Adult Sexual Attraction to Children: A Study of Paedophiles in Contemporary Society.* New York: Routledge.

Greenblatt, Stephen. 2004. "Me, Myself and I." *New York Review of Books* 51, no. 6 (8 April): 32–6.

Guappone, Nicole. 2016. "Why Isn't Pornography Part of Sex Education for Teens?" *Alternet*, 6 September. https://www.alternet.org/sex-amp-relationships/why-isnt-pornography-part-sex-education-teens.

Hajda, Sandra. 2017. "Ten Years of the Kim Kardashian Sex Tape – Paris Hilton, Kanye West, the Incredible Scandals That Followed." *Inquisitr*, 9 April. https://www.inquisitr.com/4129703/ten-years-of-the-kim-kardashian-sex-tape-paris-hilton-kanye-west-the-incredible-scandals-that-followed/.

Heller, Andrew. 2013. "Harming Children in the Name of 'Child Protection': How Minors Who Have Sex with Other Minors Are Abused by the Law and Therapy." In *Censoring Sex Research: The Debate over Male Intergenerational Relations*, edited by Thomas K. Hubbard and Beert Verstraete, 235–50. London: Routledge.

Herman-Giddens, Marcia E., J. Steffes, D. Harris, E. Slora, M. Hussey, S.A. Dowshen, R. Wasserman, J.R. Serwint, L. Smitherman, and E.O. Reiter.2012. "Secondary Sexual Characteristics in Boys: Data from the Pediatric Research in Office Settings Network." *Pediatrics* 130 (5):1058–68.

Hind, Katie. 2017. "Sext Addicts: How British Parents Are Paying £70,000 to Send Their Teenagers on Specialist Therapy Courses Abroad to Stop Them Sending Naked Photos." *Daily Mail*, 2 April. http://www.dailymail.co.uk/news/article-4371936/Parents-pay-70k-send-teens-course-stop-sexting.html.

Hoder, Randye. 2014. "Study Finds Most Teens Sext before They're 18." *Time*, 2 July. http://time.com/2948467/chances-are-your-teen-is-sexting/.

Human Rights Watch. 2013. "Raised on the Registry: The Irreparable Harm of Placing Children on Sex Offender Registries in the US." *Human Rights Watch*, 1 May. https://www.hrw.org/report/2013/05/01/raised-registry/irreparable-harm-placing-children-sex-offender-registries-us.

Influence Central. 2017. "Kids and Tech: The Evolution of Today's Digital Natives." *Influence Central*. http://influence-central.com/kids-tech-the-evolution-of-todays-digital-natives/

Jones, Gerald P. 1990. "The Study of Intergenerational Intimacy in North America: Beyond Politics and Pedophilia." *Journal of Homosexuality* 20: 275–95.

Karaian, L. and K. Van Mey. (2015) "Reframing Risqué/Risky: Queer Temporalities, Teenage Sexting, and Freedom of Expression." *Laws* 4, no. 1: 18–36. http://www.mdpi.com/2075-471X/4/1/18.

Kilpatrick, Allie C. 1987. "Childhood Sexual Experiences: Problems and Issues in Studying Long-Range Effects." *Journal of Sex Research* 23: 173–96.

Kinsey, Alfred C., Wardell B. Pomeroy, and Clyde E. Martin. 1948. *Sexual Behavior in the Human Male*. Indiana: Indiana University Press.

Klotz, Marcia. 2014. "'It's Not Really Porn': Insex and the Revolution in Technological Interactivity." In *Porn Archives*, edited by Tim Dean, Steven Ruszczycky, and David Squires, 284–99. Durham: Duke University Press.

Lamb, Sharon. 2002. *The Secret Lives of Girls: What Good Girls Really Do – Sex Play, Aggression, and Their Guilt*. New York: Free Press.

Laqueur, Thomas. 2003. *Solitary Sex: A Cultural History of Masturbation*. New York: Zone Books.

Lenhart, Amanda. 2015. "Teens, Social Media and Technology Overview 2015." Pew Research Center. 9 April. http://www.pewinternet.org/2015/04/09/teens-social-media-technology-2015/.Levine, Judith. 2003. *Harmful to Minors: The Perils of Protecting Children from Sex*. Minneapolis: University of Minnesota Press.

Malón, Agustín. 2010. "Onanism and Child Sexual Abuse: A Comparative Study of Two Hypotheses." *Archives of Sexual Behavior* 39, no. 3: 637–52.

Mamiverse Team. 2014. "The Mom Walk of Shame: Ten Ways to Handle Catching Your Son Masturbating." *Mamiverse*, 9 January. http://mamiverse.com/talking-to-boys-about-masturbation-67711/.

Miller, Michael E. 2015. "N.C. Just Prosecuted a Teenage Couple for Making Child Porn – of Themselves." *Washington Post*, 21 September. https://www.washingtonpost.com/news/morning-mix/wp/2015/09/21/n-c-just-prosecuted-a-teenage-couple-for-making-child-porn-of-themselves/.

Mitchell, Kimberly J., David Finkelhor, Lisa M. Jones, and Janis Wolak. 2012. "Prevalence and Characteristics of Youth Sexting: A National Study." *Pediatrics* 129, no. 1:1–8.

Morgan, Angus. 2017. "Pornography the Norm for Young Australians." *Burnet Institute*, 30 June. https://www.burnet.edu.au/news/852_pornography_the_norm_for_young_australians/.

Nathan, Debbie. 2007. *Groundwork Guides: Pornography*. Toronto: House of Anansi Press.

Nations Encyclopedia. 2017. "Population, Aged 13–17, Total – Population – Education Statistics." *Nations Encyclopedia*, 16 February. http://www.nationsencyclopedia.com/WorldStats/Edu-population-13-17.html.

not4urmother. 2017. "Six Things Girls Actually Think about Your Dick Pic." *FlockU*. https://www.flocku.com/articles. Link expired.

O'Leary, Amy. 2012. "So How Do We Talk about This?" *New York Times*, 9 May. http://www.nytimes.com/2012/05/10/garden/when-children-see-internet-pornography.html.

Oprah Winfrey Show. 20016. "Seduced in Cyberspace." 15 February. htttp://www.oprah.com/oprahshow/seduced-in-cyberspace/.

Owens, Eric W., Richard J. Behun, Jill C. Manning, and Rory C. Reid. 2012. "The Impact of Internet Pornography on Adolescents: A Review of the Research." *Sexual Addiction and Compulsivity* 19: 99–122.

Plummer, Kenneth. 1995. *Telling Sexual Stories: Power, Change, and Social Worlds*. London: Routledge.

Roach, Tom. 2012. *Friendship as a Way of Life: Foucault, AIDS, and the Politics of Shared Estrangement*. Albany: SUNY Press.

Rochman, Bonnie. 2011. "The Results Are In: First National Study of Teen Masturbation." *Time*, 11 August. http://healthland.time.com/2011/08/11/boys-masturbate-more-than-girls-seriously/.

Rocke, Michael. 1996. *Forbidden Friendships: Homosexuality and Male Culture in Renaissance Florence*. New York: Oxford University Press.

Romboy, Dennis. 2016. "State Senator Wants Utah to Declare Pornography a Public Health Crisis. *KSL*, 1 February. https://www.ksl.com/?sid=38354310&nid=148.

Ruszczycky, Steven. 2014. "Stadler's Boys; or, The Fictions of Child Pornography." In *Porn Archives*, edited by Tim Dean, Steven Ruszczycky, and David Squires, 399–419. Durham: Duke University Press.

Ryder, Bruce. 2003. "The Harms of Child Pornography Law." *UBC Law Review* 36, no. 1: 101–35.

Sabina, Chiara, Janis Wolak, and David Finkelhor. 2008. "The Nature and Dynamics of Internet Pornography Exposure for Youth." *CyberPsychology and Behavior* 11, no. 6: 691–3.

Saint Thomas, Sophie. 2017. "How to Take a Dick Pic That Actually Looks Good." *Allure*, 14 July. https://www.allure.com/story/how-to-take-a-dick-pic/.

Schroeder, Joanna. 2015. "What Your Kids Need to Know about Sexting." *Babble*, 8 November. https://www.babble.com/parenting/what-your-kids-need-to-know-about-sexting/

Scott, Ellen. 2017. "Sex Education Needs to Pay More Attention to Masturbation." *Metro*, 16 May. http://metro.co.uk/2017/05/16/sex-education-needs-to-pay-more-attention-to-masturbation-6641467/.

Skenazy, Lenore. 2016. "Bogus 'Sex Offender' Labels Are Ruining Lives." *New York Post*, 25 July. http://nypost.com/2016/07/25/bogus-sex-offender-labels-are-ruining-lives/

Smith, Clarissa, M. Barker, and F. Attwood. 2015. "Why Do People Watch Porn? Results from pornresearch.org." In *New Views on Pornography: Sexuality, Politics, and the Law*, edited by Lynn Comella and Shira Tarrant, 277–96. Santa Barbara: Praeger.

Snyder, Howard N. 2000. "Sexual Assault of Young Children as Reported to Law Enforcement." US Department of Justice Bureau of Justice Statistics. https://www.bjs.gov/content/pub/pdf/saycrle.pdf.

Stapleton, Adam. 2010. "Knowing It When You (Don't) See It: Mapping the Pornographic Child in Order to Diffuse the Paedophilic Gaze." *Global Media Journal Australian* 4, no. 2: 1–21.

Strohmaier, Heidi, Megan Murphy, and David DeMatteo. 2014. "Youth Sexting: Prevalence Rates, Driving Motivations, and the Deterrent Effect of Legal Consequences." *Sexuality Research and Social Policy* 11, no. 3: 245–55.

Sullivan, Andrew. 2016. "America Has Never Been So Ripe for Tyranny." *New York Magazine*, 1 May. http://nymag.com/daily/intelligencer/2016/04/america-tyranny-donald-trump.html

Sullum, Jacob. 2011. "A Life Sentence for Possessing Child Pornography." *Reason*, 7 November. http://reason.com/blog/2011/11/07/a-life-sentence-for-possessing-child-por/.

– 2017. "Dick Pic Makes Teenager Guilty of Sexually Exploiting Himself, High Court Says." *Reason*, 18 September. http://reason.com/blog/2017/09/18/dick-pic-makes-teenager-guilty-of-sexual/.

Taormino, Tristan, and Celine Parrenas Shimizu, Constance Penley, and Mireille Miller-Young, eds. 2013. *The Feminist Porn Book*. New York: Feminist Press at the City University of New York.

UK Database. 2012. "'Child Abuse Images' (Copine Scale)." https://theukdatabase.com/uk-child-abusers-named-and-shamed/childhood-abuses/paedophile-party-members/.

Viglianco-VanPelt, Michelle, and Kyla Boyse. 2009. "Masturbation." University of Michigan Health Service. http://www.med.umich.edu/yourchild/topics/masturb.htm.

Weinstein, James. 2016. "The Context and Content of New York v. Ferber." In *Refining Child Pornography Law: Crime, Language, and Social Consequences*, edited by Carrisa Byrne Hessick, 19–56. Ann Arbor: University of Michigan Press.

Westwood, Rosemary. 2016. "In the Age of Sexting, Feminism Is the Anti-Chill for Teens, and That Is Chilling." *Metro News*, 21 March. http://www.metronews.ca/views/metro-views/2016/03/20/in-the-age-of-sexting-feminism-is-the-anti-chill-for-teens.html

Williams, Linda, ed. 2004. *Porn Studies*. Durham: Duke University Press.

Wood, Heather, 2013. "Internet Pornography and Paedophilia." *Psychoanalytic Psychotherapy* 27, no. 4: 319–38.

Wyatt, Wendy, and Kristie Bunton. 2009. "Perspectives on Pornography Demand Ethical Critique." In *Handbook of Mass Media Ethics*, edited by C. Christians and L. Wilkins, 149–61. Mahwah, NJ: Erlbaum.

Ybarra, Michele L., and Kimberly J. Mitchell, 2014. "'Sexting' and Its Relation to Sexual Activity and Sexual Risk Behavior in a National Survey of Adolescents." *Journal of Adolescent Health* 55, no. 6: 757–64.

Zamosky, Lisa. 2011. "Caught Your Kid Masturbating?" *WebMD Discover Motherhood*, 4 January. https://www.webmd.com/parenting/features/caught-your-kid-masturbating/.

MEDIAGRAPHY

9 Sexts. n.d. Image. Original files unknown; image constructed by source.

Awards (2016) [BV4]. 2016. Video. (173,923 KB) 26m37s.

Beilinson, David, Suki Wahley, and Michael Galinsky. 2014. *Who Took Johnny?* Film. 120 min. https://www.youtube.com/watch?v=KU87XziW5CM. USA.

how to wank. n.d. Video. (34,086 KB) 2m14s.

IMG_1941. n.d. Video. (50,462 KB) 49s.

L2TC 28/4/2014 Gimme some fuckin requests! n.d. Image.

9 Sexts. n.d. Image. Original files unknown; image constructed by source.

OWE [Collection]. *OWC 11yo Gay Boy Plays – 20m27s.* n.d. Video. (39,513 KB) 20m27s.

Ruggli, Tamer. 2012. *Hazel.* Film. 8 min. https://vimeo.com/59415937. Switzerland.

13yo – Homemade Anus with Diaper – Fucking, Peeing, Moaning, Dirty Talking (Sound) HOT. n.d. Video. (22,257 KB) 7m41s.

Tommy13Snapchat. n.d. Video. (35,338 KB) 3m35s.

YuroTube – Hot Dutch (or Belgian) with good dick. n.d. Video. (1,365 KB) 19s.

Part Two
Ars Erotica

Pornographies

11

Like a Prayer: Confessing My Beatific-Cum-Demonic Visions of Men (and God?)

CONNOR STEELE

> So then, with my mind I am a slave to the law of God, but with my flesh I am a slave to the law of sin.
> • Paul of Tarsus, Rom. 7: 25, NRSV

Every good quasi-secular confession must contain several pieces of offensive blasphemy.[1] Hence, let me begin this one by expressing my affectionate and impious agreement with queer biblical scholar Stephen D. Moore, when he notes that the Judeo-Christian God is the archetypical "muscle jock," based on the weightlifting he enjoys as well as the amount of animal protein he likes to consume by way of sacrifice – and "power top," given his near pathological proclivity for misogyny (1996). Yahweh also seems to have much anxiety concerning his penis, else why insist so strongly upon (Israelite) circumcision? (Eilberg-Schwartz 1994).

The epigraph to this paper arguably initiated the western genre of sexual confession. Even as a good Christian boy, I always detested Paul. The apostle too wanted to be a power top, although he was likely physically disabled, and he urged his male followers to achieve the same goal (II Cor. 12:7–9). Yet his turmoil, pride, shame, sexism, and ableism still command my attraction and repulsion, in a manner far surpassing the charisma of "gentle Jesus," no matter how buff Christ was on the cross, at once crippled and celestial in his crucified and castrated masculinity. Paul, along with Augustine of Hippo, who made much of this passage when developing his doctrines of Original Sin and the Divided Will ([AD397–400] 1998, 5 [1.10] and 30 [2.6]) – in addition to giving us the genre of sexual confession, arguably spawned the sodomite, that nefarious progenitor of "the gay" (Jordan 1997). For these things, I owe these men a great, albeit profoundly ambivalent, debt. Paul and Augustine wanted to confess every prurient detail of their innermost thoughts, including, likely, desire for men and how such sordid yearnings brought them into a dialectical relationship between *porneia* (pornography, sexual exploitation, concupiscence, enjoyment) and beauty. I propose the same enterprise, confessing my sins of pride and shame.

Like them, I know what it is to be paralyzed before a hypostatized super-human whom one must love but not *too much*, and certainly not in *that way*. I know the pain of being divided, disabled, and sinful, except that I expect no salvation. Having become a somewhat (dis)reputable recovering Christian homo, I have, I think, discovered Christ in porn. Before you rebuke me, God is everywhere, especially among the fallen. Idolatry is, incidentally, the very thing that the apostle connects to "dishonourable [i.e., homosexual] passion" in Romans. 1: 27. I, like Paul and Augustine before me, desire(d) to negate my own finitude through (comm)union with and worship of a perfect male (demi)god, whose (imagined) existence is both *fabulous* (in both senses) and violently traumatic. The reason I feel the need to confess my desire for gay porn is because many men who have sex with men are often thought of as disabled in relation to ideas of sex and masculinity. We also are condemned for being queer by a very naughty God, whose Trinitarian structure means that he engages in an incestuous, not to mention homoerotic, threesome. This interdependent threesome means that he is both all powerful and disabled.

Consequently, my confession answers Robert McRuer's challenge to dissect the intersection between queer and disability studies by comprehending pornography as a key site for understanding unrealistic messages concerning what the gay male body can and ought to be *able* to do (2006). When I watch videos from sites such as SeanCody, Bromo, Men, GuysInSweatpants, Manhandled, BrokeStraightBoys, CorbanFisher, Randyblue, and so forth, in addition to the perfectly chiselled, predominantly white bodies, I see the following: performers who thrust at superhuman speed, who are unnaturally flexible, who are able to bottom (read: receive a penis in their anus) without effort or preparation, perform fellatio nearly without breathing, have sex in awkward positions, endure extreme amounts of discomfort, and perform for long periods without ejaculation. Naturally, because gay porn is all about the cock, much of my theoretical framework comes from Jacques Lacan, who is arguably obsessed with its more rarefied brother, the phallus (Irigaray 1985a).

The work of Leo Bersani (2009), Tim Dean (2009), and Lee Edelman (2004) (disciples of Lacan), or what is called the antisocial thesis in queer theory, is crucial to my theoretical understanding of my own sexual enjoyment/trauma (Bersani 2009). Bersani says that though we often long for *jouissance* (desire, enjoyment,

11.1 "Greater love hath no man than this, that he lay down his life for his friends" (John 15: 13). Connor Steele and friend. Photo by friend.

and/or orgasm) arising from erotic activity, men feel the loss of control that attends it as disquieting. In our misogynist society, he argues, the feminine, and therefore disabled, "sodomite" is a potent symbol. This theoretical position explains my (in the words of Bersani) suicidal desire to be excessively penetrated and filled with semen like a woman. My desire for "promiscuity," especially sex without condoms and other forms of masculinity, daring, and endurance, perverts traditional forms of safety, intimacy, and kinship, disobeying the contemporary injunction to health and ability (Bersani 2009, 18). Hence, much of the unacknowledged eroticism that comes from contemporary gay porn has little to do with sex *itself* – if there ever were such a thing – and very much to do with the fantasy of a self-contained, self-possessed, and extremely powerful body that is capable of limitless enjoyment. And every time I masturbate, what I think I implicitly fear is that I actually enjoyed the experience in a way that would compromise my very tenuous masculinity.

My erectile (dys)function begins to make tragic sense when one considers the following quotation from Tobin Siebers: "The ideology of ability is at its simplest the preference for able-bodiedness. At its most radical, it defines the baseline by which humanness is determined" (2008, 8). I am often symbolically castrated and rendered asexual because I am believed to be unable to reproduce. My body disrupts the narrative temporality of hegemonic sexuality and explores different erogenous zones, belying the fantasy of control and self-possession that accompanies many idealized images of sex. Indeed, as someone with Cerebral Palsy, which causes spasms, comparable to those of orgasm, frequently but, alas, without the neurochemical response – I am constantly reminded of this idea, and doubly so in my most autoerotic moments. This is especially disquieting when I ask what is sadly a very existential question in a gay man's life: "Am I a top or am I a bottom, and what does this mean for my gender identity?"

Though, knowing the effort it takes to bottom well, I acknowledge the athleticism required of both partners, in most porn the bottom is depicted as more feminine. He is often smaller in stature and body type, with a smaller (or, more accurately, less emphasized) penis. By means of camera angles, positioning, body language, facial expression, lighting, focus, and dialogue, the penetrative partner (or top) is represented as the one in charge. He is more able. He has both the symbolic phallus and the bigger cock. Because the representation of orgasm relates to fears concerning masculinity and ability, the differences between the two partners become all the more pointed. Frequently, the bottom is "more disabled" during intercourse because he is not in control of his passions and/or sensations, whereas the top is far more stoic and self-possessed. On the one hand, the ability to "shoot" semen, through its masculinist reliance on metaphors of marksmanship and excess, safeguards manhood through a Big Bang, as it were. On the other hand, no matter how explosive the cum shot, persons relinquish control of their bodies at the moment of orgasm (Dean 2009, 107–11). If my readers think that I have gone balls deep into theoretical abstraction, it is only to corroborate the sad point that virtually every man who knows me, regardless of his sexual orientation, has said something along the lines of, "Well naturally, you would be the bottom," when the topic of sexual intercourse arises. While I recognize that both performers have near super-human ability, as a disabled viewer I have a mixture of empathy and disgust for the bottom and his quest to rejuvenate his lost masculinity. Hence the genesis of the humorous and fascinating post-coital shower scene (that my second confession parodies below), in which the two partners engage in homosocial jocularity, often about what they just did. They gently cleanse each other, adopting a confident tone as though reviewing last night's hockey game. They perform this banter to reassure one another, despite the feminine and extreme pleasure they allegedly underwent, that they are still able-bodied "straight" men.

Here is the crucifying nexus of my desire. Consistent with the findings of other scholars (Downes 2012, 9–18; Lanzieri and Hildebrandt 2011, 280), I observe that my disability seemed to have interacted with gender nonconforming behaviour to elicit distance from and desire for the approval of my dad. Regrettably, my young (and sometimes contemporary) (un)conscious mind struggles with a notion of femininity associated with disability and lack. In my dad, I saw the two faces of manhood, and I fell in love with them both, even as I was a terrified child. It would probably help the reader to know that my father was an amateur bodybuilder who remains deeply conflicted about his own masculinity. He is also extremely tender, fun, and by virtue of his physical ability, better able to take care of a highly dependent person. It seems tragically obvious to me that my young mind created a dichotomy between the cold and unforgiving Yahweh, the male God of the Hebrew Bible, who, like my dad on a bad day, understands disability and non-normative sexual orientation as a curse, and the allegedly more compassionate and feminine Jesus of the New Testament. This embracing and healing hippie did not compromise his masculinity but cherished disabled and gay persons and did practical things to help them – like my dad on a good day. So I think that to unite with men sexually, and bonding homosocially more broadly, is a partial way of mending this psychic and physical wound. In a culture that constantly objectifies me by dint of a medicalized gaze, through pornography I can objectify others and participate in their sexuality, thereby somewhat regaining a crucial part of humanity denied to the disabled.

To show the psychodynamics at work, I would like to end with two confessions. These will lead me to my final and most shocking yet mundane confession. Frustrated, in every sense of that word, and inexperienced, I learned the perils of bringing home the office (I also volunteer at a sexual health clinic) with me when I had sex with a man who was overweight, to a greater degree than I am, and unfit, despite falling into the category of able-bodied. Like a good academic, I did a lot of prep work and research, I was *ready, willing, and able* to be a "power bottom." I wanted to embody heresy and incarnate the sodomite. He was willing too, but despite his desire, his back, knees, weight, and so forth, combined with my physical limitations, made this very difficult. This queen was unimpressed! Narcissistically obsessed with my own perceived sexual failures, I could not comprehend an able-bodied person failing in this way.

About a month later, I swam in a public pool with one of my attractive and athletic friends, whom I am attracted to precisely because I find his able-bodied masculinity heartbreaking and unattainable. This is even more difficult because he identifies as partially asexual. I had to behave like "a good Christian boy," though my lust/love is at times overwhelming. How could it not have been? The adorable jerk, God bless him, rock climbs, does backflips, bareknuckle-boxes, weight lifts, is kind, reads philosophy, is highly intelligent, and has a six-pack! I laughed in his face when he said my body was adorable precisely *because* my scoliosis and third nipple made it asymmetrical. I constructed him as the gentle Christ/Father (a)sexualized Adonis I still crave, giving him just enough aggression to be interesting, all the while feeling desperately unworthy of his (im)perfection. Exemplifying internalized misogyny, ableism, and homophobia, I gave a dramatic performance of ability, complete with several long laps of the pool, standing, walking, and stretching. Seeing that I was quite exhausted, he offered me a break. I said, regretting it immediately, "Breaks are for wimps!" He said, "YEAH! That's my kind of guy!"

Beaming with pride, I continued my exhausting performative exercise, feeling like a "Macho Man" indeed. Then we "danced" to "Material Girl" by Madonna, and I felt "like a virgin, touched for the very first time." Once out of the pool, he struggled to get my shirt back on. The gentle person that he is, he, like most persons, was concerned about hurting me. Because he is so strong and also suffers from chronic pain, he touches me with a firm softness that is disarming yet not condescending. Playing on my obvious fantasy, with characteristic humour he said, "YES! SHIRT IS ON! RECORD TIME! GO TEAM!" I asked for a high five and a hug.

Even though our friendship has now ended, in part because he could not take the pressure of embodying my conflicting hopes and ideals, at the time there was little I valued more than his embrace. Though our interactions never surpassed these types of transient yet precious moments, I can say, aware that this is both extremely corny and true, that they were as close to the "Beatific Vision" – to use the phrase (Aquinas [1265–74] 2017, supp. Q. 92) coined by my favourite bromo (forgive me, Pope Francis), Thomas Aquinas – as I may ever be. So perhaps my greatest virtue/vice as a queer sexuality studies scholar is in fact (dis)avowed belief in something as ideologically pedestrian as love "that moves the sun and all the other stars" (Alighieri [early fourteenth century] 2007, canto 33.34) (forgive me, Dante!), by which I am both annihilated and "resurrected" to idyllic life. My greatest and most ignominious confession, therefore, is that I am an oxymoronic, crippled, queer, wannabe-muscle-jock, postmodern, failed (a)sexualized power bottom, porn-addicted Augustinian-Thomist, body-shaming, misogynist nerd, against, or perhaps because of, my better judgment. Forgive me, father; for I have sinned! I (sometimes) know not what I do (Luke 23: 34) or whom I have truly loved.

NOTE

1 The tenor of this work takes inspiration from a fascinating and underappreciated book by Richard Rambuss, *Closet Devotions* (1998). This work begins with a discussion of gay pornography and then moves to a discussion of homoeroticism in sixteenth- and seventeenth-century English metaphysical poetry. Though the topic may, at least at first, appear frivolous and self-indulgent, I want to explore the complicated ways we try to reach what is sacred to us by profane means and the inherent link between sexuality, transgression, and violence. Consult, for example, Georges Bataille ([1962] 1977). I would also like to acknowledge support for this paper from the Humanities and Social Sciences Research Council of Canada, the generous assistance of the editors, and the continuing friendship of Eric Raymond Cramer Baxter. All mistakes are my own.

REFERENCES

Alighieri, Dante. [Early fourteenth century] 2007. *Paradiso*. Translated Robert Hollander and Jean Hollander. New York: Doubleday/Anchor. Princeton Dante Project 2.0. http://etcweb.princeton.edu/cgi-bin/dante/campuscgi/mpb/GetCantoSection.pl.

Aquinas, Thomas. [1265–74] 2017. *Summa Theologiae*. Translated by Fathers of the English Dominican Province. Edited by Kevin Knight. New Advent. http://www.newadvent.org/summa/5092.htm.

Augustine. [AD 397–400] 1998. *The Confessions*. Translated by R.S. Pine-Coffin. New York: Penguin Books.

Bataille, Georges. [1962] 1977. *Death and Sensuality: A Study of Eroticism and the Taboo*. Translated by Mary Dalwood. The Literature of Death and Dying series. New York: Arno Press.

Bersani, Leo. 2009. *Is the Rectum a Grave? and Other Essays*. Chicago: University of Chicago Press.

Dean, Tim. 2009. *Unlimited Intimacy: Reflections on the Subculture of Barebacking*. Chicago: University of Chicago Press.

Downes, Alan. 2012. *The Velvet Rage: Overcoming the Pain of Growing Up Gay in a Straight Man's World*. 2nd ed. New York: Da Capo Lifelong Books.

Edelman, Lee. 2004. *No Future: Queer Theory and the Death Drive*. 2nd ed. Durham: Duke University Press.

Eilberg-Schwartz, Howard. 1994. *God's Phallus and Other Problems for Men and Monotheism*. Boston: Beacon Press.

Irigaray, Luce. 1985a. *This Sex Which Is Not One*. 1985. Translated by Catherine Porter and Caitlyn Burke. Ithaca: Cornell University Press.

– 1985b. *Speculum of the Other Woman*. Translated by Carol Gilligan. Ithaca: Cornell University Press.

Jordan, Mark D. 1997. *The Invention of Sodomy in Christian Theology*. Chicago: University of Chicago Press.

Lanzieri, Nicholas, and Tom Hildebrandt. 2011. "Using Hegemonic Masculinity to Explain Gay Male Attraction to Muscular and Athletic Men." *Journal of Homosexuality* 58, no. 2: 275–93.

McRuer, Robert. 2006. "Compulsory Able-Bodiedness and Queer/Disabled Existence." In *The Disability Studies Reader*, edited by Lennard J. Davis, 29–301. New York: Routledge.

Moore, Stephen D. 1996. *God's Gym: Divine Male Bodies of the Bible*. New York: Routledge.

Rambuss, Richard. 1998. *Closet Devotions*. Durham: Duke University Press.

Siebers, Tobin. 2008. *Disability Theory*. Ann Arbor: University of Michigan Press.

12

Camming and Erotic Capital: The Pornographic as an Expression of Neoliberalism

ÉRIC FALARDEAU

TRANSLATED BY JORDAN ARSENEAULT

> Everything in life is an act.
> • John C. Holmes[1]

Since the early 1980s, we have seen how pornographic aesthetics have been borrowed by and incorporated into various artistic and commercial milieus. From advertising to television series, contemporary art to music videos, "pornographic" imagery seems omnipresent. This pollinizing of the mainstream by "X-rated" elements is not unrelated to the genre's newfound "legitimacy." Indeed, the past forty years have seen audiovisual pornography slowly earn its stripes in the public eye, moving from the underground to large-scale online availability, and from the counterculture to the halls of academia. Along with this shift, porn has simultaneously become an institution with its own strict codes and a unique cultural industry that makes billions of dollars in profits annually.[2]

Several authors have proposed their own terms to describe this global trend of the "pornification of culture."[3] One of the more famous of these definitions might be Claudia Attimonelli and Vincenzo Susca's concept of *pornoculture*, in which the current era of the genre has completely overcome the notion of pornography, "in the sense that we are no longer talking about a niche section of media products, but rather about a symbolic through-line, an aesthetic paradigm, a sensibility that has permeated the contemporary western context" (Attimonelli and Susca 2017, 9–10).[4]

In this context, porn stars have experienced a similar story arc from margins of the genre to the spotlight of mass media. In his introduction to porn studies, Philippe Dubois points out that "in the now wider domain of the porn star system, both male and female lead actors have become experts on sexuality in the public eye, like those sexologists who are invited to speak on talk shows" (Dubois 2014, 97). Moreover, the very notion of the porn star has been undermined by the proliferation of technologies for constructing the self, i.e., through social media, prosumer web cams, and the like. Since the beginning of the twenty-first century, the democratization of communication media, including production and online distribution, has created unprecedented forms of confessional and auto-objectivating media output; thenceforth, the representation of sexuality has no longer been the prerogative of professional makers alone but rather also that of users generating their own material.

In this essay, I try to outline this new configuration of the pornographic that has inaugurated what Brian McNair calls "striptease culture": i.e., a culture that focuses on exposure, confessionality, and self-disclosure (McNair 2002). This lens allows me to examine in a new way the neoliberal logic that would have all individuals become at once entrepreneurs and their own business. To do this, I borrow from London School of Economics professor Catherine Hakim's concept of erotic capital (Hakim 2010), applying it to a phenomenon that has taken on ever greater importance in the porn industry, to such an extent that it is expected to become the industry's main revenue source in the coming years: camming.

Mise-en-scène of the Self: A Technological Redefinition of Desirability

In recent years, the study of popular culture has looked at the issue of sexualized imagery in mass media as an attempt by women to claim their sexual autonomy (Attwood 2007). Proclaimed as a revolutionary turn, a new tool for the empowerment movement, this unabashed sexual subjectivity employs a set of affects and, above all, a panoply of "skills" that simultaneously reveal the subject's agency and her/his desirability. In this perspective, erotic power is reconceived as a form of capital.

Furthering the categories outlined in the 1980s by sociologist Pierre Bourdieu – social, cultural, and economic capital – Hakim proposes a fourth form of capital based on the power of sexual attraction, i.e., erotic capital. In her view, this form of capital has been too long overlooked and must be taken into account in any analysis of interpersonal relations. She defines it thus:

> Erotic capital is thus a combination of aesthetic, visual, physical, social, and sexual attractiveness to other members of your society, and especially to

> members of the opposite sex, in all social contexts. In some cultures, fertility is a central element of women's greater erotic capital. We use the terms "erotic power" and "erotic capital" interchangeably, for stylistic variation. Erotic capital includes skills that can be learnt and developed, as well as advantages fixed at birth. Women generally have more of it than men, even in cultures where fertility is not an integral element, and they deploy it more actively. (Hakim 2010, 501)

Erotic capital may manifest itself differently from one culture to the next, and is not synonymous with physical capital, since desire is not reducible to the valuing of mere physical beauty: such desire is contextual and subjective, no matter how discernible or discriminatory given cultural criteria may be, Hakim reminds us. Erotic capital refers to an assortment of skills, physical attributes and relational knowledge that insinuates itself into a hierarchy within pre-existing social hierarchies. Like other forms of capital, it can be accumulated, exchanged, performed, and spent. It is at once tangible or measurable, and intangible in its affects.[5]

This new paradigm of self-representation and erotic capital raises questions about the role of professionalization in the porn industry. In his foundational essay in which he analyses the process of star-making at work in the cinematic medium, sociologist Edgar Morin notes that "a star is a total commodity: there isn't a single inch of the star's body, not a shred of her soul, not a single memory of her life that cannot be flung onto the market" (Morin 1972, 100). Since one of the characteristics of being a star is to be a consumable product in every sense, I'm tempted to say that the "porn star," whether professional or amateur, is the star *par excellence*. Filmed from every angle, exposed in the minutiae of his or her intimate moments, the adult film star is further considered in the popular imagination to be a commodity that exists only to be consumed by the public gaze. Ever balancing the real and the fake, an entity in perpetual motion whose body and actions are at once fantasy and reality, the star's very being is paradox incarnate. Performer or actor? Object or subject? What, then, makes a porn star?

If we take up sociologist Mathieu Trachman's ethnographic study of the pornographic milieu in France, in which he isolates and theorizes a set of pornographic capacities or skills, we can redefine porn's "profitability" in terms of erotic capital:

> While it may appear at first glance to involve a set of bodily and aesthetic properties, [erotic capital] is also about how the body is used and about self-presentation more broadly. [Porn stars] who are able to make a name for

themselves achieve what we could call a transfiguration of their body, however ephemeral that may be: their value is no longer determined merely by how their own set of bodily characteristics is seen, but rather, according to their reputation, which guarantees them a place in upholding their success on the porn "scene." These successive operations are the result of collective labour, by ever-growing audiences who contribute to creating this figure of exception in the marketplace of fantasy. (Trachman 2013, 200)

The notion of the "newcomer," that label applied to young actresses and potential stars who fill the genre's perpetual need for novelty, is one that the internet economy has rendered obsolete. New technologies redefine [porn-makers'] capacities, their value, and the location of their performance. These technologies engender new ways of making and doing, as well as new spaces in which to make and do them, and above all, to consume them: they erase the boundaries between public and private. New kinds of "amateur" porn become absorbed into a neoliberal economic logic – were they ever otherwise? – that of the entrepreneurial self, a new embodiment of *homo economicus*.

It goes without saying that in the age of the *tubes,* the categories of amateur and professional have been blurred. What defines being a professional? Is it the structures of production and distribution? Is it about remuneration? What is the value of the pornographic body? Trachman furthers his description of what he calls pornographic labour by specifying that

> it is difficult to precisely define what factors underlie differences in value … We can see that these differences are not reducible to mere variations in physical attributes, but rather to how specific bodies are utilized; the distinctions [between amateur and professional] are produced collectively by the pornographic world, which is to say, that they are dependent on reputations. (2013, 196)

In a context where pornography seems more popular than ever, but is facing the crisis of free content affecting every other cultural industry,[6] can the concept of erotic capital explain the growing popularity of so-called amateur videos and of these new entrepreneurs of the self who profit from their erotic capital?

As media and communication technologies become more widely understood as part of the fabric of ordinary life, there has been a general blurring of the "real" and the "representational," reinforced by the dramatic expansion in forms of online self-presentation and social networking ... New communication technologies have also become part of people's sex lives, facilitating homemade DIY sex media and new types of sexual encounter in virtual environments. The new visibility of commercial sex, and in particular, porn, has worked to make it appear less disreputable and "other," while the availability of technologies has helped to elide the distinctions between sex producer and consumer and between sex as a set of practices and sex as a set of representations. (Attwood 2010, 6)

Hence, the very meaning [*signification*] of sexuality, and of its symbolic and ontological "value," has been transformed. The practices of production pertain to a different discourse altogether.

The process by which we have arrived at this juncture is rooted in the proliferation of amateur films starting in the 1960s, made possible by the commercial availability of cameras intended for at-home use, from Super8 to the digital. A further contributing factor is that this new kind of work gets shared in specialized networks (swingers' magazines, classified ads, among others) and then via the web. Hence, the professionalization of sex and sexuality surpasses the purview of the porn industry by finding expression in daily life, i.e., in interpersonal relationships. Which leads us to the world of camming.

The Economic Model of Camming

The advent and growth of user-generated online content is a function of several emerging paradigms. Economically, this trend is connected to the notion of "crowd-based capitalism" as outlined by Arun Sundarajan in *The Sharing Economy* (2016). While sharing between individuals and the fact of non-professional production are themselves nothing new, the difference is that it is now possible to make money from this "sharing" of such services. One major impact of this new reality is that being paid is no longer part of what defines professionalism. "Digital labour" calls into question not only the idea of labour in the larger sense but also its value and meaning. The same can be said of its manifestation in the porn industry.

Camming is an illustrative example of digital labour in the sharing economy because it belongs to a specialized form of marketed services. A cluster of stakeholders (websites, models, etc.) must come together to satisfy the demand of user-spectator-consumers.[7] But in the place of a traditional model of labour (and

250 | Éric Falardeau

12.1 Screen capture of *Chaturbate*'s opening web page illustrating the design and layout displaying the cammers' accounts. Chaturbate.com, 2017.

product) that relies on the employer-employee dyad, camming involves the voluntary participation of a "self-employed" or autonomous worker. As the *sine qua non* of self-representational technology, camming consists of models (either individual or a couple) filming themselves using a web camera that is connected to their computer. The model addresses the viewer directly, in real time – a viewer who is no longer confined to the role of mere voyeur vis-à-vis the sexual act displayed because he/she/they can interact with the model using the website interface. The interface allows the viewer to interact with the model using a keyboard or microphone connected to the program used for viewing the performer.

Chaturbate (fig. 12.1), launched in 2001, is one example of an online chat platform. The site allows amateur users to livestream erotic or pornographic performances (i.e., "cam shows"). The site was generating an estimated 4.1 million monthly visitors according to figures from March 2017. Chaturbate is (of course) a portmanteau of the words "chat" (meaning real-time text communication via the web) and "masturbate," as if to suggest a possible use to make of the site. User-viewers can watch the videos of the site's user-performers for free.

In order to have private access to a user-performer's videos, or to request a specific sexual act to be performed, user-viewers are required to make a financial transaction; all of this is at the discretion of the models, who chooses how or if they wish to monetize their performances. As such, a "webgirl" or "webboy" chooses which aspects of their shows remain free and which require payment.[8] The objective is simple: to create demand for services by offering some of them for free, gaining network effects and reach by association with the site (Bomsel 2007). Models' "reach" (gained from posting free content) is rewarded by the site's algorithms, which place the most popular cam performers at the top of their "grid" or list, making it easier for popular models to generate income from their content.[9] Simultaneously, these sites encourage user communities by offering free community forums that are open to anyone to join. User-viewer comments further rank a model's status on the site by showing a given cammer's rating by the community.[10] Here again, user-generated comments impact a model's ranking on the site.

Chaturbate is based on the "hyper-outsourced" (labour) model, in which "workers are outsourced, fixed capital is outsourced, maintenance costs are outsourced, and training is outsourced. All that remains is a bare extractive minimum – control over the platform that enables a monopoly rent to be gained" (Smicek 2017). In other words, users are furnished with a site that is maintained and controlled by a third party. This party "rents out" user-performers' space on the platform, a distribution outlet, in exchange for a portion of the revenues generated by the models' cam shows, which in the case of Chaturbate amounts to about 40 per cent of the artists' earnings. As to the scale of earnings the average cammer tends to make, an industry site specializing in advice to new models, *Webcam Startup*, gives this prosaic answer:

> This is always the first question people ask. It's also a very difficult question to answer. The earnings are performance-based. There is no set salary or hourly wage. The various sites will provide the platform for streaming and generate tons of traffic for the models. From there, it's up to the models to get tipped or taken to private chat (charged per minute). The networks will take a cut to cover expenses and their profit margins. That percentage varies from site to site. (*Webcam Startup* 2018)

Essentially, wages are at once direct – garnered proportionately from user purchases – and indirect, from advertising inserted into various boxes on the site. The system is based on the figure of the "infomediary," such that "regardless of how wages are determined, whether from user contact, commission, paid search engine optimization by key word, or through the sale of information acquired from given transactions, they're eventually earned from standard advertising as well" (Moeglin

2008, 10). It is worth pointing out that production costs for infomediaries are quite low, given that content is made by user-performers who procure all of their own equipment necessary to do the work – which amounts to a rather small investment given that all cammers need is a web camera – in addition to a computer and internet access, which together are a given in most home environments.

Camming: Intimacy as Erotic Value

Using webcam girl VicAlouqua (fig. 12.2) as a case study allows us to delineate the techniques for production and publicity that help construct a camming site's public "face" – and from there, to understand how erotic capital is marketed and expressed. VicAlouqua, aka Victoria, is a twenty-two-year-old French woman and one of the rare stars of the camming scene. She started out on the American site Cam4, where she posted videos and performed in 2015 (VicAlouqua 2018a), before moving on to posting on PornHub (VicAlouqua 2018b). An average of 14,000 users watched her videos daily, an audience base that earned her between 3,000 and 5,000 Euros per month. Her social media clout consisted of 85,000 Twitter followers, 40,000 Instagram followers, and 30,000 Facebook fans. One of her specialities is public exhibitionism.

Victoria is a prime example of this new type of neoliberal entrepreneurship of the self. Her erotic capital is what she supplies, i.e., is her product. On the one hand, she activates a set of mostly bodily skills, such as performance, teasing, public exhibitionism, and beauty. On the other hand, her skill set is more germane to that of a business owner: community management (social media functions), content production, payment and transactional tasks, accounting, etc. What makes her stand out from the competition are her unique services (i.e., nudity in public places), and moreover, her "unique" quality.

In order to succeed at camming, models have to break down the boundary of the screen and give their viewers the feeling that they are a part of each other's lives. In an interview, Victoria points out that one of the keys to her success is that she is present on numerous social media platforms, which allow her customers to "*suivre ma vie d'un peu plus près*," i.e., "to follow my life a little more closely" (Doucet 2016, 42). In so doing, she gives her user-viewers more than just an erotic or pornographic performance: she gives them the impression that they're sharing intimate moments of her daily life. "With each camera angle, users get the feeling of entering into her private world, a fantasy that involves seeing her sheets, her bedroom trinkets, books, or even her kitchen" (42). Her self-direction in scenes

Camming and Erotic Capital | 253

12.2 Screen capture of Vicalouqua's account on *Cam4*.com, 2017.

from daily life and in other intimate moments is highlighted through her use of social media sites, those loci of the private-as-public in the popular imagination: here is where her digital persona, her supposedly authentic and true iteration, is expressed. The "real" has taken on a symbolic value.

This kind of intimacy is synonymous with allowing her clients to get close to her. Her private conversations in chatrooms and Facebook interactions give her customers the feeling that she is accessible, that's she's just a "girl next door." Her exhibitionism is far more than just exposing her body. Consumer participation is not only encouraged, it is essential: the camgirl's job is to find her customer's way of participating, and to then to personalize his experience.

This virtual relationship is carried over to her merchandising. Victoria also sells autographed DVDs and even underwear, which of course is pre-worn. It is also possible to send her gifts, such as sex toys and lingerie, in exchange for which Victoria will send personalized photos or videos in which she puts the gifts to use.[11] Such direct contact with the consumer is a form of relationship marketing in which the affect of apparent intimacy between model and viewer becomes the product. Customers become brand ambassadors by participating in building the model's brand: the user-viewer's actions, interactions, and online views contribute to Victoria's network effects (i.e., "reach"). Product distribution is also user-generated in this scenario.[12]

Victoria is more than a nude body. Although her much sought-after skills as a model are the basis of the product she supplies, those of a "community manager" come equally into play. The combination of these two skill sets are essential elements in the camgirl's success and market share. Audience engagement is a quintessential component of creating and maintaining the desirability of her product. *Webcam Startup* is once again helpful in summarizing this notion:

> A model personality impacts the earnings ... Personality is key. It is probably the most important element to camming. Even more important than looks even [*sic*]. Camming is highly interactive. It's a lot more than just getting naked on webcam. You're going to be interacting with your entire chatroom, or with a single individual in private chat. Warm, bubbly and eccentric personalities usually perform better than others. Especially when it comes to getting regular customers and longterm profits.
>
> The earning potential is based on a wide number of things. Personality, attractiveness, streaming quality and type of shows/ performances all impact the earning potential. Camming is highly interactive, so models that do better with people typically earn more. It's also important to note that once you build up a fan-base and some good regular customers, you'll enjoy better earnings. (*Webcam Startup* 2018)

A series of factors are involved in the perceived quality or success of a camgirl or camboy as entrepreneurs of the self.[13] Personality becomes a value-added feature that singles out models who would otherwise be indistinguishable on such websites. A complex marketing nexus is at play that involves the body, intimacy, and relationality.

Current modes of content creation and digital distribution have a direct impact on the reception and production of this material. As such, camgirls and camboys are paradoxical figures in that they function in a sea of hyper-available pornographic content on the web, where both free and paywalled videos and photos are just a click away. Indeed, the digital era of porn is characterized by an exponential increase in the quantity rather than the quality of productions and products available, and by a concurrent hyper-specialization of practices and products. So, while they appear interchangeable – one glance at the homepages of Chaturbate or Chatroulette will show just how many amateur and professional performers there are out there – user-viewers seek out uniqueness and individuality. The product to be consumed is not necessarily made for mass distribution. Rather, every performance is unique, occurring at a specific time, for a particular duration, and is interactive.

As such, what the user-viewer seeks out seems more and more like a kind of aura, or what Walter Benjamin calls "the here and now of the original" in his famous 1935 essay, "The Work of Art in the Age of Technological Reproducibility." While Benjamin posited that recording technology (the ability to replay included) leads to the loss of the aura in reproduction, the camming apparatus (webcam, internet connection, website, etc.) brings us back, unexpectedly, to the unique and unpredictable quality of the original. The mirage of reproduction (and repetition) is replaced by the possibility of contact with a real person. The webcam performance is unique, because it is live and interactive. Benjamin's analysis of authenticity – comparing the original and its reproduction – does not fully apply here because there is no longer a dichotomy between real and fake when it comes to live camming.

> The whole sphere of authenticity eludes technological – and of course not only technological – reproduction ... The authenticity of a thing is the quintessence of all that is transmissible in it from its origin on, ranging from its physical duration to the history to which it testifies. Since the historical testimony is based on the physical duration, the historical testimony of the thing, too, is jeopardized by reproduction, in which physical duration has been withdrawn from human activity. Admittedly, it is only the historical testimony that is jeopardized; yet what is really jeopardized thereby is the authority of the thing, the weight it derives from tradition. (Benjamin [1935] 2008)

The reader may raise objections to this assessment in that camming is not in itself exempt from reproducibility. It is perfectly possible to save and replay these performances as videos on sites like PornHub or elsewhere. However, what the user-consumer seeks in these models' performances is a live experience with participatory and affective realness, where nothing is scripted and the viewer can influence the series of events. In other words, the value of camming for the user is bound up in a ritual of the mise-en-scène of the self: the scheduled event (the performance's temporal specificity), its real-time delivery, and the communication between parties involved. Furthermore, livestreaming can be understood in terms of the influential critic and visual-studies theorist André Bazin's notion of the "erotology" of television's directness. In a 1954 essay, he described the incursion of unpredictability, duration, and intimacy in a medium that is otherwise highly formatted [*formatté*]: "Indisputably, our awareness of the simultaneity of an object's existence with our perception of it constitutes the pleasure principle specific to television and the only thing it offers that cinema cannot" ([1954] 2014, 106).

Camming therefore transforms our way of perceiving the erotic and the pornographic. The space of the mise-en-scène is simultaneously real and virtual, private and public. We are in "pornspace":

> It could be said that our social space has *become* a digital space. It's this gradual conversion that takes on traits akin to those that define pornography. As with pornography, the digital problematizes the structure of our environment, and by extension, the structures of social norms and rules – moral, political, aesthetic. These new rules seem unacceptable from the standpoint of non-digital environments, or more precisely, *pre-digital* ones. (Vitali-Rosati 2016, 313–14)

Victoria elicits sexual desire by engaging her erotic capital as expressed not only by her body but also by the times between her performances when viewers are left anticipating fresh access to her daily life, in much the same way that lovers might anticipate intimate moments through a series of interactions. Here the distinction between the amateur and the professional is no more. Pornographic labour is now a form of leisure, the domestic setting of which is the primary fact of its eroto-pornographic economics. The economics of this labour are a function of the user-performer's agency and the value that the user-consumer accords to it. Such subjective value is a product of each individual's erotic capital, as expressed not only in live videos but also in paratextual elements such as profile photos, confessional posts, personal thoughts in posts, link-sharing, and the like. The model-user relationship evolves through a constant supply of intimate and personal details as well as through the routine performance of sexual acts; recall that models post the times of their livestream performances to allow users to adjust their schedule to match that of their favourite model, adding both intimacy and liveness to the anticipation itself. This exchange contributes to the culture of intimacy and authenticity that results from the radical change in how we consume [this material], facilitated by these twenty-first-century tools. "Better equipped, more curious, and more actively engaged, consumers seek out materiality [*le concret*] and truth [*la vérité*]" (Henrard and Pierra 2015, 21).

The intimacy and connection that create desire, the ultimate expression of erotic capital, are predicated, however, on distance. Distance requires the ritualization of the model-viewer connection: the subject constructs expectations (i.e., demand) and becomes for the viewer an object within a mise-en-scène. These pornographic somersaults share many similarities with ritual practices – namely, the use of the body as a tool for communication, the significance of costume and preparing/grooming the body, sex as a physical performance intended to achieve a form of ecstasy, and the fact of an aesthetic experience that involves a spectator (Falardeau, 2018). Here we see how the "mise-en-scène of gestures and poses choreograph a randomized mechanics, a technique of spontaneity, of realism and abstraction" (Rauger 2000, 271). Pornographic labour underlies it all.

Victoria is a master of contemporary content-marketing rules. Since she is her own content, her online presence is itself proof of how well she understands these online marketing mechanisms. Content equals brand. Public communications experts Pascal Henrard and Patrick Pierra point out that in this paradigm, quality is prioritized over quantity, and the timing of online posts and streaming is of the essence. "On Facebook, as on Twitter, each individual is a medium unto her/himself, with their own brand, content, and audience" (2015, 29). The nature of content marketing is that sales are dependent on supplying information. Rarity is as important as hyper-availability (Anderson 2006). Entertainment is the quality that links these two factors. The keywords of this marketing strategy are the same as those of self-directed performance: searchability, relatability, credibility, long-term coherence, connection, history (interpersonal and as storyline), and intimacy. Victoria's public "life" follows a specific storyline: what she produces is always already a calculated media construct. She exposes herself to her audience so that she can create a unique connection with them; her customer is the focus of her concerns because their viewership is co-synchronous with her income, proportionally, and hence each viewer counts!

Victoria is a prime example of this new pornographic paradigm that has emerged from a larger movement within post-industrial capitalism. Indeed, "the world of pornography clarifies the contemporary evolution of capitalism, and how the latter is connected to sexuality" (Trachman 2013, 10).[14] While previously the world of "adult films" created a particular relationship to sexuality typified by a stark separation between the viewer and the filmed subject, contemporary networked technologies abolish that separation. Victoria is selling herself, earning real income from her erotic capital. Nonetheless, as Trachman points out again, "the display of images from the realm of fantasy are presented not only for potential profit, they also activate knowledge and skills that produce a kind of sexual expertise, and above all, a way of defining the self as a sexual subject" (11).

Conclusion

Camming is a type of sexual representation technology that has turned pornography at once into labour, leisure, and sex. It is not merely a case of hypervisibility but rather a manifestation of the excess, intensity, immediacy, acceleration, hyperaccumulation and authenticity-seeking proper to hypermodernity. The scant boundary between image and its simulacrum becomes erased, and in its place an artificial intimacy emerges (Baudrillard 1983). Camming is a sophisticated example of a new affective means of production that is expressed through an overflow of intimacy that in turn relies on erotic capital – an erotic capital that is at once cause and consequence of the individual success of this new generation of entrepreneurs of the self.[15]

Not to be overlooked is the fact that everyone in this milieu is selling an image first and foremost. The culture of connectedness predisposes the mise-en-scène of the self, which for some, allows for increased erotic capital. In this digital age, we are no longer simply individuals: we are also individual brands [*personnes-marques*] (Kapferer 2013). The marketing logic of neoliberalism has extended to the private and intimate spheres of existence such that these environments themselves become the erotic or pornographic product. It is in this sense that pornography can be seen as an aesthetic paradigm for western societies characterized by such an inability to separate ourselves from the screen, to liberate ourselves from these techno-social prostheses that we wear and that wear us – as seen in the tyranny of *always being on*, of geolocation and tagging, these functions through which we choose to be constantly subject to the gaze and grasp of the other – as less akin to a return to a primordial herd mentality and more like the triumph of a permanent orgy that brands, swells, and intoxicates the social body (Attimonelli and Susca 2017, 104).

In this two-way movement of affirmation, confession and self-objectivation, our *pornotopia* is brought about in *pornspace*. The myth of abundance as described by Steven Marcus – the imaginary land where seduction is valued, the refusal of a carnal encounter deemed impossible, and where it's always "time to go to bed" ([1966] 2008, 269) – is embodied by these constructions of the self. "Any person today can legitimately lay claim to being filmed," Walter Benjamin wrote ([1935] 2008). Nothing is real, and yet everything is true.

NOTES

1 John C. Holmes is considered the adult film industry's first male star. Between 1969 and 1988, the year of his death from AIDS-related complications, Holmes performed in approximately 2,500 films and loops (i.e., short porn films approximately ten minutes in length, filmed on Super8 and distributed underground or sold to individuals). He was the first star to be invested in the X-Rated Critics Organization Hall of Fame, in 1985.

2 In 2007 the publisher of industry monthly *Adult Video News* confirmed that porn retail sales amounted to approximately US$6 billion, while a television report from CNBC estimated global sales at closer to US$14 billion. The proliferation of online content does not help attempts to accurately estimate the porn industry's revenues, let alone the profits from merchandising such related products as sex toys. As such, no study has managed to accurately assess the real earnings of the porn industry with adequate sources. Sarah Tarrant summarizes the situation: "Among the reasons for miscalculations and skewed statements about the financial aspects of the adult industry is the fact that multiple revenue streams fall under the pornography umbrella, there are countless online content providers, and sometimes-sloppy record-keeping" (2016, 42).

3 English language literature has opted for "pornification" (Paasonen, Nikunen, and Saarenmaa 2007), while the French have preferred "*pornographication*," the author notes.

4 Unless otherwise noted, the translation of this quotation and all other translations in this chapter are provided by the co-editors.

5 The difference between erotic capital and bodily capital varies from author to author. Both expressions (*capital érotique*; *capital corporel*) are used interchangeably in English and French texts alike to describe a similar concept. We employ the term "erotic capital" as proposed by Hakim.

6 This trend may be even more apparent in the adult industry, given that its astronomical pre-internet profits were made in spite of a series of moral, social, and legal barriers that required consumers to procure material only in proscribed contexts (video stores, porn theatres, magazines behind store counters, etc.). The internet has removed these often-intimidating obstacles that required at least some human contact; now, in the comfort of one's private space, free from any third-party judgments, we can access the objects or content of our desires without any obvious barriers.

7 We use various combinations and formulations for these amalgams: user-spectators, user-consumers, spectator-consumers, and so on. The same goes for their counterparts, i.e., the models they watch, whom we refer to as user-performers, performers, and so on. The synonyms used in both cases designate the same thing.

8 Users pay using a virtual currency, i.e., "tokens," which have an equivalent in real dollars; e.g., twenty tokens might equal an American dollar.

9   Regarding the categorization of cams by keyword, Chaturbate is divided into five categories: female, males, couples, trans, and stars. After choosing a category, one can refine searches based on specific traits: hair colour, height, sexual practices, and so on. The two levels of searchability lead to a specific ranking for models and define their desirability. Terminology and keywording are two major issues in online porn. The concepts of the "*porneme*" (Paveau 2014) and "carnal indexing" (Keilty 2017) are useful in better understanding the function and searchability of online platform content and its categories.
10 For an analysis of the content of online chats and their impact on users, see Lindgren 2010.
11 Obviously Victoria receives a percentage of the profits for lending her name to merchandising, since she becomes a spokesmodel for the brand, vouching directly or indirectly for its products. It's a win-win relationship. See https://www.espacelibido.com/mywishlist/vicalouqua.
12 For an analysis of the user's role in online porn, see Mowlabocus 2010.
13 The semi-professional, semi-amateur aesthetic is a major part of what lends believability to the performers' self-direction. The flaws in the image presented, whether it be the low-quality web camera, the static framing, natural lighting, or even an untidy apartment in the background can lend a degree of authenticity to the image.
14 It is worth noting that pornographers have not always been seen as sexual entrepreneurs. Pornography had long been a prime tool for social critique among the working classes. As with many other forms of art, "over the course of the nineteenth century, pornography transformed from critical mode to a capitalist one, founded on the onus of profit accumulation" (Trachman 2013, 8).
15 This paradigm is not exclusive to pornography. Youtubers, Instagrammers, and other "influencers" work the same way. Online porn has not emerged from a vacuum but rather from a nexus of social, cultural, and economic developments within neoliberalism.

REFERENCES

Anderson, Chris. 2006. *The Long Tail: Why the Future of Business Is Selling Less of More*. New York: Hyperion.

Attimonelli, Claudia, and Vincenzo Susca. 2017. *Pornoculture: Voyage au bout de la chair*. Montréal: Liber.

Attwood, Feona. 2007. "Sluts and Riot Grrls: Female Identity and Sexual Agency." In *Journal of Gender Studies* 16, no. 3: 233–47.

– ed. 2010. *Porn.com: Making Sense of Online Pornography*. New York: Peter Lang.

Baudrillard, Jean. 1983. "The Ecstasy of Communication." In *The Anti-Aesthetic: Essays on Postmodern Culture*, edited by Hal Foster, 126–33. Seattle: Bay Press.

Bazin, André. [1954] 2014. "A Contribution to an Erotology of Television." In *Andre Bazin's New Media*, edited and translated by Dudley Andrew. Berkeley: University of California Press.

Benjamin, Walter. [1935] 2008. "The Work of Art in the Age of Technological Reproducibility." In *The Work of Art in the Age of Its Technological Reproducibility and Other Writings on Media*, edited by Michael W. Jennings, Brigid Doherty, and Thomas Y. Levin, 19–55. Cambridge: Harvard University Press.

Bomsel, Olivier. 2007. *Gratuit! Du déploiement de l'économie numérique*. Paris: Gallimard.

Cossette, Claude, and Nicolas Massey. 2002. *Comment faire sa publicité soi-même*. Montreal: Éditions Transcontinental.

Doucet, David. 2016. "La reine de la cam." In *Les Inrockuptibles*, nos. 1078–80 (27 July–17 August): 40–3.

Dubois, François-Ronan. 2014. *Introduction aux porn studies*. Paris: Les impressions nouvelles.

Falardeau, Éric. 2018. " La pornographie cinématographique comme rituel. " In *Intérieurs du rituel: Approches, pratiques et représentations en arts*. Proceedings of the 4th Colloque Arts et Médias de l'Université de Montréal, 24–25 November, Montreal, Université de Montréal. https://www.colloqueartsmedias.ca/actes/2016/transes-extatiques-la-pornographie cinemato-graphique1.

Hakim, Catherine. 2010. "Erotic Capital." In *European Sociological Review* 26, no. 5 (October): 499–518.

– 2011. *Erotic Capital: The Power of Attraction in the Boardroom and the Bedroom*. New York: Basic Books.

Henrard, Pascal, and Patrick Pierra. 2015. *Guide du maketing de contenu. Du journalisme de marque à la publicité native: Pourquoi et comment transformer une marque en média*. Montreal: Éditions Infopresse.

Kapferer, Jean-Noël. 2013. *Ré-inventer les marques: La fin des marques telles que nous les connaissions*. Montreal: Groupe Eyrolles.

Keilty, Patrick. 2017. "Carnal Indexing." In *Knowledge Organization* 44, no. 4: 265–72.

Lindgren, Simon. 2010. "Widening the Glory Hole: The Discourse of Online Porn Fandom." In Attwood, *Porn.com*, 171–85. New York: Peter Lang.

Marcus, Steven. [1966] 2008. *The Other Victorians: A Study of Sexuality and Pornography in Mid-Nineteenth-Century England*. Cambridge: Routledge.

McNair, Brian. 2002. *Striptease Culture: Sex, Media and the Democratization of Desire*. Cambridge: Routledge.

Moeglin, Pierre. 2008. "Industries culturelles et médiatiques: Propositions pour une approche historiographique." In *Société française des sciences de l'information et de la communication: Actes du 16ᵉ Congrès* 14. http://www.sfsic.org/congres_2008/spip.php?article147.

Morin, Edgar. 1972. *Les stars*. Paris: Éditions du Seuil, Points Essais.

Mowlabocus, Sharif. 2010. "Porn 2.0? Technology, Social Practice and the New Online Porn Industry." In Attwood, *Porn.com: Making Sense of Online* Pornography, 69–88.

Paasonen, Susanna, Kaarina Nikunen, and Laura Saarenmaa, eds. 2007. *Pornification: Sex and Sexuality in Media Culture*. Oxford: Berg.

Paveau, Marie-Anne. 2014. *Le discours pornographique*. Paris: La Musardine.

Perel, Esther. 2007. *L'intelligence érotique: Faire vivre le désir dans le couple*. Paris: Robert Laffont.

Rauger, Jean-François. 2000. "La mise en scène de l'acte sexuel: focalisation/fuckalization." In *La mise en scène*, edited by Jacques Aumont, 265–78. Paris: De Boeck Supérieur.

Smicek, Nick. 2017. *Platform Capitalism*. Cambridge: Polity Press.

Sonnac, Nathalie. 2013. "L'écosystème des médias: Les enjeux socioéconomiques d'une interaction entre deux marches." In *Communication* 32, no. 2: 22.

Stenger, T., and A. Coutant. 2010. "Les réseaux sociaux numériques: Des discours de promotion à la définition d'un objet et d'une méthodologie de recherché." *Hermes* 44 (February): 209–28.

Sundarajan, Arun. 2016. *The Sharing Economy: The End of Employment and the Rise of Crowd-Based Capitalism*. London: MIT Press.

Tarrant, Sarah. 2016. *The Pornography Industry: What Everyone Needs to Know*. New York: Oxford University Press.

Trachman, Mathieu. 2013. *Le travail pornographique: Enquête sur la production de fantasmes*. Paris: La Découverte, Genre & Sexualité.

Van Dijck, J. 2013. *The Culture of Connectivity: A Critical History of Social Media*. Oxford: Oxford University Press.

VicAlouqua. 2018a. *Cam4*. https://fr.cam4.com/vicalouqua74.

— 2018b. *Pornhub*. http://www.pornhub.com/users/vicalouqua.

Vitali-Rosati, Marcello. 2016. "Pornspace." *Medium* 1, nos. 46–7: 306–17.

Vörös, Florian, ed. 2015. *Cultures pornographiques: Anthologie des porn studies*. Amsterdam: Éditions Amsterdam.

Webcam Startup. 2018. "How to Get Started as a Camgirl/ Male Performer." http://webcam-startup.com.

13

Confessions of a Masked Pornographer: Reorienting Gay Male Identity via Bodily Confession

BRANDON ARROYO

> Man is least himself when he talks in his own person. Give him a mask, and he will tell you the truth.
> • Oscar Wilde ([1891] 1982, 389)

Pornographic Confessions

Voice off-camera: Antonio, how you doin'?
Antonio Cervone: I'm doin' pretty well.
Voice: Are you nervous at all?
Cervone: Umm … this is the first time I've done this before, I mean …
Voice: You've done cam work though, right?
Cervone: Yeah.
Voice: Are you horny?
Cervone: Yeah.
Voice: Okay, all right, cool.
Cervone: Usually am.
Voice: Well, let's get your stats. How old are you?
Cervone: I'm twenty-four years old.
Voice: And what do you weigh?
Cervone: I'm 145 pounds.
Voice: Okay, how tall?
Cervone: Six feet.
Voice: Do you know how big your dick is?
Cervone: Eight feet. Oh!
Voice: Eight feet!?!?

Cervone: (*laughing*) Eight inches.
Voice: You like the boys, right?
Cervone: Yeah, I like guys.
Voice: Okay, what kind of guys do you go for?
Cervone: I usually like guys with little ... thicker set, or something ... or like a little bigger, stockier than I am.
Voice: Okay, so like a daddy type, or ... (*fading out*) otter?
Cervone: Yeah, I like daddies. I like guys with chest hair. Like, umm ... I don't know ... what was the one you said?
Voice: Like an otter?
Cervone: Yeah, I like otters, yeah! Umm ... yeah.
Voice: And are you a top or bottom?
Cervone: I'm a bottom.
Voice: Okay, all right. Do you have to have a big cock or just ...
Cervone: Umm ... I don't know, I mean not necessarily. I mean I like a big cock, but, I mean, it depends on what you can do with it, I guess.
Voice: Right, exactly! All right, cool! And umm ... how often do you jerk off?
Cervone: Umm ... usually like three, or four, or five times a day, you know.
Voice: Okay, all right, so a pretty horny guy! Where you at when you're doing that?
Cervone: Umm ... I am ... I don't know, I'm usually, like...I don't know, it's when I wake up I'll jerk off like in my bed. Umm ... I do my own work, umm ... like by a computer, and when I need a break I'll jerk off. And in the shower, yeah.
Voice: All right, nice! Well, let's check out your body and check out your jerkoff skills ... ("Antonio Cervone Solo" 2016)

This exchange between pornographic performer Antonio Cervone and the owner/cameraman of the website ChaosMen is a prototypical example of how confession has become a foundational aspect of gay male internet pornography. This should not come as a surprise considering that confession solves many production problems. Its currency lies in its ability to act as a substitute for a narrative script and to circumvent the budgeting required for an expansive feature shoot. Utilizing confession as the primary narrative mode of contemporary pornography allows internet studios to produce as many videos as they can in a shorter amount of time, while showing that they are still interested in offering a compelling story to anchor each scene. Confession is also understood as the primary marker of genuineness, and since pornography's primary motif is to convey the idea that its viewers are witnessing *genuine* sex, confession serves as an ideal complement to the intentions of the genre.

Opening this chapter with Cervone's confession also serves a couple of different purposes. Firstly, he performs genuineness quite well – the impulsive laugh upon making the mistake of saying "eight feet" instead of "eight inches" is a dead giveaway – and secondly, it provides an apt example of the habitual and benign nature of pornographic confessions. Perhaps what is most striking about describing pornographic confession this way is that these adjectives are antithetical to the ways in which we typically think about pornography: *Exciting! Erotic! Stimulating!* Instead, this confessional exchange between the Voice and Cervone is routine and boring and reveals little about the inner life of the confessant. The tone of the Voice suggests he is tiredly reading these questions from a prepared script, and additionally, he does not infuse his voice with the sexual excitement that the questions are seemingly trying to tap into. Cervone deserves credit for trying to enliven the exchange by rubbing his genitals through his pants while answering the questions – and retaining a sense of humour while making his professional pornographic debut – but the physical attention he draws to his penis only makes the words he utters that much more perfunctory. Ultimately, asking about the performer's physical proportions seems redundant considering that we already see what he looks like, and that most viewers are familiar with the fact that the camera distorts their perception of scale. And even with the promise of an eight foot – sorry, I mean eight inch! – penis, when Cervone eventually reveals it, it does not match up to the length and girth of those of most other prominent performers. Of course, there are other examples where performers testify about their first time having sex, or the "wildest" place where they have had sex, and sometimes those testimonials are more erotic than whatever sex takes place afterwards. However, more often than not, pornographic confession plays out like Cervone's. So, if one considers pornographic confession as being a provocation toward sexual excitement, these types of confessional exchanges feel like a failure.

Pondering this contradiction between the unstimulating nature of these confessions and the erotic excitement that pornography provokes, one is left to conclude that their utilization within pornographic texts must serve another purpose. To think of pornographic confessions, or the genre itself, as only an orgasmic stimulant would be to miss its role as one of the primary moving-image modes showcasing and validating gay sociality, material conditions, and sex. That is no small burden for any text to bear! Towards that aim, one can understand the genre's intent to include a wide range of elements, practices, and actors composing what we understand as an assemblage of gay identity formation. Gay male pornography's inclusion of characteristics from other media platforms like music,[1] social media,[2] and stories culled from newspaper headlines[3] testifies to the genre's eagerness to situate itself as part of the continuity of a mediasphere aimed at the varied interests of gay men. The primary trait linking both pornographic and non-pornographic texts within this mediasphere is the freedom that these platforms allow for people to express themselves via the act of confession. Here sexual freedom is linked to the freedom to confess the "truth" about oneself. Of course, confession's prominence within gay communities stems from its position as the most recognizable act confirming one's homosexuality. We can understand its importance via the practice of "coming out of the closet." The essentialism of coming out is not only marked by a National Coming Out Day (celebrated each year in North America on 11 October to commemorate the 1978 National March on Washington for Lesbian and Gay Rights) but also affirmed year-round by rhetoric endorsing the idea that the confession of coming out confirms the notion that gay people are born with an inherent sexual inclination. So, while confession is situated as a liberatory act, the narrowness with which it is interpreted within gay communities constrains confession's potentiality before it has a chance to resound in ways that might contradict these assumptions of sexual determinism. What is lost when we fail to think beyond the limitations of "the closet" (a severely bifurcated understanding reducing us to either *in* or *out*) is articulated by Cesare Casarino when he writes about the "sublime of the closet," and that to attain it, the key is "*not* a coming out. It is rather, an overcoming of the closet" (2002, 187, original emphasis). He goes on to explain,

> To come out of the closet also reaffirms the effectiveness and *raison d'être* of the closet ... This is to say that if to come out of the closet may turn out to be also the proverbial solution that feeds back into the very problem it was meant to solve, as it locks one into the vicious circle of a perpetually self-reproducing dialectical relay, other types of solutions need to be pursued at the same time. (188)

So, while confession is commonly associated with the idea of freedom, the confession itself is not free to contradict the scripted nature of the coming-out narrative. Reinforcing the discourse around the idea of "the closet" only limits our potential to think of confession outside of this mindset.

The importance of confession fitting into a mould is explained by Ken Plummer when he writes about the formation of "social memories," which he describes as growing out of "gay and women's movements" that "come to develop their own folklore of stories which get transmitted from generation to generation, complete with ritualistic days and marches – Stonewall, Gay Pride, AIDS Awareness, etc. – which help to provide a sense of shared history" (1995, 41). In this way Plummer helps us to understand how confessing one's persecution, pride, and suffering makes up the building blocks of gay identity. And because of confession's outsized role in legitimizing gay identity, the aesthetics of confession maintain a position of prominence in all types of media looking to be incorporated within a gay-identified assemblage. This is the reason for the obligatory way that confession is used in these pornographic texts. Pornography's use of confession signals its aspiration to be a fully incorporated piece of the assemblage composing gay identity. And it is precisely because confession and the coming-out narrative have become a matter-of-fact aspect of gay identity within both our networked pornographic landscape and our contemporary social media environment that their implications regarding our understanding of gay identity need to be investigated.

In addition to articulating the desires composing a gay identity, confessions add to the erotic sense that we as viewers can not only see every physical aspect of someone but can also access a piece of their interior emotional life. Pornographic performance is a totalizing experience. This is how we can understand pornography as a mode eroticizing the concept of exhaustion. Being centred on the "money shot," pornography fetishizes the idea of exhaustive finality embodied within the exploration of the physical body, the conclusion of the orgasm – and, via confession – the entirety of the interior life of the performers. What is so satisfying about the idea of *la petite mort* is an understanding that one has figuratively reached out and touched the bodily limits of one's desires. The physical orgasm for a man is desire's finality at that moment. Pornographic confession rarely distracts from pornography's aim of urging the viewer to get off/finish. To that end, pornographic confessions must align with conventional notions of gay male sexuality in terms of relationality and identity, and never undercut the journey to the orgasm. And while participants occasionally expand the boundaries of "normal" sexual practice when they regale viewers with a story about having sex with someone while they were underage, or confess to having sex with their brother (just before they literally have sex with their brother on camera!), these stories are examples of highly controlled experiences, consensual couplings, and merely reinforce the erotic scenario taking place. Pornographic confessions are a means to an end.

However, if confession is to be considered a point of analysis, then we must posit these confessions as a starting point rather than an endpoint. Instead of thinking about eroticism within the scope of finalities, Claire Colebrook reminds us, we must recognize that in fact "the world is *not* an object to be known, observed or represented, so much as a plane of powers to unfold or express different potentials of life" (2010, 97, emphasis mine). By enacting Deleuze's concept of "the fold" (*le pli*), Colebrook pinpoints how we might come to understand confession within the mould of the fold, where the act does not reveal a hidden interiority but instead exposes the degree to which we understand ourselves more through exterior affective intensities. Within this context, pornographic confession does not so much reveal the degree of one's "true" sexual desire (those confessions are performed corporeally for the sake of the camera) as hint at one's urge to be perceived as sexual, which reveals a performer's desire to tap into the wellspring of sexual affects composing the history and practice of a wider pornographic assemblage. One can read more into an intent than into a practice. And it is the intent to tap into these affects that offers us an opportunity to think about confession beyond the limits of performative verbal discourse. By invoking the idea of "the fold," we can also begin to conceive of the role that the body[4] plays in connecting with a wider range of affective registers. Deleuze connects the idea of "the fold" to the body and hints at its "animal" characteristics: "Life is not only everywhere, but souls are everywhere in matter. Thus, when an organism is called to unfold its own parts, its animal or sensitive soul is opened onto an entire theater in which it perceives or feels according to its unity, independently of its organism, yet inseparable from it" ([1988] 2006, 12). Thinking of confession in terms of the fold allows us to conceive of the practice's potentiality in a more expansive way. The fold is inherently linked to Deleuze and Guattari's concept of becoming, due to the fold's ability to account for a multitude of experientials within affective expressions.

The fold is a process of becoming. Deleuze writes, "The new status of the object, the objectile, is inseparable from the different layers that are dilating, like so many occasions for meanders and detours. In relation to the many folds that it is capable of becoming, matter becomes a matter of expression" ([1988] 2006, 41). Importantly, Deleuze describes an idea of eradicating conventional notions of emotional interiority via the fold through the resonance of affective forces. Situating the body as existing within a relational mode allows us to think of his notion of "becoming animal" as a recognition of how the body facilitates affect through embodying confession. This is how we can understand confession as an attempt to tap into something beyond the limits of verbal discourse.

The aim of this chapter is to expand upon the idea of "becoming animal" to conceive of pornographic confession as more than just a routine, and instead consider it within an affective body. Outlining the dynamics of bodily confession within gay pornographic texts also forces us to productively reconsider the role of confession within our constructions of gay identity and a queer sensibility. To draw a contrast to the type of limited verbal confessions exhibited by the likes of Cervone for professional studios, I will analyze the work of independent producers and performers like Colby Keller and the Black Spark who pointedly de-emphasize the role of verbal discourse and instead embed confession within their bodily pornographic aesthetic. Both performers de-emphasize the voice and the face by utilizing masks as a visual trope within their work. Their doing so reorients our ideas around pornographic confession from something that is verbalized to something resonating within the body. Formulating a notion of bodily confession within this context is most appropriate, considering that pornography is the pre-eminent "body genre." Compellingly, these artists use masks to trigger a crisis regarding the cohesiveness of gay identity by accentuating the abstraction of queerness. Thinking about queerness as a sensibility rather than an identity evokes the notion of "queer opacity" developed by Nicholas de Villiers. This notion strikes me as an effective way to think about how masks in pornography act as affective triggering mechanisms. For de Villiers, the idea of queer opacity "allow[s] for the possibility of non-meaning and non-knowledge as 'queer' strategies'" (2012, 15). Within this framework, pornographic masks ironically force us to read for confessional traits embodied in opacity within a genre dependent on explicit exposure.

Becoming a Confessing Animal

To be gay is to always already be in the act of confessing. Growing up gay means being confronted with questions that do not yet have fully formed (or even partially formed) answers. Because of this, the verbal exchange of confession works frustratingly to solidify the social position of a body that is actively in tune with the kinetic flows of affective intensities that are continually shaping (and reshaping) bodies and social assemblages. We can see this in action when considering the types of questions gay people encounter throughout life, and sometimes even in the course of a single dinner party: *Are you gay? Are you bi? Are you trans? When did you know that you were gay? How old were you the first time you had sex? Have you ever had sex with the opposite sex? Do your parents know that you're gay? How did your parents react then you told them? Are you "the man" or "the woman" in the relationship? Do you go to gay bars? What are they like?* The questioner's fascination with finding out about sexual practices cannot help but legitimize Foucault's presupposition that confessional exchange is about finding out if "there is something hidden within ourselves" (1988, 46). In their limited scope, these types of questions are not intended to tap into the desires of the subject but instead work to establish a foil against which to establish the questioner's parameters for what it means to be heterosexual. One gets the sense that the questioner is not so much interested in learning more about the person being questioned but that the confessions elicited are being used as a way for the questioner to situate their own heterosexual desires and practices. This leads to an unequal exchange in which the questioner is seeking confirmation about their own sexual practices, while the person answering the questions is left to continue their own sexual exploration. This is why being gay means that words typically fail, because language lacks the ability to express the expansive range of desires that defy classification.

While society impresses upon us that the act of confession is the primary way in which we reveal the "truth" about ourselves, confessing conversely activates a social pressure to conform by forcing us to be more conscious about what we are about to say, to account for the sensibilities of our audience, and to confess in a manner that will emphasize our best qualities. It is astounding if we can recognize ourselves at all after confessing! It strikes me that this is what Foucault meant when he wrote that "nothing in man – not even his body – is sufficiently stable as the basis for self-recognition or for understanding other men" ([1971] 1977, 153). Foucault's assertion that one cannot even rely on one's own body for a sense of "self-recognition" acknowledges the degree to which one's physicality is incorporated as part of the affective intensities of social assemblages, an actively modulating force that speeds past the boundaries erected by the narrowing practice of verbal confession. Brian Massumi makes this point clear when he writes that "the skin is faster than the word," and this is why a verbal confession fails to capture a coherent notion of the self, identity, or the body (1995, 86).

This disconnect between the stagnant verbal confession and the kinetic and affective body emphasizes the dissociative nature of "truth" and identity in the negotiation of the difference between verbal and bodily communication. In short, words are always playing catch-up to the body. Perhaps this is why Foucault felt compelled to associate confession with the animal kingdom, a population that does not rely on linguistic cues and can only use their bodies and howls to express themselves. Foucault does this when he declares that "Western man has *become* a confessing animal" (*devenu une bête d'aveu*) ([1976] 1990, 59, emphasis mine). Foucault's figure of a confessing animal here situates becoming as a passive experience, prioritizing the role that confession plays within power relations over any affective desire passing through the subject. Foucault's use of *bête* emphasizes this passivity with dismissive connotations of "stupidity." Once again, Foucault's dismissal of the affective potentiality of desire is lost due to not thinking of the subject beyond power relations. Black Spark's aesthetic defiance of these mainstream concepts of gay identity might be understood as a visual representation of the frustration felt by Foucault when he writes about the struggle against subjection, or what "categorizes the individual, marks him by his own individuality, attaches him to his own identity, imposes a *law of truth* on him that he must recognize and others have to recognize in him" (1983, 212, emphasis mine). For Dreyfus and Rabinow, we *become* confessing animals in the sense that we become classified, demarcated, and situated within an evolutionary chart via verbal confession. Importantly, this classification prompted by confession emphasizes a sense of disassociation from the lived reality of the confessing body. The confession is not connected to desire; it is always already incorporated within mechanisms of power. Within this formation, our verbal discourse is being classified alongside our "stupid" primitive bodies. Here, desire is lost to power.

I utilize the word "primitive" here to highlight Ludwig Wittgenstein's notion that our "language-game is an extension of primitive behaviour. (For our *language-game* is behaviour) (Instinct)" ([1953] 1958, 545). Wittgenstein's argument that "words are connected with the primitive" evolves from his allegory of the hurt child: as he gets older, "adults teach him," instead of simply crying, to use "exclamations and, later, sentences. They teach the child new pain-behaviour" (244). This learned behaviour leads to our normative condition where "the verbal expression of pain replaces crying and *does not* describe it" (244, emphasis mine). While language remains the primary practice through which we conceive of confession, Wittgenstein (perhaps unwittingly) taps into the affective characteristics of language, where its inadequacy in describing pain reveals the wide scope of affective intensities that poetically transcend the mechanics of language. Therefore, one can only understand the full affective scope of confession by understanding language's inability to fully describe it. In the same way that language can only hint at describing the affective life of pain, it is equally incapable of encompassing the totality of the self. Therefore, when it comes to confession, verbal discourse is merely a primitive "language-game," a game that must be judged against the actions of the body.

From Confessing Animal to Becoming Animal

The "game" is over once the person confessing has released their words and is subsequently left to contemplate their own body without discourse. It is at this moment that the confessing individual is confronted with what Gerald L. Bruns identifies as one of the primary "regulating questions of recent European thinking: 'who comes after the subject?'" (2007, 703). In search for an answer, one would find some possibilities in returning to the animal motif, which is picked up by Deleuze and Guattari after Foucault. One can see a through line from Deleuze and Guattari's idea of *becoming animal* to Foucault's analogy of *becoming a confessing animal*. The notion of *becoming* – which can be understood as a point of distinct classification in Foucault's usage – is more of an abstract process for Deleuze, who writes that "becoming" is a pure event "whose characteristic is to elude the present. Insofar as it eludes the present, becoming does not tolerate the separation or the distinction of before and after, or of past and future. It pertains to the essence of becoming to move and to pull in both directions at once" ([1969] 1990, 1). For Deleuze and Guattari, what comes after the subject is desire, affect, and intensity. Subjectivity happens in starts and stops, like affect. Therefore the "animal" within Deleuze and Guattari's formation is just another field of intensity that an affective body can resonate with. Foucault's formation stresses the animal (a loss of subjectivity to power relations), while Deleuze and Guattari stress becoming (individuation and affective resonance). For Deleuze and Guattari, the lines of demarcation for subjectivity, desire, and power are not as impenetrable as they are for Foucault. In their understanding of becoming, the "animal" has affective autonomy and can "move and pull in both directions at once." This is how one can come to understand how the figure of the animal for Foucault and Deleuze and Guattari operates.

For Bruns, this type of awareness of existing in between affective registers is what provokes a sense of "deterritorialization" in which "a subject no longer occupies a realm of stability and identity, but is instead folded imperceptibly into a movement or into an amorphous *legion* whose mode of existence is nomadic or, alternatively, whose 'structure' is rhizomatic" (2007, 703–4, original emphasis). This is the essence of what becoming animal means: a recognition of the futility of subjectivity via language, which translates into a desire to be a part of virtual planes of intensities. The root of this desire for desubjectification is articulated by Deleuze and Guattari when they write that "language is not life; it gives orders. Life does not speak, it listens and waits" ([1980] 1987, 76). Hence, language has the tendency to turn questions like *Are you gay? Are you bi? Are you transgender?* into emphatic statements – *You are gay. You are bi. You are transgender* – that are exemplary of the ways that language hails us into subjectivities and quashes queer sensibilities. This inevitability of subjectification is due to the gay community's inherent relationship with confession. As an example, the rhetoric and practice of coming out – the liberatory "truth" that this confessional act offers – has become a foundational aspect of what it means to identify as gay. Considering the strength of this bond between confession and gay identity – which is reinforced by hetero and homosexual neoliberal and nationalist factions – it is no surprise that this linkage is being challenged by subsequent queer ruptures within media texts, exemplified by the use of masks in the work of Keller and Black Spark.

These ruptures represent a recognition within the gay community of the radical potentiality of becoming animal. Shifting the concept of identity from the realm of stability to that of instability through the use of masks is an active aesthetic process of becoming. This process can be understood as part of a political strategy intended to counteract a mainstream media environment fetishizing the cohesiveness of gay identity via confession. This approach is also connected to a longer history of masks signifying political subversion (e.g., Guy Fawkes masks worn today by anti-capitalist activists). And in this instance, becoming animal subverts the stability of the homonationalist and homonormative identity utilized by the state to show just how *progressive* contemporary North American society has become regarding homosexuals. Here one can see the connection between the purposefully contrarian political intentions behind queer opacity (e.g., *not* coming out of "the closet," *not* verbalizing confession, *not* revealing one's face) coinciding with the tropes of becoming animal when Deleuze and Guattari write that "there is no longer man or animal, since each deterritorializes the other, in a conjunction of flux, in a continuum of reversible intensities" ([1975] 1986, 22). And while the use of *becoming* for Foucault and for Deleuze and Guattari exemplifies their differing theoretical intensions (Foucault using *becoming* to illustrate the mechanisms of disciplining categorization, and Deleuze and Guattari utilizing *becoming* as a way to emphasize the flux of a control society), each use the idea of *animal* as a way of emphasizing the body. For Deleuze and Guattari, their affective body represents an enduring impulse to circulate within non-verbal planes of intensities signalling a rupture in the established social structures of identity. For Foucault, the primitive body takes primacy over linguistic games, and for Deleuze and Guattari, speaking of Kafka, "the animal essence is the way out, the line of escape, even if it takes place in place, or in a cage. *A line of escape, and not freedom. A vital escape and not an attack*" (35, emphasis in original). Hence, for the purposes of this chapter, the idea of becoming animal focuses on how the idea of bodily confession actively works to utilize the idea of queer opacity to upset the structures of gay identity formation held in place by the practice of verbal confession. This chapter delves into the most marginalized form of media – pornography – in order to find these moments of animal rupture.

Pornography Becomes Animal

Just like queerness, becoming animal is about movement and stripping away the markers of a fixed identity. Deleuze and Guattari expand on this point:

> To become animal is to participate in movement, to stake out a path of escape in all its positivity, to cross a threshold, to reach a continuum of intensities that are valuable only in themselves, to find a world of pure intensities where all forms come undone, as do all the significations, signifiers, and signifieds, to the benefit of an unformed matter of deterritorialized flux, of nonsignifying signs. ([1975] 1986, 13)

Perhaps spurred by the era of the selfie – and overexposure exacerbated by social media generally – a countermovement has emerged within gay pornographic media embracing the aesthetics of transience, opacity, and erasure. And while the overexposed nature of pornography could not exist without fetishizing what is hidden (a fetish that is only satisfied once what is hidden is revealed), some texts within gay pornography are experimenting with enacting the erotic traits in what insistently remains hidden. A performer who embodies this ideal is Colby Keller.

Keller began appearing in studio-produced scenes in 2004, and in 2014 he started fundraising for a pornographic art project titled *Colby Does America* (CDA). Keller describes his project: "[I'll] buy a van, a mattress and a camera and travel across the country. I'll meet all my amazing fans, blog my adventures, collaborate with other artists and make videos in every state … I plan to make a porn in every state (and whatever they call states in Canada – jk! jk!)" (Keller 2014). He later explains that the process of creating each of these three- to six-minute videos requires him to shoot the footage himself on site, and then offer that footage to any artist who is willing to edit it for him before he posts it on the project's site, ColbyDoesAmerica. The highly collaborative nature of the project assures that no two videos share the same feel, though of course the inclusion of Keller, gay sexuality, and cheap hand-held cameras ensure that there is aesthetic continuity. Keller's random journey (scenes are released erratically, and he does not provide a map where viewers can follow him) exploring the exoticism of the forests and lake locales hidden in states and provinces that one presumes to know, literalizes Deleuze and Guattari's non-prescriptive invitation to "participate in movement." Keller's engagement with amateur performers – many of them discovering their sexual desires on camera for the first time – and his practice of shooting scenes with an amateur aesthetic prioritizing camera placement conducive to the parameters of the locale instead of utilizing ideal angles to complement the best sex positions – help him to "stake out a path" of his own artistic and sexual desires. However, the practice that best embodies the tropes of becoming is seen in the videos in which his co-performers wear a mask. The "path" staked out with this choice is where traditional identity forms "come undone." The use of masks in pornographic texts is less common in the post-stag era – which makes its contemporary use in a pro-am production particularly disruptive.[5] Seizing on this opportunity to explore the dynamics of the pornographic mask as a "matter of deterritorialized flux," we can work towards de-emphasizing the prominence of the face and instead situate the body as a primary site of confession.

CDA itself emerges from a context of confession – and some might say desperation! Understanding its origins gives insight into the aesthetics of movement, of stripping away of identifying traits, and of the sense of deterritorialization that encompass the project. In an interview where Keller speaks about what prompted him to start the project he explains:

> I really needed a radical solution. So I'm just going to get rid of every little thing that I own in an art piece, anyone, anyone off the street, anybody. I can't make exceptions, I need to follow this rule. To the point to where everything that I own someone has taken. Or I've gifted it to them … I got rid of the stuff. [Everything] no shoes, no socks, no underwear. I was completely naked at the end of this project. I was really struggling with how to address my career, and the way most people recognize me, which is though porn. [And] how to incorporate that though my art practice. And you know, part of that is about, you know, exposure, and vulnerability, and nudity. [And] in kind of a jokey, metaphorical way, getting to that place. Really! … It was a really transformative, really moving experience … I ended in this cave in Tennessee, completely naked. Emerging like a five-year-old child from the cave. (Keller 2017)

Invoking the figurative idea of being reborn is a theme throughout Keller's work. There has always been a sense that he is uncomfortable with being known only for his pornographic performances. Hence, he consistently seems to be reborn into different public personas. In his Twitter blurb, he describes himself as an "artist, sex activist, actor." On the blog that brought him notoriety beyond pornographic circles, BigShoeDiaries, he documents his appreciation of the fine arts, and his own art practice cultivated at the University of Maryland, where he earned a master of fine arts degree. He captured social media notoriety within gay circles by originating the hashtag #ISeePenis, where Twitter and Tumblr users have accumulated a series of pictures of seemingly non-sexual objects (like mushrooms, bottles, newspapers, and children's slides) that just happen in some way to take the shape of a circumcised penis. The hashtag shows that Keller does not want to abandon explicit sexuality as a part of his extracurricular non-pornographic work. While all his media incarnations can be read as expanding his personal "brand," emphasizing his face and his dick, his performance in a music video for the song "After Dark" by the band Undercover (2012) hints at some of the motifs of erasure he later explores in CDA. Donning a glittering silver eye mask, he looks into the mirror, contemplating the fragility of his own identity and the ease with which it can be obscured. Interestingly, Keller does not wear a mask in CDA, but the two performers who do don masks are black. This decision is regressive in terms of racial representation but dynamic in terms of how confession works in these texts to expand the parameters of how we think about the nature of gay black pornographic performers.

In the video *Colby Does Kentucky* (2015a), Keller has sex with a burly black man wearing a knitted ski mask (fig. 13.1). Throughout this two-minute video, a non-diegetic soundtrack of a horse race plays in the background. While this is an obvious reference to Kentucky's most famous annual event, the Kentucky Derby, associating a black man's penis with that of a horse cannot be considered as much more than a lazy visual trope recalling a long racist history of comparing the nature of black men's sexuality to that of a wild animal. The scene of the men having sex is intercut with an image of an animated donkey ("donkey dick" being an even cruder variation of "horse dick"), and in an attempt to interject "artistry" into the scene, there are continual cuts of horses and nude men culled from the photographic experiments of Étienne Jules Marey and Eadweard Muybridge (fig. 13.2). This intercutting not only emphasizes the connection of a black man and a "horse dick" but also reduces the sexual experience taking place on screen to that of a science experiment. Linda Williams contextualizes this type of early photographic experiments as part of pornography's prehistory when she equates the fascination with Marey and Muybridge's work with part of the "unprecedented cinematic pleasure of the illusion of bodily motion emerg[ing], partly as a by-product of the

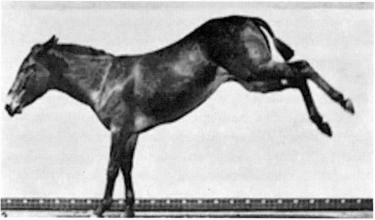

13.1 *Top* Keller engaging with a passive black performer in *Colby Does Kentucky*, 2015.

13.2 *Bottom* Intercutting Muybridge's donkey into a gay sex scene in *Colby Does Kentucky*, 2015.

quest for the initially unseeable 'truths' of this motion" (Williams [1989] 1999, 39). So while this tongue-in-cheek editing gesture might have been intended to amuse, it subtly recalls a time when film was understood as a medium for speaking the "truth" of both science and sex. It is a history that does not aid in contemporary racial understanding. The clinical way in which the both the horses and men jump in these scenes mimics the emphatic bouncing of Keller on this performer's penis. The absence of any verbal exchange between the two – due to a lack of on-location sound recording in this scene – robs the encounter of any eroticism outside of a fetish to see a black man have sex with a white man. Within this context, the mask strips the performer of any humanity or agency and adds to the continuing erasure of complex black sexuality by not allowing it to exist outside of a white perspective.

Thankfully, there is a marked change in the understanding of contemporary racial dynamics in *Colby Does Virginia* (2015b), even though the black performer in this scene also wears a mask (fig. 13.3). This change is most likely due to the editor of the video, Ulysse St-Pierre, who writes that he "wanted a counter-intuitive edit that would create a story and a mood" (St-Pierre 2015). I assume what he means by "counter-intuitive" is that the video is far more contemplative than erotic. The ominous notes of Erik Satie's *Gymnopédie No. 1* play loudly and emphatically throughout, sometimes drowning out the verbal exchange between the performers. Certainly, it is not a track that seeks to excite its listeners erotically. However, despite the uneven volume, the music connotes a sense of class and refinement that much of contemporary gay pornography rarely bothers with.[6] This is striking considering that a black performer is featured in the scene: within gay pornography, the characteristics that black performers play up most are their street-wise accents, hip-hop attire (backwards baseball caps, bandanas, and do-rags), and ferocious dominance over their white co-performers. Sites like BlackDickFever, ThugVids, and FlavaGold are pre-eminent examples showcasing these traits. This type of aesthetic is not one that works in harmony with one of the most iconic pieces within the canon of "serious" music. And while the music seems to conjure a sense of refinement, it eventually works as a point of contradiction when set against the performer's apartment where the video is shot: apparently a basement apartment with dorm-room-style mismatched clutter, giving the impression of a working-class occupant. The viewer is immediately confronted with this aesthetic opposition that mirrors the contrast of the racial depiction seen here in comparison to both *Colby Does Kentucky* and the websites mentioned above. What sets this unnamed performer apart from other black performers are the ways in which he incorporates his personal history, educational accomplishments, and living space as part of his erotic makeup.

He starts off his confession to Keller by explaining that he was a competitive gymnast and cheerleader. He then talks about attending Harvard University, and explains that despite the clichés about Harvard cultivated in movies and television, that "90 per cent" of his time there was a "good experience." Later, in what would typically be a throw-away line, Keller asks if it is okay if he "moves some of [his] stuff." This allows the audience to know that Keller is moving into this performer's personal space. This line is important because a sense of ownership is lacking for

13.3 A more engaged black performer in *Colby Does Virginia*, 2015.

black people on both sides of the camera in the gay pornography industry. None of the top studios is run by black people, and just as in *Colby Does Kentucky*, black performers are often still silenced, cordoned off into their own segregated sections of websites, and problematically objectified when they have abnormally large penises. In asking about moving his "stuff," Keller shows a degree of respect rarely granted black performers and in the process empowers the mise-en-scène in a way that threatens the pre-eminence of the sex taking place. The camera angles used in the scene reinforce this idea by using medium and long shots to capture as much of the whole bodies and their surroundings as possible instead of utilizing any close-ups of genital insertion. A prominent picture of Jesus Christ hanging on a tall cabinet that the performer leans against while he is being anally penetrated by Keller encourages us to think of the mask as a wearable type of confessional (fig. 13.4). The voice-over of the performer's confessions to Keller while he is facing away from Keller literalizes the Catholic practice of not facing one's confessor and also empowers the mask itself as a reflection point where a range of affective registers can emanate as a result of the obscurity that it provides.

While the bodily confession here relies on verbal discourse, this example is a productive starting point for thinking about this concept because of what the body of this performer – the first documented black graduate of Harvard to appear in gay pornography –represents. The strength embodied in the muscles, the pleasure expressed via moaning, and ownership of the apartment represent a

13.4 A makeshift pornographic confessional with Christ looking on in *Colby Does Virginia*, 2015.

counter-narrative to the imagery of tortured gay black men that are given such prominence in North America. The cohesiveness of this body in *Colby Does Virginia* stands in stark contrast to mainstream media narratives promoting *haunting* stories of the black experience in Ivy League schools (Pitterson 2011), the image of blacks living amongst the *shattered* ruins of formerly prominent cities (Philip 2017), the idea of black people as habitually producing *broken* families (Barras 2015), and the notion that the black community engages in *disjointed* political responses as a result (Moran, Nark, and Serpico 2016). So, while Keller attempts throughout CDA to regain ownership of his queer narrative by stripping away his identity signifiers and accumulating new ones, racial minorities conversely work to attain bodily integrity by enacting their own historical heritage, which this performer does here by recounting his time at Harvard and taking ownership of the pornographic space. The integrity of this black body is ironically fortified here by an aesthetics of opacity that denies projected readings of pain and trauma onto his face.

In both of these videos we can begin to understand the multitude of factors and events that resonate throughout Keller's journey: the black experience, film history, a particular state's identity, classical music, video-making, sex, and even the politics of attending Harvard. These varying intensities coalesce into a "map of intensity" that Keller actively creates with this project. By invoking the idea of a map of intensity, I am guided by Deleuze's outline of the concept when he writes: "It is the libido's business to haunt history and geography, to organize formations of worlds and constellations of universes, to make continents drift and to populate them with races, tribes, and nations" ([1993] 1997, 62). Here we can understand Deleuze making a divide between libido and desire. While desire is affective and becoming, Deleuze's use of psychoanalytic terminology like "libido" speaks to the ego's need for subjectivity, identity, and nationhood to satisfy a lack. Libido here represents the insistence of the body within our imagination. To tap into the map of intensity, one must scale the libido to an appropriate proportion. However, such a process of proportioning is not prescribed. By invoking the idea of "haunting," Deleuze recognizes how libidinal resonance does not transcend the realities of our understanding of the world but in fact does "[follow] world historical trajectories" (62). This is how one can gain productive insight into the racial dynamics of *Colby Does Virginia*. To situate this black performer as being in an active state of becoming one must acknowledge both his active libido via discourse and his mask, which disrupts the coherence of identity formation. This active borrowing from both fields – libido and desire – connotes becoming. Recognizing libido enacts the entrenched history of blackness in the United States and imbues his contradictory mask with disruptive force. Here we can understand how the visceral nature of affects and becoming are always dependent on their context.

Of course, the most provocative aspect of affects is the ways in which they help us see a world of potentiality beyond the scope of our immediate reality. However, it is impossible to acknowledge the exciting potentiality they conjure without recognizing the destructive ways in which they have been manifested in the past. As Clare Hemmings points out, "The delights of consumerism, feelings of belonging attending fundamentalism or fascism, to suggest just several contexts, are affective responses that strengthen rather than challenge a dominant social order" (2005, 551). So, while Massumi argues that today the power of a dominant ideology is diminished because we live in an era where a multitude of ideologies are practised and recognized, writing that "it no longer defines the global mode of functioning power … [but] is now one mode of power in a larger field that is not defined, overall, by ideology" (1995, 104), it is essential to remember that the charge of becoming stems from its ability to simultaneously enact both identity (libido) and potentiality (desire) within the same field. In this respect, one can never completely escape the legacies of one's history.

Therefore, while it is important to recognize Hemmings's declaration that "power belongs to the past" (2005, 561), a Deleuzian perspective cannot go so far in this respect (power can always be overthrown because power is never so unidirectional). Deleuze recognizes the role that history plays in maps of intensities when he explains:

> We see clearly why the real and the imaginary were led to exceed themselves, or even to interchange with each other: a becoming is not imaginary, any more than a voyage is real. It is becoming that turns the most negligible of trajectories [e.g., the past, race], or even a fixed immobility, into a voyage [e.g., the mask] ... each of these two types of maps, those of trajectories and those of affects, refers to the other. ([1993] 1997, 65)

Here we can understand how Hemmings's critique of race and power is not as clear-cut as she would like us to imagine. Deleuze never abandons gender, race, or nation. Becoming is the in-between space where the past resonates with the future; each enlivens each other, each map refers to the other. In this understanding, both history and potentiality are activated and enlivened by new generations and ideologies. But even given our instinct to continually construct new social maps, we can feel the intensities of the past, especially gender, racial, and sexual minorities, haunt us in new ways. However, it is these intensities of the past that enliven our contemporary affective maps. Therefore, when we consider the small number of black people today involved in competitive cheerleading, or who compose a graduating class at Harvard, the black performer's mask in *Colby Does Virginia* embodies a type of becoming that encompasses both the uniqueness of his social position and his active displacement from the widely accepted historical narratives about black lives. Our understanding of the pornographic black experience is modified because of the affective mapping occurring in *Colby Does Virginia*. And the rupture in our racial understanding here can only be understood via the history embedded in maps of intensity.

The affective resonance of Keller's maps of intensity across America lies in the accumulation of affective residue throughout the journey. The events from state to state cannot help but guide, change, and influence Keller's experience. As Keller explained in his confession about the project's origin, its purpose was to set out to engage in a range of genuine sexual experiences to make up for the stripping away of his superficial consumerist goods and personal emotional baggage. Hence, accumulation is a key aspect of CDA. This point is somewhat in conflict with one of the foundational aspects of affect theory as understood by Massumi: that affects are autonomous. However, as Deleuze makes clear in his articulation of libido, escaping the framework of history is nowhere near as simple as one might imagine. And for racial minorities who are essentially defined by an educational and structural apparatus defined by a white hegemony, history is both inescapable and an actor in the social construction of racial understanding. So, while affect theory enlivens queerness by counteracting neoliberal ideology, it would be naive to suggest that the ways in which the ideas of affect play out in theory are so easily applied in the real world. No theory is strong enough to erase racial difference in reality. Looking back to Deleuze, we can understand that such erasure was never a part of his theoretical goals, and critiques such as Hemmings's are essential for addressing criticisms (like her own) that affect theory attempts to erase racial difference. For affect to be relevant to our understanding of race and sex, there needs to be an acknowledgment that the reception of affective forces (and not the affects themselves) are particular, cumulative, and of course individuated. This is what accounts for racial difference. Hemmings speaks to this point when she writes that this type of reading "indicates a return to Tomkins' *affect theory* too, where it is the reinvigoration of previous affective states and their effects, rather than affective freedom, that allow us to make our bodies mean something that we recognize and value" (2005, 564, original emphasis). This is part of what remains fascinating about CDA: the journey taken would carry no meaning and lose all worth if there were not some stickiness to the intensities experienced along the way. So yes, while affect is initially autonomous, libido accounts for our conception of affect's ability to linger within the body and allows us to map its trajectory. These masked porn performers in CDA help us to understand that racialized gay identity is perhaps a little sticky, but certainly never stagnant.

The Politics of the Faceless Pornographic Image

Examining Keller's social and political intentions in his work are necessitated by the fact that he positions himself as a politically engaged artist. He is a self-described communist, claims to have worked for a lobbyist in Washington, DC, and articulates his political viewpoints for the express purpose of provoking a reaction. He did so in 2016 during an interview with *OfficeMagazine*, when he declared his commitment to vote for Donald Trump in that year's US presidential election. Keller explained his reasoning by saying that while he didn't "support or endorse any of his policies," he thought that Trump would be a productive "destabilizing force" that would "escalate the problem" of our corrupt two-party system, and help lead it to its downfall (Silver 2016). Of course, there is no need for me to rehash the obvious negative reaction that Keller's declaration evoked throughout the gay blogosphere. I will just say that the response was swift, angry, and hostile. While there is nothing particularly interesting about Keller's voting preferences, what was compelling about this hiccup within the seemingly linear narrative of universal support for Trump's opponent amongst "rational" gay men was that it hinted at a wider rupture within our understanding of "appropriate" behavioural practices for sexual minorities. Keller's confession disrupts a social class valorizing the tenets of identity politics as a measuring stick for acting "respectably" within "civilized" social circles. And he was not the only gay pornographic performer to publicly declare support for Trump (Sire 2016; Sunderland 2016). It is at times like these where wearing a mask turns into a necessity if one chooses to vote for the "wrong" candidate or follow an ideology outside of the parameters supported by identity politics. Even women were warned not to step out of line during the election when former secretary of state Madeleine Albright told a crowd at a New Hampshire rally for Hillary Clinton that "there's a special place in hell for women who don't help each other" (McCarthy 2016).

What makes Keller's confession so jarring is that it contradicts the seemingly "progressive" public face of the pornographic industry that typically coalesces around ideals like freedom of speech, gay rights, and racial equality. But of course there are limits to tolerance when it comes to political party association. The swiftness with which Keller was universally denounced on social media illustrates that the idea of freedom of speech within the industry is only legitimized by those expressing more liberal viewpoints. And while professional pornography maintains its consistent political viewpoint via its cadre of performers who typically skew towards a Democratic ideology (Harlan 2015) – and express as much on social media (*TMZ* 2015) – it is mostly only through the diffuse and haphazard realm of amateur pornography that one finds alternative platforms for expressing viewpoints frustrating this "liberal" groupthink narrative.

A platform that does this provocatively well is the social smartphone app Grindr (see Roach, chapter 29). Grindr is a geolocation-based app where gay men post pictures of themselves and fill in a descriptive profile to socially or sexually meet other men in their immediate location. While the idea behind Grindr is to facilitate physical meetings between men, in my experience it is most often used to trade nude pictures with other users, regardless of whether we intend on meeting in person or not. In this way, Grindr has become a primary platform for gay men to circulate their self-pornographic imagery. It is against the terms and conditions of the app to post a nude image of yourself as your profile picture, so all nude pictures are traded via private messaging with other users. Instead, it is through the textual content of the profile where the subversive political nature of the app is on display – and subsequently archived on the website DouchebagsOf-Grindr. This site is a collection of Grindr profiles showcasing the most politically incorrect, racist, fem-shaming, and fat-shaming descriptions of the kind of people these users are not looking to meet. As you can tell from the site's name, the comment sections are filled with people shaming these users for their short-sighted and racist perspective on their own sexual desires. It is a space where one goes to shame shamefulness. Typical entries on the site feature profiles that read:

> "I'm a gay GUY! If I wanted to date someone feminine I would be straight and with a girl" (24 August 17).
> "I block more Asians than the Great Wall of China" (24 August 17).
> "18-25 if your [sic] old enough to be my dad don't bother" (22 August 17).
> "Avg guy, masculine, happens I like guys. If you open your mouth and a purse falls out please save yourself the rejection. Not looking for a headless torso or a friend with no pic" (21 August 17).

While the site offers a comforting venue to shame others as a way towards social progress, it simultaneously exposes the ugly underbelly of the false foundation that our contemporary understanding of identity politics is built upon.[7] A common sexuality does not connote a common political cause. Keller's confession about voting for Trump only brought this level of honesty beyond the pages of DouchebagsOfGrindr and exposed it to a wider audience.

The entry by the user who is "not looking for a headless torso or a friend with no pic" highlights a crucial aspect of Grindr, and connects us to the masked performers of CDA. While my overall description of Grindr might give the impression that the app is as photocentric as Instagram, much of it is populated with headless profile pictures of torsos, blank profiles, memes, and even pictures of non-sexual objects. The prominence of faceless profiles throughout Grindr should perhaps not be too surprising considering that the app's logo is a mask (fig. 13.5). In describing the original yellow minimalist hockey goalie style mask with four square teeth jutting out at the bottom, Grindr founder Joel Simkhai explains, "We looked at this notion of meeting people and the idea is very much a basic human need to relax and to socialize. I went back to primitive tribal arts in Africa and Polynesia. One of the things I saw was these primal masks. It brings us back to basics, primal needs. Socialization is the basis of humanity" (Salerno 2011).

This romanticizing of the "primitive" and "primal" brings us back to Wittgenstein, which helps us recognize the rhetorical game Simkhai is playing here. He attempts to valorize the genuine "simplicity" of these masks by erecting a foil made up of the signifying discourse of our corrupt contemporary capitalist mode. By doing so he is hoping to exploit an inbred nostalgia for a "simpler" past. While his intentions are mostly admirable – even Foucault romanticized the East with his formulation of *ars erotica* – Simkhai's failure lies in his attempt to essentially trade one mode of signifying traits for another, and in doing so he legitimates both. Ultimately, the question here cannot be the futile search for the "proper" set of signifiers that will bring us back to a healthy "primitive" state; one must instead recognize the futility of signifiers themselves, and their inability to access the affective potentiality beyond the mask or the face. For Deleuze and Guattari, both the mask and the face are not standalone or oppositional signifiers but part of the same signifying regime. They remind us that "the mask does not hide the face, it *is* the face" ([1980] 1987, 115, emphasis in original).

What Deleuze and Guattari are referring to here is their belief in the futility of signifiers: "There is not much to say about the center of significance, or the Signifier in person, because it is a pure abstraction no less than a pure principle; in other words, it is nothing" (114–15). In fact, it is the signifier's propensity for a type of pornographic repetition that accounts for this hollowness of meaning: "The sign refers to other signs ad infinitum" (115). Understood within this context, it is fruitless to try to organize a kind of aesthetic hierarchy of profiles with faces and faceless profiles. There is no facelessness without the presence of the face anyway. Additionally, Grindr's value lies less in its ability to feature "real" pictures of users and is more invested in a regime of potentiality as a way of keeping long-time users hooked and attracting future users. Regular users of the app are already aware of the futility of the profile picture. Pornographic performers often tweet pictures of Grindr profiles using their images, doing so to either warn people about the fake profile or to point out the humour of the co-optation. It is common knowledge that the strength of the profile picture's indexicality has never been strong. This is why exchanging additional pictures via private messages remains a crucial part of the experience. *How many years ago was this picture taken? Does this person look this good in all types of lighting? Are they just sucking in their stomach for an ideal profile picture?* Such questions typically go through one's mind in analyzing profiles that provide a face picture.

The precarious indexicality of the Grindr profile picture coincides with the app's happenstantial role in exposing the fragility of a gay identity politics movement based on the social status of coming out of "the closet." While coming out has long been recognized as a strategy for formulating a type of *public face* of a sympathetic gay body, this strategy has seemingly lost much of its social energy now that inclusion in the institutions of the military, marriage, and hate-crime legislation have become norms in the United States. More nebulous struggles like racial understanding, class consciousness, and even gender fluidity are harder to stay plugged into and have met active resistance from many gay people who benefit greatly from the racial, class, and gender inequality fostered by the country's neoliberal ethos. Therefore, if we are to conceive of a contemporary gay body after it has been fully incorporated into the US neoliberal legal structure, we must also reconceive the role of its *public face* in this new makeup. This is how Grindr's platform for queer opacity via faceless profiles becomes instructive. By actively resisting facial exposure in a gay culture centred around public declarations of coming out of "the closet," these profiles enact a version of queer opacity that productively ruptures the illusion of political unity.

These faceless Grindr profiles also highlight Deleuze and Guattari's ideas about the futility of signifiers themselves. For Deleuze and Guattari, the face represents an area on the body that is over-imbued with signifiers, to the point of rendering it meaningless.[8] For philosophers prioritizing a body moving through planes of intensities, the idea of a part of the body acting as a facilitator for entrenched political and emotional signification is anathema to their project. Deleuze and Guattari go as far as saying that the face is so "overcoded" and entrenched with projected signification that it is no longer a part of the head and represents "the inhuman in human beings: that is what the face is from the start" ([1980] 1987, 171). They explain this phenomenon as "faciality" and describe it as a practice through which we go about conceiving of the entirety of the body within identity and ideological frameworks.[9] Therefore, the faceless Grindr profiles can be understood as an active retrenchment from our established modes conceiving of identity via the face, and can help us realize just how prevalent our use of faciality is in this process. Because only through recognizing our reliance on faciality will we be able to transition into realizing the affective potentialities of becoming. As Deleuze and Guattari note, "To the point that if human beings have a destiny, it is rather to escape the face, to dismantle the face and facializations to become imperceptible, to become clandestine, not by returning to animality, or even by returning to the head, but by quiet spiritual and special becomings-animal" (171).

The Faceless Aesthetic of the Black Spark

The inciting incident for this chapter occurred in late 2010, when a performer calling himself Black Spark began premiering his self-produced pornographic music videos on Xtube. Most of the songs chosen for the videos are contemporary

13.5 *Right*
The Grindr logo (original version reproduced here) illustrates how opacity has always been a foundational part of interacting within the app.

13.6 *Below*
The Black Spark shows so much yet hides his face. http://theblackspark.tumblr.com/.

with a healthy dose of digital sound pulsating listeners into trance-like states (e.g., "Woods" by Bon Iver in *Black Spark Art #12* [2013b]), with occasional pops of bouncy dance tracks (e.g., "Cards to Your Heart" by Groove Armada (2012) in *Dance in My Heart Now* [2015]). The prominence and relevance of the music alone would have been enough to mark a monumental change in pornography aesthetics that for decades relied on the monotonous droning of uninteresting background music; then in the internet era, individual scenes abandoned music altogether, preferring the diegetic sounds of the body to provide the soundscape. However, the videos' most intriguing aspect is that Black Spark wears a bandanna or mask over his mouth and nose, hiding at least half of his face – and he never reveals his identity (on or off camera) throughout his productions (fig. 13.6).

When he or his fellow performers wear an ornate mask, it is in the style of the ones featured in the mysterious costume-ball scenes in the Kubrick movie *Eyes Wide Shut* (1999). With this series of pornographic music videos, suddenly the genre that exists explicitly to exploit every crevice of the body was provocatively hiding the body's primary transmitter of affect and pleasure.

There were strategic reasons why Black Spark made the decision to cover his face. Perhaps because of the mystery it caused – and the resulting sensation throughout the gay blogosphere – he gave a series of interviews explaining some aspects of his videos to clarify his intentions. His reasons given for wearing a mask ranged from the functional (he did not "want the Black Spark to hinder [his] large-scale future plans in film") to the emotional (his "work is driven by what [he] feel[s]") (Crook 2011). The latter is an important point, because while the mask immediately connotes a sense of performativity and artifice, the mise-en-scène consistently builds up an inventory of sexual desires being fantasized and acted out in front of the camera. Black Spark's aesthetic assemblage is both consistent and revealing. Besides the familiarity of the music's tone from scene to scene, the videos are populated by a recurrent cavalcade of men with physiques seemingly ripped out of an Abercrombie & Fitch catalog, all white, young, and hairless, with rolling abs going on for as far as the eye can see! This assemblage is actually quite a feat because of the way it bucks trends in an age of amateur pornography increasingly populated by the most diverse range of body types and racial match-ups in the history of the genre, brought about by the accessibility of internet-connected cameras. The insistence on a body type typically reserved for those who make professional use of their local gym and health-food store could surely point to Black Spark's preference in men. (Who would not want to have sex with someone in such great physical condition, at least once [e.g., *Sunday Faith* (2012)]?)

In the same way, Black Spark's approach to lighting emphasizes what is hidden as a way of opening up a multitude of avenues for interpretation and confession. He uses variously coloured LED lights in otherwise darkened rooms to create strikingly half-lit figures that reorient familiar body types into new shapes and illuminated patterns (e.g., *Black Spark Art #4* [2013a]). This lighting is antithetical to the typical intense key lighting shone on all pornographic performers in professional productions, leaving very little to the imagination. The lighting in the Black Spark's videos provocatively gives us permission to question the typical lighting scheme of pornography, something that is typically taken for granted in videos that strive for a professional look. Because of how the Black Spark breaks the taken-for-granted approach to lighting, we are subsequently invited to question the indexicality of both his own partially lit performers and the fully lit figures we are accustomed to seeing throughout the genre. In Black Spark's videos, we instead think about his sparse lighting as a motif intended to connote that the genre can actually be one in which bodies are gradually discovered as performers slowly and erratically emerge out of the shadows, instead of being figures that are always already exposed. He challenges us to see that even pornography can be a site of potentiality, that there is still something about the body yet to be explored. The effect is an exciting sense of discovery in which we can feel what Black Spark might be feeling about sexual excitement and experience, feel that we are discovering new aspects of the director's sexual desires as he is realizing them on camera with his wandering LED light. This feeling aligns with his admission that the videos served as "an outlet to share my innermost desires. I had secrets that were eating me alive, and at one point I wanted to go to therapy. But I found my own therapy through making these movies" (Sire 2011).

While Black Spark's sexual satisfaction is evident through his direction, erections, and "money shots," he testifies that he found therapeutic salvation through his impulse to "share" part of himself with a wider community. That impulse is less about conforming to the conventionality of confession and more about sharing the experience of sexual and self-discovery. It is here that the role of the mask becomes evident. In positioning the videos as a type of therapy, we can understand them as a type of self-exploration. Black Spark's subjectivity has been ruptured due to the secrets "eating him alive." His sense of alienation implies a need to rediscover the self. The mask represents this drive to explore the self as if it were new – there is no *old* (face) to return to. And the bodily confession as manifested within the pornography shares this process of becoming. The dark lighting in many of the scenes also emphasizes the process of discovering the mysteries of someone else's body during sex. In addition to sharing the feeling of discovery with a lighting strategy that links his own erotic curiosity to his viewer's, Black Spark also engages in a more literal type of sharing when he shifts his sexual performance from the intimacy of his apartment to the public places of Chicago, as when he shoots in an adult video store or in snowy alleyway. Situating pornography within a cityscape taps into a longer history of gay pornography that channels a neorealist practice of utilizing the city to emphasize the wider range of affects intersecting within a sexual assemblage (Escoffier 2017; Strub 2016).

One might wonder if Black Spark is betraying his anonymous persona by giving away the specificities of his hometown, the financial means behind the equipment he uses, and the places he shoots in, and by granting interviews describing his work. However, because of the ephemeral nature of pornography, I think a case can be made for the need to explain the motivation behind one's work if there is a desire to have the public pay attention to it within a floodtide of texts and to pique an audience's interest in the work's aesthetic motivation. Elucidation does not nullify anonymity. If it were not for the interviews, we would have missed out on one of the most important insights for Black Spark's videos: his declaration that in fact his work is "not porn" (Crook 2011). Of course, we could reject this claim with the judicial definition of pornography – "I know it when I see it" – but I think there is a more essential aim embedded in this statement. Sure, while the oral and bareback sex featured in the videos testify to the normalized aesthetics of pornography, the insistence that these videos do not belong to the wider genre of pornography – along with the masked performers – contributes to an aesthetic of opacity that is in a dynamic interplay with a confessional assemblage. Black Spark strips away the markers of identity to tap into a more personalized and affective notion of confession that is not reliant on the politicized articulation of words within the text. For him, music, places, lighting, and bodies provide just enough indexicality to hint at relatable assemblage of gay male iconography, while also aspiring to create something beyond those parameters.

Queer Opacity as Confessional Aesthetic

While Black Spark's verbal confessions reliably situate his videos as a therapeutic strategy, his directorial strategy conversely utilizes the aesthetics of opacity as a confessional strategy compellingly challenging conventional notions of gay identity formation. By robbing the audience of the opportunity to know his identity via his face, he upends the foundational Balázsian notion that the "psychological interiority" of a person is to be found primarily within the physicality of facial movements (Balázs 1952). By doing so, Black Spark encourages us to heed Eugenie Brinkema's idea that the totality of mise-en-scène includes "reading for what is put into the scene," but additionally reading "for all of its permutations: what is *not* put into the scene; what is put into the *non-scene*; and what is *not enough* to put into the scene" (2014, 46). This type of reading allows us to tap into both the queer and affective identity traits that are evident in the video but *does* necessitate our venturing into paratexts to contextualize Black Spark's aesthetic of opacity.

Emerging from a media environment fostering a reactive and juvenile understanding of gay identity exemplified by YouTube's "It Gets Better Campaign" and Lady Gaga's rhetoric that gay people are "Born this Way," Black Spark's debut on the gay scene reintroduced a sense of mystery about what it means to be gay by

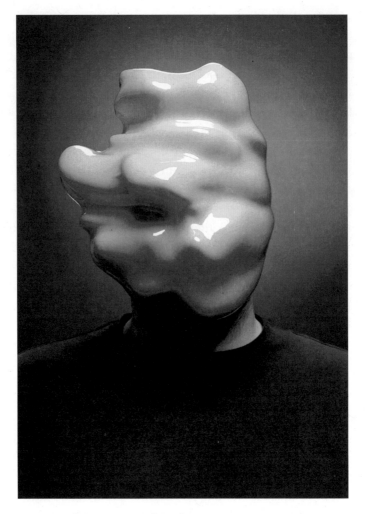

13.7 Zach Blas brings queer opacity to life. *Facial Weaponization Suite: Fag Face Mask (20 October, 2012, Los Angeles, CA.* Photograph, Christopher O'Leary.

emphasizing a queer aesthetic of opacity. Black Spark's aesthetic defiance of these mainstream concepts of gay identity might be understood as a visual representation of the anger felt by Foucault when he spoke of the struggle against subjection, or what "categorizes the individual, marks him by his own individuality, attaches him to his own identity, imposes *a law of truth* on him that he must recognize and others have to recognize in him" (1983, 212, emphasis mine). These "laws of truth," or the stability required by social pressures to maintain a coherent identity formation, are antithetical to the mode of queerness. And while "It Gets Better" and "Born This Way" rely precisely on this type of fixed, declarative, and stagnant notion of what it means to be gay – just look at how the public act of coming out is framed as announcing the "truth" of one's sexuality – Black Spark emphatically works to obscure, hide, and keep secret his identity to cultivate an aesthetic of queer opacity. De Villiers situates the concept of queer opacity as a reappropriated notion of a "style of living" standing in stark contrast to rhetoric like "Born This Way," which relies on the idea of an overdetermined way of living. This idea of queer opacity is crucial considering that we have entered a social-media age of overexposure, which means that simply making the gay experience visible is no longer a queer act.

As a reaction against the indexical "truth" of the face, artist Zach Blas literalizes this idea of queer opacity in his art project *Facial Weaponization Suite* (2011–14). In it Blas has created a series of masks meant to counteract facial recognition technologies installed as part of security cameras, retina scans, Facebook, Google facial identification, and, of course, the largest deposit of facial images in the world – at the US State Department. As you can tell from the title of this mask (fig. 13.7) – the "Fag Face Mask" – there is a particular queer aspect to this project. Blas's interest in this project stemmed from a 2008 Tufts University study in which ninety subjects were shown pictures of ninety faces against a white background – hiding distracting identification traits like hair, tattoos, and glasses. It turned out that the subjects were highly successful in identifying which faces were classifiable as "gay," even when shown a face for only 50 milliseconds (Bering 2009)! Blas's project situates queer opacity as a way of counteracting corporate and nationalist rhetoric about willingly subjecting one's face to recording for commercial and security purposes for the sake of "convenience" and "safety." Blas articulates that his project "weaponize[s] the face through masks," and in doing so adopts an "anti-politics, anti-state, anti-recognition … politics of escape" (Blas 2013). He notes that there is a "burgeoning political investment in opacity, imperceptibility, and escape" and that he is "exploring a queerness that invests and takes seriously such refusals of recognition and visibility; here, queerness is an illegibility or opacity, a refusal that remakes visibility and regimes of recognition outside of standardization through speculative and utopian experimentation and fantasy" (Eler 2013).

It is interesting that Blas utilizes the word "fantasy" within this highly politicized context. Pornography is also founded on the idea of fantasy. And while the contrast between the highly politicized nature of Blas's work stands in stark contrast to the apolitical and at times problematic politics of Black Spark and Keller, each is an example of how fantasy can help us traverse sexual and political "lines of flight" beyond what we can imagine in our physical world. These artists' examples illustrate how tapping into these potentialities depends on deconstructing the pre-eminence of the face. By exposing how the face is connected to the verbal and emotional regime of discourse, these artists reposition the body at the forefront of sexual fantasy and help us understand the primacy of the confessional body as a vehicle for navigating a wider range of affective potentialities.

NOTES

1 Who could forget Jeff Stryker singing over the title sequence of his pornographic debut in *Bigger than Life* (1986)?
2 Like YouTube viral sensation Chris Crocker performing in a video with the pornographic duo known as the Maverick Men (*Chris Crocker Fuck It!!!* 2012).
3 See Chris Steele's parody about Levi Johnston – the man who impregnated former vice-presidential candidate Sarah Palin's daughter – titled *Getting Levi's Johnson* (2010).
4 "Body" in this chapter is not understood within our conventional notions of a physical body, but instead as an affective *body* as conceived by Deleuze and Guattari. They describe this "body" as "not defined by the form that determines it nor as a determinate substance or subject nor by the organs it possesses or the function it fulfills. On the plane of consistency, *a body is defined only by a longitude and a latitude:* in other words the sum total of the material elements belonging to it under given relations of movement and rest, speed and slowness (longitude); the sum total of the intensive affects it is capable of at a given power or degree of potential (latitude). Nothing but affects and local movements, differential speeds" (1987, 260, original emphasis).
5 Throughout the history of existing stag films (1915–68) there is no consistency regarding the ways in which masks were utilized. Considering the straight male audience most of the films tried to cultivate, it is unsurprising that most of the masked performers in these stags are men. Joseph W. Slade argues that this analog strategy for hiding the face could be a byproduct of an overall effect to emphasize the erotic nature of the medium's genuineness by accentuating "ineptitude" over technological mastery (2006, 37). For Thomas Waugh, masks signal markers of delineation. In photos meant for gay male audiences the split in mask wearing is "less common" among the "amazingly brazen" amateurs who pose for nude pictures intended for private circulation as opposed to photos meant for the commercial market (1996, 342). And in stag films for straight audiences, masks emphasize the divide between amateur men looking to hide their identity contrasted against the professional female sex workers they were oftentimes performing with (2004, 136). And while Linda Williams does not address the use of masks within stags directly, she cites an important point by Beverley Brown who writes that pornography is the "erotic organization of visibility" (1999, 49). Williams goes on to explain that "hard core is the one film genre that

always tries to strip this mask ['masquerade of femininity'] away and see the visible 'truth' of sexual pleasure itself" (1999, 49–50). This is the structuring logic of William's book *Hard Core*, that pornography's strategy for erotic enticement revolves around an "involuntary confession of bodily pleasure" on behalf of the female (1999, 50). This need for visible evidence of female pleasure is fetishized within pornographic texts specifically because of its hidden nature; in contrast to the externalized ejaculating male penis. So, if what is hidden embodies an erotic charge within pornography, then the use of masks by male performers beyond their functional use should be understood as an attempt to tap into this well of eroticism. After all, a mask draws attention to the mystery of the face rather than to the obviousness of what is exposed. Of course, the political implications behind a masked straight face versus a masked gay face are radically different. However, despite the differences, the erotic allure of what is hidden behind the mask remains the same.

6 The exception to this rule is the gay pornography studio CockyBoys, whose owner and primary director Jake Jaxson frequently evokes an aesthetic closely resembling the tropes of contemporary art cinema, especially that of Terrence Malick. Jaxson went so far as to include Bedrich Smetana's "Vltava (The Moldau)" as part of his production *A Thing of Beauty* (2013) – a composition that was also featured in Malick's *Tree of Life* (2011).

7 Our popular and contemporary understanding of "identity politics" perverts the term's original purpose. It is either interpreted as meaning that racial or sexual minorities are selfishly fighting only for their own interests and abandoning the wider project of intersectional liberation (Lilla 2016). Or, as the mainstream gay-rights movement would have us believe, the term is about having all identities be a fully incorporated part of the political mechanisms of state power. However, while this chapter focuses on the political limitations of identity, it is essential to remember that the original definition of identity politics is a productively radical way of thinking that does in fact deal with the "implications of race and class as well as sex." This notion of identity politics as defined by the Combahee River Collective also makes it clear that governmental politics is anti-liberatory, writing that the "liberation of all oppressed peoples necessitates the destruction of the political-economic systems of capitalism and imperialism as well as patriarchy" (Combahee River Collective 1977).

8 "The head is included in the body, but the face is not. The face is a surface: facial traits, lines, wrinkles, long face, square face, triangular face; the face is a map, even when it is applied to and wraps a volume, even when it surrounds and borders cavities that are now no more than holes. The head, even the human head, is not necessarily a face. The face is produced only when the head ceases to be a part of the body, when it ceases to be coded by the body, when it ceases to have a multidimensional polyvocal corporeal code – when the body, head included, has been decoded and has to be *overcoded* by something we shall call the Face" (Deleuze and Guattari [1980] 1987, 170, original emphasis).

9 "But the operation does not end there: if the head and its elements are facialized, the entire body also can be facialized, comes to be facialized as part of an inevitable process" (Deleuze and Guattari [1980] 1987, 170).

REFERENCES

Balázs, Béla. 1952. *Theory of the Film: Character and Growth of a New Art*. Translated by Edith Bone. London: Dennis Dobson.

Barras, Jonetta Rose. 2015. "Broken Families Lead to Broken Communities." *Washington Post*, 8 April. https://www.washingtonpost.com/opinions/broken-families-lead-to-broken -communities/2015/04/08/041768c8-dca0-11e4-a500-1c5bb1d8ff6a_story.html.

Bering, Jesse. 2009. "There's Something Queer about That Face." *ScientificAmerican*, 23 February. blogs.scientificamerican.com/bering-in-mind/something-queer-about-that-face/.

Brinkema, Eugenie. 2014. *The Forms of the Affect*. Durham: Duke University Press.

Bruns, Gerald L. 2007. "Becoming Animal (Some Simple Ways)." *New Literary History* 38, no. 4: 703–20.

Casarino, Cesare. 2002. *Modernity at Sea: Melville, Marx, Conrad in Crisis*. Minneapolis: University of Minnesota Press.

Colebrook, Claire. 2010. *The Deleuze Dictionary: Revised Edition*. Edited by Adrian Parr. Edinburgh: Edinburgh University Press.

Combahee River Collective. 1977. "The Combahee River Collective Statement." *Circuitous*. circuitous.org/scraps/combahee.html.

Crook, Phillip B. 2011. "Need to Know: Black Spark." *Out*, 18 January. out.com/entertainment/ movies/2011/01/18/need-know-black-spark.

Deleuze, Gilles. [1969] 1990. *The Logic of Sense*. Translated by Mark Lester. New York: Columbia University Press.

— [1993] 1997. *Essays Critical and Clinical*. Translated by Daniel W. Smith and Michael A. Greco. Minneapolis: University of Minnesota Press.

— [1988] 2006. *The Fold: Leibniz and the Baroque*. Translated by Tom Conley. London: Continuum.

Deleuze, Gilles, and Félix Guattari. [1975] 1986. *Kafka: Toward a Minor Literature*. Translated by Dana Polan. Minneapolis: University of Minnesota Press.

— [1980] 1987. *A Thousand Plateaus: Capitalism and Schizophrenia*. Translated by Brian Massumi. Minneapolis: University of Minnesota Press.

De Villiers, Nicholas. 2012. *Opacity and the Closet: Queer Tactics in Foucault, Barthes, and Warhol*. Minneapolis: University of Minnesota Press.

Dreyfus, Hubert, and Paul Rabinow. 1983. *Michel Foucault: Beyond Structuralism and Hermeneutics*. Chicago: University of Chicago Press.

Eler, Alicia. 2013. "The Facelessness of Tomorrow Begins Today." *Hyperallergic*, 24 June. https://hyperallergic.com/73888/the-facelessness-of-tomorrow-begins-today/.

Escoffier, Jeffrey. 2017. "Sex in the Seventies: Gay Porn Cinema as an Archive for the History of American Sexuality." *Journal of the History of Sexuality* 26, no. 1: 88–113.

Foucault, Michel. [1976] 1990. *The History of Sexuality Vol. 1: An Introduction*. Translated by Robert Hurley. New York: Vintage Books.

– 1977. *Language, Counter-Memory, Practice: Selected Essays and Interviews*. Edited by Donald F. Bouchard and translated by Donald F. Bouchard and Sherry Simon. Cornell: Cornell University Press.

– 1983. "The Subject and Power." In Dreyfus and Rabinow, *Michel Foucault: Beyond Structuralism amd Hermeneutics*, 208–28.

– 1986. "The Discourse on Language." *Critical Theory since 1965*. Edited by Hazard Adams and Leroy Searle. Tallahassee: University Presses of Florida.

– 1988. *Technologies of the Self: A Seminar with Michel Foucault*. Edited by Luther H. Martin, Huck Gutman, and Patrick H. Hutton. Amherst: University of Massachusetts Press.

Harlan. 2015. "First Adam Ramzi, Now Gavin Waters: Hillary Has the Gay Porn Star Vote." *GayPornBlog*, 10 October. gaypornblog.com/gay-porn-stars-for-hillary.html.

Hemmings, Clare. 2005. "Invoking Affect: Cultural Theory and the Ontological Turn." *Cultural Studies* 19, no. 5: 548–67.

Keller, Colby. 2014. "Big Shoe Adventure 1: Colby Does America … and Canada Too." IndieGoGo. indiegogo.com/projects/big-shoe-adventure-1-colby-does-america-and-canada-too#/.

Lilla, Mark. 2016. "The End of Identity Liberalism." *New York Times*, 18 November. nytimes.com/2016/11/20/opinion/sunday/the-end-of-identity-liberalism.html.

Massumi, Brian. 1995. "The Autonomy of Affect." *Cultural Critique* 31, no. 2: 83–109.

McCarthy, Tom. 2016. "Albright: 'Special Place in Hell' for Women Who Don't Support Clinton." *Guardian* (UK), 6 February. theguardian.com/us-news/2016/feb/06/madeleine-albright-campaigns-for-hillary-clinton.

Moran, Robert, Jason Nark, and Erin Serpico. 2016. "In Philly Area, Disjointed but Peaceful Marches against Violence." *Philly*, 9 July. http://www.philly.com/philly/news/20160709_In_Philly_area__disjointed_but_peaceful_marches_against_violence.html.

Philip, Drew. 2017. "In 1967, They Watched Their City Erupt. Fifty Years On, How Has Detroit Changed?," *Guardian* (UK), 6 August. https://www.theguardian.com/us-news/2017/aug/06/detroit-riots-1967-protests.

Pitterson, Leslie. 2011. "Black UPenn Student Blasts Ivy League Racism, Says School Is Hostile for Students of Color." *ClutchMagOnline*, April. http://clutchmagonline.com/2011/04/black-upenn-student-blasts-ivy-league-racism-says-school-is-hostile-for-students-of-color/ https://goo.gl/LVs5UV.

Plummer, Ken. 1995. *Telling Sexual Stories: Power, Change and Social Worlds.* London: Routledge.

Salerno, Rob. 2011. "Twenty Questions for Grindr Creator Joel Simkhai." *DailyXtra*, 27 July. dailyxtra.com/twenty-questions-for-grindr-creator-joel-simkhai-33729

Silver, Jocelyn. 2016. "American History xxx." *OfficeMagazine.* officemagazine.net/interview/american-history-xxx.

Sire, Zachary. 2011. "Who is the Black Spark." *Sword*, 13 January. https://www.thesword.com/black-spark.html.

— 2016. "Gay Porn Stars Who Support Donald Trump." *Str8UpGayPorn*, 3 March. http://str8upgayporn.com/gay-porn-stars-who-support-donald-trump-ranked/.

Slade, Joseph W. 2006. "Eroticism and Technological Regression: The Stag Film." *History and Technology* 22, no. 1: 27–52.

Strub, Whitney. 2016. "From Porno Chic to Porno Bleak: Representing the Urban Crisis in 1970s American Pornography." In *Porno Chic and the Sex Wars: American Sexual Representation in the 1970s*, edited by Carolyn Bronstein and Whitney Strub, 27–52. Amherst: University of Massachusetts Press.

Sunderland, Mitchell. 2016. "Make America Hairless Again: Sensual Photos of Twinks for Trump." *Vice*, 21 July. https://broadly.vice.com/en_us/article/ypaab7/make-america-hairless-again-sensual-photos-of-twinks-for-trump.

TMZ. 2015. "I Got the Porn Vote in the Big D." *TMZ*, 10 October. tmz.com/2015/10/10/hillary-clinton-porn-star-photo/.

Ulysse St-Pierre. 2015. "Colby Does Virginia." *ColbyDoesAmerica.* colbydoesamerica.com/VA.html.

Waugh, Thomas. 1996. *Hard to Imagine: Gay Male Eroticism in Photography and Film from Their Beginnings to Stonewall.* New York: Columbia University Press.

— [2001] 2004. "Homosociality in the Classical American Stag Film: Off-Screen, On-Screen." In *Porn Studies*, edited by Linda Williams, 127–41. Durham: Duke University Press.

Wilde, Oscar. [1891] 1982. "The Critic as Artist." *The Artist as Critic: Critical Writings of Oscar Wilde.* Edited by Richard Ellmann. Chicago: University of Chicago Press.

Williams, Linda. [1989] 1999. *Hard Core: Power, Pleasure, and the "Frenzy of the Visible."* Berkley: University of California Press.

Wittgenstein, Ludwig. [1953] 1958. *Philosophical Investigations.* Translated by G.E.M. Anscombe. Oxford: Basil Blackwell.

MEDIAGRAPHY

"Antonio Cervone Solo." 2016. *ChaosMen*, June. chaosmen.com/ showgal. php?g=content/CM/video/2016/1787antonio_cervone_solo/8288/7_1&s=31.

Black Spark, dir. 2015. *Dance in My Heart Now.* Theninthspark. *PornHub*, pornhub.com/view_video.php?viewkey=136932721.

"Black Spark Art #4." 2013a. XHamster, xhamster.com/videos/black-spark-art-4-1809979 #mlrelated.

"Black Spark Art #12." 2013b. XHamster, xhamster.com/videos/black-spark-art-12-1837560 #mlrelated.

Blas, Zach. 2013. "Facial Weaponization Communiqué: Fag Face." Vimeo. https://vimeo.com/57882032.

Cervone, Antonio. 2016. "Antonio Cervone Solo." *ChaosMen*, 13 June. https://www.chaosmen.com/showgal.php?g=content/CM/video/2016/1787-antonio_cervone_solo/8288/7_1&s=31.

"Chris Crocker Fuck It!!!" 2012. *Maverick Men*. Video. maverickmen.com/mmwp/?p=4530.

Groove Armada. 2012. "Cards to Your Heart." *Black Light*. Album.

Iver, Bon. "Woods." 2009. *Blood Bank*. Album.

Jaxson, Jake, dir. 2013. *A Thing of Beauty*. CockyBoys. Video.

Keller, Colby, dir. 2015a. "Colby Does Kentucky." *Colby Does America*. Video.

– dir. 2015b. "Colby Does Virginia." *Colby Does America*. Video.

– dir. 2017. "A Man I Love Named Colby Keller." *TheLoveBomb*. 3 January. Podcast. thelovebomb.us/episodes/e17-a-man-i-love-named-colby-keller/.

Kubrick, Stanley. 1999. *Eyes Wide Shut*. Warner Brothers. Film.

Malick, Terrence, dir. *Tree of Life*. 2011. Fox Searchlight Pictures. Film.

Steele, Chris, dir. 2012. *Getting Levi's Johnson*. Jet Set Men. Video.

Sterling, Matt dir. 1986. *Bigger than Life*. Huge Video. Video.

Sunday Faith. 2012. PornHub. Vidoe. pornhub.com/view_video.php?viewkey=1465955307.

Undercover. 2010. "'After Dark' Official Music Video." YouTube, 14 October. Video. youtube.com/watch?v=lHU3e5Csk7w.

14

Sadean Confessions in Virginie Despentes's Punk-Porn-Feminism

VALENTINA DENZEL

Virginie Despentes is, according to Natalie Edwards, one of "the most transgressive writers in France today." She provocatively incorporates in her work "fictional and autobiographical accounts of pornography, sex work, desire, sexual violence, rape, lesbianism and drug culture" (2012, 12). Writing from the standpoint of a former sex worker and a rape survivor, Despentes describes "female sexuality in all of its myriad variations" (2012, 11), thereby inscribing herself in a larger literary trend of twenty-first-century transgressive francophone literature.

This chapter seeks to elucidate the "shamelessly confessional tone" (Edwards 2012, 13) with which Despentes depicts female sexuality (incest and sex work) and sexual violence (rape and sado-masochism) in her books *Baise-moi* (1993), *Les Chiennes savantes* (1996), and *King Kong Théorie* (2006) by stressing the link between her work and the "enfant terrible" of the Enlightenment, the Marquis de Sade. Like Despentes, Sade portrays sexual violence and transgressions, incorporating in his works pro-sex manifestos where his libertines confess and proclaim their transgressive pleasures. This concept of erotic confession in Sade is enlarged in Despentes by a social dimension that uses the vulnerability and subaltern status of her protagonists, mostly working-class women, to turn gender and social hierarchies upside down.

The chapter analyzes first the common points between Despentes and Sade, then examines the role that confession plays in the works of each author, and finally explores how Despentes adapts Sadean philosophy, thereby creating a new feminist approach through which the subaltern can counter the hegemonic discourse.

14.1 *Baise Moi*. This image was used on several DVD covers for film adaptation in anglophone countries. Dir. Virginie Despentes and Coralie Trinh Thi, 2000 (Video Detective, 2001).

Virginie Despentes and the Marquis de Sade

The analogies in Despentes's and Sade's works are based on the fact that both authors question authoritative norms, even though they do it in different ways. Sade is promoting eighteenth-century materialist philosophy where "nature is the paradigm for everything: this means that everything, from science to art, is, should be an equivalent if debased copy of nature" (Warman 2002, 41). Consequently, Sade's philosophy is based on the supremacy of nature that is constantly recycling and reshaping matter into new forms. According to this philosophy, there are no crimes nor virtues: both are merely man-made superstitions (Sade [1795] 1965, 238). As Caroline Warman explains, Sadean libertines "should do nothing else, they must obey their natures, so much so, that to counter natural desire is to be immoral … The libertine follows his or her feelings which instruct them to inflict cruelty; this causes pleasure which is nature's message that what they are doing is good" (2002, 71; 79). This approach allows for all sorts of transgressions, sexual and criminal.

Despentes's punk-porn feminism is influenced by American gender and queer studies, as well as by a materialist approach criticizing capitalism (Edwards 2012, 13), and lastly by the radical punk movements, which saw in Sade the icon of transgression. According to James A. Steintrager (2005, 362), "Sade's status in the 1960s was underwritten by the fact that the man and his writings seemed to confirm already existing and increasingly disseminated theories that posed sexual liberation as the key to liberation tout court." Sade became a "pop icon" (2005, 365), appealing to, amongst others, the punk and post-punk movements from the early 1980s up until now.[1]

In her work, Despentes references punk culture in order to underline gender performativity and transgressions of norms (Schaal 2012, 49–51), which are also to be found in Sade's work (Edmiston 2013, 70–2).[2] While Despentes does not proclaim the sovereignty of nature as does Sade in his materialist philosophy, she questions, as Sade does, the normative representations of human behavior. Like Sadean heroines Juliette or Madame de Saint-Ange, Despentes's two heroines in *Baise-moi* (fig. 14.1), Nadine and Manu, link sexual pleasure to violence, wondering if they prefer "fucking or carnage," and coming to the conclusion that carnage is "as good as fucking" (2002, 125, 126). Manu's and Nadine's sexual liberation functions as a liberation of social norms *tout court*.

Nicole Fayard has already pointed out the link between female eroticism in Despentes and sexual representations in Sade. Despentes's "novels are filled with a voluminous body of obscene experiences which seem to look back to Sade. There are floggings and torture, lesbian scenes and orgies, incest, infantilism [sic], and murder, all described in crude and graphic terms" (2005, 103). The close link between sexuality and death in both authors underlines the transgressive aspect of the obscene and advocates for rebellion against social and moral norms "that pollute the individual [and] deserve to be broken under the lash of the whip for emancipation to come true" (104).

Despentes's and Sade's views on marriage, prostitution, and rape represent the keystones in their opposition to sexual norms. In her feminist manifesto *King Kong Théorie*, Despentes links the concept of female dignity, according to which women do not transgress normative discourses on sexuality and gender identity, to the bourgeoisie and the marriage contract. This contract entails precise gender roles: men work, while women take care of the domestic space (2006, 61–2). The idea of women selling sex, confusing thereby the "clear" distinction between gendered spaces and the links between sex, procreation, and marriage promoted by the bourgeoisie, is inconceivable (2006, 86–7).

Yet the heterosexual marriage contract is based on the same monetary service exchange as the contract between clients and prostitutes. Echoing a similar argument by Angela Carter (1978, 9), Despentes goes so far as to say that if the working conditions for prostitutes were not constrained by legal pressure, prostitution would be for women far more lucrative than marriage, in which women engage in sexual activities for free but depend financially on their husbands (2006, 63, 80). The myth of female dignity also silences and victimizes sex workers, who are a global phenomenon in today's societies (75). Despentes counters this silencing through her autobiographical confession as former prostitute who felt empowered by making fast money and considered her profession an act of "paid charity" towards her lonely clients (70–1).

Though Despentes depicts in her works the downsides of the sex business,[3] it would be wrong to see the female protagonists in her novel *Baise-moi* (1993) as victims. Contrary to Sophie Bélot's analysis, porn actress Manu is not merely "the epitome of women's sexual exploitation" (2004, 9). Instead, she seems to enjoy her work, just like Nadine who considers prostitution to be "a good profession for her" (Despentes 2002, 57). As experts in the sex business, Nadine and Manu even engage in an analysis of different pornographic esthetic features (2002, 88), which redirects the discussion of porn away from victimization and towards artistic conceptions.

The apology of prostitution and sexual relationships freed from marriage contracts and childbearing, as well as the exploration of new sexual activities, is also a common topic in Sade. Even though Sade did not shy away from mistreating prostitutes and women of inferior social status in his real life,[4] he praised prostitutes in his fictional works.

In Sade's *Philosophy in the Bedroom* (1795) (fig. 14.2), for example, Madame de Saint-Ange confesses that she worked as "a perfect whore … during an entire week." She "satisfied the whims of a goodly number of lechers" and "beheld the most unusual tastes displayed" ([1795] 1965, 234). Marriage to her is nothing more than the "handiwork of men" (223), and women should not give into it, since they only desire to have themselves "fucked from morning to night" (222). She also gives advice on contraception (230) and advocates infanticide (249). These confessional statements that she makes in her private rooms to the young Eugénie, an apprentice of libertinism, as well as to her brother and the materialist philosopher Dolmancé, denigrate "the fictitious honor of women [that] is bound up with their anterior integrity" (251). The political manifesto "Yet Another Effort, Frenchmen, If You Would Become Republicans," included in *Philosophy in the Bedroom*,

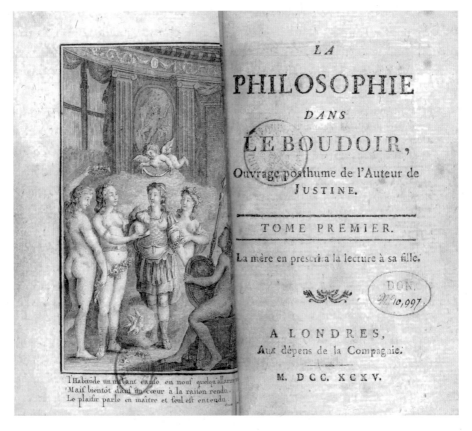

14.2 Sade's *Philosophie dans le boudoir* (*Philosophy in the Bedroom*), first edition, 1795, title page.

even suggests the creation of public houses for women, furnished with "all the individuals of either sex women could desire, and the more constantly they frequent these places the higher they will be esteemed" (322).

As for rape, both Despentes and Sade describe it as ubiquitous. According to Despentes, rape is the foundation of heteronormative societies, in which women are supposed to be weak and men to be aggressors. Yet even though rape is common, the myth of female dignity is so pervasive that rape survivors avoid identifying as "damaged goods" who lose their attractiveness on the *marché sexuel* (sex market) (Despentes 2006, 52). Hence, rape becomes a taboo, which reinforces the ideology of female dignity (38–43) and female culpability, since rape survivors are considered responsible for their fate: they transgressed, for example, the unwritten rules that women should avoid public spaces (48).

Therefore for Despentes the key for emancipation lies in the unmasking of the myth of female dignity without downplaying the traumatizing effects of rape. Despentes defines rape as common experience that women risk facing, but that they can overcome (2006, 44–6), as she did herself. Despentes was raped at the age of seventeen, yet she continued to live her life as she did before the rape, travelling alone to concerts, sleeping outside until the next train that would take her home, risking a hundred times being raped again (47).[5] *Baise-moi* also underlines the ubiquity of sexual violence in the description of the brutal gang rape of Manu and her friend Karla. The two women manifest opposite reactions to their rape. Karla accuses Manu of passivity, because she did not try to defend herself. Ironically, Karla is killed in the end when she defies her aggressors. Manu, on the other side, represents Despentes's standpoint in *King Kong Théorie*. She states that she "can't keep assholes from getting into [her] pussy," so she hasn't "left anything valuable there." Rape is just something that happens "when you're a girl" (2002, 52). Despentes thus erases the dichotomy of victimization and culpability that keeps rape survivors in a state of vulnerability (Sauzon 2014, 152).

As in *King Kong Théorie*, rape is described in Sade's *Philosophy in the Bedroom* as a common experience for women. "It cannot be denied that we have the right to decree laws that compel woman to yield to the flames of him who would have her; violence itself being one of that right's effects, we can employ it lawfully" ([1795] 1965, 319). Yet, women, due to their "violent penchants for carnal pleasure," are equally allowed "the enjoyment of all sexes and, as in the case of men, the enjoyment of all parts of the body" (321). This radical view of rape and female pleasure aligns with Despentes's, inasmuch as women avoid categorization into the binary system of victimization and culpability.

Sade's concept is obviously linked to the patriarchal family construction of the Ancient Regime. He opposes the principles of absolutist monarchy where the king figures as the "good father," as well as the "fantasy of family romance of fraternity," which is typical of the French Revolution (Hunt 1992, 52; 128). Sade parodies the concern of republicans regarding female modesty by declaring that all women should be prostitutes (Hunt 1992, 139). According to Donna Landry, "Sade challenges the familial and domestic ideology of the French Revolution" by "quantifying orgasms, advocating sodomy and other forms of non-reproductive sexual practice" (1989, 64).

Even though the historical and political circumstances of Sade's and Despentes's works differ, they share overlapping views regarding marriage, prostitution, and rape.

"Let's Talk About Sex": Confessing Unconventional Desires

Sade's and Despentes's representations of transgressive desires are expressed most efficiently in the confessional mode, thereby subverting confession as a control of human behaviour in order to create a counter-discourse that opens up new possibilities. The subversive power of the confessional mode in Sade and Despentes is highlighted by the fact that the church long monopolized the discourse on sexuality, promoting as well the idea of female dignity, which Sade and Despentes both oppose. From the Early Middle Ages through the eighteenth century, the church dominated the culture of the time through theological knowledge, doctrines that defined taboos and sins, and a vast literature on moral philosophy that used a specific narrative: confession (Kozul 2011, 4). Confession is therefore not only a way of admitting desire but also of knowing and defining it, by creating and exposing different sorts of pleasures that are categorized into legitimate sexual encounters or into sins.[6]

Due to its monopoly on the discourse on sexuality, the church influenced the medical and literary discourse of the eighteenth century that imitated but at times also contested and subverted the official ecclesiastic mode of narration. *Thérèse the Philosopher* (1748), generally attributed to Jean-Baptiste de Boyer, the Marquis d'Argens, and based on a true story, describes the pleasures of young penitents as well as their sexual abuse by their confessors. Sade, an admirer of the book and a fervent critic of the church (Seifert 1983, 24), parodied in his pamphlet "Dialog between a Priest and a Dying Man" ([1782] 1926) the confessional discourse promoted by the church. In this pamphlet, a priest tries to convince a libertine of God's existence and pushes him to confess his sins before he dies. But the libertine counter-argues, using logic and reason, promoting a materialist atheism based on the idea that nature is a "reprocessing machine" of matter (Warman 2002, 82). Creative powers are therefore removed from the divine and invested in nature. The only confession the dying man is ready to make is that he has not sinned enough, and after having persuaded the priest of his materialist philosophy, both men engage in an orgy with six beautiful women to forget "the vain sophistries of superstition" (Sade 1965, 175).

While Sade imitates in his confessional mode the church's imperative on exhaustivity regarding detailed descriptions of various sins, so much so that Foucault thinks of Sade as a follower of "treatises of spiritual direction" (Foucault [1976] 1990, 21), it would be wrong to overlook the subversive character in Sade's works. In Sade, analysis and categorizations of sexual acts are not "inserted into systems of utility, regulated for the greater good of all" (24), but serve their own purpose, namely the pleasure of violence and demonstrative reason that lead to pure negation and destruction (Deleuze 1971, 26).[7] Sade thereby creates a new model for the confessional mode that opposes itself to the hierarchical Catholic confession, in which the interlocutor represents the authority that "intervenes in order to judge, punish, forgive, console, and reconcile" (Foucault [1976] 1990, 61–2). As previously shown, Madame de Saint-Ange's confessions of unorthodox pleasures in her conversation with Eugénie are another example of Sade's subversion of the confessional mode.

During the eighteenth and nineteenth centuries, the discursive power of modern sciences controlled the notion of self through the creation of new categories of "perverts," such as the hysterical women, the masturbatory child, and the homosexual. According to Foucault ([1976] 1990, 45), the discursive creation of "perversions" links pleasure to power: the pleasure of monitoring sexuality, as well as the pleasure of evading and fooling this normative power. Sade's "Dialog" is an example of this link between regulating and transgressive pleasures. By inverting the discursive mode of confession – the sinner converts the priest to acts of debauchery – Sade uses the confessional mode to gain pleasure through transgression and to reset the hierarchical relation between the speakers.

As Sade does in "Dialog," Despentes in *King Kong Théorie* uses confessional statements to defy traditional views on marriage, prostitution, and rape to undermine the normative representation of gender roles based on the ideal of female dignity. According to Edwards, this confessional aspect has a double function: it "emphasizes the proximity of its arguments to lived experience," making it therefore even more convincing, yet it "also makes it so intimate that it is at times disturbing" (2012, 17), which underlines the subversive power of her discourse. As in "Dialog," Despentes uses confession to promote "unorthodox" sexual pleasures.

Despentes's novel *Baise-moi* also uses the confessional mode to describe unconventional pleasures, such as the incestuous relationship between a young Muslim woman, Fatima, and her father. In a conversation with the protagonists of the novel, Nadine and Manu, Fatima relives her first sexual encounters with her father when she was eleven years old: "Me and my father were together all the time, it just happened all by itself, really easy. I think I was the one who came on to him. I know that I'd wanted it a lot, thought about it for a long time" (2002, 177). What is transgressive in this passage is that Fatima describes her incestuous relationship as "the consequence of a genuine desire." Her female sexual agency subverts male heterosexual prerogatives (Fayard 2005, 112). Despentes seems to echo here Sade's defence for incest in *Philosophy in the Bedroom* (1795). According to Sade, incest ties family members together and is a natural desire that is also to be found at the origins of every society.

As Edwards described the reader's reaction to *King Kong Théorie*'s intimate, confidential atmosphere, Fatima's confession makes Manu feel uncomfortable. She "lets out a loud exhale" and adds, "When little girls fall in love with their dad, it flips me out" (2002, 178). Manu's reaction, however, is not a critique of Fatima's relationship with her father but reflects her own relationship with her father, whom she describes as a "son of a bitch" (178) who neglected her. In the end, one could interpret Manu's reaction to Fatima's confession as envy for a missed opportunity to connect (sexually) with her father.

Besides incest, sado-masochism is another sexual pleasure that the female characters in *Baise-moi* describe in a confessional mode. The prostitute Nadine confesses to porn-actress Manu the thrill of being bound, beaten, whipped, and humiliated by a client during a sado-masochistic encounter that left enormous welts on her back. As with her reaction to Fatima's confession, Manu's comments and questions serve to elicit more elucidations on sexual practices that Manu (and possibly the reader) do not understand. When Manu sees Nadine's injured back, she invites her to share her experience. "It's obvious you have no intention of talking about it, but I'd really like you to talk about it. I don't get it, you got to enlighten me" (2002, 97). Nadine "enlightens" Manu and the reader as to her sado-masochistic pleasures. "One day – by 'chance' – you run into a client who wants you tied up … With time you get into it. When I was a kid, I'd imagine myself tied tight to the table of a bar, my ass wide open, a lot of men whose faces I couldn't see were doing sick things to me. Real degrading stuff. That felt good" (97). Even though Manu does not share Nadine's sado-masochistic pleasures, she does not condemn them – "we all got childhood fantasies, I respect that" (97). In so doing, Despentes creates a panoply of female sexual desires that coexist without judgment and where the "agency of domination" resides in the one who speaks, not in the one who listens, thereby inverting the hierarchy of traditional confession (Foucault [1976] 1990, 62).

All these confessions of unconventional sexual desires are made by women to other women in a safe environment. All the women are subalterns due to their social class, gender, profession, race, or religion. Nadine, a member of the middle class, and Manu, a proletarian, are both sex workers; Fatima lives at the margins of society because of her Arabic origins and her incestuous love for her father. Despite the plurality of female identities that Despentes describes in her texts (Louar 2009, 83–4), these women are aware that they all have something in common: they share "unusual" sexual desires as well as the status of outsider, even though they endure different types of discriminations (Sicard-Cowen 2008, 69).[8]

Despentes contrasts these safe spaces to the condemnatory and disapproving reactions or to forced confessions extorted by representatives of normative authority, such as doctors and police. In the novel *Les Chiennes savantes*, for example, sex-worker Louise describes her sexual excitement while performing a striptease, which horrifies her boss Gino. According to Gino, sex workers should detest their clients and focus solely on their financial gain. To enjoy a profession that, according to Gino, is "humiliating" is an outrageous transgression (1999, 80). In *Baise-moi*, Despentes opposes Fatima's confidence to Nadine and Manu[9] to her forced confession that a doctor extorted from her. He examined her after she became pregnant by her father and "duped" her by telling her that "he was bound by some kind of secret" (2002, 177). As a consequence of this extorted confession, Fatima was forced to abort her child and her father was sent to prison, where he died. As Fatima states, she had no say in the matter; the authorities decided what was best for her. She clearly states her suffering and grief over the loss of her father and her child, as well as her "tireless strength" (176) in facing those who do not understand and approve of her incestuous love.

This opposition between the official representatives of societal norms (law and medicine) on the one side and Nadine and Manu on the other is highlighted by the fact that the two women embody the Sadean ideal of total transgression. As mentioned earlier, this transgression is also celebrated in punk culture. In 2013, for example, the American post-punk group Crocodiles released, an album called *Crimes of Passion* dedicating a song to the Marquis de Sade and S/M with the refrain "For your crimes (I wanna die) of passion (under your fists tonight)." It is no coincidence that Nadine and Manu listen to punk and metal music to celebrate their crimes of murder and theft. After killing a couple and stealing their car, for example, they listen to the song lyrics "no red lights, no speed limit" (134), a possible allusion to the lyrics "no stop sign, no speed limit" of AC/DC's "Highway to Hell" (1979).

The link in *Baise-moi* between (post)-punk, no-wave music and transgressions of societal norms is also highlighted when Nadine and Manu come to rescue Fatima while the police stop and search her. Before the two women meet Fatima for the first time, Nadine complains that she has forgotten her Sonic-Youth cassette in the BMW they stole from a man before killing him by running over him. This complaint emphasizes the importance of music as a way of expressing the strong bond between Nadine and Manu and their transgressive lifestyle. For example, the last song that the two protagonists listened to before they switched cars was

"Cotton Crown" by the American post-punk group Sonic Youth. The lyrics of this song describe a strong emotional relationship between two people, like Manu and Nadine's friendship. The lyric "angels are dreaming of you" that appears in the French text (1999, 162) might also foreshadow their future encounter with Fatima and Nadine's fascination with this young woman.[10]

When Nadine and Manu come upon Fatima being attacked by the police, they start shooting before the police have a chance to shoot back (2002, 162). Nadine and Manu are portrayed as modern female "Robin Hoods" who protect outlaws from oppressive forces. Fatima says that she only opened up to the two women because they were "cop killers" (177). Nadine, Manu, and Fatima oppose the same oppressive discourse that is not only promoted by the authorities but by common people. Manu states, "The worst thing about people today isn't their narrow minds" but that they "don't want anybody to have too good a time or they get confused" (177). This confusion arises if women transgress normative discourses on sexuality and gender identity based on the monolithic notion of "female dignity." In her works, Despentes unmasks this discourse as being oppressive.

Despentes's Sadean Feminism

Several feminists have reproached Sade for his "sexploitation" (Landry 1989, 64) and for advocating a false liberation of women. They criticize the misinterpretation of Sade by second-wave feminists, since "the sexual freedom offered women by the sexual revolution was not in itself but for men" (Gallop 2005, 90, 92). Yet Sade has inspired other feminists who adapted his materialist philosophy to promote new gender relations. Angela Carter, for example, sees in Sade a "moral pornographer ... who uses pornographic material as part of the acceptance of the logic of a world of absolute sexual licence for all the genders, and projects a model of the way such a world might work" (1978, 19). Donna Landry and Michèle Vallenthini underline the "potentially liberating gestures" (Landry 1989, 65) of analyzing power relations in Sadean pleasures and pornography and of investigating the complexity of his heroines who transcend the dichotomy of victimization and demonization. According to Vallenthini, the female character Léonore from *Aline et Valcour* (1795) embodies, for example, a "third Sadean sex/gender," representing the successful incarnation of the hybridity (feminine/masculine, conservatism /revolution) of the post-Revolutionary period. In this regard, Despentes's female heroines are Sadeian women inspired by Sade's utopia of gender equality and fluidity, robbing "the heterosexist system of its claims to gendered coherence and naturalness" (Fayard 2005, 118).

Because Despentes promotes a "proletarian feminist discourse" (Schaal 2012, 39), Sade's upper-class women in *Philosophy in the Bedroom* (Gallop 2005, 93; Carter 1978, 133) become in Despentes's work proletarian and middle-class women. This allows her to "restore the social dimensions of the sexual act, displaying relations of domination within sexuality" (Fayard 2005, 107), as exemplified in the murder scene of a bourgeois architect in *Baise-moi*. This "nonchalant, affected" (Despentes 2002, 212) man, who possesses the complete works of Sade (214) represents the upper-class interpretation of Sadeian philosophy. While Sade's principles are for Nadine and Manu a way of life, the architect confines Sade's thinking to a literary phenomenon and to sado-masochistic encounters that he controls. Hence when Manu and Nadine point their guns at him to make him open up his safe, he mistakes the threat for a sado-masochistic play of seduction, which he believes is under his control. He even asks Nadine to tie him up: "He holds out his wrists, finds the afternoon quite exciting" (219). Until the very last moment, he is convinced the "two furies" will spare him (220). Yet Nadine decides that killing the architect will be more pleasurable to her than sparing his life. While he is begging for his life, she hits him with her gun, kicks him in the face, and shoots him to death.

This reversal of roles is not only linked to gender and social class: it expresses itself also in the appropriation of the discourse of power. Nadine, the middle-class prostitute who is used to getting "fucked by some refined types" (217), now adopts the discursive power of legal authorities. She plays the role of the "good cop" (213) who is eliciting a confession of sexual pleasure and submission from an upper-class architect. He admits to trusting her blindly (218); he does not understand that he is not contracting a pact in a masochistic game in which he could negotiate with his female torturer "a precise point in time and for a determinate period [where] she is given every right over him" (Deleuze 1971, 58). On the contrary, Nadine embodies Sadeian power that aims at omnipotence and total destruction (18). As in Sade's "Dialog between a Priest and a Dying Man," Despentes inverts the hierarchy of the confessional mode between the powerless (Nadine and the dying man) and the powerful (the architect and the priest).

Despentes's work is similar in this sense to that of other pro-sex feminists and sex workers like Morgane Merteuil, a member of the sex-workers syndicate STRASS (Syndicat du travail sexuel), who unmasks the patriarchal foundation of bourgeois mainstream feminism that is based on the myth of female dignity

(Merteuil 2010, 94–104). Merteuil mentions, for example, one of France's most prominent feminist movements, Ni putes ni soumises (Neither Whores nor Submissives). As its name says, Ni putes ni soumises clearly states its take on prostitution and promotes a fixed and fixating representation of normative gender. On its Facebook page, Ni putes ni soumises posted on 6 April 2016 an article by *Le Monde* about the adoption of the law penalizing clients of prostitutes. In the same post, the group applauded these measures against prostitution that would help victims escape from this economic system of oppression.

On her Twitter page, Merteuil reacted to the implementation of the new law. On 27 June 2016, she posted an article by the French newspaper *20 Minutes* that stated that more than ten clients had been arrested by the police since 14 April 2016, when the law took effect. Merteuil commented ironically that it is unclear whether prostitutes are now saved from their misery, alluding also to Ni putes ni soumises's standpoint on the importance of rescuing victims of prostitution.[11] Merteuil avails herself of modern technology that promotes "confession through media and online communities to others" (Fejes and Nicoll 2014, 3) to shape her self-representation and to counter normative representations of sexuality.

The one-sided Facebook statement by Ni putes ni soumises opposes Merteuil's and Despentes's positive portrayal of prostitution and their insistence on feminist movements promoting a multitude of gender identities and sexual practices that should not be silenced by a totalitarian discourse (Merteuil 2010, 14; Despentes 2006, 9–14). Merteuil's and Despentes's takes on feminism are similar to Iris van der Tuin's generational feminism, which promotes a "non-linear, durational logic of differing [and] allows for feminism to exist in constant transformation" (2015, xix). According to van der Tuin (xii), the "logic of One" develops "into a norm and marks all the rest as deviant," which is the case when mass media and mainstream feminism represent rape survivors and prostitutes.

Even though Despentes does not use social media like Facebook or Twitter to comment on current events, her fan groups created a Facebook page[12] and a Twitter feed[13] under her name where they post news, interviews, and events related to her. It is striking that several fans cite her statements on rape[14] or quote her when advocating the legalization of prostitution.[15] Her fictional and theoretical work has had an impact on the discussion of these topics in social media.

The importance of appropriation of discursive power by subalterns is also a main concern of sex worker and prostitute activist Carol Leigh, also known as Scarlot Harlot. In Despentes's documentary *Mutantes* (2009), Harlot underlines the necessity of decriminalizing prostitution and implementing labour regulations. The film shows Harlot during her Interstate Solicitation Tour on Wall Street in 1991 confronting (male) representatives of the bourgeoisie and upper class. According to Harlot, most of them have "cousins, brothers or golf partners who've partaken of the services of prostitutes"; she exhorts them to join her in a gesture of civil disobedience against the laws proscribing prostitution, while insulting the crowd as being "hypocrites." Harlot's gesture is certainly less aggressive than Nadine and Manu's, who not only insult but also torture and kill representatives of the bourgeoisie and upper class. Yet the message is the same – namely, the unmasking of an unequal power relationship between prostitutes on one side, and their clients and the legal system on the other, while the clients also depend on the services provided by prostitutes. This hypocritical situation is equally unveiled by Morgane Merteuil who mentions in one of her tweets that a police agent had contacted her for a free sex service to which he felt entitled because he works for the law enforcement.[16]

Using the confessional mode, Despentes denounces unequal power relations between authorities and upper-class citizens on the one side and subalterns marginalized by their social class, gender, profession, race, and religion on the other. Like other sex workers and activists, Despentes opposes mainstream feminist representations of rape survivors and sex workers, instead promoting a sex-positive feminism and criticizing the myth of female dignity, as well as affirming sexual pleasures like sado-masochism and incest that go against normative representations of sexuality. In so doing, Despentes is influenced by queer and gender studies as well as by Sade who, according to Carter, "put pornography in the service of women" (1978, 37). His iconoclasm in relation to authority and normative representations of sex and gender enables Despentes's twenty-first-century feminism, in which confessional statements serve the appropriation of the public space and advocate alternative life styles. This appropriation is achieved by the use of social media like Despentes's Facebook page and the Twitter feed created by her fans, as well as by literature and cinema. As in Sade's work, Despentes's questioning of existing power relations in the confessional mode is a political action.

NOTES

1 William Bennet and Steven Stapleton, band members of the British post-punk groups Whitehouse and Nurse with Wounds, respectively, made a recording in 1981 inspired by the *120 Days of Sodom* (1785) by Sade called *150 Murderous Passions, or Those Belonging to the Fourth Class, Composing the 28 Days of February Spent in Hearing the Narrations of Madame Desgranges, Interspersed amongst Which Are the Scandalous Doings at the Château during That Month* (1981).

2 "Gender transitivity, then, at least in terms of sexual behavior, is one of the most important transgressions of Sade's fiction ... What is new in Sade is the detachment of this binary from the male/female ... In sum, Sade does not queer gender by opposing male domination and violence against women, but only by allowing women and men to change gender roles during sexual activity" (Edmiston 2013, 70–2).

3 In *Baise-moi*, Nadine wonders if it is worth "getting used by everybody ... It is true, it's a lot of money. But their cocks really stink when she puts them in her mouth. It's less of a drag than going to a job, but it's not easy, going to bed with them without making a face. In the beginning, you figure it's enough to have three holes to get fucked in and think of something else as it's going on. But then it lasts long after; taking a shower and slamming the door doesn't get rid of it" (2002, 56). Yet in the end she comes to the conclusion that "she really likes this kind of work" (2002, 56). In *King Kong Théorie*, Despentes compares prostitution to taking drugs. It is hard to stop, as well as difficult to combine prostitution with monogamous relationships (2006, 79–80).

4 As Maurice Lever, one of Sade's biographers, reminds us, Sade had a tendency to live his fantasies of whipping, blasphemy, and sodomy with women from the lower classes and prostitutes. The affair Jeanne Testard and the Marseilles Affair are two examples. On 18 October 1763, Sade kidnapped the fan maker Testard and had her whip him and masturbate on a crucifix. On 27 June 1772, Sade whipped and had intercourse with five prostitutes in Marseilles, giving them anise candies, which made them sick to the point that the police believed that Sade had poisoned them (Lever 1993, 119–20; 194–202).

5 "Et si je n'ai plus jamais été violée, j'ai risqué de l'être cent fois ensuite, juste en étant beaucoup à l'extérieur" (2006, 47). (And if I have not been raped since, I risked being raped a hundred times, just by spending a lot of time outside [my translation].)

6 According to Foucault, the transformation of sex into discourse started in the seventeenth century, when penitents were not only obliged "to admit to violations of the laws of sex, as required by tradition penance; but of the nearly infinite task of telling – telling oneself and another, as often as possible, everything that might concern the interplay of innumerable pleasures, sensations, and thoughts which, through the body and the soul, had some affinity with sex" (1978, 20).

7 According to Deleuze (24), Sade seeks pleasure in reason that allows him to imagine the power of total destruction that distinguishes itself from simple negation.

8 According to Foucault, it is important to ask "who does the speaking, the positions and viewpoints from which they speak, the institutions which prompt people to speak about it [sexuality] and distribute the things that are said" (1978, 11). In the case of Despentes's female protagonists, they all share the exclusion and the silencing of their voices.

9 "She has no trouble confiding in them [Nadine and Manu], which shows her trust. And the fact that she has nothing to fear" (2002, 177).

10 Nadine's attraction to Fatima is best shown in the following lines: "Nadine doesn't tire of watching Fatima in the rear-view mirror. For the first time in her life, she sympathizes with those boys who fall madly in love with a girl just because of her eyes" (165).
11 Morgane Merteuil, accessed 22 August 2016, https://twitter.com/morganemerteuil.
12 Virginie Despentes, accessed 22 August 2016, https://www.facebook.com/Virginie Despentes.
13 Virginie Despentes on Twitter, accessed 22 August 2016, https://twitter.com/despentesactu.
14 Agnes Poirier@agnespk posted on 22 March 2016 a quote by Virginie Despentes saying that rape is a political tool to make people feel vulnerable. Accessed 22 August 2016, twitter.com/agnespk/status/712175654637277184.
15 #UEmata@inmapefe97 posted on 14 August 2016 a passage from *King Kong Théorie* on the importance of legalizing prostitution. Accessed 22 August 2016, twitter.com/search?q=despentes%2C%20prostitucion&src=typd.
16 Morgane Merteuil@MorganeMerteuil 2016b.

REFERENCES

AC/DC. 1979. "Highway to Hell." *Genius Song Lyrics and Knowledge.* https://genius.com/Ac-dc-highway-to-hell-lyrics.

Bélot, Sophie. 2004. "Baise-moi: From a Political to a Social Female Friendship Film." Studies in European Cinema 1, no. 1: 7–17.

Carter, Angela. 1978. *The Sadeian Woman and the Ideology of Pornography.* New York: Pantheon Books.

Crocodiles. 2013. "Marquis de Sade." *Genius Song Lyrics and Knowledge.* https://genius.com/Crocodiles-marquis-de-sade-lyrics.

Deleuze, Gilles. [1967] 1971. *Masochism: An Interpretation of Coldness and Cruelty.* New York: George Braziller.

Despentes, Virginie. 1999a. *Baise-moi* (French version). Paris: Éditions J'ai lu.

– 1999b. *Les chiennes savantes.* Paris: Éditions J'ai lu.

– 2002. *Baise-moi* (Rape me). New York: Grove Press.

– 2006. *King Kong Théorie.* Paris: Grasset.

– dir. 2009. *Mutantes.* Documentary film. Blaq Out.

Despentes, Virginie, and Coralie Trinh Thi, dirs. 2000. *Baise-moi* (Rape me). Feature film. Pan-Européenne.

Edmiston, William F. 2013. *Sade: Queer Theorist.* Oxford: Voltaire Foundation.

Edwards, Natalie. 2012. "Feminist Manifesto or Hardcore Porn? Virginie Despentes's Trangression." *Irish Journal of French Studies* 12: 9–26.

Fayard, Nicole. 2005. "Sadean Sisters: Sexuality as Terrorism in the Work of Virginie Despentes." In *Love and Sexuality: New Approaches in French Studies*, edited by Sarah F. Donachie and Kim Harrison, 101–20. Oxford: Peter Lang.

Fejes, Andreas, and Katherine Nicoll. 2014. "An Emergence of Confession in Education." In *Foucault and a Politics of Confession in Education*, edited by Andreas Fejes and Katherine Nicoll, 1–3. London: Routledge.

Foucault, Michel. [1976] 1990. *The History of Sexuality*. Translated by Robert Hurley. Vol. 1, *An Introduction*. New York: Vintage.

Gallop, Jane. 2005. "The Liberated Woman." *Narrative* 13, no. 2: 89–104.

Hunt, Lynn Avery. 1992. *The Family Romance of the French Revolution*. Berkeley: University of California Press.

Kozul, Mladen. 2011. *Le corps érotique au XVIIIe siècle*. Oxford: Voltaire Foundation, University of Oxford.

Landry, Donna. 1989. "Beat Me! Beat Me! Feminists and Sade." *Enclitic* 11, no. 4: 62–72.

Lever, Maurice. 1993. *Sade: A Biography*. New York: Harcourt Brace & Co.

Louar, Nadia. 2009. "Version femmes plurielles: Relire *Baise-moi* de Virginie Despentes." *Palimpsestes: Traduire le genre* 22: 83–98.

Merteuil, Morgane. 2010. *Libérez le féminisme*. Paris: L'Éditeur.

— 2016a. Twitter comment by Merteuil@MorganeMerteuil. twitter.com/morganemerteuil?lang=en. 25 June.

— 2016b. Twitter comment by Merteuil@MorganeMerteuil. 22 August. https://twitter.com/MorganeMerteuil/status/767804374387134464.

"Ni putes ni soumises." 2016. Facebook comment, 6 April. www.facebook.com/niputesnisoumises/?fref=nf.

Sade, Donatien Alphonse François de. [1926] 1975. "Dialog between a Priest and a Dying Man." In *The Marquis de Sade: The Complete Justine, Philosophy in the Bedroom and Other Writings*, edited by Richard Seaver and Austryn Wainhouse, 165–75. New York: Grove Press.

— *Philosophy in the Bedroom*. [1795] 1965. In Seaver and Wainhouse, *The Marquis de Sade*, 185–367.

Sauzon, Virginie. 2014. "Ni victime ni coupable: Virginie Despentes, de la pratique littéraire à la théorie." In *Aventures et expériences littéraires: Écritures des femmes en France au début du vingt-et-unième siècle*, edited by Amaleena Damlé and Gill Rye, 145–60. Amsterdam: Rodopi.

Schaal, Michèle A. 2012. "Un conte de fées punk-rock féministe: Bye Bye Blondie de Virginie Despentes." *Dalhousie French Studies* 99: 49–61.

"Third Wave French Feminism: A Short Introduction." 2011. In *Cherchez la femme: Women and Values in the Francophone World*, edited by Erika Fülöp and Adrienne Angelo, 39–55. Newcastle upon Tyne: Cambridge Scholars Publishing.

Seifert, Hans-Ulrich. 1983. *Sade: Leser und Autor*. Quellenstudien, Kommentare und Interpretationen zu Romanen und Romantheorien von D.A.F. de Sade. Frankfurt am Main: Verlag Peter Lang.

Sicard-Cowen, Hélène. 2008. "Le féminisme de Virginie Despentes à l'étude dans le roman *Baise-moi*." *Women in French Studies* 16: 64–72.

Sonic Youth. 1991. "Cotton Crown." *Song Meanings*. http://songmeanings.com/songs/view/48802/.

Steintrager, James A. 2005. "Liberating Sade." *Yale Journal of Criticism* 18, no. 2: 351–79.

Vallenthini, Michèle. 2013. "La troisième femme." In *Sade et les femmes: Ailleurs et autrement*, edited by Anne Coudreuse and Stéphanie Genand, 21–31. Paris: L'Harmattan.

Van der Tuin, Iris. 2015. *Generational Feminism: New Materialist Introduction to a Generative Approach*. Lanham: Lexington Books.

Warman, Caroline. 2002. *Sade: From Materialism to Pornography*. SVEC Oxford: Voltaire Foundation.

15

Fuck Yeah Levi Karter! *and New Authenticities*

DANIEL LAURIN

During our first shoot together I noticed that Levi was always walking around with his laptop with the screen open – it was always with him. And when he was not with me or the other models, he was outside or in his room – with his computer. I soon discovered why: he was recording his everyday goings-on, or making little video clips of his dance moves and cheer routines ... Over time he showed me more and more – him hanging out with friends, his new puppy, being with his BF, trying out his new hooks, the cinnamon challenge, sleeping, jacking-off, and even making breakfast ... Naked! Most of it just the stuff we all do everyday. And while watching I was mezmorized [*sic*] by the perfect realness of it all. Let's face it, the word "reality" has no meaning anymore, but what I was watching WAS REAL!

• Jake Jaxson, owner of CockyBoys.com and co-director of *Fuck Yeah Levi Karter!*

Fuck Yeah Levi Karter! (2013) is a forty-minute video produced by New York–based gay porn studio CockyBoys. The movie is composed almost entirely of footage shot by porn performer Levi Karter on his laptop webcam, smartphone, and point-and-shoot digital camera. The movie is marketed as a documentary but functions as a pornographic text as well, with several apparently unsimulated sex scenes. The narrative is loosely structured around three events in Karter's life: his breakup with his boyfriend due to jealousy over his scene partners, the 2013 Grabby Awards (and a live sex show with fellow CockyBoy Ricky Roman filmed at Steamworks Baths) in Chicago, and the friction between Karter and his mother over his choice of profession. The film is meant to serve as a humanizing glimpse into the life of a porn star and one of CockyBoys' most popular models, but it also operates as a sort of prestige vehicle for the studio; it is advertised with the laurel wreaths that indicate that it screened both at the Berlin Porn Film Festival and the NYC Porn Film Fest.

Most important for my analysis is how the studio positions the movie as *real*, suggesting that it offers us access to the performer in a way that his other pornographic scenes for the studio – or even pornography in general – could not. The film's description on the CockyBoys website suggests that Karter is "exposed to the world in a way no porn star has ever been before on film" (*Fuck Yeah Levi Karter!*). In my analysis of the film, I explore the various aesthetic and formal techniques – familiar from amateur video and home movies – that are understood to attest to its *realness*, and how this allows the studio to position the film as more authentic than conventional narrative pornography. One such technique is that of the confessional – the solo, direct-to-camera confession or testimony, popular in reality television and video blogs but with antecedents in documentary cinema – and I examine how the technique is marshalled both in this short documentary and in CockyBoys' other, more straightforward porn scenes. My main argument is that beyond proving the veracity of the sexual acts performed (considered a requirement of pornographic videos), *Fuck Yeah Levi Karter!* attempts to authenticate the performer and establish him as a real person whose on-screen desires and pleasures are also authentic. This move is representative of what I am calling pornography's *new authenticities*, a set of claims in reality porn that move beyond what is often considered pornography's burden of truth: proving that the sex acts are unsimulated. I examine how this is achieved in *Fuck Yeah Levi Karter!* and argue that the film itself is a form of metatextual pornographic authentication, as it serves to authenticate the performers and performances in CockyBoys' other porn scenes, thereby strengthening the CockyBoys brand and differentiating their product from that of their competitors.

Amateur Pornography, Home Movies, and the Erotics of the Real

What qualities of Karter's recordings so mesmerized CockyBoys director Jaxson? How is their "perfect realness" established in terms of image and content? Hardcore moving-image pornography[1] is already understood as having a privileged association with the real. One of the standout claims of Linda Williams's *Hard Core* is that pornography is constructed around the *principle of maximum visibility*;

maintaining "clinical-documentary qualities" so that it can clearly display "living, moving bodies engaged in explicit, usually unfaked sexual acts" (1989, 48, 30). Bill Nichols, Christian Hansen, and Catherine Needham insist that the genre depends heavily on claims to "truthful" representations of these sexual acts, because porn trades on its "evidentiary" status (1991, 201). More recent definitions of pornography still stress the same relationship to the real; Eugenie Brinkema maintains that the profilmically real in pornography is "more than significant; it is sustaining and essential" (2014, 275). Though the veracity of the *mechanics* of the sexual acts remains mostly unquestioned, commercial pornography has come to be understood by many as artificial – constructed and consciously performed. Ruth Barcan suggests that this is one of the reasons for the rise in popularity of amateur porn: "Several decades of extremely intense pressure on ordinary people to emulate the increasingly fabricated images they see around them are beginning to produce a backlash. The taste for the ordinary can be seen as a reaction to the glut of glamour media images with which we are all constantly bombarded, and reality genres are, at least in part, bound up in this" (2002, 88).

Barcan goes on to cite an amateur porn director who argues that with the proliferation of "porn style" in billboards, video games, and magazines, people are clamouring for something less manufactured than the typical tanned, bleached, silicon-enhanced porn star (102–3).[2] We can understand this perceived fakeness as a quality both of the image and the performer, and amateur pornography can be seen as a repudiation of both. Barcan also proposes that amateur or homemade/DIY porn can be seen as a rejection of the "stilted scripts" of commercial pornography; part of what contributes to the perceived realness of amateur porn is unscripted dialogue and a lack of predetermined narrative (87–8). Definitions of amateur porn differ greatly, and it is important to remember that "amateur" is not a coherent category, nor has its meaning remained stable over time. Where "amateur" once described an intent – doing something simply "for the love of it" as opposed to for a profit – it is progressively used to describe a style of pornographic video. It is also difficult to understand amateur as opposite from "professional," as increasing availability and decreasing cost of video-recording technology and editing software, in addition to free-to-use porn sharing sites, reduce production costs but also increase the potential for easy monetized distribution. Though the term "amateur" may mean different things to different people, and though there may be debates on what constitutes "real" amateur productions, what I hope to get at is how the aesthetics of amateur production connote a "realness" that escapes commercial narrative productions.

Susanna Paasonen suggests that the look and feel of amateur pornography – "marked by shaky camerawork, low image quality, poor lighting, and awkward, untrained performers" – has worked to enhance a "sense of 'truth' and authenticity that is central to the genre" (2011, 75). She also argues that online access to pornography heightens this sense because of the internet's inherent associations to directness – "the visual and auditory accessibility of physically distant people and events" (112). For Shaka McGlotten, gay amateur productions (or "DIY porn") are possessed of a vital force, a "generative aliveness," due in part to their participatory nature and their elements of self-representation (2013, 103). He highlights, among other examples, XTube user Bryanterry, whose solo masturbation videos had been viewed ten million times (109).[3] In an interview with McGlotten, Bryanterry cited the realness of the videos he had seen on sharing sites as his inspiration for recording and uploading his own (111). He also believes the sense of authenticity of his videos is a result of the fact that they are self-produced – he records them himself on his computer webcam and his point-and-shoot digital camera – and that this sets them apart from the "'fake' or 'cheesy' offerings of mainstream commercial gay pornography" (111). Of course, this allure and heightened sense of realism have been documented long before the arrival of Web 2.0. In describing Curt McDowell's underground pornographic art-house short *Loads* (1980) in his seminal article "Men's Pornography: Gay vs. Straight," Thomas Waugh praises the "spontaneity of camera twitches, the fragility of flares" and notes that the sometimes hand-held camera adds "the frisson of subjective angle." He observes, "Slickness takes away from desire" (1985, 35). This recalls a statement by Roland Barthes, who in *Mythologies* compares the "icy indifference of skilful practitioners" of the French striptease to participants in the popular contests of amateur striptease and finds that the *gauche* steps, poor dancing, and technical awkwardness of the amateurs "restores to the spectacle its erotic power" ([1957] 1972, 86). Ruth Barcan suggests that Barthes's preference for amateur performance anticipates the growing interest in the 1990s in watching "real people" (2002, 88).[4]

Characterizing Levi Karter as an "amateur" may be confusing to some, as he is in fact a professional porn star. But even a porn star can make amateur porn, and Karter's camerawork demonstrates all of the aesthetic traces described above. Further, the quality of the footage and the particular camera angles attest to his decidedly unprofessional tools. Aspect ratio is a tell-tale indicator of amateur production: several shots feature a curious 9:16 aspect ratio, a regular widescreen shot rotated 90 degrees, suggesting smartphone footage recorded with the phone in an upright, "portrait" position (fig. 15.1). In other shots, we watch Levi from

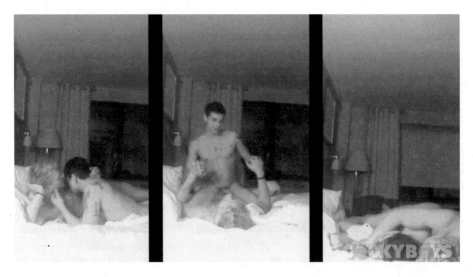

15.1 Hotel room scene composed of three "portrait" videos, successive sequences collaged. *Fuck Yeah Levi Karter!*, dir. Jake Jaxson and Levi Karter, CockyBoys, 2013.

below or from a slight low angle, signalling that the footage has been recorded via webcam on a laptop computer. Webcams, according to Jay David Bolter and Richard Grusin, operate under the logic of immediacy – a sense of transparency that rhetorically negates mediation or representation. "It is the notion that a medium could erase itself and leave the viewer in the presence of the objects represented, so that [the viewer] could know the objects directly" (1999, 5–6, 70). So in addition to being recognizable as an amateur technology, webcams purport to offer a more direct, unmediated access to their subjects, which Paasonen reminds us contributes to the "sense of realness" in online pornography (2011, 112).

Another lens through which we can interpret the footage from *Fuck Yeah Levi Karter!* is that of the home movie. Though the film is produced and distributed by a porn studio and plays in porn film festivals, only about a third of the film is pornographic.[5] The majority of the footage is much more mundane: Levi driving around his Ohio hometown, working on the computer in the CockyBoys offices, taking the "cinnamon challenge" with his friends.[6] Just like pornography, Minette Hillyer argues, home movies attempt to reveal a kind of truth: "Both show facsimiles of intimacy and revelation; they seem to ease access to those things most fundamental to our humanity" (2004, 50). In her discussion of *Pam and Tommy Lee: Hardcore and Uncensored*, Pamela Anderson and Tommy Lee's allegedly stolen vacation/sex tape, Hillyer suggests that the mundane domestic home-video footage "authenticates" the pornographic moments:

While the ratio of footage tends heavily toward the domestic, in the universe described by its movements, the domestic and the pornographic seem to work in partnership. The tape's domestic credentials serve both to establish its authenticity – in an environment populated by fake celebrity sightings and computer-generated imagery – and to add an extra charge to its pornographic appeal. (2004, 52)

The remaining forty-six mundane and domestic non-pornographic minutes of *Pam and Tommy* (out of a total of fifty-four) serve to establish what Hillyer, borrowing from André Bazin's guiding myth of cinema, terms an "integral realism" (2004, 51).

This integral realism is established in *Fuck Yeah Levi Karter!* with the inclusion of Karter's domestic footage. Though some footage is quite charming – Levi teases one CockyBoy for having never made pancakes before and teaches another how to use chopsticks – a significant amount is quite unremarkable. There is a long take of him preparing breakfast in his mom's house in Ohio, presumably recorded by placing his laptop on the kitchen counter. There are multiple webcam shots of Karter staring blankly into the camera, having recorded himself working at the computer. Further, pornographic scenes are extended so that they may once again slip back into the mundane: in one of many solo masturbation interludes, we see Karter climax, watch him breathe heavily for a few beats and assess the damage of his ejaculation, then get up and walk out of the frame as the camera lingers on the empty couch (figs. 15.2 and 15.3). Though *Pam and Tommy Lee* is advertised as being "uncensored," Hillyer points out that it is not "uncut"; the footage was edited by the video's distributor so that a sex scene occurred earlier in the narrative (2004, 67). In *Fuck Yeah Levi Karter!*, the inclusion of the domestic footage seems even more pointed; these thirty-eight minutes have been selected from the reported "hundreds of hours of footage" that Karter recorded, and the video is credited as being directed by both Karter and Jaxson. That these mundane moments were purposely selected out of such an abundance of footage (as opposed to simply not cut out, in the case of *Pam and Tommy Lee*) suggests an awareness on the part of Jaxson of their authenticating power.

In addition to authenticating the sexual performance, home movies take on an extra charge when the bodies featured are celebrities. Though I am not suggesting that Levi Karter enjoys the same status as Pamela Anderson or even Tommy Lee, he is certainly known. He was voted Performer of the Year at the 2016 Grabby awards (Chicago LGBTQ magazine *Grab*'s porn awards) and has been the subject of features in the *Huffington Post* and *Paper Magazine* and, with three other

15.2 *Above* Mundane home-movie footage: Karter films himself masturbating on a couch. *Fuck Yeah Levi Karter!*, dir. Jake Jaxson and Levi Karter, CockyBoys, 2013.

15.3 *Opposite* The camera lingers on the empty couch after Karter leaves the room. *Fuck Yeah Levi Karter!*, dir. Jake Jaxson and Levi Karter, CockyBoys, 2013.

CockyBoys, a feature for *Cosmopolitan* about the studio's huge female fan base (Wischlover 2016). At the time of writing, his Twitter followers number more than 120,000. According to Hillyer, celebrity home movies are all the more fascinating because we already know their performers as images (2004, 59). And home movies can serve to authenticate these images. Patricia R. Zimmermann singles out a moment in the 1989 Oscars broadcast in which Demi Moore and Bruce Willis share a home movie of themselves feeding their newborn: "The mawkishness of the video and its record of the daily operations of new parents authenticates Willis and Moore as a down-to-earth, average, likeable young couple who feed their baby themselves rather than as media-industry millionaires" (1995, 143). The aesthetics of amateur production combined with this traditional domestic scene thus purport to offer us unmediated images of our celebrities and serve to authenticate them in our eyes. In addition to the domestic footage of Karter, the film features footage of him at work, which serves to link the two worlds together. We see Levi pole-dancing on stage, dancing in his underwear with other CockyBoys at an event at a nightclub, and posing for photos in front of a poster advertising his live sex show with fellow CockyBoy Ricky Roman (a scene I'll return to later).

By including images of public "porn star" Levi in addition to the "private" Levi in his home movies, *Fuck Yeah Levi Karter!* establishes an equivalency between the two. This, along with the mundane domestic footage and amateur aesthetics, aims to authenticate Karter's performance and his status as a "real" person. This real-life status of the performer is conveyed through the use of the *confessional*, a popularization and vernacularization of a mode of personal direct-to-camera address that can be found in a range of media texts and is a staple of reality porn.

From Amateur to Reality: The Confessional and the Production of Truth

If amateur pornography can be understood as being more "real" than traditional narrative porn, then it should come as no surprise that the porn industry – an industry whose generic definition relies on the profilmic real – would take notice. Katrien Jacobs suggests that "commercial netporn" is adopting the tropes and aesthetics of amateur pornography to seduce viewers (2007, 47). Jacobs sees commercial netporn as separate from "real amateurs," who are "sexually driven consumers as well as media practitioners and producers who make sex scenes to explore personal desires and respond to cultural phantasms as mechanisms of power" (45). I am not personally as invested in separating "real" amateurs from the supposed fake ones, but Jacobs's point about major studios' decisions to adopt an amateur style to attract viewers is important, both because it highlights the popularity (and therefore commercial viability) of amateur-tinged productions and because it points to the notion that one consumer's amateur porn may not read as "authentic" by another. Further, it points to the development of "amateur" as an available style. This style has not remained static. Susanna Paasonen chronicles the development of "amateur" as a style of commercial pornography after the camcorder boom of the 1980s, to the rise of "gonzo" porn in the late 1980s and early 1990s (a genre that shares many aesthetic properties with amateur but is generally directed and shot by the people performing in it), to what she terms "reality porn," which emerges alongside the rising popularity of reality television in the early 2000s. Reality porn "involves staged scenes and scenarios presented as real and accidental actual events, and characters often address the camera directly. Professionally produced, it emulates the style and feel of amateur productions and lays claims to the amateur status of its performers (particularly the female talent)" (Paasonen 2011, 72–3).

Much of CockyBoys' pornographic output conforms to Paasonen's definition. If we expand this definition to include non-amateur performers (as in CockyBoys' case, porn stars), then it begins to conform more to contemporary reality television, which often features celebrities or known individuals. Though they are porn performers, CockyBoys models appear as themselves and in most scenes are understood as not playing a role. CockyBoys scenes are mostly filmed in an apartment or outdoors ("natural" locations), feature the performers in their regular clothing, and use a combination of hand-held and tripod-mounted shots filmed primarily with DSLR cameras to mimic the shallow-depth-of-field look of film. The result is naturalistic but polished.

But CockyBoys, and indeed many other producers of reality-style porn, do not simply rely on the "style and feel" of amateur productions. To back up their claim that the performances and performers (and thus their desires, pleasure, and arousal) are genuine, both *Fuck Yeah Levi Karter!* and many of CockyBoys' recent scenes rely on another staple of reality television: the confessional. Though the format of the confessional varies across genres and texts, it is called upon to serve a similar purpose in each: to deliver representations of a "real" person who registers as intimate and authentic.

In an essay first published in 1996, documentary scholar Michael Renov links the first-person video confessionals to the confession as outlined by Michel Foucault in the first volume of *A History of Sexuality* (Renov 2004, 191–215). Recall that for Foucault, the confession is the "general standard governing the production of the true discourse on sex" ([1976] 1990, 61). Renov posits the video camera as the necessary virtual presence of the authority who requires the confession, and suggests that the immediacy of video (the fact it can be self-produced and requires no other mediating contingencies) makes it particularly well suited to the confessional impulse: "No technician need see or hear the secrets confined to tape. None but the invited enter the loop of the video confession" (2004, 198). Taped self-interrogation, he argues, "can achieve a depth and nakedness of expression that is difficult to duplicate with a crew or even a camera operator present" (203). In his text he is talking specifically about independent video art produced since the 1970s by the likes of Wendy Clarke, Lynn Hershman, and Sadie Benning, but his descriptions of the truth-producing qualities of the format of video confession remain in place today. We can attribute part of this, as Renov does, to the potential of the camera itself. He cites cinéma vérité filmmaker Jean Rouch, who found the camera to function as a "psychoanalytic stimulant which lets people do things they wouldn't otherwise do":

> Very quickly I discovered the camera was something else; it was not a brake but let's say, to use an automobile term, an accelerator. You push these people to confess themselves and it seemed to us without limit ... It's not exactly exhibitionism: it's a very strange kind of confession in front of a camera, where the camera is, let's say, a mirror, and also a window open to the outside. (quoted in Renov 2004, 197)

It is these qualities of the camera, in addition to the self-production capabilities of video that require no outside intervention, that qualify the video camera as the ideal confessional tool, and why we understand these recordings to be truthful.

In our contemporary media landscape, the confessional lives on, albeit in a slightly modified version. Beginning with the first season of MTV's *The Real World* (1992), the reality TV confessional placed a performer in a space apart from the rest of the cast and provided them with the opportunity to reflect on events and feelings and to speak freely about their housemates. While these testimonies are delivered to an off-screen producer, there is an intimacy established in this setup: these reflexive moments unfold not in front of other cast-mates but in a more private setting, one that *Real World: San Francisco* housemate Judd Winick likened to "therapy without the help" (2009, 110). Confessionals have been an integral feature in reality competition series such as *Survivor* (CBS, 2000–present) and *Project Runway* (Bravo!, 2004–08, Lifetime, 2008–present), docu-soaps such as *Keeping*

Up with the Kardashians (E!, 2007–present), and the many *Housewives* franchises. Dan Udy notes that the format is updated in more recent "docu-series" such as *I Am Cait* (E!, 2015–16) and *Lindsay* (OWN, 2014) and features "a subdued soundtrack, soft lighting and multiple camera angles – often in close-up" (2016).[7] In a blog post that advocates abolishing the now tired reality-TV trope, critic Noel Murray concedes that when confessionals are done well, they serve a narrative function similar to interviews in a documentary film or in broadcast journalism, and that their function of revealing information unknown to other cast members can place the audience in a privileged position (2015).

This idea of a shared secret between confessant and viewing public is often central to *vlogging* practice. Though not explicitly labelled "confessionals," vlogs (a neologism constructed out of the terms *video* and *blog*) are formally similar and share connotations of intimacy and authenticity. Vlogs are "first-person, direct-address videos" (Horak 2014, 572) uploaded to YouTube and other social media platforms, user-created content "structured primarily around a monologue delivered directly to camera" (Burgess and Green 2009, 94). Laura Horak describes them as "talking head-and-upper-torso" videos,[8] an update to the "talking head" framing characteristic of documentary cinema and one that establishes a conversational tone via its similarities to video chat programs such as Skype (2014, 574–5). Vlogs often involve disclosure and revelation, which might seem at odds with their status as broadcast to a public. Jonathan Alexander and Elizabeth Losh, in a chapter about coming-out videos on YouTube, point out that vlogs often participate in the "public secret" phenomenon of the internet such as the "Five Things You Don't Know about Me" meme (2010, 38); Horak points out that some trans vloggers whisper to the camera to avoid being heard by their roommates (2014, 575); and Michael Strangelove highlights the hundreds of videos entitled "The Real Me" that explore the difference between vloggers' on-camera personae and their "real" selves (2010, 65). According to Horak, the authenticity of these disclosures and public secrets is validated by the formal qualities of the videos: the "close framing, a private setting, direct address, and amateur style ... make the claim that this person is real and their statements are true" (2014, 575).

Fuck Yeah Levi Karter! uses confessionals to structure the narrative of the film. Recorded primarily on Karter's laptop, they share the formal qualities of the vlog[9] and the narrative function of the reality TV confessional; they serve to introduce the major tensions of the film, often by playing directly before the home-video footage in which these tensions play out. His first entry sets up the conflict with his mother:

I'm not happy right now. My mom, she said it's not my fault or anything, but she thinks she might have to cut off her friendship with her [friend]. I didn't want the choices that I made to affect her that much that her best and longest friend is no longer going to be her friend. And it really sucks. She also wants to move because she says she can't walk on the street without thinking that someone knows everything. It's a small town and people talk, so I understand. It's also her home town, she grew up here. I didn't mean to run her out of her hometown.

The audio from this narration begins with the synchronized video of Levi recording this vlog entry to anchor the narration to this video confessional, then floats above a montage of Levi at home, playing with his puppy, sitting on a couch with a cat. Immediately following this scene is one that appears to have been filmed surreptitiously: a discussion between two women in the kitchen, with their backs to the camera. "All right, so what's going on with Luke?" one asks. "He's here," the other woman responds. "He's here, but he doesn't have a plan." In addition to revealing his real name – "Levi Karter" is his *nom-de-porn* – the sequence establishes the other side of the conflict. As the scene plays out, we learn that Karter's mother doesn't seem to think that his career in pornography and in New York will last, and that she is concerned that he won't be able to "bring his performer stuff" back to Ohio.

Another vlog segment, with the same set-up and outfit as the first, introduces Levi's troubles with his boyfriend. "I didn't really realize how I alone I was," Levi confesses into his webcam, "until after I broke up with my ex." This scene transitions into a home-video sequence in which Karter debates with his friends whether or not he should phone his boyfriend to break it off. We see Karter place the call and we hear his side of the argument before the scene dissolves to a shot of Karter with his face in his hands, his friends silently consoling him. These video confessions provide narrative framing to Karter's home movies without resorting to devices such as title cards that would remove his authorial voice or damage the confessional nature of the film, and they continue the work of authenticating Karter and his performance as honest and true.

This perceived authenticating ability of the confessional is also called upon in CockyBoys' other, more straightforward porn scenes. As I mentioned earlier, CockyBoys film most of their scenes in a reality porn style, a style that Paasonen observed emerging with the popularization of reality television. Though reality television may not present "reality" to its audiences, James Friedman argues, it does employ "real people" as opposed to professional actors (2002, 8). It is this emphasis on "real people" that I wish to stress in my analysis of CockyBoys, and one of the reasons I suggest they employ the confessional even in their non-documentary, straightforward porn scenes (fig.15.4).

In "Tegan Zayne Gets Clark'd" (2016), CockyBoys newcomer Tegan Zayne travels to Montreal for his scene with porn veteran Gabriel Clark. The opening sequence looks identical to many reality television shows and cuts between handheld footage of Zayne and Clark walking through Montreal's gay village, sitting and talking on a picturesque stoop, and a to-camera interview in the docu-series style as outlined by Udy above. In this confessional, Tegan describes the afternoon they spent together and what he has been looking forward to during his visit:

> So we went to the gay village and he showed me all the hot spots in the gayborhood, which was really cool. We went on a nice little pizza date. And if you follow either of us on Twitter, you probably saw a picture of that. So we got some quality hangout time in, played around in the village. It was nice getting to know him, but most of the time I was just thinking about that French-Canadian dick. And since I got here that's the thing I've been craving the most. Not poutine, but French-Canadian uncut dick.

Not only does this scene highlight the fact the models were spending time together prior to their shoot but it also allows Tegan to express desire for his scene partner. This confessional, though it is framed differently from Karter's self-produced video diaries, still benefits from the lingering authenticity claims of the self-produced video diaries, albeit in an updated docu-series aesthetic that brings with it associations with reality and with "real" people (fig.15.5).

These porn confessions are markedly different from the confessional nature of pornography that Linda Williams outlined in *Hard Core* (1989). Pornographic confession, for Williams, involved visible, involuntary evidence of pleasure produced by the body that would assure audiences that what they were watching was not a performance (50). The apex of this principle is the money shot – visible, external male ejaculation – "the visual evidence of the mechanical 'truth' of bodily pleasure caught in involuntary spasm; the ultimate and uncontrollable – ultimate because uncontrollable – confession of sexual pleasure in the climax of orgasm" (100–1). Though it is true that ejaculation attests to penile stimulation, it cannot guarantee sexual pleasure and is not necessarily connected to the pleasure performed on screen. Moreover, I take issue with the notion of it being involuntary.

15.4 *Top* Karter's vlog setup laptop webcam, direct address. *Fuck Yeah Levi Karter!*, dir. Jake Jaxson and Levi Karter, CockyBoys, 2013.

15.5 *Bottom* Tegan's confessional in CockyBoys' *Tegan Zayne Gets Clark'd*, dir. Jake Jaxson, CockyBoys, 2016.

I side more with Jeffrey Escoffier, who suggests that money shots should be considered forms of labour that *signify* but do not necessarily equate with pleasure: they are often choreographed after several hours of filming and require additional visual or physical stimulation (2003, 550). As such, we should be suspicious of any "truth" supposedly produced by these emissions. If we are to understand pornography's aim, as Williams does, to be to make sex speak (1989, 2), then many of the confessions produced by male orgasms would have been produced under duress. With this in mind, we can see how the confessional can serve as a new method for authenticating pleasure and assuring the viewer of the *genuine pleasure* felt by *real people* – some of porn's new authenticities.

CockyBoys and "New Authenticities"

CockyBoys fashions itself as an alternative gay porn company, releasing full-length features that range from boy-band parodies (*One Erection*, 2016), faux found-footage horror (*Meeting Liam*, 2016), reality TV-style road movies (*Max and Jake's RoadStrip*, 2013, and *Project GoGo Boy*, 2012), to more self-consciously "artistic" works such as *A Thing of Beauty* (2013), for which director Jake Jaxson was named "the Walt Whitman of Gay Porn" by a Salon.com critic (Linds 2013), and the "profoundly layered seven-part morality play" ("Watch Answered Prayers" [n.d.]) *Answered Prayers* (2015), inspired by the feelings of betrayal Jaxson felt when he believed one of his models was stealing from him (Stewart 2013). But for the most part, CockyBoys produces scenes shot in a reality style in which the only narrative set-up is that porn model A will be fucking porn model B (or A and B will flip-fuck, or A and B will take turns fucking C, and so on). The conceit of reality porn, I have argued, is that the performers are appearing as themselves, as *real people*, and that their pleasures and desires are authentic. In addition to *Fuck Yeah Levi Karter!*'s confessionals, one scene is emblematic of this approach and highlights the film's metatextual qualities.

Karter's live sex show with Ricky Roman at Steamworks Baths on the occasion of the Grabby Awards differs from the rest of the footage in the film, as it has been recorded by someone other than Karter and, it seems, with multiple cameras. Though the sequence depicts the large crowd watching the pair, it still retains a feeling of intimacy; much of the footage is in close-up and focuses on kissing, caressing, the words they whisper to each other. This scene is intercut with home-movie footage (most likely shot on Karter's laptop) of Karter and Roman having sex in their hotel room, and the editing matches up the sex acts: Levi sucks Ricky's

15.6 *Top* Footage of Karter and Roman's sex show at Steamworks Chicago. *Fuck Yeah Levi Karter!*, dir. Jake Jaxson and Levi Karter, CockyBoys, 2013.

15.7 *Bottom* Laptop recording of Karter and Roman in their hotel room. *Fuck Yeah Levi Karter!*, dir. Jake Jaxson and Levi Karter, CockyBoys, 2013.

dick on stage, Levi sucks Ricky's dick in their hotel room. Levi rims Ricky in a sling for a crowd at Steamworks, Levi rims Ricky in their bed, all alone (figs. 15.6 and 15.7). This parallel editing invites viewers to compare the two scenes, and we observe the same expressions, levels of enjoyment, and passion in both the live sex scene that both performers got paid for and the home movie presumably recorded for fun – or, we could say, "for the love of it." This sequence in *Fuck Yeah*

Levi Karter! demonstrates not only how amateur and home movie footage serve to authenticate the sex but how the film as a whole serves as a sort of metatextual authenticator for the rest of CockyBoys' oeuvre. Their models don't just fuck each other for money – they do it in their spare time too. The desire and pleasure they demonstrate on-screen manifests off-screen as well.

For CockyBoys, the ultimate goal is to claim authenticity in their performances and to establish their performers as real people with strong personalities and genuine desire for their scene partners, thereby differentiating themselves from gay porn giants like Falcon and Men.com, who produce scripted encounters between characters, and from successful "amateur" studios such as Sean Cody and Corbin Fisher, who employ mostly heterosexually identified performers. CockyBoys is "real" because the sex is "real" beyond being unsimulated. Documentary and home-movie style films such as *Fuck Yeah Levi Karter!*, itself presented as authentic with its reliance on amateur video and home-movie footage, serve to establish the studio as a creative alternative to mainstream narrative porn or amateur or reality-style porn featuring performers who don't identify as gay and therefore *perform* their pleasure or desire. If pornography can serve to highlight the existence of pleasure without desire, then CockyBoys can differentiate themselves with a product in which the two coexist. The "real" people who confess their "real" desires and pleasures are just two new authenticities being offered up by a genre that must continually reassert its reality claims against the threat of its exhaustion. Reality porn still serves as indicative of a will to knowledge about sex, but speaks to an audience whose criteria for authenticity has changed, and who desire to see "real" sex between real people. If pornography wishes to penetrate, as Tim Dean suggests, the "mysterious privacy of the insides" (2009, 111), then reality porn can be understood as a yearning for a different form of interiority: as an index of desire and not just sex, as pleasure beyond the money shot.

NOTES

1. Referred to simply as "pornography" for the rest of this essay.
2. Or, we could surmise, the enormously muscular, spectacularly endowed, fake-tanned male porn star.
3. Bryanterry's XTube channel is now defunct.
4. It should also be noted that Barthes's description also anticipates other conditions for who can be considered "amateur" or ordinary – in addition to the "sensible suits, ordinary coats" of the amateur performers, Barthes finds "far fewer Chinese or Spanish women"

(1972, 86). For further explorations of the racial construction of the category of the amateur or ordinary, see Dyer 2007 and Ward 2015.

5   I counted twelve minutes of "pornographic" footage – footage of any sex act, solo or with a partner. Even if we include all of the shots that feature nudity (Karter emerging from the shower, sleeping naked, dancing in a jockstrap, etc.) the tally only reaches fifteen minutes out of a total of thirty-eight.

6   The "cinnamon challenge" was a viral video sensation that began in 2012 and required participants to record themselves consuming a spoonful of ground cinnamon in less than one minute, without resorting to drinking water. As of 10 August 2012, more than forty thousand videos had been uploaded to YouTube, with the most popular of them gaining more than nineteen million views. A report in the journal *Pediatrics* describes the participants "coughing and choking when the spice triggers a severe gag reflex in response to a caustic sensation in the mouth and throat" and notes that it has "led to dozens of calls to poison centers, emergency department visits, and even hospitalizations for adolescents requiring ventilator support for collapsed lungs" (Grant-Alfieri, Schaechter, and Lipshultz 2013: 833).

7   Udy notes that the distinction between "docu-series" and "docu-soaps" (such as *Keeping Up with the Kardashians*, *The Hills*, *Jersey Shore*), beyond these aesthetic differences, is slight, and is more indicative of efforts of the networks to "re-orient the docu-soap away from Reality television and its implications of trash, exploitation, and entertainment."

8   This framing is particularly important to Horak as her focus is on trans men's vlogs, and the torso is therefore a very important site for trans body modification.

9   Karter refers to these segments as his "video blogs."

REFERENCES

Alexander, Jonathan, and Elizabeth Losh. 2010. "'A YouTube of One's Own?': 'Coming Out' Videos as Rhetorical Action." In *LGBT Identity and Online New Media*, edited by Christopher Pullen and Margaret Cooper, 37–50. New York: Routledge.

Barcan, Ruth. 2002. "In the Raw: Home-Made Porn and Reality Genres." *Journal of Mundane Behavior* 3, no. 1: 87–108.

Barthes, Roland. [1957] 1972. *Mythologies*. Translated by Annette Lavers. London: Jonathan Cape.

Bolter, Jay David, and Richard Grusin. 1999. *Remediation: Understanding New Media*. Cambridge: MIT Press.

Brinkema, Eugenie. 2014. "Rough Sex." In *Porn Archives*, edited by Tim Dean, Steven Ruszczycky, and David Squires, 262–3. Durham: Duke University Press.

Burgess, Jean, and Joshua Green. 2009. "The Entrepreneurial Vlogger: Participatory Culture beyond the Professional-Amateur Divide." In *The YouTube Reader*, edited by Pelle Snickars and Patrick Vonderau, 89–107. Stockholm: National Library of Sweden.

Dean, Tim. 2009. *Unlimited Intimacy: Reflections on the Subculture of Barebacking*. Chicago: University of Chicago Press.

Dyer, Richard. 2007. *White: Essays on Race and Culture*. London: Routledge.

Escoffier, Jeffrey. 2003. "Gay-for-Pay: Straight Men and the Making of Gay Pornography." *Qualitative Sociology* 26, no. 4: 531–55.

Foucault, Michel. [1976] 1990. *The History of Sexuality*. Vol. 1, *An Introduction*. Translated by Robert Hurley. New York: Vintage.

Friedman, James. 2002. *Reality Squared: Televisual Discourse on the Real*. New Brunswick, NJ: Rutgers University Press.

"Fuck Yeah Levi Karter! Porn Haus Film Fest." 2013. As of July 2019, this video is gone from CockyBoys' main page but still available on DVD (www.cockyboysstore.com). The description (8 August 2017) is still at https://web.archive.org/web/20170507004419/http://cockyboys.com/scenes/fuck-yeah-levi-karter.html.

Grant-Alfieri, Amelia, Judy Schaechter, and Steven E. Lipshultz. 2013. "Ingesting and Aspirating Dry Cinnamon by Children and Adolescents: The 'Cinnamon Challenge.'" *Pediatrics* 131 (5): 833–5.

Hillyer, Minette. 2004. "Sex in the Suburban: Porn, Home Movies, and the Live Action Performance of Love in *Pam and Tommy Lee: Hardcore and Uncensored*." In *Porn Studies*, edited by Linda Williams, 50–76. Durham: Duke University Press.

Horak, Laura. 2014. "Trans on YouTube: Intimacy, Visibility, Temporality." *TSQ: Transgender Studies Quarterly* 1 (4): 572–85.

Jacobs, Katrien. 2007. *Netporn: DIY Web Culture and Sexual Politics*. London: Rowman & Littlefield.

Linds, Justin Abraham. 2013. "The Walt Whitman of Gay Porn." *Salon.com*, 1 September. http://www.salon.com/2013/09/01/the_walt_whitman_of_gay_porn/.

McGlotten, Shaka. 2013. *Virtual Intimacies: Media, Affect, and Queer Sociality*. Albany: State University of New York Press.

Murray, Noel. 2015. "Please Kill the Reality TV 'Confessional.'" *AV Club*, 23 March. http://www.avclub.com/article/please-kill-reality-tv-confessional-215420.

Nichols, Bill, Christian Hansen, and Catherine Needham. 1991. "Pornography, Ethnography, and the Discourses of Power." In *Representing Reality: Issues and Concepts in Documentary*, edited by Bill Nichols, 201–28. Bloomington: Indiana University Press.

Paasonen, Susanna. 2011. *Carnal Resonance: Affect and Online Pornography*. Cambridge: MIT Press.

Renov, Michael. 2004. "Video Confessions." In *The Subject of Documentary*, chap. 13, 191–215. Minneapolis: University of Minnesota Press.

Stewart, Tessa. 2013. "There's Drama on Both Sides of the Camera at NYC Porn Powerhouse CockyBoys." *Village Voice*, 20 November. http://www.villagevoice.com/news/theres-drama-on-both-sides-of-the-camera-at-nyc-porn-powerhouse-cockyboys-6440187.

Strangelove, Michael. 2010. *Watching YouTube: Extraordinary Videos by Ordinary People*. Toronto: University of Toronto Press.

Udy, Dan. 2016. "Keeping It Real: Genre and Politics on I Am Cait." *Jump Cut* 57 (Fall). https://www.ejumpcut.org/currentissue/-UdyCait/index.html.

Ward, Jane. 2015. *Not Gay: Sex between Straight White Men*. New York: New York University Press.

"Watch Answered Prayers, Exclusively on CockyBoys!" n.d. *CockyBoys.com*, http://www.cockyboys.com/dvds/answered-prayers.html.

Waugh, Thomas. 1985. "Men's Pornography, Gay vs. Straight." *Jump Cut* 30 (Spring): 30–6.

Williams, Linda. 1989. *Hard Core: Power, Pleasure, and the Frenzy of the Visible*. Berkeley: University of California Press.

Winick, Judd. 2009. *Pedro and Me: Friendship, Loss and What I Learned*. New York: Henry Holt.

Wischlover, Cheryl. 2016. "'Call Us 'One Erection': Why Straight Twentysomething Women Are Obsessed with These Gay Porn Stars." *Cosmopolitan.com*, 16 May. http://www.cosmopolitan.com/sex-love/a51996/straight-women-who-love-cockyboys-gay-porn/.

Zimmermann, Patricia R. 1995. *Reel Families: A Social History of Amateur Film*. Bloomington: Indiana University Press.

16

Circuitous Pleasures, Guilt, and Pain: Nymph()maniac *and the Pornographic Hard Code*

JUSTINE T. MCLELLAN

Prologue

A vulva rendered bloody from relentless masturbation, testicles violently smashed by a log, a self-imposed excision, and a homemade abortion are but a few of the physical torments that Lars von Trier has foisted on his characters and audiences. Indeed, von Trier's filmography is crowded with "brutal and visceral images [that] appear deliberately designed to shock and provoke the spectator" (Horeck and Kendall 2011, 1). Tina Kendall and Tanya Horeck describe von Trier's mode of arthouse hard-core filmmaking as the "New European extremism" (14). Rape, mutilation, incest, and murderous rampages are some of the preoccupations of directors who follow this cinematic tendency. Fellow moviemakers of the extreme include Gaspar Noé, Christophe Honoré, Catherine Breillat, and Michael Haneke.

New Extremism and #MeToo

Perhaps unsurprisingly, the #MeToo movement is somewhat unpopular among filmmakers of the "New Extremism." Michael Haneke is of the opinion that the movement founded by Tarana Burke and the subsequent global wave of denunciations of abusers has led to a "witch hunt coloured by a hatred of men" (Mumford 2018). Catherine Breillat is "absolutely against" #Balancetonporc, the French equivalent of #MeToo, and has signed the open letter by women writers and actors attacking the movement for creating an "atmosphere of Puritanism." Ever the contrarian, von Trier believes that "the #MeToo movement is a brilliant idea" (Scharf 2018). Yet while he approves of the movement in theory, in practice he himself has been accused of sexual harassment. Filmmakers who have been accused of sexual harassment and/or rape have often been unable to resist showcasing in their work their obsession with violating people's boundaries. It is as if their entire oeuvre were one big confession, daring us to let them get away with it. Woody Allen, who was accused by his adopted daughter of sexually assaulting her, has dedicated most of his filmography to justifying his obsession with young girls. Roman Polanski, who pleaded guilty of drugging and raping a thirteen-year-old girl, wrote and directed at least three films in which a pregnancy results from assault: *Tess* (1979), *Rosemary's Baby* (1968), and *Chinatown* (1974). Comedian Louis C.K., who forced women he worked with to watch and hear him masturbate, wrote and directed a movie that includes a scene in which a character pretends to masturbate while his friend is on speakerphone with an attractive woman (*I Love You Daddy*, 2017).

Von Trier now belongs to this deplorable brotherhood of men who seem incapable of separating their art from their behaviour. In 2017, Björk wrote on a public Facebook post that von Trier sexually harassed her on the set of *Dancer in the Dark* (2000): "While filming in Sweden, he threatened to climb from his room's balcony over to [hers] in the middle of the night with a clear sexual intention, while his wife was in the room next door." In the second volume of *Nymph()maniac* (2013), which von Trier wrote and directed, a character acts out the director's threat to Björk. After an evening of listening to the tales of the titular Nymphomaniac, and professing feminist rhetoric to her, the celibate intellectual Seligman slips into her bed after she has fallen asleep and tries to rape her. In order to address the "individual and systemic abuses as part of the histories of auteurist works" (Marghitu 2018, 493), I will look at von Trier's intermixing of his work with the allegations against him in the closing arguments of this article.

Body Genres and the Hard Core Imagination

Von Trier toys with genre boundaries, and experiments in combining art cinema aesthetics with "shock tactics traditionally associated with gore, porn, and horror" (Beugnet 2007, 36). His filmography relies heavily on the body genres outlined by Linda Williams (1991); *Breaking the Waves* (1996) reimagines the sacrificial themes of the melodrama, *Antichrist* (2009) takes on horror, and *Nymph()maniac* is von Trier's foray into hard core. While the latter film does everything but arouse, it is nonetheless in constant dialogue with the pornographic imagination, including Sadean literature, porno-chic tales of female insatiability, pornotopic fantasies of bodily efficiency, and the dehumanization of black men through "big black dick" scenarios.

Bigger and Better Orgasms: Insatiability and Bodily Efficiency Narratives

Aside from one notable exception,[1] *Nymph()maniac*, volume 1 (2013), shows sex as vigorous, playful, generally joyful, and, most importantly, pleasurable. This depiction reproduces the fantasy of bodily efficiency found in porn: when she reaches adulthood, Joe indefatigably has sex daily with seven to ten men without ever appearing to need lube or a break. Despite no visible condom use or birth-control methods, she successfully avoids sexually transmissible infections and unplanned pregnancies. Moreover, her many enthusiastic partners are entirely dedicated to her pleasure. For example, Joe narrates that "F"[2] knows "without words … exactly what [she] wanted, where he should touch [her] and what he should do. The most sacred goal for F was [her] orgasm." Volume 1 shares many commonalities with pornographic utopias as described by Linda Williams (2014). While *Nymph()maniac* is by no means a "problem-free" pornotopia (74), von Trier's film is nonetheless, like the porno-chic *Insatiable* (Segall 1980), a "narrative about the frequency and facility of sexual satisfaction in which an active, sexually liberated woman pursues her own pleasure" (176). Furthermore, volume 1 and *Insatiable* both very clearly "construct its female protagonists as subjects, and not just as objects, of desire" (176). From climbing onto knotted ropes during physical education class in search of "the sensation," to, as Joe narrates, "the complicated logistics involved with arranging up to ten daily sexual satisfactions" with as many men, the overall arc of volume 1 looks at the discovery and achievement of "more and more circuitous pleasures" (Williams 2014).

BBDs

Beyond insatiability and bodily efficiency, the various acts performed in *Nymph()maniac* have been fragmented by web users as porn-streaming categories; compilations of all the sex scenes in the film were uploaded onto Pornhub shortly after the film's release. Scenes of teenaged Joe, played by Stacy Martin, are tagged with terms like "Celeb," "teen," "Euro," "Pussy Licking," "Ass fuck." Adult Joe's scenes, interpreted by Charlotte Gainsbourg, are dubbed "Milf," "Blowjob," "Handjob." Joe's threesome scene with two black men stands alone as a clip named "Deleted Scene." Predictably, the video is tagged "3some" and "interracial." A commenter on the site whose username is Jacobmorrisseyx expressed his frustration with the clip: "I gave a thumbs down the black men here are not central to the plot just a

Nymph()maniac and the Pornographic Hard Code | 341

16.1 Joe listening as two men argue before attempting double penetration. *Nymph()maniac*, dir. Lars von Trier, Zentropa Films, 2013.

sex scene to sexualized [*sic*] and stereotype black men" (2017). On another popular streaming site, YouPorn, the clip featuring the threesome is described as "Charlotte Gainsbourg have [*sic*] sex with two black dicks" (2016). As Jacobmorrisseyx astutely points out, this scene (fig. 16.1) echoes the dehumanizing white supremacist stereotype of danger and sexual excess that has been projected onto the bodies of black men in movies since *Birth of a Nation* (D.W. Griffith 1915).

Let us note that these two men are the only characters of colour in over five and a half hours of screen time. In this segment, Joe narrates that she sought a "sexual situation in which verbal communication was impossible." From her window, she watches a group of black men who meet in the park in front of her apartment. Presuming that they are unable to speak English, she hires a (very white) translator who, she says, "masters the African languages." Through the negotiations of the translator, a meeting between Joe and one of the men is settled. They will rendezvous in a cheap hotel the next day. Joe is surprised when her date, whom she nicknames "N," brings someone else along with him.

Before (and during) what will turn out to be a very short-lived attempt at double penetration, the two men argue in a language that the subtitles identify as an "African dialect" without bothering to translate their dialogue. The scene emphasizes how unintelligible the two men are and denies them any defining traits beyond their "foreignness" while literally foregrounding their large genitalia. Of course, Joe has a tendency to objectify her male partners, black or white. However, white men have a better chance at being humanized by the narrative. For example, Joe describes "F" as a kind, punctual man who made her smile when she saw him, and she portrays the dominant "K" as a mysterious, skilful, and creative person. By contrast, the two men in the cheap hotel room are, bluntly, a monocultural mass of otherness. For Wesley Morris, to be seen as "a savage," "a walking schlong … renders black men desired on one hand and feared on the other" (2016). Von Trier is fully aware of these myths and has filmed the threesome scene with tongue firmly in cheek. Nonetheless, sarcastic racism is still racism. As Kobena Mercer suggests, such scenes reveal "more about the desires of the hidden and invisible white man behind the camera than they reveal about the black men whose beautiful bodies we see depicted" (1994).

A Sadean Heroine

Beyond its ties to audiovisual porn, *Nymph()maniac* engages heavily with the eighteenth-century pornographic discourse of the Marquis de Sade. Joe's meticulous pursuit of all the pleasures her body can take, combined with the emotional *froideur* with which she goes about life, is akin to female Sadean libertines:

> Charming sex, you will be free; like men, you will enjoy all the delights that nature has made your obligations; you will not have to be constrained in any pleasure. Must the more divine section of humanity be clapped in irons by the less divine section? Ah, smash those chains – nature wants you to smash them! You should have no other limits than your leanings, no other laws than your cravings, no other morals than nature; stop languishing in those barbaric prejudices that caused your charms to fade and imprisoned the godly surges of your hearts. (1795, 281)

From age seven onward, Joe defiantly seeks all the polymorphous pleasures that her body allows. With her friend "B," teenage Joe co-founds a girl gang named The Little Flock. Together they commandeer their lust, reject what they call the "love fixated society," and routinely share their adventures with the other members of the group. The slogan of this little flock, "Mea Vulva, Mea Maxima Vulva," expresses the desired dispersion and expansion of their erotic capability, as well as the rejection of the age-old connection between women's sexuality and guilt. When "B" breaks The Little Flock's oath and falls in love, describing with tenderness the object of her affections, Joe objects contemptuously, stating that "the way you describe it, which should be full of lust, is just a nauseating analysis of his future abilities as father of your child." Joe is embarrassed by and disdainful of romantic feelings. For Joe, like many Sadean heroines, tenderness is "false, a deceit, a trap" (Carter 1976, 25).

The construction of Joe's femininity is part of a wider set of strategies that manipulate the way she is perceived by others in order to reach her goals. Like the sexually voracious and unscrupulous Juliette in Sade's *Les Prospérités du Vice*, Joe "knows how to do her own soliciting and is never the sexual prey, except for the sake of a ruse or a game" (Carter 1976, 80). During her teenage years, for example, she consciously dons porno-normative garb when pursuing sexual partners. Calculating that a schoolgirl outfit will facilitate the loss of her virginity, she dons a pleated skirt and white blouse and wears her hair in braids. Later on, in a competition with her friend "B" to determine who will succeed in having sexual contact with the most men in a short period of time, she wears tiny red vinyl shorts over fishnet tights. It is worth noting that, when she is not hunting for sexual partners, Joe's preferred outfits are large sweaters and knee-length skirts.

Years later, Joe decides that the concept of what she calls "fuck me now clothes" is in need of revision. She therefore creates a character she calls "the piano teacher." Not unlike Michael Haneke's titular heroine in the 2001 film of the same name, Joe's piano-teacher persona carries musical scores and wears glasses, a trench coat, and a white blouse. Dressed in this seemingly wholesome fashion, she removes the spark-plug caps of her automobile in order to lure men eager to prove their virility by fixing the vehicle of a "helpless" woman who is, as she demurely utters, "such an idiot with cars." This helplessness is pure performance: Joe is an able mechanic. For Joe and her Sadean counterparts, "femininity is part of the armor of self-interest" (Carter 1976, 102). Her performance of stereotyped, at times porno-normative femininity always parodies male desire, and consistently reflects her control over the mise-en-scène of her own image.

Bodily Autonomy

Both Joe and Juliette will do whatever it takes to preserve their bodily autonomy, especially when it concerns their reproductive organs. Their devotion to this aim divides the

> threefold process whereby the feminine body was analyzed – qualified and disqualified – as being thoroughly saturated with sexuality; whereby it was

integrated in organic communication with the social body (whose regulated fecundity it was supposed to ensure), the family space (of which it has a substantial and functional element), and the life of children (which it produced and had to guarantee, by virtue of a biologico-moral responsibility lasting through the entire period of the children's education). (Foucault [1976] 1990, 104)

By actively disassociating themselves from their "biologico-ethical responsibility" toward their offspring, Joe and Juliette embody a radical form of womanhood. As in the work of Sade, fertility is an inconvenience, a hindrance to Joe's massive lust. Angela Carter describes Sade's philosophy on this matter: "Since he seeks a complete divorce between sexuality and reproduction, he does not see any value in physical mothering at all. Moral mothering, the care and education of children, is a different matter and should be left to those who have shown themselves competent at it" (Carter 1976, 88). The idea that the maternal instinct is not biological but social appears when Joe explains her reason for leaving her partner, Jerome, and her son, Marcel. Conscious that she does not want to prioritize the needs of her child over her own, she places her son in foster care.

According to Carter, the desacralization of women's reproductive functions frees them so that they can be the determining agents of their own fertility. While there are definite pagan overtones to Joe's sexuality, she vehemently denies the "bankrupt enchantments of the womb" and the "deluded priesthood of a holy reproductive system" (110). Like Sade's Juliette, Joe will insist on separating her sexuality from her fertility. In contrast with *Nymph()maniac*, volume 1, which was characterized by a certain insouciance surrounding the risks of pregnancy, volume 2 is characterized by a heightened awareness about this issue.

Von Trier once suggested in an interview that his films are all about the "clash between ideal and reality" (Smith 2000, 22). I have argued that volume 1 of *Nymph()maniac* borrows the insatiability narratives and fantasies of bodily efficiency of the pornographic genre. The much darker volume 2 displays the tensions between the heroine's unappeasable search for lost pleasure, the limits of her own body, and the social isolation that results from her heterodoxy.

Linda Williams has criticized von Trier for what she considers his punitive approach to Joe's sexuality. She argues that *Nymph()maniac* "has found a way to violate one of the first rules of the genre of pornography: that the pursuit of pleasure should not lead to the punishment of the women who seek it. Even pornography's sadomasochistic variants are only about the achievement of more circuitous pleasures" (2014, 22). Indeed, while volume 1 and porn zealously champion sexual voraciousness, volume 2 shows that Joe's lust leads her to a harrowing experience; her quenchless thirst for pleasure is, in her words, a trajectory "from joy and light" toward "guilt and pain."

When Joe goes to a doctor for the abortion she ardently wants, he forces her to be evaluated by a psychologist to determine if her request is valid. Insulted and humiliated by the lengthy, condescending process, Joe uses her knowledge as a med-school dropout and performs the abortion herself. This brutal and methodical scene expresses how "the truth of the womb is that it is an organ like any other organ, more useful than the appendix, less useful than the colon but not much use to you at all if you do not wish to utilize its sole function, that of bearing children" (Carter 1976, 76). Indeed, at this stage in Joe's life, her uterus is no more useful to her than her tonsils. Worse, the mere possibility that sexual activity may lead to a second pregnancy is tremendously anxiety-inducing for her. Joe's motivation to carry out her own abortion, this excruciating and stubborn attempt to take control over her own flesh, is akin to the reasons why she visits the BDSM dominant she calls "K." Both instances are Joe's way to regain mastery over her own her body and bodily reactions. Unfortunately for Joe, she is not entirely a Sadean heroine. In Sade's philosophico-pornographic worldview, a protagonist prospers as long as she misbehaves – but to thrive as a leading lady in a von Trier film is a nearly impossible feat.

Women in Sade's novels, like Mme de St-Ange in *La Philosophie dans le boudoir* ([1795] 1983) or Juliette in *Les prospérités du vice* ([1797] 1969), preserve or even elevate their social status thanks to their sins. Not unlike these two, Joe does well financially when she leaves her straight job and, thanks to what she calls her "rather unscrupulous" nature, gets hired as an extortionist. With her "considerable experience with men and sex," she excels at her job. However, where the happily sinful women in de Sade's novels never feel negative emotions, their brains functioning like a "computer programmed to produce two results … financial profit and libidinal gratification" (Carter 1976, 79), Joe's emotional life is rather more delicate, and she will suffer from deep solitude. By choosing to chase her lust and rejecting the "obsessive sacrifices" (76) of motherhood, she ends up lonely and miserable. As the end of volume 2 reveals, after she thinks that she has made a "new, maybe first friend," her trust is bitterly betrayed (fig. 16.2).

The hardships that Joe endures in the second volume are characteristic of von Trier's work, which notoriously comprises a series of women characters who go through harrowing experiences. Indeed, nearly all of the director's films feature women protagonists who endure prodigiously intense physical and emotional suffering. His obsessive mise-en-scène of (white, cis-gendered) women in pain

16.2 Joe walking away from a car she set on fire in the context of her job as a debt collector. *Nymph()maniac*, dir. Lars von Trier, Zentropa Films, 2013.

has resulted in a number of interpretations that view his work as unambiguously misogynistic. To many, the hardships of his protagonists are the creation of a sadist who takes pleasure in simultaneously making his female characters and his audience suffer. To others, he is a provocative feminist whose films critique the patriarchal context that cause this suffering (Badley 2015; Makarushka 1998). David Gritten, in his article preceding the release of *Antichrist*, contends that "his attitude to women, or specifically the female characters he creates in his films, is bizarre, bordering on creepy. The Great Dane, we may deduce, seems to get a kick out of putting his screen women in jeopardy or in violent situations" (2009). Wendy Ide wrote after seeing *Antichrist*, "Lars von Trier, we get it. You really, really don't like women" (2009). Jonathan Romney observed after viewing *Nymph()maniac* that "in the end, von Trier does seem to be simply punishing another heroine" (2014). Others emphasize his philosophical ambivalence. According to Serge Kaganski, it is "hard to establish [if *Nymph()maniac*] is misandrist or misanthropic, feminist or misogynistic, philosexual or sexophobic … with Lars, everything is bifid, reversible"[3] (2013). Yet Damien Aubel sees in Joe a "sublime creation, his most magnificent heroine: a woman finally freed of the social, artistic, intellectual processes that have always made out the sexuality of women to be some sort of monstrosity. Here, LVT is pretty much on the side of women"[4] (Aubel 2014). For film critic Odile Tremblay, von Trier's suffering melds with Joe's. She assesses that he "is looking for himself and wanders, in palpable pain, tangled like his heroine in the Judeo-Christian hank that strangles him" (2014).

#Metoo and Martyred Femininity

Nymph()maniac adroitly juggles with feminist talking points; it's aggressively pro-abortion, addresses questions of gender performativity and slut-shaming. It consistently mocks male weakness, and Joe's "little flock" is a sex-positive coven. Seligman justifies, in terms that resemble Valerie Solanas's s.c.u.m. *Manifesto* ([1967] 2004), Joe wanting to shoot an old lover as her "[fighting] back against the gender that had been oppressing and mutilating and killing [her] and billions of women." These talking points, however, are as empty as Seligman's promise in the final scene to make sure that Joe won't be disturbed when she sleeps.

Before Björk's allegations, I leaned toward interpreting Joe's suffering as the result of the confrontation between the pornotopia that she aspires to and von Trier's "new extremist" penchant for depicting psychological and physical misery. I thought that the film expressed Louse J. Kaplan's view that there are no safe choices for women within patriarchy (1989), and that "if compliance is a form of self-destruction – a perversion – non-compliance as an indictment of normative values leads to a communal recrimination and retribution" (Makarushka 1998, 67). I saw von Trier's heroines as stumbling through the unsatisfying imbalance between conformity, revolt, and self-destruction. I firmly agreed with Linda Badley, who argued that von Trier "makes female suffering unwatchable by elevating provocation to the level of meta-commentary and meta-culture" (Badley 2010, 149). I understood his films as "psychodramas in which gender roles are metaphoric projections in a role-playing project whose core is an urgent identity politic" (70).

In light of Björk's #MeToo allegations about von Trier, the disturbing similarity between his threat to visit her hotel room at night "with sexual intent" and Seligman surreptitiously slipping into Joe's bed to rape her, understanding the on-screen misery of his protagonists as a critique of patriarchal constructs is hardly plausible anymore. Von Trier once claimed that he "is always the woman in his films" (Aftab 2009). After her experience on the set of *Dancer in the Dark*, Björk explained von Trier's identification with his women characters in this way: "You can take quite sexist film directors like Woody Allen or Stanley Kubrick and still they are the one that provide the soul to their movies. In Lars von Trier's case it is not so and he knows it. He needs a female to provide his work soul. And he envies them and hates them for it. So he has to destroy them during the filming. And hide the evidence" (Heath 2011).

When I read feminist theorists who argued that the misogynistic situations in which von Trier's leading ladies were representations of the director's hatred of women, I used to think, "Surely it's not that simple? These women feel so real!

His identification is clearly with them – how could someone make such elaborate and precise portraits of suffering without having empathy for their subjects?" Following Björk's #MeToo testimony, what I previously understood as intensely affective observations of the cruelty of patriarchal constructs turned out to be von Trier's externalization of his (very real) misogynistic urges, a mise-en-scène of his creepy fantasies. I confess, I'm embarrassed it took me this long to catch up. I suppose I was swayed by the intimacy with which he showed women in pain; I foolishly convinced myself that it came from a place of empathy when it fact, as feminist theorists like Linda Williams have eloquently pointed out all along, it came from a place of sadistic fascination.

While I've studied his work intensely for extended periods of time, I may not watch a von Trier film again. I certainly won't see his next film, *The House that Jack Built*, which follows twelve years in the life of a (male) serial killer. With no leading lady to "provide [a] soul" (Björk 2017) for the director to cannibalize, to tolerate the combination of von Trier's juggling with themes of sexual violence and his abusing of his power as an employer to sexually harass an actress is too much to ask of me as a spectator. That, and, as *Reddit* user tcex28 remarks, "The trailer look[s] like utter unmitigated wank."

I have woven a dialogue between *Nymph()maniac* and the pornographic imagination while addressing the troubling mirroring of the behaviour of one of von Trier's characters and the director's sexualized threat to a worker. In the same way that it now seems impossible to discuss Leni Riefenstahl's work without mention of fascism, or D.W. Griffith's entire oeuvre without contemplating his ties to the KKK, I can no longer look at von Trier's films and the onscreen suffering of his female protagonists without addressing his real-life penchant for sexual harassment.

If one were feeling magnanimous, one could argue that von Trier is processing his inner demons through his films, that the final scene of *Nymph()maniac* is a form of confession, and that Seligman's getting shot by Joe symbolizes his desire to eliminate this part of himself. I am not feeling magnanimous. Von Trier recently denied sexually harassing Björk and painted *himself*, of all people, as the victim of the Icelandic star's onset capriciousness, and lamented that he felt that the media insufficiently covered his denial (Sharf 2018). He went on to express how "the problem is that the internet is something that we had not imagined would affect our lives so much" (Sharf 2018). Indeed, as von Trier so astutely points out, the internet has impacted the lives of billions of people in myriads of ways. One of these ways is that social media has provided feminists across the globe with "the tools to connect, build relationships, and organize" (Soucie, Parry, and

Cousineau 2018, 223). Digital activism has led millions of women worldwide to come out with their stories of abuse. Thanks to these stories, Björk wrote in a post on social media that she was "inspired by the women everywhere who are speaking up online" (Björk 2017), and after seventeen years of silence about her ordeal, felt that she could finally be heard. For von Trier, the way the internet has changed people's lives is a "problem." For others, it's a revolution.

Afterword

Ironically, the hypocrisy, cowardice, and hubris of men is a recurring theme in the films of von Trier: "The men in my films tend to just be stupid, to have theories about things and destroy everything" (Aftab 2009). The director's frank contempt for maleness is visible throughout his filmography; the idea of male power is consistently mocked and deflated. His casting of male actors is often imbued with caustic wit that mocks conventional ideas of manliness. For example, Kiefer Sutherland, who is known for his role as a counter-terrorism agent who saves the world ad nauseam in the American TV show *24*, plays in von Trier's *Melancholia* a pedantic and cowardly patriarch. Instead of being present for his family when the end of the world approaches, he swallows the cyanide pills his wife has kept aside to offer their child a painless death should the apocalypse happen.

Stellan Skarsgard, who was cast as Seligman in *Nymph()maniac*, has not once but twice played the role of a secular confessor to a sexually voracious woman. At the beginning of his career, he starred in the blue movie *Anita: Swedish Nymphet* (1973). The plot of *Anita* resembles closely the story of *Nymph()maniac*: Erik, the character played by Skarsgard, finds a beaten and bruised woman and invites her to his home, where she tells him about the sad tale of her "nymphomania." The young man, a psychology student, decides to try to save her. His treatment initially consists of his experimenting with talk therapy, but gradually he develops feelings for his patient, and his love and devotion cure Anita of her sex addiction. The film eagerly wants us to believe in the healing abilities of Skarsgard's character; he is the "good man" who serves as a potent emotional panacea to the beautiful, damaged woman who needs rescue.

The character played by Skarsgard forty years later, Seligman, also takes the role of therapist/confessor and comes close to "healing" the sexually avid woman he has listened to. After having told her story, she is at peace, resolved to rid herself of her addiction and glad to finally have a connection with someone that doesn't revolve around physical pleasure. But after she goes to sleep, Seligman betrays her trust on the whim of his flaccid cock. This final scene self-consciously mocks the position of "deluded rationalist male figure" (Badley 2015, 198) by exposing him as a hypocritical windbag. The confessor has revealed himself as corrupt; her confession was for naught.

NOTES

1 In the scene in which Joe is "relieved of her virginity," the young man she has chosen for this task, Jerôme, penetrates her anus without her consent. She describes the experience as "hurt[ing] like hell" and says that it made her swear she'd never sleep with anyone again.
2 Most of the characters Joe mentions are identified with a single letter.
3 My translation of "difficile de dire si [Nymph()maniac] est misandre ou misanthrope, féministe ou misogyne, philosexuel ou sexophobe, hors morale (Joe) ou confit de morale (Seligman): avec Lars, tout est toujours bifide, réversible" (2013).
4 My translation of "sa plus [s]ublime création, sa plus belle héroïne: une femme enfin affranchie des procédés sociaux, artistiques, intellectuels, qui ont toujours fait de la sexualité de ces dames une monstruosité. Ici, LVT est plutôt du côté des femmes" (2015).

REFERENCES

Aftab, Kaleem. 2009. "Lars von Trier: 'It's Good That People Boo.'" *Independent* (UK), 29 May 2009. http://www.independent.co.uk/arts-entertainment/films/features/lars-von-trier-its-good-that-people-boo-1692406.html.

Aubel, Damien. 2014. "Nymphomaniac: La raison libertine." *Transfuge*, January 2014. http://www.transfuge.fr/actu-cine-nymphomaniac,270.html.

Badley, Linda. 2010. *Lars von Trier*. Urbana: University of Illinois Press.

– 2015a. "*Nymph()maniac* as Retro *Scandinavian Blue*." *Journal of Scandinavian Cinema* 5, no. 2 (June): 191–204. https://doi.org/10.1386/jsca.5.2.191_1.

– 2015b. "'Fill All My Holes': *Nymph()maniac*'s Sadean Discourse." *Ekphrasis: Images, Cinema, Theory, Media* 2: 21–39.

Beugnet, Martine. 2007. *Cinema and Sensation, French Film and the Art of Transgression*. Edinburgh: Edinburgh University Press.

– 2011. "The Wounded Screen." In *The New Extremism in Cinema: From France to Europe*, edited by Tanya Horeck and Tina Kendall, 29–42. Edinburgh: Edinburgh University Press.

Björk 2017. Facebook post, 17 September 2017. https://www.facebook.com/bjork/posts/10155777444371460.

Carter, Angela. 1976. *The Sadean Woman*. New York: Pantheon Books.

Foucault, Michel. [1976] 1990. *History of Sexuality. Vol. 1: An Introduction*. Translated by Robert Hurley. New York: Vintage.

Fuller, Graham. 2014. "No Ordinary Joe: Sex and the Single Woman in von Trier's Latest." *Modern Painters*, April.

Gritten, David. 2009. "Lars von Trier: Anti-Christ? Or Just Anti Women?" *Telegraph* (UK), 16 July 2009. http://www.telegraph.co.uk/culture/film/starsandstories/5843594/Lars-Von-Trier-Antichrist-Or-just-anti-women.html.

Heath, Chris. 2011. "Lars and His Real Girls." *GQ*, 17 October. https://www.gq.com/story/lars-von-trier-gq-interview-bjork-john-c-reilly-kirsten-dunst-nicole-kidman-extras.

Horeck, Tanya, and Tina Kendall. 2011. "What Is the New Extremism?" Introduction to *The New Extremism in Cinema: From France to Europe*, edited by Tanya Horeck and Tina Kendall, 1–17. Edinburgh: Edinburgh University Press.

Ide, Wendy. 2009. "Antichrist at the Cannes Film Festival." *Times Online* (UK), 18 May 2009. https://www.thetimes.co.uk/article/antichrist-at-the-cannes-film-festival-cxqsq2nn65j.

Jacobmorrisseyx. 2017. "*Nymphomaniac* Deleted Scene." *Pornhub*. https://www.pornhub.com/view_video.php?viewkey=ph55da42ad3d219.

Kaganski, Serge. 2013. "Nymphomaniac-volume 1, féministe ou misogyne?" *Les Inrockuptibles*, 31 December 2013. https://www.lesinrocks.com/cinema/films-a-l-affiche/nymphomaniac-volume-1/.

Kaplan, Louise J. 1991. *Female Perversions: The Temptations of Emma Bovary*. New York: Doubleday.

Makarushka, Irena. 1998. "Transgressing Goodness in *Breaking the Waves*." *Journal of Religion and Film* 2, no. 1 (April). http://www.unomaha.edu/jrf/breaking.htm.

Marghitu, Stefania. 2018. "It's Just Art": Auteur Apologism in the Post-Weinstein Era." *Feminist Media Studies* 18, no. 3 (April): 491–4.

Mercer, Kobena. 1994. *Welcome to the Jungle: New Positions in Black Cultural Studies*. New York: Routledge.

Morris, Wesley. 2016. "Why Pop Culture Just Can't Deal With Black Male Sexuality." *New York Times Magazine*, 27 October. https://www.nytimes.com/interactive/2016/10/30/magazine/black-male-sexuality-last-taboo.html.

Mumford, Gwilym. 2018. "Michael Haneke: #MeToo Has Led to a Witch Hunt 'Coloured by a Hatred of Men.'" *Guardian* (UK), 12 February 2018. https://www.theguardian.com/film/2018/feb/12/michael-haneke-metoo-witch-hunt-coloured-hatred-men.

Parry, Diana, ed. 2018. *Feminisms in Leisure Studies: Advancing a Fourth Wave*. New York: Routledge.

Romney, Jonathan. 2014. "The Girl Can't Help It." *Film Comment*, April. http://www.filmcomment.com/article/nymphomaniac-lars-von-trier/.

Sade, Donatien Alphonse François de. [1797] 1969. *Juliette, ou les prospérités du vice*. Paris: Le monde en 10:18.

– [1795] 1983. *La philosophie dans le boudoir*. Paris: France Loisirs.

Sharf, Zack. 2018. "Lars von Trier Says He 'Hugged' Björk and Did Not Sexually Harass Her, Thinks #MeToo Is 'Brilliant' If Used Correctly." *Indiewire*, 12 May. http://www.indiewire.com/2018/05/lars-von-trier-hugged-bjork-not-harassed-dancer-in-the-dark-1201966799/.

Smith, Gavin. 2000. "Imitation of Life: Gavin Smith Interviews the Great Dane." *Film Comment*, September–October.

Solanas, Valerie. [1967.] 2004. s.c.u.m. *Manifesto*. London: Verso.

Soucie, S.M.A., D.C. Parry, and L.S. Cousineau. 2018. "The Fourth Wave: What #MeToo Can Teach Us about Millennial Mobilization, Intersectionality, and Men's Accountability." In *Feminisms in Leisure Studies: Advancing a Fourth Wave*, edited by Diana Parry, 149–64. New York: Routledge.

tcex28. 2018. "Lars Von Trier's 'The House That Jack Built' Is Repulsive, Toxic Trash [Cannes Review]." *Reddit*, May 2018. https://www.reddit.com/r/GamerGhazi/comments/8jkm51/lars_von_triers_the_house_that_jack_built_is/.

Tremblay, Odile. 2014. "Portrait de Lars von Trier en nymphomane." *Le Devoir*, 22 March. http://www.ledevoir.com/culture/cinema/403181/portrait-de-lars-von-trier-en-nymphomane.

Williams, Linda. 1991. "Film Bodies: Gender, Genre, and Excess." *Film Quarterly* 44, no. 4 (Summer): 2–13.

– 2014. "Cinema's Sex Acts." *Film Quarterly* 67, no. 4 (Summer): 9–25.

YouPorn. n.d. "Charlotte Gainsbourg xxx sex." Accessed May 2018. https://www.youporn.com/watch/11793543/charlotte-gainsbourg-xxx-sex/.

MEDIAGRAPHY

C.K., Louis, dir. 2018. *I Love You, Daddy*. New York: The Orchard, 2018. Film.

Griffith, D.W., dir. 1915. *The Birth of a Nation*. Epoch Producing Corp. Internet Archive. https://archive.org/details/dw_griffith_birth_of_a_nation.

Polanski, Roman, dir. 1968. *Rosemary's Baby*. New York: Criterion, 2012. DVD.

– dir. 1974. *Chinatown*. Hollywood: Paramount, 2017. DVD.

– dir. 1979. *Tess*. New York: Criterion, 2014. DVD.

Segall, Stu, dir. 1980. *Insatiable*. Los Angeles: Caballero Home Video, 1980. Film.

von Trier, Lars, dir. 1996. *Breaking the Waves*. Santa Monica: Artisan, 2000. DVD.

– dir. 2000. *Dancer in the Dark*. Hvidovre, Denmark: Zentropa Films. Film.

– dir. 2009. *Antichrist*. New York, NY: Criterion, 2009. DVD.

– dir. 2013. *Nymph()maniac*. Vol. I. Hvidovre, Denmark: Zentropa Films, 2013. Netflix. https://www.netflix/dp/B01ARVPCOA/.

– dir. 2014. *Nymph()maniac*. Vol. 2. Hvidovre, Denmark: Zentropa Films, 2014. Netflix. https://www.netflix.com/dp/B01ARVPCOA/.

– dir. 2018. *The House That Jack Built*. Cannes Film Festival. Film.

Wickman, Torgny, dir. 1973. *Anita: Swedish Nymphet*. Swedish Film Production.

17

Porn Fast

SHAKA MCGLOTTEN

First, a trigger warning. If you are currently abstaining from porn, this essay is itself pornographic. For the rest of you, enjoy.

Confession 1: I Confess

I confess: I do not know what to make of addiction. I have sat weeping in twelve-step meetings admitting my powerlessness. As a cultural critic, I have argued that addiction is a concept with a history, a category that names, while simultaneously bringing into existence, behaviours that a culture or individual finds troubling. I am also a spiritual practitioner in a Direct Realization Tantric tradition. Not unlike some therapeutic perspectives, in my tradition, addiction names a tension in how I am relating to the world; it is symptom, not cause.

To confess to an addiction to online porn is part of the longer history of what Foucault famously called the "incitement to discourse" (Foucault [1976] 1990). Modern selves are constituted when they confess their secrets, especially the secrets of their sexual histories. But confessions also constitute a vulnerable self, one potentially open to the world, to some other way of being constituted. Abstaining from porn sets fasters on a path suspended between normative social attitudes about sex on the one hand and practices of self-making on the other.

This paper is a first endeavour toward recording some observations about porn fasts, efforts to suspend and detox from the use of online pornography. It includes confessions (my own and those of others), analysis of the claims promoted by fasting boosters, and conversations with some men from my spiritual community who together took a break from porn in the summer of 2015.

Porn Fest

When I say "porn fast," people hear "porn fest." Abundance, excess, and carnivalesque exuberance: "porn fest" isn't a surprising response, given the degree to which pornography has saturated even non-pornographic mediascapes, to say nothing of ordinary life. Indeed, for some social groups, like many gay men, the demand to participate in the increasingly user-generated economies of porn production seems nearly inescapable. Sessions on gay social media apps will nearly always include requests like "Can you send a dick pic?" Dick pics are so ubiquitous as to have almost lost their force to excite.

As I began my own porn fast in preparation for this essay, I feared the scope of the task ahead. Would I simply avoid visiting my favourite porn sites (for the record, aebn.net, pornhub.com, dudetubeonline.com)? Would I delete an increasing number of pornographic Tumblrs from my bookmarks? Would I leave the secret Facebook groups I belonged to? Would I tell lovers not to sext me? Or did porn fasting simply mean not using porn to get off? In the end, I assumed the latter, although this isn't the approach advised by the fasting resources I found, which say that one should avoid all "artificial sexual stimulation," whatever "artificial" means. It may be that I did not really do a fast at all, since my gaze repeatedly turned to this or that Grindr profile.

Confession 2: Sex Machine

Look up and listen to James Brown's song "Sex Machine." Yeah, right now. Got it? Good. You can keep it playing in the background as you read.

I got my first computer in 1999, an Apple clamshell laptop. Remember those? I bought a video camera when I picked up the computer. At first I could only jerk off to porn or with others via cam sex when my roommates were away. (I was in a house, but this problem should be familiar to anyone who has ever lived in a dorm.) But with Wi-Fi on the scene, I could go to my bedroom and edge with a cute South African teenager, or carry my laptop with its briefcase handle onto campus, where I could use the public network to arrange to meet with someone in one of the campus's many cruisy bathrooms.

The capacity to expand sexual possibilities provided by my notebook or later mobile devices are noteworthy in part for the diverse "carnal resonances" they produced, to borrow a term from Susanna Paasonen (2011). I enter into an erotic symbiosis with these technologies, neither in control nor fully subject to them (Paasonen 2011, 13). They don't only serve to provide me access to sexual encounters, or to pornography; they are sex machines unto themselves, and together we co-produce a panoply of erotic affordances (Schüll 2014, 19). They are what Paul Preciado calls techno-sexual artifacts (2013). In *Porn Archives*, queer theorist Tim Dean (2014) wonders whether sexting is "a novel kind of foreplay" (8). It is. So is swiping. But here's the question: to whom or what is the foreplay directed? A Grindr hookup, myself, or the device at my fingertips?

In *Testo Junkie*, Preciado (2013) extends Foucault's analyses of technologies of sex into the twentieth and twenty-first centuries. For Preciado, pornography and pharmacology are the unacknowledged engines of a post–World War II capitalism, which he calls "hot, psychotropic [and] punk" (2013, n.p.). Pharmacopornographic capitalism produces the "gender-sex industrial complex" (n.p.), which hails us into desiring subjectivities, expanding the possible array of these subjectivities even as they continue to bind us to binary sex/gender systems. My Apple clamshell was not merely an aid that helped me to realize my desires; rather, it fundamentally shaped my queer identity as one always already tied to a technologically enabled pornographic virtuality.[1] In "Transmaterialities," Karen Barad describes virtuality as "the ongoing thought experiment the world performs with itself" (2015, 396). This might seem like my confession, but the question of agency lingers. Perhaps my sexual sovereignty is simply some immanence in a masturbatory dance with itself.

Confession 3: The Fast Strikes Back

A former student and nascent yogi agrees to porn fast with me. Five days in, he writes to me, "Blue balls have set in," and asks, "This isn't a masturbation fast right? Please say no." I tell him no. But, again, this is not the approach recommended by most of the resources I've studied. The Nofap community advises "no PMO" ("Rebooting from Porn Addiction," 2017) – no porn, no masturbation, no orgasm. For ninety days. I've had to draw on my competitive streak to get motivated.

~~Day 1: The last porn I watch is a Max Sohl film for Treasure Island Media (TIM) video on Aebn.net called *Fuck Holes 3* (2015). TIM used to be on the cutting edge of things when it began releasing its bareback videos in the late nineties. This is an unusual video for them. Maybe the introduction of PrEP has inspired them to switch things up – the video features a straight gangbang, as well as sex between~~

~~a cis guy and a trans woman. Is this still gay porn? Are they responding to their customers' desensitization to regular old gay bareback porn? Or are they hoping to maintain their transgressive cultural cache by venturing into new territories?~~[2]

Scratch that – I have to reset. I used porn Tumblrs the next day and contributed new nudes to the secret Facebook groups I belong to. This might be harder than I thought. I add domains to the Self-Control app to block my access to certain websites, and I deactivate my Facebook account. I don't delete bookmarks, though – do you know how hard it was to find these Tumblrs? Tumblr, in case you didn't already know, is where porn lives these days, curated for your pleasure by aficionados and amateur pornoneironauts.

The first few days of my fast finds me more attuned to sex as an ambient potentiality. My friend writes to me again, this time describing a scene in the sauna at the YMCA.

> Scene: YMCA Steam Room. I sit alone, naked, sprawled, sweat seeping from everywhere. Another man enters the room. We greet each other in the reserved, knowing way men do before they know what the sexuality atmosphere is – with a nod and some garbled mumble. He sits at the opposite end of the bench from me. We do not talk the entire time after this. First, he grabs his right foot and begins stretching it. He does the same with his other foot and calf. Then he stands up, turns around to face the bench, and begins doing push-ups with his hands on the bench, so that he doesn't go all the way down to the floor. Well, his whole body doesn't go all the way down to the floor. One part of him did. I sit, seeing how far sideways I can look without moving my eyes. Pretty far. Far enough. Then he rises and returns to sitting on the towel, paying me no mind. Judging by his mustache, he was either a California Highway Patrol Officer from the late 1970s or a member in a current iteration of the Village People, which would have been more appropriate given our location.

I start to write a response:

> I have my own scene: after walking past the dry sauna in his boxers, the guy came back by sans boxers. Not obviously gay. But anyone who joins an already naked man in a sauna is at least heteroflexible. He perched himself on the edge of the bench, junk jutting forward. I pretended nonchalance as I got a semi watching him watch his rivulets of sweat roll down his torso, dripping down his cock onto the floor. When I go to the showers to cool off, he

followed me and set himself up with a clear line of sight. We watch each other get hard …

I think better of my reply, delete the draft, and then write back to him, referring vaguely to my own sauna scene and then gently scolding him for skirting the no-porn rules.

"Oh my," he replies, "I didn't even realize the implications of my story sharing for the porn fast! I think I'm still kosher because my situation just led to blue balls. Also I didn't seek it out. Ugh, now I'm justifying and rationalizing outrageous nonsense! Point taken Mr S. Point taken."

A few more days in, and I've flatlined. This, according to the FAQs at NoFap and Reddit threads, is to be expected. I feel deflated, like I don't have any desire. No matter how critical I am of the motivations behind fasters' efforts, not to mention the ways they draw on science to justify their claims, my own experiences uncannily mirror what they describe. Maybe they're right? I download Grindr, the now infamous geolocative app that presaged every other mobile dating app. I've been off of it for months (a user's profile explained why: "Grindr: the trash can of gay culture"). Just as I'm deleting the app again, I get a message from a young visitor to the area. I take him to the gym, the sauna, then my apartment.

Not too bad, I think. If giving up porn means having more sex, then that's a good thing, right?

Of course, using Grindr can look a lot like compulsive porn viewing, even if one puts to one side the constant demand to share nudes. A popular gif makes the meme rounds (fig. 17.1). It adapts a Roy Lichtenstein comic image for the age of the swipe: a man gazes into a woman's face and swipes left, swipes left, swipes left forever.

Desires, and social relations, have been gamified. Intimacy, or its potentiality, is reduced to the electrical charge of your body brushing against the capacitive screen of your smartphone.

Solitary Vice

When I was eighteen, I went to my first adult store in San Antonio, Texas. Heart racing, I bought a compilation pack – remember those? Compilation packs are sold like day-old bread – they are out-of-date porn magazines packaged together and wrapped in plastic. You can't see what you're getting beyond the magazine on the top. I used the magazines as one might expect, and I also provided myself with

17.1 "Swipe Left" GIF inspired by the art of Roy Lichtenstein. 9GAG, 2015. https:/9gag.com/gag/aGwLj5X/roy-lichtenstein-on-tinder.

an alibi (Waugh 1996). I was studying art, and so these were my models. I laid tracing paper over the images I liked the most and followed the lines of bodies, cocks, bedroom eyes. I threw the magazines away but kept the tracings for years.

I began my own intermittent porn fasts in 2009. I felt bored with porn. I'd get off and then just sit around kinda blah. Or stay up later than I meant to. I'd use it when I was lonely, at night before bed. What might happen if I didn't use porn for a bit, I began to wonder? In the summer of 2015, I undertook a fast with a group of men from my spiritual community. One of my fellow fasters' motivations echoed my own: "If I become aware of some pattern, then I want to see it and see it as clearly as I can, so I cannot be totally bound up in it and by it. There's a sense that porn fasting was part of the movement toward greater freedom. Using porn in a repetitive [way] … I didn't want to do that anymore." My first fast in 2009 hadn't really affected my anti-anti-porn stance. I viewed abstinence less as an austerity than an experiment that might open something up. More recent fasts, including the one in 2015 and the one I undertook as I drafted a version of this essay for a conference, did not result in any new certainties, a fact that speaks to the ambivalence of sex as well as to life-hacking practices of self-optimization. I went back to porn. I still felt lonely. Nothing had been transcended.

Thomas Laqueur's (2004) cultural history of masturbation, *Solitary Vice*, traces the emergence of modern anxieties about self-pleasure to the early eighteenth century. Although religious traditions frowned on the practice, it wasn't until the publication of *Onania* sometime in the early 1700s that masturbation became a cultural phenomenon; it was a tied to broader cultural concerns about the rise of other private pleasures, like reading. Anti-masturbation campaigns may have been the first sex-based meme. Others, of course, have followed.

Earlier medical quackery saw in it a range of dangers, including "spinal tuberculosis, epilepsy, pimples, madness, general wasting, and an early death" (Greenblatt 2004). We inherit this cultural baggage even as medical science has since shifted positions, arguing instead for masturbation's naturalness if not its benefits. Yet science is both appealed to and resisted – remember what happened to Surgeon General Joycelyn Elders when she dared suggest that we might talk openly to students about masturbation?

Digging into the confessional discourses of porn fasters and aspirants, one finds many of the anxieties about the solitary vice repackaged in new, digitally savvy forms that make secular appeals to scientific knowledge.

Your Brain on Porn

Yourbrainonporn.com explicitly appeals to scientific knowledge to understand how people develop addictions to online pornography, and how they might recover. In particular, they turn to neuroscience to try to understand the effects of Internet pornography on the brain, as well as how the brain's neuroplasticity offers the promise of something different. But the site also comes across as defensive – thus far, there is little scientific consensus about sexual addictions generally, much less addiction to online pornography. Efforts to include categories like sexual addiction, hypersexuality, and porn-induced erectile dysfunction in the DSM have thus far failed. Much of the difficulty has to do with the challenges in defining these pathologies, or in distinguishing them from compulsions more broadly.[3] Just to take one example, for some researchers who argue on behalf of the medicalization of sexual addiction, hypersexual disorder can be defined as having an orgasm a day for a period of six months. But for whom would such a daily practice be a problem? (Reay, Attwood, and Gooder 2013, 10).

There is also a resolute heterosexism at work here, evident even on Yourbrainonporn's current splash page, which begins with a description of the Coolidge effect: the gradual disinterest in the same sexual partner. But the examples in this experiment about bed death are straight rats, which are not exactly representative of the diverse complexities of human sexual expression.

Nofap.com began as a thread on Internet hub Reddit and has since evolved into a dedicated online community devoted to helping its members go fap-free. (Fapping is onomatopoeic internet slang for masturbation.) Nofap focuses less on the science – they acknowledge it's contentious – and instead focus on collecting reams of anecdotal data about its users' experiences. They do, however, direct fasters – whom they call "fapstronauts" – to yourbrainonporn.com. Part of what distinguishes NoFap's approach to "porn recovery" is that it seeks to gamify the experience, offering an array of challenges, as well as different "modes" – from simply abstaining from viewing porn to Hard Mode, which entails abstaining entirely from porn viewing, masturbation, and orgasm, which they abbreviate as PMO.

Another is Monk Mode, in which users not only abstain from PMO for a period of time but also abstain from sexual imagery, sexual fantasy, and sex itself. They may even add other austerities, like an intense exercise regimen – what they call "disciplines." I find Monk Mode extremely seductive: I want the no-PMO, and I want to add it to veganism, a fitness program, therapy, and an hour-long daily seated meditation practice.

I should point out that, unlike some other porn recovery programs, Yourbrainonporn and Nofap do not seek to legislate porn, but they do encourage its users to end their porn use entirely, and they say that "most people who have achieved reboot decide to cut porn out of their lives forever. There is little, if anything, redeeming about pornography. It is an unnatural superstimulus" ("Rebooting from Porn Addiction," 2017).

Fightthenewdrug is another site. This one, like those I have already described, also frames itself as secular and as not seeking to oppose porn per se. However, as Samantha Allen (2015) from the *Daily Beast* has pointed out, it is a Utah-based organization founded entirely by Mormons, so this claim is disingenuous. Jason Carroll, one of its founders, although he is no longer listed on the website, is a leading Mormon anti-gay activist who fought gay marriage all the way to the Supreme Court. One of the organization's most visible campaigns took place in

San Francisco, where they paid for billboards that read "Porn Kills Love." Allen and *Harlot Magazine*'s Lauren Parker (2015) both argue that this location was not accidental; it targets a city known for its sexually progressive attitudes. I won't spend much time on the site here, but I do recommend Parker's scathing takedown. A choice takeaway: "FTND is a fancy version of your asshole grandpa bitching about kids and their selfie sticks."

Rebooting

Yourbrainonporn and Nofap both describe the process of recovering from destructive porn use as "rebooting." The idea here is "to restore these neural pathways to factory settings, so to speak" ("About," n.d.). Both sites argue that after ninety days, you have directed the neuroplasticity of your brain toward its original, non-porn-addled state, repairing the physical and psychological harms caused by pornography addiction, like erectile dysfunction or shame or intimacy troubles. As I noted earlier, all "artificial sexual stimulation" is off limits.

In my book *Virtual Intimacies* (McGlotten 2013), I looked to the ways that digitally mediated intimacies are framed as queer, as failed forms of real intimacy. My response to these widespread beliefs was to think both about what constitutes real intimacy – normative ideas about coupling and kids, economic achievement, you know the drill – as well as to point to the ways that intimacies, including nonrelational ones, proliferate in the digital age (Roach 2015). All intimacies are virtual, and the virtual conditions the emergence of new ways of being-with oneself and others.

A couple of weeks into the fast I undertook for this project, I realize that my own factory settings might be best described as "slutty."

Rebooting promises powers that nofappers often describe as part of the appeal of fapstinence: confidence boost, increased sexual interest from others, creative mojo, and social acuity. They also argue that there are subtler signs of a successful reboot, including feeling that one has "a clearer head and [has] stopped fantasizing about pornographic sexual situations" ("Rebooting from Porn Addiction," 2017). But symptom and cure look alike – brain fog is both a sign of porn addiction and one of the experiences people describe along the road to recovery.

But superpowers are not the most important reasons people go fap-free, although, as I'll describe in a moment, they are a central focus of many, with important political implications. Most people find their way to these porn-recovery resources because they feel like something is off. For many, it is that they do not feel like they can connect emotionally with themselves and others, and often (and this is key) they have an erectile dysfunction they attribute to porn.

What becomes apparent, after spending time digging through these sites and especially the discussion forums, is that so much here is built on normative ideologies about what constitutes healthy sexuality. This is a point repeatedly made by critics of concepts of sex addiction. For example, in their 1988 article "The Myth of Sexual Compulsivity," Martin Levine and Richard Troiden argue that cultural attitudes are largely responsible for shaping what gets called compulsive sexual behaviour. They write that "sexual compulsion and sexual addiction are value judgments parading as therapeutic diagnoses" (360). In "Inventing Sex," Barry Reay, Nina Attwood, and Claire Gooder (2013) build on this work, criticizing the sex-addiction concept as "an archetypal, modern, sexual invention" (2). They argue that it is comprised of "social opportunism, diagnostic amorphism, therapeutic self-interest, and popular cultural endorsement [and] is marked by an essential social conservatism – sex addiction has become a convenient term to describe disapproved sex" (1). Whenever David Ley, author of the *Myth of Sex Addiction* (2014), weighs in on Nofap and Yourbrainonporn about their reification of the sex addiction concept and their use (or misuse) of scientific data, leaders Alexander Rhodes and Gary Wilson respond with point-by-point rebuttals that can come across as a little hysterical, going on for pages and pages (Rhodes 2015).

The persistent appeal to science to provide an explanatory framework for people to understand their experiences with porn, as well as to recover from them, is an example of the medicalization of a pathology in process. It's not my aim here to parse all of the scientific data. That is beyond the scope of this essay and my own areas of expertise. But a few points warrant mention. First, the science is contentious, as is the case with scientific knowledge production more generally. Neuroscience is still a new field, and the very notion of addiction as a brain disease remains contested. In simple terms, given the enormous variance among people, how do we determine what kinds of brains or behaviours are normal and which are culturally normative? And how can we parse these differences? How do we understand folks' problematic relationships with pornography in context, in relation to cultural conventions that continue to suture sex to shame, for example?

The normative impulse is everywhere evident across these sites, in both their official discourse and across users' comments. Men – nearly all of the descriptions describe men's experiences – express the desire to get back to biological basics.[4] They talk about what happens in nature, about alpha versus beta males, about what penises are supposed to do with vaginas. Sex is not exactly reduced to reproduction, but it's close – it's about recovering enough to get a healthy erection, and to have "real" sex. I wonder what might happen if the emphasis were instead placed on enlarging definitions of sex beyond the genital, even beyond the real. Instead of "Quit fapping and become a man of steel," how about "Quit fapping and learn how to turn your whole body into a sexual organ, learn how to become receptive, learn how to get fucked." I think of queer filmmaker Bruce LaBruce's exhortation in his *Purple Army Manifesto* to "get to know your asshole" – "Anal Liberation Now!" (LaBruce 2011).

However, even my own suggestions operate in relation to another key frame of Nofap discourse: the language of a spiritually inflected self-optimization. In *The Hermeneutics of the Subject*, Foucault ([1981–82] 2005, 15) situates his discussion of *askesis* – the disciplined modification of the self by the self – within the context of western spirituality. For the western spiritual subject, the truth is never given; it only comes at a cost. Spirituality, Foucault writes, "postulates that for the subject to have right of access to the truth he must be changed, transformed, shifted, and become, to some extent and up to a certain point, other than himself" (15). The movement of the conversion, the means by which the subject encounters the truth, is also, according to Foucault, *eros*, or love (15–16). The beneficial rebounding effects of these movements, of in-dwelling in this achieved or received truth, is fulfillment. However, fulfillment – in the form of satisfying sexual relationships or anal pleasure or whatever – isn't easy to come by. This is the whole point of a discipline, a constraint that promises greater freedom.

Addiction feels heavy; a faster from my spiritual community told me that his porn consumption was "like a social force that was acting on me. It felt, it feels, suffocating. It feels so heavy. The easiness, the access, feels suffocating. There was also this awareness that I wasn't looking at it in a vacuum but I was part of this social energy that was part of that." Fapstinence can open one up to some other set of experiences, reorienting one to everyday practices of consumption, especially those that anthropologist Natasha Schüll (2014) has called "the machine zone."

The Machine Zone

Porn fasters' approaches toward self-transformation are entangled with capitalist imperatives to effectively manage oneself, to optimize one's productivity, to achieve some other state; but this is not necessarily a state that is open, sensitive to the world. Not unlike other disordered activities – hoarding, gambling, or drug abuse – the problem is not consumption per se but the inability to complete the correct cycle of consumption, a cycle that includes disposal when referring to consumer goods, or refractory periods of rest if we are talking about fapping (see Lepselter 2011).

In *Addiction by Design*, Schüll's groundbreaking ethnography on machine gambling in Las Vegas, she describes "the machine zone" as the dark side of flow, the concept popularized by Mihaly Csikszentmihalyi. "Flow" refers to experiences of deep immersion in a fulfilling activity that mixes challenge and control; the machine zone is absent that feeling of nourishing fulfillment. Problem gambling suspends productive time and it is anti-social, an example of a death drive that aims to achieve a stasis state of desubjectification: the zero state of the machine zone (Schüll 2014, 223). People don't play to win: they play to continue. Like gambling addicts, aspirant porn fasters often understand themselves to be caught in "coercive loops."

To escape these loops of disordered consumption, internet porn addicts, turn, of course, to the internet. As twelve-steppers and cultural critics alike have noted, recovery practices are isomorphic to the addictions they seek to remedy (Reay, Attwood, and Gooder 2013). Both include, for example, practices of vigilance and self-management. The addiction, especially once it has been formally recognized, especially by medical knowledge, also produces economically driven new service industries. Recovery treatment is one example: specialists, treatment centres, and research fields. Nofap offers a premium service called Nofap Academy ($360 for a year of boot camp). Research associations form (in 2003 the more than decade-old National Council on Sexual Addiction and Compulsivity changed its name to the Society for the Advancement of Sexual Health), accompanied by journals that legitimize them. The production of academic fields is mirrored in mass culture, as a slew of films about sex addiction attest (*Don Jon*, *Thanks for Sharing*, *Shame*, among others). The medicalization of internet porn addiction, and its related harms like porn-induced-erectile-dysfunction, have made particular interpretations of experience – such as anxieties about porn consumption, about masculinity, about 'soft cocks – more likely. A "semantic contagion" (Ian Hacking in Elliott 2003, 232) magnetizes sometimes-diverse sets of experience to a narrower set of cultural frames. I wonder if this is why my own experiences of fasting seem to mirror those of other fapstronauts. Psychologists have a word for this: expectancy bias.

As I was driving a Georgia Tech student home after a hookup while working on this project, he told me he doesn't watch much porn because he heard that not watching will help him "last longer." I didn't say anything, but even without porn he was on a hair trigger.

critiquing your dick pics with love

welcome to the website where you can receive objective, honest feedback on the quality of your dick pics!

are you interested in a private review of your dick pic for $10 or — for a limited time! — a guaranteed review on the site for $25? email critiquemydickpic@gmail.com with the subject line "special review" for details!

as i am inundated with submissions, unfortunately i cannot review every dick pic i receive. please submit only your best work to critiquemydickpic@gmail.com.

submissions from trans people, people of color, and other groups who are underrepresented in the dick pic world are welcome and encouraged.

i am generally available to talk about my work for interviews, radio shows, podcasts and articles. please mark media requests clearly in the subject line of your email so that they aren't drowned out by dick pics!

FAQ | Ask me anything | rss | archive

Mar. 31, 2016 at 4:45pm with 111 notes   Iknowitwhenithitsme.tumblr.com
△ nsfw

17.2 Sexts under thoughtful review. CritiqueYourDickPic, 2016 (no longer available).

The Future of Pornography

I conclude here with a few thoughts about what porn fasts might mean for the future of pornography.

There's another way I might have framed this essay. Rather than consider fap-staining, I might have played with another implication of the term "porn fast" – namely, one concerned with speed. Porn has gotten fast. It's a ubiquitous accelerant of gender/sex systems as biotech industrial artifacts. In this sense, then, the refusal to participate in the pornographic imaginarium might be seen as resisting the interpellating call of these systems. Fasting resources and the narratives of fasters themselves, however, with their insistent focus on normative heterosexuality, belie this reading.

For now the future of porn looks like this: more porn. On Aebn.net, one of the world's most popular global streaming sites, the straight video on demand section offers "Gender Queer" as a category. Its gay section now features videos with straight gangbangs. On *Critique My Dick Pic* (fig. 17.2), a feminist critic offers generous reviews and concrete suggestions for improving practices of sexual self-representation. I regularly review my own xxx pics with her feedback in mind: lighting, non-dick body parts …

In a dialogue on the empyre discussion forum, John Stadler describes the gamification of porn compilation videos. In "Cock Hero," users stroke to electronic beats overdubbed onto videos. Stadler writes that this represents a "re-orientation of pornography as a skill-based interaction that can be trained – perhaps even won."

Maybe the future of porn is slow porn?

Or maybe fapstaining will catch on, like going gluten-free, and it won't just be superpower-seeking young single white men who haven't had sex with anyone who are into it. I imagine porn askesis spreading to the anxious repertoires of self-optimizing discourses found in the after-class banter at your next Cross Fit class, or in the recommendations for increased output that alt-academic consultants like Karen Kelsky share with aspirant tenure seekers. Porn fasting will express our desire for freedom from the hegemony of humping pixels, while simultaneously displaying our ascetic achievements.

Postscript

Meanwhile … I've stopped fasting, and my porn consumption waxes and wanes. Pleasure, dissatisfaction, ambivalence still shape my pornoworlds. I've gotten much better at sexy selfies, though. It's taken a lot of practice, and I've still got a way to go. Email me if you think you have the qualifications to review them; I'm largely relying on my partner who is a selfie guru.

He initiated me into Snapchat – this is fast porn! – and we get a little too into it. Morning masturbation sessions turn marathon as we each feed our respective stories with our sexual play, turning on strangers (and a few familiars) around the world, soliciting their interest, soliciting their shout-outs to solicit even more interest. We form groups with some, but when I check my notifications, I often see the same images and ten-second videos. I watch them anyway, although I rarely click to replay them.

I am overwhelmed with dozens of new friend requests. Since it's Snapchat, the images disappear, so I can't remember who's who anymore – is this the sexy one? Or that one? Or that one? The two of us organize a repertoire of standardized responses. "Nice!" "Fucckkk." "Show us more sexy." Cake emojis, tongue emojis,

17.3
Easter egg: the author's NSFW snapcode. spandakarikas, Snapchat, screenshot, 2018.

spritz emojis, eggplant emojis, peach emojis, and an array of goofy face emojis. We're not getting anything done. Things accelerate. Then we give it up. Our sex gets more intimate. But don't worry, we'll be back.

NOTES

1. The clamshell notebook was not unique in this sense. One could extend this analysis to broader historical periods – from the birth of the novel at least, as well as to other examples like personal advertisements, chat lines, and pornographies broadly conceived (film, video, digital).
2. Interestingly, while this video is unusual for the gay content section of Aebn, its straight section includes the category "Gender Queer," which features videos by feminist, trans*, and sex-positive filmmakers like Alyx Fox and Michelle Austin, among others.
3. Though it's not a focus of my discussion here, Schüll usefully draws distinguishes between compulsions and impulsions. The former suggests an external force operating on and against one's agency. The latter, by contrast, is an internal process of tension, gratification, and release, thereby "ego-syntonic."
4. NoFap has produced surveys of its users. In 2012, 97 per cent of respondents were men. About half had never had sex, most were single, most were white, most were straight identified.

REFERENCES

"About." n.d. *Nofap*. https://www.nofap.com/about/.

Allen, Samantha. 2015. "'Porn Kills Love': Mormons' Anti-Smut Crusade." *Daily Beast*, 1 June. http://www.thedailybeast.com/articles/2015/10/20/porn-kills-love-mormons-anti-smut-crusade.html.

Barad, Karen. 2015. "Transmaterialities: Trans*/Matter/Realities and Queer Political Imaginings." *GLQ: A Journal of Lesbian and Gay Studies* 21, nos. 2–3: 387–422.

Dean, Tim. 2014. "Introduction: Pornography, Technology, Archive." In *Porn Archives*, edited by Tim Dean, Steven Ruszcycky, and David Squire, 1–28. Durham: Duke University Press.

Elliott, Carl. 2003. *Better than Well: American Medicine Meets the American Dream*. New York: Norton.

Foucault, Michel. [1976] 1990. *The History of Sexuality*. Vol. 1, *An Introduction*. Translated by Robert Hurley. New York: Pantheon.

– [1981–82] 2005. *The Hermeneutics of the Subject: Lectures at the Collège de France, 1981–1982*. Translated by Graham Burchell. New York: Picador.

Greenblatt, Stephen. 2004. "Me, Myself, and I." *New York Review of Books*, 8 April. htttp://www.nybooks.com/articles/2004/04/08/me-myself-and-i/ 2004.

LaBruce, Bruce. 2011. "Bruce LaBruce for the Purple Resistance Army." *Vice*. 24 October. http://www.vice.com/read/bruce-labruce-for-the-purple-resistance-army.

Laqueur, Thomas. 2004. *Solitary Vice: A Cultural History of Masturbation*. New York: Zone Books.

Lepselter, Susan. 2011. "The Disorder of Things: Hoarding Narratives in Popular Media." *Anthropological Quarterly* 84 (4): 919–48.

Levine, Martin, and Richard Troiden. 1988. "The Myth of Sexual Compulsivity." *Journal of Sex Research* 25, no. 3, 347–63.

Ley, David. 2014. *The Myth of Sex Addiction*. New York: Rowman & Littlefield.

McGlotten, Shaka. 2013. *Virtual Intimacies: Media, Affect, and Queer Sociality*. New York: SUNY Press.

Paasonen, Susanna. 2011. *Carnal Resonance: Affect and Online Pornography*. Cambridge: MIT Press.

Parker, Lauren. 2015. "Fight the New Drug's Online 'Porn Rehab' Is Insidious Pseudoscience That Preys on Youth." *Medium*, 16 December. https://medium.com/@HARLOT/fight-the-new-drug-s-online-porn-rehab-is-insidious-pseudoscience-that-preys-on-youth-1c0c935bd4f3.

Preciado, Paul B. 2013. *Testo Junkie: Sex, Drugs, and Biopolitics in the Pharmacopornographic Era*. Ebook. New York: CUNY Feminist Press.

Reay, Barry, Nina Attwood, and Claire Gooder. 2013. "Inventing Sex: The Short History of Sex Addiction." *Sexuality and Culture* 17: 1–19.

"Rebooting from Porn Addiction." 2017. *Nofap*. https://www.nofap.com/rebooting/.

Rhodes, Alexander. 2015. "David Ley Attacks NoFap and Porn-Recovery: Don't Let the 'Porn Addiction' Deniers Discourage You." *NoFap*, 28 May. htttp://www.nofap.com/forum/index.php?threads/david-ley-attacks-nofap-and-porn-recovery-dont-let-the-porn-addiction-deniers-discourage-you.39162/.

Roach, Tom. 2015. "Becoming Fungible: Queer Intimacies in Social Media." *Qui Parle* 23, no. 2 (Spring/Summer): 55–87.

Schüll, Natasha Dow. 2014. *Addiction by Design: Machine Gambling in Las Vegas*. Princeton: Princeton University Press.

Waugh, Thomas. 1996. *Hard to Imagine: Gay Male Eroticism in Photography and Film from Their Beginnings to Stonewall*. New York: Columbia University Press.

Documentaries

18

"I Confess: I Was the Girl in the Shadows"

REBECCA SULLIVAN

I saw you last night. You were lurking in the dimly lit urban park looking for anyone but me. We glanced at each other and exchanged a slight smile before I slipped back out onto the street.

I saw you last night. You were at your usual post on the corner in front of my apartment building. Despite your practised stare into the mid-distance, we acknowledged each other with a slight nod before I entered the lobby.

I never thanked you for keeping that park safe for me at night, or for letting me know that you were watching the street for unwelcome interlopers to our neighbourhood. But without you, I could have never crossed those parks and those streets. More importantly, I never would have crossed through those liminal zones of underground sex culture and discovered my own sexual identity.

I had been told about these shadow worlds. Warned, more like it. In the eighties, nice, straight girls from the suburbs weren't supposed to move to downtown Toronto, much less its seedier, more crime-ridden districts populated by "queers" (it wasn't meant as a positive back then) and "prostitutes" (the term "sex workers" was still decades away). This was the era of No Means No, of rape whistles and self-defence classes. We were warned that the streets at night were not for us, underscored by some high-profile cases like the Balcony Rapist, who operated near my home.

And of course there were the porn wars. I'd seen porn already. As a child, I walked past the magazines at the same convenience store where I bought my Mr Freezie, stealing a furtive peek. Later, with the dawn of the VCR, the local video stores had poorly supervised, cordoned-off areas at the back where scratchy tapes with pasted-up covers could be rented for a premium. What I saw seemed pretty boring and monotonous. I hadn't heard the term "male gaze" yet, but it was ready-made for this early-era, mass-mediated sex culture that held little appeal for women. At the same time, I couldn't really understand the waves of anger against it all. I thought I might like sex when I got the chance to try it, so my first tentative forays into feminist spaces were confusing and a little frightening. There was a lot of heavy talk about female victimization and male power, some of which made sense to me. After all, there were serial rapists out there, and maybe one of them was that guy who followed me home last night calling me "slut." But a lot of the talk didn't feel right. And then there was the same creepy feeling from some of the older women that I was trying to avoid as from the guys. Standing too close, getting a little touchy, letting me know that they could take care of me (who said I needed to be taken care of?), telling me I deserved someone like them.

The sex zones available for straight girls in the eighties were more like no-sex zones. The spaces of smothering homosolidarity where any sex with men was called rape or the spaces of heteronormative rigidity where women who strayed from the "charmed circle" (Rubin [1984] 2014, 152) of monogamous, vanilla, relationship sex were fair game for both harassment and violence. At least that's what it felt like to me, newly liberated from family, Catholicism, high school, and everything else that kept me a good girl. Where could I go to experiment with a sexuality I didn't really understand, venture into the "outer limits" but not so far that I might risk my return to the charmed circle that still held some appeal?

The answer turned out to be gay bars. There, my friends and I could drink and dance all night, flirt safely with charming, affable men, and stumble out into the darkness towards home. But the streets were still filled with danger, especially for those of us who weren't a part of and didn't understand the rhythms of the nighttime economy. I needed to get street smart, and fast.

What I learned was that everything I had been taught to avoid was where I would be the safest. The parks, alleys, and strolls where sex was exchanged contained their own subcultural community who knew the dangers of darkness better than anyone. And so I walked alone through the parkette that cut through the gay village into the red-light district, and down the street past the hourly rate hotel, which would sometimes be my temporary haven to shake off a stalker, before entering my rundown but rent-controlled apartment building.

I belonged to the pre-postfeminist generation, too late for radical feminism, too early for riot grrrls. I was a postmodern suburban flâneuse, delighting in a juxtaposition of identities and geographies that were still relatively unknown and poorly understood. I was a temporary visitor to this part of town, and I knew it. There was no covering up the traces of middle-class status, of family security, education, and opportunity. I was also, crucially, a girl. No matter how much I resisted the imposed limitations of my gender, the fact remained that it made me a target for people I had every reason to fear. Thus, unlike the fabled flâneur of modernity, anonymity was not my intention. I wanted – needed – to be seen if I was to continue my journeys of sexual self-exploration (Wolff 1985, 41). That meant I needed to learn a different kind of gaze. The voyeuristic and sadistic gaze of the flâneur turned nighttime occupants into commodities for his pleasure. I needed to practise a kind of gaze that signalled awareness and discretion, empathy and gratitude, humility and respect. The gay men looking for sex in the park and the women selling sex on the street were knowledgeable guides who could teach me something about what it meant to be a sexual citizen in Canada at a time of intense transformation. I looked to them as teachers and protectors.

The eighties were the era of bathhouse raids, abortion-clinic attacks, porn wars, and serial rapists. Sex came out of the closet with a vengeance, catching those who wanted to keep the population divided between good and bad with their pants down. But they didn't stop trying. In high-school health class, I did my project on "Homosexuality," for which my gym teacher lamented, "Why do the nice girls want to do the dirty topics?" After the local newspaper ran a sensationalized story about a street that housed both a popular gay bar and an after-hours dance club, my father warned me never to go there. I didn't have the heart to tell him that was my haunt – I was just relieved that my face wasn't in the accompanying picture. I moved downtown the same week that I graduated from Grade 13.

I was a good girl, no doubt about that, and it wasn't so much that I wanted to be bad as I didn't really understand what was so bad about it. And in that I was not alone. Many young women were questioning the sexual double standards and not finding the answers they wanted in the largely sex-negative teachings of late second-wave feminism. Nor did burgeoning queer politics care much about straight feminine sexuality. In a time when life-or-death struggles over AIDS, police brutality, and abortion bombings were dominating sexual politics, the sexual frustration of cis, straight, middle-class white girls with birth-control pills in their purses was hardly a priority. We could march in both Gay Pride and Take Back the Night, but we did not truly belong in either. We weren't just sexually frustrated but also intellectually stymied by the options offered us, thrust to the shadows of the sex crisis.

It would be three decades before I would hear the word "consent" attached to sex. Learning it unlocked a long-buried memory of a frightening assault that some of my friends had convinced me "didn't count." Not that I blame them; few of us exited that stage of our lives unscathed, and we learned to accept that violence was the price we paid for experimentation. We would confess our risky sexual desires and our (often) unfulfilling sexual encounters to each other, supporting each other even as we mutually agreed we may have "asked for it" – whatever the unpleasant

"it" was. We covered for each other when we took jobs on the edges of the sex industry, as waitresses in strip clubs or phone-sex operators. The money was great, the stigma somewhat lessened, and the work was easy. Still, we needed alibis to explain where we were when anxious parents called or friends outside our confessional circle asked where we were working.

Likewise, we needed allies on the streets if we were to continue our nocturnal perambulations to and from work, clubs, and sex. We needed to be seen. That glance or nod was my confession to the sex criminals in my neighbourhood that I had been up to no good that night and needed safe passage home. I trusted them the way I did not trust the police or taxi drivers or even feminist security collectives who patrolled the streets looking for girls like me to warn us that we were acting stupid and asking for it. They wanted us removed from the urban night, our sexual revolution returned to the suburban bedroom, our sexual histories erased before they could be written.

"I Confess: I Was the Girl in the Shadows" | 375

18.1 *Opposite* The author in the shadows, 1980s. Photo courtesy R. Sullivan.

18.2 *Left* Happily married mom with dog, mortgage, and SUV, 2010s. Photo courtesy R. Sullivan.

By contrast, the sex workers and park prowlers generously and without judgment shared their space with us sexually questioning straight girls. And as a result, we grew more sceptical of the claims that they were not to be trusted. With all due respect to the manifestos and marches, it was also the secret exchanges of unlikely sexual comrades that helped bridge feminism and queer activism, aligned sex-worker rights with sexual violence prevention, and laid the groundwork for contemporary gender and sexual politics.

Years passed, and the charmed circle re-embraced me (figs. 18.1 and 18.2). I became exactly the person I was once so sceptical of: a happily married mom with a dog, mortgage, even an SUV. There are no more solitary midnight rambles, and although I don't miss them (gotta get up early to pack lunches), I remain grateful. Because of them, I know my life choices aren't a question of "settling" or even "compulsory heteronormativity," but honestly and self-reflexively determined. I believed those days were well behind me, but the Third Sexual Revolution made it possible to become reacquainted with my nighttime co-conspirators.

After hearing about a new sexual politics of consent, I began researching its foundations and early proponents. It wasn't available in the libraries and lecture halls, but I finally found it online. A digital network of sex workers and LGBTQ2IA+ collectives have reframed the politics of pleasure using social media to both sell their work and fight for their rights. The old anti-porn vigilantes of yesteryear may write this off as liberal consumer politics and try in vain to maintain the rigid gender and sexual binaries that undergird their arguments, but it turns out you can't selectively silence the voices anymore. Where once we were told to listen only to the victims of porn – a feminist politics of the sex confessional that privileged pain, sorrow, violence, and regret – we now have a cacophony of voices that can talk simultaneously about the problems and pleasures of twenty-first century sex (Sullivan and McKee 2015, 82). More importantly, we can engage in first-person dialogues among sex workers and university professors, trans activists and feminists, AIDS health workers, and porn professionals.

Anonymous, secretive sex isn't only on the streets but increasingly online through camming, chat sites, tube sites, social media accounts, and apps like Tinder and Grindr. This unlimited vista of digital sex may be more explicit than the stuff from the corner stores, and even in some cases, harder, but it comes with equally harder conversations about occupational health and safety, fair wages, digital piracy, performer rights, and ethical negotiations between partners in a commercial sex exchange. There is also greater diversity of bodies on display alongside an intersectional politics that includes critiques of racism, ableism, whorarchies, and an ever-growing expansion of the gender and sexual spectrum. As queer politics has gained mainstream support through heteronomative initiatives like same-sex marriage and adoption, HIV prevention agencies – with the obvious exception of Michael Weinstein's AIDS Healthcare Foundation – have begun to house and support sex-worker rights groups (HIV Equal 2015).

Our alliances and collaborations have likewise come out of the shadows. As a university professor, I have co-edited academic publications with porn performers, hosted public talks and conferences that include sex workers as experts. I am in talks with a porn production company to create educational toolkits for their films. I serve on a board for an organization dedicated to gender and sexual diversity support. Most important, every day, I publicly engage in a global network of conversations and debates about sexual politics with queer, trans, and sex-work activists through online social media. We are no longer limited to stolen smiles and guarded glances. We talk.

Thus, to be a participant in the Third Sexual Revolution is to go beyond the gaze and into the body politics of digital sex in order to demand that former and still sex criminals receive the rights of security and dignity long denied them. At the heart of that practice is removing the shame and stigma that kept all of us in the shadows (Armstrong and Reissing 2015, 931). It's time to confess our sexual desires, refuse the penance demanded, and instead claim gratitude to the second-wave revolutionaries who made pleasure political.

REFERENCES

Armstrong, Heather, and Elke Reissing. 2015. "Women's Motivations to Have Sex in Casual and Committed Relationships with Male and Female Partners." *Archives of Sexual Behaviour* 44, no. 4: 921–34.

HIV Equal. 2015. "Five HIV Activists Give the 10 Worst Offenses of AHF's Michael Weinstein." *The Body*. http://www.thebody.com/content/75994/5-hiv-activists-give-the-10-worst-offenses-of-ahfs.html?ts=pf.

Rubin, Gayle. [1984] 2014. "Thinking Sex: Notes for a Radical Theory of the Politics of Sexuality." Chap. 5 in *Deviations: A Gayle Rubin Reader*. Durham, NC: Duke University Press.

Sullivan, Rebecca, and Alan McKee. 2015. *Pornography: Structures, Agency, and Performance*. London: Polity Press.

Wolff, Janet. 1985. "The Invisible Flâneuse: Women and the Literature of Modernity." *Theory, Culture and Society* 2, no. 3: 37–46.

19

Queer Auto-Porn-Art: Genealogies, Aesthetics, Ethics, and Desire

THOMAS WAUGH

Foreplay

The Third Sexual Revolution and its vibrant landscape of queer confessional moving-image expression over the past quarter-century – not only within the arts avant-garde and the online porniverse but also in many sectors of everyday life and popular culture, whether minoritarian or majoritarian – did not self-generate spontaneously upon the gradual implementation of the internet in the 1990s. Rather, this virtual landscape of libidinous queer eruptions harnessed a flickering momentum of precursors, forebears, and ancestors who had surfaced within the first and second sexual revolutions of the analog era.

In the context of this book's survey of the seismic surfacing of the sexual "I" since the mid-1990s, this chapter zeroes in on queer autobiographical and testimonial, explicitly sexual self-representations. We could establish a whole genealogy of queer cinematic confessional sexual performance, especially during the Second Sexual Revolution of the postwar era and its wake (in roughly chronological order: Willard Maas, Shirley Clarke, James Broughton, Claude Jutra, Rosa von Praunheim, Michael Wallin, Lionel Soukaz, Curt McDowell, Barbara Hammer, Carl George, Derek Jarman, Annie Sprinkle, Mirha-Soleil Ross – to mention only the Euro-American examples that come to mind). But instead, in this too-brief chapter I will helicopter selectively first over an anonymous ancestor (the eponymous performer/"author" of the American stag film *Surprise of a Knight* [ca. 1930], "Oscar Wild"). I will then leap ahead to a handful of varied descendants from the era of the internet (or rather from its 1990s cusp onwards) and the twenty-first-century digital interactive universe, that is today's saturated virtual cosmos of sexual confession, performance and commodification. Or as Linda Williams puts it, the "present" of post-porn, post-identity digital "on/scenity"

(2004), and as this book's contributor "Intervals" puts it, "the first-person industrial complex" (chapter 10).[1] This chapter explores the rich and contradictory valences of that on/scene complex and keeps its eye on its emancipatory, even utopian potential.

My corpus from this "present" is comprised of overlapping bodies of sexually explicit queer self-presenting work – what I am terming "auto-porn-art." What I have gathered are narrative, documentary, and erotic moving-image utterances, articulated through authorial voice but also and especially through the authorial body, visualized erotic gesture and carnal performance – what Williams would call "hard core" (2008). I am focusing less on the stampede of often anonymous and variously triumphalist and abject online "tubers" than on those specific image-makers colonizing more "licit" docuporn and art-world experimentation, thereby enacting intersections, if not collisions, of porn worlds and art worlds. Although I recently lingered briefly at conferences on the case study of the notorious online auto-pornstar-artist Colby Keller, which I will briefly recapitulate here (see chapter 13 for Brandon Arroyo's more thorough and critical treatment), I will also bring into focus some exemplary though less cocky (literally and figuratively) Canadian and American contemporaries. Two groups of subject witnesses in particular interest me for their similar and overlapping moving-image discourses of erotic self-presentation, queer or LGBT men (cis, genderqueer, and trans*) and sex workers of the same gender expressions.[2] My corpus straddles the facile and increasingly obsolete and irrelevant binaries of art and porn, "underground" and marketplace, top and bottom, phallus and anus, as well as the spectrums of and between gay male and genderqueer/trans* identities and those of the digital universe and the spaces of private desire and affect. In using the word "obsolete," I wonder if I could argue that the Third Sexual Revolution has done away for all intents and purposes with the licit-illicit boundary that the Second Sexual Revolution and the era of porn chic maintained. Regardless, I am especially interested in the relational contract between auto-porn-art author (voice and body), performance, textuality and spectator, the complex and volatile relationship between confessant, confession and confessor, a relationship engaging both affect/desire/sensation and knowledge (or *ars* and *scientia*). Without daring to fetishize authorship excessively in our post-Barthesian climate, I insist that using the author's body, agency, and control as a point of departure remains productive in our minoritarian context.[3] Finally, I am interested, as is evident from my diachronically ordered corpus, in the internet's fulfilment of an almost teleological thrust palpable in the pre-digital works of the 1990s.

This reflection on historical, theoretical, political, ethical, and cultural issues sparked by the mingling of public and private spaces of desire and affect is ongoing. What are the signifying operations of explicit sexual imagery and first-person behind-the-camera subjectivity when they collide, of discursive tropes ranging from the autobiographical, the didactic and the diaristic, to on-camera sexual performance (jerkoff solos or cum shots?), solicitation (anal or phallic come-hither address?), and narrative relationality (seduction, the hand job? penetration? conjugal jouissance?). (Does my premise of the exceptional artistic and ethical status of personally performed and owned explicit sexual behaviour within the culture hold up, or is this premise curiously irrelevant in the context of our culture's flood of sexual confessionality? I say yes, resoundingly to the first question; the strange bedfellow of a jurisprudence and law-enforcement industry that sentences non-violent sex offenders more punitively than murderers would paradoxically echo my assent, but that is another essay.) Building from textual analysis, I will probe in this chapter the analogy of auto-porn-art corporeality to traditional formats of confessional utterance and reception/absolution, and engage in our ongoing conversations around political effect, play, shame, affect, desire – and utopia, of course – moving towards a parting queery as to the possibility of aesthetic and ethical applications of two enigmatic Foucauldian ideal practices, friendship and parrhesia.

Ultimately, with my stag performers and their descendants, this chapter affirms the unbroken continuum of queer sexual representation along the axis from the licit (art/documentary/science: *scientia sexualis*) to the illicit (porn/pleasure/arousal: *ars erotica*), and our urgent need, in the footsteps of scholars from Richard Dyer (1985, 1989) to Linda Williams (2008) to Nguyen Tan Hoang (2014) – and of course myself (1996, 2002, 2004, 2006a, 2006b) – to maintain this broad compass. Williams's category of "hard-core art cinema" (2008) may well preside over my inclination towards textual analysis, but not as a respectable alibi (though auto-porn-art performers to be highlighted include gender studies and fine arts graduates and curators and even an academic or two), rather as an incentive to push forward its applicability to broader swaths of visual culture in the twenty-first century than is reached by the increasingly museum-and festival-based art form of theatrical cinema, which has often been my purview in the past (2000, 2010).[4]

In this I have been inspired like so many others by queer historian Carolyn Dinshaw and her attempt to deal directly with a queer desire for transhistorical connections:

> I was trying to negotiate between alteritists (social constructionists) and those who appealed to transhistorical constants of some sort (essentialists), but this time in my analyses I found that even Foucault, the inspiration of social constructionists, connected affectively with the past. I focused on the possibility of touching across time, collapsing time through affective contact between marginalized people now and then, and I suggested that with such queer historical touches we could form communities across time. (1999)

Dinshaw's "refusal of linear historicism" and embrace of "connect[ing] affectively with the past" or "touching across time" seem a healthy way to go as we try to undermine the glib present-centrism of so much digital-era cultural studies.

The continuity through the works I have selected, spanning over eighty years of sexual revolutions, is uncanny. My materialist training will not allow me to go all the way with artist impresario Jamie Ross, originator of the *Rousings* Xtube series (to which I will return shortly), who gives very much a spiritual dimension to such connecting and touching, and cites a very felicitous reflection by Derek Jarman to flesh it out:

> An orgasm joins you to the past. Its timelessness becomes the brotherhood; the brethren are lovers; they extend the "family." I share that sexuality. It was then, is now and will be in the future. There was a night when I clicked into the ghost of one of my heroes, Caravaggio. It was an odd moment in which the past actually flashed into the present, physically – fucking with the past if you like. (Jarman [1992] 2010)

Yet I feel my fiercely materialist subjectivity being seduced into this mystic bond. My own participation in his series was not my finest moment as a performance artist, but somehow around it hovered feelings of sharing, clicking, flashing, and fucking that were clearly akin to my epiphanies over the years when an unexpected archival discovery would spark a massive shudder that was as metaphysical as it was physical (for example, in the Kinsey Institute attic in 1982, when I discovered *Surprise of a Knight*). It is uncanny that pre-internet Jarman used the word "click" as if he anticipated the logistical micro-gesture whereby his descendants could share and enter Ross's own invocation, his embodiment and orgasmic *Rousings* performance as Jarman himself; but we shall come back to the uncanny affective connections of the internet shortly.

Ancestor Worship

My first text, *Surprise of a Knight* (USA, ca. 1930), I have been writing about for more than thirty-five years, but the staggering richness and uniqueness of this simple and anonymous ten-minute silent stag movie still leave me gasping and grasping (as well as connecting me to the thirty-four-year-old me who first "discovered" it). It delivers from its abject pulpit of the anonymous and illicit stag network of furtive "smoker" supply and demand across almost ninety years an intensity that the succeeding avant-gardists, art-cineastes, and documentarists that I have listed aspired to but perhaps never acceded to. My first published description of *Surprise* in Toronto's gay lib monthly *The Body Politic* in 1983, fresh from my visit to the Kinsey archives, was joyous with a Keatsian "wild surmise":

> Despite the credit "By Oscar Wild" (*sic*), I infer that [*Surprise*] is also American because the protagonist, an elegant transvestite, has a black maid to usher in her guests. The gowned and bejewelled heroine begins by approaching the camera and poses to show off her outfit, playing with her fan, and then lifting up her skirt to show a very feminine groin. Her guest enters, also elegant in a suit, kisses her hand and lifts up her skirt. They kiss long and hard; she is outrageously coy. They dance, laughing and having fun, thrusting against each other quite lasciviously. She blows him, but he, still clothed, is not very excited. They kiss again. He touches her groin and then fucks her, she still in her gown kneeling before the sofa, he still in his shirt and boxer shorts. There are no genital close-ups, but one close image shows him kissing her shoulder while fucking her, and another shows her face in ecstasy. Then the dramatic moment of revelation that is the staple of all drag stags: she produces the cock that she has been hiding between her legs; it pops out, dangling up and down. She then dances about again for the camera, holding up her skirt. The surprise of the knight, however, is decidedly perfunctory. He helps her undress and then she poses again, this time nude, with a little wave. As a finale, she dresses again, this time as a convincing slim young man who smiles in close-up in the last shot, as coy as ever. (1983, 30)

A decade later, for a more academic audience, I offered much more detail and interpretation, as well as more informed conjectures about production and generic contexts for this clandestine legacy (1996).

In the following decade, my next definitive and final piece on the stag-film corpus focused much more – even if speculatively, given the paucity of documentation of the stag underground – on audience and exhibition. I brought up *Surprise* only in passing as belonging to that relatively small stag subgenre in which the sexual "other" (that is, "other" to the standard default ethnographic of white, cisgendered, heterosexual men and [sometimes] women) performs

> the inoculatory function and freak-show operation of queer discourses in homosocial culture. In other words, regardless of whether queers produced or performed, for the spectator who watches the sexual other perform, e.g., the drag queen in *Surprise of a Knight* (late 1920s) or the black male cocksucker in *A Stiff Game* (1930s), the meaning is "I am not like that."
> One can imagine the interactive gross-out response solicited by the playful performance of alterity onscreen, sparked within original audiences by each stage of the unfolding "surprise," along with the voyeuristic mix of prurient fascination and disavowal coloured by arousal or identification on the part of silent and shamed minority members inevitably and covertly present ... Extrapolating back through the decades, it is impossible not to imagine that difference was not present in all of those classic all-male audiences. Not only difference but also dissemblance, the deceptive performance of belonging. ([2001] 2004)

More generally, I also explored the stags as texts and social performances that actively constructed homosocial relations not only onscreen but also interactively within the male audience and between screen and spectators:

> The screenings enabled all the affective infrastructure and institutional support for that desire, from rivalry, competition and heckling to procuring, matchmaking and cheerleading, from tandem or serial sharing of women's bodies to their collective repudiation, from the mutual ego reinforcement that Gagnon and Simon identified as a main dynamic of the fraternal Elks Club settings, to the functions of instruction, mentorship and initiation that characterized the frathouse environment (1973: 266). Above all, the specularization of homosocial desire is in place, in the screening room, on the screen: men getting hard pretending not to watch men getting hard watching images of men getting hard watching or fucking women. ([2001] 2004)

Now looking at this film in the age of the internet, I wonder if the unknowable structures of the stag underground from those pre-sexual revolution decades, with their anonymity, ephemerality, fluidity, instability, and precariousness, anticipate similar dynamics within the twenty-first-century above-ground DIY tubiverse – not to mention that universe's own illicit undergrounds, the "darknet" or otherwise. One could overstate the prophetic nature of the interactive and socially constructed relationality of *Surprise*'s original exhibition moment, its anticipation of similar dynamics of the internet generations later, seated individually before the keyboard rather than in rows of folding chairs in a smoky Legion Hall basement. Still I will not disavow my intuitive, perhaps mystical recognition of parallels as a queer media historian – even if catcalls are now keyboarded rather than vocal, and audiences virtual rather than corporeal. That this playful and naughty and mock-dissembling dangler-mooner might qualify as an ancestor of our twenty-first century auto-porn-art confessants, and not only in terms of narrative or gender performance content, is truly uncanny.[5] For the purpose of this essay, I winkingly accept the film's outrageous put-on of the martyred Irish playwright (dead only a few decades at the time of its production, his name evidently still a household word, if Elks members in Omaha are presumed to recognize it) as its author (misspelled as he is). An author is needed all the same for my essay's premise, which is the thread of authorial sexual performance over the decades. Let's call the star "Wild" – for she truly is – and on an honorary basis assign her the authorship of the film that she so clearly and irrevocably steals out from under whomever the mere trenchcoat-and-suitcase metteur-en-scène/camera operator might have been.

Contemporary Corpus/Bodies

In this section I would like to flesh out the motley corpus of recent and contemporary auto-porn-art artists who are Wild's descendants: to one side, the series of hard-core autobiographical videos from the American Colby Keller, *Colby Does America* (2014 onwards), and at the centre a cluster of less notorious works from the broader hemisphere that offer additional vocabularies and questions. I use the Victorian word "motley" since my dozen or so authorial voices/bodies run a fairly diverse spectrum of (male, genderqueer, and trans*) sexual identities/corporeal presentations, as my summary of their various artistic and erotic achievements in the following pages makes clear.

My work on a contemporary corpus might seem surprising, since I'm moving away from my traditional safe and dignified stance of moving-image historian, having privileged throughout my career the study of archives from the nineteenth and twentieth centuries (1996, 2000). In effect, I don't have the habit of analyzing works diffused on XTube! This said, I hope that my qualitative and subjective analysis of a popular corpus of the internet era will serve as an antidote to the "paranoid readings" of pornography and its negative effects (to take up Eve Sedgwick's famous dyad "paranoid-reparative" [2003] in another context). This paranoia, embodied by the scandalous moral panics of wolf-criers from Gail Dines (2011) to Christopher Kendall (2005), has been critiqued by Elisabeth Mercier (2017) and explored by Corneau, Bernatchez, and Beaulieu-Prévost (2017), among others, raising the contradictions that are inherent in the consumption of a commercial pornography that is racist and sexist and everything else that is horrid. Rather, I offer here a "reparative" reading of gay pornography, one that is even hyperbolic and utopian. Hyperbolic, because I think it is important not to be shy of the affirmative and communitarian potentiality of queer hard core as we bring out its status as confessional utterance. And utopian, because I consider that the plurality of our relationships to pornography as a sexual and visual self-representation is a heritage that has been as magnificently paradigm-shifting as it is complex to understand and affirm (Waugh 1985, 1996). My idealized vision of pornography within queer culture is not new. Since Stonewall, many writers have developed the parameters of such a vision (Dyer [1985] 1992; *Gay Left* [Blachford 1978]; Patton 2014; Burger 1994; Delany 1999; Moore 2004; Mercer 2017). Let's examine what the Third Sexual Revolution and its covens of queer auto-porn-artists can add to this vision.

My diverse cohort of the horny self-imagers who are the descendants of "Wild" includes two 1990s antecedents, Phillip B. Roth and Bruce LaBruce; three millennial transitionals with their eye on the future but their feet in art-world spaces, Michael V. Smith, Isaac Leung, and Conrad Ryan; and their full-blown, twenty-first-century internet successors, Colby Keller, Jamie Ross, Derek Jackson, Branden Miller, and Viktor Belmont. The third group have transformed the bold and inventive performances of the pioneers of the earlier pre-tube, pre-webcam cusp moments into the blasé vernacular of the era of Obama and Trump. In their on-camera and off-camera roles, their corporeal and vocal performances, they are part of the conversation about aesthetics, ethics, and desire that I am urgently pushing forward. All are of course caught up in the inescapable contradictions of the neoliberal world order, whether that be the elitist pretention of the art world, the complicity of academic marketplace, the homonormativity of queer media networks, or the avaricious viciousness of the porn market; but such tensions have enlivened the texts and affects of this corpus throughout its history.

Perhaps a clarification is warranted about the relationship of my auto-porn-artists to the so-called art world I have just mentioned. No doubt because of my proudly yet selectively embraced queer essentialism – and also my admitted populist streak – I stand apart from the voluminous literature within art history/criticism on parallels and precedents within the art world historically (Warr 2000; Jones 2006), unable in this short space to trouble the problematical apartheid between art history/criticism and moving image/media studies, and never the twain shall meet. A full-length version of this study will not only fill in the gap inhabited by the filmmakers of the Second Sexual Revolution, whom I have listed above but also explore parallels between my horny self-imagers and their self-portraying analogues belonging to the art world proper from Carolee Schneemann to Cindy Sherman to Marina Abramovic, perhaps in particular those artists within academic high-conceptual and performance/body art who not only deployed their naked bodies as raw material but dared to incorporate their acts of masturbation and even fucking as idiom, ritual, provocation (erotic or otherwise), and iconography. (I am thinking not only of queer Robert Mapplethorpe, Annie Sprinkle, Ron Athey, and Charles Ray but also of straight Vito Acconci, John Duncan, Günter Brus, and Elke Krystufek [Warr 2000].)

What follows is a chronological catalogue of my selected moving-image autoporn-artists with some observations intended to bring out the textual and contextual particularity of each of the dozen or so performers.

1. "Oscar Wild," *Surprise of a Knight*, ca. 1930, 10 min. USA. (See above.)

2. Phillip B. Roth, *25 Year Old Gay Man Loses his Virginity to a Woman*, 1990, USA, 22 min.; *I Was a Jewish Sex Worker*, 1996, 72 min., USA. These two artisanal works, the first on video and the second on 16mm, gravitated around the New York City queer/ACT UP scene at the height of the Pandemic, and the former was controversially funded and then disavowed by the New York State Council for the Arts. In this collaborative performance video, pornstar-artist Annie Sprinkle (an ancestor of Colby Keller in her own way) initiates the artist into missionary-style heterocourse (with condom) and menstrual products. The latter work continues the autobiographical docu-narrative thread but in a fashion more diaristic than mise-en-scène: Roth the masseur protagonist narrates interactive episodes with both clients on his studio floor and his matriarchal family at their kitchen counters. Roth startled critical and programming circles with two such explicit queer first-person documentaries. His own sexual performance is respectively mounted centre stage before the camera and matter-of-factly followed as part of an authentic everyday, from relationships with lovers and family to bread-and-butter rub-and-tugs in New York City, presided over by a telephone-answering machine that both narrates and fills in local colour. (Does the hoary seventies-eighties shortcut plot device of voice mail–voice-over anticipate the internet in its push towards

Queer Auto-Porn-Art | 387

19.1 Anticipating the internet with shameful, lustful, and vigorous hard-core authorial thrusting. *Super 8 ½*, dir. Bruce LaBruce, 1994.

techno-interactivity and a controlling artificial intelligence?) The warm, pleasurable camaraderie with Sprinkle and the friendly and uninhibited professionalism of the happy endings both restored dignity, fun, and banality to fucking, porn, and sex work and challenged sex-phobic undercurrents that ran through the catastrophic apex of the Pandemic – acknowledged perhaps only obliquely by all that safer sex happening onscreen but without ever mentioning the friends dying off-screen.

3. Bruce LaBruce, *No Skin off My Ass*, 1991, 73 min., Canada; *Super 8 ½*, 1994, 99 min., Canada. LaBruce, as notorious as Keller in his way, surfaced from the queercore Toronto underground scene but with a cinephile streak (a degree in film studies), making a mark in the nineties with a rapid-fire series of iconoclastic art cinema/festival features. He has not let up in subsequent decades, keeping one foot in the porn world and one in the transnational art cinema and queer festival networks, with a German producer and international bums-in-seats audience – and unique among my cohort, it's in DVD distribution, digitally restored by TIFF!

All his work has retained a punk flavour, but *No Skin off My Ass* and *Super 8 ½* stand out in this respect, not the least because they star the leather-clad director-scriptwriter in explicit authorial sex scenes (their risk perhaps diminished by their conjugal narrative context within the films). LaBruce's brazen auto-fictional lead roles both inherit their film-within-a-film self-reflexivity and their lo-tech multi-platform "poverty" aesthetics from the in-your-face queercore underground of ephemeral shorts and hit-and-run performances. For all their feature-film festival positioning, the films anticipate the internet, both in DIY no-budget style and in shameful, lustful, and vigorous hard-core authorial bobbing and thrusting, a documentary aura so unique outside of the porn world at the time that critics did not know how to discuss the works.

LaBruce's belonging to the "New Queer Cinema" movement has been tenuous, perhaps because of the eroto-avoidant (if not -phobic) undercurrents in the taste-making and gate-keeping critical literature.[6] In fact this chapter's entire corpus sits uneasily on the edge or entirely outside of the canon, "new queer" or any other, mostly because of the "hard core" premise that draws me to it.

4. Isaac Leung, *The Impossibility of Having Sex with Over 500 Men in a Month – I'm an Oriental Whore*, multi-platform installation, 2003, USA, https://vimeo.com/65429303. Now based in Hong Kong academia, Leung's gallery-centred multimedia MFA project deployed chatroom diary-based documentation of tandem jerkoff encounters on webcam, exhibiting in a fine arts space and academic context. *Impossibility* incorporates auditory documents of chatroom sexual interaction between artist and contacts, while visuals are sensuously rendered abstract and oblique (strategically striptease/soft core?). Pre-Facebook, pre-Tubesites, on the cusp of the commercial popularization of the webcam, this site-specific panoply recognizes, as does Jackson (see below), the online chatroom as a significant stage in the trajectory of both virtual sexual community and racialized identity networks. "The project documents the collective experience of orgasm in virtual space. It creates a discourse of sexual politics in the context of postcolonial and interracial sexual relationships by showing my 'oriental' identity through my web camera" (cited by Jacobs 2007, 71).

5. Michael V. Smith (Miss Cookie LaWhore), *Girl on Girl*, 2004, 17 min., Canada, http://www.michaelvsmith.com/michaelv_intro.htm. This artisanal video production is rooted in the context of Smith's British Columbia–based multi-disciplinary artistic practice as novelist, columnist, poet, memoirist, teacher, activist, and public performer, including the stand-up genderfuck clown persona of Miss Cookie. The video and performance artist performs heterosexual intercourse on camera with his sex-worker gal pal Amber Dawn. Smith, in baptizing his genre

19.2 "Docuporn," or a manifesto of complicity, coalition, and friendship. *Girl on Girl*, dir. Michael V. Smith (Miss Cookie LaWhore, 2004).

"docuporn," was maybe riffing on Roth's precedent of more than a decade earlier, both artists producing a manifesto of complicity, coalition, and friendship with a female sex worker. But he was also transforming it, anchoring it in art-world cultures of iconoclastic performance art and post-Butler gender queer performative politics. The work reached festival audiences and subsequently was partially available through the artist's website.

6. Derek Jackson, *Cruiser*, 2003, video, 5 min., USA; The *Personals*, 2004, video, 5 min., USA; *Perfect Kiss*, 2007, video, 5 min., USA. Based in Portland, Maine, Jackson is a multidisciplinary artist – filmmaker, writer/critic, anti-racist, and HIV+ activist, front man for the multimedia performance art-punk band Hi Tiger (https://hitiger.bandcamp.com/) and accomplished visual artist (https://www.visualaids.org/artists/detail/derek-jackson). *Cruiser* is a hand-held diaristic saunter through Brooklyn's Prospect Park's cruising areas, focusing only on legs and feet and the heavily condom-littered ground, and includes several well-recorded conversations, both sexual and testimonial, with the artist's kindred spirits along the

way. This hyper-discreet work is sexually explicit only on the soundtrack, and even the auditory evidence of a blowjob is fleeting. Both *Personals* and *Perfect Kiss* follow instead the MTV template, animating the artist's erotic self-presentation, the first hard core, the second soft, to a song. The first erotic self-portrait is set to the vintage song "Disorder" by Joy Division, part of a larger series based on internet personals. It features the nude artist masturbating to climax in one take, seated before the camera with the frameline revealing his lively dreads and mouth and his body down to his knees, but not his identity, as per the conventions of chatroom culture (Jackson, email correspondence, 11 November 2017). All the while, he holds up title cards sharing phrases taken from a four-hour online chat session (selecting exchanges ranging from less instrumental chitchat about the weather to the more existential "I'm so lonely I could die"), echoing Leung and other artists of the millennial moment in seizing on these pre-Web 2.0 encounters as artistic raw material. Like most of my cohort, Jackson refuses to dissociate the banal everyday from erotic relationality. The later, more discreet erotic self-portrait rhythmically edits still and stop-motion "come-hither"/voguing beefcake, both domestic interior and exterior cruising landscape, to "Perfect Kiss" (New Order, 1985). The song elegiacally evokes a friend's suicide and ambiguously hints at the risk for the seropositive artist of the retrovirus, as one critic speculates (Hushka 2011), but the overall effect is incontrovertibly erotic. All three works played to queer festival and artspace audiences, specifically MIX New York. Thereafter, the artist's busy multi-platform career has regrettably enabled only sporadic and partial online and offline availability. Like others of the post-cinephile internet-era artists, Jackson has not maintained a festival presence since *Perfect Kiss*.

 7. Ryan Conrad, *Rituels queer*, 2013, 12 min. and other multiple digital and analog formats and running times, Canada. Conrad and his Super 8 cinematographer collaborator Richard E. Bump filmed Conrad and his then partner in four sessions of domestic and conjugal rituals, including grooming, bathing, kissing, sucking, fucking, and rimming, as well as a childhood game of blanket forts, much of it using in-camera superimpositions within the eight reels. Conrad's various eventual versions and formats all offered a delicate and intricate yet stirring tapestry of conjugality and sex, bringing out the eroticism of intergenerational mentoring rites (from shaving instruction and bathing to the actual setup of the filming [erotic gaze?] by the twenty-something artist's elder collaborator). Conjugality surfaces in several of my selected works, but here it is at its most intimate, lyrical and tender, which enraptures its largely queer festival and academic audiences.

 8. Jamie Ross, *Rousings*, 2014, 14 episodes, varied lengths, Canada, https://www.xtube.com/profile/rousings-24672242. This ambitious Xtube series also cir-

culated in artspace, specifically a hemispheric gallery exhibition tour (Canada, South America). There is even a hardcover tie-in catalogue, with essays by the curator and some contributors, *Rousings: A Luminous Brotherhood*, enabled by Canadian arts council funding (2015). The work's fourteen autonomous jerkoff performances are addressed to the webcam by a multinational, multiracial roster of project contributors, most wearing masks of the titular ancestor's face.

Vocal performances or voice-overs usually recite the ancestor's work as in my three selected episodes:

Arthur Rimbaud (An T. Horné, Canada): Horné's breathy, intense, and intimate performance of anal jerkoff in genderqueer period costume, otherwise unmasked, is accompanied by the sync-sound recitation of the poet's famous 1871 "Sonnet of the Asshole," perhaps the series' most literal sound-image mix.

Allen Ginsberg ("Carlos," Colombia): Carlos's jerkoff performance unfolds under an archival voice recording by the poet of an excerpt from "Howl." The encounter of Latino brown skin and cock with white North American Beat revolt has a provocative effect.

Bobby Khamvongsa (anonymous, Colombia): Another genderqueer jerkoff, this one penile and masked, in top hat and cummerbund and with only ambient sound, invokes a more obscure ancestor, a queer-of-colour martyr to 2012 police violence in Los Angeles.

Integrating a pagan spirituality and queer interdisciplinary art practice with a porn address, Ross solicited webcam jerkoff performance contributions from kindred spirits across North and South America, each to invoke through orgasm a queer ancestor, usually including a recitation of the ancestor's work. Half are signed by performers, including *Derek Jarman* by Ross, and the rest are anonymous.[7] The transcultural and transhistorical span of the series' performances affirms a global internet utopia, and Horné makes it explicit:

> I'm still amazed that Rimbaud was putting out sexual and esoteric queer poetry at the time he was, in the mid to late nineteenth century, and I see it as a building block towards creating a capacity for a queer connectivity and love to be possible and not dictated by a dominant repressive force. It was faggots like him, where creativity was essential in the attempt to experience a feeling of liberation, that have allowed me to do the same, albeit in a different form, but nonetheless I still recognize it as a sort of lineage not bound by blood persay [sic], but bound by eros. It's about liberation and being driven to creative expression that moves us further towards our visions of utopia. (cited in Ross 2015, 43–4)

9. Colby Keller, *Colby Does America*, online series, 33 episodes, varying lengths, 2014 +, USA. (See below.)

10. Branden Miller, *Pradaboiswag/ Miss Prada/ Joanne the Scammer*, 2010+, USA. Miller's multiple online personae originated on Pornhub, which originally hosted a dozen or so playful performance clips (e.g., https://www.pornhub.com/view_video.php?viewkey=298214773; Skype platform also available), fluctuating between asshole and cock focus, on-camera dildo-penetration, and jerkoff performances, between bathtub, bed, vanity mirror, and living-room carpet, often ejaculating and at least once doing so right on the lens (quickly rendering the scene rather abstract).

One clip offers unadulterated ass-shaking to music, another ass-slapping, and others extended flip-fucking with Miller's boyfriend. The Florida-based Miller eventually migrated to YouTube and Instagram, leaving behind his energized hard-core performances, segueing first towards streetside genderfuck MTV-style rap performances and finally yielding to multi-platform drag glamour fits by the aspiring genderfuck criminal Joanne on Instagram (https://www.instagram.com/joannethescammer/) – without ever entirely abandoning his former profiles – an African-American version of Chris Crocker?

11. Viktor Belmont. MSTRVKTR (series), ca. 2014+, USA, https://vimeo.com/viktorbelmontofficial. The Bay Area gay transmale escort, blogger, "curated" online persona, and porn performer's multi-platform oeuvre includes a series of twelve videos called MSTRVKTR (Mr Viktor), of which several are short, diaristic items or genre narrative shorts, MTV-style, and others "teasers" and hard-core episodes. Two of the latter are intense and ecstatic hookups with eager cisgendered white

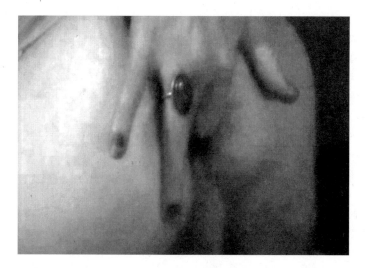

9.3 *Opposite and above* "Creating a capacity for a queer connectivity and love": channelling ancestors through vocal and corporeal auto-performance. *Arthur Rimbaud*, dir. An T. Horné, 2014; *Rousings* series, Jamie Ross, 2014.

19.4 Branden Miller (aka Pradaboiswag / Miss Prada / Joanne the Scammer), multiple online personae, pornformances, and migrations from Pornhub to Youtube and Instagram, 2010–.

male clients, told expertly with tight narrative acumen and mostly mainstream porn conventions but the aura of "authenticity." Belmont's online persona builds on an addiction-recovery, first-person narrative, "my fitness journey," and his sex-worker affirmation is explicit both on-camera and off – he even was honoured with the escort award "Hookie" in 2016 – but his Puerto Rican identity is acknowledged only indirectly. Mr. Viktor's voice and work are based in a slick website, a selfie-strewn, "curated" online persona, and larger artistic practice that includes zine production alongside film work.

His voice onscreen and online is articulate and committed:

> I have one driving life goal, and that is to make every person that I meet and every person in the world know that they belong here. I would love to spend all my time and all my resources helping my community – making sure that people have basic human rights, and get their basic human needs taken care of. I will definitely push as hard as I can to create a space where people don't have to live in fear of being who they are. Growing up, I had some access to resources with the Internet, but now there is this huge community with YouTube and everything else online that's really amazing. We can create a space where people don't have to be afraid to be themselves. Ten years from now if I could just be spending all of my time doing that, however I can directly help the most, that's really what I want to be doing. I want everyone to know that they're loved ...
>
> Now is time, more than ever, for me to create. To write it down. To show all sides. Right now its still radical for someone like me to be out and exist. So i'll do what I know and move forward ... I'm going to keep trying to make my family bigger. Take moments. Give hugs. Show kindness. I'm going to try and land johns left and right so I can continue to travel and help show the world that we out here, we've been out here, and my community is so strong, supportive, and beautiful, that we can start to heal each other. (MSTRVKTR)

Let's now come back to Colby Keller, along with LaBruce the most prolific and notorious of my auto-porn-artists, who has for a dozen years been producing online a corpus of explicit sexual self-representation with both a narrative and an erotic thrust – an oeuvre that can serve as a foil for my entire motley crew. Born in 1980 and originally from the American Midwest, Keller is a fine arts graduate from the Maryland Institute College of Art who started attracting attention in the porn milieu in his early twenties. He started out with Seancody.com, a US gay pornsite specializing in the presentation of conventionally attractive, cheer-

19.5 Colby Keller: confession plus the spectrum of desire, politics, the arts, and human relations. www.colbydoesamerica.com.

ful, wholesome, and muscled white young men, performing in both solo and narrative-conjugal scenes, with models signed up exclusively on the basis of having no prior porn history, often "gay for pay." In 2013 Keller became a red-haired and sympathetic star of CockyBoys studio, then a freshly rebranded gay pornsite that distinguished itself on the market for its greater diversity and its success in allowing arty initiatives and aspirations, leading to multiple awards. It boasts on its home page about *New York Magazine*'s appreciation of its "aesthetic" and "light," "ironic touch," and Salon.com's ultimate homage, naming director Jake Jaxson "the Walt Whitman of gay porn [that seeks to] revolutionize porn with an erotic documentary inspired by great poets and celebrating life." Now a household name in gay male community networks as pornstar, blogger, and intellectual, Keller even self-defines as communist – not an everyday American identity outside of academia!

The *Colby Does America* web series (fig. 19.5) is essentially an auto-porn-art film diary that documents the director's sexual and autoerotic adventures, usually narrated by himself. His voice touches on confession, as well as the spectrum of desire, politics, the arts, and human relations. Thirty-one episodes of ten minutes each were produced between 2014 and 2017, often displaying an artistic, even experimental flair and DIY sincerity, then uploaded and offered free for download on the artist's website, www.colbydoesamerica.com.

Keller uses a strategy of micro-crowdfunding on the net, the kind of "alternate porn economics" foreseen a decade ago by Jacobs (2007, 47), exemplary of anti-capitalist impulses within queer erotic cultures. The web series belongs more or less to its public:

> Hey, there, I'm Colby Keller … I'm an artist, a writer, and a pornstar … I have decided to turn everything I own, into art! I gave all my earthly possessions – and I mean every single thing – away for free. Here's what I need in return: Your continued support. I like to fuck, no secret there. And I'd like to fuck this great nation of ours – Canada too. So if I'm gonna be starting from scratch, I'll need a lot of help along the way. I wanna bring you with me … Watch me fuck, join in the fun, or simply help me get a bite to eat – I'll come to you. I promise to give as much I get. With your help, together, forever – or at least for a few months. (Keller 2014)

Like my entire eclectic cohort, Keller invites us to break down the separations between artist and public, director and spectator, analog contemplation and digital immediacy, to join him in a virtual, visual, and auditory adventure.

Colby Does America makes use of several narrative and erotic genres. Keller's galley of editors integrates archival documents, slow motion, jokey, self-reflexive, or "road movie" narrations, and political commentary through sound and image confrontations. As for the erotic interludes, they are inventive and versatile, sometimes borrowing commercial porn conventions from the likes of Sean Cody, etc. (as do others on my roster from Jackson to Belmont), but usually with a touch of irony, sometimes in an epistolary style, reflecting technical and aesthetic propensities of local collaborators and Keller's chemistry with them. The voices of the director and his sexual partners weave a thread through the episodes and solicit a complex but intimate bond with spectators. The onscreen sexual exchanges in almost all the episodes address the viewer on a par with the exchange of ideas, jokes, and laughter, guided tours, silent moments of camaraderie on the highway or in a forest, constructing an everyday spectrum of erotic sociality. One self-reflexive comment of a regional artist-collaborator (Oregon) is typical in highlighting the transformative potential of the triangular relationship of auto-porn-artist, onscreen erotic-artistic collaborator, and spectator: "I make short films, but I try to use dance the same way you use sexuality."

Not *all* spectators are onside, for my gay grad students are not unanimous about Keller. Does this demographic, scarred by Grindr and as blasé as fickle, find him a bit long of tooth (born 1980!) and a bit too squeaky clean? (Often romantic and childlike, he regularly invites us to bathe with him – and ejaculate – in the tubs, lakes, and streams of rustic America, in the water and under the water.) Is he paradoxically too smart and too dumb? Moreover, many of my informants are furious about his tactical support for Trump in the 2016 election (not to mention his inclusion of Israel, apparently as an honorary US state, the same year, BDS boycott or no boycott) – without really thinking through a rhetorical gesture that aimed one month before the election for a destabilization of the political landscape and catered to the peanut gallery in a manner almost as cynical as theirs. It's clear that porn stars' charms wane quickly. One of my circle hates his stylish beard, another doesn't like gingers, and a third finds him vulgar and scruffy. A few queer radicals find him simply too white, not so much in skin tone as in his default complicity with the white supremacy of a studio like Sean Cody. They are not wrong, for Keller's symbolic, contradictorily pale pinkness (as well as the problematical terms of his enrolment of a small number of queer-of-colour collaborators, as dissected by Arroyo in this volume (chapter 13), is dramatically "whitened" even further when juxtaposed to the discordant rainbow hues of much of the rest of my cohort. Moreover, his wholesome and pornonormative body stands out all the more in relation to the unconventional body types celebrated by some of my other auto-porno-artists – from stocky, squat, scrawny, and hirsute to trans* and femme, especially the potent combination of hirsute and femme (Smith and Miller). Still, I'm fascinated by his work, by the significations and self-representations of this over-the-hill cherub (not only as whore but also as artist and radical prophet) and even by his charming effort to sell his Julia Kristeva reader to finance his auto-porn-art (US$300!). In spite of everything, his flippancy – perhaps an attempt to mask a level of pain for better or worse? – does not detract from the gravity, intensity, didacticism, and risk-taking in his intervention, his productive straddling of the borders between art and porn, his political, cultural, and sexual ascesis.

Taken all together, Keller and the others, this motley corpus has offered for me an introit into an understanding of confession and testimony within gay male culture of the second decade of this century, including the explicit sexual imagery that permeates it. All of my auto-porn-art authors' testimony, voice, and image, their self-filmed and self-narrated sexual performances constitute an autobiographical discourse centred both on the self (masturbation, the cum shot) and on the relation to the other (the hand job, penetration, and a dozen other acts of reciprocal corporeal tenderness). Their work counterintuitively sets up a didactic and sober sociality that is dear to heart of this erstwhile Griersonian documentary scholar. In lieu of the Freudian/phenomenological theoretical model that has been used profitably to shed light on the not dissimilar corpus of body art in academic fine arts (Jones 1998, 103–50), the lens of Foucauldian ethics cross-pollinated by queer theory seems essential for an understanding of the auto-porn-art corpus. In the light of Foucault's central concepts of confession and parrhesia, these works highlight the corporeal and social element of the confessional enunciation, that is, "truth-telling" and erotic testimony. These artists' risk-taking truth-telling, perhaps touched by unprocessed shame (what was the affect for Roth to have his funder remove their name from his credits?), may account for a range of dynamics, from the recourse to half-hidden faces and even masks to unsustained or uneven distribution practices shared by many of them – even to the academic practice of maintaining both respectable and less respectable CVs.

Are we justified in thinking about auto-porn-art as confession? Do the institutional matrix of "interpellation-masturbation-interaction" and internet fan culture constitute a confessional relationship? Are the artists who fuck/jerk off in front of the camera – or those who document and share their online frenzy aurally, like Leung and Jackson – enacting a corporeal, gestural instance of confession? Do we, masturbators in front of the screen – or if not aroused, bored, distracted, satiated subjects or, at the other extreme, often engaged and stimulated browsers – receive their performance as a special mode of confession? Is our "arousal/erection/orgasm" before the author-whore's mediatized action – or even just our attention – a kind of confessional absolution?

Keller thinks of porn as theatre, as community storytelling:

> In a fairer world, content would be made free as a public good to be shared and valued communally. That's why I wanted to make all the videos I create for *Colby Does America* free, to mirror this idea. To see what would happen if I gave capitalism the middle finger and just gave away everything, my worldly possessions, my labour, and my body. To make it all available, for anyone who wants it … for free. For me this project is another step in the direction of revolution. Maybe I will inspire others to give themselves away for free as well. Who knows? (Keller 2014)

Many if not most of my dozen auto-porn-artists also give away their work for free (Roth and LaBruce along with his vigilant producers are positioned by default within the twentieth-century model of commercial film distribution; Leung is positioned within art-world and academic restraints; and Jackson the musician has been less committed to providing online access to his moving-image sideline than others of my case studies). Regardless of variations, all collectively join what we might call without exaggeration the creative commons of the porniverse. Belmont and Miller in particular, as well as Jamie Ross's lineup of contributor-performers, delight in the free-access dimension of the internet to circulate their work on tubesites and elsewhere (all the while, in the cases of the two Americans, making a decent living from internet merchandising, and in the case of the Canadians, funding the works through arts and academic grants!). This gesture of "giving everything" applies also to generous and articulate conversations on the multiple platforms that accompany their onscreen performances in almost every case. Their first-person voices as art/porn practitioners and public artists/personae, their supplementing of eroto-corporeal testimony and visual creation with direct address, perform a discursive relationality with spectators and collaborators alike. Their relational practices, their investments in the queer commons, go well beyond the traditional dynamics of porn, art, and confession. The direct address of the auto-porn-artistic confession – whether vocal, ocular, gestural, or monetary – even if digital and mediated – must be seen, I argue, as a "true" relation with interlocutors, whether virtual or in the flesh. These artists' rhetorical overstatements surrounding their moving images, whether trash-nihilist like Miller's, or (pretentiously?) radical like Keller's, or bordering on New Age self-help like Belmont's, are in harmony with the utopian and reparative thrusts within cultural and queer studies over the past several generations, unashamedly embracing the discourses of negation, revolt, emancipation, and community.

Cruising Saints José, Paul, and Michel

To continue in this utopian vein, I now would like to enable a little cruise between my corpus and that of José Muñoz, whose work on our need for utopia I join so many others in celebrating and using, along with bareback porn mogul Paul Morris, together at last – and I take the liberty of appropriating their voices liberally! Muñoz raised the issue of "queer optimism" in his first book *Disidentifications* (1999), which in fact is no less utopian than *Cruising Utopia*, his book that came out ten years later (2009). Here he thought about Pedro Zamora, the brave Latino reality-TV star (1972–94) who performed openly in the last year of his life as a PLWA in *The Real World: San Francisco* alongside an ensemble of roommates – as a "complicated intersectional subject" (2009, 153). Muñoz's exegesis both invoked and cited Foucault: "Zamora performed his care of the self as truth game that 'was for others,' letting them see and imagine a resistance to entrenched systems of domination" with his "care for the self ... and for the other" (144). Zamora leapt "into the social through the public performance of an ethics of the self ... a working on the self for others ... a new formation, being for others" (160). Continuing in the same vein, Muñoz describes this work as "an activity [that] implies attention, knowledge, technique." This work of video-testimony, even if it's a tacky reality-TV show, allows us to "imagine a resistance to entrenched systems of domination." It's thus a question of "an ethics around nourishing and sustaining a self within civil society," a minoritarian ethics of the self far from "socially prescribed identity narratives" (145). This "performance of Latina/o, queer, and other minoritarian ontologies – which is to say, the theatricalization of such ethics of the self – conjures the possibility of social agency within a world bent on the negation of minoritarian subjectivities" (146) ... "Representations of and (simultaneously) by that self signal new spaces within the social ... strategies that resist, often through performances that insist on local specificities and historicity, the pull of reductive multicultural pluralism ... and [that produce] 'a minoritarian space'" (146–8).

Preaching to the unconverted, Muñoz says, must be recognized as a struggle and as a priority activity. Those who engage with such an interpellation constitute a subaltern counter-public. Muñoz restructures Foucault's paradigm in the service of minority identity in the Pandemic-scarred American society of the fin-de-siècle. He reintegrates sexuality into this questioning and asks, in harmony with Foucault, "to invent from A to Z a relationship that is still formless and that is friendship," because "the problem is not to discover in oneself the truth of one's sex, but rather to use henceforth one's sexuality to arrive at a multiplicity of relations" (Foucault [1981] 1989, cited in Muñoz 2009, 159).

I much appreciate Muñoz's affective identification with both his Parisian ancestor and his Cuban-American "cousin," all the while seeking a method to expand his discourse to apply to queer public porno-art-culture of the following decades. Might I plausibly argue that my auto-porn-art personae of the twenty-first century, and their twentieth-century forebears, LaBruce and Roth, are following in the footsteps of that Pandemic-era reality-TV star as public persona and minority subject? Although one can hardly consider Keller, a cisgendered gay white man with a BFA, as minoritarian, except in a particular and nuanced way, his cohort of gender-variant and diversely racialized peers and contemporaries fill the bill. In particular, according to Keller, the combined status as whore and artist implies a greater loss of power compared to that of a masculine white gay man, and this composite public identity of whore-artist, claimed in my cohort directly or surrogately by "Wild," Roth, LaBruce, Leung, Smith, and Belmont (and at least one other, on a confidential basis), expands exponentially in their minoritarian valence in combination with their identity discourses as gendered outsider ("Wild," Smith, and Belmont) or racial outsider (Leung and Belmont). Such enunciations imply not only a reparative understanding of the internet but also a freely utopian understanding of virtual erotic, cultural, and political relations between queers, mediated and not. Utopian or not, Keller and his friends demonstrate clearly the corporeal potentialities for such relations – lively, vigorous yet tender, spontaneous, playful, and inventive, soberly engaging with ideas, spirituality, activism, affect, and desire.

Paul Morris seems to enlist Foucault to pronounce on revolution and utopia as often as Muñoz and Keller. His claims can help elaborate on their and our concept of the subaltern counter-public, as crystallized by the figures of sex worker, porn worker, and art worker:

> A cheap hotel room is the spatial analogue of a whore. And the whore is the basic identity unit of any pornographic utopia. There is nothing more politically transcendent than a cheap whore. The body of the true whore is the flint that makes a spark of revolution possible. Through representation of the whore, porn turns the world of value and wealth and possessiveness upside down. If any men can buy me, anyone can have me, but no one can own me. (Morris and Paasonen 2014, 216)

He continues, "Porn also conditions the viewer to understand and accept the net – the radically egalitarian world of the flat computer screen – as a magical habitable space, as home ... A bodily promiscuity assembled across the entire world ... the public screen of the web ... a public and massively shared imaginary ... a frontier of expression, of imagination and of aesthetics." (226)

Moreover, "queer porn identities are grouped, interdependent identities that are a 'system of opening and closing that both isolates them' – in terms of constructed temporal personae – 'and makes them penetrable' – in terms of being interpenetrating parts of a worldwide grouped, promiscuous body" (227–8).

Finally,

Imagistic thought – imagination – gets transferred from a singular and personal interior screen to the public screen of the web ... a massively shared public imagination ... Everyone everywhere is suddenly immersed in screen-life as much as 'real life.' It's a growing population of people who are thinking, musing, and interconnecting in ways that can't be controlled by power. The threat to politics is real and enormous. (228)

This "global body" and this "population" seem clearly to reverberate with Muñoz's subaltern counter-public. This shared vision, as much as the performances of Zamora and my motley crew, is part of the genealogy and corpus of auto-porn-art that I have documented through my career, the "somatic and living archives" described by Morris (321).[8]

As I've wandered selectively through the ideas and images of Muñoz and Morris and my auto-porn-art cohort, Foucault has always been in the wings, as I've repeatedly remarked. I come back now to the concept that he borrowed from ancient ethics and rhetoric – parrhesia, commonly rendered as "truth-telling." This was Plato's practice and ideal: speaking the truth to the tyrant. But it continues to be popularized in the English language, in the Trump era, thanks to Tom Roach (2012; see chapter 29) and others, more than thirty years after Foucault's death. The contrast with the traditional Catholic confession that was at the heart of the first volume of *History of Sexuality* (Foucault [1976] 1990) is elaborated in the volumes and lectures that followed: on one side, a closed relationship, codified, authoritarian, compulsive, sober, and appropriated by neoliberal power as the privileged commodity format of television and social media, or the "first-person industrial complex" already invoked in this volume (chapter 10); on the other side, an ethical relationship with the other, political and affective, playful, subjectivizing, taking risks, without limits, passionate ... In the Christian dynamic that engenders in confession a dependence in relation to the one confessed to, there is an *objectivation* of the self in the act of "truth-telling," to paraphrase Roach (2012, 25–6, 28, 34). With parrhesia, one experiences a *subjectivization* of the self, a transformation of the self. It is clear that the word "relations" is central to my constructed conversation among my motley dozen utopian perverts. One can add other words belonging to Foucault's fetish vocabulary as well, such as "work," "care," "friendship," "polymorphous," and "inventiveness." The intersection of these key concepts encounters in a surprising way the theorizations and ethics of porn, media, and the internet that we have encountered with my corpus of auto-porn-artists, as well as with Muñoz and Morris, as I've sketched out. In the face of dissidents to this gospel of porn, Morris comes back to the simple notion of truth, saying simply that "it's crucial for queer identities that the porn be true" (Morris and Paasonen 2014, 220).

Foucault and Muñoz hardly ever spoke of porn, gay or otherwise; in the only moment where the latter mentions porn in *Disidentifications*, he is on the verge of a paranoid reading of the genre (1999, 87). I would not like to insist fetishistically that the sexually explicit self-representation of the auto-porn-artist has an exceptional ethical or aesthetic status as a cinematic trope – not to mention a transcendent aura – nor to mystify masturbation as a sacramental act – though of course it cannot be denied that it is the epitomous sexual act of the digital age. Nor, of course, can this historian of pornography reify the generic boundaries between soft core and hard core. I think all the same that Foucault's, Muñoz's, and Morris's reflections engage productively with the issues I have touched on in relation to the gang of uncompromising and shameless truth-tellers I have selected. I hope I have intimated how a dialogical testimony between the two philosophers and the dozen auto-porn-artists, between ethical and political thought and public sexual performance, can be inventive, caring, friendly, and exceptionally charged in the ethical and political arena of our still sex-phobic culture … as well as confessional, parrhesiastic, flirtatious, and perhaps even arousing.

NOTES

Heartfelt thanks to my consultation, resources, and support network (in alphabetical order) Brandon Arroyo, Jordan Arseneault, Ryan Conrad, Ferrin Evans, An T. Horné, Jim Hubbard, Nicolas Hynes-Gagnon, John Greyson, Derek Jackson, Steve Kokker, Bruce LaBruce, David LeBlanc, Isaac Leung, Maria Nengeh Mensah, Gregorio Pablo Rodríguez-Arbolay Jr, Jamie Ross, Phillip B. Roth, Michael V. Smith, and Nikola Stepić, as well as Concordia University Faculty of Fine Arts, the Social Sciences and Humanities Research Council of Canada, the Kinsey Institute, and many others.

1 By coincidence the same wonderful phrase was uttered by Laura Bennett in 2015, but I have no idea who came first, "Intervals" or her.
2 I set aside for now a consideration of women's and feminist auto-porn-art, partly because this is well covered by publications from Taormino et al. (2012) to Lavigne (2014), and partly because this corpus would require a different methodology, and partly because I expose myself to it … um … less often than the boys' stuff.
3 This premise, which once might have been denigrated as auteurist in some circles, is of course complicated in relation to the usually collaborative art forms of moving-image production and pornography (even in the age of the cell-phone camera). Whatever the case, I dissociate myself from the "artist-run" fetishism of arts agencies like the Canada Council

4 This art form is nonetheless holding its own, if we witness only two recent Portuguese entries, *The Ornithologist* and *What Now Remind Me?*, autofiction and autobiographical non-fiction respectively, the latter "harder," counterintuitively, than the former.

5 Ancestor worship has its traps, of course. A recent classroom screening at Concordia sparked accusations of transphobia and unsafe space, both onscreen and among classmates. Could this lead to another essay on the relationship of the culture of heightened political sensitivity around public "identity speech" (what some would dismiss as "political correctness") and the confessional complex?

6 LaBruce is bewilderingly absent from much of the retrospective literature summing up the NQC movement, from Rich (2013) to Schoonover and Galt (2016), and is mentioned in passing by only two of the thirteen contributors to Aaron (2004).

7 Other ancestors included on the unexpectedly eclectic and unevenly queer-household-name roster are Arthur Russell, Nicky Crane, Dzi Croquettes, John Wayne Gacy, Darby Crash, Karol Romanoff, Queer Victims of National Socialism, Cris Miró, Wilhelm von Gloeden, and Francis Bacon. One inspiration for Ross had been David Wojnarowicz's famous work in which he wears a mask of Arthur Rimbaud.

8 Of course Morris is not without his critics. Arroyo is not shy to point out the contradictions in his public discourse: "Paul Morris talks a good game, but is never confronted on the amount of money he's made from these movies. He's as much a facilitator of the capitalism machine as anyone. But since he bucks the trend by embracing his performers' potential to be HIV+ as a queer act of resistance, he never gets called on it" (email correspondence, 13 November 2017).

REFERENCES

Aaron, Michele. 2004. *New Queer Cinema: A Critical Reader.* New Brunswick, NJ: Rutgers.

Bennett, Laura. 2015. "The First-Person Industrial Complex." *Slate*, September 14. http://www.slate.com/articles/life/technology/2015/09/the_first_person_industrial_complex_how_the_harrowing_personal_essay_took.html.

Blachford, Gregg. 1978. "Looking at Pornography: Erotica and the Socialist Morality." *Gay Left: A Socialist Journal Produced by Gay Men* 6 (Summer): 16–20.

Burger, John R. 1994. *One-Handed Histories: The Eroto-Politics of Gay Male Video Pornography.* New York: Routledge.

Corneau, Simon, Kim Bernatchez, and Dominic Beaulieu-Prévost. 2017. "Le Point de vue des hommes de minorités ethniques sur le racisme à travers la pornographie gaie." In *Le témoignage sexuel et intime, un levier de changement social?*, edited by Maria Nengeh Mensah, 135–44. Montreal: Les Presses de l'Université du Québec.

Delany, Samuel. 1999. *Times Square Red, Times Square Blue.* New York: New York University Press.

Dines, Gail. 2011. *Pornland: How Porn Has Hijacked Our Sexuality.* Boston: Beacon.

Dinshaw, Carolyn. 1999. *Getting Medieval: Sexualities and Communities, Pre- and Postmodern.* Durham: Duke University Press.

Dyer, Richard. [1985]1992. "Coming to Terms: Gay Pornography." *Only Entertainment.* London: Routledge.

Foucault, Michel. [1976] 1990. *The History of Sexuality.* Vol. 1: *An Introduction.* New York: Vintage.

– [1981] 1989. "Friendship as a Way of Life." In *Foucault Live*, edited by Sylvère Lotringer and translated by John Johnston, 203–9. New York: Sémiotexte.

Fruchand, Henri-Paul, and Jean-François Bert. 2012. "Un inédit de Michel Foucault: 'La Parrêsia.' Note de présentation." *Anabases: Traditions et réceptions de l'Antiquité* 16: 149–56.

Gagnon, John H., and William Simon. 1973. *Sexual Conduct: The Social Sources of Human Sexuality.* New York: Routledge.

Hushka, Rock. 2011. "It's an Image of Sex, It's Not about AIDS: The Legacy of the AIDS Crisis on American Art (It's Never Not about HIV)." *GIA Reader* 22, no. 3 (Fall). https://www.giarts.org/reader-22-3.

Jacobs, Katrien. 2007. *Netporn: DIY Web Culture and Sexual Politics.* Lanham: Rowan & Littlefield.

Jarman, Derek. [1992] 2010. *At Your Own Risk: A Saint's Testament.* Minneapolis: University of Minnesota Press.

Jones, Amelia. 1998. *Body Art/Performing the Subject.* Minneapolis: University of Minnesota Press.

– 2006. *Self/Image: Technology, Representation and the Contemporary Subject.* New York: Routledge.

Kendall, Christopher. 2005. *Gay Male Pornography: An Issue of Sex Discrimination.* Vancouver: UBC Press.

Lavigne, Julie. 2014. *La Traversée de la pornographie: Politique et érotisme dans l'art.* Montreal: Remue-ménage.

Mensah, Maria Nengeh, ed. 2017. *Le témoignage sexuel et intime, un levier de changement social?* Montreal: Les Presses de l'Université du Québec.

Mercer, John. 2017. *Gay Pornography: Representations of Sexuality and Masculinity.* London: I.B. Tauris.

Mercier, Élisabeth. 2017. "La Pornographie en ligne et l'hypersexualisation des jeunes au Québec." In Nengeh Mensah, *Le témoignage sexuel et intime, un levier de changement social?*, 67–76.

Moore, Patrick. 2004. *Beyond Shame: Reclaiming the Abandoned History of Radical Gay Sexuality.* Boston: Beacon.

Morris, Paul, and Susanna Paasonen. 2014. "Risk and Utopia: A Dialogue on Pornography." *GLQ: A Journal of Lesbian and Gay Studies* 20, no. 2: 215–39.

Muñoz, José. 1999. *Disidentifications: Queers of Color and the Performance of Politics*. Minneapolis: University of Minnesota Press.

– 2009. *Cruising Utopia: The Then and There of Queer Futurity*. New York: New York University Press.

Nguyen Tan Hoang. 2014. *A View from the Bottom: Asian American Masculinity and Sexual Representation*. Durham: Duke University Press. Patton, Cindy. 2014. *L.A. Plays Itself/Boys in the Sand: A Queer Film Classic*. Vancouver: Arsenal Pulp Press.

Rich, B. Ruby. 2013. *New Queer Cinema: The Director's Cut*. Durham: Duke University Press.

Roach, Tom. 2012. *Friendship as a Way of Life: Foucault, AIDS, and the Politics of Shared Estrangement*. New York: SUNY Press.

Ross, Jamie. 2015. *Rousings: A Luminous Brotherhood*. Montreal: Articule.

Schoonover, Karl, and Rosalind Galt. 2016. *Queer Cinema in the World*. Durham: Duke University Press.

Sedgwick, Eve Kosofsky. 2003. *Touching Feeling: Affect, Pedagogy, Performativity*. Durham: Duke University Press.

Taormino, Tristan, Celine Parreñas Shimizu, Constance Penley, and Mireille Miller-Young, eds. 2012. *The Feminist Porn Book: The Politics of Producing Pleasure*. New York: Feminist Press at the City University of New York.

Warr, Tracy, ed. 2000. *The Artist's Body*. Introduction by Amelia Jones. London: Phaidon Press.

Waugh, Thomas. 1983. "A Heritage of Pornography: Tom Waugh on the Gay Film Collection of the Kinsey Institute." *Body Politic* 90 (January): 29–33.

– 1985. "Men's Pornography, Gay vs. Straight." *Jump Cut* 30 (Spring 1985): 30–6.

– 1996. *Hard to Imagine: Gay Male Eroticism in Photography and Film from Their Beginnings to Stonewall*. New York: Columbia University Press.

– 2000. *The Fruit Machine: Twenty Years of Writings on Queer Cinema*. Durham: Duke University Press.

– [2001] 2004. "Homosociality in the Classical American Stag Film: Off-Screen, On-Screen," *Sexualities* (UK) 4, no. 3 (Fall): 275–91. Reprinted in Linda Williams, ed. *Porn Studies*. 2004. Durham: Duke University Press.

– 2002. *Out/Lines: Gay Underground Graphics from before Stonewall*. Vancouver: Arsenal/Pulp Press.

– 2004. *Lust Unearthed: Vintage Gay Graphics from the Dubek Collection*. With Willie Walker. Vancouver: Arsenal Pulp Press.

– ed. 2006a. *Gay Art: A Historic Collection*. By Felix Lance Falkon [1972]. New edition edited and updated, with introduction and captions, by Thomas Waugh. Vancouver: Arsenal Pulp Press.

– 2006b. *The Romance of Transgression in Canada: Queering Sexualities, Nations, Cinemas*. McGill-Queen's University Press.

– 2010. *Montreal Main*. With Jason Garrison. Queer Film Classics. Vancouver: Arsenal Pulp Press.

Williams, Linda. 2008. *Screening Sex*. Durham and London: Duke University Press.

MEDIAGRAPHY

Belmont, Viktor. ca. 2014–. MSTRVKTR (online series), USA. https://vimeo.com/viktorbelmontofficial.

Conrad, Ryan. 2013. *Rituels queer*. Film, 12 min., and other multiple digital and analog formats and running times. Canada.

Horné, An T. 2014. *Arthur Rimbaud*. Online short, 11 min. Canada. In Ross, *Rousings*.

Jackson, Derek. 2003. *Cruiser*. Video, 5 min. USA.

– 2004. The *Personals*. Video, 5 min. USA.

– 2007. *Perfect Kiss*. Video, 5 min. USA.

Keller, Colby. 2014–. *Colby Does America*. Online series, 33 episodes, varying lengths. USA.

LaBruce, Bruce. 1991. *No Skin off My Ass*. Film, 73 min. Canada.

– 1994. *Super 8 ½*. Film, 99 min. Canada.

Leung, Isaac. 2003. *The Impossibility of Having Sex with Over 500 Men in a Month – I'm an Oriental Whore*. Multi-platform installation. USA. https://vimeo.com/65429303.

Miller, Branden (a.k.a. Pradaboiswag/ Miss Prada/ Joanne the Scammer). 2010+. Online programs, varied lengths and platforms. USA. e.g., https://www.pornhub.com/view_video.php?viewkey=298214773.

Morris, Paul. 1998 –. Various. Treasure Island Media. USA.

MTV. 1994. *The Real World: San Francisco*. Reality television series, 20 episodes. USA.

"Oscar Wild." ca. 1930. *Surprise of a Knight*. Film, 10 min. USA.

Ross, Jamie. *Rousings*, 2014. Series, 14 episodes, varied lengths, varied platforms. Canada. e.g., https://www.xtube.com/profile/rousings-24672242.

Roth, Phillip B. 1990. *25 Year Old Gay Man Loses his Virginity to a Woman*. Film, 22 min. USA.

– 1996. *I Was a Jewish Sex Worker*. Film, 72 min. USA.

Smith, Michael V. (a.k.a. Miss Cookie LaWhore). 2004. *Girl on Girl*. Video, 17 min. Canada. http://www.michaelvsmith.com/michaelv_intro.htm.

20

On Not Seeing All: The Incomplete, *Sexual Play, and the Ethics of the Frame*

SUSANNA PAASONEN

The opening shot of Jan Soldat's *Der Unfertige* (*The Incomplete*, 2013), a documentary portrait of Klaus Johannes Wolf, begins with Wolf, a small stooped man, sitting on a bed naked except for a leather collar, wrist and ankle cuffs, and a metal codpiece. Wolf is shown preoccupied with locking first his collar and then his wrists to a long metal chain to which his ankles are already tied. Once this has been achieved, and the chain positioned to Wolf's liking, he leans back on the bed in a relaxed pose with his other leg bent up, faces the camera, and waits. The image composition is classic, with Wolf placed almost in the centre of the frame. The room is lit with natural light, and the colours are muted. The greys and browns of the prints hung on the wall echo the hue of the wall itself, as well as the shades of the fabrics spread on the bed, the red stripes of which involve the most intensity. As Soldat, who remains invisible behind the camera, asks Wolf to introduce himself, he gives a little laugh and says, "Well … ODW-Gay (Odenwald-Gay) … or Gollum … or Klaus. Sixty years old … gay … slave" (fig. 20.1).

The scene sets the tone for the rest of the film where Soldat's static camera witnesses the stories that Wolf tells about his life and follows him around in his everyday activities: arriving home, showering and changing to his preferred form of dress (as described above), cooking and eating, cleaning a master's apartment and giving him oral sex, and enrolling in a slave training class. The film's general dynamic is one of mundane "outness," of living out a sexual life where the scenes of sexual play are not marked apart from other routines or exchanges.

This chapter examines *The Incomplete* in the context of Jan Soldat's broader documentary film practice. Starting with an examination of the limited circulation of his work within film culture and the kind of publicness that this affords, it moves into considering forms of personal disclosure, sexual confession, fantasy, and play in *The Incomplete*. These strands of discussion are connected to analysis of Soldat's film style and his uses of the frame in particular.

20.1 Wolf introduces himself, *Der Unfertige* (*The Incomplete*), dir. Jan Soldat, 2013. Image courtesy Jan Soldat.

Out in the Open

Soldat's documentary films explore German sexual cultures, particularly those within the Berlin region, from the portrait of Wolf, the slave, to the activities of a gay private prison (*Haftanlage 4614/Prison System 4614*, 2015; *Hotel Straussberg*, 2014; *Die sechste Jahreszeit/The Sixth Season*, 2015; *Der Besuch/The Visit*, 2015), adult baby play (*Coming of Age*, 2016; *Happy Happy Baby*, 2016), intergenerational male sex (*Wielandstraße 20, 3.0G links*, 2012), a senior male couple's BDSM sessions (*Zucht und Ordnung/Law and Order*, 2012; *Ein Wochenende in Deutschland/A Weekend in Germany*, 2013), men living in sexual relationships with their canine companions (*Geliebt/Be Loved*, 2009), and men fantasizing about being killed and eaten "like pigs" (*Protokolle/Protocols*, 2017). These films bring onscreen practices routinely deemed obscene (literally, ones to be put "out of sight") (Williams 2004, 4; Attwood 2009, xiv) by detaching them from the frameworks of secrecy and sensationalism. In different ways, these films – and, centrally, their subjects – do not so much challenge as disregard assumptions of sex being simply a private affair or of non-normative sexual tastes being ones best hidden. Theirs is a world of mundane, unspectacular outness, "public in the sense of accessible" (Berlant and Warner 2000, 326).

Given this, there is little need in these films for sexual confession as the disclosure of secret desires and acts – let alone as disclosure of moral wrongdoing. This marks a decided departure from the tradition of *scientia sexualis* that has framed sex not as merely as an issue of bodily sensations, orientations, and pleasures but as one of truth and falsehood: "something fundamental, useful, or dangerous, precious or formidable" (Foucault [1976] 1990, 56). Here the act of confessing one's sexual desires and acts has translated as the exposure of the innermost self: "It is in the confession that truth and sex are joined, through the obligatory and exhaustive expression of an individual secret" (61). In the late nineteenth century, these truths became grounded in sexual identities, which included the discovery of novel deviant types, or "species," such as "the homosexual," "the sadist," the "masochist," and "the pervert" (see also Beckmann 2001, 66–7). Understood less as matters of practice than those of being, or even essence, sexual identities became tied in with social categorization and governance.

Routine, more or less elaborate confessions of sexual palates and deeds seem to only multiply in contemporary media culture that tirelessly zooms in, and details, sexual styles, likes, variations, and experiences of people more or less famous, on scales both local and global (Plummer 1995, 3–5, 9; Attwood 2006, 78–9). Brushing shoulders with the titillations of sensationalism, such disclosures have been associated with broader processes of "sexualization" and "pornification" of culture (see Attwood 2009; Smith 2010). Feona Attwood maps out "sexualized culture" as

> a rather clumsy phrase used to indicate a number of things; a contemporary preoccupation with sexual values, practices and identities; the public shift to more permissive sexual attitudes; the proliferation of sexual texts; the emergence of new forms of sexual experience; the apparent breakdown of rules, categories and regulations designed to keep the obscene at bay; our fondness for scandals, controversies and panics around sex. (2006, 78–9)

The increased visibility of sexual cultures, practices, and desires disturbs their association with both moral indiscretions and privacy. At the same time, sexuality and sex also remain lodged in the terrain of intimacy embedded in the social fantasy "that private life is the real in contrast to collective life: the surreal, the elsewhere, the fallen, the irrelevant" (Berlant 2000, 2). Writing on intimacy as supportive of national heterosexuality in the United States, Lauren Berlant and Michael Warner (2000, 317, 323) identify the privacy of sex as its very cornerstone, one challenged by sexual publics where sexuality is not tied in with notions of futurity, the couple format, or the imperative of monogamy, and where diverse desires and attachments abound.

Jan Soldat's cinematic practice involves a similar breaking down of the tenacious associations between sex, privacy, and intimacy. In fact, he can be understood as contributing to sexual publics in the context of film culture. Building on both Berlant's examination of intimate publics and Miriam Hansen's discussion of cinema as an alternative public sphere, Ingrid Ryberg (2012, 33–4) conceptualizes queer, feminist, and lesbian porn film culture as a public arena for articulating sexualities and coining novel experiential horizons. She is particularly interested in the safe spaces of social belonging, affective recognition, and reflection facilitated by film culture (120). Distributed in festivals, Soldat's work similarly operates within a film culture of limited yet manifest public visibility.

In Soldat's films, the persistent links between sex, privacy, intimacy, shame, and secrecy are, if not simply ignored, at least redrawn. The physical spaces involved, such as private residences and private prisons, as well as the sexual routines acted out in them are not openly accessible as such, yet they gain certain publicness through cinematic depiction. Soldat meets and contacts the people appearing in his films online on the basis of their active engagement in sexual scenes: in this sense, outness is the very premise of his film practice. The outness of sexual lives is visually echoed in the cinematic uses of natural light. The films are predominantly shot during daytime, and in one scene after another, rooms bathe in sunlight and people are shot against windows. With the understandable exception of play spaces, such as the windowless cells of a prison, the rooms are domestic. The prison in question, catering to its inmates with their forms of torture and confinement of choice, is adjacent to the home of Arwed and Dennis, the couple running it, and their relationship plays a key role in *Prison System 4614*, *The Sixth Season*, and *The Visit*.

A special power, and appeal, of Soldat's films lies in their display of everyday lives grounded in sexual play. This play is not cornered off or easily confined in specific spaces but depicted as elementary to how everyday lives get organized and lived – depicted, in fact, as what drives these lives. There are no variations in narrative rhythm or tempo between scenes focusing on BDSM play or ones documenting domestic squabbles over which frozen dishes to choose for dinner (*A Weekend in Germany*). Accounts of first meeting one's partner intersect with shots of eating their ass freshly unwrapped from diapers (*Coming of Age*), while a chat with the director on which rubber shorts to display is disrupted when a partner wants to start with the ass spanking (*Law and Order*).

The element of sensationalism might seem hard to detach from these films recording sexual play off the mainstream. Adult babies and prison play, as the subjects of the films themselves elaborate, are minor and at the margins of fetish and BDSM cultures. In fact, it might take notably little imagination to visualize these topics as parts of the late-night televisual flow of sensationalist documentaries promising titillating glimpses of extraordinary sexual lives in a framework that is either humorous or moralizing, or any combination thereof, laced with sexual norms and regulatory intent alike (see Arthurs 2004).

Many of Soldat's films place aging men at their centre of focus. Visual materials of elderly gay men's sexual practices have been circulated on the web since its early days for purposes of humour and shock, as in the well-known instance of "Lemon Party," a still image of senior men engaging in an oral sex threesome, its effect dependent on "the (homo)sexualized, elderly, or overweight body" being perceived of "in terms of disgust and amusement" (Jones 2010, 128; also Paasonen 2011, 223). Media culture is increasingly focused on the speedy circulation, spreadability, and mashability of digital content as it is linked, copied, edited, remixed, and grabbed for novel purposes. These circulations are fast and their routes impossible for those generating the content to control. In other words, the visibility of sexual cultures online also results in their vulnerability, given the impossibility of controlling the context in which their visibility unfolds, how this occurs, where, with, and for whom.

Soldat's films have not been seen on either television or online platforms, and as such the work has remained inaccessible to those wanting to freely remix it, grab clips, or craft animated GIFs. In 2019, Soldat introduced some of his films as video on demand on Vimeo, hence expanding their potential audience. As old school as the solution of primarily screening films in cinemas during festivals may seem to a director born in the 1980s, the limited circulation allows authorial control over the integrity of the work. This control also affords a degree of privacy for those appearing in the films. The images and clips openly available online are laconic and minimalist, and they generally show little of their subjects that would be identifiable. In sum, film culture can be here seen as providing an intimate and limited public for minoritarian sexual cultures and tastes of the kind that remains unavailable on open online platforms and in their circuits of constant redistribution and repurposing.

Confession and Play

In *The Incomplete*, Wolf recounts and shows photographs of his life. Occasionally pausing mid-sentence and speaking with a mild stammer, he talks of childhood and family, his work as tax advisor, and his former life in a religious confraternity. He shares autobiographical details, from the brothers of the confraternity discovering his stash of condoms – and consequently his sexual identity – to his mother's dying moments, his grandfather's sadistic streak, and the spectacle that was his father's funeral. Given the use of monologue and the format of a personal cinematic portrait, *The Incomplete* seems to set the stage for a confession of sexual identities, tastes, and acts, yet such a thing never quite unfolds. Wolf narrates no story of self-discovery or coming out. No broader, coherent narrative of the sexual self emerges. While confession is suggested, and to a degree played with, it is not acted out.

Wolf's performance of the self, while understated, is also highly self-conscious in its modes of being on display. He explains: "This is also like undressing. Like being naked. Opening up. Showing the others that 'I'm stripped down. Now you can really see everything that is me. I've taken everything off, you can see all my emotions now.'" Wolf suggests that his nakedness is literal in multiple senses. Not only is he stripped of clothing but also his emotions are out in the open for people to see and witness – in fact, *everything* about him has been put on display. In the framing suggested by Wolf, the film becomes a means of witnessing his life and persona in a seemingly transparent manner. At the same time, *The Incomplete*, edited down from fourteen hours of interviews of criss-crossing stories with many things left undisclosed (Soldat 2014, 51), can be seen as assembling "life story actions *around* lives, events and happenings" (Plummer 1995, 21) without the possibility of grasping Wolf's experience as such. The film provides markedly limited access to Wolf's life as he set firm boundaries to what Soldat could record. While shooting domestic chores was no issue, quotidian routines such as shopping or meeting up with siblings and close friends remained out of bounds (Soldat 2014, 53).

Regularly explicit in their subject matter – documenting voluntary prison inmates engaging in oral sex and an elderly man's scrotum being stroked with nettles – Soldat's films are simultaneously stylistically laconic in their delivery. Moments of fleshy intensity unfold without the rhythm, tempo, camera angle, or image size changing, and in most instances only fragments of sexual acts are shown. The camera remains static, films begin and end abruptly without an added layer of music, and editing is direct to the point of being blunt: cuts are marked with short flashes of black. All in all, the films witness what unfolds without explaining much.

20.2 Domestic routines, *Der Unfertige* (*The Incomplete*), dir. Jan Soldat, 2013. Image courtesy Jan Soldat.

In *The Incomplete*, a static camera provides shots of Wolf's mundane life largely without much of an interpretative framework. It witnesses Wolf being urinated on and spanked at the slave training camp, yet the film style remains non-intimate, and any closer, explicit details are shown as images on a screen that Wolf himself is watching. As Soldat (2014, 57) himself notes, a sense of emotional distance is pervasive throughout.

Soldat, in general, does not dwell on close-ups. The unhurried tempo of his films builds on long shots and mid shots held long enough to allow for observation. With the sole exception of a scene in *The Visit*, the camera does not follow its subjects – it does not tilt, pan, or zoom. Moving out of the frame, people also move beyond the film's visual reach. There is a specific ethical gravity to this use of frame. Drawing on Ilona Hongisto (2015, 14), Soldat's films can be characterized in terms of their ethics and "aesthetics of the frame; that is, as an aesthetics that foregrounds documentary participation in the real." The immobility of Soldat's camera makes its presence impossible to miss for either those within the frame or those watching the films. There is no aim toward the transparency or immediacy of the medium of the kind that Wolf suggests in noting that the film makes it possible to see "everything that is me." Looking at and talking directly to the camera, Wolf both recounts his life events and analyzes the practice of being a slave: "A slave is also a thing. He has no personality, he is a thing, a product. Not only is he emasculated, but you can also see the entire person, completely naked … So when I'm naked like this and telling you these things, this comes to show that what I'm saying is true. It's not some kind of fantasy."

This claim for transparency and revelation is in line with the film's placid rhythm and Wolf's constant placement in the centre of the frame. But as naked as Wolf may be, both physically and metaphorically, we can hardly see everything that he is. Speaking of how being a slave enables him to find his personal limits, push them further, move beyond them, and do more, Wolf himself later complicates and contradicts these claims of transparency and openness related to the position of the slave as one clearly detached from fantasy:

> A role play, really this role play where I can say, here I can bring my soul which has been quite a bit injured, and heal it again. It is, so to speak, a kind of psychotherapy. Without a psychiatrist. We, in our rational world that is getting more rational because everything gets more mechanical, like doing an endurance run that never ends, we are blocking the whole thing out. The whole … game. The act of playing. We can't play anymore. Our society cannot play anymore.

In this articulation, play is far from casual or random but rather something that brings purpose to life and even makes it livable. It seems to echo Foucault's ([1984] 1997, 163) discussion of sexuality as "our own creation, and much more than the discovery of a secret side of our desire," namely as "a possibility for creative life." For Foucault (165–6), the specific mixture of rules and openness in SM affords novel possibilities for pleasure and the intensification of sexual encounters through fluid, strategic relations: "Even when the roles are stabilized you know very well that it is always a game. Either the rules are transgressed, or there is an agreement, either explicit or tacit, that makes them aware of certain boundaries … It is an acting-out of power structures by a strategic game that is able to give sexual pleasure or bodily pleasure" (169).

Understood in this vein, fantasy is not the opposite of reality but rather a dynamic that contributes to the specific affective charge of individual (and social) lives and fuels acts of sexual play. In his discussion of sexual fantasies, Martin

Barker (2014, 145) critiques the Freudian framework for understanding them as either "the playback for real traumatic experiences" or "the outcome of other repressed problems released in distorted forms." For Barker, compensatory understandings of sexual fantasy reduce them to origin stories of childhood and family life in ways that efface from view later experiences of relationships, communities, bodies, and sexual cultures. It also blocks from view the productivity of fantasies "as the means through which adults might try out versions of self-in-sexual-society, reimagining themselves through others' reimaginings" (146).

Wolf describes slave role-play as personal healing and psychotherapy that necessitates no psychiatrist. This account resembles analyses of BDSM play as somatic intervention, bodily reconnection, and affective reworking of hurtful or traumatic experiences (see Barker 2005; Barker, Gupta, and Iantaffi 2007; Weiss 2011; Hammers 2014). The play of BDSM is not the opposite of serious but rather a serious game that derives some of its intensity from the incorporation of personal life experiences, attitudes, and social power dynamics into sexual scenes, which afford therapeutic possibilities of self-discovery (Weiss 2006, 236–40). As a form of trauma play, BDSM is a means to increase, or restore, the livability of bodies whose affective capacities have been truncated. The therapeutic framework of *The Incomplete* is nevertheless cut short by the fact that Wolf does not provide any further details on how his soul has been injured and what the aims of his therapy routines may be.

In *The Incomplete*, BDSM scenes and routines of everyday life are inextricably intermeshed. The role of a domestic labour slave is not something that Wolf puts on and takes off but rather his mode of being in the world and relating to himself and others. Slavehood comes across as a form of quotidian creativity and play where the sexual is quintessential to the fabric of everyday life and simultaneously provides it with its particular flavour, modality, and intensity. These dynamics can be understood through the notion of play – which Wolf discusses as the opposite of the mechanical: "The whole … game. The act of playing." Understood in this vein, role-play is seriously ludic, detached from the mandates of rationality and driven by the quest of bodily intensity (be this sexual or other). Wolf smilingly describes his heightened focus following a BDSM session:

> I need no cardiovascular agents, no coffee, nothing. My blood flow is great. It's like when Usain Bolt, the sprinter, runs one hundred metres in nine seconds. He's also in top shape. It's the adrenaline. Then everything feels right. My head is quite clear then. After that I can do my most complicated taxes. Because then your body's blood flow is at its best, it's well trained.

Soldat asks: *So, like a jump-start?* Wolf responds: "Yes! It's training. Really, it's like training. It's like training, just in a weird way."

Wolf's sexuality is not primarily of the genital kind. Rather, it involves inventing new possibilities of pleasure through an eroticization and intensification of the whole body (see Foucault [1984] 1997, 165). All of this is premised on the contractual dynamics of play that can be seen as central yet all too often overlooked aspects – not to mention thrills – of sexuality much more generally. The exploration of bodily zones of comfort, interest, and potentiality through play is part and parcel of how sexual desires, tastes, and orientations evolve across people's life spans. Sex involves bodily experimentation and a quest for intensity where the possibilities of what bodies want, do, and can do are never quite set. In other words, sex can be conceptualized as playful acts and improvisations driven by curiosity, desire for variation, openness towards surprise, and quest for bodily pleasure. (For an extended discussion, see Paasonen 2018a; 2018b.)

Anthropologist Margot Weiss writes of BDSM as complicating understandings of sexuality as based on notions of stability: "The pleasure of this play lies in its depth, in the creation and subsequent transgression of boundaries around what one is and can be, what is safe and what is dangerous and what is set aside-and what is reconnected" (2006, 240). As in Wolf's discussion of pushing his personal bodily boundaries further and intensifying his sensations and performance through controlled scenarios of slave play, Weiss emphasizes the mutability of bodily capacities. Drawing on Andrea Beckmann's (2001) study of London-based BDSM cultures, Clarissa Smith similarly argues that "for practitioners, masochism is a form of human expression drawing on sexual dissidence, pleasure, escapism, transcendence and the refusal of normal genital sexuality, allowing for safer sex explorations of the lived body and its transformative potentials" (2009, 23). For Smith, such transformations are issues of embodied capacity and affective intensity that involve potential resonance across categories of identity.

Being a slave is, for Wolf, firmly an issue of identity. His slave play is both serious and a knowing game, and its playfulness does not foreclose or undermine the gravities of identification. While exploring Wolf's personal history, *The Incomplete* does little to contextualize or narrate, let alone "solve" the question of personal desire, sexual bent, or ways of being in the world. It observes, records, and reorganizes Wolf's everyday routines and incidents into a cinematic whole that offers statements, impressions, and perceptions. And since sexuality is not seen to pose any secrets to confess or out, there is no particular underlying mystery or dilemma offered for analysis or therapeutic resolution. Slave play is depicted as being at the core of Wolf's life as that which drives him and affords him with focus. Wolf is a slave without a regular master who, moving in and out of locations and scenes, also moves in and out of arrangements with other men – including the top friend he cleans for and services, and the masters running the slave training camp. There is no cathexis to his desire: it is not directed towards a specific object such as a permanent partner. In fact, Wolf is explicitly anti-sentimental in his disavowal of emotional intimacy between men as something that he has no capacity for or interest in. His final lines in the film encapsulate much of this: "It doesn't really apply to me, seeking affection in men. What I'm looking for is understanding. The understanding to say: 'Uh-huh, he is like that.' Maybe also: 'He's like that for this and that reason, uh-huh!' This is what it means to be understanding."

This dimension, or trajectory, of understanding does not involve crossing or redrawing the boundaries of intimacy. Soldat's ethics of the frame keep the viewer firmly at a distance and allow for Wolf to disclose what he wishes, and how. Wolf describes slave play as therapeutic and central to his wellbeing; he recounts at length the legacy of the Third Reich in his family, once heavily invested in its ideology and machinery, yet the documentary portrait remains void of therapeutic goals. There is no talking cure at play. On the contrary, the depiction of a sexual life, here as elsewhere in Soldat's films, remains detached from the framework of therapy culture. Associated with the accumulations of personal confession and disclosure in the public sphere and the cultural penetration and extensive commodification of Freudian (and, more broadly, psychotherapeutic) discourse, therapy culture is premised on the notion of individual fragility (Furedi 2003; Illouz 2007). In Frank Furedi's well-known conceptualization, therapy culture involves the increasing definition of individuals through their emotional vulnerability. The pervasive language of emotionalism depicts individuals as differently traumatized, damaged, and scarred, in ways that harbour helplessness and powerlessness and that result in diminished capacities of the self (Furedi 2003, 11, 135.) In this framework, confession comes across as a therapeutic act of opening up that allows for causal explanations and possible solutions.

Soldat's films are manifestly void of psychological investigation and speculation beyond that which their subjects disclose, and there is little investment in the question of "why" people's sexual preferences and practices are how they are. Instead, the films focus on the question of "how" people are and how they act. As Soldat puts it, if, after watching *The Unfinished*, a viewer "says, 'I still don't know why he's become like that,' that's a compliment for me" (2014, 59).

Soldat's camera does not aim at inconspicuousness as much as heightened awareness of its presence: people face the camera, talk to the director behind it, and, on occasion, move away from its frame. This awareness of seeing and being

The Incomplete, Sexual Play, and the Ethics of the Frame | 419

20.3 Wolf in close-up, *Der Unfertige* (*The Incomplete*), dir. Jan Soldat, 2013. Image courtesy Jan Soldat.

seen, which unavoidably involves the question as to what cannot be seen or captured on camera, is rendered explicit in the final shot of *The Incomplete* that has Wolf facing the camera – exceptionally, in close-up and to the soundtrack of Beethoven – for thirty-two seconds. The viewer can register slight changes in his facial expression from amusement to pensiveness and back, and speculate on the possible feelings connected to these modulations, yet this visual proximity involves more than a slight sense of distance and unavailability.

With the exception of frame size, the style of *The Incomplete* is similar to that of Soldat's other film of the same year, *Beziehungsweise* (*Respectively*, 2013), which shows people sitting still in their domestic spaces together with their intimate partners and family members. Each shot lasts just over twenty seconds, during which the people do not move or speak. As in the final shot of Wolf, the duration is a little too long to be comfortable for either those in front of the camera or those viewing the film. Movement grows into a necessity, the gaze starts to wander, and a sense of uncertainty begins to set in. The film results in virtual still lives that have just a little too much life in them: dogs pant, children burst into laughter, people nervously shift positions and cannot resist the temptation of teasing one another. On one level, the shots are exceedingly intimate, recording as they do both domestic spaces and private attachments. On another level, much like the last shot of *The Incomplete*, they keep the viewer at a distance. These shots make it impossible to disregard the artificiality and awkwardness of the acts of being on display and of witnessing these displays on the screen.

The insistence on the explicit presence of the frame cuts through Jan Soldat's documentary film practice as an ethical principle that affords a degree of proximity but, even more centrally, distance and detachment. That Soldat is not himself participant in the sexual subcultures he documents adds a further ethical layer to this aesthetics of distance. Refusing to explain much of the sexual tastes, orientations, and preferences they address, his films witness sexual lives by reorganizing what people decide to show and tell of themselves.

Limited in their public circulation, the films comprise a specific cinematic sexual public that resonates beyond the arrangements, scenes, and communities documented. In their mode of mundane outness and the casual social ease with which everyday sexual lives are seen to unfold, Soldat's films veer away from scripts of therapy culture, commodified confessionality, and titillating sensationalism. Theirs is a particular ethical gravity emerging from the laconic documentation of mundane scenes of play. Framing sexual lives "as play rather than as a drama" (Berlant 2008), they manage to capture some of the complex entanglement of seriousness and play that sexual lives involve.

REFERENCES

Arthurs, Jane. 2004. *Television and Sexuality: Regulation and the Politics of Taste*. Berkshire: Open University Press.

Attwood, Feona. 2006. "Sexed Up: Theorizing the Sexualization of Culture." *Sexualities* 9, no. 1: 77–94.

— 2009. "Introduction: The Sexualization of Culture." In *Mainstreaming Sex: The Sexualization of Western Culture*, edited by Feona Attwood, xiii–xxiv. London: I.B. Tauris.

Barker, Martin. 2014. "The 'Problem' of Sexual Fantasies." *Porn Studies* 1, nos. 1–2: 143–60.

Barker, Meg. 2005. "On Tops, Bottoms and Ethical Sluts: The Place of BDSM and Polyamory in Lesbian and Gay Psychology." *Lesbian and Gay Psychology Review* 6, no. 2: 124–9.

Barker, Meg, Camelia Gupta, and Alessandra Iantaffi. 2007. "The Power of Play: The Potentials and Pitfalls in Healing Narratives of BDSM." In *Safe, Sane and Consensual: Contemporary Perspectives on Sadomasochism*, edited by Darren Langdridge and Meg Barker, 197–216. Basingstoke: Palgrave Macmillan.

Beckmann, Andrea. 2001. "Deconstructing Myths: The Social Construction of 'Sadomasochism' versus 'Subjugated Knowledges' of Practitioners of Consensual SM." *Journal of Criminal Justice and Popular Culture* 8, no. 2: 66–95.

Berlant, Lauren. 2000. "Intimacy: A Special Issue." In *Intimacy*, edited by Lauren Berlant, 1–8. Chicago: University of Chicago Press.

– 2008. "Against Sexual Scandal." *Atlantic*, 12 March. http://www.thenation.com/article/against-sexual-scandal/.

Berlant, Lauren, and Michael Warner. 2000. "Sex in Public." In *Intimacy*, edited by Lauren Berlant, 311–30. Chicago: University of Chicago Press.

Foucault, Michel. [1976.] 1990. *The History of Sexuality*. Vol. 1, *An Introduction*, translated by Robert Hurley. London: Pantheon.

– [1984] 1997. *Ethics: Subjectivity and Truth*, edited by Paul Rabinow. New York: New Press.

Furedi, Frank. 2003. *Therapy Culture: Cultivating Vulnerability in an Uncertain Age*. London: Routledge.

Hammers, Corie. 2014. "Corporeality, Sadomasochism and Sexual Trauma." *Body and Society* 20, no. 2: 68–90.

Hongisto, Ilona. 2015. *Soul of the Documentary: Framing, Expression. Ethics*. Amsterdam: Amsterdam University Press.

Illouz, Eva. 2007. *Cold Intimacies: The Making of Emotional Capitalism*. Oxford: Polity Press.

Jones, Steven. 2010. "Horrorporn/Pornhorror: The Problematic Communities and Contexts of Online Shock Imagery." In *Porn.com: Making Sense of Online Pornography*, edited by Feona Attwood, 123–37. New York: Peter Lang.

Paasonen, Susanna. 2011. *Carnal Resonance: Affect and Online Pornography*. Cambridge: MIT Press.

– 2018a. "Many Splendored Things: Sexuality, Playfulness and Play." *Sexualities* 21, no. 4: 537–51.

– 2018b. *Many Splendored Things: Thinking Sex and Play*. London: Goldsmiths Press.

Plummer, Ken. 1995. *Telling Sexual Stories: Power, Change and Social Worlds*. London: Routledge.

Ryberg Ingrid. 2012. *Imagining Safe Space: The Politics of Queer, Feminist and Lesbian Pornography*. Acta Universitatis Stockholmiensis. Stockholm: University of Stockholm.

Smith, Clarissa. 2009. "Pleasing Intensities: Masochism and Affective Pleasures in Short Porn Fictions." In Attwood, *Mainstreaming Sex*, 19–35.

– 2010. "Pornographication: A Discourse for all Seasons." *International Journal of Media and Cultural Politics* 6, no. 1: 103–8.

Soldat, Jan. 2014. *Kontrolliert einlassen – Begrenzungen und Grenzüberschreitungen meiner dokumentarischen Methode*. Schriftliche Diplomarbeit. Berlin: Hochschule für Film und Fernsehen "Konrad Wolf" Potsdam-Babelsberg.

Weiss, Margot D. 2006. "Working at Play: BDSM Sexuality in the San Francisco Bay Area." *Anthropologica* 48, no. 2: 229–45.

– 2011. *Techniques of Pleasure: BDSM and the Circuits of Sexuality*. Durham: Duke University Press.

Williams, Linda. 2004. "Porn Studies: Proliferating Pornographies On/Scene: An Introduction." In *Porn Studies*, edited by Linda Williams, 1–23. Durham: Duke University Press.

MEDIAGRAPHY

Jan Soldat, dir. 2009. *Geliebt (Be Loved)*. Germany, 16 min.

– 2012. *Wielandstraße 20, 3.OG links*. Germany, 2 min.

– 2012. *Zucht und Ordnung (Law and Order)*. Germany, 9 min.

– 2013. *Beziehungsweise (Respectively)*. Germany, 5 min.

– 2013. *Ein Wochenende in Deutschland (A Weekend in Germany)*. Germany, 25 min.

– 2013. *Der Unfertige (The Incomplete)*. Germany, 48 min.

– 2014. *Hotel Straussberg*. Germany, 27 min.

– 2015. *Der Besuch (The Visit)*. Germany, 5 min.

– 2015. *Die sechste Jahreszeit (The Sixth Season)*. Germany, 37 min.

– 2015. *Haftanlage 4614 (Prison System 4614)*. Germany, 60 min.

– 2016. *Happy Happy Baby*. Germany, 22 min.

– 2016. *Coming of Age*. Germany, 13 min.

– 2017. *Protocols*. Germany, 20 min.

21

To Queer Things Up: Sexing the Self in the Queer Documentary Web Series

SARAH E.S. SINWELL

In an era of sexting, celebrity sex tapes, and internet porn, a number of queer documentary web series are redefining the relationships between queer sexuality and confession. Following in the footsteps of the It Gets Better Project of 2010, these web series attempt to explore the constantly evolving meanings of queer sexuality via new modes of autobiography, confession, and sexual storytelling. This chapter addresses the ways in which queer documentary web series such as *Losing It with John Stamos*, *To Queer Things Up*, and *The Peculiar Kind* construct confession as queer by mapping it onto ideas of celebrity, intersectionality, and political activism.

In an effort to utilize "third and fourth screen" practices, these web series attempt to reach a new audience – viewers who watch videos on their laptops, tablets, and cell-phones. Appearing on sites such as Yahoo Screen, YouTube, and Vimeo, these series reimagine ways of telling stories about sex, desire, and the body by questioning the relationships between the verbal, the visual, and the confessional. In *Losing It with John Stamos*, celebrities like Wayne Brady, Alan Cumming, and Perez Hilton rehash losing their virginity, supported by animated sequences. In *To Queer Things Up*, queer identified people define the term "queer" in their own words. And in *The Peculiar Kind*, queer women of colour describe their sex lives and dating experiences via unscripted conversations.

Investigating terms such as "queer," "gay," "lesbian," "androgynous," "transgender," "monogamous," and so on, these web series also explore how ideas of celebrity, intersectionality, and advocacy are tied in with understandings of queer sexuality. Questioning the construction of queer identity as a single category, these web series use digital aesthetics and animated sequences to investigate visual and aural representations of sexual narratives and confessions. As Susannah Radstone argues in *The Sexual Politics of Time*, "Concern with sexuality is one of the key defining features of confession" (2007, 38). To this end, this chapter focuses on how these queer documentary web series reimagine the relationships between sexuality, the self, the other, and the camera as a means of further exploring the construction of queer sexual confessions in contemporary media culture.

Documenting Sexual Confession

Historically, confession has been considered a fundamental aspect of western identity, particularly in terms of how it contributes to the construction of sexuality. As Michel Foucault notes in *The History of Sexuality*, "Western man has become a confessing animal" ([1976] 1990, 59). Tracing the history of sexuality from the seventeenth century (when sexuality was open and free) to the increasing repression of sexuality in the Victorian era, Foucault defines sexuality as *the* open secret. He argues that in modern societies, sexuality is both obsessively talked about and condemned to prohibition, repression, and silence. In *Freakshow: First Person Media and Factual Television*, Jon Dovey argues that confessional discourse is ubiquitous, a "structuring process which generates the whole experience of individual identity" (2000, 105.) In this context, these web series explore the ways in which the confession of sexual acts becomes a means of performing the body, identity, and sexuality. Thus, queerness becomes linked not only to those subjects who identify as queer but also to those who exist outside what Gayle Rubin calls "the charmed circle" ([1984] 1993).

Within the charmed circle, sexuality that has been described as "good," "normal," and "natural" is also heterosexual, monogamous, marital, and reproductive. In the outer limits of "bad," "abnormal," and "unnatural" sex, on the other hand, are homosexuality, prostitution, promiscuity, masturbation, and cross-generational and public sex. Thus, even if the subjects of these web series do not identify as queer, their sexual acts can be described as queer. As Alexander Doty attests, "Some of the most exciting deployments of 'queer/queerness' are related to the word's ability to describe those complex circumstances in texts, spectators, and production that resist easy categorization, but that definitely escape or defy the heteronormative" (2000, 7). By extending this definition of the queer and providing new queer readings of confession, I offer an alternative means of approaching the queer.

Though Elizabeth Bruss has argued that "there is no real cinematic equivalent for autobiography" (1980, 296) and Laura Rascaroli posits "the (im)possibility of autobiography" (2009, 10), these web series on YouTube, Yahoo Screen, and Vimeo point to the continual desire to confess: to make sex, sexuality, sexual acts, and sexual identity public. YouTube in particular has become a site of confession. As Hal Niedzviecki notes in *The Peep Diaries: How We're Learning to Love Watching Ourselves and Our Neighbors*, "Peep is the backbone of [web] 2.0" (2009, 2). And Michael Strangelove notes in *Watching YouTube* that "YouTube has become a giant virtual confession booth" (2010, 72). These short documentary web series exemplify the confessing animal on screen. Exploring the ways in which the aural and the visual construct ideas of both sexuality and the self, these series also investigate how confession is intertwined with celebrity, intersectionality, and political activism.

In his essay "Stardom, Celebrity and the Paraconfession," Barry King notes that contemporary celebrity culture is obsessed with confession. Pointing out the ways in which confession is framed at the centre of television talk shows, reality television, and series such as the *Oprah Winfrey Show* (CBS, 1986–2011) and the *Jerry Springer Show* (NBC, 1991–present), he also notes that these confessions are "staged for entertainment without the deep moral consequences that are intended to follow from a confession in a church" (2011, 12). John Ellis has argued (2007) that stars are constructed as both "just like us" (the average viewer and citizen) and as objects of desire that are unobtainable (because they are stars) and yet attainable through publicity shots, tabloids, talk shows, and web series like *Losing It with John Stamos*. These celebrity confessions are framed as spectacles while at the same time constructing the celebrity as "authentic," "normal" and "everyday."

In his YouTube discussion of trans identity, Tobias Raun refers to "the autobiographical imperative," the idea that queer icons such as Ellen DeGeneres, Caitlyn Jenner, and Chaz Bono appear on talk shows to share their personal stories (2016, 29). This autobiographical imperative can also be linked to the confessional nature of the 2010 It Gets Better campaign created by Dan Savage and his partner, Terry Miller (Goltz 2013; Grzanka and Mann 2014; Hain 2016; West et al. 2013). The It Gets Better Project has inspired over fifty thousand user-created videos that have been viewed more than fifty million times (2017). Developed in 2010 to provide hope and outreach to alienated queer youth following a number of LGBTQ suicides, the project's aim was to include a variety of voices from the ordinary to the extraordinary but was critiqued as being "passive, impractical, homogenizing and exclusionary" (Goltz 2013). Though the personalized YouTube messages included in these videos were designed to create and inspire change, many critics saw these videos as ineffectual in terms of the project's activist mission. In contrast, I argue that the video confessions included in the web series *Losing It with John Stamos*, *To Queer Things Up*, and *The Peculiar Kind* push the boundaries of the idea of video confession and enable a more inclusive and radical understanding of queerness.

Losing It with John Stamos: Confessing Sexual Stardom

In September 2013, Yahoo Screen premiered its streaming web series *Losing It with John Stamos*. The series was created by John Stamos, star of *Full House* (ABC, 1987–95) and *ER* (NBC, 2005–09), and Morgan Spurlock, director of the documentary film *Supersize Me* (2004) and star of the popular FX television series follow-up *30 Days* (2005–08). Nominated for a People's Choice Award in 2014 for Favorite Streaming Series, this web series is part of Yahoo Screen's push to incorporate more original programming on its site in order to compete with other video streaming sites such as Vimeo and YouTube. Including guests such as Bob Saget, Olivia Munn, Michael Rappaport, Alan Cumming, and Perez Hilton, this series of nineteen three-to-seven-minute episodes is notable not only for its explicit content (in which celebrities recall losing their virginity) but also for its use of animation and video aesthetics.

The stars of *Losing It with John Stamos* are not from Hollywood's crème de la crème. There are no Brad Pitts, George Clooneys, or Julia Roberts. Rather, Stamos interviews a variety of celebrities who are not at all household names. Perhaps the best-known star among the interviewees, in addition to Stamos himself, is Bob Saget (also of *Full House* fame). As well as hosting *America's Funniest Home Videos* (ABC, 1989–97), he also provided the voice of the narrator on *How I Met Your Mother* (CBS, 2005–14). But other celebrities including TJ Miller of *Silicon Valley* (HBO, 2014–present), Shiri Appleby of *Roswell* (CW, 1999–2002) and *UnREAL* (Lifetime, 2015–present), and Michael Rappaport of *Zebrahead* (Anthony Drazan, 1992), *True Romance* (Tony Scott, 1993), and *Justified* (FX, 2014) are not necessarily part of the cultural zeitgeist but rather fit within a niche stardom that appeals to lovers of geek culture, science fiction, and indie cinema.

Exploring Gayle Rubin's idea of the "charmed circle," Alan Cumming of *The Anniversary Party* (2001) and *The Good Wife* (CBS, 2009–present) asks, "What do you define as losing your virginity? The first time you get penetrated or penetrate someone?" Michael Vartan of *Alias* (ABC, 2001–06) discusses "making love to her thigh and a mattress," and celebrity gossip columnist Perez Hilton talks about the appeal of Marky Mark, Calvin Klein ads, gay porn, and Grindr. In this vein, celebrity sex traverses what Michael Rappaport calls getting "the key in the keyhole" to other forms of sexual experience including kissing, masturbation, dry humping, and getting naked.

Formally, *Losing It with John Stamos* functions as a mini talk show as Stamos interviews celebrities about their "first time." However, the locations and sets of his interviews are constantly changing. From high-end bars, to coffee shops, to art galleries, to Stamos's own backyard and jacuzzi, the series plays with the use of sets as part of its narration. It also includes old photos and images of the celebrities, as well as both traditional and stop-motion animation sequences to add to its visual appeal. This type of animation has been used in a variety of YouTube video series and podcasts, including John Green's *Crash Course* (2011–present) as well as the recently released MTV series *Braless* from YouTube star Laci Green (2014–present).

In his discussion of small-screen aesthetics, Glen Creeber notes that the internet creates what he calls an "intimate screen" (2013, 121). In *Losing It with John Stamos*, this intimacy manifests itself not just through the confessional nature of the series and its explicit sexual content but also through its use of mise-en-scene, cinematography, and editing. The intimacy of the locations (in Stamos's jacuzzi, cozy by the fireplace), conversations, and dialogue are matched with close-ups on the celebrities' expressions to construct their confessions and their sexualities as normal. In this way, confession is mapped not only onto the bodies of the celebrities onscreen but also onto the motion of the camera as well as the animated bodies of puppets and dolls.

The animated sequences during the descriptions of the sex acts makes these confessions appear both ordinary and extraordinary. Celebrity confessions of the moments in which they lost their virginities stand in for the everyday experiences of the average viewer. In fact, in an interview with *SFist* magazine, Stamos calls these discussions of people's first times "the great equalizer" (Stamos 2013). Though the animation of these confessions creates a spectacle to be viewed, the everyday locations (in a café, in a kitchen, by the pool, in the NYC night club The Bowery) also contribute to the mundaneness of the storytelling. Stamos's everyday conversation starters – "Where are you from?" and "How did you meet?" – contrast with the cartoon animations of these indie celebrities' description of their sexual experiences. In this way, confession is mapped onto both the quotidian nature of the location shooting and the bizarreness of the animated sex sequences.

For instance, in the episode with Bob Saget, Saget answers Stamos's question "Who'd you lose your virginity to?" in his usual jocular fashion, answering, "the shark in *Jaws*, Eleanor Roosevelt, Beyonce, Sammy Hager." As they sit on the couch and drink their coffees, Saget describes the story of his first time as Barbie and Ken dolls appear onscreen "dry humping" in corduroys on the couch. As Saget's narration continues, the series cuts to close-ups of Saget, of Saget and Stamos on the couch, and of the Barbie and Ken dolls' antics. The intertwining of the narrative

21.1 Minor celebrity rehashes losing her virginity. Screenshot, *Losing It with John Stamos: Olivia Munn*, 2013.

as both normal (most people have worn corduroys) to the spectacular images of the Barbie dolls participating in sexual acts contributes to the construction of losing one's virginity as an everyday experience.

The revelation by Olivia Munn, *Daily Show* correspondent and *The Newsroom* (HBO, 2012–14) actress, that there were no fireworks during her first time, the admission by TJ Miller that he could not get an erection, and the description of "faking it" by *Bridemaids* (2011) director Paul Feig all contribute to the construction of losing one's virginity not as a celebrity (and celebratory) act but as one that encompasses a range of human experiences. Though the animated and puppet sequences seem raunchy on the surface, these celebrities' confessional narratives also enable viewers to imagine a variety of ways of thinking about sex, sexuality, and queerness.

To Queer Things Up and *The Peculiar Kind*: Defining Intersectional Queerness

As many critics have argued, beginning with the Combahee River Collective and Kimberle Crenshaw, theories of intersectionality recognize the need to acknowledge the intersections between racism, patriarchy, heteronormativity, and capitalism (Combahee 1982; Crenshaw 1991; Knapp 2005; McCall 2005). As Gudrun-Axeli Knapp notes, race, class, and gender are a "trilogy of oppression and discrimination"

21.2 Queer women of colour describing their sex lives and dating experiences via unscripted conversations. Cast of the web series *The Peculiar Kind*, 2012.

(2005, 255). Using feminist and critical race theory, intersectional analyses study these major systems of oppression and the multiplicity of their interconnections. Pointing out the ways in which cultural practices are also embedded in struggles for power, identity, and visibility, intersectional theories also stress the interdependence of these categories within their social, historical, and economic contexts.

In her analysis of the representation of race online, Lisa Nakamura examines the ways in which users of the internet participate in racial and gender identity formation: "Digital race formation can trace the ways that race is formed online using visual images as part of the currency of communication and dialogue between users" (2008, 11). In this context, the visual construction of race in both *To Queer Things Up* and *The Peculiar Kind* also has larger implications for the ways in which confessions are tied up with gender, class, sexuality, and nationality.

Started in 2015, *To Queer Things Up* is "a documentary web-series and running dictionary of the word queer as defined by queer identified folk" (Vimeo blurb). The series features young people who are attempting to define their own queerness and at the same time seeking to educate the public about the multiple meanings of queerness. To date, the series incorporates eight videos ranging from thirty seconds to five minutes in length. These videos exemplify the "talking head" style of documentary filmmaking, but it is through the mise-en-scene of the home and LGBTQ safe spaces that they further construct the meaning of the queer.

In "Vanessa's Definition," Vanessa begins by saying, "Queer: adjective. Strange, odd, informal, offensive, a homosexual man." She then confesses to being Latina and queer. Visually, she seems to read as a cis-gender woman, and so her aural definitions of the queer contrast her bodily personification of queer identity. This understanding of the queer continues as the camera moves from her body to focus on the clippings on her bedroom walls: Janet Mock and the "Transgender Tipping Point" *Time* magazine cover, along with images of saints, newspaper articles, and other art. She proclaims, "Queer allows for that space to deconstruct the gender binary" and argues for the need to address the intersections between trans, queer, and Latina. Her definition of the queer is one that embraces intersectionality and a multitude of differing identities and sexualities.

In her "Zaneta's Definition," Zaneta argues for the need to reclaim the queer. She says that queerness is "inclusive and exclusive, all at the same time." It is "masculinity and femininity and neither and both." As images of Blondie and David Bowie invade the screen, she addresses the limitations of the term and notes the need to expand queer narratives beyond gay and straight. She also acknowledges the racial identification associated with being queer and says that she is "black and Indian by way of Jamaica and Italy." Again, her confession that she embodies multiple genders, races, sexualities, and nationalities provides an alternative means of understanding queer identity, one that embraces all of its possibilities and complexities.

Other subjects of *To Queer Things Up* point to the idea that queer means "constantly questioning," "fluid," "always changing," "complicated," "complex," "intricate," "ambiguity." These definitions seem to be informed by both activist and academic concepts of queerness, and queer theory. They are intended to advise, educate, and inform. Yet, at the same time, they seem both deeply personal and inherently political, and, much like the videos in the It Gets Better Project, they are informed by the experiential and the "coming out" narratives that often structure queer culture.

Started in 2012, *The Peculiar Kind* is "a web series that candidly explores the lives and experiences of queer women of colour with eye-opening and unscripted conversations." The series consists of two seasons with multiple fifteen-minute episodes. In this documentary web series that "asks the questions you want answered," the subjects respond to questions like "How do you identify?"; "How do you define the term dyke?"; "Are you a flirt"; and "Have you ever experienced a hate crime?" The subjects, including Ivette, Murielle, Jade, and Sara, identify as "gay," "queer," "lesbian," "dyke." They are dating, girlfriends, married, and divorced. They "eat pussy."

Sara confesses, "I'm attracted to trans-men, and I'm attracted to cis-gendered men. I'm attracted to femme women, masculine women, androgynous women, so I don't like to pigeonhole myself in terms of my sexual orientation." She then goes on to discuss jealousy in a non-monogamous marriage. Ivette confesses, "I'm single, but I'm obsessed with someone else. I have a life partner, but I'm single." Other subjects of *The Peculiar Kind* confess to being in non-monogamous relationships, strictly sexual relationships, and aromantic relationships. In this way, the confessions in *The Peculiar Kind* make it clear that sexuality is multiple, that queerness is complicated, and that there are infinite ways of defining queer sexualities.

The talking-head documentary footage begins cutting between its subjects and the footage of a party. At first the mood is light; the subjects seem upbeat and optimistic. But the first episode takes an unexpected turn about halfway through. After the subjects answer the question, "Are you aware of the type of protection women use with other women?," the screen is suddenly filled by a quote: "To date, there are no confirmed cases of female-to-female transmission of HIV in the United States Database." The source citation is even included on the slide (CDC, March 2005). Then the subjects are asked if they have ever experienced a hate crime and if they have ever heard of an organization called RightRides. This non-profit organization offers women, transpeople, and gender queer individuals a free, late-night ride home to ensure their safe commute to or through high-risk areas. It extends to forty-five neighbourhoods in the New York City area. This reminder of the very real impact of hate crimes, hazing, and violence is thus intertwined with the entertaining and personal nature of confessions from the beginning of the episode. Though the earlier confessions of sex and sexuality may seem light and inconsequential, the last part of the episode reinforces the cultural consequences of being queer.

The episode then continues to address contemporary social issues by advocating justice for Zoliswa Nkonyana (a South African woman who was murdered for being a lesbian). Viewers are encouraged to sign a petition to end hazing and anti-gay hate crimes at change.org, and reminded of the many award nominations of *Pariah* (a 2011 film by Dee Rees featuring a black lesbian character). Though these references seem to be in direct contrast to the confessional narratives of the series' opening, they point to the necessity of intertwining the confessional with the political. For the creators of *The Peculiar Kind*, gender, sexuality, race, class, and nation are intersectional. Like *To Queer Things Up*, *The Peculiar Kind* also wishes to inform, educate, and advocate, and this movement from confession to activism serves as a reminder that one cannot separate the experiential from its cultural, societal, and political implications.

Conclusion

In "Sex in Public," Lauren Berlant and Michael Warner argue for "the queer project … [of supporting] forms of affective, erotic and personal living that are public in the sense of accessible, available to memory, and sustained through collective activity" (1998, 562). Made public on Yahoo Screen, YouTube, and Vimeo, these web series intertwine the personal and the political, the experiential and the activist, the confessional and the radical. Focusing on the ways in which confession can be mapped onto the body, the self and Other, these web series point to new possibilities of representing queerness online.

Recently, the Pop Network (previously known as TVGN) agreed to produce a TV series based on the web series entitled simply *Losing It* with John Stamos as host. This fits into the new Pop Network's focus on celebrity fandom and adults between twenty-five and thirty-five who grew up in the late 1980s and early '90s (Andreeva 2015). Though the videos from *To Queer Things Up* and *The Peculiar Kind* have received only hundreds or thousands of views rather than the millions for *Losing It with John Stamos* and the videos associated with the It Gets Better Project, one could argue that the former series' lack of visibility is due to their lack of celebrity content. However, all these series' insistence upon intersectionality and the need to address the political implications of queer confession may enable an open and public discussion of the intersections between gender, sexuality, class, race, and nationality, and the myriad ways in which queer identity can be defined in contemporary culture.

References

Andreeva, Nellie. 2015. "Pop Announces Projects with John Stamos and Elvis Duran, Touts Rebrand – TCA." *Deadline*. http://deadline.com/2015/01/john-stamos-elvis-duran-series-pop-rebrand-1201345678/.

Berlant, Lauren, and Michael Warner. 1998. "Sex in Public." *Critical Inquiry* 24, no. 2: 547–66.

Bruss, Elizabeth. 1980. "Eye for I: Making and Unmaking Autobiography in Film." In *Autobiography: Essays Theoretical and Critical*, edited by James Olney, 296–326. Princeton: Princeton University Press.

Bruzzi, Stella. 2006. *New Documentary*. 2nd ed. London and New York: Routledge.

Buckton, Oliver. 1998. *Secret Selves: Confession and Same Sex Desire in Victorian Autobiography*. Chapel Hill: University of North Carolina Press.

Busis, Hillary. 2013. "John Stamos on Gathering Celeb Sex Stories – For a New Web Series." *Entertainment Weekly*. http://www.ew.com/article/2013/09/11/john-stamos-losing-it-olivia-munn.

Chambers, Samuel. 2009. *The Queer Politics of Television*. New York: I.B. Tauris.
Combahee River Collective. 1982. "A Black Feminist Statement." In *But Some of Us Are Brave*, edited by G.T. Hull, P. Bell Scott, and B. Smith, 13–22. New York: Feminist Press.
Creeber, Glen. 2013. *Small Screen Aesthetics: From TV to the Internet*. London: BFI.
Crenshaw, Kimberle. 1991. "Mapping the Margins: Intersectionality, Identity Politics, and Violence against Women of Color." *Stanford Law Review* 43, no. 6: 1241–99.
Doty, Alexander. 2000. *Flaming Classics: Queering the Film Canon*. New York: Routledge.
Douglas, Kate. 2001. "'Blurbing': Biographical Authorship and Biography." *Biography* 24, no. 4: 806–26.
Dovey, Jon. 2000. *Freak Show: First Person Media and Factual Television*. London: Pluto Press.
Dyer, Richard. 1980. *Stars*. London: BFI.
Ellis, John. 2007. "Stars as a Cinematic Phenomenon." In *Stardom and Celebrity: A Reader*, edited by Sean Redmond and Su Holmes, 90–7. Los Angeles: Sage.
Flanagan, Mary. 2007. "Mobile Identities, Digital Stars, and Post-cinematic Selves." In Redmond and Holmes, *Stardom and Celebrity: A Reader*, 298–308. London: Sage.
Foucault, Michel. [1976] 1990. *The History of Sexuality*. Vol. 1, *An Introduction*. Translated by Robert Hurley. New York: Vintage.
Gamson, Joshua. 1994. *Claims to Fame: Celebrity in Contemporary America*. Berkeley: University of California Press.
Goltz, Dustin Bradley. 2013. "It Gets Better: Queer Futures, Critical Frustrations, and Radical Potentials." *Critical Studies in Media Communication* 30, no. 2: 135–51.
Grzanka, Patrick, and Emily Mann. 2014. "Queer Youth Suicide and the Psychopolitics of 'It Gets Better.'" *Sexualities* 17, no. 4: 369–93.
Hain, Mark. 2016. "'We Are Here for You': The It Gets Better Project, Queering Rural Space, and Cultivating Queer Media Literacy." In *Queering the Countryside: New Frontiers in Rural Queer Studies*, edited by Mary L. Gray, Colin R. Johnson, and Brian J. Gilley, 161–80. New York: New York University Press.
Hanson, Ellis 2006. "Technology, Paranoia, and the Queer Voice." In *Queer Screen*, edited by Jackie Stacey and Sarah Street, 55–79. London: Routledge.
Holmes, Su, and Sean Redmond. 2006. "Introduction: Understanding Celebrity Culture." In *Framing Celebrity: New Directions in Celebrity Culture*, edited by Su Holmes and Sean Redmond. New York: Routledge.
It Gets Better Project. 2017. "What Is the It Gets Better Project." http://www.itgetsbetter.org/pages/about-it-gets-better-project/.
King, Barry. 2011. "Stardom, Celebrity and the Paraconfession." In *The Star and Celebrity Confessional*, edited by Sean Redmond, 7–24. New York: Routledge.
Knapp, Gudrun-Axeli. 2005. "Race, Class, Gender: Reclaiming Baggage in Fast Traveling Theories." *European Journal of Women's Studies* 12, no. 3: 249–65.

McCall, Leslie. 2005. "The Complexity of Intersectionality." *Signs* 30, no. 30: 1771–802.

McCallum, Kristen. 2015. "To Queer Things Up: An Interview with Trans-Masculine Docuseries Creator Avatara Smith-Carrington." *Afropunk*. Blog. http://www.afropunk.com/profiles/blogs/feature-to-queer-things-up-an-interview-with-trans-masculine-docu.

Nakamura, Lisa. 2008. *Digitizing Race: Visual Cultures of the Internet*. Minneapolis: University of Minnesota Press.

Niedzviecki, Hal. 2009. *The Peep Diaries: How We're Learning to Love Watching Ourselves and Our Neighbors*. San Francisco: City Lights Books.

Radstone, Susannah. 2007. *The Sexual Politics of Time: Confession, Nostalgia, Memory*. London: Routledge.

Rascaroli, Laura. 2009. *The Personal Camera: Subjective Cinema and the Essay Film*. London: Wallflower Press.

Raun, Tobias. 2016. *Out Online: Trans Self-Representation and Community Building on YouTube*. New York: Routledge.

Rubin, Gayle. [1984] 1993. "Thinking Sex." In *The Gay and Lesbian Studies Reader*, edited by Michelle Aina Barale, Henry Abelove, and David M. Halperin, 3–44. New York: Routledge.

Sandberg, Elise. 2015. "Celebrities to Recount Losing Virginity in New TV Show." *Hollywood Reporter*, 9 January. http://www.hollywoodreporter.com/live-feed/celebrities-recount-losing-virginity-new-762315.

Stamos, John. 2013. "Talking Music, Saget and Losing Your Virginity with John Stamos." *SFist*, 16 September. https://sfist.com/2013/09/16/john_stamos_tells_us_how_he_lost_his_virginity/.

Strangelove, Michael. 2010. *Watching YouTube: Extraordinary Videos by Ordinary People*. Toronto: University of Toronto Press.

West, Isaac, Michaela Frischherz, Alison Panther, and Richard Brophy. 2013. "Queer Worldmaking in the 'It Gets Better Campaign.'" *QED: A Journal of GLBTQ Worldmaking* 1: 49–85.

MEDIAGRAPHY

Alias. 2001–06. TV series. ABC.

America's Funniest Home Videos. 1989–97. TV series. ABC.

Cumming, Alan, and Jennifer Jason Leigh, dirs. 2001. *The Anniversary Party*.

Drazan, Anthony, dir. 1992. *Zebrahead*. Film.

ER. 1994–2009. TV series. NBC.

Feig, Paul, dir. 2011. *Bridesmaids*. Film.

Full House. 1987–95. TV series. ABC.

General Hospital. 1982–84. TV series. ABC.

The Good Wife. 2009–present. TV series. CBS.

Grandfathered. 2015–16. TV series. Fox.

Green, John, dir. *Crash Course*. 2011–present. YouTube channel.

Green, Laci, creator. 2014–present. *Braless*. YouTube channel. MTV.

How I Met Your Mother. 2005–14. TV series. CBS.

Justified. 2010–15. FX.

Losing It with John Stamos. 2015. Yahoo Screen. Web series. https://screen.yahoo.com/losing-it-with-john-stamos/.

The Newsroom. 2012–14. TV series. HBO.

The Peculiar Kind. 2015. YouTube. Web series. http://www.thepeculiarkind.com/episodes.

Rees, Dee, dir. 2011. *Pariah*. Film.

Roswell. 1999–2002. TV series. CW.

Scott, Tony, dir. 1993. *True Romance*. Film.

Silicon Valley. 2014–present. TV series. HBO.

Spurlock, Morgan, dir. 2004. *Supersize Me*. Film.

– dir. 2005–08. *30 Days*. Film. FX.

To Queer Things Up. 2015. Vimeo. Web series. https://vimeo.com/toqueerthingsup.

UnREAL. 2015–present. TV series. Lifetime.

22

A Man with a Mother: Tarnation *and the Subject of Confession*

DAMON R. YOUNG

In D.A. Miller's "Anal *Rope*," Miller relates an exchange in a Barbara Pym novel in which one character describes another in the following terms:

– He strikes one as the kind of person who would have a mother.
– Well, everybody has or had a mother. But – I see just what you mean.

When I first read Miller's (1990) essay about the closet as a closeted teenager, I blushed with shame upon reading this quotation; though I had not yet been able to formulate the thought (far less the statement) that I might be gay, I was quite clearly somebody who had a mother, a fact whose self-evidence suddenly seemed to render evident more than just itself. (Years later, when I met D.A. Miller, we exchanged anecdotes about our mothers; mine had by that time been released back to the simplicity of self-reference.)

Jonathan Caouette, a man with a mother, made two films about her: the much-discussed *Tarnation* (2003), which is the subject of this essay, and its lesser-known sequel, *Walk Away Renee* (2011). *Tarnation* attracted a lot of attention at the time of its release, not only because of its moving portrayal of Caouette and his mother, Renee LeBlanc, but also because of its unique formal properties as the first (and possibly the last) film edited on iMovie to gain mainstream theatrical distribution. The film appeared at a pivotal moment in the transition between media paradigms. It was released the same year as the social media site MySpace, and one year before the advent of Facebook; in this synchrony as well as in the expansive practice of self-portraiture it models, the film seems to anticipate the rise of social media as a new "cultural dominant." At the same time, *Tarnation* is a feature-length, documentary film that was screened in theatres. In this essay, I argue that *Tarnation*'s historical and formal straddling of two media paradigms – cinema in its older narrative and documentary forms, and social media as a quotidian practice of self-documentation – corresponds to its straddling of two modes of subjectivity which these different paradigms may support. The subject of *Tarnation*'s self-portraiture is at once the confessional subject of a long western tradition, and a subject shaped through the particular properties of video in its analog and digital forms. Rosalind Krauss associated video, specifically, with narcissism, but in my analysis narcissism is differently at stake in each paradigm. As I use it here, narcissism is a neutral term, one that tracks the self's necessary interest in itself – narcissism is a constitutive feature, in other words, of the ego that is externalized through the work of self-portraiture, though differently inflected across transforming media platforms.

Corresponding to these different media paradigms, the narrative and form of *Tarnation* are constructed around confession in a double sense. Throughout the film, title screens that punctuate the footage unfold a story about the genesis of subjectivity within the family, whose "secrets" the film unearths: this is a confession at the level of content. Underpinning and accompanying that (confessional) account of the self's formation, a different kind of self-disclosure is at work, one that takes the form of a constant activity of recording. Here the "confession" is the documentation – not the narration – of private experience. There is some sort of pleasure at stake in the very fact or activity of that documentation, one that is attested rather than thematized within the film: Jonathan, writes Michael Renov (2008, 45), is a "compulsive and lifelong self-documenter." Indeed, *Tarnation* issues from a quotidian practice of self-documentation that far exceeds the frame of the eighty-five-minute feature into which it has been edited. It is comprised of footage in a variety of formats compiled over a twenty-year period, including still photographs, cassette recordings, Super 8, VHS, and mini-DV. As such, it offers a mini-history of media platforms and home-recording technologies, while demonstrating Jonathan's long-standing fascination with those technologies. Underpinning the explicit self-reflection that organizes the film's confessional narrative is the (pleasurable) activity of non-stop recording that constitutes, as we will see, a different form of reflexivity, a different mode of narcissism, and a different sexuality, and that constructs or discloses a different kind of subject.

Domestic Ethnography

Tarnation, I have said, is at once a self-portrait film and a portrait of Caouette's mother, Renee, her struggle with mental illness, and the domestic relations within which this illness is embedded and of whose dysfunction it might be the index.

(This is Renee's own theory: "Sick parents," she says at one moment in the film, "raise sick children.") At this level, *Tarnation* belongs to the category of what Michael Renov (2004) calls "domestic ethnography," a genre that proliferated in the 1990s, with famous examples including Mindy Farber's *Delirium* (1994) and Deborah Hoffman's *Complaints of a Dutiful Daughter* (1993). *Tarnation* is also clearly situated within a specifically gay and lesbian history of video self-documentation – which Renov calls "confessional" – in the 1980s and '90s. The works that Renov discusses involve the narrator's settling of accounts with a family member, often a mother or grandmother, one who is often, writes Renov, "ill, dead, or dying." In a later essay (2008, 45), he comments specifically on *Tarnation*, writing that here, "as in other instances of domestic ethnography, family life is shown to be the most fundamental crucible of psychosexual identity."

Confession films, in the tradition evoked by Renov, advance a model of identity in which the fantasmatic and erotic identifications of early family life condition – which is not to say determine – the orientation of desire. (A similar assumption underpins the euphemism about the kind of man who would have a mother.) The video camera, writes Renov (2004, 203), fills in for the analyst or confessor; it serves a therapeutic function which he associates specifically with video as a medium "suited to confession … a format historically joined to the private and the domestic … a vehicle of autobiography in which the reflex gaze of the electronic eye can engender an extended, even obsessive, discourse of the self." If the domestic family is positioned as what shapes the subject in this kind of confession, it makes sense that *Tarnation* should serve as the occasion for reuniting Jonathan's mother and his estranged father, Steve, who left thirty years earlier. The film reconstructs the Oedipal family for the purposes of filming it, tracking down Steve and reuniting him with Renee and Jonathan in a dreary apartment living room. It is as if the pillars of psychosexual identity (according to this model) – the mother and the father – had to be rendered present before the camera as part of this giving an account of oneself. Renee inappropriately jokes that perhaps Steve is seeking to have a "sex orgy." She thus explicitates the sense in which the family is the origin point for psychosexual identity; she desublimates Oedipal eros, making Steve, the lost and returned father, into a figure for this (momentary) erotic desublimation.

From this perspective, the video camera seems to be a technological apparatus that extends the disciplinary system of sexuality, described by Michel Foucault ([1976] 1990), that since the eighteenth century has taken the form of an "incitement to discourse." This system, formed "at the juncture between Christian confession and medicine," produces sex as a truth that, in being uttered, becomes available for interpretation, which also means for categorization and control (Foucault [1978] 2011, 391). In Foucault's famous account, psychoanalysis and psychiatry are secular heritors of the Christian tradition of confession, soliciting a discourse of the self that is at once a form of therapy and a means of pathologization and medicalization.

The medicalization that haunts confession in this sense forms an important part of the framework of *Tarnation*. The film begins with Caouette scouring medical websites for information about "lithium overdose." This medical diagnosis is the first of many that will be ventured throughout the film, which has itself internalized the logic and the language of diagnosis. However, the medical institution is also presented as violently normative: Renée's electrical shock treatment at the hands of unscrupulous doctors is identified at one point as the very cause of the illness it was supposed to treat, an illness that takes on different aspects, and is given different names, throughout the film. Later, proliferating her own diagnoses, Renee describes her own mother, Rosemary, as "schizophrenic … very neurotic, and … very psychotic." Nor does Jonathan escape the diagnostic circuit: near the beginning of the film, we learn that "between 1987 and 1993, [his grandparents] Rosemary and Adolph hospitalized Jonathan 8 times." The titles proceed to give us a medical definition of "Depersonalization Disorder," from which Jonathan is said to suffer: "Persistent or recurrent episodes of feeling detached from, and as if one is an outside observer of, one's mental processes or body." To be "an outside observer of one's own mental processes or body": this medical definition could also serve to describe the condition of the self-documenting subject. Jonathan's self-diagnosis of being "outside himself" thus unites the two kinds of subjectivity on display in *Tarnation*. But for now, let us simply note that the confessional subject that Jonathan is, and that the video camera solicits or produces, is one formed in the crucible of the Oedipal family and within a framework of medicalization and pathologization whose terms the film adopts as its own even as it documents their frequently violent effects.

The Traumatic Genealogy of the Self

The medical diagnoses that appear throughout *Tarnation* not only name static conditions but also serve, crucially, to institute a structure of division between an idyllic "before" and a dystopian "after." These diagnoses are the markers of a (shifting) temporal rupture that corresponds to the ego's fall from an ideal to a pathological state. It is in the terms of this before-and-after narrative that we are introduced to Renee. Through still images and titles, the film portrays Jonathan's grandparents, Rosemary and Adolph, in idealizing terms: "Once upon a time in a small Texas town / In the early 1950s / A very good man met a very good woman." The titles then announce the birth of their "beautiful daughter," and inform us that "Everything in their lives was / Bright / Happy / And promising." Until everything changed: "Around the time Renee was 12 years old," we learn next, "Everything in her life began to become sad / Renee was playing on the roof of her house / Renee fell / She landed on her feet without bending her knees / Renee became paralyzed / For about 6 months." The advent of this paralysis, which, it is implied, was occasioned by the jolt of landing on her feet without bending her knees, corresponds to a categorical shift: while before the fall, "everything" is bright, happy, and promising, afterwards "everything" becomes sad. I say "afterwards," but the phrasing is ambiguous: it is not clear if the fall precipitates the sadness or is perhaps precipitated by it. Nevertheless, "around the time Renee was 12 years old," a categorical shift occurred from ideality to sadness that determines the structure of Renee's subsequent struggles.

The idea of the fall from the roof as an originary moment of trauma is later repeated in a conversation between Jonathan and Renee. However, the same notion of a traumatic rupture returns at other moments with different contents. The jolt from falling off the roof is the first event that separates an idyllic past from a troubled present, but immediately thereafter, we learn that Renee was subject to electric shock treatments "twice a week / For 2 years." This series of medically administered jolts is formally rendered in the jolt-like flash cuts and electric sounds that are introduced into the sequence and will recur throughout the film. These shock treatments, designed to remedy what is presumed to be a hysterical paralysis occasioned by the fall from the roof, then themselves assume the role of traumatic cause.

Later, yet another origin story is given, which situates the original scene of trauma *prior* to the (literal) fall: Renee claims she was locked in a cupboard as a small child and beaten. At yet another moment, the original trauma is said to be a time when Renee took drugs, and then at another, a rape in Chicago that Jonathan witnessed. Even though these accounts factually differ, they are structurally consistent: each reproduces the narrative according to which a projected ideality or subjective plenitude in the past was ruptured through the advent of a traumatic event, often a form of violence suffered at the hands of others (Renee's parents, the neighbour who recommended shock treatments, the doctors who administered those treatments, the rapist). This event precipitates an illness to which various names are given throughout the film, and of which the film presents itself, from its opening images of present-day Renee singing "This Little Light of Mine," as the document.

The narrative of a traumatic event that occasions damaged subjectivity is, in the film, *Renee's* story – but it is also repeated as *Jonathan's*. I mentioned above Jonathan's self-diagnosis of "depersonalization disorder." He attributes the cause of this disorder to, variously, his witnessing of Renee's rape in Chicago, his own history of physical abuse as a foster child, and his smoking as a young teenager of a joint laced with PCP and formaldehyde, given to him by a dealer while he was visiting Renee. Each of these causes of Jonathan's "disorder" closely parallels one of the various causes the film identifies for Renee's trauma. At the same time, though each of the causes is different, Renee is somehow at fault in all of them (the PCP incident occurs while Jonathan was visiting Renee; he is placed in foster care because of Renee's inability to care for him, etc.). The protean nature of the account of trauma's origin leaves only one thing certain: that there is some trauma – located in the past – around which all subsequent experience turns, a trauma that at once marks a wound inflicted by the mother *and* a point of identification with her. What it means to have a mother is starting to seem less straightforward than we first assumed!

In one of the film's most striking scenes, a young Jonathan in drag, age eleven, performs a confessional for his own camera that reproduces the same narrative of traumatic rupture, but now in an explicitly theatrical mode and at a time that predates the film by two decades. "Am I on?" asks the young Jonathan – tautologically, since he has just turned the camera and the lights on himself. (This self-reflexive acknowledgment of the fact of recording recurs throughout the film.) What follows is a precocious and impressive performance of damaged subjectivity, from the point of view of a mother: "My name," he intones in a Southern drawl, "is Hilary Chapman Laura Lou Guerillo … My testimony is about me and my little baby, Caroline … I've been through hell. I'm kind of nervous here in front of you all … He used to beat me when he'd come home drunk at night, he used to … kick me in the stomach while I was pregnant." This emotional "testimony" video once again stages a confession – now in the mode of melodrama or camp – of the self's traumatic fall from ideality. If this moment strikes us as uncanny, it is not only because of the astonishingly mature quality of the young Jonathan's performance. It is also because it resembles something we have already seen and will see again. Formally, this theatrical performance mirrors the opening scene, in which the adult Jonathan, facing the camera in a very similar framing, sets up his own story of a rupture with past plenitude. And it anticipates at least two scenes that will follow. The first is one in which Renee "confesses" to Jonathan's camera about her childhood experience of abuse and its effects. The second is the scene at the end, in which Jonathan once again, twenty years after his performance as Hilary, stages an emotional confession with a near-identical framing, with Jonathan both behind and in front of the camera, but this time in the mode of documentary and not fiction: "I don't know if it's just because I'm a grown-up now that people tell me things like, 'Why do you look so worried? Why do you have so much stress in your face?'... or 'What the hell's wrong with you?'" Jonathan both repudiates and intensifies the identification with his mother: "I don't ever want to turn out like my mother," he tells us, followed by: "I love my mother so much ... I can't escape her. She lives inside me. She's in my hair, behind my eyes, under my skin."

This closing scene of "true" confession strikingly resembles the earlier "fictional" scene of the eleven-year-old Jonathan playing Hillary Chapman Laura Lou Guerillo, mother of Caroline. In both cases, a subject addresses the camera directly in order to confess a story of suffering, one that involves an identification with the mother (Hillary Chapman *is* a mother; Caouette at the end of the film tells us his mother "lives inside him"), and in which some violence in the domestic sphere has occasioned a fall from ideality. In other words, since many years before *Tarnation* took shape, Jonathan has been performing for the camera a fictional story that, in *Tarnation*, will be re-performed as *his* story – life copies art indeed! The story of a fall from ideality through the advent of domestic (maternal) trauma is Renee's at the outset of the film, and also Jonathan's, but before either of those, it is Hilary's, whose fictional confession provides in advance the template for all subjectivity as imagined in *Tarnation*. "My testimony" – my confession – consists in the rehearsing of a narrative whose variable details are distilled to their essence in Hilary's statement "*I've been through hell.*" Whether this is a fictional or a real hell seems of little importance; the structure of the narration transcends the distinction between Renee and Jonathan, Jonathan and Hilary, past and present, and fictional and "real" confession.[1]

In his essay "On Narcissism," Freud (who cannot be far away from this story of mothers and sons) uses the example of organic illness to describe the retraction of the libido from an object in the world back into the ego, a retraction he calls narcissism. The narcissistic libidinal withdrawal is in its paradigmatic iteration associated with illness or injury, whether real or imagined (Freud 1914). Put differently, the ego *suffers*, it makes itself known in suffering; the narcissist becomes one in imagining himself to be ill. However, there is another aspect of Freud's writings on narcissism that can further clarify the stakes of this particular model of the confessional subject. In a much-commented passage, Freud describes the

Tarnation and the Subject of Confession | 443

22.1 *Top* Jonathan, age eleven. *Tarnation*, dir. Jonathan Caouette, 2003.

22.2 *Bottom* Jonathan, age thirty-one. *Tarnation*, dir. Jonathan Caouette, 2003.

transition from an early, non-differentiated state of "auto-erotism" to the formation of the ego proper: "We are bound to suppose that a unity comparable to the ego cannot exist in the individual from the start; the ego has to be developed. The auto-erotic instincts, however, are there from the very first; so there must be something added to auto-erotism – a new psychical action – in order to bring about narcissism" (1914, 76–7).

In his commentary on Freud's narcissism essay, Jean Laplanche (1976) describes this "new psychical action" as a reflexive turn that generates the ego; later in his essay, Freud seems to associate it with the advent of an "ego-ideal imposed from without" (1914, 100). Although I must defer a longer discussion of the theoretical details, Laplanche's reading of Freud suggests that narcissism is not what accompanies the development of the ego as its sense of self-satisfaction, but rather as *the retrospective sense of a lost plenitude*. The ego, constitutively at odds with its own ideal, projects its narcissism backwards in time to a (fantasized and retroactively constructed) moment of wholeness. The "new psychical action" – the reflexivity – that is "added to auto-eroticism," as Freud puts it, generates the ego as fundamentally narcissistic. But the reflexive turn that constitutes the ego as such also constitutes it as at a remove from an ideal state it thus imagines itself to have lost. What has come between the ego and the fantasy of a prior ideality is something, in Freud's words, "imposed from without" (for Laplanche, the identification with an ideal ego, or an external mirror image).

From within this psychoanalytic framework, too briefly sketched, *Tarnation*'s reiterative confession of a temporally situated (but inconsistently specified and ultimately unspecifiable) fall from ideality illustrates a fundamental feature of the ego, and of its constitutive narcissism. The very condition of the ego is to *suffer*; its narcissistic self-investment is an investment in an ideality projected backwards, but it also seems to take a performative pleasure in recounting the traumatic break from that ideality – which is to say, in temporalizing itself ("I don't know if it's just because I'm a grown-up now that people tell me things like, 'Why do you look so worried?'"). The recording apparatus here would facilitate the pleasurable (narcissistically gratifying) confession, providing a platform for the narration of the self's painful genesis. In *Tarnation*, the narcissistic narrative of a fall from ideality embeds the identification between mother and son; if that identification is queer in the sense of the old stereotype ("he looks like the kind of man who would have a mother"), it is also the case that this Freudian narcissism is queer in a more general sense. Narcissism, which Freud at first associates with women and homosexuals, tends by the end of the essay to have annexed even the most apparently normative, "anaclitic" (other-directed) love.[2] Like the Greek myth on which it is based, narcissism names a relation to the self and the world that is queer in the sense that it complicates, competes with, or belies heterosexual object relations.

"The Medium of Video Is Narcissism"

Earlier I suggested that subtending this confessional frame, and spilling out of it, what the film *also* is, even primarily, is the material archive of Jonathan's lifelong activity of recording. Near the beginning of the film, the voice of a very young Caouette can be heard quivering with anticipation: "Oh brother, I wonder how we're going to sound on tape!" The *fascination with recording* registered in this remark is not explicitly thematized in the film, but it is the film's condition of possibility, consisting as it does of footage produced by Jonathan over a number of years and in a range of media formats. Underpinning its manifest narrative about

Renee and her relationship with Jonathan, the film is also the material archive of a history of encounters with the camera. Indeed, the narrative is so compelling that it is easy to forget that the camera not only observes but also *accounts for* each of the film's moving-image scenes; those scenes are all structured around a relation to the camera, whether resistant (as when Jonathan films his grandfather, who does not want to be filmed), compliant (Jonathan's boyfriend David, who allows himself rather passively to be filmed), playful (as when Renee sings and performs for the camera), anxious, desirous, or excited. Between family history and the film lie the recording devices that have interposed themselves, rendering that history visible and documenting it while remaining at the centre of every documented scene. This family history is thus also a history of encounters with the recording apparatus, only a fraction of which made it into the finished film. Jonathan's relation to the activity of recording, beyond merely curious or mechanical, has from the beginning been charged with the strongest affects. Recording is a passion, a compulsion, an obsession (recall Renov's description of Jonathan as a "compulsive self-documenter"). It is a recording that, whatever its object, performs a reflexive function and produces or materializes his "sense of self," which is to say, his ego.

We have all been at parties at which the documentation and instant streaming of the social event to, say, Facebook or Instagram is inseparable from the event itself. Jonathan's entire life seems to have been conducted in this way, in a constant process of self-documentation that involves the externalization or redoubling, in media form, of his perception. The footage that comprises the film is the material residue of a drive to transform (unmediated) "life" into (mediated) "representation"; from an early age, Jonathan's sense of the "private" includes a reflexivity whose position is occupied by the instrument that records it. From a phenomenological point of view, we could say that the distillation of a transcendental "I" from the morass of experience has been redoubled and externalized as a technology. Similarly, the family narrative that explains the formation of that "I" is redoubled (I would say, in some de Manian sense, ironized) by the sheer fact of recording it. The narrative is, from this perspective, merely (but truly) a convenient occasion for a recording that supersedes its (or any) object.

In this sense, Jonathan's will to record resembles the fantasy described by photobloggers interviewed by Kris Cohen (2005) in an ethnographic study conducted in 2003, the year Jonathan made *Tarnation* (which was also the moment the practice of photoblogging really took off: the psychosocial origins of what would later become Instagram). One of Cohen's interview subjects, Ed, said his ultimate fantasy would be to "go around recording, taking pictures by blinking." Cohen comments, "Blinking, as a trigger, would collapse the instant of first sight with photography itself, with the act of making [a] picture" (2005, 892). And this picture would in turn be immediately uploaded to the blog, which would thus provide a material archive of everything Ed sees.

Though Ed's fantasy involves a certain pleasure of the eye, it does not have the same structure as what Freud called *scopophilia*, which film theory elaborated in the late 1960s into a notion of cinematic looking as voyeurism. For Ed, the pleasure is not in looking per se, nor in the power relation between seer and seen, as in Mulvey's (1975) description of the structure of the male gaze, but rather in the reflexive redoubling of the look in the form of an externally displayed archive, the photoblog. Ed's fantasy is that experience would be mediated, transformed instantly into media; it is not the fantasy of a voyeuristic but more properly (though paradoxically) an *exhibitionistic* seeing, since it aims to transform perception immediately into display. Contrary to the subject of the cinematic apparatus described by 1970s film theorists – a subject who sees everything but is never in the picture – in Ed's fantasy, the image that is given is marked by my subjectivity (as the site of its production and thus its ultimate referent), meaning that I am *always* in the picture, never seen but always on display. This would be a takeover of the functions of perception by the ego, as Laplanche (1976, 83) puts it: "I perceive, just as I eat, for the love of the ego." Ed's fantasy of transforming the entire field of his perception into an accessible digital archive would be something like the technological translation of this egoistic drive.

Laplanche's formulation suggests a preliminary psychic explanation for the phenomenon of photoblogging, a practice that now seems to represent an egoic exhibitionism in which the act of perception itself, which in the bloggers' fantasy is instantaneously transformed into digital images and uploaded to the blog, is displayed "for the love of the ego." Laplanche's formulation also brings us back to the topic of narcissism. But is it the same narcissism as that of the ego narrating its fall from ideality, which is to say an ego that retrospectively fantasizes a lost plenitude? Is it the narcissism of the confessional subject caught up in a drama of the family as "crucible of psychosexual identity," to return to Renov's description of domestic video ethnography?

Rosalind Krauss (1976) advanced a theory of narcissism as a specific condition of video art in her contribution to the very first issue of *October*. Her enigmatic claim was that "the medium of video is narcissism." Later in the essay she elaborates: "The medium of video art is the psychological condition of the self split and doubled by the mirror-reflection of synchronous feedback" (55). The word "synchronous" is key here, because it names a flattened temporality that also, writes Krauss, collapses the subject-object distinction that is fundamental, for example, to the looking dynamics of traditional film. In the real-time feedback loop of video, modernist reflexiveness (which requires or produces a distance from the object) is replaced by *mere reflection*, a technologized "mirror-reflection" that, writes Krauss, has the effect of flattening temporality and "erasing the difference between subject and object" (57). The mirror-reflection, she writes, substitutes for *text* (the displacements of complex meaning) and for *history*. And "the result of this substitution is the presentation of a self understood to have no past ... as well [as] no connection with any objects that are external to it. For the double that appears on the monitor cannot be called a true external object" (55).

Krauss calls this "narcissism." (Eschewing this psychological term, her fellow *October* critics will instead tend to associate this flattened temporality and lack of critical distance with "postmodernism.") Unlike Freud, Krauss does not see this narcissism as gendered. In fact, in "erasing the difference between subject and object," as she puts it, it would also seem to effect a queer suspension of sexual difference. *Tarnation*, however, while embodying some of the attributes Krauss discusses in '70s video works by Vito Acconci, Lynda Benglis, and others, does seem to preserve the association forged in narrative cinema between femininity and what Mulvey (1975, 16) called the "to-be-looked-at." In the film, Jonathan first associates this quality of to-be-looked-at-ness with his grandmother Rosemary – whom he repeatedly tells throughout the film, even on her deathbed, that she is "pretty"; "pretty grandma" – and then with his mother, Renee, whom the titles tell us was discovered by a photographer in Houston and turned into a "very famous regional child model." A hyperbolic to-be-looked-at-ness thus seems to define Jonathan's sense of the women in the family, a to-be-looked-at-ness that, unable to contain itself in a single image, seems to impel a continuous splitting, redoubling, and vertiginous multiplication of images that veers towards infinity (fig. 22.3).

If this asymptotic sublimity of the to-be-looked-at is a specifically feminine propensity, it is also one that Jonathan assumes as his own. (It is also one that lays the foundation for contemporary selfie culture, in which there can never be enough images of the self.) In including footage from a television commercial in which he appeared in his twenties, he situates himself in the lineage of Renée as former model. Mother and son thus share not only in the narrative structure of a traumatic fall from ideality but also in a (non-narrative) propensity to-be-looked-at, to reward the gaze, as it were, by embodying an imagistic ideality that survives that fall. The film is constantly interspersed with images – both still and moving – of Jonathan's self-regard in the camera, a kind of stalling or paralysis in

the reflexive moment that recalls Mulvey's description of the to-be-looked-at as the "no-man's-land" (1975, 12) outside of narrative time and space, or Krauss's argument that the narcissistic feedback loop of video suspends temporality. A certain satisfaction in simply looking at the camera, being photographed, thus undercuts, or supplements, the temporally linear narrative of family history that the film undertakes to present, and it provides another axis of identification between Jonathan and Renee, since Jonathan's film itself fulfills the destiny that Renée's early beauty adumbrated as he assumes her photogenicity and transforms it into a way of life. The mother is the connecting figure between both the confessional *narrative* of the self's troubled formation that structures *Tarnation* and the atemporal transfixedness in and by the camera's gaze that transcends the narrative frame. This "transfixedness" is not static; it is transfixed precisely in a state of frenetic movement, driven by a proliferative, self-replicative animation, one whose primary function is not confessional – does not deliver narrative contents – but merely, though insistently, *phatic*.

On the one hand, *Tarnation* gives us a retrospective and reflexive narrative of a traumatic rupture in the genesis of the self, which connects mother to son; this

Tarnation and the Subject of Confession | 449

22.3 *Opposite* Sublime infinity of the to-be-looked-at. *Tarnation*, dir. Jonathan Caouette, 2003.

22.4 *Above* Like mother, like son. *Tarnation*, dir. Jonathan Caouette, 2003.

model dates back (as I suggested in note 1), at least to Rousseau's *Confessions*. But this reflexive, retrospective, narrative version of confession is belied – or supplemented – by the sublime of infinitely proliferating self-representations where sexuality seems to exist in the relation to the camera, not to emanate from a domain of inner truth, and where the family narrative provides simply another excuse for selfies: here we come closer to Kim Kardashian's *Selfish* (2015) than to Rousseau. The sexual and even pornographic dimension of this second mode, abundantly on display in Kardashian, seems strangely muted in *Tarnation*. The film is bookended by scenes of Jonathan with his lover, David, in their New York City apartment. This means that Jonathan is presented from the outset as gay, but in a way that structurally contains sexuality within the field of domestic conjugality. David, who seems to incarnate affirmation, comforting and cuddling Jonathan, for that reason also represents an emotional anchoring that remediates, by replacing, the fractured family life that is the subject of the film's narrative. The remedy for troubled domesticity is untroubled domesticity – put differently, the queerness of fractured family life finds its remedy in homonormativity. In Kardashian's book of selfies, the family similarly provides a justificatory frame for the profusion of images that are, in her case, strongly sexualized: here is Kim, near-naked, buttocks in the air, pouting suggestively at the camera, with the caption "#wife life." In the Kardashian archive, one gets the sense that the activity of self-portraiture generates an eroticism that finds its dramatic expression in poses that reference visual pornography, while never featuring any partner. Although the montage sequences in *Tarnation* include a number of nude or otherwise erotic shots amidst their proliferation, sexuality here, while explicitly an orientation, is generally sublimated into some more diffuse form of eros: the eros of the to-be-looked-at as a principle or state of being. In this state, there is no longer a clear projection of ideality into the past; instead there is an enclosure in the present of self-reflection, albeit with the forward momentum of an endless succession (the endlessness of the Instagram feed). This succession tends towards an effacement of the "past plenitude" model; in the succession of selfies, still and moving, we sense a limitless proliferation that turns neither around the confession of a sexual secret nor around the avowal of a traumatic fall from ideality.

This brief sketch of two models of the subject that are simultaneously on view in *Tarnation* opens onto a set of questions, which I offer in conclusion without being able for now to answer them: Does the tension in the film between a temporalizing narrative of trauma and an atemporal, technologized self-regard evidence the moment at which one paradigm supplants another – corresponding, for example, to the supplanting of the organized narrative form of the feature film by the amorphous or rhizomatic form of social media? Or does *Tarnation* demonstrate that psychoanalytic and post-psychoanalytic subjectivities today coexist in a functional alliance? In a different register: Is Jonathan's passion for self-recording related to the fact that he is "the kind of man about whom one would say that he has a mother" – in other words, is there something specifically queer about his obsession with the camera and eager inhabitation of the eroticized position of the to-be-looked-at? Or has the to-be-looked-at, now elevated to a general cultural principle, transcended the gendered distinction that was once said to produce it as a specific domain, thus effecting something like the general queering of digital culture? To the model of the queer subject organized around the psychic intensities of the Oedipal melodrama, the film counterposes that of the depthless and timeless "narcissism" that Rosalind Krauss associated with the feedback loop of video (also here effected through a maternal identification). In *Tarnation*, the figure of the mother is situated at the nodal point between these two narcissisms, these two models of subjectivity – mediating between them, the coin of which they are the obverse and reverse. In the era of the closet (already "over" by the time of *Tarnation*), a certain epistemological density accrued to "having a mother." What is the status of epistemology – and what kind of mothers will we have – in the post-cinematic century that *Tarnation* anticipates as the last and first of its kind?

NOTES

1 This same structure of an originary moment that marks a fall from ideality recurs throughout Rousseau's *Confessions* ([1782] 2000), which is perhaps the progenitor of the model I am describing.
2 For a longer discussion of narcissism's promiscuous expansion, see Warner (1990).

REFERENCES

Cohen, Kris. 2005. "What Does the Photoblog Want?" *Media, Culture and Society* 27, no. 6: 883–901.

Foucault, Michel. [1976] 1990. *The History of Sexuality.* Vol. 1, *An Introduction.* Translated by Robert Hurley. New York: Vintage.

– [1978] 2011. "The Gay Science." *Critical Inquiry* 37, no. 3: 385–403.

Freud, Sigmund. 1914. "On Narcissism." In *The Standard Edition of the Complete Psychological Works of Sigmund Freud.* Vol. 1, *1914–1916*, edited by James Strachey, 67–102. London: Hogarth Press.

Kardashian, Kim. 2015. *Selfish.* New York: Rizzoli.

Krauss, Rosalind. 1976. "Video: The Aesthetics of Narcissism." *October* 1: 50–64.

Laplanche, Jean. 1976. *Life and Death in Psychoanalysis.* Translated by Jeffrey Mehlman. Baltimore: Johns Hopkins University Press.

Miller, D.A. 1990. "Anal *Rope.*" *Representations.* 32 (Autumn): 114–33.

Mulvey, Laura. 1975. "Visual Pleasure and Narrative Cinema." *Screen* 16, no. 3: 6–18.

Renov, Michael. 2004. *The Subject of Documentary.* Minneapolis: University of Minnesota Press.

– 2008. "First-Person Films: Some Theses on Self-Inscription." In *Rethinking Documentary: New Perspectives and Practices*, edited by Thomas Austin and Wilma de Jong, 39–51. Berkshire: McGraw-Hill Education.

Rousseau, Jean-Jacques. [1782] 2000. *Confessions.* Translated by Angela Scholar. Oxford: Oxford University Press.

Warner, Michael. 1990. "Homo-Narcissism; or, Heterosexuality." In *Engendering Men: The Question of Male Feminist Criticism*, edited by Joseph A. Boone and Michael Cadden, 190–206. New York: Routledge.

Transmedia

23

Looking, Stroking, and Speaking: A Queer Ethics of MAP Desire

ANONYMOUS

[Adolescence] is something in adults' minds; something that exists for them on all sorts of levels, as a fantasy, as a segregative social practice, as a collective assemblage.
• Félix Guattari (2009)

The boy I carry about inside me smiles and is sadly amused at my being concerned with things of this world.
• Jean Genet ([1948] 1969)

"Tell me your desires, I'll tell you who you are." [I] think that people still consider, and are invited to consider, that sexual desire is able to reveal what is their deep identity.
• Michel Foucault (1997)

"You got to see this cutie. He's fucking hot," says my friend, calling me from the kitchen, as I fetch another round of beer for us.

"Yeah, love that slender, cut bod. He's got really hairy legs. How old you think he is?" I take a drag from a smouldering joint we're sharing.

"I'd say probably fifteen years old – maybe sixteen. Look at his muscle development."

"Yeah, very fucking sexy. Pull this one up." My buddy clicks on another thumbnail that reveals a rather shaky video of slender boys in their mid-teens wrestling, shirtless and in bare feet, in what appears to be a panelled basement.

"Really cute. He's got amazing feet."

• • •

First-person narratives of non-normative, challenging, and transgressive desires and erotic practices have a modern history stretching back to the eighteenth-century English and French libertines and the works of the Marquis de Sade, erotic classics such as *Fanny Hill*, and anonymous fiction and memoirs such as *My Secret Life*, and *Autobiography of a Flea* (Kendrick 1988). Denounced as prurient and scandalous by the political and religious authorities of their time, they were often the target of censors (Hunt 1993). Leaping ahead a few centuries to the past three decades, in LGBTQ and sexuality studies, analytical and confessional narratives have emerged within pro-sex feminist and lesbian literature grappling with BDSM, pornography, sex work, and dissident desires (Califia [1988] 2009; Matrix 2001; Johnson 2002; Vance 1984).

In the arena of intergenerational "queer" desires, the social-science literature is somewhat modest but growing. There are retrospective accounts by gay men of queer desires or consensual sexual activity directed at an older partner as a child or adolescent (Chase 1998; Dollimore 2017). Queer theories of childhood and youth have made their appearance on the scene (Bruhm and Hurley 2004; Edelman 2004; Stockton 2009; Janssen 2017). A contemporary tiny renaissance in scholarship on intergenerational sexualities is making its presence felt (Puglia and Peano 2018; Hubbard and Verstraete 2013; Duvert 2010; Geraci 1997), and critical (queer) readings of pedophilic themes in films have appeared in cinema and media studies (Davies 2007; Durber 2008; Waugh and Garrison 2010; Waugh 2018). Biographers have been working to uncover previous suppressed histories of pederastic desires in gay intellectual luminaries like André Gide (Sheridan 1998), Pasolini (Schwartz 1995), and Paul Goodman (Lee 2011) and reassessing the Victorian and Edwardian homosexual careers in minor figures such as Frederick Rolfe (Baron Corvo) and other "Uranian" poets (Scoble 2013; Kaylor 2009; Smith 1970), as well as gay canonical authors such as Hopkins, Pater, and Wilde (Kaylor 2006). Yet for all this scholarship, there remains a lacuna of contemporary living writers discussing their attractions to youth or children. Contemporary memoir or autoethnographic accounts by subjects inhabited by forms of desire and erotic feelings for children, adolescents, or youth, together called "minor-attraction," are scarce in sexuality studies or queer theory literature and in the social sciences generally.

In order to fill this gap, what follows are my reflections on what two teen-boy-loving friends get up to when they meet, laptops fired up, ready to desire. Inspired by Jack Halberstam's notion of "tiny archives" (2008) of queer pleasures and precarious social worlds, this is a narrative of the kind of desiring practices that are relegated to the margins, queer feelings that are disavowed, generally unknown, and thus mostly undocumented. I offer critical reflections of an erotic feeling mainly told by others, a kind of desire that has been misunderstood, severely stigmatized, and starkly channelled through psychiatric and behaviourist psychology's interpretive frameworks. Wriggling free of those paradigms, it has another story to tell by those who experience its allure.

My friend and I have encouraged each other to speak these desires, creating a space to explore the intricate nature of aspects of our sexual desires, which has more often been left to languish in the potentially shame-hidden recesses of private feeling. While looking at publicly available images of shirtless teenage boys (on Tumblr, YouTube), we have learned much about the working of our desires, their complex forms and connections, and how and why to various degrees they impinge on us, while remaining ultimately opaque, as erotic desires are to everyone, to any fulsome and "complete" understanding.

I provide an account of what our discussions have looked like as we engage in a pedagogical exchange about our desires. We critically discuss the shape of our desires and the ethics of erotic fantasy connected to teenage boys, while at the same time engaging in mutual masturbation – getting turned on by non-pornographic images of mostly shirtless male teens. I don't pretend to provide an exhaustive account, as the critical material I present, although incipient during our sessions, I later worked on alone in light of my memories of our time together. I eschew the reductionist ethos of positivist etiological approaches to desire as a substratum to a classification system of sexual identities. This medicalized approach to human sexualities has historically been disproportionately levered onto those whose desires are deemed outside the norm (Terry 1999). It is usually the stigmatized, unusual, or non-normative desires, or those deemed dangerous, that are submitted to regulatory scrutiny, often spurred by acute social and economic conditions and the corresponding panic narratives that form in their wake.

Contemporary sexual panics situate children and youth as sites of vulnerability. The space of childhood and youth has become a site of hyper-normalization and consequent social regulation. Moral panics erupt over "youth crime," over children's "appropriate" use of communication technologies, the threat of sex offenders, forms of erotic knowledge, and youthful pleasures deemed "out of place" (Payne 2008). Sex panics are queer things. The acceleration of cultural representations via new communication technologies, coupled with media-capital concentration, has made sex panics into a permanent low-intensity sex war that permeates political discourse and media outlets. An enduring component of these panic narratives involves how the public imagines and frames the experience of the Minor-Attracted Person (MAP)[1] and their erotic pleasures, or speculates in fearful ignorance on what, in fact, MAPs "get up to."

Anonymous

23.1 The ethics of erotic fantasy: "me and matt boxing," Tayyutube3, YouTube, 2008.

The introductory exchange between my friend and me punctuates the moments we have spent looking at images and seeking YouTube videos of teen boys, usually shirtless, engaged in various activities. My slightly younger friend and I are both white, early middle-aged, cis-gendered gay guys from working-class backgrounds. I have advanced university degrees from North American universities; my buddy has college training and works in the trades. I've been out, living on my own, and involved in the downtown queer community in a large urban centre since my late teens. My friend, in his mid-thirties, lives with his mother in a small town. We met during a typical gay chat-room encounter and discovered that we shared similar erotic interests in younger guys, including teenage or adolescent boys. He brings his laptop loaded with images of teenage boys drawn from publicly available (and legal) social-media websites such as Tumblr, YouTube, or Facebook. I share some of my favourite youth wrestling and boxing videos available on YouTube, and during these (at times overnight) sessions, we've become unacknowledged experts on the physical development of teenage boys. Amid laughter, heartfelt discussions, and moans and declarations of erotic delight, we decode in intricate detail what makes these shirtless teenage boys so deliciously appealing to us.

We enjoy these self-produced images for what they make publicly available to us, and consequently, set some rules for our play. We make no attempt to contact the youths in the images. Neither do we engage in any live messaging, or leave comments, or pretend to be teenagers ourselves on any teen-friendly chat site. Our activities are restricted solely to the pleasure of viewing images. We attempt no pursuit of images proscribed by child pornography laws. (When we supplement our visual fare with nude images, we use ones publicly available on legal mainstream gay porn sites, usually dubbed "twink" porn.) All the images of minor youth are ones that have been self-produced by the boys themselves and made available for public viewing on social-media platforms. As such, these images contain no nudity or sexual behaviour, as these would not be legally allowed on platforms such as YouTube or Facebook. We make no use of the so-called dark web nor do we seek a way to encrypt our web-surfing. In fact, neither of us employs nor knows much about these aspects of the web and internet security technologies. In light of the way we choose to limit our erotic pastime together, we do so primarily for our own safety from detection and do not want to give credence to the cyber-predator myth and persistent ideas of children and youth being, first and foremost, at undue risk from the internet (Payne 2008). Neither do I wish to disclaim the multiple and heterodox set of relations that can and may occur, in the culture at large, between adults and youth in organized sport, hobbies, music and art, social justice activism, community organizations, and, at times, finding one another in socially consensual erotic experiences.

Not surprisingly, we have similar tastes, although my buddy's tastes also include more commodified forms – teen pop star Justin Bieber sends him into a tizzy of erotic excitement, but I remain largely cold and indifferent to his over-determined media presence. The feeling of being nakedly manipulated by the corporate image factory leaves me cold, despite Bieber's (too obvious and overly wrought) sex appeal. I strive to maintain a critical distance even amidst my friend's moans of delight, preferring, for instance, a line of subversive irony like that found in contemporary Instagram artist Amalia Ulmans's proclamation of Bieber as "part of the universal audiovisual masturbatory mechanism" in her online piece *The Future Ahead: Improvements for the Further Masculinization of Prepubescent Boys*.[2]

Our usual fare of online videos is the ones that are shaky, self-produced, in domestic settings. A large proportion of our viewing features largely middle-class white boys with lean compact bodies; some are small, thin boys, others sport mesomorphic athletic bodies or bodies tending toward a lean and youthful mesomorphic physique. They range in age (as far as one can estimate from looking or can glean from the online comments and video descriptions) from early teens (thirteen- and fourteen-years-olds) to late teens and early twenties. These videos feature teenage boys engaged in wrestling and rough and tumble play-fighting, including earnest attempts at acquiring amateur UFC or MMA[3] sporting skills. The videos are set in front and backyards, in parks, basements, bedrooms, and living rooms. You've probably encountered these videos if only accidentally, as they seem to populate YouTube with regularity.[4] Perhaps you've dismissed them as simply forms of juvenile display, the childish hijinks that boys get up to and part of the amateur detritus that clogs social-media and sharing platforms; maybe you enjoy them for your own reasons, or you may even feel a degree of erotic *frisson* as we do.

Our erotic responses to these images involve a sense of admiration and devotion to their youthful masculinity. We respond to their displays of vigour and play, we admire their skills, or their attempts to portray themselves as actively engaged masculine subjects replete with an endearingly boyish charm. We are captivated by their attempts to impress with physical prowess and their self-conscious display of their developing bodies. Tom Reeves (1939–2012), the US gay liberationist, antiwar activist, and college teacher, and a founding member of the North American Man-Boy Love Association, reflects on his own love of and attraction to boys with a tinge of romanticism:

> My own sexuality is as little concerned with children ... as it is with women. It is self-consciously homosexual, but it is directed at boys at that time in their lives when they cease to be children yet refuse to be men. I celebrate with them their act of rebellion, their genuine emotion and authentic, self-originating actions and ideas ... I am positively turned off by the notion of molesting someone. (Reeves 1981, 27)

Any sense of aggression on our parts is also absent; instead, my friend and I have a sense of reverence for these bodies. We admire the beauty of these masculine forms – lean and strong, active and lithe, and not far removed aesthetically from the ideal images of youth celebrated in western art and ancient Greece (the *kouros*) and later reflected in similar bodies in Renaissance art. Submitting to this form of beauty and the erotic sensibility it exudes is for us an erotic devotion, a celebration of our ideal of youthful male beauty. We are also aware how this form of admiration of ideal beauty can be allied to a form of paternalistic control, in much the same way that traditional patriarchal attitudes construct the "woman on the pedestal." Although these idealizations, left unchecked, may contribute to a fantasized distancing from the real lives of teenage boys in all their lived diversity, access to that form of power has never been available to queer men as a group, especially as erotic "identification" across sexual orientation, age, and class lines. This kind of power doesn't seem available to my friend and me either, as we are wont to shrink in the face of youthful aggression and displays of homophobic violence.

The Game of Confessional Narratives

We don't live in a culture that allows the free exchange or dialogue about the full range and complexity of our own or others' erotic feelings. Narratives about desire are constrained by what contemporary norms allow and by patterns of disavowal and occlusion. Confessional narratives of sexuality, as Foucault reminds us in his epigraph, participate in a regulatory game whereby sexual desires are produced as the core truth about individual or group identity. Whereas claims to identity have produced important human-rights advances in formal liberal equalities for LGBTQ folks in primarily western countries, and have been an important aspect of expanding social justice for groups under the banner of identity, there are limitations to these hard-won advances, as Lisa Duggan (2004) has noted. One of the starker limitations on the extension of liberal rights is its failure to extend economic or material forms of distributive justice; racialized and queer and trans youth and children have been the most affected by this failure to attend to deeper structural change. On a more symbolic level, age-graded legal discourses have become more prominent as regulatory practices, and the desire to protect the young is an ever more persistent cultural trope that trades on the cultural currency of discourses of the innocence of the young and victimization (Lancaster 2011). The consequences for the young are manifold, as a plethora of new forms of social and legal regulations restrict their abilities for pleasure-seeking and gaining direct knowledge of their erotic capacities (Krinsky 2008). Moreover, those who harbour desires for the young are more hyper-visible in ways that are largely under the representational control of others whose institutional powers are almost exclusively bent on uncovering a "hidden" danger, on policing MAPs, and on diagnosing even the presence of desires for the young as pathological.

Given this context, disclosing desires related to attractions to children or youth is potentially perilous and is wrapped in a tortured skein of meaning that dispossesses MAPs of intelligibility and, consequently, viable pathways to belonging. The problem is especially poignant for those inhabited by desires for those under the age of majority. The weighty biomedical labels of pedophilia, ephebophilia, and hebephilia,[5] instead of the more neutral and non-stigmatizing term Minor-Attracted Persons, allow scientific authorities to reduce MAPs to sclerotic forms of life, as cognates of behavioural psychology. MAP desires, if not their entire subjectivity, are imagined as a triple threat: their thinking or moral reasoning is impaired ("cognitive distortions"); they harbour pathological desire; and they are marked by a disease of the will[6] (i.e., intransigent forms of addiction or the problematic concept of sexual compulsivity). An image of MAPS is produced as dangerous and unable to govern themselves, especially around the object of their erotic desires. All points of the compass are covered; non-normative desires are addressed only to delegitimate them. The triple threat of this medicalized subject is then translated and sustained by panic narratives that, on the whole, locate childhood sexual abuse and adult traumas in these desires. The result is a tight conceptual circle that resists and punishes interlopers.

My buddy and I, in our collaborative enjoyment, engage in a form of ethics as embodied resistance at its most micro level; we analyze why these images become more or less appealing and how they fit into a larger scheme of our lives. Our discussions have the potential to enlarge the framework of knowledge-production and provide a critical mode of entry into understanding MAP desires and how they are experienced by MAPS.

In looking for historical analogies for our activities, my research into the use of pornography by queer men has revealed a complex culture of meanings and responses to porn images and its utility as subcultural practices, and online archives (see Dean, Ruszczycky, and Squires 2014; Burger 1995). For instance, our enjoyment of a particular image may come down to the quality of the light and a camera angle that produces exquisite lurches of lust from a certain angle of a lithe torso. I have experienced a catch of breath and a deep lunge of excitement in the solar plexus at one of these fleeting moments. That is when our spontaneous exclamations emerge, when mute renderings of bodily excitement form barely comprehensible moans. Our exclamations are as crude and commonly available as they are deeply felt: "Holy shit! He's a sexy fucker!" we almost simultaneously utter as a keyboard click reveals the sight of a particularly exquisitely formed young teen. Baring our desires to each other, masturbating together to these images while giving our desires a narrative form, we create a queer micro counterpublic of teen-boy-loving practices. Our collaborative erotic practices contain the seeds of an ethics of pleasure, an *askesis* of MAP pleasures and the online practices that challenge the orthodox and cynical view that is taken as the truth about pederastic pleasures. Our looking, stroking, and speaking are linked to experiencing our libidos as joyful and yet limned with a degree of uneasy urgency. Our desires are framed with a deliciously anxious aura of the unacceptable and the outré. My friend and I both agree: we can't imagine what it would be like to feel jaded or cynical about our desires and their materialization as visual pleasures during these times.

Our use of pleasure allows us to explore the range and specificity of responses to the images and the meanings that these images represent to our lives and libidos in complex ways. As we allow the slippery pathways of our libidos to surge and churn, we have formulated a variety of narratives: some are partial, suspended or stuck, others rail on energies unimpeded by fears and normative categories. Narratives of our own youth emerge, tales of perceived failures of masculinity ascribed to us by a culture that sets clear markers about what constitutes appropriate and dominant forms of adult masculinity. It may be that a sense of shame in our perceived "failures" of masculinity as children or teenage boys, the difficult non-supported negotiations of an all-encompassing homophobic environment that we found ourselves in as youths, is somehow a factor in our magnetized arousal as adults to the vaunted displays of youthful hegemonic masculinity.

I'll Show You My Fantasy If You Show Me Yours

Nothing about our capacity as humans for erotic desire and fantasy is ordinary or commonplace. Everyone can benefit from the uncomfortable practice of submitting their desires, what turns them on, to critical examination. A wider understanding of ourselves results when we attempt to track down what our desires are linked to and how they are formed, including the relative berth and status they are ascribed in the symbolic and material economies to which they are inevitably attached. The myriad of feelings or experiences uncovered may involve fear, shame, discomfort, or unalloyed joy, providing insight into the complex ways erotic desire both fits into and troubles the shape our lives take. Such an exploration means asking uncomfortable questions and may produce discomfort about what we may find. It may mean facing personal histories of pain and humiliation and feelings of loss and inadequacy, and consequently, this allows us to trace aspects of how we recognize and use our own power and learn to negotiate that of others.[7]

My age-related attractions run the gamut from youth to adults my age or older. But in my heterodox ensemble of desires, there is a potent line of attraction to aspects of the youthful vigour of teenage boys. My desires rarely attach to boys who have not reached puberty. Prepubescent boys hit my erotic psyche like a blank screen. There is nothing that ensnares my libido; that generative power of arousal is missing. Rather, what excites me is masculinity coming into bloom. The increase in musculature, the growth of so-called secondary sex characteristics such as leg hair and armpit hair: these are absolutely crucial to my desire. It may sound pretentious to point to the classical adolescent forms in Greek and Renaissance sculpture, but there is a trajectory of my desire that is activated by an aesthetic apprehension of beauty. Bound up with this aspect of my desire is also a profound appreciation of aestheticized beauty that is subversive to the more commodified forms of youthful representations that crowd the visual economy of consumer culture and its exploitation of the beauty and sex appeal of youth in cynical ways. Our non-commodified backyard kickboxers coming into bloom are boys whom Donatello, Leonardo da Vinci, or Michelangelo would have befriended as models in all their real-world messiness and transformed into the timeless lines and proportions of classical aesthetics – minus the sweat and the dirty feet.

Our desires for comely youths displaying their bodies in active rituals of masculinity are caught within a cultural imperative to link these desires to feelings of shame, exclusion, and disappointment that we both experienced as queer teens existing in unsupportive homophobic environments. Ways we may have experienced our own bodies as "underdeveloped," "small," and "skinny" may be linked to our fears and erotic fascination for the hegemonic displays of youthful heteronormative masculinity and its ready-made storyline of an overweening embodied confidence. For many, this is an appealing storyline, soaked with desire. While perhaps true in some respects, these aspects of MAP desire can easily be overdrawn, as our desires for youth are also about the complex relation we have to our own adulthood and respect for youth cultures in general beyond the immediate erotic appeal they may hold for us. These more subtle, non-reductive, reflexive, nuanced, and multiple storylines of our erotic feelings for teen boys are unavailable in public discourse and often prevented from emerging. In the dominant narrative, our desires are simply the alpha and omega of harm. Thus, even if our desiring is not constituted as dangerous and made a target of security measures, we are variously deemed deficient, underdeveloped, or somehow defective, and the police and psychiatrists are installed.

Our looking and stroking practices are embedded within and to some degree rely upon the erotic power of normative social categories. These gridlines of social power are constituted by hegemonies of whiteness, dominant body morphologies, masculine heteronormativity, and largely middle-class settings and practices participating in the image of the socially connected teen subject's success in dominant symbolic economies of social power and status. Thanks to new technologies, including digital video, iPhone cameras, and internet social-media platforms, the images that form the economies of youthful social status are more disseminated and circulated today than in any other period. Yet it is in these multiple forms of online dissemination and in the multiplicity of meanings and practices that ensue that difference and unforeseen connections arise. Postmodern adolescence and Pederasty 2.0 collide, as it were, forming potentially multiple visual economies and new interchanges of age-graded erotics.

How youth represent themselves in visual media on social networking sites like YouTube or Tumblr is part of the story of my desire. The narratives that these young men want to project compete with other patterns of reality in boys' lives. These images participate in a teen male folklore, focusing on the energy and un-self-conscious display of youthful masculinity. The production of these images is a small proportion of our culture, being a skewed representation of the lived realities of youth today. What my buddy and I choose to view and make part of our desiring practices is an effluent of a culture that regulates and patrols the way boys identify, and consequently, what images and narratives are made available. Other narratives about teen males are generally unavailable – images that narrate loss, insecurity, vulnerability, shame, weakness, loneliness, and illness, sexual orientation and gender diversities, bodily differences, etc. These counter-narratives are not likely to appear or be as easily accessed as the available images, because they don't have the same cultural currency and detract from the powerful spectacle of hegemonic white masculinity.

It may be that our capacity to sensitize ourselves to the dilemmas that difficult desires can engender depends on our ability to expand our individual and social grammar of the erotic as fantasy. An enhanced ability to sensitively and compassionately interrogate our own movements of desire, especially in dialogue with others, is an ethical practice that has the capacity potentially to transform dangerous patterns that reside in all forms of desire and sexual preferences. Interrogating and talking about desire would allow us to discuss, for instance, all-consuming sexual obsessions, abuse of power and exploitation, and narcissistic and ego-driven erotic practices that subsume the other as a subject of sexual agency. A pedagogy of pederastic desire forming a reflexive ethics of pleasure can emerge here and can potentially and precariously lead the way as a more general potential social form. This is what Foucault meant when he interrogated ancient forms of truth-telling that involve an *askesis*, or a form of self-knowledge wrought through collaborating in narratives around our practices of the self, rather than internalizing codifications of behaviour into set forms or identities. As Foucault outlined in his discussions of friendship as a way of life, it was a way of developing an "aesthetics of existence, the purposeful art of a freedom perceived as a power game" (Foucault [1984] 1985,

253). As this account of our desiring practices may demonstrate, it is these very experiments in the ethics of MAP desires – a counter-practice to the persistent discourses of psychiatric normalization – that are actively erased and prevented from emerging in most erotic publics, in the clinic, the courts, and even among many groups that name themselves progressive or radical in movements for sexual liberation.

Critics and detractors of our online looking and stroking activities would say that we are the gurgling centre of real or potential erotic danger to the young. Our culture imagines the existence of MAPs as buried and unexploded armaments lying in wait on the carefully ploughed field of decent and responsible sexuality. The problem, according to these critics, is the very fact of MAPs' arousal and the consequent "sexualization" of the young.[8] Dispossessing the child or youth of capacities for desire and agency, these positions imagine that entry to erotic life occurs as harmful seduction, and so non-normative sexualities become evidence of a crime committed against an otherwise "innocent" young subject. It is these anxious imaginings of that carefully ploughed field that sustain hegemonic reproductive sexualities, obfuscate erotic difference, and retrench normative lines of power between adults and youth.

Another difficult problem that MAPs face is the imputation of social harm arriving immediately in the reader's mind. In the public mind, not only is this author in the grip of dangerous desires but – what is perhaps really intolerable – he is unapologetic about this particular mode of erotic enjoyment, and this may indeed invite extreme phobic responses. Slavoj Žižek reminds us, in a classic Lacanian formulation, how often the motivating energies of intolerance toward others is libidinally charged and negatively magnetized around how the other takes their erotic pleasures; thus "the performance of the ritual destined to keep illicit temptation at bay becomes the source of libidinal satisfaction" (Žižek 1999, 5). This negativity is itself a libidinal response to the pleasure of enforcing a law amidst the discomfiting or ego-shattering knowledge that the possibilities of the other's pleasures may bring, resulting in phobic and sometimes violent forms of disavowal (see also Bersani 2009).

These teen self-produced videos, which are, in essence, banal activities for those who produce them, help construct and stabilize the white heteronormative masculine teen boy. The production of meanings available to these videos (see the links below) range from the oft-repeated palliative "boys will be boys" and amused interest to erotic engagement such as ours (and a host of others, no doubt). In our readings, the videos display a form of controlled aggression wrought through youthful masculine rituals of display and contest that range from silly and playful to serious competition. Yet all of this is also tempered and complicated through wry performances and narratives that display marked aspects of parody and ironic detachment, displaying a knowing performance for the camera (see boyd 2014). It is also not clear who the intended audience is for their videos. Their friends are often somewhere in the frame. Perhaps girls in their lives may watch, and even parents have been at times behind the camera, but it's unlikely that they derive much pleasure from viewing these often single-note performances. It's also an open question as to how the youth accept adult gay online voyeurism. There are homophobic comments at times delivered on camera or in the comments sections, but there is evidence that these young YouTube "actors" are aware that a segment of their audience is older gay males whose viewing practices are linked to their youthful appeal. At times adulatory comments from self-identified gay men have appeared in the comments section to the videos. I have witnessed a few occasions when a friend has apologized to the audience for another friend's homophobic remarks.

Pop culture is replete with images of child and adolescent beauty, deployed for maximum market penetration, arousing heterodox desires tied to aesthetic and erotic affect, and articulating heteronormative oedipal desires (Mohr 2004). It seems to me that part of the story of the vitriolic condemnation of MAP desires has to do with the implicit challenge it poses to normative oedipalization. Popular images of youth in advertising and popular culture circulate by inciting the very desires that are used to exploit normative erotic and social hierarchies for pleasure and profit (Kincaid 1998).

Throughout the accumulating media archive of youthful images and the erotic interpretations that these teen videos allow resides the queer pederastic libido as a contemporary aspect of online cultures of queer teens and adults and youthful masculinities. As in hidden homosexual desires of the past, pederastic desires today make use of cultural productions that are inflected along a line of erotic desire as one mode of interpretation. Complex crossings and articulations occur between the performance of micro-publics of (private) queer desire and the normative public visual economy of teenage boy culture. A similar pattern of complex articulation of non-normative desires making subversive use of publicly available materials circulated during an era when gay men utilized early men's fitness magazines like Bob Mizer's *Athletic Model Guild* publications as a way of realizing desires that could not find an overt gay male public sphere (Waugh 1996). The 1960s also saw underground publishing that featured teenage boys as part of the gay male visual erotic repertoire. Cottage-industry publishers out of New York such as Media Arts and Vulcan Studio produced small-format magazines that found a ready public among gay men at a time when the boundaries between erotic desires for youth and adults were less codified as identity constructs and their representations less clearly patrolled.[9]

The multiple narratives that emerge from this fraught area of cultural production involving "normative" teen boy visual culture and their MAP admirers largely invalidates the univocal cultural story of the threatened child or youth. This universal and terrorizing discourse has been intensifying its shrill claims over the past couple of decades, seeking to extend its reach into new areas of law and life. This story mandates that the youth and the queer are very separate realms of experience, organized around a potent binary of sexual innocence versus sexual predation. The protection of normative heterosexuality, and aspects of familial homonormativity, has taken a turn toward protecting the normative boundaries of childhood and youth. This is an action in which heterosexuality (and dominant white middle-class homonormative familial sexualities) can be disavowed as a site of power and privilege that is wedded to the innocent body of the child, evacuated of desire, difference, and agency. The child and the child's body become a palimpsest allowing normative claims to settle, interweaving the normative relations between youth and adults as generative of ideas of proper citizenship, the family, and the nation (McCreery 2008). Yet, it is youth themselves and the emergence of a micro-public among MAP consumers of these videos that can expand the range of narratives and interpretations that are possible and put the lie to our culture's compulsive fixation on the Grand Guignol of innocence and corruption.

MAP desires are generally held to flit between the poles of a deliberate "choice" (a really bad or "evil" one at that) or the involuntary manifestation of a deep psychological disorder that reduces the subject of desire to a reflex akin to Pavlov's dogs salivating at the siren call of psychic food – in this case, an image of a cute boy. Our interventions in a field of meanings of youth and MAP desires not only challenge these stark medicalized conceptions but can also challenge the consolatory narratives of all sexual identities. We witness today a marked tendency for instant and uncomplicated validation for our desiring and sexual identities. This validation isn't something that we can take for granted when we are inhabited by desires that are largely stigmatized and are challenging to many. Yet we don't need to be validated once and for all. We need to work on ourselves. I mean all of us. You too. The mainstreaming of the queer has forgotten what MAP must always remember. In the wake of Foucault's work on power and discourses as productive of sexualities in the modern era, our easily confirmed erotic identities risk being an explanation for everything, or, equally concerning, the kernel of truth about who we *really* are (Foucault [1978] 1990). Socially challenging desires that we refuse to disavow can provide a standpoint from which to critique dominant modes of seeing and experiencing social and erotic life. In the era of #MeToo, all modes of desiring have the potential for danger and as sites of unethical practices. It behooves all of us to question those measures of sexual desires and identity that secure immediately consoling narratives as an all-to-easy palliative to power, or conversely, as thoroughly imbued with corrupting power and inviolably dangerous. We need to keep things *potentially* dangerous and use that ever-present potential for things to go a little bit off the rails as a way to work on ourselves – not only or simply as a private individual or ethical practice but as a social and political collective public endeavour. This is the critical queer promise of perverse pleasures.

NOTES

I'd like to acknowledge crucial dialogues and support offered to me during the preparation of this article from the producers of this anthology and two other friends and colleagues, MB and RG. I also wish to thank the anonymous reviewers of this chapter for their important input.

Anonymous authorship is absolutely necessary at this time. The revelation of cross-generational desires functions like a contemporary scarlet letter – a very real danger, that like the Nathaniel Hawthorne story of moral transgression, also contain the seeds for the transformation of shame that highlights the culture's blinkered construction of norms that the protagonist is pressured to uphold. As in Hawthorne's tale, the mere confession of non-normative desires can potentially set in motion social machinery that plunges the subject into a maelstrom of permanent suspicion and potential surveillance, pre-emptively invalidating calmer consideration, attention to counter-evidence, or entreaties to fair-minded assessments. Even though my account is a meditation on the politics of an erotic feeling – any actual acts involving a young person are entirely absent – MAPs who reveal their desires in this moment of sustained cultural panic aggravated by social-media (no-)platforming run a very real risk of being positioned as radically unintelligible and thus "colonized" by the interpretive frameworks of criminological and psychiatric discourses accompanied by pervasive popular loathing and misunderstanding.

1 The acronyms MAA and MAP, Minor-Attracted Adult and Minor-Attracted Person, respectively, emerged in the aught decade as a way to apply a "neutral," non-stigmatizing, and non-pathologizing label to those whose desires are aimed, partly or exclusively, toward subjects that we normally define as children, adolescents, or youth. One of the first researchers to utilize this non-stigmatizing label in her publicly funded research was UK sociologist Sarah D. Goode (2010; 2011). See Freimond (2013) for a recent Canadian investigation into the experiences of MAPs negotiating stigma. An organization out of Baltimore,

B4U-ACT (b4uact.org), has led the way in providing non-stigmatizing counselling and social-support programming for MAPs. Richard Kramer, the science and education director of B4U-ACT, changed "Adult" to "Person" in their use of the acronym in their programming in order to be inclusive of teenagers who may be attracted to those children younger than themselves.

2   See the wry critical deconstruction by contemporary digital-platform performance artist Amalia Ulman (b. 1989) of Bieber's commodified heteronormativity as a détourned tour-de-force in her October 2014 online film *The Future Ahead: Improvements for the Further Masculinization of Prepubescent Boys*, available in video and slide formats. For slides, https://docs.google.com/file/d/0B1ldoyQIgqA-ejlVbzgzNzFWeGs/edit; for video, https://www.youtube.com/watch?v=grpx7VW4qYU.

3   Ultimate Fighter Competition and Mixed Martial Arts, respectively. These sports have recently gained a much wider audience and have expanded their professional reach to younger audiences, including the development of mixed-gender child and youth training centres.

4   Examples of the search terms used in YouTube's search engine are "teen basement wrestle," "Backyard MMA," "teen basement UFC," "teen backyard boxing."

5   The term "hebephilia" was introduced into the DSM-V (2013) as a new subdivision of paraphilia designating those who are primarily attracted to youth aged eleven to fourteen/fifteen years and who fit other DSM criteria as set out under the section on paraphilia. Although space prevents me from a longer analysis, this new category came about at roughly the same time – and in part, relies upon – discussions in Canada that led to an increase in the basic (and heterosexist) legal age of sexual consent from fourteen to sixteen in 2008, while keeping its anal sex provisions set at eighteen years (despite legal rulings from several provincial courts pointing to its impingement on charter rights; see Hunt 2009). During discussions for the revision and update of the DSM, the professional viability and epistemological foundation of psychiatric categories of age-graded attraction have come under heavy contestation and debate. Consult the *Archives of Sexual Behaviour* 38, no. 3 (June 2009) for articles pertaining to this scholarly exchange on "hebephilia."

6   Term borrowed from Canadian social-regulation scholar Mariana Valverde's 1998 study of the history of addiction discourses.

7   This lends itself to a psychoanalytic reading that I won't attempt here, leaving it to others who are better trained in the literature. There is a lack of critical queer and/or feminist psychoanalytic accounts of age-graded desires and of deconstructionist readings of the pedophile figure. For a start, consult the work of Stephanie Swales (2012), Dave McDonald (2016), and Steven Angelides (2004).

8   A critical discussion of the contemporary doxa of the "sexualization" of the young would take me too far afield and won't be attempted here. This concept has been closely interro-

gated by several scholars in poststructuralist childhood and youth studies. See Egan and Hawkes (2009), Harper et al. (2013), and Taylor (2010).

9 Media Arts publications from the 1960s featured youthful models in their series *The Male Nude*. The first issue includes an essay on the art of Michelangelo, titled "The Masterful Nudes of Angelo." The second issue includes advertisements for other publications featuring teenage boys: *Teen Nude*, *Nudist Youth*, and *Nature Boys*. Another notable publication from this time featuring teenage boys was *101 Boys*, out of New York, published by 101 Enterprises Incorporated. Issue 11, dated August 1966, includes sexy images of boys in posing straps – none nude – ranging in age from fourteen to nineteen, and includes a description of each boy's interests. For more information on images of youth in gay male erotic representation and pornography, including its proscription in recent years under child pornography laws, see Waugh (1996) and Ruszczycky (2014).

REFERENCES

American Psychiatric Association. 2013. *Diagnostic and Statistical Manual of Mental Disorders* [DSM-V]. 5th ed. Arlington: American Psychiatric Press.

Angelides, Steven. 2004. "Historicizing Affect, Psychoanalyzing History: Pedophilia and the Discourse of Child Sexuality." *Journal of Homosexuality* 46, nos. 1–2: 79–109.

Bersani, Leo. 2009. *Is the Rectum a Grave? and Other Essays*. Chicago: University of Chicago Press.

boyd, danah. 2014. *It's Complicated: The Social Lives of Networked Teens*. London: Yale University Press.

Bruhm, Steven, and Natasha Hurley, eds. 2004. *Curiouser: On the Queerness of Children*. Minneapolis: University of Minnesota Press.

Burger, John R. 1995. *One-Handed Histories: The Eroto-Politics of Gay Male Video Pornography*. New York: Harrington Park Press.

Califia, Patrick. [1988] 2009. *Macho Sluts*. Vancouver: Arsenal Pulp Press.

Chase, Clifford, ed. 1998. *Queer 13: Lesbian and Gay Writers Recall Seventh Grade*. New York: William Morrow & Co.

Davies, Jon. 2007. "Imagining Intergenerationality: Representation and Rhetoric in the Pedophile Movie." *GLQ: A Journal of Lesbian and Gay Studies* 13, nos. 2–3: 369–85.

Dean, Tim, Steven Ruszczycky, and David Squires, eds. 2014. *Porn Archives*. Durham: Duke University Press.

Dollimore, Jonathan. 2017. *Desire: A Memoir*. London: Bloomsbury Academic.

Duggan, Lisa. 2004. *Twilight of Equality: Neoliberalism, Cultural Politics and the Attack on Democracy*. Boston: Beacon Press.

Durber, Dean. 2008. "The Paedophile and 'I.'" *Media International Australia* 127 (May): 57–70.

Duvert, Tony. 2010. *Diary of an Innocent*. New York: Semiotext(e).

Edelman, Lee. 2004. *No Future: Queer Theory and the Death Drive.* Durham: Duke University Press.

Egan, R. Danielle, and Gail Hawkes. 2009. "The Problem with Protection: Or, Why We Need to Move towards Recognition and the Sexual Agency of Children." *Continuum: Journal of Media and Cultural Studies* 23, no. 3: 389–400.

Foucault, Michel. [1976] 1990. *The History of Sexuality.* Vol. 1, *An Introduction.* Translated by Robert Hurley. New York: Pantheon.

– [1984] 1985. *The History of Sexuality.* Vol. 2, *The Use of Pleasure.* Translated by Robert Hurley. New York: Pantheon.

– 1997. "Interview with Stephen Riggins." In *Essential Works of Foucault, 1954–1984.* Vol. 1, *Ethics, Subjectivity and Truth,* edited by Paul Rabinow, 121–35. New York: New Press.

Freimond, Carin Marie. 2013. "Navigating the Stigma of Pedophilia: The Experiences of Nine Minor-Attracted Men in Canada." Master's thesis, Simon Fraser University.

Genet, Jean. [1948] 1969. *Funeral Rites.* Translated by Bernard Frechtman. New York: Grove Press.

Geraci, Joseph, ed. 1997. *Dares to Speak: Historical and Contemporary Perspectives on Boy-Love.* London: Gay Men's Press.

Goode, Sarah D. 2011. *Paedophiles in Society: Reflecting on Sexuality, Abuse and Hope.* New York: Palgrave Macmillan.

– 2010. *Understanding and Addressing Adult Sexual Attraction to Children: A Study of Paedophiles in Contemporary Society.* London: Routledge.

Guattari, Félix. 2009. "The Adolescent Revolution." In *Soft Subversions,* ed. Sylvère Lotringer, 131–40. New York: Semiotext(e).

Halberstam, Judith (Jack). 2008. "The Anti-Social Turn in Queer Studies." *Graduate Journal of Social Science* 5, no. 2 (December): 140–56.

Harper, Kate, Y. Katsulis, V. Lopez, and G.S. Gillis, eds. 2013. *Girls' Sexualities and the Media.* New York: Peter Lang.

Hubbard, Thomas K., and Beert Verstraete, eds. 2013. *Censoring Sex Research: The Debate over Male Intergenerational Relations.* Walnut Creek, CA: Left Coast Press.

Hunt, Kalev. 2009. "Saving the Children: Queer Youth Sexuality and the Age of Consent in Canada." *Sexuality Research and Social Policy* 6, no. 3 (September): 15–33.

Hunt, Lynn, ed. 1993. *The Invention of Pornography, 1500–1800: Obscenity and the Origins of Modernity.* New York: Zone Books.

Janssen, Diederik. 2017. "Queer Theory and Childhood: An Oxford Bibliography." *Oxford Bibliographies.* Last modified 27 June. http://www.oxfordbibliographies.com/view/document/obo-9780199791231/obo-9780199791231-0022.xml.

Johnson, Merri Lisa. 2002. *Jane Sexes It Up: True Confessions of Feminist Desire.* New York: Four Walls Eight Windows.

Kaylor, Michael Matthew. 2006. *Secreted Desires: The Major Uranians: Hopkins, Pater and Wilde.* Brno: Masaryk University Press.

– ed. 2009. *A Defense of Uranian Love, by Edward Perry Warren.* Kansas City: Valancourt Books.

Kendrick, Walter. 1988. *The Secret Museum: Pornography in Modern Culture.* New York: Penguin.

Kincaid, James R. 1998. *Erotic Innocence: The Culture of Child Molesting.* Durham: Duke University Press.

Krinsky, Charles, ed. 2008. *Moral Panics over Contemporary Children and Youth.* London: Ashgate.

Lancaster, Roger N. 2011. *Sex Panic and the Punitive State.* Berkeley: University of California Press.

Lee, Jonathan. 2011. *Paul Goodman Changed My Life.* New York: Zeitgeist Films.

Matrix, Cherie. 2001. *Tales from the Clit: A Female Experience of Pornography.* Oakland: AK Press.

McCreery, Patrick. 2008. "Save Our Children / Let Us Marry: Gay Activists Appropriate the Rhetoric of Child Protectionism." *Radical History Review* 100 (Winter), 186–207.

McDonald, Dave. 2016. "Who Is the Subject of Queer Criminology? Unravelling the Category of the Paedophile." In *Queering Criminology*, edited by A. Dwyer, M. Ball, and T. Crofts, 102–20. New York: Palgrave Macmillan.

Mohr, Richard D. 2004. "The Pedophilia of Everyday Life." In Bruhm and Hurley, *Curiouser: On the Queerness of Children*, 17–30.

Payne, Robert. 2008. "Virtual Panic: Children Online and the Transmission of Harm." In Krinsky, *Moral Panics over Contemporary Children and Youth*, 31–46.

Puglia, Ezio, and Irene Peano. 2018. "Tony Duvert: A Political and Theoretical Overview." *Whatever* 1: 183–97.

Reeves, Tom. 1981. "Loving Boys." In *The Age Taboo: Gay Male Sexuality, Power and Consent*, edited by Daniel Tsang. London: Gay Men's Press.

Ruszczycky, Steven. 2014. "Stadler's Boys; or, the Fictions of Child Pornography." In Dean, Ruszczycky, and Squires, *Porn Archives*, 399–419.

Schwartz, Barth David. 1995. *Pasolini Requiem.* New York: Vintage.

Scoble, Robert. 2013. *Raven: The Turbulent World of Baron Corvo.* London: Strange Attractor Press.

Sheridan, Alan. 1998. *André Gide: A Life in the Present.* Cambridge: Harvard University Press.

Smith, Timothy d'Arch. 1970. *Love in Earnest: Some Notes on the Lives and Writings of the English "Uranian" Poets from 1889–1930.* London: Routledge & Kegan Paul.

Stockton, Kathryn Bond. 2009. *The Queer Child or, Growing Sideways in the Twentieth Century.* Durham: Duke University Press.

Swales, Stephanie S. 2012. *Perversion: A Lacanian Psychoanalytic Approach to the Subject.* New York: Routledge.

Taylor, Affrica. 2010. "Troubling Childhood Innocence: Reframing the Debate over the Media Sexualization of Children." *Australasian Journal of Early Childhood* 35, no. 1: 48–57.

Terry, Jennifer. 1999. *An American Obsession: Science, Medicine, and Homosexuality in Modern Society*. Chicago: University of Chicago Press.

Valverde, Mariana. 1998. *Diseases of the Will: Alcohol and the Dilemmas of Freedom*. Chicago: Cambridge University Press.

Vance, Carole S. 1984. *Pleasure and Danger: Exploring Female Sexuality*. Boston: Routledge & Kegan Paul.

Waugh, Thomas. 1996. *Hard to Imagine: Gay Male Eroticism in Photography and Film from Their Beginnings to Stonewall*. New York: Columbia University Press.

– 2018. "Do You Like Boys? Claude Jutra's Disappearances: Confession, Courage, Cowardice." *Jump Cut* 58 (Spring). https://www.ejumpcut.org/currentissue/WaughJutra/index.html.

Waugh, Thomas, and Jason Garrison. 2010. *Montreal Main: A Queer Film Classic*. Vancouver: Arsenal Pulp Press.

Žižek, Slavoj. 1999. "You May! – Slavoj Žižek Writes about the Post-Modern Superego." *London Review of Books* 21, no. 6 (March): 3–6.

LINKS

"me and matt boxing." n.d. https://www.youtube.com/watch?v=EYlll72WTp0&index=8&list=UUdHOvoOiXzt8eZB6YIxJ3mA.

"funny wrestling match." n.d. https://www.youtube.com/watch?v=MJhf5FaMs7I.

"Youth Works Wrestling." n.d. https://www.youtube.com/watch?v=Vwx31MHqtIk.

"The Finisher vs Mighty Mouse." n.d. https://www.youtube.com/watch?v=gITSpUMmaaQ.

24

Playing Confession: Gaming, Autobiography, and the Elusive Self

STEPHEN CHARBONNEAU

In her book-length essay ZZT, indie game designer Anna Anthropy reflects on a seminal playing experience from her youth. In playing Tim Sweeney's episodic game ZZT (Potomac Computer Systems, 1991), whose title she appropriates for her book (2014), Anthropy was struck by the game's inescapably "personal" and authorial aesthetic (18). In spite of the game's assemblage of lions, tigers, "slimes," forests, and castles, Anthropy observes, Sweeney's presence stretches beyond the credits and is inscribed throughout the game's story worlds or "in the architecture itself," as she puts it (16, 18). Even when the authorial stamp is not overtly present, ZZT is a "world made of text" that renders the presence of words "indigenous" and infuses the game with an aura of personal expressivity (18). Anthropy further notes that the writerly nature of the game extends to encouraging the player to make a contribution through ZZT's in-game "scripting language" (ZZT-OOP), a limited but simple tool that allows users to create their own "worlds" (42). The game, then, not only positions itself as a work of personal expression but also holds out the potential for the player to respond, to return the volley and expand upon rather than simply explore ZZT's story universe.

Although we live in an historical moment when video games can be "as expensive and risky as movies," there is a distinct and in many ways opposite trajectory towards smaller-scale, independent game production utilizing software that is "cheap and easy to use" (Dougherty 2013). A particular cluster of notable "indie" games promote the inscription and depiction of an authorial self. As Anthropy observes in her book, the embrace of a retro or nostalgic design is often wrapped in the presence of words highlighting an overt or covert form of subjective expression. The net effect of these textual features is a sensation of intimacy in which the production of a "voice" takes hold, one that addresses players even as they play. Such games garnered mainstream attention in the early 2010s as autobiographical or "empathy games" (Dougherty 2013). In August 2013, the *Wall Street*

Journal recognized empathy games as a new trend in which designers "use the video game form to tell stories that are far more personal than the Hollywood tropes most big budget games still rely on" (Dougherty 2013). *Depression Quest*, *Papo & Yo*, and *Papers, Please* are singled out by the author as games that reflect the life experiences of their designers and are characterized elsewhere as "deeply intimate, [and] immersive, unfold[ing] more like a diary" than a video game (Rizzo 2016).

This intersection of varying forms of subjective expression with gaming, particularly games that are autobiographical, immediately raises a host of questions: What does it mean to play another's expression? What does it mean to play another's experience? Are we truly listening if we are also playing? Does playing become a form of listening? Is it an acknowledgment that I – the player – cannot in all likelihood truly understand the life experiences of the designer, and that perhaps "playing" some form of this experience is the best I or we can do? If such games can be seen as a form of self-portraiture, do they unsettle or secure the self through the playing experience? My aim over the course of this essay is to touch on these questions and consider autobiographical gaming through the prism of what Eric Freedman has characterized as the "life technobiographic," or the "the life written through technology and approximated by a data trail (a rich record of subjective presence)" (2011, 4). For Freedman, "technobiography implies a particular form of authorship and calls for an understanding of how the self is situated within social relations that inherently involve engaging with information technologies" (4). His project prompts him to query the "assumptions that underpin the exhibition of personal images, occasional photographs, and amateur video in public domains" (15). The breadth of Freedman's concept, which encompasses a wide array of platforms, can help us connect natively digital culture with the historical legacy of the essay and its privileging of subjective expression. In this sense, the life technobiographic helps us link the past with the present, in the process enabling a critique of a widespread fascination with confession in the 2010s.

Refining Freedman's concept down to the scale of this particular brand of indie games will also help us consider the unique ways in which western confessional cultures are being transformed, reinvented, and consolidated. The two specific games I discuss here are Anthropy's own *dys4ia* (2012) and Sam Barlow's acclaimed *Her Story* (2015). While *dys4ia* is a clear example of a confessional, autobiographical game, *Her Story* approaches this phenomenon from the opposite angle. Rather than express and represent some aspect of the designer's life, *Her Story* grants the player access to a fictional police video database. I argue that as the player navigates and interprets various clips of a woman being interrogated by police, the game implicitly critiques a widespread fetishistic investment in mining the interior lives of others through the life technobiographic. The two games discussed here thus allow us to consider millennial confessional cultures and gaming from the perspective of the player as well as that of the authorial "self" implied by the screen; the desire to confess and the desire to consume confession are both highlighted as ways to affectively map the life technobiographic in the early twenty-first century.

The notion of an "affective map" is taken from Steven Shaviro and his book *Post-Cinematic Affect*, in which he contrasts Fredric Jameson's "call for a cognitive mapping" with a similar but different call of his own. Shaviro points to a shared impulse between Jameson's work and the "cartographic project that [Brian] Massumi inherits from [Gilles] Deleuze and [Félix] Guattari," resulting in what Shaviro characterizes as "an aesthetic of affective mapping" (2010, 5). He writes:

> For Jameson and Deleuze and Guattari alike, maps are not static representations, but tools for negotiating, and intervening in, social space. A map does not just replicate the shape of a territory; rather, it actively *inflects* and *works over* that territory. Films and music videos, like the ones I discuss here, are best regarded as affective maps, which do not just passively trace or represent, but actively construct and perform, the social relations, flows, and feelings that they are ostensibly "about." (6)

My claim here then is that the indie games featured here – *dys4ia* and *Her Story* – both actively engage with and critique a contemporary infatuation with confessional discourses and digital practices. Both participate in a broader historical linkage between the "life technobiographic" and the essayistic while also suggesting a problem with the way in which autobiographies are produced and consumed on a daily basis. In essence, these games generate, mock, and ultimately unsettle our entitlement to the interior lives of others. This active engagement with contemporary confessional cultures renders both *dys4ia* and *Her Story* potent affective maps in a manner that parallels Shaviro's comments above.

Dys4ia: Playing the Essay, Queering the Essay

Dys4ia is an autobiographical game that charts the designer's experience with hormone replacement therapy. The player witnesses Anna Anthropy's experiences of disorientation and displacement prior to and during her transition from male to female. An Adobe flash video game released in 2012, *dys4ia* condenses Anthropy's six-month treatment of taking estrogen into a ten-minute series of mini-games distributed over four levels. With the use of arrow keys, the player traverses the various stages of Anthropy's treatment, including her initial feelings of gender dysphoria, doctor visits, and hormone replacement therapy. As Alexei Othenin-Girard puts it, "There is no 'fail state' in the game; each [level] will continue until it is completed or it ends on its own" (2012). John Sharp has noted that the "shape of the game" – its 4:3 aspect ratio – is a deliberate "aesthetic choice made by Anthropy, likely as a reference to early 8-bit games" (2012, 92). Linzi Juliano similarly reads *dys4ia*'s "retro-arcade visual style" as an homage to "games of the past ... sometimes taking on the mechanics of *Pong*, other times that of *Pac-Man* or *Donkey Kong*" (2012, 598). Juliano also emphasizes Anthropy's overall queering of the game experience, not simply in light of the autobiographical content but through its very interface (598). The relatively simple mode of "engagement" entailing the use of the arrow keys steers the player's attention toward "in-game content and design rather than mastery of a sophisticated controller system" (598). Juliano reads this as a "relational" dynamic that resists the "idealization of command and conquer" while yielding an overall more "feminine" game experience (598).

The politics of the game are also clearly trumpeted in light of its status as a work of self-expressivity. Juliano has characterized *dys4ia* as a kind of "diary" (598). Other commentators and reviewers have described *dys4ia* as well as games like *Depression Quest* as "confessional stories" (Lewis 2014, 341). Anthropy has openly insisted on the "expressive richness" of personal games, or "authored games," over the anonymity of "group design" and has bemoaned the depersonalization of most video games (Westecott 2013, 80–1). Emma Westecott notes that this aspect of Anthropy's work resonates with "feminist art practices and actualizes the feminist insistence that the personal is political for DIY games" (2013, 81). Westecott continues to emphasize the enhanced authorial credentials of so-called "indie games":

> Beyond the specifics of aesthetic style, game making as a form of personal expression is very much a handmade affair. The tools of digital game making are computational, yet the maker uses her hands to build her game and is involved in all aspects of creation. DIY game development involves shorter development times and less ornate game structures than the mainstream sector. Often the DIY maker is the sole creator, allowing for authorship of the game development process, and playable outcome. The designer's voice and values are reflected in the resulting game. (82)

In her summation of research presented at an interdisciplinary conference held at Concordia University, Cheryl MacDonald (2014) notes that some participants – specifically, Sara Breitkreutz – made a strong case for video games "as a medium for ethnographic representation and interaction" (118). According to MacDonald, Breitkreutz insisted on an alignment between the goals of ethnography and some video games "by virtue of the lived experience of telling stories ... immersing oneself into other worldviews and ways of life, and educing a deeper understanding of self and other" (118–19). Breitkreutz further notes the "marked presence" of video games at a recent Margaret Mead Film Festival as an indication of the (auto)ethnographic potential of the medium (119).

This investment in gaming formats that explicitly produce an authorial aura is a concrete instance of the life technobiographic. Command-and-conquer schemes yield to a diaristic mode of communication whereby an irreducible sense of subjectivity addresses the player. The way in which such games reject the registration of *group design* in their style and interface inevitably generates associations with confessional, polemical, and autobiographical discourses. This technological inscription of a subjective voice that is also inescapably social can be similarly characterized as *essayistic*, as a continuation of the essay's cinematic and literary legacies.[1] The essay's elastic shape, encompassing both private and public spheres, dovetails with and can help elaborate upon what it means to express a life to others through technological means. In his book *The Essay Film: From Montaigne, after Marker*, Timothy Corrigan focuses on the *cinematic* essay and intentionally sidelines "some of [the essayistic's] most intriguing contemporary transformations through the internet, other electronic media, and even museum installations" (2011, 7). *Dys4ia* gives us an opportunity to pursue this line of inquiry Corrigan has set up, to consider how the autobiographical video game might be seen to *transform* the essayistic. To help track the "evolution" of the essay "from Montaigne to the essay film," Corrigan identifies three "interactive and intersecting registers" (14). From this vantage point, the essay film often entails the coordination of "personal expression, public experience, and the process of thinking" (14). For Corrigan, it is precisely the "interactivity of these three dimensions [that] creates a defining representational shape" whose history and emergence can be traced "from the literary heritage of the essay" to the late twentieth century essay film (14).

While there is no simple or clear correlation between gaming and the essay films Corrigan highlights in his book, it is his insistence on contemporary transformations of the essayistic that is most pertinent here. In fact, elasticity is a core feature of the essay's form. For instance, Corrigan, following Adorno, highlights "unmethodical method" as "the fundamental form of the essay," one that helps "explain one of the central paradoxes and challenges of the essay: It is a genre of experience that ... may be fundamentally antigeneric, undoing its own drive toward categorization" (8). This central unruliness of the essay is one reason why Adorno insists "luck and play are essential" to it ([1958] 1984, 152). Autobiographical games could similarly be described as belonging to a genre of experience that is also anti-generic. This dialectical tension is reflected in Anthropy's own discourse about the powers of the authorial and autobiographical video game, which resist the generic rigidity of *group design* even as they inaugurate a new and tenuous categorization of self-inscribed gaming.

The treatment of the self in autobiographical gaming similarly approximates the essayistic subject. Corrigan writes "that the essayistic is most interesting not so much in how it privileges personal expression and subjectivity but rather in how it troubles and complicates that very notion of *expressivity* and its relation to *experience*" (2011, 17; emphasis in original). In films such as *Bright Leaves* (Ross McElwee, dir., 2004), *The Gleaners and I* (Agnès Varda, dir., 2000), and *Mr. Death: The Rise and Fall of Fred A. Leuchter* (Errol Morris, dir., 1999), the selves featured are often left rattled, delighted, or somehow changed by a series of experiences or encounters. The presentation of a self in the format of a game is similarly shaken, leaving the player with more questions than answers. This strange confluence inevitably ensures that the player feels somewhat outside the experiences referred to by the gameplay. In the case of *dys4ia*, a portrait of the self seems both delivered and obscured by the player's actions. These actions seem to play a part in the unfolding of the designer's experience even as they distinctly unfold across an elsewhere, in the time and space of the gameplay. And when the game is over, the player's relationship to the content is unclear. What has been learned? Does my experience as the player give me access to Anthropy's experiences in life? The frame of the game undercuts any feeling of access, but the content persists nevertheless. Relaying the experience of playing the game to others, even speaking critically about it, can feel like chasing an ever-receding vanishing point.

This unsettling of the self, which the essayistic helps us map, can be productively engaged through a Deleuzian *schizoanalysis*, which Patricia Pisters characterizes as "a mode of thinking with ... specific assemblages of desires" that look to future horizons, "producing new models, new subjectivities, with uncertain outcomes" (2012, 39). From this vantage point, *dys4ia* may be an example of what Pisters describes as a "neuro-image" that privileges "mental worlds" and "brain spaces" and yields to the *schizo* "flow" or "madness of contemporary media culture" (14, 68). From here we might consider Alexander Galloway's observation that the first person perspective is "marginalized" in film and "used primarily to effect a sense of alienation, detachment, fear, or violence" (2006, 40). By contrast, Galloway insists, games frequently embrace the "subjective perspective," using it "to achieve an intuitive sense of motion and action in gameplay" (40). The essayistic both affirms and unravels this prescription, foregrounding the self across both media as well as carrying over the problematization of the self from film to the video game, unsettling the latter's traditional alliance with the self as a facilitator of fluid action.

The avatar of *dys4ia* is represented as a figure of self-expression and speaks to us in first-person voice through the manifestation of text on the screen. To reiterate, our participation is heavily attenuated through the confinement of our movements to the arrow keys – undermining our traditional "command-and-control" gaming posture. Our ability to move the avatar and act out various scenarios is thwarted by key obstacles and by frequent shifts from one mini-game to another, often before we can completely get our bearings. The total playing time for *dys4ia* lasts approximately ten to twelve minutes, and this playing time is distributed across four levels: "Level 1 – Gender Bullshit," "Level 2 – Medical Bullshit," "Level 3 – Hormonal Bullshit," and "Level 4 – It Gets Better?" Over the course of this short playing time, we play forty-two mini-games or scenes designed to chart Anthropy's struggles with her gender dysphoria. Each of these vignettes is an opportunity to complete a task or, just as often, merely bear witness to a frustrating or humiliating scenario. But the frenetic pace as we transition from one vignette to another approximately every fifteen seconds yields a dizzying effect. We simply don't have enough time to feel as though we have a grasp on what Anthropy has experienced. The game seems to act on us more than we act on it. The "retro-arcade visual style" renders the vignettes visually abstract and undercuts or mocks our unconscious insistence on attaining visual mastery of the experiences depicted.

An overview of the first level – "Gender Bullshit" – should suffice for our purposes here. The first vignette is a recurring one and presents a broken wall with an odd-fitting fragment to the proclamation "I feel weird about my body." Next we're dodging verbal attacks as we read "These feminists don't accept me as a woman." This is followed by a mini-game in which we frantically hit the down arrow as we are reminded that, unfortunately, "girly clothes ... don't fit!" A series of additional mini-humiliations include being addressed as "sir," having to shave one's moustache (and cutting oneself), and feeling like an outsider in the women's bathroom. Our desire for a sense of victory is temporarily achieved when – after repeatedly tapping the up arrow – a rising sun disperses an ominous cloud to reveal a possible answer to the feeling of displacement: "hormones!"

24.1
"Girly Clothes Don't Fit": one of forty-two mini-games in the video game *dys4ia*, creator Anna Anthropy, 2012.

The publicness of the experiences in these scenes fades in and out as Anthropy's alter ego skips from personal spaces to public ones in which she feels judged and misjudged by various audiences. Of course, the public experience of the game itself seizes on personal experiences to render them *playable* by outsiders, even as the play is ultimately elusive and almost parodic, reinscribing our outsiderness. Furthermore, the visual distortion and disorienting pace of the game steers its essayistic features – personal expression, public experience, and the process of thinking – back towards certain elements of Pisters's neuro-image, especially the notion of the "embodied brain." For Pisters, the neuro-image

> involves a shift from considering cinema and the spectator as a "disembodied eye" defined by the look and the gaze, desire and identification, to consider cinema and the spectator as an "embodied brain," defined by perceptions (even illusory ones), selections (even random ones), memories (even fake ones), imaginations, suggestions, and above all emotions as pure affect. (2012, 71)

As an embodied brain, we are forced to "ask ourselves constantly: Where is the screen? How do I relate to it? What does it make me see, feel, grasp, do?" (71).

The player's disorientation resonates with but is not equal to Anthropy's dysphoria. The life technobiographic expressed here is fragmentary, partial, and elusive, undermining the communication of a clear and coherent knowledge effect.

Pixelated avatars and an intensified duration (four levels in ten minutes) rattle us and mirror the game's presentation of Anthropy as caught betwixt and between interpellative schemes. From this vantage point, the game reminds us that a life technobiographic is often riddled with multiplicity as vignettes, imagery, and text associated with a self are endlessly fragmentary, distributed across social media.[2] If a confession implies a sense of finality, a feeling that the confessant has been unburdened, then *dys4ia* resists this label. Its essayistic wandering or embrace of unfolding thought combats the enclosure of confession. Here the game frustrates a cisgender look that might otherwise fixate upon transgender experience and transgender bodies, mining and exploring them in pursuit of a stable categorization. The opacity of this specific game as well as the generic elements of gaming presents Anthropy's experience from a canted angle, rendering her subject position and ours off-kilter. If the subject position is difficult to evade completely, this conjunction of autobiography with gaming at least leaves us with more questions than answers in a manner that resonates with the concept of the neuro-image with its insistence on mental worlds and a productive madness. The shiftiness of Pisters's theorization of the neuro-image as an "embodied brain" dovetails here with the unruliness of the essayistic in which unmethodical methods present thoughts in process rather than wholly formed and complete. The game thwarts any initial expectation that it will feature a presence that presents itself to us and for us, leaving the life written through technology incomplete and something we must pursue rather than something to which we are entitled.

In the next section, we discuss a recent game that similarly highlights how the life technobiographic is constructed through consumption or produced from the vantage point of the audience.

Her Story: Playing the Archive, Playing the Confession

In a presentation on his award-winning video game *Her Story* (2015), game designer Sam Barlow (2015) opened by sharing with his audience photographs sent to him by his fans. These photographs feature not the fans but rather an accumulation of their handwritten notes produced as a result of playing *Her Story*. The implication here is that Barlow's latest work is not simply interactive but powerfully generative, inciting players to creatively and cognitively map a narrative whose presentation is defiantly sparse. Barlow reinforces this point in an interview with *International Business Times* when he notes that he sought to draw players in by incorporating "gaps, omissions … [and] negative space" (Laverde 2015).

Her Story (2015) is a crime-fiction game centred on a simulated police video database from 1994. The videos are drawn from a total of seven interviews in which a British woman, Hannah Smith, answers questions about her missing husband. The player performs search queries, and the game returns pertinent video clips of the woman's testimony as the narrative unfolds in nonlinear ways. More than simply an interactive fiction, *Her Story* was additionally conceived by Barlow as a commentary, a teaching tool, on the "modern phenomen[on] of the YouTube Jury, in which police forces distribute the footage of intimate suspect interviews for armchair detectives to dissect … in cases such as those of Jodi Arias and Amanda Knox" (Barlow 2014). My intent here is to amplify Barlow's ambitions and to reflect upon the significance of reading this game as a kind of commentary, as a gaming experience that does not simply invite us to participate creatively in its diegesis but also pressures us to reflect on our own experience in the digital world beyond the game. While *Her Story* is unique as a game experience, I would argue that it can be placed alongside the independent games mentioned earlier that reflect or comment upon millennial confessional cultures.

Her Story, however, is not a confessional game along the lines of *dys4ia*. Rather than presenting itself as a mode of reflection on the daily life of its designer, Barlow's game stages a fictional confession at the heart of its diegetic archive. To repeat, short video clips from Hannah's interrogation appear in response to the terms of the player's searches. The nature and the trajectory of the protagonist's "confession" depend in part on our actions, placing us in the position of the interrogator, albeit across a temporal division between the "now" of our actions and the "then" of the protagonist's taped responses. This reproduces what Jaimie Baron (2014) characterizes as an "archive effect" in which a "temporal disparity" is generated by a viewer's "perception … of a 'then' and a 'now' … within a single text" (18). Unlike *dys4ia*, which gives us access to the "inside" of a designer's life through a convergence of gaming and autobiographical expression, *Her Story* critically highlights the fascination of the user, the amateur sleuth whose actions assume centre stage. The focus, then, is on our desire to consume confession and to play an active role in eliciting or calling out confessions.

Her Story and other confessional games refer again to Freedman's notion of the "life technobiographic." While the emergence of confessional games represents another layer in technobiographical expression, a game like *Her Story* reminds us of how a life technobiographic is often the result of how we, the users, "author" or make sense of a particular data trail. The game entails a push and pull between a sense of getting closer to a master narrative – an ultimate reveal and discovery of a latent narrative twist – and a lacunary structure that requires us to build the narrative, in some sense to construct the story based on each player's unique set of search terms. This dialectical tension between creating and discovering is at the heart of the film's "commentary" and what it might be saying about historicity as well as the amateur digital sleuth.

At the outset of the game, we find ourselves seated in front of an old desktop computer reminiscent of the mid-1990s, the period in which the interrogation of Hannah takes place. The screen in front of us bears the mark of the "South East Constabulary" and is sparsely populated with icons, including two text files, a "rubbish bin," and a database checker. When we click on the database checker, another window opens, notifying us that we are logged in as a "guest." The screen invites us to "enter [queries]" in the search field "to access archived footage." When we enter a search term, the game returns pertinent "entries" or clips of Hannah's interrogation running anywhere from a few seconds to a minute and a half – or none. (Our search terms may not yield any results.) We may, if we choose, click "Add to Session" and have the video stored for future viewing as we gradually find our way through the narrative. The game also keeps track of our search history, encouraging more refined searches as the game progresses. An option of adding "user tags" similarly invites us to actively track the narrative, to find the coherent thread that ties the fragments all together.

Throughout the gameplay, the screen doubles as both an interface and a diegetic reflective surface. That is, unless we choose to turn on the "anti-glare filter," the screen "reflects" a specific spatial setting that matches the institutional aesthetic of the interface. Visually, the screen projects the glare of two fluorescent lights, signifying an office environment. Aurally, the non-diegetic soundtrack mixes with diegetic sounds from the office, including the intermittent buzzing of the lights and the subtle creaks and groans of an empty office setting. During the game, the lighting from the room produces a backlighting effect in which we can make out the faintest outline of ourselves reflected on the screen. However, at key moments or upon discovery of particular video clips, a dormant light flickers on, generating a momentary key light that presents a hazy view of our avatar in this game: a young woman who bears a strong resemblance to the protagonist, Hannah.

At the heart of this game experience, then, is the construction of a life technobiographic, a life of video fragments whose coherence must be discovered or generated through the activity of the player. We search a storehouse of twenty-year-old video clips and, in turn, assume the position of archon or collector for our own database as we add various clips to our own session. The central role of appropriation in this game is at the heart of its commentary on digital historicity and amateur digital sleuthing. As Jaimie Baron notes in her book, "If one tendency

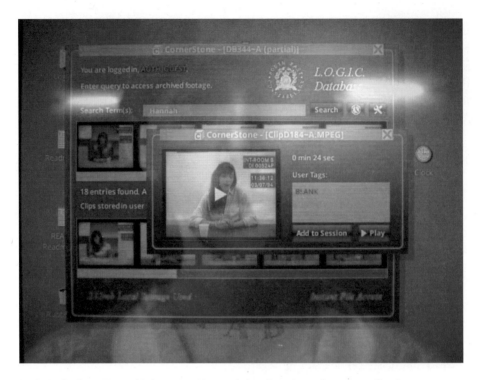

24.2 A clip from Hannah's interrogation and the player's momentary reflection, from the video game *Her Story*, creator Sam Barlow, 2015.

can be said to characterize media production in the digital era, it is appropriation" (2014, 142). Although it is fictional, *Her Story* mocks our relationship to the digital archive, albeit through the contrivance of its institutional setting. In this regard, the game – itself a digital entity – situates itself between the material and the digital archive. It simulates a material archive through the bricks-and-mortar setting of the police station in which the desired documents are housed and presumably confined. And yet the use of cutscenes in the game or video clips is reminiscent of the digital archive in which indexical moving image documents are so prominent.

The game then positions us as amateur sleuths, mining and combining pieces of testimony to uncover a life as well as a master narrative of what really happened. In this regard, the game both fits and does not fit into what is typically understood as a database narrative. To a substantial degree, players actively select and define their game experience and the direction of the story through their actions and selections. (Recall the notes shared with Barlow by the game's fans.) Nevertheless, while there are many possible pathways and queries, the interrogative momentum of the gameplay overwhelms and reaffirms the authority of the *then* of the past over and above the *now* of our retroactive machinations. The game is, simply put, interactive only to a point. Eventually the conventionality of gameplay steers us towards a melodramatic revelation. A chat window opens once a certain threshold of gameplay has been reached and reveals a surprising bond between the player and Hannah. At the outset, our position as a post-factum interrogator imparts a sense of authority, and yet by the end the inertia of the narrative takes hold, undercutting our interactivity and tipping the scales in favour of a historical revelation. Rather than bemoaning an abandonment of history in digital media, Jaimie Baron insists that "certain contemporary appropriation films" directly stage for us the "problems we currently encounter as we confront the digital archive in the pursuit of some form of historical understanding" (143). *Her Story* does something similar in this regard by mocking the consumption of confessional discourses and imparting an ultimately false sense of historical authority and empowerment. The game rechannels all our efforts, all our note-taking, towards what Barlow emphasizes is a silly and even unbelievable narrative reveal (Laverde 2015).

The game's implied commentary – its critical treatment of the impulse to dissect the confessions of others – is also reinforced through Hannah's divergent appearances and performances across the various video clips. The varying ways in which she speaks, laughs, sings, cries, and dresses encourages at minimum an attentive examination of her entire affect. A gendered dynamic takes hold, particularly as in one clip in which Hannah addresses the interrogating detective out of frame as male. To reiterate, the player is positioned early on as a future-tense extension of the detective and our evolving judgment of Hannah – what she says, how she says it, how she wears her hair, and so on – places us in a masculine position of sceptical reception and careful assessment of the feminine subject. And yet the flickering reflection of our self-image undercuts this position relatively early in the game. Our external position as interrogator is overturned through a bond with the feminine subject, who looks, we realize, like us.

Barlow's game highlights millennial confessional cultures and how confessions and self-expressions are consumed as well as produced by an active and overly discerning digital audience. A life technobiographic is one that is a boundary-crosser, not just traversing different platforms but also passing between the originating subjective presence and the anxious and excitable reader, between the temporally disparate positions of then and now. In a passage that applies to both *dys4ia* and *Her Story*, Freedman insists that the "object's original fixity (and the producer's foundational subject position), while important, is not the end of the story" (2011, 172–3).

Yet despite this movement, this flux, there still seems to be a fundamental belief that we can glue these narratives together – that our endless reading of images yields some form of progress, a continuity brought about by the insistent impulses of an integrated subjectivity and a desire to believe in development. Implicit in this act of binding is the ideological notion that our passage through time will lead to something; it will develop our knowledge, secure our well-being, strengthen our social bonds, increase our social status, and perhaps help us realize material gain. Yet progress is not a necessary state of affairs, and we seem to be opening up to this possibility as we embrace new forms of interactivity and accept the tangents that are implied by navigating the Web and the new grammatical constructs that such activity produces. (173)

Both *dys4ia* and *Her Story* – as "new forms of interactivity" – elicit and ultimately undermine this yearning for narrative coherence and the staging of a stable self. The playing on some level grants access to another's experience but also becomes an experience that resides elsewhere. The experience may follow its own logic and disturb the virtual exchange, as in the case of *dys4ia*, or assume a satirical role as it encourages and mocks the amateur digital sleuth, as in *Her Story*. As we reflect back on the pictures of the elaborate note-taking of *Her Story*'s fans, a different sensibility takes hold. Rather than simply celebrating the process of thinking triggered by the narrative's gaps, *Her Story* essentially reroutes the player's investigative efforts towards a conclusion that is, to a significant degree, autonomous; the game has its own self-determining logic. The machinic progress of the game is related to the player's progress and yet is outside it as well. The multiple meanings accommodated by the game are also directed toward a conclusion that is conventional, melodramatic, and even absurd.

Returning to Pisters, we can read both *dys4ia* and *Her Story* as advancing a "mode of thinking" that is adventurously "directed toward the future, to experimenting with producing new models, new subjectivities, with uncertain outcomes" (2012, 39). An essayistic concern with thought as a process, allied with aperture and not closure, dovetails nicely with Pisters's characterization of contemporary spectators as embodied brains. From this vantage point, the "representational shape" of the essayistic, whose impulse is often arbitrary and open-ended – and stands accused of "project[ing] meaning where there is nothing to interpret" – swells in significance, lacing empty play with meaning (Adorno [1958] 1984, 152). While not wholly representative of a broad cross-section of recent games, both *Her Story* and *dys4ia* share a distinctly critical take on how the life technobiographic is both produced and consumed. They highlight our drive as players to understand another's experience or to retroactively discover and stabilize another life through appropriation while also mocking our efforts by associating them with play.

NOTES

1 I have chosen to privilege the essay's literary and filmic legacies in order to maintain some semblance of historical perspective and critical orientation for these otherwise natively digital forms. To be clear, this chapter is speculative in spirit. I admit there is no easy correlation between the cinematic essay and the essayistic traits of games like *dys4ia*. Nevertheless, the fact that Timothy Corrigan explicitly draws a boundary in his seminal book between filmic and other electronic and digital manifestations of the "essay" communicates a few key points. The first is that the cinematic tradition should be studied on its own where filmic specificity can be accounted for. But the second point is that Corrigan's willingness to highlight this exclusion is also an affirmation of future lines of inquiry. The way in which he underscores this omission is, then, a form of intellectual honesty, suggesting that transmedial forms of the essayistic are both related to the essay film and pursuant of their own goals and medium-specific experiences.

2 Freedman argues that this very "transiency" enables a "peaceful return to the sustained experience of the individual ego" (2011, 156). "Life may be unstable and fleeting," he writes, "but the networked organism is even more so. As individuals we find refuge in biography, in the subjectivization and individualization of the world around us" (156).

REFERENCES

Adorno, T.W. [1958] 1984. "The Essay as Form." Translated by Bob Hullot-Kentor and Frederic Will. *New German Critique* 32 (Spring–Summer): 151–71.

Anthropy, Anna. 2014. *ZZT*. Los Angeles: Boss Fight Books.

Barlow, Sam. 2014. *Her Story*. http://www.herstorygame.com/about/.

– 2015. "Sam Barlow on the Origins of Her Story." *Vimeo*, 29 October. https://vimeo.com/144009779.

Baron, Jaimie. 2014. *The Archive Effect: Found Footage and the Audiovisual Experience of History*. London: Routledge.

Corrigan, Timothy. 2011. *The Essay Film: From Montaigne, after Marker*. Oxford: Oxford University Press.

Dougherty, Conor. 2013. "Videogames about Alcoholism, Depression, and Cancer." *Wall Street Journal*, 15 August. https://www.wsj.com/articles/videogames-about-alcoholism-depression-and-cancer-1376605817.

Freedman, Eric. 2010. *Transient Images: Personal Media in Public Frameworks*. Philadelphia: Temple University Press.

Juliano, Linzi. 2012. "Digital: A Love Story; Bully; Grand Theft Auto IV; Portal; dys4ia." *Theatre Journal* 64, no. 4 (December 2012): 595–8.

Laverde, Jake. 2015. "Her Story Interview: Sam Barlow on Storytelling and 'Not a Game' Claims." *International Business Times*, 6 July. http://www.ibtimes.co.uk/her-story-interview-sam-barlow-storytelling-not-game-claims-1509473.

Lewis, Helen. 2014. "A Quest for Understanding." *Insight* 1, no. 1 (October 2014): 341.

MacDonald, Cheryl. 2014. "Inscribing Context 2013: Reflections on an Annual Interdisciplinary Graduate Student Conference at Concordia University." *McGill Sociological Review* 4 (February): 116–20.

Othenin-Girard, Alexei. 2012. "Bodies, Games, and Systems: Towards an Understanding of Embodiment in Games." Master's thesis, University of California, Santa Cruz.

Pisters, Patricia. 2012. *The Neuro-Image: A Deleuzian Film-Philosophy of Digital Screen Culture*. Stanford: Stanford University Press.

Rizzo, Meredith. 2016. "How a Little Boy's Cancer Diagnosis Inspired a Haunting Video Game." *National Public Radio*, 13 January. http://www.npr.org/sections/health-shots/2016/01/13/462929457/how-a-little-boys-cancer-diagnosis-inspires-a-haunting-video-game.

Sharp, John. 2012. "Dimensionality." In *The Routledge Companion to Video Game Studies*, edited by Mark J.P. Wolf and Bernard Perron, 91–8. London: Routledge.

Shaviro, Steven. 2010. *Post-Cinematic Affect*. London: Zero Books.

Westecott, Emma. 2013. "Independent Game Development as Craft." *Loading…* 7, no. 11: 78–91.

25

From a "Disappeared Aesthetics" to a "Trans-Aesthetics": Derek Jarman and Ming Wong's Image-Based Technologies of the Self

MILAN PRIBISIC

"Modern man has become a confessing animal," Michel Foucault famously proclaimed in his *History of Sexuality*; for Foucault, this ritual of confessional discourse in which the speaking subject is also the subject of the statement ([1976] 1990, 59–61) became one of the "technologies of the self," the forms of "labor of self on self" taken in different historical periods (Bakardjieva and Gaden 2012, 153–4). While the pre-modern and modern confession that Foucault has in mind refers to the Christian tradition of private auricular confession of sins, in postmodern times, confession-seeking subjects turn to the technologies of film, video, and digital media for public confession that goes beyond sin to include desire, sexual practices, and identity. I use Foucault's terminology as a framing device through which to historicize, or fail to, the construction of the queer self as documented in contemporary moving-image culture and its genres of self – "light writing."

This essay takes as its object of inquiry a network of relations established among the film *Blue* (1993) by the late British artist Derek Jarman, the various video art and installations made between 2005 and 2015 by Singaporean artist residing in Berlin, Germany, Ming Wong, the multiple "I" voices used in their work, and the audiences that engage with these works. The works of Jarman and Wong are posited here as the extreme opposites of a queer confessional art continuum perceived as dialogical discourse among "texts," their historical contexts, and their authors, I-narrators, and audiences.

Disappeared

Blue, released in late 1993, was the last film made by Derek Jarman (1942–94), an artist working in both visual and performing arts. I saw the film for the first time at the Cleveland's Cinémathèque in the first half of the 1990s. I was familiar with

25.1, 25.2 Disappeared author reappears as disappeared aesthetics in Derek Jarman's *Blue*. Zeitgeist Films, 1993.

Jarman's films and print work, and I eagerly awaited his testimonial – and *testamentary* – film, extensively covered in both the mainstream and gay press as a seventy-eight-minute projection of the colour blue as the visual equivalent of the blindness (Jarman uses the term "sightlessness" in the film) that fell upon the artist living with AIDS.

Here is the memory of my first encounter with *Blue*: after the opening title credits, the colour blue dominates the screen, accompanied by the soft music; then a voice, in a sort of whisper, starts narrating. Different sound effects enter the now multi-layered soundtrack. The blue seemed to be unchanging, but I catch myself moving between watching the screen intensely and listening very attentively to the voice-over (after all, English is not my first language) to comprehend and follow what I am hearing. At moments, the blue and the audio narration about the blue, the current war and violence in the Balkans, the AIDS threat, and refugees come together, and then I am back to listening or to watching. I let go, allowing *Blue* to reach me in all possible ways – the experience is a mixed bag but I sit through it all (figs. 25.1, 25.2).

Then, and now as I am rewatching *Blue* on DVD (*Glitterbox*, 2008), the claims and the questions reappear and remain. First, *Blue* is a powerful, indelible confessional of an artist suffering and living with AIDS in the late 1980s and early 1990s. It is a document of a time when the destructiveness of AIDS was prevalent and seemingly unconquerable. *Blue* delivered an imminent aural testament on film about being gay, being an artist, and being an out person living with AIDS. The challenge here is, in Vivian Sobchack's words, our "naturalized attitude" toward the phenomenon we call a "film" and how it correlates to what we understand as visual perception (Sobchack 2012, 19). Since their inception in the late 1800s, moving pictures are habitually perceived as an image-based technology that records reality and preserves it on a film strip. Film is thus traditionally seen as a tool that makes us see, and re-see, the world in which we live.

Based on these long-standing views, *Blue*'s continuous cobalt screen was hastily perceived as a blank screen or an imageless film. Watching that seemingly monochromatic and unchanging imageless screen supported the notion that *Blue* is, indeed, film at its limits, the end of film as we know it, the anti-film. If early film history is often, wrongly, referred to as the "silent" film era, stressing the ocularcentrism of the medium, after the introduction and inclusion of sound, film became a medium that "catches" reality by recording both its visuals and its sounds. So, after the initial shock of the imageless *Blue*, the viewer realizes the necessity of incorporating the aural aspects into the visual, creating a "*sonorously visual* world" (Sobchack 2012, 28). The soundtrack of *Blue* is layered with several different elements – what in my personal memory was one voice-over turns out to have been four voices (the actors Tilda Swinton, Nigel Terry, John Quentin, and John Lynch read Jarman's texts, and the author himself acts as a narrator [Khalip 2010, 103n16]); the music heard was composed for the film by Simon Fisher Turner; finally, there are different sound effects, such as wind blowing, sea breezes, dog barking, and others, creating a melancholy "ambient poetics."[1] The content of the spoken words addresses issues such as the progress of the AIDS virus within the author's body and mind and considerations of life, the arts, and poetry.[2] When all these elements on the soundtrack are taken in as part of a film experience, the seemingly imageless film finds its anchor in a "moving" image of no visible thing (Sobchack 2012, 26), an image of blue darkness made visible (as is stated word-by-word by Jarman's voice-over on the soundtrack). Once this image of blue "no thing" is accepted as visible, tangible, and signifying, *Blue* comes across as a liberating experience confirming itself as a figure-less film, perhaps, but not as an image-less one (27). Out of this blue emerges the voice of the invisible narrator confessing his authorial figurative disappearance only to reappear as the medium of film itself. The artist's self-destroyed visual figure continues to live as his double in the form of his audiovisual medium of choice – the artist and its medium/double become one! With this, Jarman's queering of film art/form comes full circle.

Some of these notions were confirmed by Jarman himself a few years before *Blue* was made. In *Kicking the Pricks*, originally published in 1987, one year after he tested HIV-positive and the year in which *The Last of England* was released, Jarman declares that the act of making the film was "the battle for a cinema which … declares that experience is the basis for serious work" (Jarman [1987] 1996, 167).

On the same pages he states: "I think film-makers [sic] should bring much more of their experience to their work than they do" (196). As if to prove that his words are his action and his claim that "the film is the fact – perhaps in the end the only fact – of my life ... my life is now my films" (193–4) is true, Jarman lets his experience, thoughts, feelings, his garden, his sexuality, colour his work. From *The Last of England* to the final *Blue*, the coming-together of the artist's life experiences and his art work takes Jarman and his spectator on a search for an aesthetics of filmic representation that will both truthfully represent the unrepresentable (AIDS, the inside of the queer brain, soul) and use the moving image–based medium to its full potential. John Paul Ricco names this coming-together of disappearing life and reinvigorated art a "disappeared aesthetics" (Ricco 2002, 38).

Jarman found out he was HIV-positive on 22 December 1986. In *Kicking the Pricks*, the second in his print series of memoirs and public confessions,[3] Jarman wrote,

> The young doctor who told me this morning I was a carrier of the AIDS virus was visibly distressed. I smiled and told her not to worry, I had never liked Christmas ... I thought it was inconceivable I could have avoided the virus, though I had avoided the test for as long as was decently possible ... The finality of it seemed attractive ... I stopped at the stationers and bought a day-book for 1987 and a scarlet form to write out a will. ([1987] 1996, 16–17)

In 1987 Jarman also shot *The Last of England*, for which he decided that "the autobiographical element should come right to the fore" (190). Although his films and videos can be interpreted as confessional, for which he was praised and criticized in equal measure, the feature films made for theatrical release are a combination of fiction and confession. Jarman's artistic approach, however, makes his confessions complicated; he often shot films using his "confessional" super 8mm camera, then reshot them on video and projected them either like that or, if the financial support was obtained, transferred onto 35mm film. This technique of intervention on the existing film is similar to the layering of the palimpsest – here it starts with a document and ends in an open cinematic work. This visual palimpsest is doubled down by the layering of the film's soundtrack: writing about *The Last of England*, Jarman referred to the soundtrack as "a palimpsest" (166). If the audiovisual aspects of his films, and especially *Blue*, are "palimpsestic," their ideological composition is simpler; their modus operandi is inspired by 1960s critical theory and is operating on the Manichean principle of good versus evil, just versus unjust, natural versus artificial, pre-modern versus modern, humanistic versus commodified. Jarman's films unveil to criticism late capitalism's consumerism, neo-conservativism, and neo-conformism.

This rhetorical logic of historicization, which favours summarization of life work, has been challenged by the authenticity of the AIDS crisis emphasizing a self-destroying impulse of remembrance (Khalip 2010, 80). The result is repetition with a difference, as every film that Jarman made was always already about the self and at the end, with *Blue*, "beside oneself" (Ricco 2002, 38). In the context of the AIDS crisis and his terminal illness, Jarman's film constitutes the "becoming-disappeared of visual representation, identity, visual-based epistemologies" (45), the transformative impulse that emotionally envelopes the spectator and anticipates the heteroglossic possibilities of the (film) medium despite the disappearing act. The analog image/confessant is gone and re-emerges as "acoustic *bricolage*" (Khalip 2010, 81) in the rectangular shape of the medium's blue screen. Facing that blueness accompanied by the soundtrack "as a narrativizing force" (Singh 2016, 25), the spectator becomes the co-creator and co-confessant in the age of AIDS. "An artist is engaged in a dig," Jarman proclaimed (1996, 235), but so is the viewer, who starts to "see things" in the infinite blueness. This "seeing" is not of a visual kind but nevertheless is a perception resulting in feelings through which a spectator evaluates zir/eir whole-body viewing experience.

From 1981 through 1983, Jarman worked on a project entitled *Neutron*, never realized despite his completing several drafts of its script. In *Kicking the Pricks*, he describes it as "a love affair with the shadow, he who walks beside" (184). The project was based on C.G. Jung's *Aion: Researches into the Phenomenology of the Self* ([1951] 1959). Although *Neutron* never materialized, it is clear from Jarman's memoirs that some of the main ideas and the atmosphere from that project were part of his work starting with *The Last of England* and ending with *Blue*.

Jung's study that inspired Jarman is on the archetype of the Self as historically embodied in the figure of Christ. Jung acknowledges that the knowledge of the Self is a complicated process that should direct us toward wholeness, granted only to the divine. Perfect wholeness is quite different from the clash of opposites that constitutes human consciousness. The Self is the field of consciousness (the personality) of which ego/consciousness is only a small part; the ego is subordinate to the Self, which acts upon it. Two main elements influence the ego and contribute to the constitution of the Self – one is individual, the shadow, and the other is social and is made up of the anima and the animus. The analytic process of self-criticism starts with the integration of the shadow as the personal unconscious, the dark aspects of the personality; the anima and the animus are the personification of the collective unconscious and are rarely realized. The anima, becoming the Eros of consciousness, is the feminine inner personality of a man; the animus, the Logos of consciousness, is the male aspect of the female self.

In *Neutron*, Jarman adapts Jung's opposites as the conflict between a revolutionary and the artist, between action and contemplation; in the end, the artist kills the revolutionary and becomes zim. The disappearance of one is the reappearance of the other as both, as wholeness. This tense opposition looking for a release achieves it in *Blue* with the disappearance of the author who re-emerges as the aural blue bliss of the flickering film projection, as the audiovisual totality, both visible and invisible, made possible by the medium of film. With *Blue*, Jarman delivers his personal thanatography, a poetic and emotional study in dying. He does so, according to Nicoletta Vallorani, through "an empty blue screen" with "a cinema fighting against itself, that is a cinema without images" (2010, 90). Yet *Blue* is not without image(s), only without figures; Ricco's "disappeared aesthetics," of which Jarman's last film is an example, refers to an act of disappearing through representation. Only on the surface is *Blue* a refusal of the medium, since it is the medium itself that delivers the film as "the refusal of the acceptable refusal" (Ricco 2002, 34). By denying visibility to the spectacle of AIDS body and by making it along the way be heard, Jarman opts for the queer potentiality of visuality. In *Blue*, film, as an image-based medium of representation, ascends to "the aporetics of representation" (Ricco 2002, 43) making the paradox of the medium tangible. This aporetics engenders a complex psychological space in-between the seer and the seen, the viewer and the viewed, the subject and the object. It is in this space in-between that the meaning is created by making the "imperceptible … tangible" (44)

Paradoxes abound in Jarman's work and are productive of multi-layered, queer experiences for their viewers who become the active co-creators of meaning. Jarman's distinction between sight and vision is another paradox. Vision is greater than sight and losing sight due to AIDS-related illness is unrelated to his vision, which is neither the matter of sight nor a mode of representation. Thanks to vision, the visible streams from the invisible. This vision survives in the blindness, it persists-in-blindness (Ricco 2002, 46), it continues to go on without seeing. It is this vision as pure possibility (of visuality, of imagining, of understanding) that connects the invisible yet audible I of the confessant, the visible blue screen of the film medium, and the cinematic experience of the spectator, allowing us to see through the sound and despite the darkness and blindness. With *Blue*'s "disappeared aesthetics," the absence (of the author, of the figurative) comes back in full force as a necessary element for calculations of queer presence.

25.3 Ming Wong is Emmi, Ming Wong is Ali, Ming Wong is ... *Angst Essen/Eat Fear*, dir. Ming Wong, 2008. Courtesy Studio Ming Wong.

Trans-ing

On the other side of this disappearing aesthetics is the "confessional increment" (Goldknopf 1969, 19–20) of the many voices, narrators, and roles present in the video art installations by Ming Wong. Wong's performances of the variety of roles and characters in his video art speak directly to the postmodern notions of identity as relational self, as a set of unstable tensions and mutations at the base of queer identity, impossible to be separated from class, racial, ethnic, and national identity, and co-created with others (characters, roles, audience members) in our social existence. If Jarman's films are immersed in the artist's lived experience from the 1960s through the early 1990s and are directly confessional in form, Wong's video art installations are performance-based confessions of an artist using adaptation of popular culture in general, and national (e.g., Hong Kong, Malaysian, Hollywood, European nations) cinemas, seen inherently as "transnational," in particular as his primary method of work. If Jarman's life became his films, Wong's video art installations are commentaries on cultural and political issues, such as language and identity, that resonate on both the personal and social level. Wong uses as his source material the original work of celebrated film artists in the West (e.g., Douglas Sirk, Rainer Werner Fassbinder, Wong Kar-Wai, Roman Polanski, Pier Paolo Pasolini, Luchino Visconti, Alain Resnais) and adapts them by acting the characters from the source films without ever appearing as himself or in his own words; the viewer thus is led to perceive and interpret these as the "drag confessions" of the colonized minority mimicking the colonizing figures. We watch Wong play Petra von Kant, Emmi and Ali, Gustav von Aschenbach, and Tadzio in replicas of the original films' costumes, wigs, and makeup. So many impersonations by Ming Wong are on the screen(s) of these multi-channel installations, and yet no authentic Ming Wong Huang (his full name in Mandarin) ever shows up. Where is the artist known as Ming Wong? Has he, not unlike Derek Jarman in *Blue*, disappeared through his aesthetics, only to reappear as the medium of zis choice? Who is the "I" behind all these contrasting character impersonations? Should we understand these performances as "drag diaries" of a postmodern, transnational subject in constant flux offering one's self for public viewing even when not referencing oneself or when referencing oneself through stereotypes created by the colonizer? The rest of this essay seeks to answer these and related questions.

Ming Wong was born in 1971 in Singapore; his father's ancestors came there from China, and his mother was originally from Malaysia. Wong went to school in London and, like Derek Jarman, attended the Slade School of Art, University College London, where he received his MFA degree in visual arts. In 2005, Wong created *Four Malay Stories*, a twenty-five-minute, four-channel video installation loop inspired by the work of the Malay film icon P. Ramlee from the 1950s, '60s, and '70s. This was the first in a series of video installation adaptations based on national cinemas in which Wong acts all the roles from the film source. Wong plays sixteen different characters from four of the best-known of Ramlee's films. He also speaks some classic lines from these films in Malay, of which he has a limited knowledge. He adds a visual tool on the screen, subtitles in both Malay and English, to help the viewer understand his lines. The cross-dressing, the different genre conventions of the original films, the acting, and the spoken words delivered with an accent and accompanied by the subtitles, all suggest an over-the-top, parodic camp performance suffused with both nostalgia and a cultural critique of gender binarism and racial, national, and sexual stereotypes. The overall effect is playful, witty entertainment that, apart from all the laughs, makes one think about the issues of sex, gender, race, age and class, as well as the regulations imposed on them by the state, nation, or culture (Wong 2016).

As Wong confesses, "It's more like non-acting – I actually play myself trying to be this other person." His fascination with the cinema has to do with who he is and where he came from. Growing up in Singapore, Wong spent a lot of time watching movies: "A lot of my work is about my own identity so movies play a big part" (Uttam 2011). Statements like these bring the autobiographical into the picture, confirming the notion that the cross-dressing masquerade allows the colonized and marginalized (sexual, ethnic, aesthetic) to enter the mainstream and to obtain agency even though, perceived only on the costumes' surfaces, it perpetuates the culture's standards and stereotypes.

While still in London, Wong was invited to be an artist in residence at Berlin's Künstlerhaus Bethanien and while preparing for it he produced a video art installation of Rainer Werner Fassbinder's early film and one of the unforgettable works of the New German Cinema, *Die Bitteren Tränen der Petra von Kant* (*The Bitter Tears of Petra von Kant*, 1972, West Germany, 124 min.). This was a perfect opportunity to revisit the director he had discovered at the London's ICA (Institute of Contemporary Arts) in the late 1990s; also, it was an occasion for him to prepare for living in Germany and, with his audiences, to *Lerne Deutsch mit Petra Von Kant/Learn German with Petra von Kant* (2007) – as Wong titled this ten-minute-long video loop installation. During his residency, Wong relocated to Berlin, residing in the Kreuzberg district of the city, populated mostly by Turkish immigrants. This environment brought him back in 2008 to yet another Fassbinder early landmark, *Angst Essen Seele auf* (*Ali: Fear Eats the Soul*, 1974, West Germany, 93 min.), which became a twenty-seven-minute, single-channel video installation entitled *Angst Essen/Eat Fear*, with Wong playing up to five separate roles from the original source (Ting 2009).

For the *Lerne Deutsch mit* video, Wong selected one pivotal scene from *Petra von Kant*, based on Fassbinder's original stage play – the birthday scene in which the power dynamics among the all-female chamber-piece characters turn upside down, and the until-that-moment dominant character of the fashion designer Petra falls victim to falling in love with a working-class model, Karin. Petra's falling is literal – she is on the floor, with a glass and a bottle of booze, next to the phone waiting for Karin's call. Wong replicates from Fassbinder's original Petra's blond wig à la Kim Novak and the green gown with a red neckpiece but eliminates all elements of the setting except for the phone and the bottle. In this set-up, the focus is on Petra's monologue, which once again Wong's delivers in the source's original language, German. It is broken German, visually emphasized by the use of subtitles, both in German and English. The effect is ultimately one of distancing and alienation, punctuating, in Lilian Haberer's words, "the hybrid nature of his character," in terms of its race, nationality, gender and sexuality (Haberer 2013, 261).[4]

This distancing and hybridization become multiplied in *Eat Fear*, which is a condensed re-enactment of the original's plot, with Wong playing both protagonists, Emmi, a sixty-year-old German cleaning lady, and her new husband, a thirtysomething Moroccan guest worker, as well as a few supporting characters (fig. 25.3). The story of racism and xenophobia in post–World War II West Germany turns, in Wong's restaging, into a search for identity in a world of transnationalism. By enacting all these different characters in broken German and thus de-emphasizing the speech and accents of native Germans and foreign workers from Fassbinder's source film, Wong undermines the cultural/linguistic differences, making them all German and/or non-German; they all, in a way, become foreigners and foreign to their cultural condition. In all of this, in his performances and impersonations, Wong remains Wong, and the different characters he impersonates are perceived as his "split alter ego" (Haberer 2013, 260).[5]

The above descriptions of Wong's video adaptations based on two early Fassbinder films are adequate if they are watched on YouTube or some other streaming video platform. Jun Zubillaga-Pow reminds us that Wong's videos are video art installations and that the context in which he delivers them needs to be taken into consideration to avoid narrowing down the hermeneutic possibilities of their aesthetic meaning. Zubillaga-Pow frames Wong's installations as Wagnerian *Gesamtkunstwerk*, a total work of art (Zubillaga-Pow 2015). Wong places his video adaptations in the three-dimensional spaces of art galleries and museums where they function as trans-disciplinary, mixed media of film, theatre, sound, and visual art. The projection of the videos is just one aspect of the installation, which one can walk through or around as if entering a movie/stage set. These projections get multiplied and end up on different surfaces and with multiple angles promoting refracted perspectives and methods used by the artist to guide the viewer's perception and attention.

I experienced both of Wong's above-discussed video adaptations at the *Fassbinder NOW: Film and Video Art* exhibit at the Deutsches Filmmuseum (German Film Museum) in Frankfurt-am-Main in 2014. The installations were part of the exhibition dedicated to contemporary filmmakers and visual artists directly, or less so, inspired by Fassbinder's films, aesthetics, and ideas. This was an international group covering mostly European countries but also Bangladesh and Singapore. The influence that Fassbinder has been having on these various artists confirms the notion that film language, even when delivered within national cinemas, has always been a sort of transnational medium. Fassbinder, very much influenced by, for example, the American melodramas of Douglas Sirk, dreamed of and tried to make films about Germany and life in it that would be as beautiful as Hollywood movies but less hypocritical – he was dreaming of the German Hollywood film (Töteberg 2002, 116). Artists working today are continuing Fassbinder's impulse to work independently and, in some instances, anarchically, to create something popular and spectacular, and, at the same time, adapt to existing political and economic conditions through the process of negotiation between local, regional, national, and international trends and interests. Wong's mimicry and masquerade seen in the Fassbinder adaptations can now be contextualized as transnational cinema and as a way of including and representing a minority group and culture.

Adaptation is the key term here to frame Wong's video art installations. Wong's adaptations are interventions on the source material (a two-hour film becomes a ten-minute video loop; all roles, regardless of age, class, sex/gender, or nationality are played by an ethnic Chinese gay man) and as such involve memory, selection, and interpretation. Why is Fassbinder's *Petra von Kant* reduced to a single scene with the monologue of the inebriated heroine delivered by a Chinese man in drag speaking broken German? What kind of subjectivity is at play here? Also, who remembers what from the films we watch, and why? The answers to these questions, of course, depend on the experiences, life and cinematic, of individual viewers, some of whom are familiar with Fassbinder's films as sources and some of whom will view Wong's adaptations without previous knowledge of them. With his *Lerne Deutsch mit* video, Wong gets access to an artifact of post–World War II New German Cinema and the language of the culture that became his adopted artistic home country. Spectators, on the other hand, become privy to the self as a product of narration, which is a result of memory and adaptation. To paraphrase Suzanne Diamond, we may ask: Whose confession is it that we are witnessing anyway, in this flux of subjectivities? (Diamond 2010, 95). Is it Fassbinder's or Petra's or Ming Wong's or the viewer's, or all of the above? The video art installations are clearly an intertext, a mix of fact and fiction, and the selfhood that emerges resonates as "real" only insofar as it is always in question and perceived as collaboration stressing "the collaborative character of selfhood" (Fanthome 2006, 34).

Seeing Wong's video adaptations as part of installations, in space that one can walk through, stop and reflect, and come back to the video loop, accentuate the trans-mediality and trans-disciplinary configuration of his work. *Lerne Deutsch mit*'s set-up at the *Fassbinder NOW* exhibit made that very clear: the video loop was projected on a small television set typical of the 1970s, the time that Fassbinder's source film was made; it was placed on a white flokati rug fashionable at the time and used in the original film. The video loop on a small, tacky TV monitor with Wong as a drunk, mad Petra on the floor with a glass and bottle provides both time period and physical frame to the re-presentation. The image(s) on the TV are nostalgic, but Wong's drag impersonation gives it a contemporary shift. When the film originally appeared, the critics, helped by some of the Fassbinder's friends and collaborators, perceived the performances as always already in drag, as female actors masquerading as female characters with femininity held at a distance (Cottingham 2005, 52–5). Wong's performance, on that tiny monitor, added another mask to the masquerade and another aesthetics to the original one. The result of this "doubling" is Wong's queer trans-aesthetics, the blurring of boundaries between nature and culture, fact and fiction, gender, race, and class, movies and theatre and performance art. This is the multiplying of disciplines and media, aesthetics, and costumes "where all identities are at work" (Pérez 1999, 7) and private fantasies meet public ones to deliver a confession in public, for the public.

To enter the (inter)national art scene of Frankfurt, Los Angeles, Sydney, Beijing (etc.), the artist is "passing" as video artist, drag performer, language instructor, filmmaker, a Singaporean and non-Singaporean, nationalist and trans-nationalist, insider and outsider; "he" is using "she" to enact a trans-gender and trans-sex figure to activate the queer politics of trans-aesthetics – of trans-ing in general understood as an action across the binary divisions and labels. This amalgamation of the sexual, political, and economic within the work of art, as Jean Baudrillard describes it (Zubillaga-Pow 2015), transcends the affirmative traits of identity politics, offering instead, as in negative dialectics, the non-identitary under the aspects of identity, illusion as a promise of freedom from illusion. This is a subversive, oppositional aspect of Wong's work, of his aesthetic of doing and being trans – (Zubillaga-Pow 2015), an example of decolonial transmodern aesthetics through which "the silent gain their agency" (Pérez 1999, 33).[6] Wong's video art installations are an open invitation for audiences to go beyond the traditionally prescribed standardized notions of sex/gender/nation/class and creation/spectatorship in search of freedom and autonomy as offered by these politically charged "total works of art."

The examples of image-based media confessionals created by Derek Jarman and Ming Wong discussed in this essay are used to historicize the fifty-year trajectory of queer artists' self-reflection and creation in moving-image art. Early on within this queer journey, Derek Jarman used the analog film medium as a technology engaged in both the "archeology of soul" (Jarman [1987] 1996, 235) and "archeology of sound" (Khalip 2005). His film confessionals are entrenched in identity politics as a product of the 1960s and early '70s civil-rights and sexual and gay-liberation movements. After being diagnosed with HIV at the end of 1986, Jarman turned to the mixed media of film and video to engage "in a dig"; his seeking of the personal shadow/ unconscious and the anima and animus of the social unconscious brought him eventually to the "disappeared aesthetics" of his last work, *Blue*. On the other side of this queer journey of "labour of self on self," now using digital-media technologies, are Ming Wong's video art installations of the early twenty-first century. Wong, not unlike Jarman, in seeking the truth of his own being, arrives in the space of negotiation, the in-between space of the decolonial imaginary. This is the space of shadows, of a "trans-aesthetic" of passing and doubling that challenges audiences with destabilized, queer notions of gender, race, nation, class, and language. Wong's multiplying of identities, disciplines, and media goes beyond the identity politics of the 1960s and '70s to bring together the goals of both queer and postcolonial politics. His decolonial moving-image confessions in drag serve as a transitional phase of critical work that questions and undermines the affirmative aspects of the 1960s and '70s identity politics, understanding queer sexual politics as inextricably linked to the broader issues of ethnicity, race, nation, and class in the contemporary trans-national moment.

NOTES

1 This is Timothy Morton's term, quoted in Khalip 2010, 81.
2 For the purposes of textual accuracy, I used the text of Jarman's *Blue* as available in full at https://qcc2.org/gallery-2/derek-jarman/.
3 The memoir was originally published in 1987 under the title *The Last of England* and reprinted as *Kicking the Pricks* (the original title Jarman had in mind) in 1996; the other memoirs are *Dancing Ledge* (1984), *At Your Own Risk: A Saint's Testament* (1993), and *A Modern Nature* (1994).
4 An excerpt from the video is available on youtube.com, https://www.youtube.com/watch?v=mFHptG3dmoU.

5 A video preview of *Angst Essen* is available on Ming Wong Studio's page, http://www.mingwong.org/video-preview-angst-essen-eat-fear.
6 For differentiation in usage of the terms postcolonial and decolonial and on the technologies of decolonial desire see, among others, Pérez 1999. For Pérez, the decolonial is a time lag between colonial and postcolonial, as she perceives the latter as "a hopeful utopian project" (33).

REFERENCES

Bakardjieva, Maria, and Georgia Gaden. 2012. "Web 2.0 Technologies of the Self." In *Cultural Technologies*, edited by Göran Bolin, 153–69. New York: Routledge.

Cottingham, Laura. 2005. BFI *Film Classics: Fear Eats the Soul.* London, BFI.

Diamond, Suzanne. 2010. "Whose Life *Is* It, Anyway? Adaptation, Collective Memory, and (Auto)Biographical Processes." In *Redefining Adaptation Studies*, edited by Dennis Cutchins, Laurence Raw, and James M. Welsh, 95–110. Lanham, MD: Scarecrow Press.

Fanthome, Christine. 2006. "The Influence and Treatment of Autobiography in Confessional Art: Observations on Tracey Emin's Feature Film *Top Spot*." *Biography: An Interdisciplinary Quarterly* 29, no. 1: 30–42.

Foucault, Michel. [1976] 1990. *The History of Sexuality.* Vol. 1, *Introduction.* Translated by Robert Hurley. New York: Pantheon.

Goldknopf, David. 1969. "The Confessional Increment: A New Look at the I-Narrator." *Journal of Aesthetics and Art Criticism* 28, no. 1: 13–21.

Haberer, Lilian. 2013. "Ming Wong's Restaging of Language and Identity." In *Fassbinder NOW: Film and Video Art*, edited by Deutsches Filminstitut–DIF and the Rainer Werner Fassbinder Foundation, 258–65. Frankfurt: Deutsches Filminstitut Filmmuseum.

Jarman, Derek. [1987] 1996. *Kicking the Pricks.* London: Vintage.

– 2017. *Blue:* Text of a Film by Derek Jarman." *Queer Cultural Center.* https://qcc2.org/gallery-2/derek-jarman/.

Jung, C.G. [1951] 1959. *Aion: Researches into the Phenomenology of the Self.* Translated by R.F.C. Hull. Princeton: Princeton University Press.

Khalip, Jacques. 2010. "'The Archeology of Sound': Derek Jarman's *Blue* and Queer Audiovisuality in the Time of AIDS." *Differences* 21, no. 2: 73–108.

Pérez, Emma. 1999. *The Decolonial Imaginary: Writing Chicanas in History.* Bloomington: Indiana University Press.

Ricco, John Paul. 2002. *The Logic of the Lure.* Chicago: University of Chicago Press.

Singh, Greg. 2014. *Feeling Film: Affect and Authenticity in Popular Cinema.* London: Routledge.

Sobchack, Vivian. 2012. "Fleshing Out the Image: Phenomenology, Pedagogy, and Derek Jarman's *Blue*." *Cinema* 3: 19–38.

Ting, Celina. 2009. "Interview: Ming Wong." *InitiArt Magazine* (Summer). http://www.initiart magazine.com/interview.php?IVarchive=12.

Töteberg, Michael. 2002. *Rainer Werner Fassbinder*. Reinbek bei Hamburg: Rowohlt.

Uttam, Payal. 2011. "Ming Wong, the Chameleon Artist, on Hong Kong Cinema and Turkish Porn." *CNN.com*. http://travel.cnn.com/hong-kong/play/does-art-have-be-beautiful-025471.

Vallorani, Nicoletta. 2010. "Path(o)s of Mourning. Memory, Death and the Invisible Body in Derek Jarman's *Blue*." *Altre Modernità* 4: 82–92.

Wong, Ming. 2016. "Projects." *MingWong.org*. http://wingwong.org/projects.

Zubillaga-Pow, Jun. 2015. "Trans-Aesthetics: The Art of Ming Wong between Nation and State." *Intersections: Gender and Sexuality in Asia and the Pacific* (August). http://intersections.anu.edu.au/issue38/zubillaga-pow.html.

MEDIAGRAPHY

Jarman, Derek. [1986, 1993, 1985, 1993, 1994] 2008. 313 min. *Glitterbox (Caravaggio/Wittgenstein/ Angelic Conversation/Blue/Glitterbug)*. New York: Zeitgeist Films.

Wong, Ming. 2008. *Angst Essen/Eat Fear*. Germany, 27 min. *Fassbinder NOW* Exhibition. Deutsches Filmmuseum, Frankfurt am Main, 2013.

– 2007. *Lerne Deutsch mit Petra Von Kant/Learn German with Petra von Kant*. Germany, 10 min. *Fassbinder NOW* Exhibition. Deutsches Filmmuseum, Frankfurt am Main, 2013.

26

Writing Intimacy: Fantasy, New Media, and Confession in Marie Calloway's what purpose did I serve in your life

ELEANOR TY

Chronicling her sexual experiences and sex work from the age of eighteen to twenty-two, Marie Calloway's *what purpose did I serve in your life* has been called a "dirty YA novel" (Spiers 2013) and described as "titillating, frustrating" (Orange 2013). Because of the young age of the mixed-race Korean American author and her narrator (who is closely linked to the author), the work has generated mixed reviews; the author has been called both "jailbait" (Carver 2013) and a "narcissist" (Spiers 2013). The book is made up of a series of loosely linked short narratives told from a first-person point of view, interspersed with grainy photographs of the author and screen-caps of text messages to and from Calloway's internet clients/boyfriends. Many of the autobiographical excerpts were originally published online on sites like *Thought Catalog* and on Facebook and Tumblr. The work is personal and intimate, yet public and performative. The scenes depicted are playful, erotic, and at times painful, making it difficult to discern whether the narrator is a victim of porn culture or a media-savvy and calculating blogger.

In this essay, I examine the power dynamics in Calloway's narratives, looking at her photographs, her self-representations using images and texts, her use of social media, her confessional technique, and her repeated accounts of self-abasement. While reviewer Elizabeth Spiers calls her style "affectless realism" (2013), I suggest that Calloway's work incites strong affective responses, curiosity, and voyeurism through its seeming authenticity and familiarity. Her narratives interest us in the same way that we pore over the audacious photos of Kim Kardashian, to catch a glimpse of what lies behind the public face, of what it's like to lead a more exciting or intense life than our own. Like Kardashian, Calloway fulfills men's fantasies of the sexually compliant kitten at the same time as she is able to exercise control over the documentation and memorialization of these events. Calloway's *what purpose did I serve in your life* reveals what Smith and Watson call the "complexities of questions of agency" (2010, 55) in the way she empowers herself by exploiting her sexualized body.

As Irene Gammel observes, women's relationship to confessional writing, especially sexual confessions, has been particularly fraught:

> A history of confessional readings has created the perception of women obsessively confessing their secrets, reinforcing stereotypes of the female psyche as fragmented and, with what is perhaps, even worse, as "needy." In western society, in which the self-sufficient, self-reliable bourgeois subject remains the ideal norm, confession easily becomes a measure of mental immaturity and emotional instability. (1999, 4)

Confessions are also implicated "within a power relationship," as Michel Foucault reminds us. "One does not confess without the presence (or virtual presence) of a partner who is not simply the interlocutor but the authority who requires the confession, prescribes and appreciates it, and intervenes in order to judge, punish, forgive, console, and reconcile" ([1976] 1990, 61–2). However, with digital tools and social media, the power dynamics between the writer/creator and audience shifts somewhat because the writer can decide what is being confessed, when the confessing takes place, and the means of representation. The online addressee can respond with comments and can judge harshly, punish with "dislikes," or just simply ignore the posts. But digital confessions are less hierarchical than those of a patient to his therapist or a sinner to his priest. In addition, there is the added possibility of the writer's creating a fictionalized virtual identity. What Paul Longley Arthur notes of digital biographies applies in part to digital autobiographies: "Many of the lives we can see [online] are actually second lives, fabricated identities. One could say, in fact, that the whole realm of 'cyberbiography' is like a 'second life' in relation to the traditional field of biography" (2009, 77).

Marie Calloway's blogs, autobiographical narratives, and photos are sexual confessions, pornographic fantasies, a narrative of abjection and trauma, written in a style described by one critic as "Asperger" (Marche 2013) because of its lack of ethical and emotional filter. *What purpose did I serve in your life* challenges our expectations of the prostitute's scandalous memoir, the seduced maiden story, and fiction because it is all of these genres but does not follow their generic conventions. The first story in the collection, "Portland, Oregon 2008," is an account of Calloway's loss of her virginity at eighteen to a stranger she met on the internet. The narrator is surprisingly naïve and at the same time determined not to show

26.1 Calloway's self-representation: playful, erotic, and at times painful. Reprinted from Dawn West's review, *The Female Gaze* blog, of Marie Calloway's *what purpose did I serve in your life*, Tumblr post, 7 June 2013.

her unease and lack of experience. Meeting a man in a messy apartment with a mattress on the floor, she thinks, "I thought it looked interesting and was even pleased that this room was so far off from the romantic dreamscapes girls are supposed to want to lose their virginity in" (2013b, 3). She hides her pain in her desperation to be cool about the experience: "Two of his fingers went into my vagina and it hurt tremendously. My eyes snapped shut and I started to moan both from pain and out of feeling an obligation to make him think I was enjoying it, and feeling like I wanted to excite him by moaning and groaning" (4). Her reactions reveal her limited sexual knowledge and her vulnerability: "He started to finger me again, faster and faster and then started to roughly rub my clit and I was in so much pain I had to fight back tears. I wanted to fake an orgasm so he would stop, but I didn't know how to or what women even acted like when they came" (5). At once subject and object of desire, in her narrative she confuses our categories of seducer, victim, and the seduced maiden.

What is disturbing and original about Calloway's account is her masochistic determination to make her first time as unemotional an experience as possible. Although it seems that she initiated the encounter, her low self-esteem becomes apparent when she describes how she endures the pain, how she feels compelled to fake her orgasm. The account is clinical, complete with the way she looks at herself, watching "his cock going in and out of my vagina. It was so shocking and strange and interesting looking I wanted to keep staring at his cock going in and out" (6). Unlike confessions in front of priests, Calloway's lacks guilt and regret, yet the scene is far from titillating. Instead the story reveals the complex power relations that a woman has to negotiate in acting out desire; the ways the sexual lives of women and girls are still circumscribed, not by the teachings of the church but by the expectations set up by mass mediated culture, pornography, and social media.

Calloway's account of losing her virginity illustrates the difficulty of women's attempt to be what Gammel describes as the "self-sufficient, self-reliant bourgeois subject" (1999, 4). She fights the stereotype of the "needy" woman, but the extent of her resistance is limited. At the end of the narrative, she writes, "All day long I was in pain from my vagina being incredibly sore. I wrote furiously, obsessively in my notebook all day long about what had happened. And I couldn't get the image of his penis going in and out of my vagina out of my head" (2013b, 9). Calloway succeeds in exploring sexuality and pushing the boundaries of writing about sexuality to a different level, but the confession of her body in pain curtails the liberatory and existentialist elements of the account. Instead it leaves readers in an ambiguous affect of pity, bewilderment, and frustration at her co-optation.

In *The Body in Pain*, Elaine Scarry argues that pain is inexpressible and unshareable: "For the person whose pain it is, it is 'effortlessly' grasped ... while for the person outside the sufferer's body, what is 'effortless' is *not* grasping it (it is easy to remain wholly unaware of its existence" (1985, introduction, 2). Pain, she says, cannot be represented through language: "Physical pain does not simply resist language but actively destroys it, bringing about an immediate reversion to a state anterior to language, to the sounds and cries a human being makes before language is learned" (2–3). Pain is difficult to express because it is invisible. Despite Scarry's assertions, readers are able to understand, if not feel, Calloway's soreness and pain, as she describes how she had to "fight back tears" and how her vagina was raw all day. The kinds of situations Scarry discusses – physical pain from torture, war, illness – are those that involve unwilling participants who are subjected to pain. That Calloway's pain results from her own choices makes it more complicated; she is not simply victim but partly responsible for her bodily pain. She participates or claims to want to participate in her self-abasement and pain.

What purpose did I serve in your life uses visual as well as textual illustrations to narrate Calloway's sexual experiences. The book includes screen shots of text messages between Calloway and internet clients who often express their secret desires to her. With a schoolgirl profile picture of herself in pigtails, she gives her clients short responses that seem to encourage acts of violence and abjection. For example, she asks one text-message correspondent to "tell me what else u like to force girls to do," and he replies: "stand on your knees and keep my balls in your mouth while I masturbate on you," "choke yourself while I'm fucking you," "drink my cum" and "gargle with it." Her response is usually "K," "yes," or "mew" (2013b, "Cybersex"). As there are no comments or explanations after these screen shots or in the chapter, we do not know whether she is simply playing the role of the willing cybersex partner or if she actually would relish doing these things. In other words, it is nearly impossible to distinguish between the performance and the confession, between the fantasy and the autobiography of the prostitute. The contrast between the earlier autobiographical narratives of bodily pain and the text messages suggests that she presents different kinds of selves online and offline.

Photographs included in the book are similarly ambiguous. Most are photographs of herself, but they are not selfies that tend to be funny – "girls making pouty lips," "duckface with the photographer's arms," "bad camera angles" (Saltz 2014). Calloway's pictures of herself are grainy, sometimes with parts deliberately blurred out. They are taken by a web cam, depicting herself masturbating, showing herself in bed, a close-up of a bruised breast, blood on towels. A chapter called "criticism" contains a dozen pages with pictures of herself over-written with others' comments about her and her writing. These include scathing reviews, advice, hate mail, and insults. The text, in white font, covers her grainy photos. In one text, she is called "a female train wreck, a creeper, a woman that gets obsessed with boys and her looks, and who lacks any moral component" (Calloway 2013b, 142). Another image has a caption that reads: "I want her to be choking to death on kale leaves / I want marie calloway's body to slam to the floor, also causing blunt head trauma" (144). These captions anticipate readers' reactions and criticism of her work in a postmodern way, but they subvert rather than support her aspirations as a writer. In choosing to include these hyper-critical rather than the positive reviews, she again shows her puzzling tendency to punish and abase herself.

Both Calloway's book and Kim Kardashian's *Selfish* are forms of diary, but they are very different in tone. While Kardashian's photos are presented year by year, chronologically, and "capture her evolution" (Garber 2015), Calloway's are disjointed. Kardashian's show her experimenting with makeup, hair colour, hairstyles, looks, Calloway's are stark, wistful, wounded, and sad looking. Tanya Dalziell and Lee-Von Kim note that "*Selfish* might be read as an attempt to claim not (only) ownership of the photographs but also authorship of (selected) stories of the self" (2015, 378). We could say that Calloway also attempts to claim ownership of her images, but the result is disturbing rather than powerful or uplifting.

A number of textual narratives, accounts of her sex work, are similarly equivocal in tone and intent. In an encounter, titled "Sex Work Experience Three," she struggles between media representations of sexual experiences and reality. She writes about being "disgusted" by the "tight, dingy grey briefs" of her client and her difficulty with trying to please him:

He rubbed his penis all over my face.
　I get turned on whenever I watch this happen in porn, but now it's happening to me and I feel sick, though also slightly turned on. *I want to like this more.*
　He touched his penis to my lips and I opened my mouth mechanically.
　He placed his hands on the back of my head and gripped my hair and began to move my head wildly back and forth.
　My eyes were shut tight. I stopped thinking then and was only aware of the pain in my throat and how much I wanted to gag but I couldn't. *I can't show any weakness, I can't let him humiliate me. I can't let him win.* (2013b, 67)

The account stops short of being erotic because of the conscious interjections of the writer. During her sexual encounters, she never surrenders herself to sensual feeling. Instead, she depicts herself as constantly aware of the performative potential of these scenes, that what she says and shows will become indications of her intentions, even of her identity. In *Excitable Speech*, Judith Butler argues that "language sustains the body not by bringing it into being or feeding it in a literal way; rather, it is by being interpellated within the terms of language that a certain social existence of the body first becomes possible" (1997, 5). The passage reveals the struggle that Calloway feels between what her body experiences, how she wants to appear to her client, and her will to win what she sees as a battle. Though she is interpellated by the women in porn movies and tries to perform according to what she has seen, she is also implicitly making what J.L. Austin calls "performative utterances" ([1955/1962] 1975, 6) when she thinks "I can't let him humiliate me. I can't let him win" (Calloway 2013b, 67). These utterances, though not as

26.2
Calloway's stark, wistful, wounded, and sad-looking diary photos, attempting to claim ownership? From "Interview with 23-Year-Old Sex Memoirist Marie Calloway," *ONTD* blog post, *Live Journal*, 23 June 2013

binding as a legal vow, can be seen nevertheless as assertive and transformative. She is promising to keep her dignity at all cost.

Butler's oft-quoted insights about the relationship between words, acts, gestures, and desire and the production of an "internal core or substance" can be fruitfully used to understand the implications of Calloway's performances during sex. In her discussion of gender identity, Butler argues that "the inner truth of gender is a fabrication" and that "a true gender is a fantasy instituted and inscribed on the surface of bodies" (1990, 136). Butler's thoughts about gender can be used to discuss desire. Gender, as Butler has noted, is a "*stylized repetition of acts*" (1990, 140; italics in original). "Bodily gestures, movements, and styles of various kinds constitute the illusion of an abiding gendered self" (140). If we are what we perform, our desires also become constituted by what gestures and movements we perform during the sex act.

Calloway is conscious of how she has altered her desires to conform to what she believes men want. Thinking about sexual positions, she says: "I had never met a guy who liked doing it in missionary before. I kind of even trained myself out of liking it, because most guys are so bored by it" (2013, 117). If desires can be "trained" as Calloway articulates, the repeated performance of certain kinds of acts can become inscribed as desire. In a conversation with a writer, whom she calls "Adrien Brody," Calloway says that pornography has changed the terms of intimacy, because she observes that for the young guys she has sex with, "their whole idea of what sex is has been shaped by pornography. They're bored by sex that isn't like violent or degrading" (132).

The problem arises when she can no longer distinguish between her many internet partners' ideas of what sex should be like, what is degrading, and what she likes. She describes an encounter with "the Irish photographer": "'Good girl.' It was like I was his dog. He was humiliating me but I felt safe and warm and completely turned on. Nothing could be more enjoyable than this. To be dominated and degraded was what I wanted. Sex is just a way to get those things. I felt valued, even though I actually wasn't" (45).

It is not surprising that, based on comments and reviews on Goodreads.com, Calloway's book is liked by men more than women. She fulfills heterosexual men's desire to dominate but also expresses enjoyment at the domination. Reviewer Stephen Marche notes that Calloway submits "herself to horrific sexual experiences *in order to write about them.* That's how much she cares about writing" (Marche 2013). I am not certain that it is writing that she values so much as the ability to shock and then control her memory of the event by blogging about it immediately after.

The most infamous story is one based on her sexual encounter with New York writer, cultural critic, and editor of the *New Inquiry* Rob Horning, forty years old at the time she was twenty-one. She contacted him after reading an article he wrote to ask if he was interested in sex with her. Shortly after they spent time together, she published a detailed account of their affair, and then, after an uproar from the literary community, changed it to a short story called "Adrien Brody."

At one point with Adrien Brody, she deliberately flaunts her youth:

"Do you feel weird about me being twenty-one?"
"No. You're an adult," he shrugged. "Should I feel weird about it?"
"No, I was just wondering if you did."
I was actually trying to explore my reverse Lolita complex with him, but I backed off after that because it seemed he wasn't into it at all. (2013b, 129)

At another point, she acts as if she were the director of a film:

>   To put him at ease I decided to reenact a scene from a Japanese pornography I had once watched. I opened my eyes and looked into his and smiled up at him.
>
>   Then when he finally came on my face I moaned and moved the cum from my cheeks with my finger tips to my mouth, and then sucked my fingers. His face changed to this huge dumb grin, like he couldn't believe it, couldn't believe his luck. (2013b, 115)

She ends by asking Adrien Brody to take a picture of her with her phone and later posts the photo on the internet. It is a close-up of her lips and chin with a man's ejaculation all over. The text over image is a screenshot of an ironic text message: "Sorry I'm not good at getting u off :(" (2013b, chap. "men"). The effect is shocking, and more so because her narrative reveals that she was the one who staged it. By posting the picture, she takes control of the situation, turning degradation into a scene of playful defiance.

Calloway's *what purpose did I serve in your life* is a confessional narrative that challenges many of our preconceptions of power, control, and abjection, of the link between intimacy and privacy. Not only does the work remind us of the importance of representation and who gets to tell the story but also of the impact of the speed of communication enabled by digital technology. For through her posts, blogs, and text messages, disseminated almost immediately after her sexual encounters, Calloway is able to tell her version of the story first. It may not be the whole story, but the memorialization of the event in virtual space allows her fantasies, rather than those of the men she is with, to dominate. She creates what Halbwachs calls the "collective memory" of the event before others even have time to process the encounter (quoted in Erll 2011, 16). By giving readers details of her sexual exploitation, the pain she feels she as well as the triumph, Calloway elicits sympathy at the same time as arousing sexual excitement in her readers. The book does not wrestle with questions of morality or guilt; there is no sinner's repentance at the end. Instead, on the last page, we see a moment of self-realization: "I wonder when I would stop abusing myself for the sake of new experiences, new sensations" (2013b, 240). She echoes this query in another story about her encounter with a dom: "I wonder – how can you ever totally anticipate your boundaries? Where is the line between a woman choosing to pursue sexual autonomy, and caving to a misogynistic society that encourages the sexual degradation of women" (2013a). In many ways, her confessional writing has been an exploration of borders of various kinds: of sexuality, desire, power, female subjectivity, and social acceptability. Her work reveals the complex social, psychological, and cultural layers that shape and engender female sexuality and identity.

REFERENCES

Arthurs, Paul Longley. 2009. "Digital Biography: Capturing Lives Online." *a/b: Auto/Biography Studies* 24, no. 1 (Summer): 74–92.

Austin, J.L. [1955/1962] 1975. *How to Do Things with Words*. 2nd ed. Edited by J.O. Urmson and Marina Sbisa. Cambridge: Harvard University Press.

Butler, Judith. 1990. *Gender Trouble: Feminism and the Subversion of Identity*. New York: Routledge.

– 1997. *Excitable Speech: A Politics of the Performative*. New York: Routledge.

Calloway, Marie. 2013a. "In Which I Meet an OKCupid Dom." *Thought Catalog*, 28 September. https://www.youtube.com/watch?v=pvI9PuGorwI&spfreload=10.

– 2013b. *what purpose did I serve in your life*. New York: Tyrant Books.

Carver, Lisa. 2013. "Marie Calloway on Her New Novel and Being Called 'Jailbait.'" *Vice Reader*, 13 June. http://www.vice.com/en_ca/read/marie-calloway.

Dalziell, Tanya, and Lee-Von Kim. 2015. "Self-Regarding: Looking at Photos in Life Writing." *Life Writing* 12, no. 4: 377–81. http://dx.doi.org/10.1080/14484528.2015.1084580.

Erll, Astrid. 2011. *Memory in Culture*. Translated by Sara B. Young. Houndmills: Palgrave.

Foucault, Michel. [1976] 1990. *The History of Sexuality*. Vol. 1, *An Introduction*. Translated by Robert Hurley. New York: Vintage.

Gammel, Irene, ed. 1999. *Confessional Politics: Women's Sexual Self-Representations in Life Writing and Popular Media*. Carbondale: Southern Illinois University Press.

Garber, Megan. 2015. "You Win, Kim Kardashian." *Atlantic* 13 May. http://www.theatlantic.com/entertainment/archive/2015/05/kim-kardashian-selfish/393113/.

Losse, Kate. 2013. "The Return of the Selfie." *New Yorker*, 13 May. http://www.newyorker.com/tech/elements/the-return-of-the-selfie.

Marche, Stephen. 2013. "The New Bad Kids of Fiction." *Esquire*, 10 June. http://www.esquire.com/entertainment/books/a23000/marie-calloway-tao-lin/.

Orange, Michelle. 2013. "Men Respond to Marie: The Titillating, Frustrating Debut by Online Lit's Enfant Terrible." *Slate Book Review*, 7 June. http://www.slate.com/articles/arts/books/2013/06/marie_calloway_what_purpose_did_i_serve_in_your_life_is_a_titillating_frustrating.2.html.

Saltz, Jerry. 2014. "Art at Arm's Length: A History of the Selfie." *Vulture*, 16 January. http://www.vulture.com/2014/01/history-of-the-selfie.html.

Scarry, Elaine. 1985. *The Body in Pain: The Making and Unmaking of the World*. New York: Oxford University Press.

Smith, Sidonie, and Julia Watson. 2010. *Reading Autobiography: A Guide for Interpreting Life Narratives.* 2nd ed. Minneapolis: University of Minnesota Press.

Spiers, Elizabeth. 2013. "But Is It Good? The Problem with Marie Calloway's Affectless Realism." *Flavorwire*, 18 June. http://flavorwire.com/398643/but-is-it-good-the-problem-with-marie-calloways-affectless-realism.

27

Hentai *Confessions:* Transgression and "Sexual Technologies of the Self" in Akihiko Shiota's Moonlight Whispers

RON S. JUDY

> There is a kind of mysticism in perversion: the greater the renunciation, the greater and the more secure the gains; we might compare it to a "black" theology where pleasure ceases to motivate the will and is abjured, disavowed, "renounced," the better to be recovered as a reward or consequence, and as law.
> • Gilles Deleuze, *Coldness and Cruelty* (1991)

Late-summer cumulonimbuses intersected by power lines; a high-school couple riding a bicycle together alongside a floodway in suburban Japan; warmly lit *tatami* rooms viewed from oblique angles; a boy tied up in a dusty attic while his girlfriend has sex with her *kendo* instructor. All but the last of these scenes would seem to mark Akihiko Shiota's *Moonlight Whispers* (*Gekko no Sasayaki*, 1999) as a fin-de-siècle nostalgia film. However, as an adaptation of a 1980s manga, the film relies on a stylized visual strategy that is sharply ambivalent: the nostalgic world of daily high-school life is interrupted by explosions of "perverse" sexual passion. As in many twentieth-century Japanese film masterpieces, however, the coexistence of traditional life and erotic pathos is quite common, as if Japanese cinema were meant to be about an alliance between the pleasure and reality principles.[1] On the other hand, Shiota also pays tribute, like many of the filmmakers of his generation (post–New Wave directors like Kurosawa Kiyoshi, Takashi Miike, Tsukamoto Shinya, and Sion Sono), to the *ero guro nansensu* (erotic-grotesque nonsense) tendency in late twentieth-century Japanese visual culture. This tradition or tendency embraces the shocking, absurdist sexual imagery of manga, *Pinku* (soft-core) film and combines it with "grotesque" characters and "nonsensical" situations in a manner reminiscent of 1930s popular culture.[2] Skirting the boundaries of these genres, *Moonlight* focuses on the bare, "realistic" visual beauty of its subjects while showing us the "perverse" (*hentai*) identities evolving at the centre of the film. This chapter relies on Gilles Deleuze's reflections on the "black theology" of perverse artistry and Michel Foucault's "technologies of the self" to consider how the film imagines perversion in terms of visual style.

Perverse Confessionalism

A few words about the title of the film are in order before we try to understand its inner thematic dimensions and visual workings. The "moonlight whispers" alluded to are evidently the sporadic voice-over of the male protagonist's perverse alter-ego, or his "true self." As many scholars have noted, modern "confession" is a distinctly post-Enlightenment literary form, one strikingly imagined in the first book of Jean-Jacques Rousseau's *Confessions*, in which the philosopher admits that already in early adolescence "to fall at the feet of an imperious mistress, obey her mandates, or implore pardon, were for me the most exquisite enjoyments" ([1765–70] 1945, 14). Rousseau regards this initial confession of his perverse desire as "the first, most difficult step, in the dark and painful labyrinth of my Confessions," because as an adolescent he felt a deep sense of difference within himself – a dark maze of desires considered socially taboo (15). Arousing himself verbally, in the confessional world the adult Rousseau gains mastery over his experience (whether true or not) by (re)constructing it from erotic, vividly described episodes of adolescent wonder.

Rousseau's frankness about his deepest desires and the realistically described misadventures they entailed had enormous impact on later philosophical, legal, and psychological discourse, deeply influencing the theoretical work of the great nineteenth-century German psychiatrist Richard von Krafft-Ebing. In his groundbreaking work on the science of sex, *Psychopathia Sexualis*, Krafft-Ebing diagnosed numerous "abnormal" patients who described how truly life-altering it was to read of Rousseau's "exquisite enjoyments." As Amber Musser has pointed out, however, Krafft-Ebing regarded Rousseau and Leopold von Sacher-Masoch as literary figures – creators of fictional discourses about sex and masochism. In the latter's novel, *Venus in Furs*, "masochism" appears as an erotic joy at being humiliated by a Slavic dominatrix – making it an "inversionary" disorder of the supposedly normal heterosexual power dynamic (Musser 2008, 208). For Krafft-Ebing, a shared affinity for a type of sex observed in reference to books was important because it suggested that his middle-class (predominantly male) patients and readers were all "on the same page" when it came to ideas about the private bedroom. According to Musser, consuming these erotic works, imagining these private spaces, and internalizing their confided pleasures, his patients were forming new identities through an obsession with confessional discourse. Moreover, as Musser points out, readers of the *Psychopathia Sexualis* were further prompted to confide their own tales of submission and sadomasochism after reading it, demonstrating a further shared affinity (or identity motif?) for male-to-female submission among the subjects. Adopting Michel Foucault's terminology, Musser considers this form of subject-formation to be the by-product of a particular masochist "technology of the self" (hereafter ToS) – that is, a "practice of identity formation that disrupts the traditional top-down models of power" and instead comes about in self-imposed practices (217). Foucault himself defines the ToS as techniques that "permit individuals to effect by their own means or with the help of others a certain number of operations on their own bodies and souls, thoughts, conduct, and way of being, so as to transform themselves in order to attain a certain state of happiness, purity, wisdom, perfection, or immortality" (1988, 18). Starting from these reflections about confessional, self-disciplinary practices and ideas from Foucault during his later period (after the publication of *History of Sexuality*) about sexuality and technologies of the self, in what follows I wish to suggest that *Moonlight Whispers* is a film about cinema's connection to these strict "operations on the body" and the fashioning of new selves.

Like the eponymous Japanese manga of the 1980s, *Moonlight Whispers* is an extreme coming-of-age story that interrogates the idea of perversion in bourgeois Japanese society by depicting a "first love" romantic relationship that seems to go awry between two high-school students, the male "masochist" protagonist Takuya Hidaka (Kenji Mizuhashi) and his sadistic female mistress Kitahara Satsuki (Tsugumi).[3] Adolescence is depicted as a vacillation between the extremes of sexual passion and peaceful bourgeois life; however, direct sexual imagery is virtually absent from the film. Instead, by the emphasis on scenes of school routine, teens travelling across suburban landscapes, warmly lit interiors, and the like, Hidaka and Satsuki seem to live in a moment of perfect equilibrium. The film begins with a visual exploration of the teenagers' shared love of competitive *kendo* and quickly moves from the sparring hall to the innocent bike-riding and quiet walks in the suburbs.

In the opening *kendo*-hall scene, we see Hidaka and Satsuki squaring off against one another in practice armour with their *bokken* raised. Shouts and blows are delivered. Hidaka is struck fiercely on the head by the much faster Satsuki. Cut to the pair putting their shoes on: they share a brief exchange laden with deep im-

27.1 A disturbing voice-over confession. Frame grab, *Moonlight Whispers* (Gekko no Sasayaki), dir. Akihiko Shiota, 1999.

plications for what is to come: "[*Kendo*] depends on keeping the right distance," says a bashfully smiling Hidaka, rubbing his head. "Actually, I like it when you strike me on the head … It gives my dull life a shake. I like the jolt to my head." Satsuki's curt, off-handed reply foreshadows all that will come: "In that case, you're a pervert" (*hentai*).[4] Hearing the "truth" of his identity spoken aloud by her, the young man experiences a psychic breakthrough in the form of another smack on the head.

The above scene reveals one of the central motifs and antinomy of *Moonlight Whispers*: "perversion" and "normalcy" are an unstable, wayward binary that repeatedly cross and intersect like Japanese street wires. For example, Satsuki's repeated, violent insistence on "having a normal relationship" produces a girl becoming a *hentai* herself. Whereas Hidaka's perversion produces a normalization of the abnormal, Satsuki's produces a denormalization of the "normal." For example, shortly after the start of their romance, Hidaka falls ill, suffering in bed from a severe fever. Still in her school uniform, Satsuki arrives to comfort the boy, lying stiff and unfamiliar under his mother's blankets. When she offers to remove her clothes, Hidaka seems overawed by the sudden availability of Satsuki's body; he stops short of consummating the act of sexual love. It not entirely clear from the scene, but it appears that Hidaka is heterosexual but impotent when it comes to real women. In any case, very little is said before, during, or after this overwrought scene, but as the couple lie in bed afterward, a silent Hidaka makes a disturbing confession in voice-over: "This is what you have always wanted. You're happy now. I tried to convince myself. But inside a different voice kept whispering ... 'Liar'" (fig 1.).

The "moonlight whispers" of the title, then, are the inward conversations of these voices, a confessional self that externalizes a denial. After the aborted sex scene, when Satsuki asks to use the bathroom, Hidaka hops up and goes in first, where he installs a tape-recorder behind the toilet bowl. Later that night, with cool blue moonlight streaming in his window, we see Hidaka at the foot of his bed, masturbating to the audio playback of Satsuki urinating in his bathroom. As literally as the *kanji* characters indicate, Hidaka is a *hentai*, for his pleasure has always to be diverted, delayed, distanced from its original, presumably "normal," condition of carnality.

Naming the "Pervert" and the Confessional Self

Not long after their aborted attempt at love-making, a determined Satsuki returns to Hidaka's home, only to be unexpectedly met by the boy's mother. Calling to him from the kitchen to help her prepare lunch, the mother insistently tears her son away from his girlfriend. In a pivotal scene, left alone in Hidaka's bedroom, Satsuki discovers one of her gym socks, stolen from her school locker, beneath the bed sheets; then, in a locked drawer, she finds several voyeur photos taken of her in gym uniform; finally she comes upon the secretly recorded urination tape. Outraged, she storms from the house, calling Hidaka a "pervert" (*hentai*) even as he implores her to understand – which of course means to accept and forgive – his fetishes. Needless to say, she does not. Even though speech is strictly limited in this film about voyeurs and the pleasure of witnessing pain, clearly it is the element of language that both frees and restricts the action: there is little difference between Satsuki's repeated reprimand "Pervert!" and Hidaka's periodic confessional voice-overs. Disparagement and inward narrative, the definitive act of naming, and confessional speech are used to develop and formalize a process of self-understanding that lies at the foundation of love and sexual desire. Going beyond this foundation to the fundamental id would seem to mean discovering the limit of the self/other relation, a restless search for perverse enjoyment, or *hentai jouissance*, in an enabling *technic* or power relation.[5]

Hidaka may be a liar and a pervert, but at least these things are not erotically disabling – he is not an impotent, false player in the game he so seriously plays.

Instead, he is a fetishist who gains significantly more pleasure from the auratic objects associated with the girl's body – her socks, her pictures, the urination tape – than he does with her body. His obsession with these "fetishes" seems to define his relations with her, but later, with their increased intimacy, comes an attraction to the escalating degradation she inflicts on him. As Deleuze suggests in his study of masochist works like *Venus in Furs*, this is because "beneath the sound and fury of sadism and masochism the terrible force of repetition is at work," a force he likens to "a 'black' theology where pleasure ceases to motivate the will and is abjured, disavowed, 'renounced,' the better to be recovered as a reward or consequence, and as law" (1991,120). Moreover, in this "formula of perverse mysticism," Deleuze claims, the promise "is coldness and comfort (the coldness of desexualization, on the one hand, and the comfort of resexualization)" (120). Through personal rituals of dominance and submission, staged and restaged by her as "scenes" of disavowed erotic pleasure, Satsuki develops a kind of erotic skill at coldly controlling and keeping Hidaka "awake." *Moonlight Whispers* conveys this coldness most vividly in nighttime scenes in the boy's room, where all alone he experiences sex as a fundamental void to be filled with confessional words. Thus, whereas Shiota suggests the only way to avoid this coldness is for the couple to share their mutual perversion, Deleuze believes what is most significant about "pornological" works like this is that they are "aimed above all at confronting language with its own limits, with what is in a sense a 'nonlanguage' (violence that does not speak, eroticism that remains unspoken)" (22).

In erotic (not pornographic) films, the non-language of perversion is everywhere present. For example, if we look at a work like David Lynch's *Blue Velvet* (1986), we see, in a segment similar to the dusty attic scene described above, Dorothy (Isabella Rossellini), an older woman with masochistic tendencies, put young Jeffrey (Kyle MacLachlan) in a closet while she and Frank (Dennis Hopper) have kinky sex in the bedroom. In Slavoj Žižek's view, Lynch's film presents us with the basic question: For whom (and by whom) is this scene staged? It appears to be aimed at Jeffrey, but in a brilliant reversal, Žižek reveals that for Lynch the "original fact" is the masochist woman's depression, Dorothy's "sliding into the abyss of self-annihilation, of absolute lethargy" (1994, 121). This depressive slide is what causes the sadist, Frank, to repeatedly exhibit himself to her "as the object of her gaze. Man 'bombards' her with shocks in order to arouse her attention and thereby pull her out of her numbness – in short, in order to reinstate her in the 'proper' order of causality" (121). "Woman" – here the passive-aggressive force of Dorothy – must be forever reanimated and shocked back into participation in the social order and the life she is constantly trying to slip out of – and thus male confessions are invariably about how we cope with this Other.

If we apply Žižek's logic to Shiota's film, the roles must be changed somewhat, but as we do so, things begin to look clearer: Satsuki stages tawdry scenes of lovemaking with Uematsu, an upper-classman and *kendo* instructor, as a means to "shock" Hidaka out of his passive, manic-depressive spiral into oblivion. However, it is Hidaka (boy) who has with his "perverse" behaviour foisted this role onto Satsuki (girl) in the first place; when she accepts and begins to wield her power, she finds it satisfying to the point where she becomes a "pervert" herself. Staging her painful spectacles and exploring their outcomes, after she lets Hidaka out of the attic she herself has changed, and it becomes increasingly difficult to discover where causality begins and effect ends. Is Satsuki also "impotent" without the "real" Hidaka? Has their love substantially changed in anything other than degree? In the scene in which Satsuki instructs the boy to follow her in the rain on his bicycle while Uematsu takes her bowling, we become voyeurs also, watching Hidaka watch the two teenagers from afar as they have a seemingly "normal" date. Cut to a rain-soaked Hidaka standing outside the window, smiling at Satsuki. She glares furiously at him and excuses herself from the table with Uematsu. In the lobby, after slapping him hard on the face, she asks, "Why are you smiling at a time like this?" Hidaka confides, "Getting soaked in the rain, I realized you know me, Satsuki. The real me I can't show anyone. You're the only one who knows. It was a real relief to realize that." In telling her this, he is suggesting that she knew her sadistic game of voyeurism was exactly what would turn him on. As we have seen, *kendo hentai* identity develops, like *kendo* sparring, out of rituals of "awakening" that bring the couple dangerously close together in ways that keep them apart.

"Perversion" and the Disavowal of (Visual) Enjoyment

To briefly recapitulate, as soon as Satsuki begins to have sex with another boy, her pleasure irrevocably involves tormenting and trying to control Hidaka even further. However, for the boy, it is precisely Satsuki's staged sex scenes with Uematsu that are arousing to him as well – at first because he thinks they demonstrate how much she thinks about him – so his "perversion" is partly an enjoyment of the repetition of passive distancing. Then, in the sadistic rituals imposed on him, he discovers what Deleuze would describe as a "primal disavowal," a self-overcoming that "challenges the superego and entrusts the mother with the power to give birth

27.2 A *hentai* practice of the self. Frame grab, *Moonlight Whispers* (Gekko no Sasayaki), dir. Akihiko Shiota, 1999.

to an 'ideal ego' which is pure, autonomous and independent of the ego" (1991, 127).[6] The masochist fundamentally relinquishes control of his fate, going outside of himself for the first time and seeing himself as the Other does. Thus, for example, in the crucial attic scene, where Hidaka agrees to be stashed while Satsuki and Uematsu make love, we see how absolute his "disavowal" has become, entrusting his ego to her in the hopes that he will be granted absolution. When he begs her forgiveness afterward, however, she becomes even more furious, kicks him, accuses him of still only thinking of himself, and again calls him "pervert!" (*hentai*!). Proclaiming him a deviant, Satsuki also names her lover's perversion as selfishness; then, in a flash she realizes, "Watching you cry like that … I'm starting to feel really great. I'll make you cry plenty, and I'll just feel better and better." Discovery of her own will to punish is part of Satsuki's great inner transformation into a full-fledged "pervert" who has finally accepted Hidaka and her own need for control. From here on, everything is performance and acting out roles, for in ceding control to her Hidaka has also imposed his *Ideal-Ich* on her: the two are in a mirror relation that now reflects back on itself (fig. 27.2).

My contention that *Moonlight Whispers* imagines a *hentai* practice of the self rests not just on psychology, however, as not only do the pair learn their own "erotic arts" in parallel to the martial arts but their bodies come to rely on "whacks on the head" for not "keeping the proper distance." That is, their courtship is developing more toward an "ontological" than a psychological condition. Satsuki is admired by her female peers as a formidable *kendo* competitor, someone with speed and agility who wins matches for her team, while Hidaka achieves at best a mediocre ranking. Although we were unaware of it at first, it was already clear from this *kendo* sparring who would dominate whom in this story. This is not to suggest that Shiota implicates Satsuki's sadism with her skill at *kendo* but rather that *ars erotica* and *kendo* are natural counterparts in many cultures due to a certain reverence for body rites as vehicles for achieving personal transcendence. Although Hidaka's masochistic voyeurism is a means of testing the absolute limits of his devotion, Shiota's representation of sex also reveals "the limit of language, since it traces that line of foam showing just how fast speech may advance upon the sands of silence" (Foucault, in Sheridan 1990, 164–5). The making of the *hentai* requires silent rituals of transgression that allow it to pass beyond these limits of thought, word, and even action to arrive at a new power dynamic and a new way of being in the world.

In an interview, Shiota also reflects on the role of *hentai* ambivalence in his work:

There is this ambivalence in my films, but it's this ambivalence that is most interesting to me. That means there is a contrast in a character, a harsh one even. They have a weak point and a very powerful point. When these two points come together, there is a kind of explosion … I have an interest in this kind of person. She [Satsuki] thinks of herself as normal and that she can have a normal relationship with a normal man. But she is with a masochistic man and actually she becomes a sadist herself. Even if she didn't think of herself as being a sadist, she changes little by little. Then there's this kind of explosion when she says, "Why, if I'm normal, do I have to be with a man like you?" (Mes and Sharp 2005, 267–8)

These weak/powerful "points" that Shiota highlights, I suggest, represent the "limits" that Foucault writes about in connection with the ethics of self-care and the ToS.[7] Likewise, Satsuki's moment of "explosion" is her moment of transgression, her passing beyond the person she once was, for in that experience she goes from being a "normal" high-school student to one who perceives herself anew as a different, relational self tied to Hidaka. In a striking passage from his essay on the subject, Foucault writes that transgression "is not related to the limit as black to white, the prohibited to the lawful, the outside to the inside, or as the open area of a building to its enclosed spaces. Rather, their relationship takes the form of a spiral which no simple infraction can exhaust" (1977, 35). This spiral can serve as an apt metaphor for Hidaka and Satsuki's relationship, for in becoming free of "false" conceptions of sexuality, the two plummet into a vortex of transgression that almost leads to Hidaka's death. And thus because of (and not in spite of) the self-discipline they enjoy in *kendo* training, Satsuki and Hidaka come also to enjoy experiencing different forms of pain and pleasure. That is, although their relationship emerges from and temporarily reflects the stable, competitive power dynamic of *kendo*, it soon goes far beyond that when Uematsu unwittingly becomes involved in their relationship.

Shiota's abrupt shift near the end of the film from steady close-ups and warm interiors (orange-lit houses) to movement around a hot-spring resort, replete with rushing waterfall and steamy forest, embodies the theme of transgression developed in the film. From here we finally get broader, distanced views of the characters – Satsuki has called both boys to her – in the mists of terrible, uncanny nature. If the former mood emphasized Hidaka's quiet, secret sense of sublime perversion, this latter outdoor view suggests the tumultuous out-flowing of Satsuki's passion. The waterfall, she tells the boys as they walk beside it, is a place she was deathly afraid of when her father brought her here as a child. For her the place is shrouded in an aura of fear and death, so when we suspect her intention is to have Hidaka commit suicide by jumping off it, we see this as her final attempt to master the relationship and conquer her fear of losing control. "Once you die, everything will be fine," she tells him, no doubt meaning "normal."

Hidaka consents. "I will die for you," he says, but "I have one request. Remember me always, until the day you die." His words infuriate Satsuki, who realizes Hidaka is again laying claim to her, imprinting his death on her mind as an emblem of love and fanatical devotion but also proving Deleuze's insight that if "possession is the sadist's particular form of madness," then "the pact is the masochist's" (Deleuze 1991, 21). Hidaka takes Satsuki's silence for agreement as the camera focuses in extreme close-up on her face, which is turned away from him as he disappears into the woods and over the waterfall.

Fashioning the *Hentai* Self

According to Steven Allen, the cinematic spectator's enjoyment in scenes like the one described above derives from "witnessing the deployment of control and the loss of control, not merely the either/or scenario of enjoying sadism or masochism"

(2014, 21). Japan is home to a rich *ars erotica* body aesthetics and is often associated with the art of erotic bondage (*kinbaku-bi*, or "aesthetic binding") that developed there.[8] From a comparative standpoint, Allen's association of visual pleasure with "witnessing" gains/losses of control seems useful, for like *kendo*, *kinbaku-bi* is an art or self-discipline that focuses on the performance of restraint and eroticism. However, Allen also develops the view that "films of the controlled body disclose our anxiety over being increasingly remote from the experience of pain. But they also reflect a desire to continue the process of mastering it, no longer in a medicalized sense, but through making these traumatic events sites of significance" (198). This "anxiety" about achieving "mastery" over pain could account for the perverse pleasure we gain from *Moonlight Whispers*, but our interest is not really aroused by the tension between bound and unbound but by the drama of destruction/creation that plays out in the couple's relationship. Will they be set free from the "fetish" ideas that seem to bind them, or will they be destroyed by them? In the case of Satsuki, for example, what will she do to her own body in order to humiliate her lover? Will her *hentai*-esque obsession with the boy ultimately drive her mad, or will she return to the *kendo* practice that seems to balance her?

Thus although we only see Hidaka bound in loose wires in the attic scene, it appears we are witnessing a ritualized erotic performance in which Satsuki is the exhibitionist and Hidaka the powerless voyeur. However, as Foucault would remind us, power is not simply "held" by the dominant or the submissive role: it is rather the basic, vacillating form (or structure) of their relationship. For example, as we look down on him lying on his back in the dust, licking sweat from Satsuki's leg, we should notice that we're actually looking at him from the gaze of the "whisperer," from his true *hentai* self. In this way the film collapses the scopophilic gaze into the narcissistic, so that we are actually watching the boy from his alter ego point of view. It turns out that we are watching someone who is forced to watch himself. Hidaka and Satsuki participate in the perverse "black theology" that Deleuze describes in the epigraph to this chapter – a quasi-religious belief that their renunciation of pleasure expresses some pure devotion that will finally be recognized by the maternal superego.

Another way to understand the "perverse" modes of seeing developed in Shiota's film would be by way of a comparison with western film and theory. As we have already seen, in *Blue Velvet* Lynch triangulates the viewer's gaze among Jeffrey, Frank, and Dorothy, going one step beyond the strictly male voyeurism of Hitchcock of *Vertigo*. In that film we see, according to Laura Mulvey's famed reading, the perverse, fetishized gaze of the male ex-detective Scottie (James Stewart). What is sadistic about Scottie's male gaze, according to Mulvey, is that the woman he is hired to follow, Madeleine-Judy (Kim Novak), is significant only because her "exhibitionism, her masochism, make her an ideal passive counterpart to Scottie" (2009, 66). Thus when we follow the protagonist and voyeur Scottie, we enjoy imagining ourselves in his position as a male stalker who spies on the passive but comely Madeleine and her twin, Judy. The problem with Mulvey's thesis, as many critics have since pointed out, is that Hitchcock makes us constantly aware that we are watching Scottie watch Madeleine-Judy. The camera obsessively draws our attention to the her body and the neurotic behaviour we witness in Scottie as the film progresses, but it also makes us aware of the perspective of Scottie's female friend, Midge. A former lover, she is the one character in the film who sees what we in the audience see: Scottie's downward spiral into a pathologic obsession with Madeleine-Judy. According to Gaylyn Studlar (1985) we should think of the cinematic gaze in terms of this kind of helpless third-person standpoint because "cinematic pleasure is much closer to masochistic scopic pleasure than to a sadistic, controlling pleasure" that critics like Mulvey think is determinant (2009, 274). For Studlar, focusing only on the sadism of voyeurs like Scottie would mean overlooking a key component of narrative visual pleasure – namely, that "cinema encourages a regression characterized by all possibilities of identification and projection resembling the infantile mechanisms operative in perversions" (1985, 277).[9] In other words, although we may enjoy watching Scottie watch Madeleine-Judy, we are also keenly aware of how infantile Scottie's idolatrous relationship to this woman is. Similarly, when we watch Lynch's regression of Jeffrey watching Dorothy and Frank, we are also aware of the numerous perverse "identifications" the scene sets up – not just between the characters but also between the camera and the audience.

In Shiota's film, things are perhaps more straightforward. Satsuki's "sadist voyeurism" is clearly aimed at staging Hidaka's punishment for their mutual pleasure, and perhaps ours. Thus, in a crucial sex scene Uematsu commands Satsuki to look at him when at that instant she is looking at Hidaka's tearful face and bound form. Having sex with someone else, she is nevertheless exhibiting herself for her lover's humiliation, torturing him with what he cannot have. From this moment, we begin to identify with the clueless Uematsu, for his active role is blind, negated by the formalized *hentai* ritual of the pair. Moreover, the sense of *ero guro nansensu* (and sheer embafflement) is strongest at the end of *Moonlight Whispers*, in the penultimate scene at the hospital, where we see Hidaka's bandaged, heavily plaster-casted body laid out in bed some time after his failed suicide attempt. We cut away from the white desert of Hidaka's broken body to a sudden view of Satsuki's thighs sitting warmly beside his bed. The pervert's gaze is never where it should be – on her eyes – because that imperious face is turned away, seemingly in a deep reverie. We are both stunned and pleased to see him alive and still able to hobble on crutches down several flights of stairs to buy a soft drink for Satsuki. Wounded and broken, his efforts seem heroic in some sense, which is undercut by the existential absurdity of his act, especially because when he finally gets back to Satsuki with the soft drink, she glances at it and says, "Actually, I wanted ginger ale." This would seem cruel had we not seen Hidaka smiling at the vending machine, delighted to be able to fulfill the wishes of his mistress once more. To make matters more surreal, Satsuki is wearing a square, theatrical-looking patch over one eye – an anomaly from the scene at the waterfall where she was somehow injured.

In the final scene of the film, Shiota creates an iconic parable of *hentai* romance. As Satsuki and Hidaka and sit together on the riverbank, she drops her arm into his lap, saying, "A bug bit me," upon which the boy holds the proffered limb with a look of dumbfounded joy. Then, for the sake of perverse symmetry, she adds, "We should go to the beach when your cast comes off. We will invite Maruken too." Invoking the name of his best friend, Satsuki simultaneously affirms her own *hentai* nature and breaks the boy's will, reminding him of his original "disavowal" of her by not making love to her. We are thus led to believe that more voyeuristic masochism is to come, perhaps more painful falls, definitely more shame, but our wistful, ironic happy ending has arrived with a look to the future selves they will encounter. The spectator's reward is an upbeat ending that "reanimates" the spark of love between Hidaka and Satsuki, only now, instead of the naïve sparring partners, we have maturing perverts. Hidaka has developed into the person whom Satsuki, the dominant maternal superego, has tacitly agreed to help create – that is, by accepting the "contract" to become the coauthor of his fate (and plan an end for it, no matter how tragic). Finally the "moonlight whispers" have emerged in the less enraged voice of Satsuki, for she too has abandoned her desire for normalcy in favour of an erotic self-fashioning – what some theorists describe as a "return to bodies and pleasures" that "promote an 'economy of pleasure' not based on 'sexual' norms nor on the liberation of a constructed 'sexdesire'" (Beckmann 2014, 192). There is both a destructive and a creative dimension to romantic relationships like the one imagined here; however, it can only be imagined within a non-liberationist setting.

Are Perverts People Too?

One answer to this question would be, "Not quite, but then who is?" Hidaka's fetishism, his ritualized worship of Satsuki's most private "things" (originally, her sock), reminds us of a parallel scene in Jean-Jacques Rousseau's *Confessions*. In a memorable scene early in the Book 1, the first time the adolescent Rousseau is spanked for breaking one of Mme Lambercier's personal hair-combs, he describes his first painful encounter with injustice. Although he utterly denies ever touching the comb, he admits that he has trouble "disentangling and following up the least trace of what then took place within me," so that afterwards "the tranquility of my childish life was over. From that moment I ceased to enjoy a pure happiness" (1945, 16). This loss of innocence cannot be disentangled, but readers feel it must somehow be connected to the author's adult obsession with spankings and masochist rites. Although Hidaka's first punishment in the rain centres on a sock taken from Satsuki's locker, it leads to a similar discovery of pleasure in pain. Furthermore, the sadist's fascination with possession is evidenced by the fact that Satsuki's elaborate theatre of pain is staged in or around her own home. Thus almost exactly insofar as their world is "perverse," it also remains traditional and bourgeois as it emphasizes home, possessions, ritualized education, and mainstream normative values. The camera leads us to wonder with Rousseau if the tranquil happiness of "childhood" is not an illusion conjured by its counterpart, an adult self nostalgically recalling (if only in confessional whispers) its earlier, unbound self. Thus while the "code of conduct and practices of consensual 'SM' seem to be able to foster an experience-oriented approach to ethics as the conscious practice of freedom," it nevertheless does so using the apparatus of nostalgic confessionalism (Beckmann 2014, 242).

In Shiota's other major works from this period, *Harmful Insect* (*Gaichu*, 2002) and *Canary* (*Kanaria*, 2005), we also see an adult fascination with the seemingly "abnormal" lives of adolescents and delinquents.[10] In *Gaichu* we follow a middle-school student, Sachiko, whose mother has attempted suicide and abandoned her duties as a parent. Nonetheless, Sachiko tries to attend school and act like a "normal" student – "normal," except that she has had an affair with her former science teacher, a man with whom she continues to exchange letters about tropical fish and daily life. Gradually she only pretends to go to school. The climax of that film sees Sachiko hurling homemade firebombs at the apartment where her mother's boyfriend attempted to rape her, a lone individual who becomes radically disillusioned with her world, which she finally renounces and attempts to destroy.

Gaichu ends as *Moonlight Whispers* does too: the perverse gaze of the film has objectified these "harmful insects" (*gaichu*) and then gradually made us empathize with them – the adolescents we once might have been.

Despite their troubles, there is much to admire in these devoted young *hentai* figures, and Shiota's fascination with them as a group forces us to ask whether the director is trying to suggest that a different method of seeing and/or mode of voyeuristic learning is in order: one in which the truth and radical sincerity of youthful passion is "realized" only because "the objective is no longer to get prepared for adult life, or for another life, but to get prepared for a certain complete achievement of life" (Foucault 1988, 31). The adolescent, who, like neurotic modernity itself, must undergo a Kantian self-imposed maturity to achieve Enlightenment, is compelled to imagine herself as an "adult ego" capable of renouncing all extreme passions and of purging disruptive or unproductive sexual *pathos*. Thanks to fantasy, for Shiota's young people it often *appears* there may be another way, a path that leads not to total disavowal but to a "complete achievement of life" and away from dull, repressive adult society.

NOTES

1 In Donald Richie's assessment, "candor created the realism of the Japanese film style … that has always insisted that life be seen as it is. This honesty created the films about ordinary people, about the lives of the unhappy, about life as it really is" (1971, xviii). This insistence on candour is what fosters the continued attention to tradition's conflict with modernity. For example, Yasujiro Ozu's *Late Spring* (1939) is a film about the unusually close relationship between an aging college professor and his marriage-resistant daughter; similarly, Shohei Imamura's *The Insect Woman* (1963) offers a frank, "realistic" depiction of sexual relations in modern Japan – not only prostitution but also premarital sex and interracial relations with an American GI.

2 For more on the connection between *ero guro nansensu* and Japanese film, see Miriam Silverberg's brilliant *Erotic Grotesque Nonsense* (2004, 108–42).

3 The heroine's name is difficult to render in English because of the use of familiar/non-familiar names in Japanese. For Hidaka, she remains the familiar Satsuki; but for her sexual partner, Uematsu, she is always referred to more formally as Kitahara (implying their relationship never got very far).

4 The word for pervert, *hentai* (変態), has a critical etymology: it only enters the Japanese language through a translation of Krafft-Ebing's *Psychopathia Sexualis* (*Hentai seiyoku shinrigaku*), first translated in 1894. See Nathen Clerici's thesis, "Dreams from Below:

Yumenko Kyusaku and Subculture Literature in Japan" (University of British Columbia, 2013), 50. For a more concise history of *hentai*, see McLelland 2006.

5 What Foucault finds interesting in confessional discourse is that it is one of subjectivity's formative techniques for transcoding sexual behaviour into language and for bodily desires and energies to be converted into language means that they generate power. Thus in the first volume of *The History of Sexuality* he writes that, by the seventeenth century in the West, "an imperative was established" in the church: "Not only will you confess to acts contravening the law, but you will seek to transform your desire, your every desire, into discourse" ([1976] 1990, 21).

6 In one sense, Hidaka is like Howard, the IRS auditor in *Stranger Than Fiction*, directed by Marc Foster (2006), who one day awakens to a female voice narrating the story of his every action and decision – which is actually the dull repetitive tale of how he has renounced every possible desire (music and love) to achieve order and stability in his life. As Howard discovers, this outside authorial voice is what put him in his predicament in the first place: he is the creation of an unhappy author of tragically beautiful novels who is famous for killing off her characters at book's end. Like Howard, Hidaka's ego is subordinated to that of a domineering female (superego) who in turn refashions him as a masochist whose purpose is to hate himself and eventually die. Hidaka is much less fortunate than Howard, however, in that he gains pleasure from the process of being tortured.

7 Foucault's ideas about sexual self-fashioning are clearly explicated in Lynne Huffer's "Foucault's Ethical *Ars Erotica*" (2009, 125–47).

8 A growing but still underground erotic art scene, in Japan *Kinbaku-bi* (緊縛美) and *Shibari* (縛り) are not part of a traditional *ars erotica* tradition but rather have roots in *Hoj jutsu* (捕縄術), the martial art of tying prisoners up.

9 See also Marian E. Keane's "A Closer Look at Scopophilia: Mulvey, Hitchcock, and *Vertigo*," (2009, 231–48). For an up-to-date review of Mulvey and current *Vertigo* scholarship, see Klevan's "*Vertigo* and the Spectator of Film Analysis" (2014: 147–71).

10 Shiota discusses his fondness for the theme of adolescent rebellion at length in a Tom Mes interview for *Midnight Eye* (2001).

REFERENCES

Allen, Steve. 2014. *Cinema, Pain and Pleasure: Consent and the Controlled Body*. New York: Palgrave Macmillan.

Beckmann, Andrea. 2014. *The Social Construction of Sexuality and Perversion: Deconstructing Sadomasochism*. New York: Palgrave Macmillan.

Deleuze, Gilles. 1991. *Coldness and Cruelty*, and *Venus in Furs* [1870] by Leopold von Sacher-Masoch. In *Masochism*, translated by Jean McNeil and and Aude Willm. New York: Zone Books.

Foucault, Michel. 1977. "A Preface to Transgression." In *Language, Counter-Memory, Practice: Selected Essays and Interviews*, translated by Donald F. Boucher and Sherry Simon, 29–52. Ithaca: Cornell University Press.

– 1988. *Technologies of the Self*. Edited by Luther H. Martin, Huck Gutman, and Patrick H. Hutton. Cambridge: University of Massachusetts Press.

– [1976] 1990. *The History of Sexuality*. Vol. 1, *An Introduction*. Translated by Robert Hurley. New York: Vintage.

Huffer, Lynne. 2009. "Foucault's Ethical *Ars Erotica*." *SubStance*, 38, no. 3: 125–47.

Keane, Marian K. 2009. "A Closer Look at Scopophilia: Mulvey, Hitchcock, and *Vertigo*." In *A Hitchcock Reader*, edited by Marshall Deutelbaum and Leland Poague, 231–48. New York: Wiley-Blackwell.

Klevan, Andrew. 2014. "Vertigo and the Spectator of Film Analysis." *Film Philosophy* 18: 147–71.

Krafft-Ebing, Richard von. [1894] 2014. *Psychopathia Sexualis*. Internet Archive. https://archive.org/details/PsychopathiaSexualis1000006945.

Masahiko, Kikuni. 1994–97. *Gekko no Sasayaki*. 6 vols. Tokyo: Shogakukan.

McLelland, Mark. 2006. "A Brief History of 'Hentai.'" *Intersections: Gender, History and Culture in the Asian Context* 12. http://intersections.anu.edu.au/issue12/mclelland.html.

Mes, Tom, and Jasper Sharp. 2001. "Moonlight Whispers" Review. *Midnight Eye*: *Visions of Japanese Cinema*. http://www.midnighteye.com/reviews/moonlight-whispers/.

– 2005. *The Midnight Eye Guide to New Japanese Cinema*. Berkeley: Stone Bridge.

Mulvey, Laura. [1975] 2009. "Visual Pleasure and Narrative Cinema." In *Film Theory and Criticism*, edited by Leo Braudy and Marshall Cohen, 711–22. Oxford: Oxford University Press.

Musser, Amber Jamilla. 2008. "Reading, Writing, and the Whip." *Literature and Medicine* 27, no. 2: 204–22.

Richie, Donald. 1971. *Japanese Cinema: Film Style and National Character*. New York: Anchor.

Rousseau, Jean-Jacques. [1765–70] 1945. *The Confessions of Jean Jacques Rousseau*. New York: Modern Library. https://archive.org/details/confessionsjean10rousgoog.

Scott, A.O. 2000. "Masochists Always Hurt the Ones They Love." Review of *Moonlight Whispers*, directed by Akihiko Shiota. *New York Times*, 22 November.

Sheridan, Alan. 1990. *Michel Foucault: The Will to Truth*. London: Routledge.

Silverberg, Miriam. 2006. *Erotic Grotesque Nonsense*. Berkeley: University of California Press.

Studlar, Gaylyn. 1984. "Masochism and the Perverse Pleasures of the Cinema." *Quarterly Review of Film Studies*, 9, no. 4: 267–82.

Williams, Linda. 1991. "Film Bodies: Gender, Genre, and Excess." *Film Quarterly* 44, no. 4: 2–13.

Žižek, Slavoj. 1994. *Metastases of Enjoyment: on Woman and Causality*. New York: Vertigo.

MEDIAGRAPHY

Foster, Marc, dir. 2006. *Stranger than Fiction*. Los Angeles: Sony Pictures.

Hitchcock, Alfred, dir. 1958. *Vertigo*. Hollywood: Paramount Pictures.
Lynch, David, dir. 1986. *Blue Velvet*. Hollywood: De Laurentiis Entertainment Group.
Ozu, Yasujiro, dir. 1949. *Banshun / Late Spring*. Tokyo: Shochiku.
Shiota, Akihiko, dir. 1999. *Gekkou no Sasayaki / Moonlight Whispers*. Tokyo: Nikkatsu.
– dir. 2002. *Gachu / Harmful Insect*. Tokyo: Nikkatsu.
– dir. 2005. *Kanaria / Canary*. Tokyo: Nikkatsu,.

28

Porno-Graphing: "Dirtiness" and Self-Objectification

ANNAMARIA PINAKA

Drying sex of its juices has been a primary theme in my lens-based art, along with the use of sexual exposure and vocabularies of confessionality, autobiography, and diarism.

Exposure for me, rather than concerning representation, has to do with destabilization – the artist's and the viewer's – through (for example) the overlaying, complication and suspension of signifiers of truth and non-truth. Similarly, by "drying sex of its juices," I mean the deliberate reduction and withdrawal of the aspects of sex and sexuality that have to do with enjoyment, passion, satisfaction, reproduction, and repair. My focus is not the trashing of sexual or other joy but the emptying or "dirtying" of notions of value.

The central theme of this chapter is my notions of "dirty" and "dirtying." My use of inverted commas around these words aims to signal that I don't attribute fixed meaning to them; instead, I use them precisely to denote an investigation that concerns the attribution of meaning and value onto certain sexual subjectivities and artworks that involve these subjectivities. As I understand and frame "dirty" sexual subjectivity, a person's subjectivity is "dirty" in relation to another's subjectivity. "Dirty" does not stand as binary opposite to a sharply defined or homogenous "clean," as I consider "dirty," "clean," "healthy," "pathological," etc. as notions that, if ascribed to subjectivity, rely on the personal judgment (strongly dependent on cultural/social context) of the individual who is doing this ascribing. Therefore "dirtiness" depends on the arbitrary judgment of individuals, as this is informed according to social norms and values and then incorporated into the subject's own sense and understanding of their self.

By "dirtying" notions of value, I refer to processes of "dirtying" the art-value of a piece of work,[1] not so much through the sexual content or the aesthetics of the image but by contextually complicating and disordering the meaning of sexual content and aesthetics. Such processes of meaning and value disordering involve the artist's own destabilization, in the way of doubting the value of their work – doubting, for instance, that they can perceive correctly the meaning and value of their work while making it.

During my earlier work I was using detachment and distance to approach the use of sex in art and anxiously felt that doing so was wrong and that feeling it was wrong was in itself wrong as it betrayed a lack of confidence in my artistic authorship. I experimented with creating dry reports of my sexual and romantic encounters in writing and later reading these reports to the camera while introducing obstacles to inhibit a clear or engaged reading. I used to strip sex of its joyful characteristics and administrate it to the furthest extents I could think of. I made domestic micro video-performances where I extensively used interior landscapes and the camera to explore agency, performativity, and the ability that I attributed to the camera to reveal. To do so, I hid things from the camera to see what the image revealed through my performance of half- or quasi-concealment. For example, between 2006 and 2009 I created numerous masturbation video-performances in which I would try to hide my orgasms from the camera by keeping myself as silent, still, and expressionless as possible. Similarly, I set up situations such as calling a close friend or relative as I lay naked on a bed, keeping my back to the camera so that the camera would autonomously reveal in the form of shapes, for example, aspects of my relationship to that person through my processes of exposing and withdrawing. I was aware of being reductive because while I was using my unarranged domestic setting to negotiate truth and matter-of-factness, I was at the same time doing so to imply a lack of creative attention or of creativity altogether. I was questioning the truthfulness of my own artistic intention by detaching, or appearing to detach, from it.

Such use of one's subjectivity (self-doubt, destabilization, etc.) may find a theoretical grammar in "the anti-social turn" (or "anti-relational turn") in queer theory – a theoretical field that critically examines queer negativity. While Leo Bersani is "credited for first questioning the desire to attribute an ethical project to every kind of gay sex" (Halberstam 2011, 149), the agency of negativity can be found to be shaping, forming, and informing various political projects, processes, and artifacts, "from anticolonialism to punk" (Halberstam, in Caserio 2006, 824). Working within the spectrum of the anti-social turn, Lee Edelman coined the term "reproductive futurism" to question political value, rejecting the "future" by rejecting the "Child," since for him the "Child remains the perpetual horizon of every political intervention" (Edelman 2004, 3). Scholars such as José Esteban Muñoz and Judith Jack Halberstam have widely and soundly criticized Edelman's theoretical formation; Muñoz, for instance, points out that to reject the future, one needs to be privileged with it, whereas queer people of colour are not granted it. Calling out the anti-relational turn in queer studies as "the gay white man's last stand," Muñoz argues for "the essential need for an understanding of queerness as collectivity" and therefore for "queerness as primarily about futurity" (Muñoz, in Caserio 2006, 825). Similarly, Halberstam underlines the anti-social turn's own shortcomings, arguing that "negativity might well constitute an anti-politics but it should not register as apolitical" (Halberstam 2008, 148), because "the apolitical anti-social agenda ... cuts both ways and while it mitigates against liberal fantasies of progressive enlightenment and community cohesion, it also coincides uncomfortably with a fascist sensibility" (143).

Lauren Berlant and Lee Edelman in *Sex, or the Unbearable* argue that "much of contemporary critical thinking (and much of contemporary activist practice)" regard sex as "negative" – carrying "the odor of anachronism, narcissism, or something irreducibly and disconcertingly personal" as if it indicates "a refusal to move on." Yet, they note, such are the attributes of sex, the personal, that render it crucial to contemporary thought concerned with normativity and antinormativity. In Lacanian terms, negativity foregrounds how sexual desire "remains fixed to a primal attachment" that remains elusive and that makes the object "appear as desirable." In these terms, desire is stubborn and resists its own liberation from itself in the form of clarity and resolution. Sex, deliberated through the scope of negativity, concerns "our nonsovereign status as subjects" (Berlant and Edelman 2014, 63–4), how we undo each other and how we become undone.

If the personal can be considered anachronistic and irrelevant, the use of sexual and autobiographical material to make art may lead to the dismissal of the work, by the viewer or the artist, as valueless – for instance, due to appearing apolitical. Yet, as I hope to demonstrate through this article by discussing the work of another artist, Leigh Ledare, working from positions of non-sovereign subjectivity (that state of subjectivity in which one is not able to explain one's self to one's self) can challenge patterns of meaning-making and thus offers fresh ground from which subjectivity and its value can be negotiated.

Rather than seeing self-doubt as a sign of authenticity, I consider that working from positions of non-sovereignty is a strategy that is used to negotiate notions of value attached to authenticity and subjectivity. This strategy can be demonstrated through the art methodology I call "porno-graphing."

I use the term porno-graphing to investigate contemporary lens-based artworks in which artists take on a sexual situation or sets of sexual dynamics present in their life independent from and outside their art practice and act upon it to make art. I considered that this "acting upon" involves negativity: for example, artists acting upon sex to "deprive" it of its everyday private enjoyment and "reduce" it to art-making. An example of the use of negativity in the methodology of porno-graphing lies in how artists approach the frames of meaning and representation they seek to critique by appropriating them, as I do here while referring to sex by using the words "deprive" and "reduce," appropriating the negative connotations of these words.

Artists who create porno-graphing actions self-objectify into roles that they themselves understand from the outset as "dirty" from the potential perspective of others. Insofar as sexual dynamics and subjectivities in works that involve porno-graphing may be perceived as "dirty," their "dirtiness" relies on the heterogeneity of opinions, morals, and perceptions that vary between times, cultural contexts, and individuals' own projections onto other individuals and groups. On the one hand, my use of terms such as "dirty" does not aim to frame this sort of moralism as irrevocable but seeks to underline that value (and lack of value) attributed to subjectivities (e.g., the value of a "natural" identity) is constructed and reproducible. On the other hand, I claim a permanence of "dirtiness" with the aim of arguing that its use in porno-graphing actions does not aim toward its catharsis.

In using the term porno-graphing, my aim is to approach elements of sex and sexual dynamics that I consider unspeakable – that is, difficult to approach through language and understanding – and to investigate how these elements can negotiate subjectivity, its meaning, and its value when used in lens-based art. Most importantly, my focus is on how these sexual situations and dynamics are acted upon to make art from them: how sexual subjectivity and sexual dynamics are reflected on by the artists; how the artists then orchestrate and strategically frame them to make art. In other words, I do not seek to reveal the nature of the sexual practices involved in porno-graphing; rather, my focus is to investigate the "dirtiness" of their framing.

Considering that "whereas the high art body signifies reason, cleanliness and order, the porn body connotes passion, dirtiness and disorder" (Attwood 2002, 96), porno-graphing is an approach willing to open itself to scrutiny regarding its status as art or porn – by showing the work. The particular creative conjuring that involves negativity in porno-graphing implicates a broad but stable and continuous process of presenting sexual dynamics that can potentially be perceived as taboo, transgressive, "dirty," and "improper" – for example, in the way that "the incest taboo" is considered by Rosi Braidotti as "the fundamental law of our social system" (Braidotti 1994, 82).

Through the rest of this article, I discuss porno-graphing methodologies, taking as an example two works of artist Leigh Ledare, *Pretend You're Actually Alive* (*Pretend*) (2000–08), and *Double Bind* (2010). I first discuss *Pretend* and illustrate foundational premises of porno-graphing processes, such as acting upon sexual situations with the aim to make art. I briefly overview what can currently be thought of as the art/porn debate in order to explain how porno-graphing strategies of self-objectification have the capacity to intervene in contemporary discourses cornering subjectivity and representation. To examine how in *Double Bind* Ledare creates open-ended frameworks regarding subjectivity, art, and value, I circle back to *Pretend*.

Ledare's *Pretend You're Actually Alive* is primarily made up of images of Ledare's "aging mother, who offers herself with disarming graphicness to her son's camera and to the unknown public who will then see the images" (Filipovic 2012, 16). The first information given to the viewer via the titling of the pictures is that the woman portrayed is the photographer's mother: "Mom and Me in Mirror," "Mom with Wrist Brace," "Mother Tied to Catch 22," "Mom with Scepter," "Mom Pulling Down Panties with Purple Chair," "Mom Spread with Red Heels," etc. *Pretend* started when Ledare arrived home after not having seen his mother, Tina Peterson, for over a year: "She knew I was coming and opened the door naked. A young man, almost exactly my age, was sprawled out naked." He sees this moment as his mother's "way of announcing to me what she was up to, at this period of her life – almost as to say 'take it or leave it.' I had a camera and began making photos of her then. She was the catalyst" (O'Hagan 2013). The porno-graphing methodology at work is that of taking on a situation that when seen from an outsider position (not the participants') has the potential of being received as taboo, "improper," and "dirty," and then acting upon it to make art from it.

The "improper" or "dirty" situation is the one of a mother answering the door to her son naked, as her lover, who is her son's age, lies on her bed also naked. The acting upon this situation involves the process of the artist's (her son) reflection of the possibility of how this situation could be received as sexually "dirty" and taboo. He acts upon this possibility, using the camera and further activating the "dirtiness" of the situation. In doing so, he introduces his (and her) agency into the frame under which such a situation would be considered taboo to begin with.

Ledare hints towards the possibility of desiring his mother sexually. Alongside photographs and videos, texts are presented in frames on the walls: handwritten and typed notes, journal entries, and magazine pages. One of them, "Girls I Wanted to Do," is a note written by the ten-year-old Ledare to himself about all the girls he would like to have sex with, which includes "all of my brother's girlfriends" and "mother." "Me and Mom in Photobooth" is a piece composed of sixteen small-scale black and white photobooth pictures placed in a single frame in which we see Ledare posing with Peterson. First they look at the camera, then they hug, cheek-kiss, lip-kiss, and eventually embrace in a seemingly passionate tongue-kiss. These are some of the most suggestive moments of the project regarding the sexual dynamic between Ledare and his mother.

Presented as the central focus of the images in *Pretend* is Peterson's sexual persona, echoing through possible roles and stereotypes regarding aging, womanhood, femininity, motherhood, and daughterhood. For example, while the majority of pictures in the exhibition feature Peterson "*au naturel*" – a term that Filipovic (2012) provides, which describes both Peterson's nudity and the diaristic, often low-tech aesthetics of some of the images – Ledare invites the viewer to consider her sexual subjectivity through other details of her life. Through visual and written material, he gives information about Peterson's personal and professional past, her relationship to other members of their family, the various ways she addresses her agency and authorship through the photographic lens, and her ways of using outfits to express her creativity. For example, Ledare positions his mother as a subject inscribed socially through her attachments to her family members by including images of her parents (for example, "Grandma and Me in Hospital") and images of her other son (such as "Brother Pressed Charges"). Ledare displays a portrait of her as a sixteen-year-old "award-winning ballerina" entitled "Mom's Profile in Seventeen Magazine, 1966," photographed diagonally from above in a pink dress and wearing her hair in a ponytail with a ribbon. Peterson as a teenager was a ballet prodigy, later a model, an aerobics instructor, and a stripper, and she participated in soft-core porn films. In making all this information available visually and textually – Peterson's "clean" and "orderly" side as the ballerina teenager and her "dirty" and "disorderly" side as a mother who is a stripper letting her son photograph her while having sex – Ledare invites the viewer to build their own relationship to the material by presenting "discourses that typically are seen as binaries" alongside each other (Ledare, personal communication, 2015).

In using "dirty" sexual subjectivities and dynamics, porno-graphing artists don't seek to ground the value of their works on the basis of rhetorics of liberation or celebration of difference per se but to expose how sex and sexuality are subjects of discourse and the normative and anti-normative structures through which discourse is made. In these terms, artists such as Leigh Ledare can appear apolitical. By "appearing apolitical," I don't mean that these artists are not politically motivated; I mean that they resist defending the value of their work on the basis of their political beliefs and political contribution, doubting their work's purpose, claiming at times to not know or own it – or, to use Halberstam's term, "unknowing" it. By not signposting their political position, thus underlining the "dirtiness" of the sexual subjectivities involved in these works, they question the structures that assign value, or lack of value, to these subjectivities and to these works. In the ways that Ledare uses and displays lens-made images in *Pretend*, he suggests specific complications regarding the relationship between image and meaning that confront the viewer's own lens of perception. For example, he invites the viewer to recognize their own patterns of meaning-making and to build their own relationship to the work by using discourses that can be thought of as binary to each other. He uses pornographic and autobiographical rhetorics not as binaries to each other per se but in order to bring up discourses regarding subjectivity that can be thought of as binary and contradictory (fig. 28.1).

Ledare uses elements of autobiography in ways that, seen through the antisocial thesis, operate as "an unwriting, an undoing, an unraveling of self" – "an unbecoming, a cleaving to that which seems to shame or annihilate" (Halberstam 2008, 149–51). For to produce *Pretend* he performs (especially given that he does visually participate in the project) "a double persona: a sleazy participant suspended between complicity and bewilderment, and a detached, transgressive artist," and marks his image with the "mustache of the pornographer, which is also the artist's trademark" (Guagnini, in Filipovic 2012, 62–4) (fig. 28.1). These open-ended gestures that Ledare orchestrates to "model binaries and contradictions" (Ledare, personal communication, 2015) – contradictions, for example, between art and pornography, success and failure – are tricks of the porno-graphing action. It is an enigmatic (in how it remains elusive, moving between explicitness and implicitness) marking of the space of art-making with elements associated with pornography – here, for example, "the mustache of the pornographer."

Ledare and Peterson use and comment on a wide range of "dirty" sexual and artistic subjectivities, such as the sexual and therefore "bad" mother, the pornographer son, or the male artist who objectifies his female subjects. The term "Oedipal complex" has frequently been applied to this work by online authors.[2] By framing *Pretend* as the expression of an "Oedipal complex," such articles project a first reading of the situations that *Pretend* uses as involving psychologically "troubled," pathological individuals and relationships. Ledare attests that such quick readings that frame *Pretend* into an Oedipal narrative ignore Peterson's agency – how "she was performing a self-objectification as a negation." He further maintains that such readings either "charge" him for "enabling her to fulfill something that people

28.1 "An unwriting, an undoing, an unraveling of self." Leigh Ledare, "Me and Mom in Photobooth," 2008. Courtesy Leigh Ledare.

may regard in light of a narrow morality" (Anastas and Ledare 2015, 94) or cast him as a victim of their relationship (224).

On one level, Ledare himself challenges pathological readings through his other art-projects, his writing, and his public speaking. More crucially, it is the porno-graphing actions and the artworks themselves that challenge such readings, because the artist is prepared for this sort of reception. Being prepared doesn't mean that such readings don't personally affect him but mean that he opens himself and the work up strategically to such scrutiny so as to complicate and challenge the viewer's patterns of meaning-making. Therefore, the impact of works that involve porno-graphing actions is shaped by how the artist acknowledges and structures the making and presentation of their work through techniques of self-objectification: their use of identity and subjectivity. In turn, this puts porno-graphing methodologies in a unique place to unsettle the art/porn debate.

The art/porn debate can be thought of broadly as concerning the relationship between pornography and art – the two as defined against each other for reasons of legality and political and aesthetic value. As Gary Needham observes, the sides of the debate that claim that a certain artwork is not pornography but "just art" often not only sidestep the artists' identities but also negate them. For instance, drawing from the debate surrounding Robert Mapplethorpe's work, Needham notes that the defences of his work against charges of pornography come "at the expense of identity, context and agency, which are necessary political conditions of both queer and feminist art practice" (Needham 2017, 168).

A foundational methodology of porno-graphing actions is that they do not defend themselves against the accusation of being pornography; furthermore, they rely on the specificities of the artists' identities to invite them to be measured as pornography in a negative sense, and therefore potentially as not art or at least not valuable art. They do so by negotiating and performing their identities and subjectivities (for example, as queers, women, mothers, sons) in ways that may potentially be perceived as sexually transgressive or "dirty." By relying on material present and evident in the artists' lives prior to their deciding to make art from them, they signal forms of autobiographical authenticity. For example, Ledare, I argue, decides to produce, gather, and present autobiographical material such as "Me and Mom in Photobooth" and "Girls I Wanted to Do" exactly because he conceived, conceptualized, and framed his project as dealing with issues of "dirty" sexual subjectivity and representation.

Ledare's *Double Bind* is a piece that writes back into the reception of *Pretend* in ways that exemplify porno-graphing tactics of self-objectification into "dirty" roles. Ledare created *Double Bind* "making use of a select set of social facts from his lived experience." He asked his ex-wife, Meghan Ledare-Fedderly, to join him for a three-day trip in upstate New York "and to participate in photography work during the trip." He subsequently produced five hundred black-and-white photographs of Ledare-Fedderly. He then invited her to take the exact same trip with her current husband, Adam Fedderly, and paid for it. Fedderly is a photographer, and Ledare asked him to shoot the same volume of photographs; upon his return, Fedderly handed Ledare fourteen rolls of unprocessed film. Ledare then "produced the other elements of *Double Bind*: a print-media collection of some six thousand pages appropriated from a wide variety of magazines, newspapers, and other periodicals, and forty-eight panels of imagery that arranged and montaged his and Fedderly's photographs with these mass-media materials." Ledare positions signifiers of meaning (e.g., a woman being photographed by her husband and ex-husband) and signifiers of value and discourse (e.g., pornography, advertisement, art) within a seemingly open-ended framework. The overwhelming volume of material in *Double Bind* generates an "abundance" or "abyss of meaning" (Anastas and Ledare 2015, 88) (fig. 28.2). In turn, this abyss of meaning "may recast the genre of realism that *Pretend* locates" (223). *Double Bind* suggests that the autobiographical language the artist employed in *Pretend* is staged and adopted from the conceptual outset of *Pretend*.

Similarly, Ledare centres issues regarding subjectivity, "how as singular subjects we're submitted, and submit ourselves, to systems" (28), by self-submitting into certain positions (fig. 28.2). Along these lines, it can be assumed that in *Pretend* Ledare intentionally enacts and presents certain sexualities and subjectivities to the world. He is consciously playing with the possibility that his relationship with his mother could be read as incestuous, in this way "calling forward and complicating the judgments of other people" (223–4).

In Ledare's view, the fact that he staged *Pretend* without dictating meaning nor favouring or contextually underlining one particular judgment regarding his and his mother's subjectivities "interferes with viewers' desires to categorize." In this sense, the viewer's sensationalizing of the work as taboo" and reducing it to "this absurd Oedipal reading" are essentially hurried categorizations so that the viewer does not encounter traits of Ledare's relationship with his mother which "in reality were highly ambiguous" (93–4). While Ledare attests that he "certainly played with assumptions like these" (such as the pathology of their relationship) and "complicated them as well as exploited them" (224), he also explains that for him the reception around *Pretend* "was particularly difficult to manage" (93). Viewers or critics would take any fragment from the project and would present it to fit their

"Dirtiness" and Self-Objectification | 543

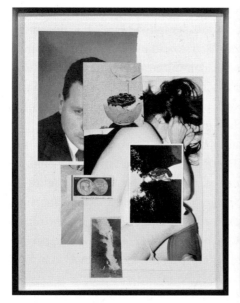

28.2 An overwhelming volume of material generates "abundance" or "abyss of meaning." Leigh Ledare, *Double Bind (diptych #6/25)*, 2010. Courtesy Leigh Ledare.

own agenda, taking it out of context, or "people were writing without even having seen the work. Just moralistically dismissing it as pathological" (Ledare, personal communication, 2015).

Bringing together these thoughts of Ledare's demonstrates that the artist's investment in giving ground to readings that are pathologizing on multiple levels works in dialogue with how such readings, or the possibility of such readings, destabilize him. Or, that in order to push beyond categorization and the viewer's desire for order and clear-cut meaning-making, he first allows himself to be open to such readings, so that he can "complicate" and "exploit" them. The fact that this process involves his own destabilization, his non-sovereignty, and the deliberation of his apparent contradictions – for example, that he finds it difficult to manage a reception to which he knowingly exposed himself, and, in fact, self-objectified into – further reveals the porno-graphing nature of his methodology. His personal destabilization (e.g., frustration, fear, contradictions) functions methodologically to pose the question of "Where does meaning reside inside an artwork?" (Ledare, personal communication, 2014). While working from this position of non-sovereignty runs the risk that the viewer may dismiss the work altogether (decide that it is not art/has no meaning or value because it solely demonstrates a narrative of pathology or a pornographic rhetoric), it also offers the possibility for the viewer to perform an "active reading" of the work, to build a personal relationship to it (Ledare, personal communication, 2014). This in turn allows the potential for engagement and connection between the viewer and the wide spectrum of complexities that the work presents. These complexities involve the production of subjectivities and their manifestation, and so require the viewer's participation in creating and trading subjectivities.

To examine the "dirty" subjectivities that the artist occupies in *Double Bind*, as well as their effects, it is important to first acknowledge that for the creation of the project Ledare deliberately acted on the private life of a heterosexual married couple in order to make art from it. Ledare acts on the sex between the couple, altering it for the purposes of his project: he makes himself part of the sexual life of the husband and wife – an intrusion that can potentially be seen as inappropriate and exploitative. For example, it is because of Ledare's artistic initiation that the couple went on this trip and had sex in this location, resulting in Fedderly taking post-coitus and "trophy" pictures of his wife. Ledare interprets those post-coitus pictures as partly addressed to him, that through them he is told that he doesn't have sexual access to Ledare-Fedderly anymore, as Fedderly is the one who gets to take these after-sex photographs (Ledare, personal communication, 2014). Through his physical distance, his non-possession, his *lack*, Ledare makes himself present in the married couple's sex. This position can potentially be received as inappropriate and "dirty" due to the very distance through which Ledare acted on this sexual dynamic (which didn't include him to begin with), not even merely for his own personal and private sexual pleasure but for the purpose of artistic production. Furthermore, aware that the images of *Double Bind* would be read in relation to *Pretend* – a sexually explicit piece – the artist underlined the sexual activity in *Double Bind*. For example, he stigmatized the legitimacy of the heterosexual married couple through the "Oedipal complex," the "pathological" sexual dynamics that *Pretend* presented. This exemplifies how porno-graphing actions involve the "dirtying" of personal dynamics that would regularly be seen as "normal," such as the institution of heterosexual marriage. At the same time, this particular method of "dirtying" isn't solely aimed at what could be considered "normal" but at the very structures of thinking that, in their determination for order, reproduce notions of "normality."

Furthermore, Ledare self-objectifies into the "dirty" role of the exploiter – he exploits the subjectivities of both Ledare-Fedderly and Fedderly, as well as their marriage and his own divorce. He orchestrates their roles by anticipating how the viewer will read them. For example, further to objectifying his ex-wife as a female, a wife, an ex-wife, and an icon and sexualizing her marriage for his own artistic agenda, he strategically and knowingly frames Fedderly in the heteronormative position of the straight, male photographer who objectifies his female subject, as ultimately it is Fedderly who takes naked and sexualized pictures of Ledare-Fedderly.

> And despite *that*, I work out of the project with dirtier hands than Adam because I have orchestrated the loop through which I have distanced myself from the very thing that I am orchestrating. Which functions as an allegory of the viewers' own distancing from the excess that is in the project. That is what I mean about the work working back into the discursive positions that people take in order to regard the work. (Ledare, personal communication, 2014)

Ultimately, to engage with the images of *Double Bind*, which do not make claims to representation but on the contrary are "anti-photographs" or "negative models" (Ledare, personal communication, 2015) and therefore concern the unrepresentability of the subject, the viewer has to participate in a "negative encounter" – to borrow a term of Edelman and Berlant. This encounter can manifest as the viewer feeling unable to stand the work (Anastas and Ledare 2015, 28), the work being "unbearable," a term that Edelman and Berlant use to describe "what cannot be borne by the subjects we think we are." For them, what is unbearable in terms of one's subjectivity is not merely the opposite of who one thinks one is but the "vertiginous nonidentity" of negativity – what remains incoherent and unknowable no matter how "much we think we know of our own and the world's incoherence" (Berlant and Edelman 2014, 121). In the ways that Ledare's work challenges categories and order, the viewer is invited to endure their participation in determining meaning.

Ledare's "undoing" of himself functions to tempt the viewer to endure what may remain unknowable – for example, in the relationship between Ledare and his mother in *Pretend* – or irresolvable – for example, in the interrelationships between people, images and discourses in *Double Bind*. Participation in such "intensified encounters" nurtures the awareness that as subjects we find and lose our own sense of value by ascribing value and lack of value to other subjects, and highlights the structures we use, employ, and exploit to do so. Within the instability of not seeking easy clarity or the safety of assured knowing but instead enduring incoherence, enduring doubt, lie "enigmatic" opportunities for connection and communication.

In this chapter I have developed a new terminology I have called "porno-graphing" to think about artists who act on a sexual situation to make art from it. It is important that this (sexual) situation may exist in the artists' life before their decision to make art from it; additionally, they may choose it as art material because they consider that if it is seen from an outsider position, it has the potential of being perceived as "dirty." This course of decision-making regarding the art material is important because it is through this potentiality (of being considered as "dirty"), and its ambiguity, that artists form their processes of self-objectification and self-submission into sexually and artistically "dirty" positions. Thus one way in which artists act upon sex to make art is by the strategies through which they self-objectify into such "dirty" positions, which also involves their being open to (even inviting) their works to be seen and measured as pornography or the documentation of a pathology rather than art. A question that keeps arising is: Who considers or may consider someone (such as an artist) or something (such as a sexual situation) as "dirty?"

The questions of who is doing the considering, who is it that attributes value and meaning, whose authority I am assuming and recalling when I speak of a subject's "dirtiness," link to a series of other questions regarding contexts of viewing. Such were the questions I was frequently asked as part of my art-making training as an art student: "Who is this art for?" "Who is the audience?" "Who is your *ideal* audience?" To me these were scary questions that I couldn't and can't answer, not because I don't want my work to be seen but because the unknownness, so to speak, of the viewing subject is crucial to the type of work I make, which is work involving porno-graphing actions. This ambiguity is important because if the artworks' aims were framed within the works, or strictly framed within the artist's conscious process of making these works, then possibly they wouldn't invite the viewer to search for them and thus not know how to enter them or "stand" them.

I have argued that *Pretend* and *Double Bind* require detailed critical attention that does not simply either dismiss as problematic (i.e., pathological) or celebrate its sexual explicitness and the ways that the artist explores and uses taboo – in terms of both the images and the context of their making. Instead, I argue that the artist's use of certain "dirty" subjectivities through the form of self-objectification can be regarded and analyzed on the basis of the artist's "negative" tricks.

Such an approach can negotiate artistic value by attending to how an artist strategically self-objectifies into the very contradictions of what art may or may not be.

NOTES

1 By "value" and "art-value," I don't mean financial value; I consider that the art-value of an artwork concerns its status as art precisely independently of its place in the market.
2 Two examples of such articles: M. Carpentier (2008), "Leigh Ledare's Oedipal Complex Is Not Our Gain," *Jezebel* (blog), 30 July, http://jezebel.com/5031205/leigh-ledares-oedipal-complex-is-not-our-gain/; F. Mathieson (2013), "Does Photographing Your Mother Having Sex Really Qualify as Art?," *Refinery29* (blog), 11 October, http://www.refinery29.com/2013/10/55129/leigh-ledare-mother-having-sex-photo/.

REFERENCES

Anastas, Rhea, and Leigh Ledare. 2015. *Double Bind*. New York: Art Press.
Attwood, Feona. 2002. "Reading Porn: The Paradigm Shift in Pornography Research." *Sexualities* 5, no. 1: 91–105.
Berlant, Lauren, and Lee Edelman. 2014. *Sex, or the Unbearable*. Durham: Duke University Press.
Bersani, Leo. 2010. *Is the Rectum a Grave? and Other Essays*. Chicago: University of Chicago Press.
Braidotti, Rosi. 1994. *Nomadic Subjects: Embodiment and Sexual Difference in Contemporary Feminist Theory*. New York: Columbia University Press.
Caserio, Robert L., Tim Dean, Lee Edelman, Judith Halberstam, and José E. Muñoz. 2006. "The Antisocial Thesis in Queer Theory." *PMLA* 121, no. 3: 819–36.
Copjec, Joan. 2015. *Read My Desire: Lacan against the Historicists*. London: Verso.
Dean, Tim. 2015. "No Sex Please, We're American." *American Literature History* 27, no. 3: 614–24.
Doyle, Jennifer. 2006. *Sex Objects: Art and the Dialectics of Desire*. Minneapolis: University of Minnesota Press.
Edelman, Lee. 2004. *No Future: Queer Theory and the Death Drive*. Durham: Duke University Press.
Filipovic, Elena, ed. 2012. *Leigh Ledare et al.* Brussels and Milan: WIELS Contemporary Art Centre/Mousse Publishing.
Halberstam, Judith. 2008. "The Anti-Social Turn in Queer Studies." *Graduate Journal of Social Science* 5, no. 2: 140–55.
– 2010. "The Artist Is Object – Marina Abramovic at MOMA." *Bully Bloggers* (blog), 5 April. https://bullybloggers.wordpress.com/2010/04/05/the-artist-is-object-%e2%80%93-marina-abramovic-at-moma/.

– 2011. *The Queer Art of Failure.* Durham: Duke University Press.

Kunst, Bojana. 2015. *Artist at Work, Proximity of Art and Capitalism.* Alresford: Zero Books.

Muñoz, José Esteban. 2009. *Cruising Utopia: The Then and There of Queer Futurity.* New York: New York University Press.

Needham, Gary. 2017. "'Not On Public Display': The Art/Porn Debate." In *The Routledge Companion to Media, Sex and Sexuality*, edited by Clarissa Smith, Feona Attwood, and Brian McNair, 163–73. London: Routledge.

O'Hagan, Sean. 2013. "Oedipal Exposure: Leigh Ledare's Photographs of His Mother Having Sex." *Guardian* (UK) 10 October. https://www.theguardian.com/artanddesign/2013/oct/09/leigh-ledare-photographs-mother-having-sex.

29

Shut Me Up in Grindr: Anti-confessional Discourse and Sensual Nonsense in MSM Media

TOM ROACH

The Age of Nonsense

It is difficult these days to believe in the power of rational argument, coherent speech, and logical consequence. In "the age of Trump," as mainstream US media have taken to calling it – thereby validating the troll-in-chief's megalomania – nonsense, inarticulacy, and bald-faced dishonesty prevail. The weight of history and the factuality of events or statements appear to matter little: to misquote, or at best misrepresent, Marx and Engels ([1848] 1978), "All that is solid melts into air" (476). Of course, Marx and Engels are not referring here to inauguration attendance numbers, the alleged millions of illegal American voters, fictional massacres, presidential wiretapping, or any of the other 2,140 falsehoods concocted, packaged, and tweeted by the Trump administration in its first year in office (Kessler and Kelly 2018). No, in this famous quip from the *Manifesto*, Marx and Engels praise, however backhandedly, the bourgeoisie's revolutionary capacity to obliterate the instruments of production and social relations of an earlier industrial era. And though Marx and Marxism have seemingly been reduced to a footnote in the neoliberal rewriting of history, "all that is solid melts into air" resonates in Trump's pseudo-revolutionary and denialist nihilism, a force that lays waste to claims grounded in the scientific method and humanities-based, critical analysis alike. Amplified in the social-media vortex and shat out of alt-right news outlets, Trump's "alternative facts" gain traction and contribute to the destruction of the moderately progressive gains achieved during the Obama presidency – not to mention the destruction of the planet.

Nonetheless, US news media would better serve the public by rebranding "the age of Trump" with the catchier and farther-reaching "age of nonsense." This slogan more accurately designates a moment when facts and history dematerialize or mutate into magical reality, when reasoned argument fails, and when astute analysis competes for airtime with wilfully ignorant claptrap. This age, of course, predates the political rise of the short-fingered man with the immoderately long and pathetically overcompensatingly phallic necktie. Number Forty-Five is at least in part the logical consequence of neoliberal *ressentiment* and despair – a condition itself that is the result of massive income inequality, a news and social-media culture that traffics in conspiracy theory and misinformation, systemic racism, and institutionalized misogyny, among other factors. Try as progressives might to counter Trump's bilious nonsense with non-alternative facts and investigative reports that reveal the emperor's nakedness, it is folly to wait for Hegel's heroic rational spirit to swoop in to right the wrongs of the world anytime soon. Indeed, the Trump problem cannot be countered with reason because reason has become part of the problem.

Gilles Deleuze's (1995) thoughts on the corruption of rational communication in contemporary "control societies" are here illuminative. In control societies, communication is a principal commodity, a primary force of economic production. Education, the erstwhile training in rational thought, functions chiefly as the accumulation of marketable skill sets. Although at first glance control societies seem more open – especially in contrast to disciplinary societies, which operate on the principle of confinement in spaces like factories, schools, barracks, and hospitals – the foremost technology in a control society is incessant monitoring; one's productivity, effectiveness, and health (i.e., human capital) must be known and evaluated so as to be optimized. Deleuze asserts in his essay "Control and Becoming" that discursive politics, representational politics, are compromised once communication is subsumed by capital. In response to Antonio Negri's techno-optimistic speculation that communism may be "less utopian" (i.e., more realistic) in a context in which new communication technologies permit individuals to "speak out and thereby recover a greater degree of freedom," Deleuze muses,

> You ask whether control or communication societies will lead to forms of resistance that might reopen the way for a communism understood as the "transversal organization of free individuals." Maybe, I don't know. But it would be nothing to do with minorities speaking out. Maybe speech and communication have been corrupted. They're thoroughly permeated by money – and not by accident but by their very nature. We've got to hijack speech. Creating has always been something different from communicating. The key thing may be to create vacuoles of noncommunication, circuit breakers, so we can elude control. (1995, 175)

Put differently, all the communicative freedom in the world cannot topple the billion-dollar industries – and lapdog governments – invested precisely in the commodification of communication. Gently squashing Negri's dream of a communicative communism, Deleuze makes clear here that resistance in the form of "speaking out" – specifically, the creation of a reverse discourse by minority groups, or, in the current political context, speaking truth to power via reasoned debate – is not the guarantor of greater freedoms in a control society. A liberatory politics grounded in resistant discourses will only go so far: like all systems of representation, language is inevitably commodified and corrupted; as in all dialectical struggles, reverse discourse is merely a stepping stone to future becomings. Instead of investing in a discursive politics of representation, then, "eluding control" might involve the creation of sites of non-communication, perhaps the creation of nonsensical communication, that work as "circuit breakers" in the capitalist consumption/subsumption of ideas. In other words, perhaps it is time again, or, at last, to heed David Byrne's directive from the Reagan 1980s: *Stop Making Sense*.[1] Trump's nonsense, and, by extension, the neoliberal commodification of communication, might best be negotiated, thwarted, and ultimately vanquished by "better" nonsense: not a smarter nonsense per se, but a *sensual* nonsense that, however unwittingly and however ironically, might pave the way for an exodus from these nonsensical times.[2]

Which leads me to MSM (men-seeking-men) media. One need only read the words of a Grindr spambot[3] to ascertain the absurdity of a typical MSM media exchange. To clarify, a bot is only as effective as it is convincingly human; the moment a user realizes that a "conversation" is in fact a phishing scam is the moment the bot fails. Hence, "ive have a really nice dick broand i love showing it off" is a perfectly credible statement in MSM media, a statement that many would follow down the rabbit hole (fig. 29.1). And yet precisely because of such absurd enticements and inarticulate gobbledygook, geosocial MSM apps might be understood as "circuit-breakers" creating a discursive nonsense that brushes against both the neoliberal commodification of communication and the reified, sexological classifications of sexual identity. Although dominated by transactional exchanges that would make any salesperson (or phisher) proud, the post-articulate call and response prevalent in media like Grindr simultaneously resists two hegemonic discursive forms: 1) the language of transparency so valued in corporate and governmental settings, and 2) a confessional discourse so necessary for the invention and perpetuation of modern sexuality. Indeed, in the world of MSM hookup apps, the revelation of an interior life – emotions, intellect, eloquence – is more

29.1
Grindrbots are deployed to mine user data. After flirty small talk, users are typically asked to share credit card info, email addresses, etc. In this screenshot of a Grindrbot "conversation," the user is clearly aware of being drawn into a phishing scam. Joseph Patrick McCormick, "WARNING These Grindr Profiles Are Actually Robots Trying to Steal Your Info," *Pink News*. 2015. http://www.pinknews.co.uk/2015/08/11/warning-these-grindr-profiles-are-actually-robots-trying-to-steal-your-info/.

often than not a liability. On Grindr, for instance, users are encouraged to identify not as singular individuals but as members of a "tribe" or type: bear, twink, daddy, jock.[4] This subjective deferral de-emphasizes the psychic life of sexuality and arguably works to de-link erotic desire from social identity: a link forged fundamentally through the confession "I'm gay." The type, then, serves as a mask, even a puppet, that deflects the significance and deep-seatedness of sexual desire. Users become ventriloquists of a sort, speaking not primarily of their personal histories or "deep thoughts" but rather the clichéd lexicons of the porn star, the bro, the businessman, the tribe.[5]

The logical conclusion of this anti-confessional and ventriloquial subjective deferral comes in the form of (my personal favourite) Grindr user "Emily Dickinson."[6] While the poet died over a century ago, her poetry is indeed immortal, thanks in part to a Grindr user who responds to potential suitors exclusively in Dickinsonian verse (fig. 29.2). The silliness of this gesture not only brings levity to the typically transactional, often woefully banal MSM media scripts but also underscores the fact that there are no "people" on Grindr, that everyone, in one way or another, is speaking through an avatar and negotiating the discursive norms

29.2
Grindr conversation with user "Emily Dickinson," screenshot, GrindrTextsFromEmily Tumblr account, 25 November 2014. http://grindrtextsfromemily.tumblr.com.

of the platform. Be they the bluntest of porn-esque pickup lines or hetero-erotic slang ripped from hip-hop and sports cultures, the language of MSM media emanates from the broader cultural milieu more so than from any authentic, singular voice. In short, Grindr nation, we are all, to some degree, "Emily Dickinson."

In the pages to come, I explore the ethical and political potential of MSM media's sensual nonsense, focusing on three main points: first, the confession as the discursive crux of identitarian sexuality, itself the nexus of disciplinary and biopolitical power in modernity; second, human capital trumping depth-psychological models of sexuality in neoliberalism and its influence in MSM media; and third, the sublime digital closet of MSM media, a space in which users practice an anti-identitarian ethics of impersonality that opens onto non-dialectical, post-representational political imaginaries.

The Fantastic Confession

Before I begin, a note of clarification: I do not believe MSM media are any sort of "training grounds" for a resistant politics. I understand resistance as a force intrinsic to dialectical struggle, ultimately subject to the discursive terms of that struggle. Without diminishing the importance of a politics of resistance – acting up, fighting back, and working to expand the scope of civil rights and political representation are perhaps more imperative than ever in the "age of Trump" – I glimpse in MSM media a nascent, immanentist political project "growing sideways."[7] In these media, I discern relational practices that circumvent or stray from the push and pull of representational political power. Such relational practices – imperceptible or perhaps superfluous from the vantage point of a resistant politics – contain the germ of a queer erotics beyond the discursive frameworks of sexuality as we have come to know it. That said, a "post-sexual" erotics is by no means an inevitability: media born of and steeped in neoliberal logics might in the end merely affirm contemporary sexual and neoliberal conventions. However, it is worth running the risk to think otherwise. For the remainder of the essay, I explore MSM media cruising as a form of sensual training for a post-representational, non-communicative politics that seeks relational and ethical freedoms beyond those afforded in neoliberal (control) societies.

This exploration begins with the confession, a discursive rite historically inextricable from the conceptual implantation of a sexual essence in individuals and the population at large.[8] Foucault, of course, credited this "perverse implantation" to a *scientia sexualis* that secured a link between sexual desire and subjective truth.

Forged primarily by forcing sex to speak through confession, this link becomes paramount in the functioning of modern biopolitics.[9] In his late interviews, Foucault repeatedly, almost polemically, instructs readers to distrust this link. He counsels against investing in a concept of sexuality created to substantiate, and thereby manage, bodies and pleasures. In terms of sexual politics, the declaration of one's truth via the sexual confession – for example, coming out – not only validates but arguably celebrates the "imprisonment" of erotic desire in a marked subject and a manageable demographic. A political project erected on the basis of the sexual confession is, then, at best a reactive and quite limited strategy because it remains ensnared within a rigged discursive/dialectical struggle set in motion by biopolitical administrates. As an alternative, Foucault suggests that a creative exodus from biopolitical administration begins with the severance of the link between sexual desire and self-truth. In his lived friendships, work, and politics, he strove to prompt such an exodus by, among other things, minimizing the psychological and identitarian significance of sexual desire and avoiding the confessional register altogether.[10]

Unfortunately, despite the valiant efforts of feminist and queer theory professors worldwide, the belief that humans are born with a core, intractable sexual orientation – one invested with enormous identitarian and social significance – has gained in popularity since the publication of Foucault's seminal work.[11] Aided by mainstream LGBT political efforts, the work of the *scientia sexualis* is indeed implanted, perhaps more firmly than ever, into the psyches, laws, and censuses of the US citizenry. No matter how often we stray from our sexual "home" via drunken, experimental, or ritualized (homo)sexual behaviour, many of us are now confident that a solid foundation – a biological substructure of genes, hormones, and chromosomes – grounds the frisky sexual self. Especially for dominant social groups, being "born this way" is a comforting, even liberating fact. In *Not Gay: Sex between Straight White Men*, Jane Ward (2015) notes that medical/scientific conceptions of sexuality, both past and present, grant straight-identified white men more than a few queer freedoms. Confident in the biological certainty that they are "not gay," men create elaborate rituals (fraternity hazing, military "bonding," *Jackass*-style tomfoolery) to touch one another. Outrageous rationalizations, frequently backed by the medical/psychiatric community, follow: the *unheimlich* behaviour is justified as circumstantial (in prison, for example), homosocial (in the frat house and barracks), or pure accident (intoxication). Through it all, not-gay men remain devoted to a stigma-free heterosexual identity and a heteronormative politics frequently peppered with misogyny and racism. In this mindset, heteronormativity has little to do with sexual practice. As long as "authentic" gays wilfully occupy the role of the sexual Other, as long as "authentic" gays continue to validate the deep-seatedness and identitarian significance of (homo)sexuality, straight white men can do what they please with their bodies and remain politically and socially in the driver's seat.[12]

Compounding the irony, in the age of "born this way" sexuality, "gay love" comes to emblematize ideal, romantic love; in what might cynically be deemed just deserts, the conjugal gay couple is held captive in a house of its own making. This unexpected plot twist is one consequence of same-sex marriage legalization: "love wins" only when it is domesticated, dyadic, and nuptial. Marriage becomes the compulsory *telos* of all romantic love, and the new poster children for this toxic myth are those fresh-from-their-honeymoon husbands. The upshot of the bait-and-switch is that queer sex is appropriated by straights, rebranded as heteroflexibility for white women and "str8 dude sex" for white men,[13] and queer public cultural spaces become playgrounds for bachelorette parties and (often barely) gay-friendly bros. The script, at its best, goes something like this: "I'm straight, but I totally support gay rights and marriage. You guys are a cute couple; you should definitely get married. Now move aside and allow me to invade your bars, co-opt your sex, and colonize your culture. You can stick around to provide style advice and entertainment."

In sum, the popular notion that there exist "authentic" gays – those born with a homosexual essence – works to the benefit of straight white male hegemony and hetero-/homonormative politics. Coming out as gay, consequently, is not necessarily an anti-normative or countercultural act insofar as it is consistent with the sexual logic serving the status quo.[14] For this reason, Ward places a great deal of emphasis on the current importance of cultivating or *choosing* a queer political identity. Regarding this choice, she writes:

> Certainly to imagine that queerness is an option for all people – to consider that anyone could, technically, choose to get off the tired, beaten path of heterosexuality or homonormativity and relocate him- or herself among the freaks and perverts, among the leather daddies and fat dykes in San Francisco ravenously filling each other's orifices with organic squash – is to highlight that most straight-identified people are "straight" not because they don't ever want to have a same-sex encounter, but because, in their view, queer modes of homosexual relating do not constitute an appealing way of life. Because their allegiance, ultimately, is to normativity. (2015, 208)

The idea of queerness being "an option for all people," of queerness defined solely as a cultural and political affiliation, returns us to an issue that plagued early queer theorists: is queerness merely anti-normative politics? If so, are we back in the conceptual realm of the "lesbian continuum" or the "straight but not narrow?"[15] What happens to bodies and pleasures – to queer sex practices – that might ground a queer politics? Ward, fully aware of this conundrum, closes her book with a call to "re-center sex acts themselves" (211), to invest queer sex with a sincerity and a significance shrugged off by (straight white male) practitioners of not-gay sex. Nonetheless, questions remain: Is *more* significance in sex acts a canny strategy? Will not a reinvestment in the meaningfulness of queer sex place us squarely within the jaws of the trap set by the *scientia sexualis*? What happens to Foucault's call to de-emphasize the social and subjective significance of sex? To delink sex from identity? What becomes of the sincere (homo)sexual confession if it ultimately works to enhance the power of a seemingly intractable power bloc?

Because the *scientia sexualis* has persuaded the majority of Americans with its concepts and categories, the sexual confession is simultaneously more banal and more loaded. If sexual behaviour and social identity are essentially biological destiny, speaking our sexual truth seems at once like reading aloud the results of a DNA test and handing out a life sentence. Although many folks sleep more soundly knowing that homosexuals are "born this way," the political investment in this essential truth affects not only individual life trajectories but also the future of sexual politics. Regardless of whether one embraces a hetero-/homo-normative ideology bolstering the status quo or a resistant, anti-normative stance, the terms of the debate have been established as a dialectical back-and-forth. Lest we forget, it was the biopolitical administrates, not queers, that set this struggle in motion; the best we can do within this debate is react. In this regard, the sexual confession, while crucial to gay rights campaigns, might be considered a trap for a queer politics seeking freedoms beyond the scope of a dialectical, sexual-political struggle. So what power, if any, does the confession hold for a contemporary queer politics?

This question becomes more interesting when considered in relation to neoliberal policies and practices. As the editors of this collection note, "Confession has become the last space for individual self-actualization, the enduring fantasy where we can imagine that we exist outside of the neoliberal ethos" (7). According to this neoliberal ethos, the self is merely a bundle of activities, a collection of skill sets, and a fungible vessel of human capital whose personal history and interior life matter little.[16] By assertively bringing to the foreground issues concerning subjective interiority, the sexual confession potentially disrupts a neoliberal "business as usual" that wilfully overlooks personal histories and thus purposefully exacerbates social inequalities based in race, gender, class, and sexuality. In highlighting the importance of the interior life and identitarian histories, then, the confession humanizes and diversifies an increasingly automated workplace and public sphere … or so the story goes. The key word in Waugh and Arroyo's previously quoted statement is "fantasy": the confession offers the *fantasy* that we can actualize ourselves beyond the constraints of neoliberal subjectivity. Shannon Winnubst (2012), however, reminds us:

> Once the principles of neoliberalism are absorbed into a culture, as they increasingly are in the U.S., we are all succumbing to the social rationality of neoliberalism: despite ideological or political differences, we are all speaking the same language, drinking the same Kool-Aid, breathing the same air. Consequently, the question of identity, which involves laying claim to a substance, is turned inside out, becoming a matter of process that is absorbed into this neoliberal grammar of success. One does not ask, "who are you?" in neoliberalism. Rather, one asks, "how good are you at what you do? How successful are you?" And the true bottom line: "*how much and how well do you maximize your interests?*" (86)

The diversity so celebrated in neoliberal publics – specifically, a diversity of sexual orientations that rests on confessions – is hence purely formal, "a matter of process." Success, be it financial, health related, or popular, is constituted as the fundamental evaluative principle for all social identities. Although the subjectifying confession might superficially diversify a social milieu, it is in the end merely a stage in the process of neoliberal self-actualization – most certainly not a break from it. And while the sexual confession "I'm gay" might augment one's social interest and more readily translate into an anyone-can-do-it, rags-to-riches success story, it does little to unsettle the underlying conceptual premise of neoliberalism: radical individualism and cutthroat competition will produce a society of few "winners" and innumerable "losers."

One need only look to the success of Donald Trump to understand the social hierarchy that neoliberal theorists had in mind. Born with a silver spoon, obsessed with self-brand marketing and maximization of self-interest, committed to intensifying political, economic, and social divisions, Trump, the quintessential neoliberal "winner," will ensure that the so-called free world he leads remains riven by the obscene social inequalities wrought by thirty years of neoliberal policy. "Losers" like the poor, the elderly, and the undocumented will be sadistically punished because they weigh down a trickle-up economic system. People of colour will continue to be murdered by Trump-backed storm troopers, whose witness-stand tears will be rewarded with exoneration, police protection, and a pension. Emergent within this social wreckage, indeed in the very romantic heart of it, are media that arguably distil the zero-sum, winner-take-all imperatives of neoliberalism: Grindr, Scruff, Jack'd. Counterintuitively, these media might also prepare us for finding a way out of this mess.

Shut Me Up in the Digital Closet

To summarize, the sexual confession is historically instrumental to the formation of identitarian sexuality and, by extension, the functioning of a biopolitical governmentality. At present, the scientific notion that sexual orientation is biologically hard-wired into our psyches is more popular than ever. We have apparently become the docile subjects that biopolitical administrates wished to create. However, in a neoliberal context, human capital trumps any depth-psychological model of subjectivity. The confession and identitarian sexuality become increasingly insignificant in neoliberalism: both are "absorbed into the neoliberal grammar of success," as Winnubst so aptly puts it. Instead of subjective truth and personal history, then, a neoliberal conception of sexuality emphasizes surfaces, visuals, skill sets, and branding. A neoliberal sexual subject works to optimize and maximize his or her sexual interest: sex is less a question of who one is than how successful one is in practising it, less an expression of a deep-seated essence than a marketing strategy to achieve profitable returns.

Two distinct concepts of sexuality, therefore, currently compete for our attention: a neoliberal sexuality evaluating how well we "employ" our sexual desires, and an identitarian sexuality concerned with how authentic we are in our sexual being-ness. Depending on the context, whom or what we desire paradoxically reveals nothing and everything about who we are and what we are capable of. We daily navigate a course between the rock of scientific sexuality and the hard (work)place of neoliberal sexuality. We adapt, somewhat schizophrenically, to the illogical and incommensurate demands of relational norms and romantic myths on the one hand and an unforgiving marketplace in which such norms and myths are liabilities on the other. Our lives as striving individuals and biopolitical subjects become more manageable knowing "who we are," and yet we are encouraged to check our self-truth at the office door lest we risk playing the "gay card," the "race card," the "gender card." In this age of being and not being then – in this age, that is, of nonsense – what might we glean from MSM media to help chart a course through this sexual-political Scylla and Charybdis?

For starters, in MSM media we can witness neoliberalism stripped bare, so to speak. The discursive, relational, and self-presentation norms of these media exemplify some social ideals of neoliberalism: hyper-individualism, self-branding, anti-confessional, transactional exchange, and the instrumentalization and commodification of intimacy.[17] Yet in this hotbed of neoliberal sexuality, new subjective and relational freedoms, however negatively conceived, also emerge. These include: 1) freedom from a deep-seated, psychic sexual core, substantiated historically by linking erotic desire to self-truth; 2) freedom from a confessional imperative inextricable from identitarian sexuality; 3) freedom from romantic myths shackling sex to love to marriage; and 4) freedom from corporate/workplace communicative norms that demand expressivity, transparency, articulacy, and team building. As a result, I discern in MSM media a restlessness with essentialist, scientific models of sexuality and a yearning for connection beyond romantic and neoliberal relational norms. Specifically, the former two freedoms afford an escape from the trap laid out by the *scientia sexualis*, whereas the latter signal a longing for intimacies beyond romantic and neoliberal limits. Thinking optimistically, we may have here the basic rudiments of both a Foucauldian exodus from biopolitical sexuality and a Deleuzian circuit breaker in the commodified communicative flows of control societies. If not, then MSM media at least express disenchantment with the present. But do they offer more than a desire to escape these bleak times?

The sage verse of Emily Dickinson ([ca. 1862] 1999), wittily appropriated by Grindr user "Emily Dickinson," is illuminative here. Specifically, the following Dickinson poem, surely quoted by "Emily Dickinson" in one Grindr exchange or another, speaks to the limited discursive confines of MSM media and the ecstatic excess produced precisely because of such confinement:

They shut me up in Prose –
As when a little Girl
They put me in the Closet –
Because they like me "still" –

Still! Could themself have peeped –
And seen my Brain – go round –

They might as wise have lodged a Bird
For Treason – in the Pound –

Himself has but to will
And easy as a Star
Abolish his – Captivity –
And laugh – No more have I –

Countering common understandings of closets as dark, even shameful sites of punishment and personal misery, Dickinson's poem emphasizes the enraptured imagination and unbridled willpower a closet might produce. Forced into "Prose," a genre deemed more appropriate for "a little Girl" by the masculinist literary gatekeepers of the nineteenth century (Galvin 1999), the narrator refuses to let this (gendered) "Closet" contain her poetic creativity. In defiance of her jailers' wishes, her imagination ("Brain") flies like a bird through the bars of its prison; her "will" shines like a "Star" to reveal the boundaries of "Captivity" abolished. This "little Girl" surely has the last laugh.[18] The poem thus sheds light on the artistic invention and affective production taking place in the "Closet": artistry and affect perhaps birthed *only in* the closet. If we were to commit the dreaded biographical fallacy and interpret this work as Dickinson's own plight, the poem itself becomes Dickinson's closeted production, one might say her secret weapon: the rebellious poetry written in the "Closet" of "Prose" is made visible and public in this verse. In this regard, the poem is also, in the Austinian sense, performative (Austin 1962): in its generic form, it abolishes the "Prose" closet Dickinson was relegated to; through its form, Dickinson herself not only exits the closet but destroys it altogether by becoming-poet in the poem's utterance. Although the "experts" of her day attempted to shut her up – that is, to silence Dickinson's poetic voice – that voice "comes out," declares itself, and speaks loudly and proudly of its being-ness. Or does it?

It is tempting to appropriate this poem for a sexual or feminist liberationist project: to read the poem as evidence of unruly women making history, as the public confession of a closeted secret, a coming-out narrative, even an ode to the moral necessity of coming out. Indeed, it is tempting to compare the performative utterance "I am gay" to Dickinson's performative enactment of "I am poet." But might these words instead be a paean to the sublime pleasures, affects, and intellects produced *in* the closet? Might it be a song of praise *for* the closet, a space productive of an imaginative and sensual potential that knows no bounds? Is the closet a jail ultimately inaccessible to the jailers themselves, in that it explodes dualistically conceived notions of in/out and incarcerated/liberated altogether?

Cesare Casarino (2002) interprets the poem precisely in this manner: "For (Dickinson's poem seems to be saying) you can 'shut me up in' the 'Closet,' but then you no longer have control over the blazing and star-like *potentia* that can be produced within it, thus effectively exceeding it and abolishing it from the inside" (186). For Casarino, the sexual closet is the "privileged locus of an as yet untapped excess of same-sex desire" (186) that "marks the threshold of an other-becoming" (187). This "becoming" is more than a transformation into an identifiable (gay) subject because the closet itself, like Walt Whitman, contains multitudes: molecular desires, sublime pleasures and affects, a potential to become anything.[19] Dickinson herself exemplifies this multitudinous becoming: in her Closet of Prose, she becomes a bird, a star, and, indeed, a poet. Using Dickinson as a starting point, Casarino thus complicates sexual-political understandings of being "in" or "out" of the closet by arguing that the immanent excesses of being "in" serve no purpose for – in fact, overcome the limitations of – a dialectically conceived "out" politics. Like Foucault, however, Casarino is adamant about the "dire necessity" (188) of coming out: although a resistant gay politics might ultimately affirm a heteronormative dialectical social order in which anti-heteronormative resistance was conceived and foretold, it is nonetheless imperative to participate in such dialectical struggle, to embrace and cultivate a public LGBTQ social identity despite the risk of affirming precisely what that identity theoretically opposes. Nonetheless, coming out will not ultimately afford an escape from the quagmire of dialectical sexual politics: "Just because the act of coming out is necessary and inevitable at a given conjuncture in both the life history of particular sexual subjects and in the larger-than-life history of modernity, it does not necessarily follow that such an act is the solution to the problem that produced the closet in the first place" (189).

So, what might the closet offer that a public "outness" cannot? Unnamed and unclassified libidinal energies, affective sensualities, and molecular sexualities; invisibility, imperceptibility, fraught with and intensified by anxiety, loneliness, and other ecstatically unbearable somatic sensations; the pleasures of enclosure, a finite space yielding to an imaginative infinity, a claustrophilia; the welcoming security of finitude itself, of finality, a tomb, extinction. All such excess cannot be assimilated into a manageable social identity or recognized as a coherent political stance. Casarino goes so far as to argue that the closet ultimately houses the waste of modernity's dominant mode of production, the dialectic itself, including its primary product, the homo-/heterosexuality binary:

> In the sublime of the closet one confronts nothing less than the excess of the onto-epistemological production of modernity. Such an excess constitutes an escape from modernity as we know it – a cunicular network of a subterranean history of the body threatening suddenly to erupt through the ground of modernity and to materialize that which never would or will be modern. (192)

That which "never would or will be modern" is precisely that which is unrecognizable and unrepresentable from the standpoint of "out" politics: the sensual *potentia* that exceeds social identity and escapes demographical, economic, or quantitative evaluation; a *potentia*, in other words, that forges a course between and beyond identitarian and neoliberal sexualities.

It requires now only a small conceptual leap to understand MSM media as a contemporary digital manifestation of Casarino's, or Dickinson's, sublime closet. First, in MSM media, one need not "come out" of or as anything: although providing virtual space for men to connect with other men (an activity, like poetry writing), these media are not necessarily or solely for "gay men" (a social demographic). Non-identitiarian desires circulate freely in this space, some surely inassimilable to the sexual codes and categories created "in real life" to represent them. Second, the discursive conventions of MSM media encourage anti-confessional, crassly sexual exchanges – typically *not* proud declarations of gay identity or cultural affinity. One discovers in the stammering and inarticulate chatter instead a sensual, depersonalized, even *impersonal*, discourse. If we neoliberals are shut up in a closet of discursive transparency and personal accountability, that closet also produces its opposite in MSM media: opacity and unreliability.[20] Just as Dickinson's Closet of Prose unintentionally produces poetry, the MSM media closet, ostensibly created to connect users at least preliminarily through conversation, inadvertently generates an impersonal discourse of ventriloquists. The form of intimacy emergent in this discourse, long familiar to queers, is what I understand as shared estrangement.[21] Manifest historically in practices such as anonymous cruising, friendships emergent in the AIDS crisis, and, arguably, bareback subcultures (Dean 2009), shared estrangement finds its contemporary home in the digital closet. Here, the ache of longing, the loneliness of isolation, even the "shame" of desiring non-marital, unromantic intimacies, are (un)shared in a non-dialectical, disconnected mingling. If "vacuoles of non-communication" are needed to circumvent the commodified communicative forms in control societies, then an anti-relational, queer ethic of shared estrangement might be one such "circuit-breaker." Its past implementation in queer culture has proven prescient, resilient, and politically strategic; as cultivated in MSM media, it may hold the capacity, like Dickinson's wilful imagination, to abolish our captivity in dialectical struggle.

Third, MSM media require users to create a profile: a digital self-representation that characteristically features an invented name, photos of faces or body parts, lists of sexual preferences or skills, and references to a type or tribe. As with the dialogic norms, profiles typically steer clear of personal history and emotional interiority. They are often perfunctory when it comes to (non-sexual) self-description and cautious in terms of socially identifying markers. Since "out" politics has rendered same-sex desire so blindingly visible and thoroughly individualized, becoming "invisible" in profile creation can be understood as a (re-)enactment of the anxious anonymity of the closet as well as form of self-dissolution. More than simply nostalgia, however, such imperceptibility lends itself to the establishment of unconventional communal forms.[22] The Grindr grid, for instance, can be understood as the visual representation of a non-identitarian collectivity affirming a common, asubjective substance that seethes beneath identifiable individuals – libidinal energies, affective intensities, molecular desires.[23] Such sensual *potential*, as Casarino reminds us, threatens to explode the very conceptual framework in which the closet was conceived in modernity.

Finally, claustrophilia: it is gratifying, even liberating, to feel in control of one's confines, no matter how oppressive that imprisonment may be, no matter how illusory such control is. Within that finite space, one can likewise dream up fantasies, scenarios, and worlds unimaginable – or more often than not, unrealizable – outside of it. The unbridled imagination produced in and by Dickinson's Closet finds its complement in MSM media in flights of fancy and fugitive desires.

Of course, the above descriptions of MSM media protocols and conventions might also likely appear in a self-help book entitled "How to Brand Yourself and Find a Mate in Neoliberalism," or "How to Repudiate the History of Struggle and Sacrifice That Paved the Way for MSM Media." In other words, we cannot simply ignore the ways that MSM media affirm neoliberal logics and potentially belittle the agonizing, life-threatening work of queer activists. However, I also discern in these media an ambivalence that signals a desire for something more: alternative presents, other-than-neoliberal futures. Unlike Jane Ward's not-gay men who want homosexual sex without the stigmatizing label "homosexual," we can, of course, experience the sublime pleasures of the digital closet *and* embrace a public queer identity. In cultures for which "gay" increasingly signifies domestic, dyadic love, however, the lure of MSM media lies in the "shame" of returning to the closet. The shamelessly crass, dehumanizing, and transactional discourse typical of MSM media is not only often shamefully erotic but also surges with affective, nonsensical, and sensual *potentia*.[24] The abject, self-negating pleasures produced in this digital closet are anathema to both rights-seeking politics and neoliberal injunctions to self-optimize. And in this space, we might be training for a politics that exceeds rights-seeking and neoliberal "winning," a politics beyond the dialectical trap set by the *scientia sexualis* and incomprehensible to quantitative, neoliberal metrics. The sensual nonsense coursing through MSM media might be, like Dickinson's poem, a secret weapon that explodes sensible politics altogether: using an imagination produced only in the closet, we too might become astral, avian – indeed, poetic. If all systems of representation – linguistic, scientific, political – are, at best, artistic renderings of a finally unrepresentable outside, then the conversion of the closet's sublimity into a representational form may, at best, be a poetic politics.[25] For this translation and transition, let the verse of "Emily Dickinson" be our guide.

NOTES

MSM is an abbreviation of "men-seeking-men" or "men-who-have-sex-with-men," and is often used in HIV-prevention campaigns to destigmatize male same-sex behaviour. The logic is this: even though a man has sex with other men, he might not identify as "gay" due to the social stigma attached to that label. Prevention campaigns nonetheless strive to reach this "not-gay" man to provide safe-sex information. I use "MSM" instead of "gay" in this essay first and foremost because one need not identify as "gay" to post a profile on, for example, Grindr. Also, as I will argue, I observe in MSM media, for better and for worse, a delinking of erotic desire and social identity.

1 David Byrne is the lead singer and lyricist of the post-punk/rock group Talking Heads. I am referencing here the group's 1984 concert film, *Stop Making Sense* (Jonathan Demme, dir., 1999, Palm Pictures). The film's title, a command, seems both prescient and astute, given the American political-economic context of the early '80s. Neoliberal policy (e.g., Reagan's trickle-down economics and the gutting of the welfare state) and ideology (Reagan's celebrity and spectacle carrying more weight than his political experience or education) were both beginning to take hold in the United States at this time. Given this context, the film's title seems a clarion call to resist the neoliberal tendency to quantify, rationalize, and measure – so as to commodify – all aspects of human life. Thirty-plus years later, diving into the wreck of neoliberalism, I find Byrne's command more relevant than ever.

2 By "sensual nonsense," I am referring to the haptic practice of cruising MSM media as well as the typically inarticulate, post-grammatical discourse circulating therein. Hunter Hargraves (2013) emphasizes the tactile sensuality of the iPhone in his dissertation chapter "iTouch Therefore iAm: The iPhone as Masturbation": "What I am envisioning here is a

total explosion of tactile vision into a synthesis of hand/iPhone sexual contact: when hand and phone become inextricably tethered to each other, the iPhone becomes a masturbatory aid, a blurring of flesh and cellular technology that demands immediate gratification of both tactile and visual pleasure" (3). According to Hargraves, the sensual and masturbatory fusion of human/machine, enhanced by geosocial cruising apps, restructures queer social relations and communities (22). It is the *form* of this restructured, post-human community that interests me most here. In "Becoming Fungible" (Roach 2015), I designate this form "whatever-belonging," a community in which "difference becomes identical yet remains discreet; units "touch" but do not violate; similitude unbinds subjects, yet singularity remains intact; relating is not a Venn diagram but bounded" (71). I discover in MSM media an ethics of (non)relation circulating in this communal form. I understand MSM media cruising as a practical training in an anti-intersubjective and incommunicative ethics.

3 Grindr (2017) is, according to the company's promotional material and app download data, "the world's largest social networking app for gay, bi, curious and queer men." A spambot is malicious software designed to lure users to websites that infect phones with malware or steal personal information. Grindr has been plagued in recent years by spambots, or, what users call "Grindrbots," causing much frustration and at times defection from the app. For data regarding Grindr's popularity, see Karlan, Feder, and Rial (2015). For more information on Grindrbots, see McCormick (2015).

4 To date, there are twelve Grindr tribe classifications: Bear, Clean-Cut, Daddy, Discreet, Geek, Jock, Leather, Otter, Poz, Rugged, Trans, and Twink.

5 For more on the "circuit-breaker" of post-articulate communication and the ethical promise of trafficking in fungible types in MSM media, see Roach 2015.

6 "Emily Dickinson" is not, in fact, the handle of the Grindr user who responds only in Emily Dickinson verse. I chose this pseudonym in order to, as they say, "protect the innocent." An archive of Grindr texts from "Emily Dickinson" can be found at http://grindrtextsfromemily.tumblr.com.

7 A brief historical example to clarify the distinction between resistant and immanentist political strategy: the legalization of same-sex marriage is without question an enormous achievement for a resistant sexual politics grounded in political representation. However, friendships immanent to queer cultural formations, ones that breech boundaries of normative political, ethical, and relational classification systems, erupt in innovative activism and artistic creation that contribute to a perhaps farther-reaching political project beyond dialectical struggle. I argue in previous work (Roach 2012) that the friendships of shared estrangement cultivated in the AIDS crisis form the backbone of AIDS activism. As in these queer friendships, I see in MSM media the germ of a powerful political project – one that will not perforce blossom into a resistant politics but one whose form and development are

notable for "growing sideways" and retreating from neoliberal logics. The concept "growing sideways" appears in Kathryn Bond Stockton's book *The Queer Child, or Growing Sideways in the Twentieth Century* and concerns "a mode of irregular growth involving odd lingerings, wayward paths, and fertile delays" (promotional description, https://www.dukeu press.edu/the-queer-child-or-growing-sideways-in-the-twentieth-century). In contrast to a resistant politics that works progressively and linearly towards a *telos*, MSM media cruising is typically meandering, repetitive, circular, unproductive – arguably, more of a thumb-twiddling time sink than a motivated, goal-oriented form of engagement. In a very basic sense then, such cruising brushes against the grain of neoliberal productivity norms. Moreover, this "sideways" practice, as I will argue, might also be a practical training in a form of non-communicating that defies neoliberal relationality. For more on growing sideways, see Bond Stockton 2009.

8   To avoid rehashing a story likely told many times in this volume, I offer this quotation from my previous work (Roach 2012) summarizing the intrinsic link between confession and modern sexuality: "When in the nineteenth century sexuality was constituted as a problem of truth, the confession became the lynchpin between sexuality and truth, the discursive rite that provided the subject a knowable, manageable self. Historically rooted in the Christian pastoral, the ritual has become so familiar in modern Western life that 'we no longer perceive it as the effect of a power that constrains us' (Foucault 1990, 60). We view confessions instead as liberatory, redeeming, and purifying rather than as systems of regulation and surveillance" (2012, 21). As I argue in the pages to come, I view the anti-confessional register typical of MSM media as brushing against the grain of a modern (homo)sexual identity grounded in a confession.

9   See Roach 2012, 78–80.

10 See ibid., 17–42.

11 Jane Ward notes, "The number of Americans who believe that sexual orientation is biologically determined has been steadily increasing from 13 percent in 1977, to 31 percent in 1998, to 52 percent in 2010" (2015, 83).

12 Ward argues that the desire for heteronormativity is itself a socially constructed erotic desire, just as much, if not more, as compulsory heterosexuality. She writes: "The investment in heteronormativity is itself a *bodily desire*; in fact, I believe it is *the* embodied heterosexual desire ... It is the desire to be sexually unmarked and normatively gendered. It is a desire that people may well feel in their genitals" (2015, 35).

13 Ward (2015) elaborates on Str8 dude sex and female heteroflexibility on 119–52 and 12–21, respectively. On a side note, the popularity of the *50 Shades of Grey* franchise likewise speaks to the appropriation of queer sex cultures by the heterosexual mainstream. Only in a cultural context in which heterosexuality is authenticated by science can kinky sex be so utterly disengaged from the queer sex cultures in which it blossomed. As long as it is

not *gay* sex, the expression of a biologically incongruent essence, queer sex is permissible, even popular, among the straight-identified.

14 I complicate this statement in this chapter's third section. Although coming out is not a solution to the problem of dialectical sexual politics, it remains necessary to do so at this historical juncture.

15 I refer here to the pioneering work of Adrienne Rich (1982) and a common "LGBT ally" slogan from 1990s activism. Rich's concept of the lesbian continuum includes the "range … of woman-identified experience, not simply the fact that a woman has had or consciously desired genital sexual experience with another woman" (239). Both Rich's concept and the ally slogan run the risk of desexualizing queer politics so as to increase the ranks of a feminist and LGBT political bloc. This conceptual move was met with much resistance, most notably by Leo Bersani (1995).

16 Here I am summarizing important work on Foucault's concept of *homo economicus* – the theoretical subject of neoliberal philosophy – in Brown 2003, Read 2009, and Dilts 2011.

17 For more on MSM media's affirmation of neoliberal subjective and relational ideals, see Roach 2015, 55–7 and 59–60.

18 Cesare Casarino's chapter section "Preliminary Remarks on Emily Dickinson's Last Laugh" deeply informed my interpretation of both Dickinson's poem and the digital closet of MSM media. See Casarino 2002, 186–95. I discuss his work in detail in the following paragraphs.

19 Gilles Deleuze (1986) distinguishes molecular sexuality from molar sexuality. The molecular involves multiple desires of radical difference that are irreducible to the molar, binary code of sexual opposition. The molecular is reined in and territorialized by the molar into representational forms, primarily hetero- and homosexuality. He writes: "But always … a molecular sexuality bubbles away beneath the surface of the integrated sexes" (76). Although most MSM hookup apps attempt to "molarize" sexuality by offering specific identity categories (orientation, tribe, type, etc.), preferences (top/bottom), and a host of other markers that users are encouraged to assign themselves, I nonetheless find in these media the circulation of molecular desires exceeding the codes created to represent them. I discuss this point further in relation to Casarino's concept of the sublime of the closet.

20 For more on opacity and unreliability as queer strategies, see de Villiers 2012, especially "'What Do You Have to Say for Yourself?': Warhol's Opacity," 89–116.

21 Shared estrangement is the affective register of historically queer practices of impersonal intimacy. A relation of shared estrangement refuses a discourse of transcendence that assimilates difference into an identity. Regarding MSM media cruising, the phone screen mediates user interaction. However sensually caressed, it stands as a persistent reminder that inter-subjective fusion is impossible. Tarrying in this uncomfortable relational space can provoke, as it has throughout queer history, unconventional affective ties that form the

22 In figure 29.2, "Emily Dickinson" proclaims that she is "nobody" and welcomes another "nobody" into her closet. The mental image of a closet full of anonymous, perhaps invisible "nobodies" mingling sensually not only calls to mind the queer sex space of the dark room but also envisages the communal form of whatever-belonging I define above: "a non-identitarian collectivity affirming a common, asubjective substance that seethes beneath identifiable individuals." In this sense, the work of "Emily Dickinson" is useful for more than a laugh.

23 For more on the Grindr grid as a visualization of whatever-belonging, see Roach 2105, 70–4.

24 Of course, like Trump's Twitterverse, such media frequently traffic in racist, misogynist, ageist, ableist (and every other "ist") discourse. For more on race and racism in MSM media, see McGlotten 2013, "Feeling Black and Blue," 61–78; on racism and misogyny in Craigslist hookup ads, see Ward 2015, "Average Dudes, Casual Encounters," 119–52.

25 Here I have in mind Friedrich Nietzsche's (1873) critique of Cartesian dualism, perhaps best encapsulated in this quotation: "On the whole it seems to me that the 'right perception' – which would mean the adequate expression of an object in the subject – is a nonentity full of contradictions: between two utterly different spheres, as between subject and object, there is no causality, no accuracy, no expression, but at the utmost an *aesthetical* relation, I mean a suggestive metamorphosis, a stammering translation into quite a distinct foreign language, for which purpose however there is needed at any rate an intermediate sphere, an intermediate force, freely composing and freely inventing" (263).

REFERENCES

Austin, J.L. 1962. *How to Do Things with Words*. William James Lectures series, 1955. Cambridge: Harvard University Press.

Bersani, Leo. 1995. *Homos*. Cambridge, MA: Harvard University Press.

Bond Stockton, Kathryn. 2009. *The Queer Child, or Growing Sideways in the Twentieth Century*. Durham: Duke University Press.

Brown, Wendy. 2003. "Neo-Liberalism and the End of Liberal Democracy." *Theory and Event* 7, no. 1. https://muse.jhu.edu/article/48659.

Casarino, Cesare. 2002. *Modernity at Sea: Melville, Marx, Conrad in Crisis*. Minneapolis: University of Minnesota Press.

Dean, Tim. 2009. *Unlimited Intimacies: Reflections on the Subculture of Barebacking*. Chicago: University of Chicago Press.

Deleuze, Gilles. 1986. *Foucault*. Translated and edited by Seán Hand. Minneapolis: University of Minnesota Press.

— 1995. "Control and Becoming." In *Negotiations, 1972–1990*. Translated by Martin Joughin. New York: Columbia University Press.

de Villiers, Nicholas. 2012. *Opacity and the Closet: Queer Tactics in Foucault, Barthes, and Warhol*. Minneapolis: University of Minnesota Press.

Dickinson, Emily. [ca. 1862] 1999. "They Shut Me Up in Prose (445)." In *The Poems of Emily Dickinson*, edited by Ralph W. Franklin. Cambridge, MA: Harvard University Press. https://www.poetryfoundation.org/poems-and-poets/poems/detail/52196.

Dilts, Andrew. 2011. "From Entrepreneur of the Self to Care of the Self: Neoliberal Governmentality and Foucault's Ethics." *Foucault Studies* 12: 130–46. https://rauli.cbs.dk/index.php/foucault-studies/article/view/3338/3643.

Foucault, Michel. [1976] 1990. *History of Sexuality*. Vol. 1, *An Introduction*. Translated by Robert Hurley. New York: Vintage.

Galvin, Mary C. 1999. "Poltergeist of Form: Emily Dickinson and the Reappropration of Language and Identity." In *Queer Poetics: Five Modernist Women Writers*, 1–20. Westport, CT: Greenwood Press

Grindr. 2017. http://www.grindr.com/about/.

Hargraves, Hunter. 2015. "iTouch, Therefore iAm: The iPhone as Masturbation." In "Viscerally Uncomfortable TV: Affective Spectatorship and Televisual Neoliberalism." PhD dissertation, Brown University.

Karlan, Sarah, J. Lester Feder, and Michelle Rial. 2015. "Here Are the World's Most Popular Dating Apps for Gay Dudes." *BuzzfeedNews*. https://www.buzzfeed.com/skarlan/here-are-the-worlds-most-popular-hook-up-apps-for-gay-dudes.

Kessler, Glenn, and Meg Kelly. 2018. "President Trump Made 2,140 False or Misleading Claims in His First Year." *Washington Post*, 20 January. https://www.washingtonpost.com/news/fact-checker/wp/2018/01/20/president-trump-made-2140-false-or-misleading-claims-in-his-first-year/.

Marx, Karl, and Friedrich Engels. [1848] 1978. "Manifesto of the Communist Party." In *The Marx-Engels Reader*, edited by Robert C. Tucker, 473–500. New York: W.W. Norton.

McCormick, Joseph Patrick. 2015. "WARNING: These Grindr Profiles Are Actually Robots Trying to Steal Your Info." *Pink News*, 8 November. http://www.pinknews.co.uk/2015/08/11/warning-these-grindr-profiles-are-actually-robots-trying-to-steal-your-info/.

McGlotten, Shaka. 2013. *Virtual Intimacies: Media, Affect, and Queer Sociality*. Albany: State University of New York Press.

Nietzsche, Friedrich. [1873] 2005. "On Truth and Lying in the Extra-Moral Sense." In *Literary Theory: An Anthology*, edited by Julie Rivkin and Michael Ryan, 262–6. Malden, MA: Blackwell Publishers.

Read, Jason. 2009. "A Genealogy of Homo-Economicus: Neo-Liberalism and the Production of Subjectivity." *Foucault Studies* 6: 25–36. https://rauli.cbs.dk/index.php/foucault-studies/article/view/2465/2463.

Rich, Adrienne. [1982] 1993. "Compulsory Heterosexuality and Lesbian Existence." In *The Lesbian and Gay Studies Reader*, edited by Henry Abelove, Michèle Aina Barale, and David M. Halperin, 227–54. London: Routledge.

Roach, Tom. 2012. *Friendship as a Way of Life: Foucault, AIDS, and the Politics of Shared Estrangement*. Albany: State University of New York Press.

— 2015. "Becoming Fungible: Queer Intimacies in Social Media." *Qui Parle: Critical Humanities and Social Sciences* 23, no 2: 55–87.

Ward, Jane. 2015. *Not Gay: Sex between Straight White Men*. New York: New York University Press.

Winnubst, Shannon. 2012. "The Queer Thing about Neoliberal Pleasure: A Foucauldian Warning." *Foucault Studies* 14: 79–97. https://rauli.cbs.dk/index.php/foucault-studies/article/view/3889/4235.

Figures

Foreword
Ken Plummer
00.1 Publicity still, Johnnie Ray, 1952 | x
00.2 Poster for *Victim*, dir. Basil Dearden, 1961 | xii

Introduction
Thomas Waugh and Brandon Arroyo
0.1 Poster for *I Confess*, dir. Alfred Hitchcock, 1953 | 4
0.2 Poster for *Le Confessionnal*, dir. Robert Lepage, 1995 | 4
0.3 *Boy with Machine*, oil on canvas, Richard Lindner, 1954 | 12
0.4 "Leave Britney Alone," Chris Crocker, YouTube, 2007 | 14

PART ONE SCIENTIA SEXUALIS
Activism

1 The Treachery of Rape Representation
Tal Kastner and Ummni Khan
1.1 *The Treachery of Images*, oil on canvas, René Magritte, 1928–29 | 30
1.2 *Ceci n'est pas un viol* (This Is Not a Rape), Emma Sulkowicz, 2015 | 36
1.3 *Ceci n'est pas un viol* (This Is Not a Rape), Emma Sulkowicz, 2015 | 36

2 More Than Just Selfies: #Occupotty, Affect, and Confession as Activism
Andie Shabbar
2.1 Michael Hughes, #Occupotty tweet, Twitter, 2015 | 50
2.2 Brae Carnes, WeJustNeedToPee, Instagram, 2015 | 57

2.3 "Trans Women Belong Here (in this bathroom and in world)," Instagram, 2017 | 61

3 Against Authenticity: The Feminist Turn in N. Maxwell Lander's Video Work
Naomi de Szegheo-Lang with N. Maxwell Lander
3.1 Aesthetic overload, *'98 Bit*, dir. N. Maxwell Lander, 2012 | 71
3.2 Disruption via multiple screens, *Porn Game*, dir. N. Maxwell Lander, 2014 | 75

4 Blogging Affects and Other Inheritances of Feminist Consciousness-Raising
Ela Przybylo and Veronika Novoselova
4.1 *xoJane* online magazine, 2016 | 94
4.2 *Jezebel* online magazine, 2016 | 98

5 "YES I'M GAY": The Mediality of Coming Out
Silke Jandl
5.1 "I'm Bisexual," Shane Dawson TV, YouTube, 2015 | 111
5.2 Dawson and prom date, "I HATE MYSELFIE 2," Shane Dawson TV, YouTube, 2015 | 117
5.3 Dawson and Monson, "IT GETS WORSE," Shane Dawson TV, YouTube, 2016 | 119

Author, Subject, and Audience

6 "Aren't You Worried about What People Might Say? What People Might Do?": Lady Gaga and the "Heeling" of Queer Trauma
Jacob Evoy
6.1 Jacob Evoy, February 2013 | 131

7 Letters to Nina Hartley: Pornography, Parrhesia, and Sexual Confessions
Ingrid Olson
7.1 Letter from Robert, 19 August 1997 | 146
7.2 Letter from Trace, p. 1, 17 March 1998 | 148
7.3 Letter from Trace, p. 2, 17 March 1998 | 149
7.4 Letter from Carole, undated | 151
7.5 Letter from Davey One Step, undated | 153

8 Femininities of Excess: The Cinematic Confessions of Rituparno Ghosh
Shohini Ghosh
8.1 Rituparno Ghosh, the public intellectual | 159
8.2 The young Rabindranath Tagore, in *Jeevan Smrit*, dir. Rituparno Ghosh, 2013 | 170
8.3 Ritu and Shohini Ghosh | 172

9 The Videomaker and the Rent Boy: Gay-for-Pay Confessional in *101 Rentboys* and *Broke Straight Boys TV*
Nicholas de Villiers
9.1 Poster for *101 Rent Boys*, dir. Randy Barbato and Fenton Bailey, 2000 | 179
9.2 Advertisement for *Broke Straight Boys* TV, Here TV, Twitter post, 2 December 2014 | 184

10 Confessions: Watching the Masturbating Boy (Excerpts)
Intervals, an anonymous collective
10.1 Hazel sexting us, *Hazel*, dir. Tamer Ruggli, 2012 | 207
10.2 Hazel erased, *Hazel*, dir. Tamer Ruggli, 2012 | 209
10.3 Cutout image, unidentified frame | 215
10.4 *L2TC 28/4/2014 Gimme some fuckin requests!* | 220

PART TWO **ARS EROTICA**
Pornographies

11 Like a Prayer: Confessing My Beatific-Cum-Demonic Visions of Men (and God?)
Connor Steele
11.1 Connor Steele and friend | 239

12 Camming and Erotic Capital: The Pornographic as an Expression of Neoliberalism
Éric Falardeau
12.1 Chaturbate.com, 2017 | 250
12.2 VicAlouqua, Cam4.com, 2017 | 253

13 Confessions of a Masked Pornographer: Reorienting Gay Male Identity via Bodily Confession
Brandon Arroyo

13.1 Keller and black performer, *Colby Does Kentucky*, dir. Colby Keller, 2015 | 277

13.2 Intercutting Muybridge's donkey in *Colby Does Kentucky*, dir. Colby Keller 2015 | 277

13.3 Keller and black performer, *Colby Does Virginia*, dir. Colby Keller 2015 | 279

13.4 Makeshift pornographic confessional, *Colby Does Virginia*, dir. Colby Keller 2015 | 280

13.5 Original Grindr logo | 288

13.6 The Black Spark | 288

13.7 *Facial Weaponization Suite Fag Face Mask*, 20 October 2012, Los Angeles | 292

14 Sadean Confessions in Virginie Despentes's Punk-Porn-Feminism
Valentina Denzel

14.1 DVD cover image, *Baise Moi*, dir. Virginie Despentes and Coralie Trinh Thi, 2000 | 301

14.2 Sade's *Philosophie dans le boudoir*, first edition (1795), title page | 304

15 *Fuck Yeah Levi Karter!* and New Authenticities
Daniel Laurin

15.1 Hotel room scene collage, *Fuck Yeah Levi Karter!*, dir. Jake Jaxson and Levi Karter, CockyBoys, 2013 | 322

15.2 Karter's home movie, *Fuck Yeah Levi Karter!*, dir. Jake Jaxson and Levi Karter, CockyBoys, 2013 | 324

15.3 Karter's couch, *Fuck Yeah Levi Karter!* | 325

15.4 Karter's vlog setup, *Fuck Yeah Levi Karter!* | 331

15.5 Tegan's confessional, *Gabriel Clark Fucks Tegan Zayne*, dir. Jake Jaxson, Cockyboys, 2016 | 331

15.6 Sex show at Steamworks, *Fuck Yeah Levi Karter!* | 333

15.7 Hotel room scene, *Fuck Yeah Levi Karter!* | 333

16 Circuitous Pleasures, Guilt, and Pain: *Nymph()maniac* and the Pornographic Hard Code
Justine T. McLellan

16.1 Joe with two black performers, *Nymph()maniac*, dir. Lars von Trier, 2013 | 341

16.2 Joe torches a car, *Nymph()maniac*, dir. Lars von Trier, 2013 | 346

17 Porn Fast
Shaka McGlotten

17.1 "Swipe Left" gif, 9GAG, 2015 | 358

17.2 CritiqueYourDickPic, 2016 | 365

17.3 Screenshot, spandakarikas, Snapchat, 2018 | 367

Documentaries

18 "I Confess: I Was the Girl in the Shadows"
Rebecca Sullivan

18.1 The author in the shadows, 1980s | 374

18.2 Happily married mom with dog, mortgage, and SUV, 2010s | 375

19 Queer Auto-Porn-Art: Genealogies, Aesthetics, Ethics, and Desire
Thomas Waugh

19.1 Vigorous authorial thrusting, *Super 8 ½*, dir. Bruce LaBruce, 1994 | 387

19.2 Docuporn manifesto, *Girl on Girl*, dir. Michael V. Smith (Miss Cookie LaWhore), 2004 | 389

19.3 Channelling ancestors, *Arthur Rimbaud*, dir. An T. Horné, 2014 | 392–3

19.4 Branden Miller (aka Pradaboiswag / Miss Prada / Joanne the Scammer), Instagram, 2010– | 393

19.5 Colby Keller, in *Colby Does America*, 2015 | 395

20 On Not Seeing All: *The Incomplete*, Sexual Play, and the Ethics of the Frame
Susanna Paasonen

20.1 Wolfe introduces himself, *Der Unfertige* (*The Incomplete*), dir. Jan Soldat, 2013 | 409

20.2 Domestic routines, *Der Unfertige* (*The Incomplete*) | 414

20.3 Wolf in close-up, *Der Unfertige* (*The Incomplete*) | 419

21 To Queer Things Up: Sexing the Self in the Queer Documentary Web Series
Sarah E.S. Sinwell
21.1 *Losing It with John Stamos*, Yahoo!, 2013 | 428
21.2 Cast of *The Peculiar Kind*, 2012 | 429

22 A Man with a Mother: *Tarnation* and the Subject of Confession
Damon R. Young
22.1 Jonathan, age eleven, *Tarnation*, dir. Jonathan Caouette, 2003 | 443
22.2 Jonathan, age thirty-one, *Tarnation* | 443
22.3 Sublime infinity of the to-be-looked-at, *Tarnation* | 448
22.4 Like mother, like son, *Tarnation* | 449

Transmedia

23 Looking, Stroking, and Speaking: A Queer Ethics of MAP Desire
Anonymous
23.1 "me and matt boxing," Tayyutube3, YouTube, 2008 | 456

24 Playing Confession: Gaming, Autobiography, and the Elusive Self
Stephen Charbonneau
24:1 "Girly Clothes Don't Fit," mini-game from Anna Anthropy's *dys4ia* video game, 2012 | 480
24.2 Hannah's interrogation, Sam Barlow's *Her Story* video game, 2015 | 484

25 From a "Disappeared Aesthetics" to a "Trans-Aesthetics": Derek Jarman and Ming Wong's Image-Based Technologies of the Self
Milan Pribisic
25.1 *Blue*, dir. Derek Jarman, 1993 | 490
25.2 *Blue*, dir. Derek Jarman, 1993 | 490
25.3 *Angst Essen/Eat Fear*, dir. Ming Wong, 2008 | 495

26 Writing Intimacy: Fantasy, New Media, and Confession in Marie Calloway's *what purpose did I serve in your life*
Eleanor Ty
26.1 Dawn West's online review of Marie Calloway's *what purpose did i serve in your life*, 7 June 2013 | 506

26.2 "Interview with 23 Year Old Sex Memoirist Marie Calloway," ONTD blog post, 23 June 2013 | 510

27 *Hentai* Confessions: Transgression and "Sexual Technologies of Self" in Akihiko Shiota's *Moonlight Whispers*
Ron S. Judy
27.1 Voice-over confession, *Moonlight Whispers*, dir. Akihiko Shiota 1999 | 518
27.2 *Hentai* practice of the self, *Moonlight Whispers* | 522

28 Porno-Graphing: "Dirtiness" and Self-Objectification
AnnaMaria Pinaka
28.1 Leigh Ledare, "Me and Mom in Photobooth," 2008 | 540
28.2 Leigh Ledare, *Double Bind (diptych #6/25)*, 2010 | 543

29 Shut Me Up in Grindr: Anti-confessional Discourse and Sensual Nonsense in MSM Media
Tom Roach
29.1 Grindrbot conversation, Joseph Patrick McCormick, "WARNING: These Grindr Profiles Are Actually Robots Trying to Steal Your Info," 2015 | 552
29.2 Grindr conversation, GrindrTextsFromEmily, Tumblr, 25 November 2014 | 553

Contributors

ANONYMOUS is a social scientist, writer, researcher, and teacher in a major North American city.

BRANDON ARROYO is a PhD graduate of Concordia University, film and moving image studies. His dissertation, "Becoming Pornographic: Identity, Affect, and Networked Assemblages," uses the framework of affect theory to analyze the circulation of pornography within gay social assemblages and its utilization within identity construction. He has been published multiple times in the journal *Porn Studies* and is a member of its editorial board. He has also written for *MediaCommons* and *Textual Overtures*. The recipient of a Student Writing Award from the Society for Cinema and Media Studies, he is also the creator and host of the Porno Cultures Podcast, where he interviews scholars focusing on sexual representation in the media: pornocultures.podomatic.com. Twitter: @brandrroyo. arroyo.brandon@gmail.com.

STEPHEN CHARBONNEAU is associate professor of film and media studies at Florida Atlantic University, where he is also the director of the MA program in communication studies, School of Communication and Multimedia Studies. His work on media pedagogy, youth media, and documentary film has been published in *Jump Cut*, *Journal of Popular Film and Television*, *Framework*, *Spectator*, and several anthologies. His first monograph, *Projecting Race: Postwar America, Civil Rights, and Documentary Film*, was published in 2016 (Wallflower Press). He is currently editing an anthology on global media activism, entitled "InsUrgent Media" (with Chris Robé, under review), researching essayistic digital cultures, and writing a biography of George C. Stoney. scharbo1@fau.edu.

VALENTINA DENZEL is associate professor of French at Michigan State University. She received her doctoral degree at Paris Diderot University (Paris 7) in comparative literature. Her primary field of research is seventeenth- and eighteenth-century French literature. In her book *Les mille et un visages de la virago: Marfisa et Bradamante entre continuation et variation* (Garnier Classique 2016), she analyzes the evolution of the representation of the woman warrior in French and Italian literatures from the Middle Ages to the Enlightenment by taking into consideration the political and historical context of this evolution and the symbolic value of the woman warrior in each specific time period. Her second book project analyzes the representation of violence, gender, and pornography in Sade's oeuvre, and its link to his own time period as well as his legacy in popular cultures. She is the co-PI for the HWW-sponsored project "Legacies of the Enlightenment." vdenzel@msu.edu.

NAOMI DE SZEGHEO-LANG is a PhD graduate of gender, feminist, and women's studies at York University. Her research analyzes representations of intimacy in online public cultures and in responsive forms of queer and feminist art. Her dissertation, "Queer Feeling: Affective Bonds, Intimate Possibilities," looks to queer and/or unexpected forms of intimacy that have taken hold of the public imaginary in recent years – professional cuddling, feminist pornography, interspecies friendships, and object-oriented sexualities. Her writing on affect, intimacy, and queer representation has appeared in *Atlantis* journal and *Disrupting Queer Inclusion* (UBC Press 2015). Naomi is also a professional editor and an academic writing coach. naomilang.ca.

NICHOLAS DE VILLIERS is associate professor of English and film, University of North Florida. He is the author of *Opacity and the Closet: Queer Tactics in Foucault, Barthes, and Warhol* (University of Minnesota Press 2012) and *Sexography: Sex Work in Documentary* (University of Minnesota Press 2017). He is currently writing a book on spatial and sexual disorientation and cruising in the films of Tsai Ming-liang. He would like to acknowledge the generous support of the 2016 Florida Blue Ethics Fellowship. n.devilliers@unf.edu.

JACOB EVOY is a PhD candidate at Western University in Canada completing a collaborative degree in women's studies and feminist research, and transitional justice and post-conflict reconstruction. Their doctoral research examines the roles of non-normative sexualities within rebuilding processes following genocide through an oral history of LGBTQ children of Holocaust survivors entitled

"Queering the Post-Holocaust Experience: An Oral History of LGBTQ Children of Holocaust Survivors." Their research interests include queer theory, trauma studies, Holocaust and genocide studies, and queer history. jacobevoy2@gmail.com.

ÉRIC FALARDEAU is a PhD candidate in communication studies at the Université du Québec à Montréal. His research examines the representations of the male body in pornographic online audiovisual production. He holds an MA in film studies (Université de Montréal) in which he wrote about the depiction of bodily fluids in gore and pornographic movies. His first feature film, *Thanatomorphose* (2012), won fifteen awards at international festivals and is distributed in a dozen countries. Falardeau was the guest curator at the exhibition Secrets and Illusions: The Magic of Special Effects, presented at the Cinémathèque québécoise (2013–17). He co-edited with Simon Laperrière the anthology *Bleu nuit: Histoire d'une cinéphilie nocturne* (Éditions Somme Toute 2014) and wrote *Une histoire des effets spéciaux au Québec* (Éditions Somme Toute 2013). His most recent book is *Le corps souillé: Gore, pornographie et fluides corporels* (L'instant Même, 2019), http://www.instantmeme.com/ebi-addins/im/ViewBooks.aspx?id=3282. He is currently working on his second feature film. www.ericfalardeau.com.

SHOHINI GHOSH is Sajjad Zaheer Chaired Professor at the AJK Mass Communication Research Centre at Jamia Millia Islamia, New Delhi. She is the director of *Tales of the Night Fairies* (2002), a documentary on the sex workers rights movement in Calcutta and the author of *Fire: A Queer Classic* (Arsenal Pulp Press, Vancouver / Orient Publishing, New Delhi 2010). Ghosh has been visiting professor in a number of universities within and outside India and has had a long association with CREA's Sexuality, Gender and Rights Program. She writes on contemporary media, speech and censorship, popular cinema, visual cultures, documentary and issues of gender and sexuality. She is currently working on a book titled "Violence and the Spectral Muslim: Action, Affect and Bombay Cinema at the Turn of the 21st Century." sghosh1@gmail.com.

INTERVALS is an anonymous collective with many decades of combined intellectual, professional, and activist experience, in LGBTQ and other movements. Intervals researches, publishes, and presents on the topic of intergenerational sexuality and politics in journalistic and academic contexts. They choose to be anonymous due to the current political climate and maintain no persistent public digital identity, social-media presence, or email account, and do not participate openly on any website or forum.

SILKE JANDL received her BA and MA in English and American studies from the University of Graz, Austria. As part of her alma mater's joint master's degree program, she studied for a semester at the University of Roehampton, London. During the 2013–14 academic year, she served as a teaching assistant at the University of Minnesota and enrolled in the PhD program in English and American studies in the fall of 2014, defending her dissertation in 2019. In March 2015, she assumed a part-time position at the Centre for Intermediality Studies in Graz and began teaching classes in the American Studies Department. She was awarded the dean's prize of the University of Graz for her publication "The Lizzie Bennet Diaries: Adapting Jane Austen in the Internet Age." silke.jandl@uni-graz.at.

RON S. JUDY is associate professor at National Chung Hsing University in Taiwan. His research focuses on East/West comparative literature and culture. ron_judy@nchu.edu.tw.

TAL KASTNER is acting assistant professor at New York University School of Law. Her research focuses on contracts and on the intersection of law, culture, and society. Her work has appeared in *Law and Social Inquiry*, *Law and Literature*, and the *Indiana Journal of Global Legal Studies*, among other publications. She holds a PhD in English from Princeton University and a JD from Yale Law School and has practised as a transactional attorney in New York. tal.kastner@nyu.edu.

UMMNI KHAN is associate professor in law and the joint chair in women's studies at Carleton University and the University of Ottawa. Her research addresses the legal and cultural construction of sexual deviancy in relation to gender, racialization, class, and disability, along with other axes of difference and identity. She has recent publications in *Studies in Gender and Sexuality*, *Oñati Socio-Legal Series*, *Canadian Journal of Law and Society*, and *Current Sexual Health Reports*. ummni.khan@carleton.ca

N. MAXWELL LANDER is a photographer, designer, VR-maker, and MDes student in digital futures at OCAD University in Toronto. His recent work critically engages with masculinity in ways that range from subtle and playful to brutal and unnerving. His artistic interests include nudity, queer sex, bold images, and overly ambitious projects. He is part of the queer trash collective Only Dead Men and an active member of the feminist video-game organization Dames Making Games. Will take headshots for money. max@maxwellander.ca.

DANIEL LAURIN is a PhD candidate at the Cinema Studies Institute and a member of the Collaborative Graduate Program in Sexual Diversity Studies at the University of Toronto. His dissertation, supported by the Social Sciences and Humanities Research Council of Canada (SSHRC), focuses on straight performers in online gay pornography and how the genre uses confession and the aesthetics and conventions of amateur video and reality television to support its claims to authenticity. His research interests include gay pornography, pre-AIDS sexualities and identities, and the queer personal archive. d.laurin@mail.utoronto.ca.

SHAKA MCGLOTTEN is associate professor of media studies at Purchase College-SUNY. Their research focuses on sexuality, race, and emergent media technologies. They are the author of *Virtual Intimacies: Media, Affect, and Queer Sociality* and co-editor of *Zombie Sexuality: Essays on Desire and the Living Dead* and *Black Genders and Sexualities*. shaka.mcglotten@purchase.edu.

JUSTINE T. MCLELLAN is an audio producer and independent researcher based in Montreal and Brooklyn. She teaches literacy through film at the Brooklyn Public Library, and produces *The Oldest Profession*, a podcast about the history of sex workers, theoldestprofessionpodcast.com. Her master's thesis contrasted the evolution of psycho-medical discourse on BDSM with twenty-first-century onscreen representations of kink. Her research interests include pornography, queer spectatorship, the representation of BDSM in pop culture, sex-workers' rights activism, and witches. justine.mclellan@gmail.com.

VERONIKA NOVOSELOVA has a PhD from York University's Gender, Feminist and Women's Studies program. Her dissertation identifies, contextualizes, and analyzes responses to verbal violence on digital media platforms across Canada and the United States. Located at the intersections of media studies and feminist theory, her most recent research explores how digitally mediated confessions reveal negotiations of privilege and difference in feminist blogging cultures. In addition to teaching and research, she has served as a managing editor at *Feral Feminisms*, a peer-reviewed multimedia journal based in Toronto. veronika.novoselova@gmail.com.

INGRID OLSON is a PhD graduate in the Centre for Cross-Faculty Inquiry, University of British Columbia. Her doctoral research examines the concept of "speaking sex" through an analysis of pornography star Nina Hartley's fan-mail archive. Her areas of research include pornography studies, BDSM studies, sexuality studies, sexuality and the law, sexual archives, and trans and gender studies. Academic publications include "Long Jeanne Silver: Dis/ability, Agency, and Porn" and "Too 'Extreme': Gonzo, Snuff, and Governmentality" in *Porn Studies*; "Abduction in the Public Sphere: Sadomasochism, Surveillance, and Counterpublics" in *Sexuality and Culture*; "Asking for It: Erotic Asphyxiation and the Limitations of Sexual Consent" in *Jindal Global Law Review*; and the chapter "Disidentifications: Alternative Sex/Gender Identities through Sadomasochistic Praxes" in *Queer Sexualities: Staking Out New Territories in Queer Studies*. She acknowledges the Center for Sex and Culture in San Francisco for access to the Nina Hartley fan archive. ingrid.olson@alumni.ubc.ca.

SUSANNA PAASONEN is professor of media studies at University of Turku, Finland. With an interest in studies of popular culture, sexuality, affect, pornography and media theory, she is most recently the author of *Carnal Resonance: Affect and Online Pornography* (MIT Press 2011) and *Many Splendored Things: Thinking Sexuality and Play* (Goldsmiths Press 2018), co-editor of *Networked Affect* (MITP 2015, with Ken Hillis and Michael Petit) and co-author of *Not Safe for Work: Sex, Humor and Risk in Social Media* with Kylie Jarrett and Ben Light (MITP 2019). Her work has appeared in journals such as *Sexualities, Porn Studies,* GLQ, *New Media and Society, Feminist Theory, European Journal of Cultural Studies, International Journal of Cultural Studies, Velvet Light Trap,* and *Television and New Media*. susanna.paasonen@utu.fi.

ANNAMARIA PINAKA is a visual artist, performer, and writer. The focus of her work is the use of life material in art and the relationship between sex, sexuality, and image making. Using the self as source of performance, she creates a visual language that borrows from the rhetorics of pornography but relates also to the domestic realm, the mundane, banal, low-tech, and lived ordinary. In 2017 she completed her practice-led PhD thesis, "Porno-Graphing: 'Dirty' Subjectivities and Self-Objectification in Contemporary Lens-Based Art," at the Department of Theatre, Drama and Performance at Roehampton University, London (UK). An element of her PhD has been published as *Porno-Graphing: What Do 'Dirty' Sexual Subjectivities Do to Art?* (Onomatopee, Eindhoven, NL, 2017). annamaria.pinaka@gmail.com.

KEN PLUMMER is emeritus professor in the Department of Sociology at the University of Essex, where he taught between 1975 and 2005. He is the author of *Telling Sexual Stories* (1995), was the founder editor of the journal *Sexualities*, and has researched and published widely in the fields of critical humanism, narrative, and critical sexualities studies. His most recent books are *Cosmopolitan Sexualities: Hope and the Humanist Imagination* (Polity Press 2015) and *Narrative Power: The Struggle for Human Value* (Polity Press 2019). plumkessex@gmail.com.

MILAN PRIBISIC is adjunct instructor in media history and theory at the School of Communication, Loyola University Chicago, researching, presenting, and publishing in the areas of intermedia dialogism, adaptation studies, and queer representations. He has contributed to the 2009 anthology *Playing with Memories: Essays on Guy Maddin*, edited by David Church. His book-length study *Sveti Fasbinder: Queer Mu itelj i Mu enik* (Saint Fassbinder: Queer Martyr and Torturer) was published in 2014 by Film Center Serbia in Belgrade. mpribis@luc.edu.

ELA PRZYBYLO is an assistant professor in the Department of English at Illinois State University. Her forthcoming book *Asexual Erotics: Intimate Readings of Compulsory Sexuality* (Ohio State University Press 2019) draws on Audre Lorde's conceptualization of the erotic to rethink the role of sex for feminist and queer thought and practice. Ela's work on asexuality has appeared in GLQ, *Sexualities, Psychology and Sexuality, Feminism and Psychology* and in *Asexualities: Feminist and Queer Perspectives*, and *Introducing the New Sexuality Studies* (3rd ed.). She is co-editor of *On the Politics of Ugliness* (Palgrave 2018). https://przybyloela.wordpress.com/.

TOM ROACH is professor of literary and cultural studies and coordinator of women's, gender, and sexuality studies at Bryant University, Rhode Island. His most recent book is *Friendship as a Way of Life: Foucault, AIDS, and the Politics of Shared Estrangement* (State University of New York Press 2012). He is currently completing his second monograph, tentatively titled *Screen Love: Queer*

Intimacies in the Grindr Era, also to be published by SUNY Press. His work has appeared in *Qui Parle*, GLQ, *Cultural Critique, New Formations, Theory and Event*, and *Quarterly Review of Film and Video*. Most of his scholarship is available at bryant.academia.edu/TomRoach. troach@bryant.edu.

ANDIE SHABBAR is a PhD candidate in the Department of Women's Studies and lecturer in the Faculty of Information and Media Studies, Western University. Her dissertation, "Queer Autonomous Zones: Surveillance, Art, and the Politics of Imperceptibility," examines the creative means by which queer and Indigenous activism subverts contemporary state-capitalist practices of sexual surveillance in the twenty-first century. She is particularly interested in the affective relationship between art, activism, and philosophy and how they can be brought together to form new images of thought along with unconventional modes of protest. Her primary objects of analysis include glitch art, queer bathroom graffiti, the NoDAPL movement at Standing Rock, and public installation artwork. She teaches courses in sexuality, media, queer theory, and virtual worlds. Her research has been published in *Rhizomes* and *Studies in Visual Arts and Communication*. On Twitter: @andiedentata. ashabba@uwo.ca.

SARAH E.S. SINWELL is assistant professor in the Department of Film and Media Arts, University of Utah. She has published essays on Kickstarter, *Green Porno*, and *Mysterious Skin* in *A Companion to American Indie Film* (Wiley 2016), *Women's Studies Quarterly*, and *Asexualities: Feminist and Queer Perspectives* (Routledge 2014). Examining shifting modes of independent film distribution and exhibition on YouTube, Netflix and SundanceTV, her current book project redefines independent cinema in an era of media convergence. sarah.sinwell@utah.edu.

CONNOR STEELE is a PhD student supervised by Lori G. Beaman and Peter Beyer in the Department of Classics and Religious Studies at the University of Ottawa. He has previously published in the *Religion and Diversity Project Ejournal* (2017) on depictions of messianism and heterosexist violence in the Netflix series *Orange Is the New Black*. His research, which received the Joseph Bombardier award from the Social Science and Humanities Research Council (SSHRC), focuses on the role of shame in Canadian constitutional culture particularly with respect to the contested and unfolding boundaries of religious freedom and sexual-orientation equality rights. After completing his PhD, he desires to go to law school. He strives to be an engaged academic, and his advocacy was responsible for the proposed bill of the current Canadian federal Liberal government that would repeal the last anal sex law from the Criminal Code of Canada. cstee005@uottawa.ca.

REBECCA SULLIVAN is professor of Women's Studies at the University of Calgary. Her book, *Pornography: Structures, Agency and Performance* (co-authored with Alan McKee, Polity Press 2015), was called "a model of nuanced thinking … that breaks the stalemate and provides important avenues for constructive conversation." She is currently leading a Social Science and Humanities Research Council (SSHRC) funded project entitled "The Legacy of Studio D for Canadian Feminist Media Activism." Sullivan is the author/co-author/co-editor of seven books and a member of the *Porn Studies* editorial board. rsulliva@ucalgary.ca.

ELEANOR TY is professor of English and film studies at Wilfrid Laurier University. She has published eleven books, on cultural memory, Asian North American issues, and eighteenth-century British literature. Author of *Asianfail: Narratives of Disenchantment and the Model Minority* (University of Illinois Press 2017), *Unfastened: Globality and Asian North American Narratives* (University of Minnesota Press 2010), and *The Politics of the Visible in Asian North American Narratives* (University of Toronto Press 2004), she has recently co-edited two volumes on cultural memory, *Canadian Literature and Cultural Memory*, co-edited with Cynthia Sugars (Oxford University Press 2014), and *The Memory Effect: The Remediation of Memory in Literature and Film*, with Russell J.A. Kilbourn (Wilfrid Laurier University Press 2013). ety@wlu.ca.

THOMAS WAUGH is distinguished professor emeritus, film studies and sexuality, Concordia University, Montreal. His books include the anthologies *Show Us Life: Towards a History and Aesthetics of the Committed Documentary* (1984), *Challenge for Change: Activist Documentary at the National Film Board of Canada* (with Michael Baker and Ezra Winton, 2010), and *The Perils of Pedagogy: The Works of John Greyson* (with Brenda Longfellow and Scott MacKenzie, 2013); the collections *The Fruit Machine: Twenty Years of Writings on Queer Cinema* (2000) and *The Right to Play Oneself: Looking Back on Documentary Film* (2011); the monographs *Hard to Imagine: Gay Male Eroticism in Photography and Film from Their Beginnings to Stonewall* (1996), *The Romance of Transgression in Canada: Sexualities, Nations, Moving Images* (2006), *Montreal Main* (2010), and *The Conscience of Cinema: The Films of Joris Ivens* (2016, SCMS

Kovacs Book Award); and the edited art books *Outlines: Underground Gay Graphics from before Stonewall* (2002), *Lust Unearthed: Vintage Gay Graphics from the Dubek Collection* (with Willie Walker, 2004), and *Gay Art: A Historic Collection* (scholarly edition, with Felix Lance Falkon, 2006). He is also coeditor with Matthew Hays of the Queer Film Classics book series (2008–19, Arsenal Pulp). Thomas.Waugh@concordia.ca.

DAMON R. YOUNG is assistant professor of French and film and media at the University of California, Berkeley, and a faculty member in the Program in Critical Theory. He is the author of *Making Sex Public and Other Cinematic Fantasies* (Duke University Press 2018) and co-editor, with Nico Baumbach and Genevieve Yue, of a special issue of *Social Text* titled "The Cultural Logic of Contemporary Capitalism." damonyoung@berkeley.edu.

Index

'98 Bit, 71–5
101 Rent Boys, 177–92
1950s, ix–x
1960s, x–xv, 9, 83–7, 249, 302, 465, 469n9, 501
1970s, xiv–xv, xvii, 86, 137, 327
1980s, xv, xviii, 6, 91, 302, 326, 371, 373, 551
1990s, xvii, 6, 145, 197, 321, 355, 379, 387, 497; 1995, 3–4, 9
2000s, 84, 92, 173n5
2010s, 375, 473–4

abjection and self-abasement, 504–5, 508, 512, 565
able-bodiedness. *See* disability
academia, 15–18, 20, 22, 23, 66, 194, 241, 364, 385, 388, 398; academic freedom, 18
ACT UP, xviii, 134n1
activism, xiii–iv, xviii, 49–64, 147, 174n5, 189–90, 194, 312–13, 423–5, 431, 535, 564, 566n7; digital, 349
adaptation, 108, 116, 496, 498–500, 515
addiction, 353, 355, 359–64; addiction industries, 364
adolescence, 19, 107–28, 453, 456, 517
Adorno, Theodor, 477–8, 486
aesthetics: amateur, 95; of excess, 71
affect, 49–64, 130; affective body, 294n4; affective geography, 9; affective intensity, 51, 268, 417; affective map, 281, 282, 475; affective tool, 50–1; theory, 83–106, 263–99
African Americans, 21, 274–80, 389–90, 392
African arts, 285
African characters, 340–1, 431
age of consent, 21, 225n5, 468n5
agency, 194, 202, 355, 505, 534, 537–9, 541
aging, xvi–xvii. *See also* seniors

Ahmed, Sara, 88, 90, 97, 130
AIDS pandemic, xvii–xviii, 387, 490–4
Alexander, Jonathan, and Elizabeth Losh, 328
alibi, 357
Alighieri, Dante, 242
Allen, Pamela, 89, 90
Allen, Steven, 524–5
Allen Ginsberg, 391
alternate public sphere, 411
alt-right, 549
amateur photography and video, 94–5, 458, 474; pornography, 248–50, 254, 256, 275, 284, 289, 294n5, 319–34, 334n4
America Online, 3, 9
anal sex, 139–40, 152, 155n2, 279, 350n1, 363, 380, 391, 468n5
analog, 6–7, 378
Angst Essen/Eat Fear, 495, 497
animation, 423–8
anonymous authorship, 17–21, 61, 382, 391
anthropology, 203, 213, 223
Anthropy, Anna, 473–81
Antichrist, 346
"apolitical," 538–9
Aquinas, St Thomas, 242
archives, 22, 93, 137–8, 144–5, 154, 196, 206, 212, 221, 224, 382, 436–52, 402, 454, 460, 465, 482; digital, 484–5; archival footage, 396, 481–7
Arekti Premer Golpo, 162
Arroyo, Brandon, 3, 7, 8, 9, 10, 24n1
ars erotica, 15, 286, 523, 525
art: art-making, 536, 539, 546; "art-value," 533, 547n1; art world, 379–9; "art/porn debate," 541; cinema, 387; gallery and art-house panics, 16. *See also* sex panics; video
Arthur, Paul Longley, 505

Arthur Rimbaud, 391–3
asexual, 239, 241
Ashookh, 168
Asian American, 504–14
askesis, 363, 366, 460, 463
aspect ratio, 321, 476
assemblage, 51, 54–5, 59–60, 266–7, 289; social or technological, 13, 269
Athletic Model Guild, 465
audience, 15, 30–42, 71, 133, 254, 383, 423, 465
Augustine of Hippo, St, 31, 44nn2–3, 143, 237–8
aura, 255
Austin, J.L., 509, 561
authenticity, 31, 67–9, 72–4, 111–22, 255–6, 260n13, 394, 425, 504, 535, 541, 555–6, 559, 567n13; "new authenticities," 318–38
author and authorship, 379, 403n3, 534; authorial self, 473
autobiography, xvi, 92, 94, 109, 114–15, 120–1, 158, 300–3, 424–5, 492, 497; autobiographical games, 473; auto-fiction, 388; "auto-porn-art," 378–407
autonomy, 140–54
auto-porn-art, 378–407
avant-garde, 378
Aviance, Kevin, 134

baby boomers, xvi
Bacon, Francis, 63n3
Bailey, Fenton, and Randy Barbato, 178–82
Baise-moi (novel), 300–17
Baise-moi (film), 301
Balázs, Béla, 291
Barcan, Ruth, 320, 321
Barlow, Sam, 474, 481–5
Barnard Conference on Sexuality, xvii, 7
Baron, Jaimie, 482–5
Barthes, Roland, 177, 181, 321, 334n4
bathrooms, 49–64, 216–17
Baudrillard, Jean, 258, 500
Bazin, André, 255–6, 323
BDSM, 74, 300, 308, 311, 313, 344–5, 408–22, 511–12, 515–32
becoming, 268–9, 281–90; becoming animal, 269–75, 287
Belmont, Viktor, 392–3
Bengal, 158–76
Benjamin, Walter, 255, 258
Berlant, Lauren, 61, 84, 95, 411, 432, 535, 545

Berlin, 409–22
Berry, Justin, 204
Bersani, Leo, 238–9, 534
Bhaduri, Chapal, 162–3, 173n4
Bible, 237, 241
Bieber, Justin, 457
bisexuality, 108–28, 181, 185
Björk, 339–47
blackmail, xi–xii
blackness, 87, 89–90, 96, 101nn1–2, 189, 276–82, 339–42, 382–3, 431. *See also* African Americans; African arts; African characters
Black Spark, 269, 271, 273, 287–92
"black theology," 515, 520, 516, 525
Black Women's Liberation Group, 87
Blas, Zach, 292–4
blogging, 49–64, 83–106, 107–28, 504–14; blogosphere, 289; photoblogging, 445–6. *See also* vlogging
Blue, 489–96, 501
Blue Velvet, 520–1, 524
BluMedia Group, 185–6
Bobby Khamvongsa, 391
body, 171, 216, 247, 257, 401, 517, 563; "bodies without organs," 10–13, 55; bodily confessions, 263–98; body genres, 269, 339; whole body, 305, 417
Bogarde, Dirk, xi–xii
books, 107–28
"Born This Way," 8, 129–35, 291–3, 555–7
Bourdieu, Pierre, 246
Boy with Machine (painting), 12–13
"boy without sex," 12–13
boys and boyhood, ix–xi, 453–72; masturbating, 193–232; puerile desire, 194
Boys in the Band, The, xiii, xxn2
Braidotti, Rosi, 536
Breillat, Catherine, 338
Breitkreutz, Sara, 477
Brinkema, Eugenie, 291, 320
Broke Straight Boys TV, 177–92
Bruns, Gerald, 272–3
Bruss, Elizabeth, 424
Bryanterry, 321
Butler, Judith, 130–1, 183, 509–10
Byrne, David, 551

Calcutta, 158–76
Calloway, Marie, 504–14

camming: cam sex, 245–62, 354; Cam4, 252
camp, 132, 180
Canada, 19, 20–1, 63n1, 133, 194, 210–14, 218, 373, 387–92, 399, 468n5
Caouette, Jonathan, 436–51
capitalism, 7, 99, 182, 257, 295n7, 302, 355, 398, 404n8, 493; crowd-based, 249; pharmaco-pornographic, 355
carceral state, 19
"carnal resonances," 354
Carnes, Brae, 55–63
Carr, John, 222–3
Carter, Angela, 310, 343–5
Casarino, Cesare, 266, 562–4, 568n18
Ceci n'est pas un viol, 29–48
celebrity, 14, 122, 138, 165, 323–4, 326, 423–8, 432
cell-phone, 56, 204, 423
censorship, 204, 209, 218
Center for Sex and Culture, 137
Cervone, Antonio, 263–4, 269, 287
"charmed circle" (Rubin), 372, 375, 424–6
chatrooms, 7, 9, 253–4, 388, 390, 456
Chaturbate, 250–4
Chicago, 290, 318, 323, 333
Chiennes savantes, Les, 300, 309
child pornography, 22, 195–6, 200, 201–3, 205, 209–11, 212, 213, 217–19, 222, 224
children: child sexuality, 194, 455, 457–9, 461, 464–6, 534; innocence, 195, 202, 204, 219, 459, 466
Children's Hour, The, xii
Chitrangada, 160, 162–3, 166–7, 168, 172
Christianity, 117, 237–44
cinéma vérité, 180, 183, 327
cinnamon challenge, 335n6
"circuit breakers," 550–1, 560, 563, 566n5
cisgender, 49, 56–8, 86, 88, 91, 392, 400
cityscapes, 290
civil disobedience, 18, 58, 313
civil liberties, 190
civil rights movement, 85, 501
class, 86–90, 93, 181–4, 189, 278, 284, 287, 295n7, 310–11, 371–7, 428–9, 431–2, 456, 457–9, 466, 516–17
click bait, 99, 110
Clift, Montgomery, x, 3–4
closet, 184–5, 266, 561
cocksucking. *See* oral sex
CockyBoys, 295n6, 318–37, 395

coercion, 30–2, 39–42, 66, 70
Cohen, Kris, 445–6
Colby Does America, 274–80, 384, 392, 394–9
Colby Does Kentucky, 276–80
Colby Does Virginia, 278–82
Colebrook, Claire, 268
collaborative media making, 65–82, 124n9, 274, 386, 499
collage, 86, 322
collective: authorship, 92; feelings, 89; politics, 49–64
colonialism, 87; anticolonial, 534; decolonial, 500–1, 502n2; postcolonial, 388, 501
Columbia University, 29–48
Combahee River Collective, 295n7, 428
Comella, Lynn, 195
coming out (of the closet), xi, 8–14, 107–28, 131, 266, 273, 286–7, 293, 328; closeted, 436; coming-out stories, xiv, 430; National Coming Out Day, 266
commodification, 74, 99, 550–1
community, community activism, 49–64
confession: anti-confessional discourse, 141, 154, 549–71; Christian sacrament, 11, 44n2, 51, 143, 398; confessant, 265; confessing animal, 269–74; confessional (sacrament/trope in porn and TV), 183, 265, 319, 325–2, 425; confessionality, 3, 485; confession in law, 30–2, 38–9; confessor, 60, 62; counter-confessional performance, 178; dangerous, 193; digital, 505; as disciplinary/individualizing, 51–2, 88; drag, 496; as movement, 53; sexual, 136–57, 378–406, 408–22, 424–35, 557–9; verbal, 270; visual, 21, 68–9; voice-over, 519, 279
Confessionnal, Le, 3–4
conjugality, 388, 390, 395, 449, 556
Conrad, Ryan, 385, 390
consciousness raising, 83–106
consent, 35, 39–43, 45n9, 45n10, 45n11, 45n15, 46n21, 144, 200, 218, 373, 376, 457, 528; age of consent, 225n5, 468n5
control society, 11, 273, 550–1
Corrigan, Timothy, 477–8, 487n1
counter-publics, 400, 402, 460
creative commons, 399
criminalization, 19; incrimination, 21
Crimp, Douglas, xviii
Crocker, Chris, 8, 14, 294n2, 392

Crowley, Mart, xiii
Cruiser, 389
cruising, 389–90, 563; media cruising, 554, 565n2, 566n7, 568n21
culture: cultural studies, 66, 203, 381; queer, xviii, 132, 385, 430, 563–4, 566n7; visual, 15, 380, 466, 515
cum shot, 72, 220, 240, 267, 290, 330, 332, 380, 398
Cumming, Alan, 425
"cutout" technique, 208–9, 214–5, 223
Cvetkovich, Ann, 129, 132–4

daily life. *See* everyday life
Dalziell, Tanya, and Lee-Von Kim, 509
Dancer in the Dark, 339, 347
Dawson, Shane, 108–23
de Villiers, Nicholas, 269, 293
Dean, Tim, 334
death and dying, xvi, xviii, 302, 494, 524
Deep Throat, 7
Deleuze, Gilles, 307, 311, 314n7, 515–16, 520–1, 524–5, 550–1, 568n19; and Félix Guattari, 10–13, 53–5, 63n3, 180, 268, 272–5, 281–3, 286–7, 294n4, 295n8, 296n9, 475
desire, 281; desiring-machines, 13
Despentes, Virginie, 300–17
détournement, 22, 468
dialectics, 60, 140, 154, 238, 266, 500, 551–65, 566n7
Diamond, Suzanne, 499
diary, 92, 330, 380, 386, 388–9, 392, 395, 474, 476–7, 496, 508, 533, 538
dick pic, 200, 216, 354, 365
Dickinson, Emily, 549–69
digital: biography, 505; economy, 93, 101
dildo, 72
Dines, Gail, 197–201, 385
Dinshaw, Carolyn, 380–1
direct address, 49, 328, 331, 399
directness, 255
"dirtiness," 533–48
disability and, able-bodiedness, 152–4, 237–44
"disappeared aesthetics," 490, 492, 494, 501
discipline, 143, 363; disciplinary society, 438. *See also* control society
disidentification, 58–62, 187–9, 399
distribution, 217; theatrical, 436
DIY, 94–5, 249, 320–1, 387–8, 476

documentary, 177–92, 423–35; documentary effect, 187
Doty, Alexander, 424
Double Bind, 537, 541–7
DouchebagsOfGrindr, 285
Dovey, John, 424
drag, 382–4, 392, 441, 496–501
DSM (Diagnostic and Statistical Manual of Mental Disorders), 359, 468n5
Duggan, Lisa, 459
DVD, 387, 490
Dyer, Richard, 334n4, 380, 385
dys4ia, 474–81, 485–6, 487n1

Edelman, Lee, 238, 534, 535, 545
elderly. *See* aging; seniors
Elders, Joycelyn, 197, 359
Ellis, John, 425
Emile, 71–5
"Emily Dickinson," 552–4, 560, 565
emojis, 366–7
emotion, 37, 53–4, 63n3, 83–5, 88–90, 96, 101, 113, 130, 134, 208, 221, 225n4, 281, 289–90, 294, 345, 413–14, 418, 454–5, 462, 479, 509
empowerment, 70, 92–3, 109
England, ix–xxi, 222, 226n10
erections, 197, 208, 215–17, 218, 363, 398; erectile dysfunction, 359, 361–2, 364
Erickson, Mark, and Damian McKnight, 178, 185–6
erotic capital, 245–63
Escoffier, Jeffrey, 186–7
essay, 100, 474, 477, 486; essay film, 487n1
ethics, xiv, 18, 22, 67, 91, 140–5, 378–407, 453–72, 523, 528, 554, 563, 565n2; of documentary, 177–9, 189, 408–22; of MAP desire, 453–72; of porn production, 74
ethnography, 247, 383, 445, 477; autoethnography, xv, 454, 477; domestic ethnography, 437–9
everyday life, xx, 17, 56, 74, 86, 93, 129, 132, 180, 203, 318, 363, 386, 390, 396, 408, 411, 416–17, 420, 425, 427–8; daily life, 92, 249, 252–3, 256
exhibitionism, 252–3, 327, 446, 525–6
exploitation, 59, 66, 70, 194, 200–3, 210–13, 217, 223–4, 303, 505, 512, 544; sexploitation, 310

face and faciality, 269, 273, 276, 280, 283, 287, 291–3, 295n8, 296n9

Facebook, 252–3, 257, 312–13, 354–6
"Fag Face Mask," 292–3
failure, 171–3
fall from ideal, 439–44, 446–7, 450, 451n1
fans and fan culture, 109–10, 114, 119, 120, 123n6; fan letters, 136–57; porn fans, 136–57
fantasy, 67, 70, 74, 76, 77, 79, 145–7, 206–7, 239–42, 247–8, 252, 257, 293–4, 340, 415–16, 445–6, 455–6, 461–3, 504–14, 557–8
Fassbinder, R.W., 496–500
fat, 96, 113, 285, 556
fathers, 208, 240–2
feelings. *See* emotion
female: excessive femininity, 158–76; myth of female dignity, 302–7, 310–13
feminism: bad girl, 7, 371–7; black, 87, 89; digital, 83–106; and feminist art practices, 476; and feminist porn, 65–82, 136–57; Feminist Porn Awards, 65–6, 78–9, 79n1; feminist spaces, 372; generational, 312; postfeminism, 93; "punk-porn feminism," 300–17; Second Wave, 92, 101, 310, 373; sex-negative, 199–200, 372–3; sex-positive, 7, 65–6, 300, 311, 313, 347, 367n2, 454; Third Wave, 101n1; white, 87, 88
Feminist Porn Book, The, 19, 195
fetish, 152, 181, 267, 274, 408–22, 519–20, 525, 528
fighting, 458, 468n3
fightthenewdrug, 360–1
film festivals, 16, 411–12
films, 115–23, 408–22
Finkelstein, Joanne, 114
First Amendment, 209, 212
"First Person" (Rituparno Ghosh column), 158, 161
"first person industrial complex," 6, 84, 99, 193, 224, 379, 402
first-person media: narratives and voices, 6–7, 15, 92, 101, 326, 376, 380, 386, 394, 399, 424, 454, 478–9, 504–14; pornography, 208. *See also* autobiography; auto-porn-art; vlogging
fisting, 151–2
"fold, the," 268b
Foucault, Michel, xiv, 6, 11, 33, 44n1, 44nn6–7, 136, 140, 152, 154, 381, 402, 453, 459, 523, 560–2; on the child, 194–5; *History of Sexuality*, vol. 1, xvii, 51–2, 60, 85–8, 270–3, 286, 306–8, 314n6, 314n8, 326, 344, 353, 410, 424, 438–9, 466, 489, 505, 530n5, 554–5, 567n8; late work

on the self, 91, 136–57, 183, 292, 363, 380, 398, 400, 402–3, 415, 417, 463, 467, 515–32, 557
Four Malay Stories, 496–7
fragmentation, 69–70, 77, 79
frame (cinematic), 408–22
Franta, Connor, 109–12, 118
Freedman, Eric, 474, 485–6
French Revolution, 305
Freud, Sigmund, 442–4, 446–7
Friedman, James, 329–30
friendship, 67, 120, 141, 154, 164, 242, 310, 380, 389, 400, 402, 463–4, 555, 563, 566n7
Fuck Yeah Levi Karter!, 318–38
funding, 23, 174n7, 226n11, 386, 391, 398, 399, 403n3; crowdfunding, 83, 274, 396
Fung, Richard, 144, 152
Furedi, Frank, 418

Gaichu (Harmful Insect), 528–9
Gallop, Jane, 18, 23, 310–11
Galloway, Alexander, 478–9
gambling, 364
games, 415–17, 459, 473–88; gamification, 78, 357, 360, 366; indie games, 473–6
Gammel, Irene, 505, 507
Gay Liberation Front, xiii–xvi
gay male, 177–92, 207, 237–43, 263–300, 354, 356, 257, 372–3, 379, 395, 397, 400–1, 408–12, 436, 449; gay-for-pay, 177–92, 318–37; internet pornography, 263–99, 318–37
gaze: female, 506; forensic, 208–9; male, 371, 446, 525–6
Gekko no Sasayaki, 515–32
gender: distinctions, 199; non-conformity, 159, 165–6, 310–11, 338–52; roles, 65–82, 83–106, 139–40, 504–15
genderqueer, 78, 379, 384, 388–9, 391–4
generations, xvi–xx, 84, 267, 312, 372; intergenerational relations, 7, 17–19, 390, 399, 452–72; and mentoring, 390
Genet, Jean, 453
Germany, 495–503
Ghosh, Rituparno, 158–76
Girl on Girl, 388–9
girls and girlhood, 198–201, 213, 219–20, 225n3
Goode, Sarah D., 224, 467n1
Graceffa, Joey, 109, 112, 124n16
graffiti, 58, 61–2
Griffith, D.W., 341, 348

Grindr, 284–8, 354, 355, 357, 376, 397, 549–69
"growing sideways," 554, 566n7
Guattari, Félix. *See* Deleuze, Gilles
Guide to Alternative Sex, 139

Haberer, Lilian, 498
Hakim, Catherine, 246–7
Halberstam, J.J., 133, 173, 454, 534–5
Haneke, Michael, 338, 343
Hansen, Christian, 320
Hansen, Miriam, 411
happiness, unhappiness, 87–8, 90, 101, 130, 528
hard core art cinema, 338–52
Hart, Hannah, 109, 123n1
Hartley, Nina, 136–57
Harvard University, 278–80, 282
hashtags: #balancetonporc, 338; #MeToo, 4, 338, 347–8; #Occupotty, 49–64
hate-reading, 97
Hazel, 206–9, 226n11
Hefner, Hugh, 5–6
Helbig, Grace, 112
Hemmings, Clare, 281–3
hentai, 515–32, 529n4
Her Story, 474–5, 481–6
heterosexuality, 117, 133, 136–57, 188–9, 199, 219, 245–62, 270, 303, 383, 388–9, 410–11, 424, 466, 504–14, 516–17, 544; heteronormativity, 58, 61, 88, 133, 139, 218, 304, 372, 424, 428, 462–5, 468n2, 555, 562, 567n12
high heels, 129–35
Hillyer, Minette, 322–3
Hilton, Perez, 426
Hitchcock, Alfred, 3–4, 142–3, 525–6
HIV. *See* AIDS
home movies, 322–5, 329, 333–4, 436–52
homophobia, 129–35, 162–6, 188, 462
homosexuality, 107–28, 129–35, 177–92, 237–44, 263–99, 318–37, 378–407, 423–35, 549–71; homonationalist and homonormative, 273, 466, 556; situational, 187. *See also* LGBTQ2I+
homosociality, 22, 383–4
Hongisto, Ilona, 414
hooks, bell, 89, 91, 99
Horak, Laura, 328, 335n8
hormone replacement therapy, 5, 475–6, 479
Horning, Rob, 511–12
Hughes, Michael, 49–64

humour, 79, 113, 120, 200, 242, 265, 286, 412
Hutcheon, Linda, 108, 116

identity, 281–4, 287–8, 291–3; identity politics, 51, 62, 284–6, 295n7, 500–1; nonidentity, anti-identitarian, 62, 545, 554, 569n22; "oriental identity," 388; psychosexual identity, 438, 446, 466; queer porn identities, 401
ideology, 281–4
illicit materials, 21
illness, xv
incest, 300, 302, 307–9, 313, 536
Incomplete, The (*Der Unfertige*), 408–22
indexicality, 209, 286, 290, 291, 293
India, 158–76
Insatiable, 340
Instagram, 49, 57–61, 252, 392, 445, 450, 457
"integral realism," 323
interactivity, 75–7, 107–28, 141, 154, 249–58, 481, 486
interdisciplinarity, 15
International Megan's Law, 20
internet, xvii, 9–14, 197, 200, 202, 222, 259n6, 348, 381; safety, 222
intersectional, 74, 87, 88, 94, 97, 99, 238, 295n7, 376, 400, 423, 428–32
intertextuality, 32–9
interviews, xiv–xv, 67, 177–92, 264–91, 328, 330, 413, 426–7, 482
intimacy, 68, 70, 72, 90, 93, 115, 122, 136, 158–9, 169, 180, 186, 252–8, 307–8, 322, 327, 328, 332, 348, 357, 410–11, 412, 418, 420, 473–4, 520, 560, 563, 568n21; intimate public, 61, 95, 100, 411; intimate screen, 427; virtual intimacies, 361–2; writing intimacy, 504–14
It Gets Better, It Gets Worse, 291, 423, 425, 430, 432

Jackson, Derek, 385, 388–90, 396, 398–9
Jacobs, Katrien, 325–6
Jagoda, Patrick, 77–8
Jameson, Fredric, 475
Japan, Japanese, 515–32
Jarman, Derek, 378, 381, 391, 489–503
Jaxson, Jake, 295n6, 318, 319, 322, 323, 332, 395
Jeevan Smriti, 160, 162, 168–73, 174n12
Jenkins, Henry, 108, 119
Jesus Christ, 237–8, 241–2, 279, 493

Jezebel, 84–106
Juliano, Linzi, 476
Jung, C.G., 493–4

Kahana, Jonathan, 180
Kaplan, Carla, 91
Kaplan, Louise J., 347
Karaian, L., and K. Van Meyl, 218, 220
Kardashian, Kim, 449–50, 504, 508–9
Karter, Levi, 318–38
Keller, Colby, 263–99, 384–92, 394–8
kenbaku-bi (aesthetic binding), 525
Kendall, Christopher, 385
kendo, 517–18, 521, 523–5
Kennedy, Flo, 87, 89
King, Barry, 425
King Kong Théorie, 300, 302, 305, 307–8
Kinsey, Alfred, 3, 19, 194, 381–2
Kipnis, Laura, 138, 145
Klein, Bonnie Sherr, 178
Knapp, Gudrun-Axeli, 428–9
knowledge and knowledge-making, 86, 89, 92, 95, 136, 142, 155; self-knowledge, 138, 141
Kolkata. *See* Calcutta
Krauss, Rosalind, 437, 446–8, 450
Kroker, Arthur, 10–13

labour, 332; affective, 181; digital, 84, 93, 99
LaBruce, Bruce, 387–8, 399–1, 404n6
Lacan, Jacques, 238
Lady Gaga, 129–35, 291
Lander, N. Maxwell, 65–82
Laplanche, Jean, 443–6
Laqueur, Thomas, 197–8, 359
Last of England, The, 491–3, 501n3
Latinx, 101n1, 391, 399–400, 429–30
law, 29–48, 209–12, 287, 459, 468n5, 556; contract, 31, 39–42; and illegality, xiv, 20, 49, 201–3, 217–18, 222; "legitimate purpose" defence, 209–14
"Leave Britney Alone," 14
Ledare, Leigh, 535, 537–47
Lepage, Robert, 3–4
Lerne Deutsch mit Petra von Kant, 497–8
lesbians, 65–82, 116–17, 153, 423–35, 568n15; butch/femme, 68; dyke sex, 78
letters, 136–57
Leung, Isaac, 388, 390, 398, 399

LGBTQ2I+, 111–13, 132, 174n5, 190, 376, 379, 423–5, 438, 454, 459, 555, 562
libertines, 300, 301, 342, 454
libido, 281–3
lighting, 68, 110–11, 180, 260n13, 286, 289–91, 408, 411, 483
Lindner, Richard, 12
liveness, 256
London, ix–xx, 181
Losing It with John Stamos, 426–8

MacDonald, Cheryl, 477
"machine zone," 363–4
MacKinnon, Catherine, 35–6
Madonna: Truth or Dare, 185–6
Magritte, René, 29–34, 44n6
manga, 515, 517
Mapplethorpe, Robert, 386, 541
Marche, Stephen, 505, 511
Marcus, Steven, 258
marriage, 302–3, 544–5
martial arts, 22, 515–32
Marx, Karl, and Friedrich Engels, 549
Marxism, 549
masculinity, 22, 458, 464–5; hegemonic, 461–4; male characters, 349–50; toxic, 199, 225n4
masks, 263–99, 391, 398, 404n8; masquerade, 497
masochism, 515–32
Massumi, Brian, 7, 11, 53, 270, 281–2, 475
masturbation, 22–3, 93, 391, 534; jerk porn, 73, 79; masturbating boy, 22, 193–233
"Mattress Performance" (*Carry That Weight*), 29–48
Maybe He's Gifted, 66–71
McDowell, Curt, 321
McGlotten, Shaka, 321
McNair, Brian, 246
McRuer, Robert, 238
media: generations, xvii–xviii; mediality, xx, 107–28; mediasphere, 266; new, 101, 504–14; platforms, 12–13, 49–64, 78, 92, 108, 252, 266, 328, 437; transmediality, 500
medicalization, 241, 359, 362, 364, 439, 455, 460, 466
memory, 373, 512; queer, xviii–xix; social memories, 267
mental illness, 437
Mercer, John, 17, 20, 21

Mercer, Kobena, 342
merchandising, 253, 259n2, 399
Merteuil, Morgane, 311–13
Miller, Branden, 392–3
Miller, D.A., 436
minor-attracted adults (MAPS), 19–20, 436–52, 453–72
minoritarian identities, ethics, and subjectivities, 62, 400–1, 412
minorities: sexual, gender, and racial, 6, 12, 22, 60, 224, 280, 282–4, 295n7, 383, 412, 496, 550–1
minors, 22, 193–236, 453–72
misogyny, 38, 239, 242, 346, 347–8, 512, 550
models and modelling, 65, 73, 178, 185, 250–7, 260n9, 318–19, 326, 330, 332, 334, 395, 447, 469n9
monetization, 78, 84, 93–4, 99, 249–62
money shot. *See* cum shot
Monk Mode, 360
monologue, 328, 413, 498–9
Monroe, Marilyn, ix, 137, 139
Montreal, 330
Moonlight Whispers, 515–32
Moore, Stephen D., 237
Morin, Edgar, 247
Mormons, 360–1
Morris, Paul, 399–403, 404n8
mothers, 202, 328–9, 344, 436–51, 533–48
MSM media, 549–69
Mulvey, Laura, 446–8, 525–6
Muñoz, José Esteban, 58–62, 134, 399–403, 534–5
music video, 68, 72, 109, 123n2, 276, 287, 289; MTV, 327
Mutantes, 312–13
Muybridge, Eadweard, 276–7

Nakamura, Lisa, 428
narcissism, 119, 142, 437, 442–8, 450, 504, 535
Needham, Catherine, 320
Needham, Gary, 541
Negri, Antonio, 550–1
neoliberalism, xvii, 7, 13, 100, 245–62, 273, 283, 287, 549–65, 565n1, 566n7
neuro-image, 478, 480–1
"New European Extremism," 338–9, 347
New Queer Cinema, 388, 404n6

New York, 7–10, 134, 386–7, 389–90, 431, 449, 465–6, 469n9
New York Radical Women, 85–6
New York v. Ferber, 211
Nguyen Tan Huang, 380
Ni putes ni soumises (Neither Whores nor Submissives), 312
Nichols, Bill, 320
Niedzviecki, Hal, 425
Nietzsche, Friedrich, 569n25
nineteenth century, 39–40, 260n14, 391, 410, 561, 567n8
Nkonyana, Zoliswa, 431
NoFap, 355–7, 360–4, 367n4
non-binary identities, 56, 58, 109–10
non-heterosexual, 107–28
nonsense, age of, 549–71
North American Man-Boy Love Association (NAMBLA), 458
Not a Love Story, 178
nyakaa (affectation), 167
Nymph()maniac, 338–52

obesity. *See* fat
Oedipal narrative, 539, 542, 544, 547n2
oral sex, 139, 150, 207, 238, 332
orgasm, 67, 69, 72, 76, 194–5, 198, 221–2, 225n3, 238–40, 267, 330, 332, 340, 359–60, 381, 388, 391, 398, 534; faking, 506–7
Othenin-Girard, Alexei, 476
"outness," 408, 410–11, 420
outsourcing, 251–2

Paasonen, Susanna, 321–2, 326, 329, 354–5, 401–3
pagan, 344, 391
Page, Ruth, and Bronwen Thomas, 107–8
pain, 504, 506–9, 512, 525
painting, 12–13, 29–30
palimpsest, 466, 492
Pam and Tommy Lee: Hardcore and Uncensored, 322–3
paranoid reading, 403
parody, 71, 77, 165, 184, 240, 305–6, 343, 480, 497
parrhesia, 136–57, 398, 402–3
past, the, xvi, xix–xx, 281–2, 381, 440–1, 450, 485
pathologizing readings, 533, 539, 541–4, 546
Paul of Tarsus, St, 237–8

Peculiar Kind, The, 428–32
pedagogy, 7–8, 455, 463
pederasty, 224n1, 454, 460, 463, 465
pedophile, pedophilia, xiv, 194, 204, 211, 224n1, 226n15, 454, 459
peer review process, 17–23
penis, 220, 240, 263–5, 276
performance art, 29–48, 386; autobiographical, 506, 509; confessional, 179, 190; video, 534
performative discourse, 142
"personal is political," 92, 476
perversion and "perverts," 141, 145, 307, 347, 410, 515–32, 554, 529n4
Peterson, Tina, 537–9
Philosophy in the Bedroom, 303–5, 308, 311
photography, 49–64, 78–9, 95, 115, 145–7, 200–1, 212, 215–17, 285, 504–5, 508–9, 512, 533–48; photoblogging, 445–7; photobooth, 538, 540, 541
Pinku film (soft core), 515
Pisters, Patricia, 478, 480–1, 486
Playboy, 3
Plummer, Ken, ix–xxi, 5, 193, 267, 413
Polacheck, Jen, 96–7
police: police state, 194, 224; policing and law enforcement, x, 200, 203, 208–9, 217, 221, 309–10, 312–13, 481–6
Pop Network, 432
Porn Game, 75–9
Porn Studies (periodical), 16
pornography: amateur, 6, 150, 188, 247–50, 254, 256, 260n13, 275, 284, 289, 294n5, 319–32, 334, 334n4; art, 69, 338–9, 378–407; chic, 379; child, 457; confession, 184; consumers, 187–8, 257; documentary, 318–22; "evidentiary" status, 320; genres, 332; gonzo, 326; hard core, 69, 72, 220, 294n5, 379–406; industry, 246, 279; and intimacy, 511; literacy, 74; "porn fast," 353–69; "pornification," 245, 259n3, 410; pornoculture, 245; porno-graphing, 533–49; pornspace, 256, 258; porn studies, 195, 178; public domain, 219; reality porn, 319, 325, 326, 329, 332, 334; "realness," 255, 265; stars, 19, 136–57, 183–4, 245, 247, 248, 252, 326, 397; "twink," 455. *See also* feminism
Pornhub, 252, 340–2
PornResearch.org, 218
Porter, Cole, 3

post-ideological era, 7
postmodern, xv, 11, 77, 133, 372, 447, 489, 495, 508
Preciado, Paul, 354–5
PrEP, 5, 355
present-centrism, 381
Pretend You're Actually Alive, 537–9, 541–2, 544–6
priest, 3, 142, 279, 306
"primitive," 271, 285–6
private sex, 409
prostitutes. *See* sex workers
prosumers, 246
protest, xiii, 85
psychiatry, psychology, and psychoanalysis, 195, 201–2, 416, 439, 455, 462, 464, 467n, 468n5, 555
Puar, Jasbir, 100
puberty, 225n2
public, 133–4; public intellectual, 159; counterpublics, 400, 402, 460
punishment, 344–6
punk music, 309

queer, 423–35; ethics, 453–73; icon, 165; opacity, 269, 273–4, 280, 287–8, 291–3; optimism, 399; queerbaiting, 110, 118, 121; queers of colour, 58, 60, 388–94, 430; space, 133; time, 220
queer theory, 178, 237–44, 263–99, 534–5, 559; antisocial turn, 238, 534–5, 539

race, 428–32; interracial sex, 189, 340–1
racism, 86–7, 90, 96, 189, 340–1, 342, 498, 550, 555
Radstone, Susannah, 423–4
Rambuss, Richard, 243n1
rape, 203, 300, 302, 304–5, 312–13, 371–3; representation of, 313; survivors, 300, 304–5, 312–13
Rappaport, Michael, 426
Rascaroli, Laura, 424
Raun, Tobias, 60
Ray, Johnnie, ix–xiii
Ray, Satyajit, 166–8, 174n12
"Real World, The," 327, 400
reality TV, 95, 178
"rebooting," 361–3
Redstockings, 85–6

Reeves, Tom, 458
reflexivity, xiv–xv, 119, 327–8, 388, 396, 436–52
relationships and relationality, 136–57, 181, 189, 216, 246, 249, 254, 267, 303, 363, 379, 380, 384, 388, 390, 396, 398, 400–1, 402, 431, 466, 515–32, 554
religion and spirituality, 140, 161, 237–44, 306–7, 353–70, 381, 391
Renov, Michael, 326–7, 438, 445–6
Rentboy.com, 189–90
reparative reading, 385, 399
"reproductive futurism," 534
rhizome, 53–4
Ricco, John Paul, 492–4
Riggs, Marlon, 21
RightRides, 431
Rimbaud, Arthur, 391–2
Rinaldi, Cirus, 181
rituals, 5, 44n2, 89, 143, 255–7, 267, 386, 390, 462, 464, 520–8, 555, 567n8
Roach, Tom, 141, 145, 154, 220
Roman, Ricky, 332–3
Romney, Jonathan, 346
Ross, Jamie, 381, 385, 390–3, 399
Roth, Phillip B., 385–7, 389, 398, 399–401
Rouch, Jean, 327
"rough trade," 184
Rousings, 381, 390–3
Rousseau, Jean-Jacques, 449, 451n1, 516, 528
Rubin, Gayle, 19, 372
Ryberg, Ingrid, 411

Sade, Marquis de, 300–17; Sadean, 300–17, 339, 342–3
sadism, 348, 520–1, 523–6, 527
safe spaces, 371, 411
Saget, Bob, 426–7
San Francisco, 137, 327, 360–1, 400
Sarachild, Kathie, 83–9
sauna, 356–7
Savage, Dan, 425
Scarlot Harlot (Carol Leigh), 312–13
Scarry, Elaine, 507
schizoanalysis, 478
scientia sexualis, 15, 410, 554–5, 557, 560, 565
scopophilia, 446
Seancody.com, 394–5

second sexual revolution. *See* sexual revolutions
secondary sexual characteristics, 461–2
self, the, making of, 7, 67, 93, 353; entrepreneurs of, 254, 258
self-representation and self-documentation, 6, 158–76, 215–21, 284, 378–406, 437–9, 445, 463, 504–14; selfies, 49–64, 216, 365–6, 447; self-objectification, 533–48; self-portraiture, 437; self-produced videos, 457–8
Sen, Aparna, 161, 164–5, 165, 174n7
seniors, 409, 412–13, 559
sentencing, 205, 380
sex: "boy without sex," 12–13; child sexual abuse, 193–232, 460; digital sexualities, xx, 377; education, 136–57, 201; industry, 249, 374; machine, 354–5; and negativity, 545, 635; offenders, 20; sex offender registries, 19, 201; sexology, 178; sexual assault (*see* rape); sexual awakening, 207; sexual compulsion, 359, 362, 367n3; sexual cultures, 409–22; sexual harassment, 5; sexual labour, 66, 248; sexual minorities (*see* minorities); sexual networks, 219; sexual play, 408–22; sexual stories, ix–xx; sexual stigma, xv, 20, 374, 455–9, 564; sexual subject/ivity, 257; sexual technologies of the self, 515–32; "sex wars" (aka "porn wars"), xvii, 6, 66, 371, 455; underground sex cultures, 371; sex work (*see* sex worker)
sex panics, xvii, 5, 7, 19, 174n5, 194, 197–8, 202, 210, 385, 455, 460
sex workers, xix, 7, 19, 66, 177, 181, 190, 300–16, 371–7, 379, 388–9, 401, 504–14; male (hustlers, rent boys), 177–92, 386–8, 397–8, 401; self-employed, 250; trans*, 392–3
sexism, 85–6, 91, 97, 347
sexting, 19, 197–8, 200–1, 204–6, 207–8, 210–11, 213–21, 223, 225n7, 225n9, 354–5, 365
sexual revolutions, 3–5; first sexual revolution, 3; second sexual revolution, 3–7, 19, 378–9, 386; third sexual revolution, 5–7, 11, 13, 376–7, 378–9, 379
sexuality studies, 18, 242, 454; scientific language of, 196
shame, 130, 132, 398, 455, 461–2, 463, 467n
"shared estrangement," 563, 566n7, 568n21
Sharp, John, 476

Index | 601

Shaviro, Steven, 475
showers, 240, 314n3, 356–7
Siebers, Tobin, 239
signifiers, 280, 286–7
Simkhai, Joel, 285–6
Simondon, Gilbert, 10
slaves and slavery, 40, 237, 408–22
slut-shaming, 347
smartphone, 75, 284, 318, 321, 357
Smith, Michael V., 385, 388–9, 401
Snapchat, 219, 366
Sobchack, Vivian, 490–1
social media, 5–7, 40, 49–64, 78, 92, 101, 108, 120, 186, 195–7, 205, 221, 246, 252–3, 274, 276, 284, 293, 312–13, 348, 354, 376, 436, 450, 456–8, 462, 504–5, 536, 549–71
social sciences, xiv–xv, 15, 225n6, 454
sodomy, 237, 239, 241, 305
Soldat, Jan, 408–22
Sonic Youth, 310
sound: music, 278, 288, 419; soundtrack, 68–73, 76–7, 169–71, 180, 276, 288, 390–1, 396, 419, 483, 490–3, 501
"spambots," 551–2, 566n3
Stadler, John Paul, 188
stag films, 294n5, 378, 381–3, 386
stars, 107, 129–35, 425–6
statistics, 205
Stepić, Nikola, 132
Stewart, Potter, 196
Steyerl, Hito, 95
Stop Making Sense, 551, 565n1
stories and storytelling, xiii–xxi, 93–6, 99, 107–28, 206, 266–7, 398, 416
straight. *See* heterosexuality
Strangelove, Michael, 425
Stranger Than Fiction, 530n6
"striptease culture," 246
Studlar, Gaylyn, 526
subalterns, 300, 308, 312–13, 402
subject and subjectivity, 136–43, 154, 436–52, 460–1, 463, 466, 473–88, 489–503, 533–48
suicide, xi–xii
Sulkowicz, Emma, 29–48
Sundarajan, Arun, 249
Super 8mm, 390, 437, 492
Supreme Court of Canada, 218

Surprise of a Knight, 378, 381, 382–4, 386
surveillance, 15, 20, 29–48, 141, 200, 225n7

Tagore, Rabindranath, 160–3, 168–72, 175n13
"talking head," 328, 429, 431
Tarnation, 436–51
Taylor, Chloë, xxn3, 84–5, 87–8, 91–2, 143, 154
technology/ies, 204, 248–9, 355; global connectedness via, 9–10; home-recording, 436–52; new communication technologies, 249, 455, 550–1; of the self, 489–503, 515–32; technobiographical, 474, 481; techno-optimistic, 551
teenagers. *See* adolescence
"Tegan Zayne Gets Clark'd," 330
television, ix–xi, 255–6
Telling Sexual Stories, xv
therapy and therapists, 19, 133, 144, 201, 206, 290–1, 327, 349, 353, 362, 438–9; therapeutic, 438–9; therapy culture, 415–20
There's No Business Like Show Business, ix–x
Thérèse the Philosopher, 306
third sexual revolution. *See* sexual revolutions
time: diachronic vs synchronic, xix; queer time, 220
to-be-looked-at, 447–50
To Catch a Predator, 20
To Queer Things Up, 428–32
Tolentino, Jia, 85, 94, 99–101
tomboy, 158
top/bottom, 240
Toronto, 371–7
totalitarian, 18, 224, 312
Trachman, Mathieu, 247–8, 257, 260n14
Tracy, Linda Lee, 178
Trahison des images, La, 29, 32
trans*, 382–4, 388, 391–4; transgender, 49–64, 90, 429–30; transitioning, 475–81; vlogs, 335n8
transaction, 179
trans-aesthetics, 500–1
transgression, 300–4, 306–7, 309–10, 314n2, 515–32
transmedia and transmediality, 107–28
transnationalism, 100, 387, 496, 498, 499
trauma, 84, 96, 99, 100, 129–35, 193, 195, 439–42, 444, 447–8, 450

Treachery of Images, The, 29–30, 32
Treasure Island Media, 355
tribes (Grindr), 552, 564
trigger warning, 33, 353
Trump, Donald, 283, 284–5, 397, 549–51, 558–9
Tumblr, 115, 276, 288, 354, 356, 455–6, 463, 504, 506, 553
Twitter, 5, 220

utopia, 5, 188, 399; internet utopia, 391, 401

Vallorani, Nicoletta, 494
van der Tuin, Iris, 311
Venus in Furs, 516, 520
Vertigo, 525–6
VicAlouqua/Victoria, 252–7, 260n11
Victim, ix–xi
victims and victimization, 303, 305, 310, 312, 459
video, 444–50; video art, 327, 446; video art installation, 495–501
videogames, 75–9
viewer. *See* audience
viral media, 96, 100
virginity, 423–8
visibility, xi, xiii, xviii, 17, 49, 60–3, 69–70, 73, 101, 197, 200, 215–17, 249, 258, 293–5, 319–20, 330, 342, 410–12, 491, 494, 561–4
vlogging, 54, 60, 107–28, 328
von Krafft-Ebing, Richard, 516
von Sacher-Masoch, Leopold, 516
von Trier, Lars, 338–52
voyeurism, 37, 41, 69, 250, 373, 383, 446, 465, 504, 519, 521, 523, 525–7, 529

Walk Away Renee, 436
Ward, Jane, 177, 188–9, 555–8, 564, 567n11, 567n12, 567n13
Warner, Michael, 432
Waugh, Thomas, 7–9, 190, 294n5, 321, 358, 454, 558
web (World Wide Web): Web 2.0, 107–28, 321, 390; webcam, 110, 204, 208, 219, 221, 251, 252, 254–5, 318, 321–3, 331, 354, 388, 391; web series, 384, 395–6, 398, 423–35. *See also* internet

Weeks, Jeffrey, xvii
WeJustNeedtoPee, 49, 55, 57, 63n6
West, Donald J., 181–2
West Bengal. *See* Bengal
Westecott, Emma, 476
"western" world (Judaeo-Christian/Euro-American/global north), 22, 31, 44n2, 174n7, 237, 245, 258, 270, 363, 424, 437, 458, 474, 505, 525, 567n8
what purpose did I serve in your life, 504–14
white supremacy, 397
Whitman, Walt, 332, 395, 562
Who Took Johnny?, 221
Wild, Oscar (pseud.), 382–4
Wilde, Oscar, 263
Williams, Linda, 16, 69, 136, 177–8, 188, 195, 276–7, 294n5, 319–20, 330, 332, 339–40, 344, 348, 378–80, 409
Winfrey, Oprah, 204, 425
Wittgenstein, Ludwig, 271
women of colour, 93–4; queer, 423, 429–30
women's movement, 83–106. *See also* feminism
women's studies, 66, 91
Wong, Ming, 489–503

xoJane, 84–106
Xtube, 287, 321, 381, 385, 390

YMCA, 356–7
Young Physique, 9–10
yourbrainonporn.com, 359–62
youth protection industry, 19, 202, 222–3
YouTube, 13, 60, 107–28, 328, 423–32

Zamora, Pedro, 399–400
Zimmerman, Patricia R., 324
Žižek, Slavoj, 464, 520–1
Zubillaga-Pow, Jun, 498